The Silent Cinema Reader

The Silent Cinema Reader offers a wide-ranging and accessible guide to the development of cinema from its emergence in the 1890s to the introduction of sound in the late 1920s. Combining key essays from leading scholars in the field with extensive introductory chapters written by the editors, the reader covers international developments in film aesthetics, the growth of the American film industry and its interaction with foreign competitors at home and abroad. It also discusses the wider cultural, social and political contexts of film production and consumption in the United States as well as Britain, Russia, France and Germany.

The *Reader* includes in-depth case studies of:

- the pioneering work at the studio of American inventor Thomas Edison
- the international operations of the French Pathé company
- the emergence of film editing
- the rise of nickelodeons
- controversies about the movies
- the importance of film stars such as Pearl White, Charles Chaplin, Buster Keaton, Gloria Swanson and Rudolph Valentino
- the work of major directors like D. W. Griffith, Cecil B. DeMille and Sergei Eisenstein
- the distinctiveness of film culture in Tsarist Russia and Weimar Germany

Essays by: Richard Abel, David Bordwell, Ben Brewster, Joseph Garncarz, Frank Gray, Lee Grieveson, Tom Gunning, Sumiko Higashi, Peter Krämer, Charles J. Maland, Charles Musser, Roberta E. Pearson and William Uricchio, Ben Singer, Shelley Stamp, Gaylyn Studlar, Kristin Thompson, Yuri Tsivian, Ruth Vasey, Linda Williams.

Editors: **Lee Grieveson** is a Lecturer in the Film Studies programme at King's College London. He is author of *Policing Cinema: Movies and Censorship in Early Twentieth Century America* (2004) and a former winner of the prestigious Katherine Singer Kovacs Essay Award from the Society for Cinema and Media Studies.

Peter Krämer is a Lecturer in Film Studies at the University of East Anglia (UK). He has published widely on American film and media history, and on the relationship between Hollywood and Europe. Together with Alan Lovell, he co-edited *Screen Acting* (1999).

The Silent Cinema

Reader

Edited by

Lee Grieveson and
Peter Krämer

Routledge
Taylor & Francis Group

LONDON AND NEW YORK

First published 2004
by Routledge
2 Park Square, Milton Park, Abingdon, Oxon, OX14 4RN

Simultaneously published in the USA and Canada
by Routledge
711 Third Avenue, New York, NY 10017 (8th Floor)

Routledge is an imprint of the Taylor and Francis Group, an informa business

Typeset in Perpetua and Bell Gothic by
Florence Production Ltd, Stoodleigh, Devon

British Library Cataloguing in Publication Data
A catalogue record for this book is available from the
British Library

Library of Congress Cataloging in Publication Data
 The silent cinema reader / edited by Lee Grieveson and Peter Krämer.
  p. cm.
  Includes bibliographical references.
  1. Silent films – History and criticism. 2. Motion pictures – History.
 I. Grieveson, Lee, 1969–. II. Krämer, Peter, 1961–.
 PN1995.75.S547 2003
 791.43′09 – dc21   2003013504

ISBN10: 0–415–25283–0 (hbk)
ISBN10: 0–415–25284–9 (pbk)

ISBN13: 978–0–415–25283–6 (hbk)
ISBN13: 978–0–415–25284–3 (pbk)

Contents

Illustrations

Notes on contributors

Richard Abel is Robert Altman Collegiate Professor of Film Studies at the University of Michigan. His most recent books are *The Red Rooster Scare: Making Cinema American, 1900–1910* (University of California Press, 1999), and, co-edited with Rick Altman, *The Sounds of Early Cinema* (Indiana University Press, 2001). Currently, he is editing the *Encyclopedia of Early Cinema* (Routledge, 2004) and writing a book entitled *The 'Imagined Community' of US Cinema, 1910–1914*.

David Bordwell is Jacques Ledoux Professor of Film Studies and Hilldale Professor of Humanities at the University of Wisconsin-Madison. He has written several books on film theory, aesthetics and critical analysis, most recently *Planet Hong Kong: Popular Cinema and the Art of Entertainment* (Harvard University Press, 2000). He is at work on a book-length study of staging in cinema.

Ben Brewster is Assistant Director at the Center for Film and Theatre Research at the University of Wisconsin-Madison. He is co-author, with Lea Jacobs, of *Theatre to Cinema: Stage Pictorialism and the Early Feature Film* (Oxford University Press, 1997).

Joseph Garncarz, Privatdozent in Film Studies at the University of Cologne in Germany, has published numerous articles on German film history in English, American and German journals and edited collections. He is the author of *Filmfassungen* and a forthcoming book on the emergence of cinema in Germany.

Frank Gray is Director of the South East Film & Video Archive and a Principal Lecturer in Art & Media History at the University of Brighton, England. His research and his publications are devoted in general to late Victorian and Edwardian film culture and in particular to the filmmakers G. A. Smith and James Williamson.

Tom Gunning is Edwin A. and Betty L. Bergman Distinguished Service Professor in the Art History Department and the Cinema and Media Committee at the University of Chicago. Author of *D. W. Griffith and the Origins of American Narrative Film* (University of Illinois Press, 1991), and *The Films of Fritz Lang: Allegories of Modernity and Vision* (BFI, 2000), he has written numerous essays on early and international silent cinema, and on American cinema, including Hollywood genres and directors as well as the Avant Garde film. He has lectured around the world and his works have been published in a dozen different languages.

Sumiko Higashi is Professor Emerita in the Department of History at SUNY Brockport. She is the author of *Cecil B. DeMille and American Culture: The Silent Era* and numerous works on American film history, especially the silent period; women in film and television; and film as historical representation.

Charles J. Maland is a Lindsay Young Professor of American Studies and Cinema Studies at the University of Tennessee. He is the author of, among others, *Frank Capra* and *Chaplin and American Culture: The Evolution of a Star Image*. The latter book won the Theater Library Association Award for excellence in writing about film, television or radio.

Charles Musser is Professor of American Studies and Film Studies at Yale University where he co-chairs the Film Studies Program. His film *Before the Nickelodeon: The Early Cinema of Edwin S. Porter* (1982), now available on DVD, premiered at the New York Film Festival, then at the London, Berlin, Sydney and New Delhi film festivals. Carrie Rickey of the *Village Voice* called it one of the year's best documentaries. His history *The Emergence of Cinema: The American Screen to 1907* (1990) was awarded the Jay Leyda Prize, the Katherine Kovacs Prize for outstanding book on Film and Television as well as the Theater Library Book Award. His other books on early cinema include *High-Class Moving Pictures: Lyman H. Howe and the Forgotten Era of Traveling Exhibition, 1880–1920* (with Carol Nelson, 1991) and *Thomas A. Edison and His Kinetographic Motion Pictures* (1995).

Roberta E. Pearson is Reader in Media and Cultural Studies at Cardiff University. With William Uricchio, she is the author of *Reframing Culture: The Case of the Vitagraph Quality Films* (Princeton University Press, 1993). She is also the author of *Eloquent Gestures: The Transformation of Performance Style in the Griffith Biograph Films* (University of California Press, 1992).

Ben Singer is an Associate Professor in the Department of Communication Arts, University of Wisconsin-Madison. His book *Melodrama and Modernity: Early Sensational Cinema and its Contexts* was published by Columbia University Press in 2001.

Shelley Stamp is the author of *Movie-Struck Girls: Women and Motion Picture Culture after the Nickelodeon*, a Choice Outstanding Academic Book, and co-editor of two anthologies, *American Cinema's Transitional Era: Audiences, Institutions, Practices* (with Charlie Keil) and *Women and the Silent Screen: Cultural and Historical Practices* (with Amelie Hastie). She is Associate Professor of Film & Digital Media at the University of California, Santa Cruz where she won the Excellence in Teaching Award.

Gaylyn Studlar is Rudolf Arnheim Collegiate Professor of Film Studies at the University of Michigan, Ann Arbor, where she has directed the Program in Film and Video Studies since 1995. She is the author and co-editor of several books, including most recently, *Titanic: Anatomy of a Blockbuster* (1999), co-edited with Kevin Sandler, and *John Ford made Westerns* (2001), co-edited with Matthew Bernstein. She is currently working on a history of classical Hollywood's representation of female transition.

Kristin Thompson is an Honorary Fellow at the University of Wisconsin-Madison. Her books include *Exporting Entertainment: America in the World Film Market 1907–1934* (British Film Institute, 1985), *Breaking the Glass Armor: Neoformalist Film Analysis* (Princeton University Press, 1988), *Storytelling in the New Hollywood: Understanding Classical Narrative Technique* (Harvard University Press, 1999) and *Storytelling in Film and Television* (Harvard University

Press, 2003). She is co-author, with David Bordwell and Janet Staiger, of *The Classical Hollywood Cinema: Film Style and Mode of Production to 1960* (Columbia University Press, 1985).

Yuri Tsivian has a PhD in film studies from the Institute of Theatre, Music and Cinema, Leningrad, 1984. His recent books are: *Silent Witnesses: Russian Films, 1908–1919* (BFI, 1989), *Istoricheskaja recepcija kino* (Zinatne, 1991), translated as *Early Cinema in Russia and its Cultural Reception* (Routledge 1994; paperback edition published in 1998 by Chicago University Press), and, in collaboration with Yuri Lotman, *Dialogues with the Screen* (Tallinn, 1994). His most recent work includes *Ivan the Terrible* (BFI, 2002) and the CD-ROM *Immaterial Bodies: Cultural Anatomy of Early Russian Films* (University of Southern California, 2000). He is professor of film in the Art History Department of the University of Chicago.

William Uricchio is Professor of Comparative Media Studies at MIT in the US and professor of Comparative Media History at Utrecht University in the Netherlands. He has held visiting professorships at Stockholm University, the Freie Universität Berlin, and Philips Universität Marburg and he currently leads a five-year cultural identity project within the European Science Foundation's 'Changing Media Changing Europe' initiative. His broader research considers the transformation of media technologies into media practices, in particular, their role in (re-) constructing representation, knowledge and publics. A Fulbright and Humboldt research fellow, Uricchio has written extensively on both 'old' and 'new' media, popular cultures and their audiences.

Ruth Vasey has written extensively about the American cinema over the last fifteen years. Her book, *The World According to Hollywood 1918–1939*, was awarded the Kraszna-Krausz Moving Picture Book Award for Culture and History in 1997. She lives in Adelaide, South Australia, with her husband, film scholar Richard Maltby, and their son Ben, and she teaches at Flinders University.

Linda Williams is Professor and Director of the Film Studies Program at the University of California at Berkeley. Her books include *Figures of Desire: A Theory and Analysis of Surrealist Film* (University of California Press, 1981), *Hard Core: Power, Pleasure and the Frenzy of the Visible* (University of California Press, 1989, second edition 1999), and *Playing the Race Card: Melodramas of Black and White, from Uncle Tom to O. J. Simpson* (University of Princeton Press, 2001). She is also editor of *Viewing Positions: Ways of Seeing Film* (Rutgers University Press, 1993), and co-editor of *Reinventing Film Studies* (Arnold, 2000).

Editors

Lee Grieveson is Lecturer in Cinema Studies at King's College, University of London. He has taught silent cinema at undergraduate and graduate levels and is author of *Policing Cinema: Movies and Censorship in Early Twentieth Century America* (University of California Press, 2004) and co-editor of *Mob Culture: Essays on the American Gangster Film* (Rutgers University Press, forthcoming) and *Inventing Film Studies* (Duke University Press, forthcoming). His essay 'Fighting Films: Race, Morality, and the Governing of Cinema, 1912–1915' won the Society for Cinema Studies Katherine Singer Kovacs award for outstanding essay in English language media studies.

Peter Krämer teaches Film Studies at the University of East Anglia (UK). He has published essays on American film and media history, and on the relationship between Hollywood and Europe, in *Screen*, *The Velvet Light Trap*, *Theatre History Studies*, the *Historical Journal of Film, Radio and Television*, *History Today*, *Film Studies*, *Scope* and numerous edited collections. Together with Alan Lovell, he co-edited *Screen Acting* (Routledge, 1999). He has also co-authored a children's book entitled *American Film: An A–Z Guide* (Franklin Watts, 2003).

Acknowledgements

We would like to thank Rebecca Barden at Routledge for her support and incredible patience. Likewise, Kate Ahl, Helen Faulkner and Donna Gregory have been helpful and wonderfully efficient. Thanks also to the authors collected here, who have helped considerably with the production of this book and whose work on silent cinema has inspired us and kept us interested in this project during the time it has taken to complete it. We are grateful to have had the chance to work with them. Lee Grieveson would like to thank Vanessa Martin and Lauren and Riley Martin-Grieveson for their good humour and patience, and Robin Abrahams for expert computer support at a crucial moment. Peter Krämer would like to thank Thomas Elsaesser for introducing him to the study of early cinema. He also wishes to acknowledge the support he received from the Arts and Humanities Research Board.

Most of the chapters in this book have previously been published (for details see below). We indicate in the text where we have edited them. Some chapters have been revised by their authors.

Abel, Richard, *The Ciné Goes to Town: French Cinema, 1896–1914* (Berkeley: University of California Press, 1998), 59–101. Copyright © 1994 The Regents of the University of California. Reprinted by permission of the University of California Press.

Abel, Richard, *The Red Rooster Scare: Making Cinema American, 1900–1910* (Berkeley: University of California Press, 1999), 48–80. Copyright © 1999 The Regents of the University of California. Reprinted by permission of the University of California Press.

Bordwell, David, *The Cinema of Eisenstein* (Cambridge, Mass.: Harvard University Press, 1993), 61–78. Copyright © 1993 by the President and Fellows of Harvard College. Reprinted by permission of Harvard University Press.

Brewster, Ben, 'Traffic in Souls: An Experiment in Feature-Length Narrative Construction,' *Cinema Journal*, vol. 31, no. 1 (1991), 41–54. Copyright © 1991 by the University of Texas Press. All rights reserved.

Grieveson, Lee, 'Fighting Films: Race, Morality, and the Governing of Cinema, 1912–1915,' *Cinema Journal*, vol. 38, no. 1 (Fall 1998), 40–72. Copyright © 1998 by the University of Texas Press. All rights reserved.

Gunning, Tom, '"Now You See It, Now You Don't": The Temporality of the Cinema of Attractions,' *The Velvet Light Trap*, no. 32 (1993), 3–12. Copyright © 1993 by the University of Texas Press. All rights reserved.

Gunning, Tom, 'From the Opium Den to the Theatre of Morality: Moral Discourse and the Film Process in Early American Cinema,' *Art and Text*, no. 30 (1988), 30–40. Reprinted with permission of the author and *Art and Text*.

Higashi, Sumiko, *Cecil B. DeMille and American Culture: The Silent Era* (Berkeley: University of California Press, 1994), 142–178. Copyright © 1994 The Regents of the University of California. Reprinted with permission of the University of California Press.

Krämer, Peter, 'The Making of a Comic Star: Buster Keaton and *The Saphead*,' in Henry Jenkins and Kristine Brunovska Karnick (eds), *Classical Hollywood Comedy* (New York: Routledge, 1995), 190–210. Reprinted by permission of Routledge.

Maland, Charles J., *Chaplin and American Culture: The Evolution of a Star Image* (Princeton: Princeton University Press, 1989), 1–24. Copyright © 1989 by Princeton University Press. Reprinted by permission of Princeton University Press.

Musser, Charles, 'Before the Rapid Firing Kinetograph: Edison Film Production, Representation and Exploitation in the 1890s,' from Charles Musser, *Edison Motion Pictures, 1890–1906: An Annotated Filmography* (Washington: Smithsonian Institution Press, 1997), 19–50. Copyright © 1997 by Charles Musser and Le Giornate del Cinema Muto. Used by permission of the author and publisher.

Musser, Charles, *Before the Nickelodeon: Edwin S. Porter and the Edison Manufacturing Company* (Berkeley: University of California Press, 1991), 235–290. Copyright © 1991 The Regents of the University of California Press. Reprinted by permission of University of California Press.

Pearson, Roberta E., and Uricchio, William, 'How Many Times Shall Caesar Bleed in Sport: Shakespeare and the Cultural Debate About Motion Pictures,' *Screen*, vol. 31, no. 3 (Autumn 1990), 243–262. Reprinted by permission of Oxford University Press.

Singer, Ben, 'Manhattan Nickelodeons: New Data on Audiences and Exhibitors,' *Cinema Journal*, vol. 34, no. 3 (Spring 1995), 5–35. Copyright © 1995 by the University of Texas Press. All rights reserved.

Stamp, Shelley, *Movie-Struck Girls: Women and Motion Picture Culture After the Nickelodeon* (Princeton: Princeton University Press, 2000), 102–153. Copyright © 2000 by Princeton University Press. Reprinted by permission of Princeton University Press.

Studlar, Gaylyn, *This Mad Masquerade: Stardom and Masculinity in the Jazz Age* (New York: Columbia University Press, 1996), 150–198. Copyright © 1996 Columbia University Press. Reprinted by permission of the publisher.

Thompson, Kristin, 'The International Exploration of Cinematic Expressivity,' in Karel Dibbets and Bert Hogenkamp (eds), *Film and the First World War* (Amsterdam: Amsterdam University Press, 1995), 65–85. Reprinted by permission of the publisher.

Thompson, Kristin, 'Early Alternatives to the Hollywood Mode of Production: Implications for Europe's Avant-Garde,' *Film History*, vol. 5, no. 4 (December 1993), 386–404. Reprinted by permission of John Libbey publishers.

Tsivian, Yuri, 'Early Russian Cinema: Some Observations,' in Richard Taylor and Ian Christie (eds), *Inside the Film Factory: New Approaches to Russian and Soviet Cinema* (London: Routledge, 1991), 7–30. Reprinted by permission of author and publisher.

Vasey, Ruth, *The World According to Hollywood, 1919–1939* (Exeter: University of Exeter Press, 1997), 29–62. Reprinted with permission of the publisher.

Williams, Linda, *Playing the Race Card: Melodramas of Black and White from Uncle Tom to O. J. Simpson,* (Princeton: Princeton University Press, 2001), 96–128. Copyright © 2002 by Princeton University Press. Reprinted by permission of Princeton University Press.

LEE GRIEVESON AND PETER KRÄMER

INTRODUCTION

'LAST NIGHT I WAS IN THE KINGDOM OF SHADOWS', Russian novelist Maxim Gorky wrote in July 1896, reflecting on the experience of seeing for the first time a demonstration of projected moving pictures. 'If you only knew how strange it is to be there', he told his readers, to witness 'not life but its shadow . . . not motion but its soundless spectre', an experience that was for Gorky 'an intimation of life in the future'.[1] Like Gorky, other audiences and commentators at the inception of projected moving pictures were conscious of the novelty and strangeness both of film technology and of the films themselves. One of the prevalent responses was astonishment at the realism of film, at its vivid images of what the British *Strand Magazine* described as 'astounding actuality and life' provided by machines with names that frequently drew attention to their ability to represent life in compelling detail.[2] *Vitascope*, *Biograph* and *Animatograph* exhibitions were, then, greeted with a response that registered fascination with the technology and its products, a response that insistently commented on the strangeness of film as either a hyper-realistic medium or, for Gorky and others, a shadowy, unrealistic space of fantasy and projection of 'impalpable phantoms'.[3]

Likewise, our response, across the divide now of two centuries, to the surviving images that still flicker on various kinds of screens can frequently be a perplexed one, for these images seem distant but strangely present and modern, lifelike and recognizable yet also ghostly and fantastic, confusing and perhaps frustrating as well as fascinating and compelling – and worthy, we think, of the various kinds of explication pursued by the scholars gathered together in this book. Why have these scholars been so interested in silent cinema? To begin with, the very strangeness of early films demands an explanation, requiring us to situate them in the historical context – so different from the present – in which they emerged. Second, the length, style and subject matter of early films, their exhibition, audiences and social function changed with great speed from the 1890s to the 1920s, the period covered in this book, and such rapid and dramatic change provides rich material for historians to study and raises many questions for historians to answer. Third, the cinema as it developed during this time became – and continues to be – extremely important to many people and in many ways (influencing, for example, how people see themselves and others). Finally, in understanding past media developments such as this one we might be better positioned to understand and perhaps influence the development of new media taking place today and those that will happen in the future.

Before offering a brief overview of major developments in silent cinema which we will explore in depth in the remainder of this book, let us linger briefly on that moment in the late nineteenth century when collective audiences came into contact with the projection of photographic moving images for the first time. What was this new invention? Where did audiences watch moving pictures? What did they see?

International efforts to present ever more lifelike images on big screens gathered pace in the nineteenth century, linked on the one hand to scientific endeavours and on the other to a thriving popular screen entertainment culture exemplified by magic lantern shows.[4] Late in the nineteenth century the twin imperatives of science and entertainment led to the projection of photographic moving images. The initial exploration of film technology by assistants working for and with Thomas Edison from 1888 resulted in a camera recording photographic images in quick succession, the so-called *Kinetograph*, and a device called *Kinetoscope* which allowed individuals to watch films through a peephole. Arcades filled with kinetoscopes spread rapidly in large and small cities throughout 1894 and 1895, charging people for the pleasure of peeping at moving pictures.[5] Edison films, as Charles Musser shows in Chapter 1, were brief scenes filmed inside a purpose built studio, often featuring performers from popular variety theatre.

Louis and Auguste Lumière, amongst others in Europe and the US, developed what they called the *Cinématographe* throughout 1894 and 1895, a machine that allowed the *projection* of photographic moving images on a screen to bigger audiences and hence the development of what later came to be called *cinema*, defined loosely as film projection to paying audiences.[6] Initially, though, Lumière exhibitions were for free as they took place at relatively high-brow photographic congresses and conferences of learned societies from March 1895, including a public demonstration for the magazine *La Revue Générales des Sciences*.[7] Other shows featuring film technology were seen at large-scale international expositions or at high-brow institutions like the Brooklyn Institute of Arts and Sciences.[8] Motion picture technology was presented here as a scientific development. However, this was a popular science which presented technological developments like the X-ray machine or the telephone as technological wonders and as entertaining spectacle. Lumière films (and indeed many of the films made up until about 1903) tended accordingly to be brief records of actual events or real-life scenes, so called *actualities*, a form aided also by the relative lightness of the camera developed by the Lumières.

Visual entertainment was tied here to the re-presentation of real life, evident for example in *L'Arrivé d'un Train en Gare de la Ciotat* (*Train Arriving at a Station*, Lumière, 1895), the countless travel films produced by Lumière operators, or in the recording of important participants at a photographic congress in Lyon, France, cleverly presented to flatter the congress members in the film *Arrivée des Congressistes á Neuville-sur-Saone* (*Arrival of Congress Members at Neuville-sur-Saone*, Lumière, 1895). Lumière exhibitions thus initially presented a different kind of entertainment than that associated with the kinetoscope, suggesting a possible public role and social function for film which went beyond straightforward entertainment. Here cinema could be imagined as providing educational and/or scientific displays in non-theatrical surroundings.

Later though, in December 1895, the Lumière brothers arranged a public commercial screening of the cinématographe at the Grande Café on the Boulevard des Capucines in Paris.[9] In the midst of several actualities was the comedy *Le Jardinier et le Petit Espiegle* (*The Gardener and the Bad Boy*, Lumière, 1895), one of the first films to present a minimal, yet complete story in showing a young boy stepping on the hose being used by a gardener who, surprised to find that the flow of water has stopped, unwisely looks down the hose only for the boy to lift his foot and to douse the gardener. The gardener catches the boy and spanks him. Similar to the actualities in many respects – it is a brief, one-shot film with no camera movement, frontally and centrally staged – the film is, though, a staged fiction film, creating an amusing incident rather than representing real life, and doing so in the form of a story which was derived from other media.[10]

Like the Lumière exhibition in a café in Paris, other exhibitions of moving picture technology were increasingly located in commercial, theatrical contexts. Vitascope shows in the US from April 1896 took place principally in variety theatres which presented a number of separate and unrelated acts (singers, comic sketches, one-act dramas, and so on) to audiences seeking amusement and excitement. Likewise, the cinématographe premiered in London in April 1896 at a variety theatre and at a similar theatre in New York City in June 1896, where it was advertised as 'the greatest fashionable *and* scientific fad of London, Paris, Vienna, Berlin and the entire continent'.[11] Variety theatres, together with travelling shows, became the dominant exhibition context for early films in the US, the UK and other European countries, consistent with the growing sense that the short-term future of moving pictures was less that of a scientific device and more that of a popular entertainment medium.

Gorky had in fact suggested as much when he responded to the Lumière films in July 1896. He was viewing them in a morally dubious café that seemingly doubled as a brothel run by entrepreneur Charles Aumont as part of the All Russia Nizhi-Novorod Fair. Gorky acknowledged that the Cinématographe could be 'applied to the general ends of science' but was also conscious that this was not 'to be found at Aumont's where vice alone is being encouraged and popularized'.[12] Vice was the future of this invention, Gorky anxiously predicted – assuming it had a future at all, of course, a fact that many doubted. Louis Lumière himself predicted, in 1896, that film was an invention 'without a future' and the following year the Lumière family withdrew from exhibition altogether and began to scale down film production. Auguste Lumière would devote much of the rest of his life to science and medicine, turning his back on the now corrupted cinema.[13]

Let's fast forward some thirty years beyond the initial exhibition of projected moving pictures and Louis Lumière's gloomy prognosis, to another response to the exhibition of films at one of the estimated 20,500 screens in the US in the mid-1920s that were attended by some 60 million people a week in 1927 and that made the film industry one of the country's fifty largest industries.[14] Here is the by then quite familiar scene of an opening night for a new feature at the Rivoli Theatre in New York City, one of the ornate movie palaces built in the teens and twenties. 'Gloria Swanson's most ambitious screen achievement, the film version of *Madame Sans Gene*, was presented last night at the Rivoli theatre, and its presence caused a remarkable demonstration', the *New York Times* reported on 18 April 1925. 'Long before the hour fixed for the opening of the film, the streets in the neighbourhood were all but blocked by a crowd of literally thousands of the curious' eager for a view of Swanson, who was attending the premiere with her new French husband.[15] Crowds inside the theatre were treated to an orchestral rendition of the Marseillaise before the film began, part of the stage entertainment and balanced programme common to movie palaces. Exhibitions at the Rivoli usually included an overture, a newsreel, a short comedy film, a song or other live act, and an organ solo alongside the main feature.[16]

Madame Sans Gene itself was produced by Famous Players-Lasky in Hollywood, directed by a Frenchman, Léonce Perret, and featured a mixture of American and French performers.

It told a story about the French revolution and Napoléon. *New York Times* reporter Mordaunt Hall observed that 'ghosts of the Napoleonic days seemed to come to life and tread once more the floors, staircases and lawns of the Chateaux of Fontainebleau and Compeigne' in the film.[17] Like Gorky's unsettled response to the moving shadows provided by the Lumière films at Aumont's café, Hall regarded the film he saw as in some way 'ghostlike' – but for him these ghosts were evidence of the realism and believability of the film, of its ability to revive the (European) past. These 1920s ghosts do not represent a challenge or potential threat like their 1890s predecessors, but instead are a measure of the cinema's power to entertain people by transporting them into another world.

A lot had changed, then, between 1895 and 1925. To begin with, in 1925 audiences no longer got excited about the technology that brought pictures to life on the screen; indeed they were no longer aware of it (although this would change again when synchronized sound was successfully marketed the following year). The show still consisted of a range of entertainments, as it had done in the variety theatre, but now film was not simply one item among many, but the main attraction, heading the bill. Clearly the films being watched in the mid-1920s were considerably different from those watched by astonished audiences in the mid-1890s. Instead of lasting a minute or so like the earliest movies, feature films now constituted an evening's entertainment. Rather than presenting brief snippets of mainly real-life scenes, feature films were primarily telling fictional stories designed to engage audiences in the on-going action. The range of different forms of scientific, educational, informative, spectacular and entertaining displays in the 1890s had been narrowed down to a focus in the main on entertaining stories. To be sure, other kinds of entertainment like, for example, visual spectacle or the pleasure of seeing foreign lands were frequently still present as part of the experience of cinema, whether in a feature film like *Madame Sans Gene* or in a newsreel or travelogue, but these were now overshadowed by the feature film's capacity to absorb audiences in its story.

Visual displays, as for example in the sumptuous scenes revealing the splendour of the palaces, costumes, staircases and lawns of *Madame Sans Gene* – loaned to the production company by the French authorities – were subordinated to the story, to narrative suspense and to the creation of a consistent fictional world. Important here were complex forms of characterization absent from the earliest films. We know more, for example, about the motivations of the central characters in *Madame Sans Gene* than we do about those of the gardener or the bad boy in *Le Jardinier et le Petit Espiegle*. Linked to this was the presence of film stars like Gloria Swanson or, as we shall see in later chapters, Rudolph Valentino, Charlie Chaplin and Buster Keaton, who played the main characters in films and attracted spectators to see their films while also becoming the subject of much publicity and speculation about their off-screen lives.

Film stars played an important role in attracting audiences for the large industry that had grown up around moving pictures worldwide by 1925, an industry that produced ever more expensive films in vast studio complexes and exhibited them in movie palaces like the Rivoli (a total of 967 cinemas, for example, were constructed in the United States in 1926; over 4200 cinemas existed in Germany in 1926).[18] While large film industries grew in the US and a number of European countries, the American film industry – known as Hollywood – was, after the First World War, more successful than any other in exporting films worldwide. In sharp contrast with the enormous impact made by American exhibitions of the cinématographe in the mid-1890s, by the mid-1920s the American market was effectively closed to foreign competition. European subject matter and creative personnel continued to be important in American cinema – as *Madame Sans Gene* shows – but European films did not circulate freely.

L'Arrivé d'un Train en Gare de la Ciotat watched by conference delegates in March 1895, *Le Jardinier et le Petit Espiegle* watched in a café in 1895 or a bar beneath a brothel in 1896 and *Madame Sans Gene* shown at a movie palace in 1925 – here we can see in stark outline some of the dramatic developments of the first 30 years of cinema history, transformations that make this one of the most exciting periods of cinema history. Like other scholars, we think that by the 1920s many – if not most – of the important decisions about what cinema would be, what films would be like, where they would be seen and how they would be produced and experienced, had been made and that those important decisions have a longevity which stretches to the present day and beyond.[19] In this book, then, we are going to examine the important transformations taking place during the first three decades of cinema, asking a fundamental question: Why did cinema take the shape it did? The essays collected here and our introductions to the various sections of this book will offer wide-ranging and complex, but by no means exhaustive answers to this question.

The following chapters avoid the easy explanations that have often been offered in the past. One way of explaining why cinema took the shape it did is to say that the changes it underwent during the silent period were inevitable. A number of historians, writing in the immediate aftermath of the transformations we want to describe and explain in this book, suggested this. Film, they argued, was inherently a narrative medium and its early history was merely a matter of prescient filmmakers taking the technology and finding the right way to use it for telling stories able to engage spectators.[20] Like many other film historians writing more recently, we do not think this *teleological* account (which assumes an inherent goal, or telos, for historical developments) is correct for it fails on at least two important counts. First, it does not acknowledge that early filmmakers, exhibitors and audiences understood cinema in ways which differed radically from the understanding developed in later periods; ideas about cinema's social role, its mode of exhibition, and audiences' responses to films were distinctive in this early period. Labelling or castigating early cinema as 'primitive' because it did not tell stories the way we now expect is wrong because it did not aim to do so. We may as well castigate tea for not being like coffee. Second, a teleological explanation fails to account for the complex factors that shaped cinema. Economic, technological, cultural and ideological forces impinged on the way cinema developed, and it is the historian's task to describe these forces and their interaction with each other as precisely as possible, and thus to explain how modern cinema came about.

This book, then, is based on the assumption that it is necessary to engage with seemingly strange forms of filmmaking on their own terms, placing them in the contexts in which they were made, exhibited, and understood, and that the ultimate shape cinema took was not inevitable but contingent, a result of diverse pressures. Underlying this position is a belief that the best film historiography is conscious of the intricate play of forces at work in cultural events and tries to describe the generative mechanisms that produce observable events.[21] Consequently, much of the work that follows seeks to situate films and film historical developments in relation to broader social and political contexts. These include, to take just two examples, transformations in the roles of women (and their impact on female spectatorship) and the Russian Revolution (and its impact on film form and content in the Soviet Union) addressed, respectively, by Shelley Stamp, Gaylyn Studlar, Sumiko Higashi and David Bordwell.

Linked together, the section introductions and the essays in this book tell a story about the emergence and development of cinema, primarily in the US yet with frequent references to Europe, up until the beginning of the sound era in the late 1920s. This story covers key textual and institutional transformations and relates them to the contexts in which films were made and seen. Why end the book with the introduction of synchronized sound in 1927? On the one hand, this time frame allows us to include a consideration of the establishment of a stable industrial configuration in the US in the early 1920s, and of important developments within European cinemas in the mid-1920s. On the other hand, the coming of sound marks a major shift in the experience of cinema-going. Most cinemas throughout the so-called silent period were not silent and movies were usually accompanied by music, provided in the movie palaces by large orchestras and in other theatres by smaller bands or individual pianists.[22] Audiences in fact often stated that they chose which cinema to visit on the basis of the music played.[23] The innovation of synchronized sound meant that the musical accompaniment present in the theatre largely disappeared; from then on, the films on the screen were no longer mediated through live performance in the auditorium. Even so, this technological change did not cause a fundamental shift in the basic identity of cinema, which by then had been given a stable textual and institutional shape.

Why focus principally on America? Lumière technology and films were, as we have seen, important to the emergence of cinema and, slightly later, films produced in France by the Pathé company and others were crucial to the development of cinema in the US, as Richard Abel shows in Chapter 6. Likewise, the example of *Madame Sans Gene* shows the interaction between European personnel and subject matter, on the one hand, and Hollywood on the other. Throughout the 1910s and 1920s, however, European films were marginalized from the mainstream of American film exhibition, and national traditions and strategies of differentiation from American production informed the development of European cinemas. We will pay considerable attention in this book to European developments and the interactions between Europe and the US, as we have in this introduction. Even so, the principal thread of our narrative is the development of American cinema. This is due to practical concerns – it is crucial that we narrow our focus down to a manageable level – but there are also intellectual reasons. Developments in America were to some extent representative of general developments in Western filmmaking; what happened in the US also happened – and for similar reasons – in other countries. At the same time, US developments no doubt influenced international filmmaking due to Hollywood's pre-eminent role in exporting films from the 1910s onwards. Consequently this book does not include a substantive engagement with many European cinemas or with important cinemas outside the West. However, we have compiled references to the growing literature on silent cinema all around the world in our bibliography, which may serve as a starting point for further investigations. We hope that looking closely at the factors shaping the development of American cinema will provide something of a model for the way other cinemas could be studied – but that model will need to be tested and revised in relation to particular cases.[24]

A few final words here about the organization of this book and the sections and chapters that follow. Each section has its own introduction, sketching in historical contexts and referencing the relevant scholarly work so as to situate the chapters that follow. In doing so, we have drawn on our own research and on the research of other scholars. The *Prologue* is concerned with the development of moving image technologies and film production in the early

1890s, focusing on the kinetograph and kinetoscope in the US. Leading on from this, we shift our attention to the international development of film projection from the mid-1890s onwards in the section *Film Projection and Variety Shows*. This section traces the shift from a technology based industry to the emergence of an entertainment based industry and maps out the various exhibition contexts in which films were shown until the early 1900s as well as the form and content of the films themselves, both in the US and in Europe. We take up this story in the following section, entitled *Storytelling and the Nickelodeon*. Here we cover the years 1903–08, which saw the increasing importance of story films and the rise of 'nickelodeons' – cheap, small theatres in the US that showed predominantly moving pictures and can be seen as the beginnings of modern cinema. This section focusses again on the US, yet takes into account the crucial role played by French films in the success of motion pictures in America. Leading on from this, the section *Cinema and Reform* considers how the rise of the nickelodeon brought forth a series of official interventions into cinema in the US in the period 1907–15 and, in turn, how these interventions had important effects on the kinds of films being produced and on the definition of the public role of cinema.

Feature Films and Cinema Programmes addresses key developments in film form, production and exhibition in the 1910s. These include the rise of multiple-reel features – an important departure from the earlier one-reel standard – and of movie palaces, which soon offered a balanced programme combining feature films with shorts, amongst which serials and slapstick comedies were the most prominent genres. We focus mainly on the US but again reference international developments, especially in the increasing complexity and expressivity of filmic storytelling. The section *Classical Hollywood Cinema* takes up these questions of film form, industrial organization and social context, tracing out the establishment of the relatively stable formal and industrial system which emerged from the developments of the 1910s and which, within its stable framework, was responsive to social and cultural transformations in the surrounding society. Our focus here is on the years 1917–27 and again closely on America. However, the section also explores how Hollywood's commercial strategies and self-regulatory procedures took account of the world market, especially Europe. Finally, *European Cinemas* deals with developments in three countries between the mid-1910s and the late 1920s. Rather than trying to provide a wide-ranging overview as the other sections do, here we concentrate more narrowly on specific issues. These include differences in the mode of production between the French, German and Russian film industries on the one hand, and Hollywood on the other; the characteristics of films made in Russia before and after the Russian Revolution, and their relationship to the country's cultural traditions; and the specificity of German film culture in the 1920s.

A number of themes are foregrounded across the sections of this book. These include: the role of nationalism and nationally specific cultural traditions; questions of changing gender roles, particularly in relation to women and shifting configurations of the public sphere; the importance of ethnicity and race, notably in debates about cinema and the social order; and the influence of class on the makers and consumers of moving pictures. Thus, in addition to tracing the emergence and development of cinema as a powerful mass medium, the following chapters also offer insights into the political, social and cultural transformations which shaped the twentieth century.

Notes

1　I. M. Pacatus (pseudonym for Maxim Gorky), *Nizhegorodski Listok* (4 July 1896), translated in Jay Leyda, *Kino: A History of the Russian and Soviet Film* (London: George Allen and Unwin, 1960), 407; 'Gorky on the Films, 1896', trans. Leonard Mins, in Herbert Kline (ed.), *New Theater and Film: 1934 to 1937, An Anthology* (San Diego: Harcourt Brace Jovanovich, 1985), 228. An insightful discussion of Gorky's response and the response of others in Russia can be found in Yuri Tsivian, *Early Cinema in Russia and its Cultural Reception*, trans. Alan Bodger (London: Routledge, 1994), 5–7.

2　'The Prince's Derby: Shown by Lightning Photography', *The Strand Magazine*, vol. 12 (1896), 140.

3　Tom Gunning, ' "Animated Pictures," Tales of Cinema's Forgotten Future', *Michigan Quarterly Review*, vol. 34, no. 4 (Fall 1995), 468.

4　Late nineteenth century scientific experiments with photography and the reproduction of movement are discussed in Charles Musser, *The Emergence of Cinema: The American Screen to 1907* (Berkeley: University of California Press, 1990), 48–54; and Marta Braun, *Picturing Time: The Work of Etienne-Jules Marey* (Chicago: University of Chicago Press, 1992). On the broad parameters of what Musser calls 'screen practice' in the nineteenth century, see, for example, Musser, *The Emergence of Cinema*, 15–48; and Deac Rossel, 'Double Think: The Cinema and Magic Lantern Culture', in John Fullerton (ed.), *Celebrating 1895: The Centenary of Cinema* (London: John Libbey, 1998); Laurent Mannoni, *The Great Art of Light and Shadow: Archaeology of the Cinema*, translated and edited by Richard Crangle (Exeter: University of Exeter Press, 2000).

5　Musser, *The Emergence of Cinema*, 55–90; David Nasaw, *Going Out: The Rise and Fall of Public Amusements* (Cambridge, Mass.: Harvard University Press, 1999), 130–4.

6　Various nations can (and have) laid claim to the invention of moving picture technology but the cinema has no precise originating moment and owes its birth to no particular country or individual. Important developments by Max Skladanowsky in Germany or William Friese-Green in the UK, for example, could equally be the focus here. Likewise, developments in celluloid technology were important, as was the application of precision engineering to projector design by people working in various countries. See Deac Rossell, *Living Pictures: The Origins of the Movies* (Albany: State University of New York, 1998).

7　Alan Williams, *Republic of Images: A History of French Filmmaking* (Cambridge, Mass.: Harvard University Press, 1992), 24–5.

8　Charles Musser with Carol Nelson, *High-Class Moving Pictures: Lyman H. Howe and the Forgotten Era of Travelling Exhibition, 1880–1920* (Princeton, NJ: Princeton University Press, 1991).

9　Williams, *Republic of Images*, 26–30.

10　See Williams, *Republic of Images*, 27, 408; and Peter Krämer, 'Bad Boy: Notes on a Popular Figure in American Cinema, Culture and Society, 1895–1905', in Fullerton (ed.), *Celebrating 1895*.

11　*New York World* (28 June 1896), 14 (emphasis added); *Black and White* (4 April 1896), 441–2; *New York Dramatic Mirror* (4 July 1896), 17; Robert C. Allen, *Vaudeville and Film, 1895–1915: A Study in Media Interaction* (New York: Arno, 1977), 81–109; Musser, *The Emergence of Cinema*, 135–45.

12　Gorky, *Nizhegorodski Listok* (4 July 1896), in Leyda, *Kino*, 409.

13　Georges Sadoul, *Lumière et Méliès* (Paris: Editions Pierre Lherminier, 1985), cited in Lisa Cartwright, *Screening the Body: Tracing Medicine's Visual Culture* (Minneapolis: University of Minnesota Press, 1995), 1–3.

14　Richard Koszarski, *An Evening's Entertainment: The Age of the Silent Feature Picture, 1915–1928* (Berkeley: University of California Press, 1990), 9, 26; Robert C. Allen and Douglas Gomery, *Film History: Theory and Practice* (New York: McGraw-Hill, 1985), 38.

15　*New York Times* (18 April 1925), 19:1.

16　Koszarski, *An Evening's Entertainment*, 34–56.

17　*New York Times* (18 April 1925), 19:1.

18　Koszarski, *An Evening's Entertainment*, 17; Joseph Garncarz, 'Exhibition', in Thomas Elsaesser with Michael Wedel (ed.), *The BFI Companion to German Cinema* (London: British Film Institute, 1999), 80; the Rivoli was built in 1917.

19　See here in particular David Bordwell, Janet Staiger and Kristin Thompson, *The Classical Hollywood Cinema: Film Style and Mode of Production to 1960* (London: Routledge, 1985).

20　See, for example, Robert Grau, *Theatre of Science* (New York: Broadway Publishing Co., 1914); Terry Ramsaye, *A Million and One Nights* (New York: Simon and Schuster, 1926); and the discussion of these historians in Allen and Gomery, *Film History*, 51–60.

21 Allen and Gomery, *Film History*, in particular 104–5, 213–15.
22 On the diversity of sound practices in early cinema, see Richard Abel and Rick Altman (eds), *The Sounds of Early Cinema* (Bloomington: Indiana University Press, 2001).
23 Koszarski, *An Evening's Entertainment*, 31.
24 For exemplary accounts of how to conceptualize the specificity of a country's cinema, see Richard Abel 'Booming the Film Business: the Historical Specificity of Early French Cinema', *French Cultural Studies*, vol. 1, no. 1 (1990); and Joseph Garncarz, 'Art and Industry: German Cinema in the 1920s', in this volume.

Prologue

INTRODUCTION

LATE IN 1888 THE WELL KNOWN INVENTOR and entrepreneur Thomas Edison, who had previously made his name with a variety of inventions including the light bulb, improvements on the telegraph and telephone, and a sound recording device called the phonograph, wrote: 'I am experimenting upon an instrument which does for the Eye what the phonograph does for the Ear, which is the recording and reproduction of things in motion, and in such a form as to be both Cheap practical and convenient. The apparatus I call a Kinetoscope "Moving View"'.[1] Let's begin by asking a simple question: What use did Edison and other people working on moving picture technology envision for it? Whilst we cannot answer this question in full, by tracing developments at Edison's laboratory and examining Edison's public statements we can get a sense of the distance between initial ideas and the actual uses that were later made of the new technology.

Experiments from early 1889 by Edison and his assistants William Kennedy Laurie Dickson and William Heise, including a significant exchange between Edison and the French inventor Jules Etienne Marey, succeeded by May 1891 in producing a moving picture system that created the illusion of movement by displaying a rapid succession of photographs inside a box to be viewed by individuals through a peephole.[2] Invited delegates of the convention of the National Federation of Women's Clubs witnessed the first public exhibition of the kinetoscope in May 1891.[3] In the same month Edison gave an interview for an issue of the *World's Columbian Exposition Illustrated* and together these events generated massive publicity for the invention that, with the important patents Edison took out three months later, underpinned the technical possibility and industrial development of what later came to be called cinema. Various technical refinements were carried out over the following two years and the first film studio was built by Edison in late 1892, leading to the production of 15-second films from 1893 and the first showing of the kinetoscope outside the Edison laboratory in May 1893 at the prestigious annual meeting of the department of physics of the Brooklyn Institute of Arts and Sciences.[4]

Imagining the future of this medium, Edison and other commentators described the new invention not in terms that clearly prefigured cinema – photographic moving pictures projected for a paying audience – but rather, quite misleadingly, as an instrument of instantaneous transmission of audiovisual signals, which today we would call television. Interviewed in May 1891, Edison said:

> I hope to be able by the invention to throw upon a canvas a perfect picture of anybody, and reproduce his words ... And when this invention shall have been perfected ... a man will be able to sit in his library at home, and, having electrical connection with the theatre, shall see reproduced on his wall or a piece of canvas the actors, and hear anything they say.[5]

In fact, what Edison and others envisioned was the future integration of existing media technologies, merging the capacity to record sounds and images of the phonograph and motion picture device with the long distance transmission of signals provided by the telegraph and the telephone. The aim was to bring the theatre and indeed the whole world into people's homes, and to allow domestic users to move imaginarily into whatever surroundings they desired to be in. An article in *Harper's Weekly* concluded in 1891: 'We seem to be nearing a time when every man may realize the old philosophical idea of a microcosm – a little world of one's own – by unrolling in his room a tape which will fill it with all the forms and motions of the habitable globe'.[6] Not until the development of television, video and the Internet several decades later did this grandiose vision come even close to realisation.[7]

The initial commercial exploitation of moving pictures by the Edison Manufacturing Company from April 1894 onwards was a much more modest affair. Instead of using a big screen, Edison marketed kinetoscopes, that is peephole devices, and instead of targeting the mass market of domestic consumers with an affordable product, he sold expensive coin-in-the-slot machines for $200–$300 through several agents to entertainment entrepreneurs. Edison was economically interested in the hardware, the machine, rather than the software that was the films. In doing so, Edison followed the example of the commercial exploitation of phonographs, which had, after unsuccessful marketing as an office dictaphone, been used briefly as a concert attraction but more successfully as an attraction in phonograph parlours from 1890 where individuals would pay to listen to a recording of music or speech.[8]

Following the model of phonograph parlours, entrepreneurs placed the kinetoscope in public premises, beginning on 14 April 1894 with a kinetoscope parlour on Broadway, New York City, which had ten machines each with a different film.[9] This is the beginning of the history of commercial motion pictures. Other parlours were started in downtown locations in major cities, including Chicago in May and San Francisco in June 1894. Exclusive rights to market kinetoscopes in particular territories were organized from July 1894, led by Norman Charles Raff and Frank R. Gammon, and kinetoscope parlours and temporary exhibitions spread to large and mid-sized cities in the US by the end of 1894 and indeed to major European cities, opening, for example, in Paris in September and London in October.[10]

Admission to kinetoscope parlours initially cost 25 cents and enabled customers to use a selection of machines with different films in them. This made film a relatively expensive experience that was evidently aimed at well-to-do audiences like those who attended the legitimate theatre or respectable vaudeville. Novelty guaranteed a quick profit, as the public flocked to see the latest technological marvel, and film production at the Edison studio accordingly gathered pace throughout 1894, when overall 75 films were made. Charles Musser considers some of these films in his chapter in this section, asking a series of important questions: What representational strategies did the filmmakers use? What kinds of meanings were attached to these films and how did they imagine the world? What was their relationship to the larger culture and society? And what impact did they have on subsequent motion picture practice and American life? In his analysis of these brief films, Musser suggests that they teeter on the edge of tradition and modernity, and art and science. They were principally rooted in the homosocial (all-male) world of work, yet increasingly represented a vibrant urban popular culture. Their cosmopolitanism was largely abandoned with the shift to film projection, when Edison's films came to represent American identity in more narrowly nativist terms. Women were frequently marginalized in these films, rendered as an erotic spectacle. Alternative acts of reception were available, though, such as when women went to see images of semi-clad male bodies fighting, a moment that was suggestive of the friction between a traditional homosocial world and an emergent heterosocial culture.[11] Looked at in the ways Musser outlines, kinetoscope films provide a suitable introduction to many of the issues – modernity, popular culture, gender, race and nationalism – that animate much of the scholarship on silent cinema collected in this book.

Late in 1894, however, the professional market for kinetoscopes was reaching saturation point. By the summer of 1895, despite the introduction of the kinetophone (a combination of kinetoscope and phonograph), machine sales had slumped badly and audiences had dwindled. Kinetoscopes spread to other locations like saloons, becoming increasingly associated with a risqué sporting male culture a long way from Edison's initial presentation to the National Federation of Women's Clubs. It seemed possible, then, that the kinetoscope would fade away as just another technological novelty or would become a source of entertainment shunned by respectable people. Moving picture technology was, though, rescued by film projection – a story we take up in the following section.

Notes

1   Thomas Edison, 'Motion Picture Caveat I', October 1888, reprinted in Gordon Hendricks, *The Edison Motion Picture Myth* (Berkeley: University of California Press, 1961), 158. A 'caveat' is a description of an invention that the inventor wishes to develop further before applying for a patent.
2   Charles Musser, *The Emergence of Cinema: The American Screen to 1907* (Berkeley: University of California Press, 1990), 62–72; Deac Rossell, *Living Pictures: The Origins of the Movies* (Albany: State University of New York Press, 1998), 79–83; Laurent Mannoni, *The Great Art of Light and Shadow: Archaeology of the Cinema*, translated and edited by Richard Crangle (Exeter: University of Exeter Press, 2000), 387–415.
3   Hendricks, *The Edison Motion Picture Myth*, 111–18; Musser, *The Emergence of Cinema*, 68–71.
4   Musser, *The Emergence of Cinema*, 72–81; Rossel, *Living Pictures*, 86.
5   *World's Columbian Exposition Illustrated*, May 1891, quoted in Hendricks, *The Edison Motion Picture Myth*, 104.
6   George Parsons Lathrop, 'Edison's Kinetograph', *Harper's Weekly* (13 June 1891), reprinted in Gerald Mast (ed.), *The Movies in Our Midst: Documents in the Cultural History of Film in America* (Chicago: University of Chicago Press, 1982), 8–12.
7   See here Peter Krämer, 'The Lure of the Big Picture: Film, Television and Hollywood', in John Hill and Martin McLoone eds., *Big Picture, Small Screen: The Relations Between Film and TV* (Luton: University of Luton Press, 1996).
8   Musser, *The Emergence of Cinema*, 56–62; Krämer, 'The Lure of the Big Picture', 17–18; David Nasaw, *Going Out: the Rise and Fall of Public Amusements* (New York: Basic Books, 1993), 120–9. Ian Christie and Tom Gunning consider the cultural roots of the development of the phonograph and kinetograph in their essays 'Early Phonograph Culture and Moving Pictures' and 'Doing for the Eye What the Phonograph Does for the Ear', both in Richard Abel and Rick Altman (eds), *The Sounds of Early Cinema* (Bloomington: Indiana University Press, 2001).

9 Musser, *The Emergence of Cinema*, 81.
10 Musser, *The Emergence of Cinema*, 81–4; David Robinson, *From Peep Show to Palace: The Birth of American Film* (New York: Columbia University Press, 1996), 48–50; John Barnes, *The Beginnings of the Cinema in England* (London: David and Charles, 1976), 12–17.
11 Musser, *The Emergence of Cinema*, 200; Miriam Hansen, *Babel and Babylon: Spectatorship in American Silent Film* (Cambridge, Mass.: Harvard University Press, 1991), 1; Dan Streible, 'A History of the Prizefight Film, 1894–1915' (Ph.D. diss, University of Texas, 1994), 420.

Chapter 1

CHARLES MUSSER

AT THE BEGINNING
Motion picture production, representation and ideology at the Edison and Lumière companies

T HIS ESSAY COMES OUT OF MY RESEARCH for *Edison Motion Pictures,*
1890–1900: An Annotated Filmography.[1] It re-examines the beginnings of modern motion
pictures, focusing on those films intended for exhibition in the peep-hole kinetoscope and
produced at the Edison Laboratory in West Orange, New Jersey, between 1893 and 1895. It
also comments on the shift to projection (to the cinema) in the United States and briefly
considers aspects of Edison production through the end of the nineteenth century in light of
these earlier activities.[2] Finally it compares the emergence of a representational system in Edison
kinetoscope films to its equivalent in the first Lumière productions.

Films for demonstration purposes: spaces, real and constructed

One area in which *Edison Motion Pictures* departs from the chronology offered by Gordon
Hendricks—and by me in *The Emergence of Cinema* and *Before the Nickelodeon*—has to do with
the extent of Edison motion picture production during 1893, the year before motion pictures
were introduced on a commercial basis.[3] After the experimental process had been completed
but before the onset of commercial production, William Kennedy Laurie Dickson and William
Heise, members of Edison's laboratory staff, made several demonstration films that included
Blacksmithing Scene (1893), *Horse Shoeing* (1893) and *The Barber Shop* (1893). A news article in
the *Brooklyn Eagle*, which Hendricks and I both somehow managed to overlook, describes the
showing of *Horse Shoeing* at the Brooklyn Institute of Arts & Sciences on 9 May 1893.[4] At least
two films were presented on that occasion: *Blacksmithing Scene* (mentioned in an article appearing
in *Scientific American*) and *Horse Shoeing*.

What kinds of spaces were depicted in Edison's demonstration films, made in 1893? In
contrast to the experimental subjects made before this trilogy and the vast majority of kinetoscope pictures made afterwards, Edison filmmakers chose to construct simple if meticulous
sets that represented well-developed and self-consciously chosen spaces. These locations were
not taken from life: the camera was not moved outdoors to shoot the local blacksmith shop
that did, in fact, exist at the Edison Laboratory and continued to serve its needs. Nor was an
exhaustive replica assembled inside the Black Maria itself. These locales are rendered schemat-
ically; they are suggested by the inclusion of carefully chosen props—an anvil and forge, or a
barber's chair, a barber's pole and sign. The self-conscious rendering of these spaces was, in

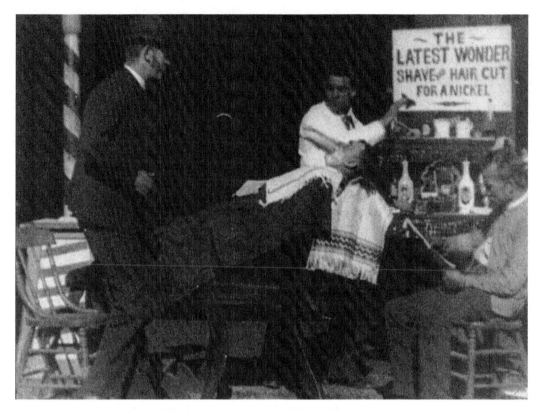

Figure 1.1 The Barber Shop (1893)

fact, foregrounded by their placement against the simple black walls of the studio interior. These were not casual, quickly-done productions. If their running time was brief (about 15 seconds) and quite simple, their forum and place in the Edison production chronology requires us to take them seriously.

What is the relationship among 1) these mock spaces (blacksmith shop and barber shop), 2) the more substantive studio space in which they had been constructed (the Black Maria), and 3) the enclosing and essential milieu of the Edison Laboratory itself? Like Russian wooden folk dolls, the depicted spaces are contained within the studio space, which is set neatly within the larger laboratory. Yet these overlapping spaces have many similarities. Edison employees appearing in the films were simultaneously performing work in the real spaces of the Black Maria and the Edison Laboratory as well as in the mock space of the blacksmith shop where they worked by pretending to work, in short by acting. The world of the Edison Laboratory— perhaps the ultimate center for modern, innovative technology in 1893—was humorously transfigured in ye olde fashioned blacksmith shoppe. The fictive work carried on with anvil and forge became a kind of play.

For Edison and his employees the newly built Black Maria enabled play to be considered work, and work to become a kind of play. In many respects this is the subject of *Blacksmithing Scene*, the more revealing of the two films that premiered at the Brooklyn Institute. Three blacksmiths work together, shaping a piece of metal in a single work cycle that includes not only hammering the iron but passing around and imbibing from a beer bottle. Work, pleasure and socializing are integrated within this view that can accurately be described as nostalgic.

Figure 1.2 Blacksmithing Scene (1893)

Roy Rosenzweig has remarked that work and socializing were increasingly separated by the late nineteenth century, with drinking on the job considered part of a bygone era.[5] This film already reveals a kind of historical impulse, a looking backwards that feeds the ultimate technological novelty—a taste of things to come. Nostalgia continued to be rampant in Edison film production: whether filming Buffalo Bill, Annie Oakley and Sioux Indians after the close of the frontier; ritual ceremonies that eulogized America's heroes such as Ulysses S. Grant and George Dewey; or short bad boy comedies which were designed to recall the carefree days of male youth (e.g. *Wringing Good Joke*, April 1899). With *Blacksmithing Scene*, the newest and most modern technology is used to prop up and document a past that it is quickly making obsolete. As André Bazin has remarked, film embalms time.

If *Blacksmithing Scene* points to a receding past, it also suggests that the interpenetration of work and leisure still characterized the Edison Laboratory, depicting it in some respects as a utopic, non-alienated space. More accurately, filmmaking was a break from the everyday demands of work and experimentation. This shifted form during the following year when professional entertainers began to perform at the studio. The Black Maria became a profitable distraction from Edison's financially disastrous and ultimately unsuccessful efforts at iron ore milling—a project that exhausted the inventor and demoralized his staff. Edison, Dickson and other employees soon found themselves socializing with stars of the variety stage—and "Wizard Edison" was a vaudeville fan. The famed inventor also apparently attended at least some of the boxing exhibitions staged in the Black Maria, a throw back to his youth when he had attended fights in the rougher spots of Manhattan's night life. *Blacksmithing Scene* and *Horse Shoeing* hint at the complex interrelationships—perhaps impossible to pin down either in these films or in the culture of the Edison Laboratory—among work, play and creativity.

Blacksmithing Scene can be contrasted to the Lumières' "first film," *Sortie d'usine*, known in English as *Employees Leaving the Lumière Factory*. In its single-shot, the Lumières filmed a complex, transitional space that encompasses both the space of work (the factory) and the space of leisure (the space outside).[6] It is a film that focuses on the boundary between work and play, rather than on their interpenetration. As Noël Burch has pointed out, the Lumières filmed *their* employees leaving *their* factory after a day of productive toil.[7] Serious work is not interrupted so the Lumière employees might play with this newest novelty. Nor is labor treated in an ironic, mocking way. There is the world of work inside, and the realm of rest and relaxation outside. The two realms, though dependent on each other, are carefully separated. It is a well-regulated and apparently happy world—testimony to the beneficence of Lumière paternalism. Employment by the Lumières does not appear unduly burdensome and there is a certain esprit that is generated by the very act of filming, one that is communicated by the gestures and movements of the employees as they head home (indeed, as Alan Williams has suggested, this scene was probably carefully staged).[8] *Sortie d'usine* is a film made by a self-consciously "enlightened" owner of a large business enterprise. Designed for demonstration purposes (it was shown at various lectures prior to the cinématographe's official premiere), the film served the practical role of self-promotion. *Blacksmithing Scene* was created by Edison's employees working independently of their boss' supervision. However, it was not made by the poorly paid wage earners who labored in Edison's factories (the inventor-entrepreneur would soon break the strike of their fledgling union),[9] but by the cherished members of his laboratory staff— employees who enjoyed considerable latitude to strike a more independent, anarchic attitude.

This then is the first point about *Blacksmithing Scene* and *Horse Shoeing*: as representations they are at once nostalgic and modern, serious and self-mocking, ambiguous and finally contradictory. They are about spaces, particularly that eccentric, almost carnivalesque space that very early on was called the Black Maria, named after the black paddy wagons that brought prisoners to jail. Yet in this topsy turvy world of representations and naming, this Black Maria offered escape into nostalgia and play rather than the likelihood of imprisonment.

Connecting theater to film

Until March 1894, the Edison Laboratory was not only the site of motion picture experimentation and production, it was also the film's subject. Low level employees such as G. Sacco Albanese, James Duncan (a day laborer), and Fred C. Devonald (who worked in the supply room) as well as Dickson and Heise served as subjects for the early experiments. Edison employees continued to serve as performers in the demonstration films of 1893. The making of *Sandow* on 6 March 1894 represented an important break from past efforts. It initiated commercial production with a new kind of subject matter and introduced a relationship between the world of performance culture and the world of motion pictures which has continued in some form to this day.[10]

Eugen Sandow first appeared in the United States at New York City's Casino Theatre in June 1893 and then went on to become one of the stars of the 1893 World's Columbian Exposition in Chicago, with assistance from his manager Florenz Ziegfeld.[11] During the winter of 1893–94, he had become a headline attraction at the nation's foremost vaudeville house, Koster & Bial's Music Hall, located on 34th Street and Herald Square just a short distance from the place where the first kinetoscope parlor would be opened.[12] How did Dickson and Heise decide what to film and how to film it? Not surprisingly they selected a portion of Sandow's act, since it was a well-established and successful routine. At Sandow's New York debut:

The curtain went up, revealing the stage steeped in gloom. Then, suddenly, two curtains at the back of the stage were drawn aside, in a blaze of light stood the "Strong Man," with his mighty muscles standing out in bold relief in the white glare of an electric light. After performing a number of "tableaux vivants," to the accompaniment of slow music and much perspiration, Mr. Sandow left his cabinet, the lights were turned up, and the show began in earnest.[13]

Sandow began the earnest part of his act by lifting a large dumb-bell: the spheres at each end were then opened to reveal two men curled up in tight balls. After demonstrating a few additional feats of strength, he did several somersaults with his eyes blindfolded and his legs tied. Then two horses were led in and played see-saw, using his chest as a pivot.

Despite the possibilities of filming Sandow's more entertaining shenanigans, Dickson chose to film the introductory moment of Sandow's stage act—in which the strong man moves through a sequence of held poses. We can only speculate about the reasons for this choice. Posing allowed the strong man to show off his body with a variety of angles and postures while the camera could be moved closer to capture a more intimate view. Weight lifting would have kept the camera at a distance. Perhaps also the film's credibility as an objective recorder of a spectacular feat of this kind would have been undermined in the absence of direct physical verification by the spectator. But Sandow's introductory series of "tableaux vivants" is echoed by the experience of watching the first motion pictures as a series of still images become animated as the familiar static photograph comes to life. As Sandow moves from one pose to the next, alternating back and forth between arrested motion and fluid movement, the film indulges the viewer in a game of fort-da. The viewer's experience when peering into the peep-hole parallels

Figure 1.3 Sandow (1894)

the story of Pygmalion and his statue of Galatea which is brought to life.[14] With this film, Dickson plays Pygmalion to Sandow's Galatea. Indeed, the ways in which motion pictures bring the static or death-like photographic image to life became a virtual cliché in nineteenth-century discussions of motion pictures. It also became the subject of various early films: not only Georges Méliès' own film of the Pygmalion and Galatea story, but the Edison film *An Artist's Dream* (March 1900).

Sandow offers a nonnarrative moment in which the emphasis is on the body as a spectacle. The rapid succession of poses has no particular order and no tension or climactic moment, which would have been the case if Sandow had chosen to execute a feat of strength. The film's presentational methods, with a powerful emphasis on erotic display, yielded an example of what Tom Gunning has called "the cinema of attractions." And cinema was still almost two years in the future. Yet at the same time, as Brigitte Peucker has suggested in her remarks on tableaux vivant artist Emma Hart, "by framing the body as an aesthetic object and placing it against a funeral backdrop of black velvet, [s]he conversely played on the body's death into representation."[15] Indeed filmmakers displayed an only slightly later fascination with the extinguishing of life in such films as *Rat Killing* (September 1894) and *The Hanging of William Carr* (December 1897). In these instances, the trajectory is in the opposite direction—from moving bodies to dead ones. Yet in both cases the life-like and death-like quality of images collide in ways that are troublesome. With *The Hanging of William Carr*, the spectator witnesses Carr's final moments of life, even as the same film demonstrates that he has been dead for some time. The act of extinguishing life is re-enacted, potentially obsessively, in the most life-like of representational modes. Sandow's poses repeatedly burst forth into life, resulting in a film that suggests cinema's triumph over stasis and death. At the same time, Sandow's perfect body cannot be perfect for very long. Indeed, it will soon cease to exist except as representation. The ways in which Edison's motion picture system thus acts as a time machine—to evoke the title of H.G. Wells' book, published in 1895—becomes foregrounded.[16]

Sandow was a carefully selected and staged example of "filmed theater," an approach to subject matter that proved common in the kinetoscope period and beyond. However, it was filmed theater of a particular kind. If the filmed sequence of poses corresponded in some loose way to the opening of Sandow's routine, the strong man did not bring his posing cabinet. In this instance the Black Maria's dark background focused attention on the star's body much as the cabinet was intended to do. For this production and many that followed, Dickson and Heise dispensed with the sets and backdrops, concentrating viewer attention on performance and movement instead.

Filmed theater (or more accurately filmed performance) as an approach to representation was only a starting point for the development of a multi-faceted relationship between the amusement world and film in this period. *Sandow* inaugurated an impressive mapping of American performance-based popular culture during the 1894–95 theatrical season. It encompasses everything from Hoyt's musical farce *A Milk White Flag* to African-American buck and wing dancers in *The South Before the War*, from Buffalo Bill's Wild West and Barnum & Bailey's Circus to boxing matches, female duelists and a dog performing a skirt dance. This focus should not be seen as the negative result of a lack of ideas for subject matter. Rather Dickson was tapping into a rich vein of material; and his exploration had its own logic and momentum. Kinetographic practices were representing popular amusements—using them as raw material for this new technology-based form of popular amusement. While this redundancy may seem reductive and lacking in "originality," the social and cultural impact of this approach would be profound.

If a Lumière counterpart to Edison's *Sandow* exists, it involves a very different trajectory. In the Edison imaginary, the world of commercial amusements stood in opposition to the world of work. It filled the leisure realm. For the Lumières, in contrast, family and domestic life were offered as complements to the work-a-day world. In this respect, *Repas de bébé* (July 1895), for which Louis filmed Auguste and his wife feeding their young child, is emblematic.[17] It is the perfect expression of the numerous domestic scenes made in this early period including *Pêche aux poissons rouges* in which a Lumière toddler tries to catch a gold fish in a small aquarium; *Partie d'écarté*, which features Antoine Lumière and Louis' father-in-law; and even *Arroseur et arrosé*. The Lumières generally avoided filming performance culture à la Edison until quite late, while the family unit is not really shown in an Edison film until the summer of 1896, well after the Lumières' impact was felt on American production.[18]

The presence or absence of theater in early motion picture production has been noted by historians in various ways. Georges Sadoul has seen the filmed theater of Edison leading to the fantasy trick films of Méliès and the sterile productions of Pathé Frères. In ways that have been widely celebrated by commentators of documentary film, the Lumières were said to engage the world more directly, rather than retreating to the studio.[19] Although scenes in early Lumière films are frequently staged, there is little acting in the sense that those people in front of the camera do not create fictional personae or play roles: they do not *dissemble*. The Lumières' avoidance of theater, traditionally seen as a positive *aesthetic* choice by many historians, was also an expression of their anti-theatrical prejudice that came out of well-established uses of the stereopticon, illustrated lecture, and amateur photography.[20] Perhaps then, this provides some insight into the Lumières' withdrawal from film exhibition early in 1897: it required them to pursue the film-theater connection in ways that made them uncomfortable. In contrast, faced with a similar kind of crisis about 1900, Thomas Edison finally decided to open a glass-enclosed studio in the heart of New York City's theater district.

Homosocial space, affirmed yet upended

The earliest Edison films were shot in the male, homosocial world of the Edison Laboratory.[21] When Dickson and Heise began to create imaginary spaces that were both located in and counterparts to the Edison Laboratory, they chose spaces that men exclusively occupied—a smithy and a barber shop. The Edison Laboratory was a bastion of masculinist culture. When work was done by women, it was often done by wives, at home and then brought to the Laboratory (for example, Fred Devonald's wife made a screen or Edmund Kuhn's wife hand tinted kineto-scope films). When men were working on a project, they were expected to put in long hours, perhaps like their boss catching naps in the lab rather than going home. The Edison Laboratory was an alternative to the family as much as or more than its complement. Women were not so much excluded from these earliest Edison films: they were simply not present in the larger space from which the casts was drawn.

Throughout 1894–95 Dickson, Heise and their colleagues continued to make a wide range of films that appealed to this culture of rugged masculinity. In the months immediately after *Sandow* was filmed, light-weight boxing champion Jack McAuliffe visited the Black Maria (*Boxing*, May 1894).[22] Known to be a brawler who was as ready to fight outside the ring as in it, McAuliffe nonetheless declined to participate in a serious exchange of blows in the limited space of the enclosed studio. "Mike" Leonard and Jack Cushing had fewer qualms and fought a bout of six abbreviated rounds in June (*Leonard-Cushing Fight*, June 1894). Additional fights followed. Other films involving man-to-man combats included *Mexican Knife Duel* (October 1894) and *Gladiatorial Combat* (January 1895). In addition there were depictions of blood sports such as *Cock Fight* (December 1896); *Rat Killing*, in which a terrier kills six or so rats; and *Dogs Fighting* (May 1894).[23]

Women did eventually find their way into Edison films. One works behind the counter as a barmaid in *Bar Room Scene* (May 1894), made shortly after the opening of the New York kinetoscope parlor and the fourth Edison film to present an elaborated space. This bar room may no longer be an all-male preserve, but it unquestionably remained a homosocial one dominated and regulated by men—one in which nineteenth-century masculine values were firmly entrenched. Not surprisingly, kinetoscopes showing fight films were sometimes located in bar rooms.

The female bartender was not the first woman to appear in an Edison film, however. This honor belonged to Spanish dancer Carmencita, who was filmed at the Black Maria in mid-March 1894, approximately two weeks after Sandow (*Carmencita*, March 1894). Carmencita debuted on the New York stage in 1889, performing Spanish dances between acts of a musical. She rose to fame under the management of John Koster and Albert Bial, who put her in their original music hall on 23rd Street, commencing 10 February 1890. Carmencita communicated an intense sexuality across the footlights that led male reporters to write long, exuberant columns about her performance (several such articles appear in the document section for the entry on Carmencita in *Edison Motion Pictures, 1890–1900*).

Following *Carmencita*, Dickson and Heise made numerous pictures featuring women engaged in performances that had an erotic component. Women were often scantily dressed and executed sexually suggestive poses or movements. *Trapeze* (April 1894) featured a female trapeze artist. *Bertoldi (Table Contortion)* (April 1894) presented contortionist Ena Bertoldi who displayed her body in ways that could readily trigger male fantasies of sexual availability. The sexually explicit *danse du ventre* and the slightly more refined Serpentine dance, particularly as rendered by Annabelle Whitford who cavorted before Edison's kinetograph many times between 1894 and 1898, were mainstays of Edison production throughout this period. When women appeared before the camera it was typically to appeal to male voyeurism, to the interests of the men behind the camera and the men assumed to be looking into the kinetoscope—men like those making the films. In short these films of sex and violence had a strong commercial sense, but the filmmakers tended to imagine an audience consisting of men like themselves.

As Dickson and Heise prepared for the kinetoscope's debut, they belatedly recognized that the kinetoscope's audiences would often be mixed sex ones that included middle-class women who typically saw the burlesque show, music hall or boxing ring as inimical to their domestic values. Edison's "scientific experiments" would interest these women—as it had interested the heads of women's clubs who had been the first members of the public to see Edison's experimental kinetoscope in May 1891. But what could they see that might be considered acceptable? When the first kinetoscope parlor opened in New York, the only film in those ten machines which was designed to appeal to this more general public was *Highland Dance* (April 1894). Significantly it also served as an exemplary film for an article on Edison's new motion picture system appearing in a journal for adolescents, *Harper's Young People*.[24] Other films such as *Organ Grinder* (May 1894) and *Trained Bears* (May 1894) were soon made to address this shortage. Films of trained animals, bronco busting and a fire rescue appealed to a more heterosocial audience that included children. Nor is this an esoteric point. Films of Annabelle were banned from exhibition in Asbury Park and other locales.[25] But even though scenes of fire rescues and bronco busting appealed to a mixed sex audience, they came out of the quintessentially masculinist culture of fire companies and wild west shows.

As should already be evident, the Lumière imaginary was gendered in quite different ways. If Edison's earliest films depicted a homosocial world, theirs was resolutely heterosocial, even feminine in its emphasis on the domestic sphere. As Tom Gunning has suggested they had strong ties to amateur photography, which emphasized the family.[26] Even the factory, located immediately behind the Lumière mansion, was in many ways an extension of this filmic universe. In any case, the departing Lumière employees included women as well as men. Dickson and Heise did move toward gender diversity, first by filming women who performed in these homosocial spaces and then by filming scenes of commercial amusement that included women and were intended to appeal to a more general public. The depiction of heterosocial space, however, remained a weaker impulse throughout the kinetoscope era.

If Edison production expanded from depicting an all-male world to include women, a parallel can be found in the expansion of Lumière filmmaking, in moving outward from the private realm to incorporate the public sphere. This had two related trajectories. First the Lumières began to shoot public places such as *Place des Cordeliers* in Lyons, then gradually expanded their selection to include symbolic spaces associated with different nations: Hyde Park in London, the Brooklyn Bridge in New York and the Geneva Exposition in Switzerland. Public space was still heterosocial space. Somewhat later, the Lumières expanded their repertoire in a second direction by filming scenes involving the armies of France and then other nations. Their movement backwards into the all-male world of soldiering resulted from the decision to film the military and other representatives of state power. The Lumières came to depict a world in which family, nation and state were among the most prominent features. All three were largely ignored if they were not actively lampooned in Edison pictures of the kinetoscope period. (Dickson took many films of Charles Hoyt's *The Milk White Flag*, a musical comedy that mocked the state militias.)

By some standards, the Lumière films can appear more progressive and enlightened. In Edison kinetoscope films, women are on display. Their status as objects of the male gaze is further heightened by the process of peep-hole viewing itself. Screen entertainment, which the Lumières pioneered, was a form of public viewing that was more proper and allowed for other kinds of subject positions for its spectators. In the world constructed by the Lumière camera, women may not be objects of salacious male voyeurism, but they also have little definition outside the family. As Alan Williams has observed, the Lumières depict an orderly, contented world where bourgeois values have triumphed and are made permanent as representations.[27] The world on screen and the refined, mixed-sexed audiences who came to see these representations were more comfortably matched.

If Edison films were cruder and more shocking than their Lumière counterparts, they were also more disruptive and dynamic, often in ways that were not anticipated. The disjunctions between the semi-illegal, hidden, masculine world of blood sports and heterosocial spectatorship were powerful. Because this performance culture had been reduced to representations, women could, for instance, more freely view Sandow's almost naked body. And they were allowed to see two perfectly conditioned male fighters, stripped down to their togs. Female voyeurism was unexpectedly mobilized, within a socially acceptable framework, in ways that have been discussed by Miriam Hansen.[28] They gained access, however limited, to the male homosocial world from which they had been either excluded or kept at the periphery. Motion pictures thus contributed to the breakdown of two discrete and complementary realms—that of rugged masculinity and feminine domesticity—by pulling the veil from the former and exposing it to the latter. Kinetoscope films and their exhibition were involved in a breakdown and curtailment of an older homosocial world and the emergence and expansion of a newer heterosocial culture.

Art and science, eroticism and ethnography

Although Edison and his associates were using film in a way that disrupted the cultural status quo, the inventor nevertheless appropriated familiar and reassuring discourses about science and art when talking about his new invention. Edison often promised to bring opera, the epitome of high art, to the masses for a reasonable price.[29] Motion pictures, it was promised, would preserve great performances of Shakespeare.[30] In truth, the gap between promise and practice was great: the actual subject matter was of a much more popular kind. Science helped to bridge the gap. Sandow, it was asserted, was taking part in a disinterested scientific experiment. Edison was said to be perfecting his invention—"the latest development of Edison's genius in the line of photography, on which he had been working for the past five years."[31] The *New York World* and *Harper's Weekly* both published sequences of Edison motion pictures which analyzed actions—the successful and unsuccessful somersaults of an amateur gymnast and the sneeze of Edison employee Fred Ott. Black backgrounds focused attention on the isolated events which were themselves reduced to single cycles of action.

In their approach to representation, Dickson and Heise were evoking and reworking aspects of Eadweard Muybridge's serial photography, which also depicted subjects against plain black backgrounds and showed complete cycles of actions, such as walking, jumping, or pouring a bucket of water. Muybridge, who often photographed his subjects in a state of partial or complete undress, claimed the right to take and exhibit (life-size via projection) his highly eroticized photographs of naked or semi-naked men and women because he was doing so for scientific purposes. He was teaching people about human and animal locomotion, or so he claimed. When Muybridge came to lecture on serial photography in Orange, New Jersey, in October 1888, these images scandalized some members of the audience who found them to be pornographic in character.[32] Scientific purpose provided sufficient justification for many but not all patrons.

In the Edison film of Eugen Sandow, the strong man is all but naked; and like many films that followed, it is erotic in its content. Dickson and Heise, like Muybridge, combined a reputedly scientific approach with eroticism. If people were aware that this evocation of science was self-serving, however, Edison's subject matter was finally less controversial.[33] Dickson and Heise played with the periphery of acceptable commercial entertainment, with scantily clothed dancers rather than naked bodies. The staging of so-called scientific experiments, however, also provided opportunities for concealing or at least minimizing the commercial nature of Edison's latest venture into the amusement world, one that would complement the phonograph. Contra Edison's public statements, not science and art but technology and amusement were being forged into a new, explosive combination that would provide the foundation for what has generally come to be called the culture industry.

There was always a certain comic potential in applying the kinetograph's "scientific" method or attitude to an inappropriate object. The *New York World* did this, no doubt intentionally, in April 1896, when it published a sequential series of photographs showing a kiss by John C. Rice and May Irwin. The first film kiss (and the first depiction of a kiss to be published in a newspaper, according to the *World*) was analyzed with a scientific eye. "The first section was devoted to what apparently was a kiss, but was really only the preparation for one. These pictures show very distinctly how easily a person watching a couple might think they kissed when they didn't," observed Mrs McGuirk of the *World*. When she examined the next and final section of the film, the journalist concluded that "the real kiss is a revelation."[34] This mocking of the scientific stance toward films of sex and violence apparently brought this particular strand of scientific discourse to a halt, though it would re-emerge somewhat later in slightly altered form.

Another way in which Edison's kinetoscope films could be taken seriously in their "scientific" aspirations was as ethnographic "documents." In many respects these films extended the emphasis on displaying cultures offered at the 1893 World Columbian Exposition of Chicago, both in the Anthropological Building and on the Midway Plaisance.[35] In many cases these World's Fair exhibitions involved the presentation of ethnic types "in situ." There was Franz Boas' Skidgate village of Kwakiutl Indians, a Samoan village and the Street of Cairo. As Barbara Kirshenblatt-Gimblett has observed in relation to ethnographic displays of human beings:

> Human displays teeter-totter on a kind of semiotic seesaw, equipoised between the animate and inanimate, the living and the dead. The semiotic complexity of exhibits of people, particularly those of an ethnographic character, may be seen in reciprocities between exhibiting the dead as if alive and the living as if they are dead, reciprocities that hold as well for the art of the undertaker as they do for the art of the museum preparator.[36]

As already suggested, motion pictures were ideally suited for playing this seesaw between living and dead. The images were "life-like" and yet the people appearing in the films were not actually present. In fact, shot at some earlier point in time, they could be and perhaps might as well be dead. Film more or less quickly became a form for presenting ethnographic information; in fact, it was one of the first uses to which Dickson and Heise put the new medium.

The early kinetoscope films offered a "gallery of nations," similar to the one being employed by Charles Willson Peale as early as 1797 using wax works. Peale's museum presented "a group of contrasting races of mankind" which featured peoples from China, the Pacific Islands and North and South America.[37] When shown in a battery of kinetoscopes, Edison's early films encouraged patrons to compare people from different nations, cultures and races. Such analyses could proceed along gender lines as men and women engaged in characteristic actions in the areas of dance, feats of strength, and combat. With the proper scientific attitude, a spectator might contrast the American Serpentine dance to the *dance du ventre* of the Middle East, the English *pas seul* of Lucy Murray or the Sarachi dance of the Japanese *mako*. Different notions of feminine beauty could also be compared. The same held true for the films of male combats: Mexican knife duels, Irish-American boxing, Buffalo Bill's rifle shooting and Romanesque gladiatorial jousting could be contrasted to each other and to the animal combats of cock fights and rat baiting. Certainly these films as a group conform to a hierarchy of types that was consistent with popular prejudices of the period.

From cosmopolitan internationalism to jingoistic nationalism

Kinetoscope films were often ambiguous in their meanings and genres. Although many were ethnographic in their impulse or could be made to function in this manner, most depicted a self-confident commercial popular culture that was international in its scope and orientation. Dickson and cameraman William Heise filmed a vast array of theatrical performers whose geographic, racial and cultural diversity is striking: German strong men Eugen Sandow and Louis Attila; Italian acrobat Luis Martinetti; Columbian tightrope walker Juan Caicedo; French trapezist Alcide Capitaine; Japanese tumbler Toyou Kichi; English dancers Lucy Murray and May Lucas; Arab gun twirler Sheik Hadj Tahar; and Mexican rope performer Vincente Oropeza. And the silent nature of early motion pictures, which effaced the barrier of language, helped to forge this sense of a shared, fluid world. Motion pictures from their earliest moments, whether in the peep-hole kinetoscope or projected onto the screen, provided this sense of a world that could transcend national identity but also a world where performers and viewers could play with, and enjoy cultural particularity.

This international cast was balanced by an American one—Annie Oakley, Buffalo Bill, scenes from Hoyt's musical farce *The Milk White Flag*, Irish-American boxers James Corbett and Peter Courtney, African-American dancers such as James Grundy, and Sioux Indians.[38] Although the approximately 135 known kinetoscope films hardly functioned independently of racist and culturally elitist preconceptions, they display a consistency in depiction that marks this as a remarkable moment. They offered a cosmopolitan vision that admittedly embraced stereotyping but generally avoided demeaning depictions (Robetta and Doretto in *Chinese Laundry Scene* perhaps being an exception). Like the vaudeville stage (notably Koster & Bial's) from which many of these performers came, these films articulated a vision of American identity which was polyglot, self-confident and, within limits, fluid.[39]

These kinetoscope films offered a space apart, a fantastic space removed from daily life and its constraints. People of all cultures and races appeared on the same vaudeville stage, enjoying the same basic forms of compensation and attention. At the Black Maria, the camera also treated these subjects approximately the same: camera distance was one of the few variables and it operated within the pragmatic goals of best capturing a performance.[40] As performers who construct their own image (admittedly constrained by performance categories and cultural preconceptions) and compete in the marketplace, they could destabilize established hierarchies of culture and what were often considered scientific categories of race. Each had his or her own specialty or talent which demanded fascination and respect. Here was an alternative rather than an obviously oppositional vision of a world. Racial and economic hierarchies may not have been upended but they were potentially effaced, flattened out, offered up as equivalents or otherwise subverted. These films, like many of the performers who appeared in them, were part of a global culture that operated outside localized social norms. They became part of "The Family of Man," to evoke a photographic exhibit that would juxtapose some of the same kinds of images some 60 years later.[41]

There is a noticeable shift in the nature of filmic representations with the onset of projection. Not unlike Edison, the Lumières offered up an array of international images, but ones with an emphasis on the family, state and nation. These easily provoked or constructed national rivalries. Of course, Edison and other American filmmakers participated actively in these shifts in the United States. The Edison group moved from a cultural stance that was cosmopolitan to another that could be, and was probably intended to be, constructed as "American" in a much more narrow, nationalistic sense. Raff & Gammon's choice of films for the vitascope's Koster & Bial premiere in April 1896 was hardly random. Of the three or four films that had been made for the kinetoscope in 1894–95, all were of white, American performers: the Leigh sisters in *Umbrella Dance; Band Drill* from *The Milk White Flag*; and *Walton & Slavin*, showing a burlesque boxing match from *Little Christopher Columbus*. New subjects within the familiar genre of dance films included films of toe dancer Amy Muller and a skirt dance by an unidentified performer (the film may well have been an old one): here again the performers were white, native-born Americans. The two most novel films were *The Monroe Doctrine* (April 1896) and Robert Paul's *Sea Waves at Dover*—duly credited as an English subject but without acknowledging its true author. It suggested not only the geographic mobility of the American machine, but its ability to keep the heart of the British Empire within its vision. And as the waves crashed on the cinematic shore and failed to sweep away its vaudeville spectators, did not this film hint that British power in the Americas was only an illusion? Or that British waves (and John Bull) should stay on British shores?

The order of the films was 1) *Umbrella Dance*, 2) *Sea Waves at Dover*, 3) *Walton & Slavin*, 4) *Band Drill*, 5) *The Monroe Doctrine* and 6) Serpentine or Skirt Dance.[42] The program thus started off by showing two young female dancers, asserting a continuation between stage and screen. (According to one critic, "It seemed as though they were actually on the stage, so natural was the dance, with its many and graceful motions.")[43] The proscenium arch established by this first film was then broken in *Sea Waves at Dover*. The British waves metaphorically wash away the stage and the Leigh Sisters even as they assault American patrons, causing initial consternation and excitement. This is followed by a familiar subject that reasserted the proscenium. The burlesque bout was between "the long and the short of it," featuring lanky Charles Walton and the stout John Slavin. According to some sources, *The Monroe Doctrine* also featured Walton as Uncle Sam, as well as Slavin's replacement, John Mayon, as John Bull. In any case, Walton and Slavin visually evoked, at least subliminally and retrospectively, Uncle Sam and John Bull engaging in a fistic encounter. The fourth film showed a marching band in uniform: suggesting a mobilization of the American military, it "elicited loud cries of 'Bravo!'."[44] *Band Drill* thus prepared the way for *The Monroe Doctrine*, which "twinned" *Sea Waves at Dover*. The British bombard the shoreline of another American nation—with guns instead of cinematic waves. Uncle Sam forces John Bull to stop. According to one report, "This delighted the audience, and applause and cheers rang through the house, while someone cried, 'Hurrah for Edison.'"[45] With this victory there was a return to the status quo as patrons again viewed a dance film, one similar in style and subject matter to the opening selection. The program began and ended with films of women that indulge male voyeuristic pleasures. A masculinist-nationalist (English-American) confrontation thus forces these pleasures aside until an American triumph is achieved (on the screen), and audiences are returned to their sensual pleasures. Hardly a miscellaneous collection of films, this opening night program was a sophisticated achievement indicating that Raff & Gammon had consciously chosen to fight the expected influx of international machines (English as well as French) by appealing to American patriotism with American subject matter—even as they (like Maguire & Baucus) had marketed the kinetoscope on the basis of a cosmopolitan internationalism.[46]

Here again the Lumières had a unique and crucial impact on the cultural landscape of cinema's novelty year. Edison's camera crew emulated their subject matter and began to take scenes on location with a portable camera on 11 May 1896. By the time the cinématographe had its New York City debut in late June, the Kinetograph Department had a reasonably large selection of outdoor scenes—including pictures of New York, Brooklyn, Coney Island, and Niagara Falls. Edison cameramen had also filmed horse races and parades well before the cinématographe's premiere at Keith's. The erasure of the Edison/stage versus Lumière/outdoor difference, however, meant the creation of another that was at least as profound. Because the Edison crew took its films in the New York area, the vitascope inevitably showed essentially American subjects (views of American cities and tourist landmarks, and of American performers such as May Irwin and John C. Rice in *The Kiss*). The Lumière cinématographe showed foreign, essentially European views (not only of France, but of Italy, Switzerland, Russia and other distant locales). The differences in terms of subject matter were Edison/American versus Lumière/International even as "authorship" distinctions, both of films and the respective technological systems, were Edison/American versus Lumière/French.

If the Lumière cinématographe ran counter to the American nationalism of the vitascope, it also provided the necessary term that made such opposition clear cut and vital. Moreover, its programs foregrounded nation-states as an ongoing principle for depicting and understanding the world. Once unleashed, this jingoism proved powerful. Two years after making *The Monroe Doctrine*, the Edison Manufacturing Company was providing a war-inducing array of films showing the sunken battleship "Maine," Spanish fortresses in Cuba and American arma-ment ready to acquire an overseas empire. And to the extent that the cinématographe featured a rich array of military scenes, its internationalism was of a very particular kind—one that easily fostered national rivalries. In these films, the absence of presence suggested power (the cavalry charging the screen) without consequence—the clash of real armies off-screen. The move from peep-hole to projection brought with it new kinds of subject matter and a greater visceral impact on audiences, but this achievement was not without its costs. It also produced a new dialectic: between a patriotic even jingoistic nationalism, which saw American identity in narrow nativist terms; and a cosmopolitanism with a fluid, easy going sense of American identity. These were poles around which United States and even European cinemas fluctuated in the 1890s and beyond. It was a tension strikingly absent from the films of the kinetoscope period.

Notes

1. This chapter is a substantially condensed version of the essay "Before the Rapid Firing Kinetograph: Edison Film Production, Representation and Exploitation in the 1890s" in Charles Musser, *Edison Motion Pictures, 1890–1900: An Annotated Filmography* (Washington: Smithsonian Institution Press, 1997), 19–50, with a small amount of additional material that can be found in "Nationalism and the Beginnings of Cinema: The Lumière Cinématographe in the United States, 1896–1897," *Historical Journal of Film, Radio, & Television* 19, no. 2: 2 (June 1999), 149–176.
2. In referring to this pre-cinema motion picture work, I certainly do not want to limit our concerns to activities at the Edison Laboratory. The work of Robert Paul and Birt Acres is equally relevant and of considerable international significance. In the United States and possibly Australia, production for peep-hole machines was pursued quite independently of Edison. Nor is this an effort to marginalize the impact of other cultural influences on the beginnings of cinema. Newspapers, popular theatre, photography and other cultural forms had profound influences on cinema's initial formation, but we must adequately conceptualize the structure of influence that produced this new but hardly unformed phenomenon.
3. Gordon Hendricks, *The Edison Motion Picture Myth* (Berkeley: University of California Press, 1961); Gordon Hendricks, *The Kinetoscope: America's First Commercially Successful Motion Picture Examiner* (New York: The Beginnings of the American Film, 1966); Charles Musser, *The Emergence of Cinema: The American Screen to 1907* (New York: Charles Scribner's, 1990); Charles Musser, *Before the Nickelodeon: Edwin S. Porter and the Edison Manufacturing Company* (Berkeley: University of California Press, 1991).
4. "Department of Physics," *Brooklyn Daily Eagle*, 10 May 1893.
5. Roy Rosenzweig, *Eight Hours for What We Will: Workers and Leisure in an Industrial City, 1870–1920* (Cambridge: Cambridge University Press, 1983).
6. Edison's motion pictures not only required the development of a new technology and new equipment, it required the construction of new spaces to house them. There was the Photographic Building constructed in August 1889 to house motion picture experiments, the Black Maria studio built in late 1892–early 1893 to support commercial production, and the kinetoscope parlor at 1155 Broadway, in New York City, which opened on 14 April 1894. Yet it was not strictly necessary to create these spaces in the way it was necessary to build the technology. The Lumières, for instance, not only made do with simpler technology—a single piece of equipment that served as camera, printer, and projector—but they were much more efficient in their film-related architectonics. They shot outdoors and located their first commercial exhibitions in a café that needed little renovations. (It seems that Lumière père was more interested in building homes, the brothers in building factories.)
7. Noël Burch, *Life to Those Shadows* (Berkeley: University of California Press, 1990).
8. Alan Williams, *Republic of Images* (Cambridge, Ma.: Harvard University Press, 1992), 28–29.
9. "Striking at Edison," *New York Journal*, 18 July 1893.
10. My analysis has admittedly ignored a number of films using members of the Newark Turnverein. These films were made, most likely, to stimulate subsequent commercial production with its need to accom-modate outside performers with reasonable speed and reliability. In short, the German-American athletes, who can be understood as modest counterparts to Sandow, were being used for a dry run. These films represent a transitional moment.

11. David L. Chapman, *Sandow the Magnificent: Eugen Sandow and the Beginnings of Bodybuilding* (Urbana: University of Illinois Press, 1994).

12. Many of the performers in Edison's kinetoscope films had their American vaudeville debut at Koster & Bial's Music Hall and later appeared in houses with "popular prices" such as Keith's Union Square Theatre and Proctor's 23rd Street Theatre.

13. "The Strong Man Appears," *New York Times*, 12 June 1893, 5.

14. Brigitte Peucker, *Incorporating Images: Film and the Rival Arts* (Princeton: Princeton University Press, 1995).

15. Brigitte Peucker, "Looking and Touching: Spectacle and Collection in Sontag's *Volcano Lover*," unpublished paper given at the Modern Language Association Conference, December 1994.

16. Terry Ramsaye discusses the relationship between cinema and Wells' time machine in *A Million and One Nights: A History of the Motion Picture* (London: Simon & Schuster, 1926), 152–162.

17. The Lumières' *Repas de bébé* is open to a somewhat similar symptomatic interpretation as *Sandow*—as an allegory of regeneration and life.

18. The Lumières, particularly the father, did have some ties to performance culture, for example Félicien Trewey. In this respect, the films of Trewey's performance must also be seen as the filming of a family friend. Likewise one might argue that some early Edison films do depict families—for instance *Cupid's Dance* of the Ewer sisters—but they occur within the framework of performance culture.

19. Erik Barnouw, *Documentary: A Short History of the Non-Fiction Film*, rev. ed. (1974; New York: Oxford University Press, 1983), 2–22.

20. Jonas Barish, *The Antitheatrical Prejudice* (Berkeley: University of California Press, 1981).

21. Kathy Peiss developed and popularized the concept of homosocial space in *Cheap Amusements: Working Women and Leisure in Turn of the Century New York* (Philadelphia: Temple University Press, 1986).

22. "Griffo and M'Auliffe Fight," *New York Herald*, 17 May 1894, 9.

23. For a study that situates the world of boxing within the context of "the cult of masculinity," see Michael T. Isenberg, *John L. Sullivan and His America* (Urbana: University of Illinois Press, 1988).

24. *Harper's Young People* 15 (22 May 1894), 500.

25. Hendricks, *The Kinetoscope*, 78–79.

26. Tom Gunning, "A Mischievous and Knowing Gaze: The Films of the Lumière Company and the Culture of Amateur Photography," Congrès Lumière, Lyons, France, 7–10 June 1995.

27. Williams, *Republic of Images*, 32.

28. I first discussed this idea at the May 1987 Society for Cinema Studies conference in Montréal, in relation to the exhibition of Corbett-Fitzsimmons fight films. Several of these types of disjunctions are also analyzed in *The Emergence of Cinema*. The idea of a public sphere where the dynamics of a new medium generate unexpected contradictions of this kind has been theorized within a Frankfurt School perspective by Miriam Hansen in *Babel and Babylon: Spectatorship in American Silent Film* (Cambridge: Harvard University Press, 1991). I have been trying to grasp the depth and diversity of this phenomenon both here and in essays such as "Passions and the Passion Play: Theater, Film and Religion, 1880–1900," *Film History* 5, no. 4 (1993), 419–456.

29. "The Kinetograph," *New York Sun*, 28 May 1891, 1–2.

30. *New York World*, 3 June 1888, 16.

31. "Edison Perfects His Kinetoscope," *New York Herald*, 7 March 1894, 9. The idea that Sandow was participating in an "experiment" is mentioned in almost every news report.

32. *Orange Journal*, 3 March 1888, 2. The day following his controversial exhibition in Orange, NJ, Muybridge met with Edison at the inventor's near-by laboratory. In the course of their discussions, the two promised to collaborate by combining Edison's phonograph with Muybridge's serial photography. Muybridge thus spurred Edison to develop his motion picture systems. But his work also influenced the subject matter and representational strategies adopted for these early films.

33. The sexual proclivities of both Muybridge and Dickson merit further study. Dickson's fascination with Sandow goes beyond the depiction of a homosocial space to one that is homoerotic. This becomes quite obvious when one looks at the highly charged photographs of Sandow, which Dickson included in his *History of the Kinetograph, Kinetoscope and Kineto-Phonograph*.

34. "Anatomy of a Kiss," *New York World*, 26 April 1896, 21.

35. Curtis M. Hinsley, "The World as Marketplace: Commodification of the Exotic at the World's Columbian Exposition, 1893," in Ivan Karp and Steven D. Lavine, eds, *Exhibiting Cultures: The Poetics and Politics of Museum Display* (Washington, DC: Smithsonian Institution Press, 1991), 344–365.

36. Barbara Kirshenblatt-Gimblett, "Objects of Ethnography," in Karp and Lavine, eds., *Exhibiting Cultures*, 398.

37. Kirshenblatt-Gimblett, "Objects of Ethnography," 399.

38. A certain amount of more or less intentional confusion accompanies any effort to identify the ethnic and national identity of vaudevillians. Despite her Italian sounding stage name, Ena Bertoldi was English. Likewise, despite their Italian stage names, Robetta and Doretto (Phil Lauter) were of British descent. In playing an Irish cop and Chinese laundryman, they were playing somewhat anarchically across racial and ethnic lines.

39. Alan Trachtenberg, "Conceivable Aliens," *The Yale Review* 82, no. 4 (October 1994), 42–64; Werner Sollors, *Beyond Ethnicity* (New York: Oxford University Press), 149–173.

40. So far as we know, Dickson and Heise employed closer views (camera framings approaching a medium shot in today's terminology) only with European and European-American performers.

41. Edward Steichen, *The Family of Man* (1955; New York: Museum of Modern Art, 1986), 3.

42. For newspaper accounts of this screening see Musser, *The Emergence of Cinema*, 116. I misidentified *Band Drill* as *Finale of 1st Act of Hoyt's "Milk White Flag,"* in Musser, *Before the Nickelodeon*, 62.

43. "Wonderful is the Vitascope," *New York Herald,* 24 April 1896, 11, in Musser, *Edison Motion Pictures, 1890–1900*, 200–201.

44. Ibid.

45. Ibid.

46. Reports of the cinématographe reached Raff & Gammon from England. London screenings destroyed their hope for a sale of considerable size and importance. Also British systems as well as the Lumière cinématographe were in use by this period. In this respect Great Britain was an appropriate if somewhat misplaced object of Raff & Gammon's barbs.

PART I

Film projection and variety shows

INTRODUCTION

L ATE IN 1894 A NUMBER OF INDEPENDENT experiments to develop a film projection system began more or less simultaneously in France, England, Germany and the US, often in response to kinetoscope technology and in any case consistent with earlier projection technology like the magic lantern and with Edison's stated goal to develop film projection.[1] In this introduction we pose a number of questions about the emergence and development of film projection so as to better situate the following chapters on the films produced during the late 1890s and early 1900s. Why was projection technology developed? Who developed it? How did these people conceptualize the use of projection technology? What kinds of films did they produce? And how successful were these films with audiences?

In 1894 Edison was not interested in public film projection for simple economic reasons because his film business was centred on the selling of kinetoscope machines. As we saw in the last section, film projection entered into Edison's plans only insofar as it could be used in the home. Projecting films to audiences in theatres was undesirable because it would cut down on the number of machines that could be sold. Edison continued to pursue the goal of domestic projection for a number of years, notably with the development of a domestic projection system in 1911, but the high cost of this to consumers militated against widespread use.[2]

Looked at from a different perspective, one that saw the film business less as a technology based industry and more as an entertainment based industry, film projection was extremely desirable. It would enable showmen to buy just one machine to exhibit to large paying audiences and also to be increasingly mobile, so that they could move to find new audiences in different locations. Initial efforts to develop film projection in the United States proceeded from this logic, beginning with the successful attempt of kinetoscope parlour owner Woodville Latham and his sons to adapt the kinetoscope to projection; later developments included the licencing and marketing of a successful projection system by the important kinetoscope distributors Norman Charles Raff and Frank R. Gammon.[3]

Latham and his sons Otway and Gray ran a kinetoscope parlour in New York City and had quickly realized the commercial desirability of film projection. Edison, though, rejected their request to work together to this end. Latham, a former chemistry professor, pursued the project anyway, enlisting the help of William Laurie Kennedy Dickson, who was increasingly dissatis-fied with his work at Edison's laboratory, and former Edison employee Eugéne Lauste.[4] Together the group succeeded in producing a viable projection system that was demonstrated on 21 April 1895 in the first public demonstration of projected moving pictures in the United States. Late the following month a storefront theatre was opened on Broadway, New York City, showing films of a boxing match arranged on the roof of Madison Square Garden. 'It is all realistic, so realistic, indeed', reported the *New York World*, 'that excitable spectators have forgot themselves and cried "Mix up there!" "Look out, Charlie, you'll get a punch"'.[5] Boxing films were particularly important for the Lathams and their audiences, partly it seems because they replicated similar kinetoscope entertainments and because the films were able to repre-sent boxing matches to audiences (such as women) who for various reasons could not attend the actual events.

The Lathams' machine, the *Eidoloscope*, as it came to be called, was, however, techni-cally flawed, for it basically copied the kinetoscope system which featured a constantly moving strip of film rather than an intermittent mechanism that momentarily stopped each frame of film in front of the lens (which is the basis of all modern projection). Image quality was conse-quently variable.[6] Crucial advances were made here by a young government clerk and inventor called C. Francis Jenkins and his partner, real estate entrepreneur Thomas Armat. Late in 1894 Jenkins and Armat began working on film projection and they developed an intermittent mechanism in mid-1895.[7] On the threshold of commercial success, the partnership dissolved and Armat arranged with the kinetoscope entrepreneurs Raff and Gammon to commercially exploit the machine which came to be called the *Vitascope*. Raff and Gammon in turn contracted with Edison to manufacture the projectors and the films and, indeed, to pretend that the machine had been devised by Edison, so capitalizing on his celebrity. He agreed, presumably because he saw that the kinetoscope business was clearly nearing its conclusion and was conscious that other projection systems were being developed, in particular the Lumières' cinématographe which was scheduled to make its American debut in June 1896. Pre-emptively, 'Edison's Vitascope' premiered at Koster and Bial's Music Hall on Broadway on 23 April 1896, with Edison in the audience.[8] It was, the *New York Dramatic Mirror* observed, 'a success in every way and the large audience testified its approval of the novelty by the heartiest kind of applause'.[9]

The successful premiere helped Raff and Gammon sell exhibition rights to a number of entre-preneurs who would exploit the vitascope at a range of exhibition sites in different localities. The initial programme of six films was similar to earlier kinetoscope exhibitions in content, including a serpentine dance and a burlesque boxing bout, but it also featured an 'actuality' film made in Britain called *Rough Sea at Dover*, described by the *New York Mail and Express* as 'by far the best view shown', so much so that it 'had to be repeated many times'.[10] Like in the kinetoscope, each film was spliced end to end to form a continuous loop so that a brief film could be shown over and over, like *Rough Sea at Dover* evidently was. Vitascope exhibitions, then, emphasized lifelike images and movement rather than the development of narrative. The brief programme of films of different genres suited the principle of variety entertainment, which was the dominant theatrical entertainment form of the turn-of-the-century period consisting of a range of very different acts (singers, magicians, comedians, brief dramas and so on).

Important parallel moves towards film projection had taken place in Europe. Late in the summer of 1894, the French businessman Antoine Lumière is reported to have interested his sons Louis and Auguste in the problem of motion picture projection by showing them a piece of kinetoscope film given to him by one of Edison's concessionaires: 'This is what you have to make, because Edison sells this at crazy prices and the concessionaires are trying to make films here in France to have them cheaper'.[11] Interested in expanding their photographic goods business, the brothers worked on the idea through late 1894 and succeeded in producing the cinématographe, a simple multi-purpose camera that could be used as a projector and printer, by February 1895. Exhibitions at various scientific congresses took place, as we have seen, from March 1895, and the first commercial exhibition occurred in a café in Paris in December 1895.[12]

Lumière films tended to be actualities, brief scenes of real life, often travel films showing views of, initially, European cities like Venice, Paris, London and Moscow, enabling spectators to travel vicariously via what Noël Burch has called 'celluloid tourism' and, as Tom Gunning suggests, to 'consume' the world in a way hitherto impossible.[13] Late in 1896 some films of American towns and cities were produced. Important also to the Lumière output were films about the Lumière family such as *Feeding the Baby, M. Lumière Receiving Guests, Children at Play, The Children's Seaside Frolic*. Such scenes of middle class domestic life differed from the variety theatre acts filmed by the Edison Manufacturing Company and marked a critical shift from the homosocial world of the kinetoscope and, to a lesser extent, the early eidoloscope and vitascope films, to an address of a broader heterosocial public. Women, children and middle-class audiences became increasingly important.

Late in 1894 also, Robert W. Paul, a scientific instrument maker from London, began to experiment with moving picture technology, inspired by the kinetoscope and by reports about the cinématographe and conscious of the money to be made from the sale of hardware and the entertainment of audiences. He was able to copy and manufacture his own kinetoscopes because Edison had declined to take out world-wide patents, allegedly because of their cost. It is more likely, though, that it was due to his belief that the broadness of his patents would not be recognised in Europe.[14] Paul developed a camera in collaboration with photographer and inventor Birt Acres, initially to produce films for the copied kinetoscopes. On hearing of the development of projection by the Lumières, Paul and Acres, having dissolved their partnership, rushed to produce their own projection systems. Acres gave the first demonstration of film projection in Britain at a meeting of the Royal Photographic Society in January 1896. Paul's system premiered at Finsbury Technical College in London on 20 April 1896, the very same day that the cinématographe premiered in London. One of Paul's projectors was bought by George Méliès, who, as Richard Abel's chapter in this section shows, went on to become an important French filmmaker. Later, phonograph exhibitor Charles Pathé also bought one prior to developing the biggest film company of the early period (discussed by Richard Abel in the following section). Like the cinématographe, the display of Paul's *Theatrograph*, as it was initially called, was quickly moved from the original scientific and educational context to music halls like the Olympia and Alhambra in London's Leicester Square and in other cities later in the summer.[15]

Variety theatres in cities were commonly among the first places to show projected moving pictures because variety theatre impresarios were always interested in exploiting the latest visual novelties and because the modular nature of the variety theatre bill, typically including a series of 10- to 20-minute acts with no narrative or thematic connection, suited the use of moving pictures as an isolated number. Vitascope exhibitions began at Koster and Bial's, one of New York City's most popular vaudeville theatres (an upmarket form of variety theatre for a broadly based middle class audience). Likewise, the cinématographe was shown at the

Empire Leicester Square in May 1896 and premiered in America at Keith's Union Square Theatre on 29 June; vaudeville impresario Benjamin Keith obtained the US rights of the ciné-matographe for the first few months of its exhibition.[16] The *Biograph* projector, developed by a group including Dickson and one of the most technically impressive machines, toured vaude-ville theatres in the summer of 1896 as part of a show featuring the strongman Eugene Sandow.[17] Other projectors were used at variety theatres across Great Britain, the US and other countries, introducing moving pictures to millions of spectators.

Diverse audiences saw films in this way, their composition depending on the kind of theatre in which the projector was set up. In the US, for example, risqué burlesque houses attracted boisterous working class males, whereas vaudeville theatres like Koster and Bial's and Keith's charged from 25 cents to $1.50 for admission and mainly attracted a middle class family audi-ence.[18] The pleasures the first film audiences gained from the projection of moving pictures in these settings were diverse. As with the kinetoscope, some of the attraction was related simply to the exhibition of a novel technology. Various genres also seemed to be particularly import-ant, a topic Richard Abel considers in his chapter here: actualities were popular, so were brief comic and trick films and, slightly later, longer dramatic films. The cultural resonances of train films are explored in Frank Gray's chapter, while Tom Gunning outlines the distinctive formal and stylistic features which underpinned the powerful impact of this 'cinema of attractions'.

Variety theatres in cities were only one of an assortment of exhibition venues for projected moving pictures. Itinerant exhibitors were particularly important in introducing moving pictures to small towns and rural areas.[19] Moving pictures were often shown in community or town halls or local theatres or as part of country fairs, fairgrounds and amusement parks. Many of these sites charged so little that even working-class audiences could gain admittance. Lexington, Kentucky, a small city in the American south, provides a useful example of the diversity of exhibition contexts. Gregory Waller's research has shown that moving pictures were exhibited in the city's opera house, in churches, at a summertime theatre in a local park, at various large-scale fairs visiting the city (including the Colored A&M Fair in 1897, an important site for black audiences to engage with moving pictures in a segregated culture), at street fairs and at Chautauqua assemblies (high-minded cultural gatherings).[20] Popular and commercial contexts existed side by side with highbrow and non-commercial contexts.

Lyman Howe, a prominent touring lecturer and purveyor of 'genteel' entertainment, incor-porated moving pictures into his slide and phonographs programmes from December 1896, integrating films into a respectable entertainment form seen by middle class and elite audi-ences at venues like the Brooklyn Institute of Arts and Sciences.[21] Lovers of refined culture sometimes saw moving pictures, notably those made by the Lumières, as part of a lecture or lecture series which often focused on travel. These audiences also saw versions of themselves in the on-screen images of middle class life which, as we have seen, was the subject of many of the films.

Often the interest in travel reflected an imperialist sense of the primitive nature of other cultures and deeply embedded views about ethnic and racial difference. Charles Musser has described this as a 'cinema of reassurance' and for Alison Griffiths these films commodified alterity (otherness) in a way that could function as a legitimation of colonial projects.[22] Travel lecturer E. Burton Holmes began to integrate filmed material of his own journeys around the world. Lecturing on 'Manila and the Philippines', the filmed material helped emphasise Holmes's arguments about the primitive conditions of life on the islands and the heroic actions of American soldiers.[23]

Important also to this sense of cinema as part of genteel culture were the various versions of the Passion Play that were filmed from 1897, for these self-consciously linked cinema to religious ideals and were often exhibited in churches.[24] Religious groups, particularly Protestant ones, increasingly sponsored film programmes in the late 1890s. Located in various exhibition contexts, then, cinema from the outset 'drew its audiences from across the working, middle, and elite classes', becoming part of the life of audiences who looked for education and entertainment.[25] This was the case in Europe as well as in the US.[26]

Despite the initial popularity of film shows with a broad swathe of society, the film industry encountered significant problems. Late in 1897 American film companies were locked into a long-running legal battle over patent rights initiated by Edison. Edison's litigation was the first of many attempts to establish a monopoly over the American film industry, and it severely restricted the operations of his competitors. There is also evidence to suggest that audiences in variety theatres in cities in the US were tiring of moving pictures, or at least that the novelty of projected moving pictures had worn off and interest levels had decreased accordingly.[27]

Events in the broader socio-political sphere helped arrest the downturn in audience interest, when the sinking of the *USS Maine* in Havana Harbour sparked a flurry of nationalistic sentiment in the US that was sustained through the brief Spanish–American war and conflict in the Philippines. Audiences wanted to see realistic images of the conflicts. Scenes of American troops leaving for the front, camp life in Cuba, the burial of American soldiers and the triumphant return of the war's heroes were widely seen. Films came to fulfil an important role as visual newspaper and, importantly, as a propaganda tool and shaper of a sense of national identity. Exhibitors frequently renamed the cinema apparatus the *Wargraph* or the *Warscope* and organized individual films into sequences that culminated with a display of the mastery and power of US imperialism.[28] Links between cinema and colonial projects were also visible in European film culture.[29]

Visual depictions of news events like the Spanish–American war, Queen Victoria's Diamond Jubilee celebrations, the funerals of Queen Victoria and President McKinley, the Russo-Japanese war or the Dreyfus Affair in France tied filmmaking to broader debates about controversial public events and national ideologies, and helped to foster a sense of nation-hood.[30] Interest in films tended to be high when significant news events were taking place or in their immediate aftermath; in the absence of such events, however, the appeal of film programmes often declined. This fluctuation meant that the future of the new medium was by no means guaranteed at this point.

How, finally, can we characterize the films seen by audiences between 1896 and 1903? How did they engage audiences? The essays gathered here offer some answers to these questions. Variety theatres encouraged the production of brief films that were visually arresting and offered a diversity of appeals, ranging across different genres like the variety bill itself.[31] The exhibition context of most film shows therefore helped produce a 'cinema of attractions', characterized by Gunning as a cinema that tended to show or display the technical possibilities of the medium (including all manner of tricks) or the spectacle of human figures, natural landscapes and constructed decors as visual attractions. This was predicated on engaging the viewer with a variety of competing spectacles rather than absorbing him or her into a coherent narrative. Attractions were derived from documentary scenes, from the technical possibilities of cinema like close-ups and those demonstrated in trick films (one of the genres analysed here by Richard Abel), and from staged scenes showing brief gags or variety acts. Gunning argues that this mode of representation was dominant until about 1908, though he notes that attractions and narrative frequently co-existed in a dialectical interplay – and indeed, frequently still do in a contemporary cinema often invested in the presentation of exciting visual spectacles.[32]

One important aspect of the early cinema of attractions worth noting here is how frequently women were positioned as an erotic spectacle, a point made by Richard Abel in his chapter and also forcefully in work by Linda Williams, Lauren Rabinovitz and Constance Balides.[33] Women's complicated position in the films of the cinema of attractions and in the various exhibition contexts where they were shown has been linked by Miriam Hansen to broad shifts in the organisation of public and private space characteristic of modernity in many Western countries in the turn-of-the-century period.[34]

Like Hansen, Gunning has increasingly sought to contextualize the cinema of attractions in relation to the broad social, political and cultural configuration of modernity, characterized by rapid advances in industrialization, urbanization, consumerism and in America at least, immigration at the turn of the century. The accelerated pace of life and increased use of visual spectacle brought about fundamental changes in perception and subjectivity which were reflected and refracted in the films produced at this moment, Gunning and others have argued.[35] This so-called 'modernity thesis' has been a source of considerable debate amongst film scholars, crystallizing questions about the significance of early cinema's mode of representation, about the relationship between film viewing and visual experiences of modern urban life, and about the effects of social and cultural transformations on vision and subjectivity.[36]

One other issue is worth exploring in relation to Gunning's justly influential concept of the cinema of attractions. Charles Musser's work has shown that exhibitors and showmen often put together a programme of films according to narrative principles. Lyman Howe, for example, created a programme in late 1898 from various films of the Spanish–American war that in combination told a story about preparation, conflict, and victory.[37] Lecturers also frequently commented on films as they were being shown, providing information to audiences and functioning effectively as 'cinematic narrators'.[38] In this sense, the creative role of exhibitors shaped films into narratives and thus lessened their status as exhibitionist attractions divorced from narrative in the period after the 'novelty year' of 1896–97.[39] Here, then, we find an important difference in the analysis of early cinema between two of its most important historians, who are adopting different perspectives: Gunning focuses closely on the films and, increasingly, on the broader contexts in which they were made and seen whilst Musser looks at film programmes and extra-filmic aspects of their exhibition.

A popular genre within the cinema of attractions was the train film. There were countless films of onrushing trains or of train crashes, films taken from moving trains (so-called 'phantom rides') and travel films involving trains. These two important technologies of modernity were frequently linked together to provide visual spectacle (with both films and trains being capable, it is worth noting, of annihilating space and time and figuratively or literally *moving* people). Frank Gray analyses some of the early train films made in England in his essay here, demonstrating the international impact of film production in England and outlining the contexts in which it emerged. Gray's chapter focuses on the films of G. A. Smith which both presented attractions and moved beyond them by beginning to combine shots to tell a story in a way that much later came to be known as continuity editing.

Like Gunning and Gray, Richard Abel in his chapter in this section is interested in a close examination of early films, focusing on important French productions from 1896 to 1904 and tracing out the interplay between attractions and narrative across a range of genres. French films were popular both in France and internationally. Indeed, they were, as Abel shows in the following section, crucial to the expansion of cinema in the US. All three chapters unpack the complexity of the films under consideration, showing that what at first sight might seem to be simple artefacts were in fact intricately constructed texts that drew on other entertainment forms and were often responsive to social, political and cultural trends.

By the end of the period covered in this section, the success of story films together with important developments in film distribution set the stage for the emergence of the nickelodeon, which both secured the future of film as a mass medium and dramatically increased its reach – subjects we consider in the following section.

Notes

1 The magic lantern was a sort of slide projector and had been used from the seventeenth century onwards as a form of visual entertainment. Photographic images could be projected from the 1850s onwards. See here Charles Musser, *The Emergence of Cinema: The American Screen to 1907* (Berkeley: University of California Press, 1990), 17–38; Deac Rossell, 'Double Think: The Cinema and Magic Lantern Culture', in John Fullerton (ed.), *Celebrating 1895: The Centenary of Cinema* (Sydney: John Libbey, 1998); Laurent Mannoni, *The Great Art of Light and Shadow: Archaeology of the Cinema*, translated and edited by Richard Crangle (Exeter: University of Exeter Press, 2000), in particular 28–135.

2 Ben Singer, 'Early Home Cinema and the Edison Home Projecting Kinetoscope', *Film History*, vol. 2 (1988), 37–69.

3 Raff and Gammon had, as we noted in the introduction to the previous section, been central to the commercial exploitation of the kinetoscope. Likewise, Otway Latham had formed the Kinetoscope Exhibition Company in May 1894 for the express purpose of exploiting films of prizefights. He was joined by his father Woodville and brother Gray. Gordon Hendricks, 'The History of the Kinetoscope', in Tino Balio (ed.), *The American Film Industry* (Madison: The University of Wisconsin Press, 1985), 51; Musser, *The Emergence of Cinema*, 82–3. Showmen from other backgrounds also moved into film projection. William Selig, for example, was a former stage magician. William Paley had previously worked as an X-ray projector when X-rays enjoyed a short-lived vogue as visual entertainment.

4 Musser, *The Emergence of Cinema*, 91–100; Deac Rossell, *Living Pictures: The Origins of the Movies* (Albany: State University of New York Press, 1998), 123–7.

5 *New York World* (28 May 1895), 30, quoted in Musser, *The Emergence of Cinema*, 99.

6 Even so, the so-called Latham loop would prove to be very important for future cameras and projectors. Most cameras and projectors up to this point could only use a short stretch of film, lasting less than three minutes, since the tension created by a longer, heavier roll would break the film. The Lathams added a loop to relieve the tension, allowing much longer films to be made. It has been used in most cameras and projectors ever since.

7 Musser, *The Emergence of Cinema*, 100–05; Rossell, *Living Pictures*, 119–21.

8 Musser, *The Emergence of Cinema*, 109–12, 115–18.

9 *New York Dramatic Mirror* (2 May 1896), 19, quoted in Musser, *The Emergence of Cinema*, 116.

10 *New York Mail and Express* (24 April 1896), 12, quoted in ibid., 116.

11 David Robinson, *From Peep Show to Palace: The Birth of American Film* (New York: Columbia University Press, 1996), 60–1.

12 Alan Williams, *Republic of Images: A History of French Filmmaking* (Cambridge, Mas.: Harvard University Press, 1992), 24–5.

13 Noël Burch, *Life to Those Shadows*, trans. Ben Brewster (London: British Film Institute, 1990); Tom Gunning, 'The World as Object Lesson: Cinema Audiences, Visual Culture and the St. Louis World's Fair, 1904', *Film History*, vol. 6 (1994); Tom Gunning, 'The Whole Town's Gawking: Early Cinema and the Visual Experience of Modernity', *The Yale Journal of Criticism*, vol. 7, no. 2 (1994).

14 Michael Chanan, 'Economic Conditions of Early Cinema', in Thomas Elsaesser (ed.), *Early Cinema: Space, Frame, Narrative* (London: British Film Institute, 1990), 174; Musser, *The Emergence of Cinema*, 71–2, 504.

15 John Barnes, *The Beginnings of the Cinema in England* (Newton Abbott: David and Charles, 1976), 47. Numerous other inventors were also important. We have focused our attention on France, Britain and the United States so as to introduce the following essays which deal with those countries.

16 Barnes, *The Beginnings of the Cinema in England*, 89; Musser, *The Emergence of Cinema*, 135–45. Lumière's cinématographe was particularly well suited to exploitation in variety theatres, for the camera functioned as a printer and projector and was light and mobile. Important also was the fact that the ciné-matographe was hand cranked and did not run off electricity like the vitascope, for example, did. This was helpful because the electricity supply in towns and cities was not standardized and so the vitascope was unable to run in some places.

17 Musser, *The Emergence of Cinema*, 145–57. Biograph went on to become one of the most important film companies, as we will see in later sections.

18 Vaudeville had in fact grown out of various risqué variety theatre traditions in the 1880s and had estab-lished itself as a 'respectable' entertainment form. See Robert C. Allen, *Vaudeville and Film, 1895–1915: A Study in Media Interaction* (New York: Arno Press, 1980); Robert C. Allen *Horrible Prettiness: Burlesque and American Culture* (Chapel Hill: University of North Carolina Press, 1991). Two kinds of variety theatres in Germany, the so-called Folk Theatre and International Variety Theatre, similarly attracted different audiences in terms of class, the former largely working class and the latter largely middle class. In Britain, Music Halls were predominantly attended by working class audiences. Joseph Garncarz, 'The Origins of Film Exhibition in Germany', in Tim Bergfelder, Erica Carter and Deniz Göktürk (eds), *The German Cinema Book* (London: British Film Institute, 2002); Roberta Pearson, 'Early Cinema', in Geoffrey Nowell-Smith (ed.), *The Oxford History of World Cinema* (Oxford: Oxford University Press, 1996), 22.

19 Charles Musser with Carol Nelson, *High-Class Moving Pictures: Lyman H. Howe and the Forgotten Era of Traveling Exhibition, 1880–1920* (Princeton: Princeton University Press, 1991); Kathryn H. Fuller, *At the Picture Show: Small-Town Audiences and the Creation of Movie Fan Culture* (Washington: Smithsonian Institution Press, 1996); Vanessa Toulmin, ' "Local Films for Local People": Travelling Showmen and the Commissioning of Local Films in Great Britain, 1900–1902', *Film History*, vol. 13, no. 2 (2001); Garncarz, 'The Origins of Film Exhibition in Germany'.

20 Gregory Waller, *Main Street Amusements: Movies and Commercial Entertainment in a Southern City, 1896–1930* (Washington: Smithsonian Institution Press, 1995), in particular 23–64.

21 Musser with Nelson, *High Class Moving Pictures*.

22 Musser with Nelson, *High Class Moving Pictures*, 197; Alison Griffiths, ' "To the World the World We Show": Early Travelogues as Filmed Ethnography', *Film History*, vol. 11 (1999), 285. See also Alison Griffiths, *Wondrous Difference: Cinema, Anthropology, and Turn of the Century Visual Culture* (New York: Columbia University Press, 2002).

23 Musser, *The Emergence of Cinema*, 222–3.

24 Charles Musser, 'Passions and the Passion Play: Theater, Film, and Religion in America, 1880–1900', in Frances G. Couvares (ed.), *Movie Censorship and American Culture* (Washington, DC: Smithsonian Institution Press, 1996).

25 Musser, *The Emergence of Cinema*, 193.

26 See, for example, Joseph Garncarz, 'Exhibition', in Thomas Elsaesser with Michael Wedel (eds), *The BFI Companion to German Cinema* (London: British Film Institute, 1999); and Barnes, *The Beginning of Cinema in England*.

27 Musser, *The Emergence of Cinema*, 263.

28 Ibid., 226–61; Kristen Whissel, 'Uncle Tom, Goldilocks and the Rough Riders: Early Cinema's Encounter with Empire', *Screen*, vol. 40, no. 4 (Winter 1999).

29 See, for example, Guido Convents, 'Documentaries and Propaganda before 1914: A View on Early Cinema and Colonial History', *Framework*, no. 35 (1988); John Barnes, *Filming the Boer War* (London: Bishopsgate Press, 1992), republished as *The Beginning of Cinema in England: Volume Four, 1899* (Exeter: University of Exeter Press, 1996).

30 See, for example, Stephen Bottomore, 'Dreyfus and Documentary', *Sight and Sound*, vol. 53, no. 4 (Autumn 1984).

31 David Bordwell, Janet Staiger and Kristin Thompson, *The Classical Hollywood Cinema: Film Style and Mode of Production to 1960* (London: Routledge), 159–61.

32 Other scholars have argued that the dominance of attractions subsides earlier. Abel's analysis in Chapter 4 suggests this, as does Charles Musser in his essay, 'Rethinking Early Cinema: Cinema of Attractions and Narrativity', *The Yale Journal of Criticism*, vol. 7, no. 2 (1994).

33 Linda Williams, 'Film Body: An Implantation of Perversions', in Philip Rosen (ed.), *Narrative, Apparatus, Ideology: A Film Theory Reader* (New York: Columbia University Press, 1986); Lauren Rabinovitz, 'Temptations of Pleasure: Nickelodeons, Amusement Parks, and the Sights of Female Sexuality', *Camera*

Obscura, no. 23 (1991); Constance Balides, 'Scenarios of Exposure in the Practice of Everyday Life: Women in the Cinema of Attractions', *Screen*, vol. 34, no.1 (1993).

34   Miriam Hansen, *Babel and Babylon: Spectatorship in American Silent Film* (Cambridge, MA: Harvard University Press, 1991).

35   Tom Gunning, 'The Whole Town's Gawking'; Ben Singer, *Melodrama and Modernity: Early Sensational Cinema and Its Contexts* (New York: Columbia University Press, 2001).

36   Concerns about the 'modernity thesis' have been raised by David Bordwell and Charlie Keil. See David Bordwell, *On the History of Film Style* (Cambridge, MA: Harvard University Press, 1997), in particular 141–6; Charlie Keil, ' "Visualized Narratives": Transitional Cinema and the Modernity Thesis', in Claire Dupré la Tour, André Gaudreault and Roberta Pearson (eds), *Cinema at the Turn of the Century* (Lausanne: Éditions Nota Bene, 1999). For a thorough account of, and response to these concerns, see Singer, *Melodrama and Modernity*, 101–30.

37   Musser with Nelson, *High Class Moving Pictures*, 87–90.

38   Musser, 'The Nickelodeon Era Begins: Establishing the Framework for Hollywood's Mode of Representation', in Thomas Elsaesser (ed.), *Early Cinema: Space, Frame, Narrative* (London: British Film Institute, 1990), in particular 257–63.

39   Musser, 'Rethinking Early Cinema'.

Chapter 2

TOM GUNNING

"NOW YOU SEE IT, NOW YOU DON'T"
The temporality of the cinema of attractions

T HE REVISION OF EARLY FILM HISTORY that began in the late 1970s was only partly a process of correcting the scholarship of previous generations of scholars (who had not had easy access to film archives) through more careful film analysis and a thorough winnowing of secondary material, such as trade journals, film catalogs, and business records. The possibility of seeing and analyzing a large number of films from the period before World War I certainly inspired the transformation. But the new discoveries also created and were guided by new schemata through which the history of early cinema was (re)constructed. Inspired in a central way by certain insights of Noël Burch, other scholars and I began to envision early film as less a seed bed for later styles than a place of rupture, a period that showed more dissimilarity than continuity with later film style.

This sense of rupture and difference contrasted with previous assumptions about the beginnings of film style and practice. Although the history of early cinema had never been thoroughly theorized, I believe one can isolate three assumptions that underpinned what I will call the continuity model. This model sees early cinema as a preparatory period for later film styles and practices, the infancy of an art form. The first assumption appeared earliest historically and remained the least theorized because it was seen as a natural assumption. We could call this the evolutionary assumption, and it motivates the structure of early film histories such as those of Terry Ramsaye and Lewis Jacobs. This assumption sees cinema before WWI as primitive, an early stage in which later potentials are sketched out but imperfectly realized. Following a biological and teleological logic, this assumes that the later styles of cinema are a sort of natural norm that early cinema envisioned but was not yet capable of realizing because of technological and economic immaturity and a natural need for a period of development guided by a method of trial and error. This assumption sees film history as a linear evolutionary process in which the earliest stage is by definition a period of less development.

A second assumption can be seen as growing out of the evolutionary assumption, giving it more specificity and defining the goals of the development of film art with more precision. I will call this the cinematic assumption. The work of classical film historians Lewis Jacobs, Georges Sadoul, and Jean Mitry all show its influence. In this assumption, the development of film came from a discovery and exploration of its true cinematic essence. This development usually takes the dramatic form of a liberation of film from a false homology that restricted it to the technological reproduction of theater. In this assumption, editing usually plays the key role, but other inherently "cinematic" devices of camera mobility and freedom of shooting angle also help define a uniquely cinematic essence. Within this scenario, early cinema makes the initial error of simple reproduction and theatricality and then dramatically discovers its own nature.

The third assumption is perhaps the most subtle and was the last to be articulated, appearing in the semiological writing of Christian Metz. Metz reworked the assumption of a natural cinematic essence by highlighting the narrative function, declaring that cinema only truly appeared when it discovered the mission of telling stories: "The very nature of the cinema rendered such an evolution if not certain at least probable."[1] Mitry had already formulated the cinematic assumption by seeing early cinema as a struggle between theatricality and narrativity,[2] and Metz extends this formulation into what we could call the narrative assumption. All three assumptions can function together to form a tightly knit understanding of the continuity of early cinema with its later development. The telling of stories supplies the goal of the evolutionary assumption (cinema must evolve as a better and more efficient teller of stories) as well as a motive for its differentiation from theater (since silent cinema was mute, it had to compensate with other regimes of signifiers to carry narrative information and therefore developed its own language).

When André Gaudreault and I introduced the term *cinema of attractions* in the early 1980s, we were trying to undo the purchase these assumptions had on conceptualizing early film history.[3] Of course, these assumptions are not simply illusions to be dispelled; they do contain schemata that have been important for certain periods of film history. In particular, my own work on the early films of D. W. Griffith reexamined the narrative assumption and found that the function of storytelling was determinate for stylistic transformations in Griffith's Biograph films.[4] But my historical work also questioned Metz's theoretical assumption of a natural match between cinematic form and the mission of narrative. The dedication of film form to a narrative task that rules Griffith's early work was hardly the outcome of a previous evolution or gradual discovery of film's essential nature. Griffith and his contemporaries (and some immediate predecessors) were engaged in a redefinition rather than a discovery of film – a redefinition shaped by an economic reorganization attempting to regulate the film industry in the wake of the enormous expansion of nickelodeon exhibition. It was at this point in history and within this intersection of economic and social forces that film "discovered" its narrative vocation.

However, cinema before 1908 (or so) presents a different landscape. Here the assumption of narrative primacy becomes more of a barrier to understanding than a useful hypothesis. While storytelling is not totally foreign to cinema before the nickelodeon boom (1905–1909), a number of apparent stylistic anomalies and an often radically different mode of exhibition lead us in another direction. Rather than early approximations of the later practices of the style of classical film narration, aspects of early cinema are best understood if a purpose other than storytelling is factored in.

Cinema as an attraction is that other purpose. By its reference to the curiosity-arousing devices of the fairground, the term denoted early cinema's fascination with novelty and its foregrounding of the act of display. Viewed from this perspective, early cinema did not simply seek to neutrally record previously existing acts or events. Rather, even the seemingly stylistically neutral film consisting of a single-shot without camera tricks involved a cinematic gesture of presenting for view, of displaying. The objects of this display varied among current events (parades, funerals, sporting events); scenes of everyday life (street scenes, children playing, laborers at work); arranged scenes (slapstick gags, a highlight from a well-known play, a romantic tableau); vaudeville performances (juggling, acrobatics, dances); or even camera tricks (Méliès-like magic transformations). But all such events were absorbed by a cinematic gesture of presentation, and it was this technological means of representation that constituted the initial fascination of cinema.

My emphasis on display rather than storytelling should not be taken as a monolithic definition of early cinema, a term that forms a binary opposition with the narrative form of classical cinema. Rather, films that precede the classical paradigm are complex texts that occasionally interrelate attractions with narrative projects. My point is not that there are no narrative films before the nickelodeon era but rather that attractions most frequently provide the dominant for film during this period and often jockey for prominence until 1908 or so (and even occasionally later). The desire to display may interact with the desire to tell a story, and part of the challenge of early film analysis lies in tracing the interaction of attractions and narrative organization. The ambivalence that Noël Burch found in the work of Edwin Porter may be partly explained by this interaction, with the famous close-up of the outlaw firing the pistol at the camera in *The Great Train Robbery* functioning as a fairly autonomous attraction while most of the film strives for a sort of linear narrative.[5] In classical cinema, narrative integration functions as a dominant, but attractions still play a role (moments of spectacle, performance, or visual pyrotechnics) with their subordination to narrative functions varying from film to film. Similarly, I do not want to identify narrativity exclusively with the classical paradigm. There are many ways of telling a story in film, and some of them (particularly in cinema before the 1920s or, obviously, in avant-garde work) are clearly nonclassical. In some genres (musicals, crazy comedies) the attractions actually threaten to mutiny. By describing narrative as a *dominant*[6] in the classical film, I wish to indicate a potentially dynamic relation to nonnarrative material. Attractions are not abolished by the classical paradigm, they simply find their place within it.

I propose attractions, therefore, as a key element of the structure of early film rather than as a single-tracked definition of filmmaking before 1908 (although it may, particularly in the earliest period, function as a defining element). It can only be defined with precision through contrast, however, and I want to further specify some of the ways attractions differ from the cinema of narrative integration that comes after it, as well as from most forms of cinema based on a narrative dominant.

As a new way of approaching early cinema, attractions foreground the role of the spectator. Cinematic attractions can be defined as formal devices within early film texts. However, they can only be thoroughly understood if these devices are conceived as addressing spectators in a specific manner. This unique spectatorial address defines the cinema of attractions and its difference from the classically constructed spectatorial address of later narrative cinema. While I am not sure that the metapsychology of the spectator devised in the seventies is truly adequate to the complexity of even the classical style of narrative (let alone a revision which recognizes the continued role of attractions within classical Hollywood cinema), certain basic contrasts are apparent.

Narrative invokes the spectator's interest (and even desire, in a psychoanalytical model) by posing an enigma. The enigma demands a solution and, as Roland Barthes and the Russian Formalists have shown, the art of narrative consists in delaying the resolution of that enigma, so that its final unfolding can be delivered as a pleasure long anticipated and well earned. Further, in classical narrative cinema this pursuit of an enigma takes place within a detailed diegesis, a fictional world of places and characters in which the action of the narrative dwells. From a spectatorial point of view, the classical diegesis depends not only on certain basic elements of coherence and stability but also on the lack of acknowledgment of the spectator. As the psychoanalytically shaped theory of Metz claims, this is a world that allows itself to be seen but that also refuses to acknowledge its complicity with a spectator. In the classical diegesis, the spectator is rarely acknowledged, an attitude exemplified by the stricture against the actor's look or gestures at the camera/spectator. As Metz says, the classical spectator becomes modeled on the voyeur, who watches in secret, without the scene he watches acknowledging his presence.[7]

Attractions pose a very different relation to the spectator. The attraction does not hide behind the pretense of an unacknowledged spectator (in this respect it recalls Thelma Ritter's line as Stella in Hitchcock's *Rear Window* – "I'm not shy, I've been looked at before"). As I have stated elsewhere, the attraction invokes an exhibitionist rather than a voyeuristic regime.[8] The attraction directly addresses the spectator, acknowledging the viewer's presence and seeking to quickly satisfy a curiosity. This encounter can even take on an aggressive aspect, as the attraction confronts audiences and even tries to shock them (the onrushing locomotive that seems to threaten the audience is early cinema's most enduring example).[9]

The metapsychology of attractions is undoubtedly extremely complex, but its roots could be traced to what St. Augustine called *curiositas* and early Christianity condemned as the "lust of the eye."[10] We could list a number of inherently "attractive" themes in early cinema: a fascination with visual experiences that seem to fold back on the very pleasure of looking (colors, forms of motions – the very phenomenon of motion itself in cinema's earliest projections); an interest in novelty (ranging from actual current events to physical freaks and oddities); an often sexualized fascination with socially taboo subject matter dealing with the body (female nudity or revealing clothing, decay, and death); a peculiarly modern obsession with violent and aggressive sensations (such as speed or the threat of injury). All of these are topoi of an aesthetic of attractions, whether of the cinema, the sensational press, or the fairground. Attractions' fundamental hold on spectators depends on arousing and satisfying visual curiosity through a direct and acknowledged act of display, rather than following a narrative enigma within a diegetic site into which the spectator peers invisibly.

Rather than a desire for an (almost) endlessly delayed fulfillment and a cognitive involvement in pursuing an enigma, early cinema, therefore, *attracts* in a different manner. It arouses a curiosity that is satisfied by surprise rather than narrative suspense. This different temporal configuration determines its unique spectatorial address as much as its acknowledgment of the spectator's gaze, and it is the explosive, surprising, and even disorienting temporality of attractions that I want to explore in the rest of this essay.

First let's consider the temporality of narrative. Beyond stylistic devices of temporal manipulation any narrative implies a development in time. In addition to the base of simple temporal progression and change, this implies what Paul Ricoeur has called a configuration of time, time assuming a sort of shape through the interacting logic of events.[11] As Ricoeur argues, it is through this configuration that events become a story and narrative moves beyond the simply chronological. Time in narrative, therefore, is never just linear progression (one damn thing after another), it is also the gathering of successive moments into a pattern, a trajectory, a sense. Attractions, on the other hand, work with time in a very different manner. They basically do not build up incidents into the configuration with which a story makes its individual moments cohere. In effect, attractions have one basic temporality, that of the alternation of presence/absence that is embodied in the act of display. In this intense form of present tense, the attraction is displayed with the immediacy of a "Here it is! Look at it."

While this temporality is most apparent in the many one-shot films, it also determines the temporal structure of films that include more than one shot, such as the early multi-shot films of Méliès. The odd temporality of Méliès has been noted by John Frazer:

> The causal narrative links in Méliès films are relatively insignificant compared to the discrete events. We experience his films as rapidly juxtaposed jolts of activity. We focus on successions of pictorial surprises which run roughshod over the conventional

niceties of linear plotting. Méliès' films are a collage of immediate experiences which coincidentally require the passage of time to become complete.[12]

Frazer here contrasts two types of temporality: the linear progression of plotting and causality, and the staccato jolts of surprise that characterize Méliès films. While the simple linear model may do a disservice to the possible complexities of narrative structure, Frazer's invocation of jagged rhythm catches the irruption of a different, nonconfigured temporality, that of the attraction.

The temporality of the attraction, therefore, is greatly limited in comparison to narrative, albeit possessing its own intensity. Rather than a development that links the past with the present in such a way as to define a specific anticipation of the future (as an unfolding narrative does), the attraction seems limited to a sudden burst of presence. Restricted to the presentation of a view or a central action, the cinema of attractions tends naturally toward brevity rather than extension. Such restricted focus on a simple action is beautifully indicated by an Edison catalog description of its famous one-shot film *The Kiss:* "They get ready to kiss, begin to kiss, and kiss in a way that brings down the house."[13]

This does not necessarily mean that the act of display was always restricted to the surprise burst of the instant or could not play with its temporality. Certain attractions – most obviously extended landscape panoramas or the railway journeys of the Hale's tours sort – take longer to unfold without creating the patterning expectations that narrative implies. The Biograph 1904 film within the New York subway constantly renews its sense of revelation as the change of light and shadow. The passing structures of subway supports, the appearance of stations, and turns in the track make the film frame a location of seemingly endless visual patterns.[14]

Likewise the very moment of display can be manipulated into a scenario of suspense unique to the aesthetic of attractions. Founded on the moment of revelation, the cinema of attractions frequently redoubles its effect of appearance by framing the attraction with a variety of gestures of display. The most common of these are the literal gestures of the magician in magic films who through a sweep of the hand or a slight bow directs the audience's attention to the transformation that then takes place. This gesture sets up a hierarchy between the magician as displayer and the transformation as the event displayed. Beyond enframing (and therefore calling attention to) the act of display, it also performs the important temporal role of announcing the event to come, focusing not only the attention but the anticipation of the audience.

The temporality of the attraction itself, then, is limited to the pure present tense of its appearance, but the announcing gesture creates a temporal frame of expectation and even suspense. It differs from diegetic suspense, of course, in being concerned less with *how* an event will develop than with *when* an event will occur. Early showman exhibitors were keenly aware that such focused anticipation played an important role in putting an attraction over. Since this temporality need not refer to diegetic unfoldings, the framing gesture could occur outside the actual film, embodied in the way the film was presented. The exhibitor's role as a showman presenting an attraction embodies the essential gesture of the cinema of attractions and could be dramatically intensified through temporal manipulation. For instance, Albert Smith recalled his early days as a traveling exhibitor at the turn of the century with his partner, John Stuart Blackton, and the startling effect of Blackton's lectures that accompanied their films. To emphasize the novel illusion of motion, the first frame of their most popular film, *The Black Diamond Express*, a shot of a locomotive barreling toward the camera, was projected first as a frozen image. Over this curiosity-provoking suspended moment, Blackton would intone: "Ladies and Gentlemen, you are now gazing upon a photograph of the famous Black Diamond Express.

In just a moment, a cataclysmic moment, my friends, a moment without equal in the history of our times, you will see this train take life in a marvelous and most astounding manner. It will rush toward you, belching smoke and fire from its monstrous iron throat."[15]

The act of display on which the cinema of attractions is founded presents itself as a *temporal irruption* rather than a temporal development. While every attraction would have a temporal unfolding of its own and some (a complex acrobatic act, for instance, or an action with a clear trajectory, such as an onrushing train) might cause viewers to develop expectations while watching them, these temporal developments would be secondary to the sudden appearance and then disappearance of the view itself. In this sense Méliès' transformations become emblematic examples of the cinema of attractions, endlessly replaying the effect of surprise and appearance, as would a series of brief actualities of the Lumière sort, appearing one after another.

The suspense created by Blackton in the delay of the moving image of the locomotive may have similar effects to suspense within a narrative, such as the sharpening of expectation and even the growing anxiety as an event is announced but withheld. But it is not absorbed into a diegetic world of cause and effect, it has no relation to the fate of characters or the course of events. Rather, it simply redoubles the basic effect of an attraction, cathecting curiosity through delay and creating a satisfying discharge by unleashing the suspended rush of time. Not all gestures of display need to be so violent or shocking, but the shock effect highlights the attraction's disjunctive temporality. Such disjunction could also be used to an erotic effect, as the scopophilia implied by this mode becomes thematized. Edison's *What Happened on Twenty Third Street, New York City* provides a complex example.

This film from 1901 seems to transform itself from a street scene actuality to an erotic scene in the course of its single-shot. Shot on the eponymous New York City street, our original attention is, as in so many early actualities, diffused across the shot, solicited by many little events, none of which seem to have any narrative purpose. Rather, we are simply absorbed in the act of viewing, responding to the display of a moment of big city life. As the shot progresses, a couple emerges from the background of street life detail, soliciting our attention as they move toward the camera. As they near the foreground, an air current from a sidewalk grate lifts the woman's dress, and the film ends after the couple reacts to this moment of disclosure and moves on through the frame. Certainly this transformation from a decentered view to a gag centered on specific characters and a moment of erotic display possesses some temporal development. In fact, Judith Mayne in *The Woman at the Keyhole* sees it as moving toward a narrativization of the display of the female body.[16]

I would not dispute Mayne's insightful reading or deny the presence of a sort of temporal development in this film, which shows how difficult it might be to find moments even in early cinema that are totally bereft of narrative development. Particularly when dealing with a film in which the issues of gender (and the relations of power and exploitation they imply) are so clearly inscribed, it is difficult to articulate such relations outside of a narrative framework. However, I would emphasize that while the film can be viewed as a proto-narrative, it is still largely under the sway of a cinema of attractions. The act of display is both climax and resolution here and does not lead to a series of incidents or the creation of characters with discernible traits. While the similar lifting of Marilyn Monroe's skirts in *The Seven Year Itch* also provides a moment of spectacle, it simultaneously creates character traits that explain later narrative actions.

The film's title also sheds light on the structure of attractions. Its precision of location seemed to me simply documentary overkill until Brooks MacNamara explained its significance. Twenty-third Street near the Flatiron Building drew crowds of male loiterers during the turn of the century not only for the sight of New York's famous skyscraper but for less exulted visual pleasures as well. Known as the windiest corner in New York City, it was also known among the lascivious as a place where women's dresses were frequently lifted by the breeze.[17] The immediate cause of such indecent exposure (in an era where a glimpse of stocking was worth an afternoon of idleness) in this film is a hot air grate (described in the Edison Company publicity as coming from one of the large newspaper offices on the block).[18] To local audiences, at least, the title instead of connoting dull documentary precision would set up an atmosphere of titillation. Such playing with expectations recalls the structure of Blackton's locomotive show: announcement of what is to come, a delay in its revelation, followed by a diminuendo as the display ends and the attraction moves out of the frame.

A similar interaction between narrative structure and the specific temporality of attractions is found in Biograph's 1904 film *Pull Down the Curtain Susie*. Another one-shot film, *Susie* uses a multileveled set of an urban street front with residential windows to stage its drama of revelation. At the opening of the film, a man and a woman walk into the frame together. The shot is framed to focus on a second-story window so that only the heads and busts of the couple are included at the bottom of the frame as they walk (presumably on the street in front of the building). The woman gives the man a kiss, and they exit left. The woman reappears framed in the window of the set as the man reenters the street below. As the man watches excitedly, the woman begins to undress, taking off her skirt and blouse. She starts to remove her shift, then suddenly yanks down the curtain. The man throws up his arms in frustration and the film ends.

Susie unfolds a drama of sexual exhibition with an intradiegetic voyeur. While our involvement with the attraction is certainly mediated by the character of the man who shares our expectation and frustration (assuming, of course, the patriarchal ideology and sexual attitudes the film implies), and the disrobing entails some temporal development, the film nonetheless basically restricts itself to a demonstration of the simple temporality of the attraction: now you see it, now you don't. The climax here (as well as the event announced by the film's suggestive title) comes more from the disappearance of the view than its revelation. The basic structures of attractions, then, revolve around the act of display and the anticipations that can be heightened by delaying or announcing it (or both) and its inevitable disappearance (which can be gradual or sudden and dramatic). Therefore attractions do show a sort of temporal structure, but the structure consists more of framing a momentary appearance than an actual development and transformation in time. The attraction can appear or disappear and generally needs to do both. While present on the screen, it may in fact change, but insofar as these changes begin to entail further development, we move out of the structure of attractions and into a narrative configuration.

But this does not necessarily mean that the cinema of attractions was restricted to single-shot films. A Méliès transformation film provides the most obvious model for the longer film of attractions with its succession of magical appearances, transformations, and disappearances. One may string a series of attractions together as a magic film or a Lumière program might. The construction of such suites of attractions displays a highly paratactic structure with no attraction preparing the way for the next, but a simple rule of succession functioning. However, as with the vaudeville show, which would exemplify this variety format, a number of non-narrative logics might determine the arrangement of attractions.

This was a consideration not only in the production of a film but in the arrangement of a program of films. As Charles Musser has shown, the distinction between film and program was a vague one in this period in which the showman exhibitor asserted as much control over the final form of the film projected as the production company that issued the individual bits of celluloid with which he worked.[19] One basic consideration of such showmen was whether to opt for a basic thematic consistency (for instance, assembling films dealing with similar topics, such as military actualities) or going for its opposite and maximizing variety (following an actuality film with a gag film or trick film). Another structure of attractions relevant for both an exhibitor's program and an actual multi-shot film involved orchestrating the intensity, elaborateness, and emotional tone of the attractions. The obvious example of this (evident in many trick films) would be ending the film with a particularly spectacular attraction or with a gag. Or, alternatively, attractions could be crossbred with narrative forms, but with attractions still dominating, so that narrative situations simply provided a more naturalized way to move from one attraction to the next. This is clearly evident in Méliès' or Pathé's early extended trick films in which a well-known fairy tale might provide a logical connection between a series of tricks and spectacular effects, the famous "pretext" of a story line on which Méliès would hang his attractions.[20]

This capacity of an attraction to create a temporal disjunction through an excess of astonishment and display rather than the temporal unfolding essential to narrative explains one of the most interesting interactions between narrative form and the aesthetic of attractions, the apotheosis ending. This ending, which entered cinema from the spectacle theater and pantomime, provided a sort of grand finale in which principal members of the cast reappear and strike poses in a timeless allegorical space that sums up the action of the piece. The apotheosis is also the occasion for scenic effects through elaborate sets or stage machinery, as well as the positioning of the performers (often in the form of a procession, or an architectural arrangement of figures, with actual characters often supplemented by a large number of extras precisely for their spectacular effect). Such endings are frequent in the *ferrique* films of Méliès and Pathé, and examples can be found in Méliès' *The Kingdom of the Fairies* and *The Impossible Voyage*, Porter's *Jack and the Beanstalk*, and Pathé's *Le Chat botté*, *La Poule aux oeufs d'or*, and *Aladin du lampe merveilleuse*. Occasionally they also appear in more realistically but still spectacularly conceived dramas, such as Pathé's *Policeman's Tour of the World*, which ends a tale of a worldwide pursuit with an allegorical image of detective and thief shaking hands over an image of the globe, while extras parade by in native costumes of the various countries through which the course of the pursuit ran.[21] What is striking about these apotheosis endings is the way more complex narrative films make use of their "show-stopping" nature to produce a nonnarrative form of closure. Although often integrating the narrative outcome of the action (Jack with the giant's treasure, Azurine and Belazor's connubial bliss and assembled offspring, the rapprochement between thief and detective), they effectively halt the narrative flow through an excess of spectacle, shifting spectator interest from what will happen next to an enjoyment of the spectacle presented to them. In other words, a change in spectatorial registers and temporality takes place with the nondevelopmental time of a crowning attraction closing off the narrative and guaranteeing spectator satisfaction on two levels: the resolution of narrative action and the satiation of visual pleasure.

The apotheosis ending demonstrates once again that in spite of (indeed because of) the structural differences between the temporality and visual pleasure offered by attractions and those structured by narrative, the two ways of addressing spectators can frequently interrelate within the same text. Rather than a developing configuration of narrative, the attraction offers a jolt of pure presence, soliciting surprise, astonishment, or pure curiosity instead of following the enigmas on which narrative depends. However, this burst of presence can itself be structured by playing with or delaying its act of presentation and disappearance. Further, it can interact with narrative structures either by dominating them or by submitting to their dominance and assuming circumscribed roles within a narrative logic.

If we consider the sorts of attractions I have examined here in order to investigate their temporality, certain insights into the metapsychology of the spectator of early cinema suggest themselves. The sudden flash (or equally sudden curtailing) of an erotic spectacle, the burst into motion of a terroristic locomotive, or the rhythm of appearance, transformation, and sudden disappearance that rules a magic film all invoke a spectator whose delight comes from the unpredictability of the instant, a succession of excitements and frustrations whose order cannot be predicted by narrative logic and whose pleasures are never sure of being prolonged. Each instant offers the possibility of a radical alteration or termination. As one perceptive reader of an earlier draft of this essay pointed out, the title of this essay, a familiar phrase from midway ballyhoo and magic shows, implies precisely this discontinuous succession of instants: *now* you see it, *now* you don't. In contrast, narrative temporality moves from *now* to *then*, with causality as a frequent means of vectorizing temporal progression. My title phrase stresses both the spectator awareness of the act of seeing and the punctual succession of instants, while narrative temporality moves through a logic of character motivation ("First she . . . , *then* she . . ."). [. . .]

If the classical spectator enjoys apparent mastery of the narrative thread of a film (able to anticipate future action through her knowledge of the cues and schemata of narrative space and action), the viewer of the cinema of attractions plays a very different game of presence/absence, one strongly lacking predictability or a sense of mastery. In this sense we can see the relevance of Lynne Kirby's description of the early film spectator as a victim of hysteria.[22] The cinema of attractions truly invokes the temporality of surprise, shock, and trauma, the sudden rupture of stability by the irruption of transformation or the curtailing of erotic promise. Like the devotees of thrill rides at Coney Island, the spectator of early film could experience the thrill of intense and suddenly changing sensations.

This strongly discontinuous experience of time may be seen as an ideal form of early cinema's difference from later classical narrative. Certainly not all early attractions sought to shock their spectators. But rather than a purely passive recording of theatrical acts or slices of life, we see that the act of display in early film also carried at least the possibility of an experience of a time of pure instance. It was partly this temporality that explains the enthusiasm the early avant-garde had for the aesthetic of attractions, whether in variety theater, the fairground, the circus, or early cinema. The gesture of display figured a time that seemed to escape from a linear or successive configuration of time. The potential shock of the cinema of attractions provided a popular form of an alternative temporality based not on the mimesis of memory or other psychological states but on an intense interaction between an astonished spectator and the cinematic smack of the instant, the flicker of presence and absence.

Notes

The author would like to thank Lucy Fischer for her comments on an earlier draft of this essay.

1. Christian Metz, *Film Language: A Semiotics of the Cinema* (New York: Oxford University Press, 1974), pp. 44–45.
2. Jean Mitry, *Histoire du cinéma*, vol. 1 (1895–1914) (Paris: Editions Universitaires, 1967), p. 370.
3. André Gaudreault and Tom Gunning, "Le Cinéma des premier temps: Un défi a histoire du film?" in J. Aumont, A. Gaudreault, and M. Marie, eds, *Histoire du cinéma: Nouvelles approches* (Paris: Publications de la Sorbonne, 1989), pp. 49–63 (first presented at Cerisy Colloquium in 1985). See also Tom Gunning, "The Cinema of Attractions: Early Cinema, Its Spectator and the Avant Garde," in Thomas Elsaesser, ed., *Early Cinema: Space Frame Narrative* (London: BFI, 1990), pp. 56–62.
4. See Tom Gunning, *D. W. Griffith and the Origins of American Narrative Film* (Champaign: University of Illinois Press, 1991).

5. Noël Burch, "Porter or Ambivalence," *Screen* 19 (Winter 1978–79), 91–105.

6. The concept of the dominant comes from the Russian Formalists. For good summaries, see Victor Erlich, *Russian Formalism: History and Doctrine* (New Haven, Conn.: Yale University Press, 1981), pp. 212, 233; Peter Steiner, *Russian Formalism: A Metapoetics* (Ithaca, NY: Cornell University Press 1984), pp. 76–77, 104–106, 111. Kristin Thompson has used the concept in a number of fruitful ways in film analysis in *Breaking the Glass Armor: Neoformalist Film Analysis* (Princeton, NJ: Princeton University Press, 1988), pp. 43–45, 89–131.

7. Christian Metz, *The Imaginary Signifier: Psychoanalysis and the Cinema* (Bloomington: Indiana University Press, 1975), pp. 61–66, 91–97.

8. Gunning, "The Cinema of Attractions," p. 57.

9. For a fuller discussion of the relation of the cinema of attractions to the experience of shock touched on here, see Tom Gunning, "An Aesthetic of Astonishment: Early Cinema and the (In)Credulous Spectator," *Art and Text* 34 (Spring 1989), 31–45.

10. St. Augustine, *The Confessions* (New York: New American Library, 1963), pp. 245–247.

11. See Paul Ricoeur, *Time and Narrative*, vol. 1 (Chicago: University of Chicago Press, 1984), pp. 66–77. I want to thank Vicente Benet of the Universitat Jaume, Castello, Spain, for pointing out to me the relevance of this concept to early film.

12. John Fraser, *Artificially Arranged Scenes: The Films of George Méliès* (Boston: G. K. Hall, 1979), p. 124.

13. "Edison Film Catalogue" in Charles Musser, ed., *Motion Picture Catalogs by American Producers and Distributors. 1894–1908: A Microfilm Edition* (Frederick, MD: University Publications of America, 1985).

14. The unfolding of a landscape may imply a different spectator reception than the shock of display found in many typical films of the cinema of attractions. However, as constantly changing views they still possess the essential nonnarrative emphasis on display that defines the cinema of attractions. Further, early catalogs for films taken from trains also stressed the experience of speed and sudden changes in terrain and other experiences of shock and surprise. I thank Janet Staiger for her comments on this issue at a presentation of a shorter version of this paper at the 1991 SCS Conference at USC.

15. Albert E. Smith with Phil A. Koury, *Two Reels and a Crank* (New York: Garland Publishing, 1985), p. 39.

16. Judith Mayne, *The Woman at the Keyhole: Feminism and Woman's Cinema* (Bloomington: Indiana University Press, 1990), pp. 162–164.

17. This information can be found in print in the WPA 1939 *Guide to New York City*. Policemen assigned to scatter such loiterers coined the later familiar catch phrase "Twenty Three Skidoo." My intense thanks to Brooks MacNamara for the information and the source and to Ben Singer for further confirmation.

18. Musser, *Motion Picture Catalogs*, p. 86.

19. Musser makes this point in a number of his writings; see *The Emergence of Cinema*, vol. 1 of *History of the American Cinema* (New York: Charles Scribner's & Sons, 1990), pp. 179–181, 258–261.

20. Georges Méliès, "Importance du scenario," in Georges Sadoul, *Georges Méliès* (Paris: Segher, 1961), p. 118.

21. An insightful discussion of this final shot can be found in Phil Rosen, "Disjunction and Ideology in a Preclassical Film: *A Policeman's Tour of the World.*" *Wide Angle* 12:3 (1990), 20–37.

22. Lynne Kirby, "Male Hysteria and Early Cinema," *Camera Obscura* 17 (May 1988), 113–131.

Chapter 3

FRANK GRAY

THE KISS IN THE TUNNEL (1899), G. A. SMITH AND THE EMERGENCE OF THE EDITED FILM IN ENGLAND

I N 1920, LEV KULESHOV, the Russian film-maker and theorist, wrote a treatise on the nature of film. Entitled 'The Banner of Cinematography,' it articulated his theory of film montage/editing and what he described as the "essence of film art." He said, "the artistic vehicle of the cinema lies in the composition, in the way filmed pieces succeed each other. What matters most in terms of the screen impression is not what each piece represents but how the pieces are arranged. The essence of film art should be sought not within a single-shot but in the succession of shots! . . . the essence of cinema, its own vehicle of impression, is montage."[1] Kuleshov probably never saw a film by the pioneer English film-maker George Albert Smith (1864–1959), but it was Smith who played an essential role in the early evolution of the edited film in Europe and America.

Kuleshov's understanding of 'film art' applies directly to our understanding of Smith's films in 1899 and 1900 and in particular to his *The Kiss in the Tunnel* (1899) as it represents his first attempt to produce a multi-shot narrative. This three shot film is in fact the combination of Cecil Hepworth's single-shot film *View From an Engine Front – Train Leaving Tunnel* (1899) and Smith's one shot film *The Kiss in the Tunnel* (1899). Hepworth's film constitutes shots one and three and Smith's film serves as the inserted second shot of the railway carriage interior. Their unification introduced Smith's new understanding of continuity film editing, a concept that would have a profound impact on the development of editing strategies and become a dominant practice. Accordingly, the purpose of this essay is to use this film by Smith as a vehicle for an analysis of the development of editing strategies in the late 1890s, in particular Smith's contribution to the development of continuity editing. I will first outline the early history of the edited film in relation to the magic lantern before introducing Smith and exploring the specific histories of the phantom ride and the long film in relation to the production of Smith's film. The essay concludes with a consideration of *The Kiss in the Tunnel* in terms of its representation of late Victorian culture, its influence on Smith's work in 1900 and on the English film-maker James Williamson.

Editing the projected image

The embryonic concept of the edited film, as developed by Smith and some of his contemporaries around 1900, established that editing was a post-production activity and involved the selection and editing/cutting of individual shots together into a form determined by a narrative and the visual content of each shot. Crucial to this activity, both then and now, was the recognition of the film shot as a unit of meaning designed to be added to other shots/units in order to produce a film. The emergence of this concept signalled the end of the unedited, single-shot film that had been the dominant mode of film production since 1893.

However, this editing consciousness did not first emerge with the rise of film in the late 1890s as its origins are found within the history of the magic lantern. With lanternists who produced their own slides, individual lantern slides would be prepared, selected and arranged to accompany particular lectures. Each slide was designed to serve a particular function within the delivery of a linear, spoken narrative. With the industrialisation of the lantern in the late nineteenth century, commercially produced sets of slides could be purchased in which each slide was assigned a prescribed role within a set lantern reading. In performance, with either hand-made or purchased slides, the lecturer determined the order in which the slides appeared and the duration of their projection, following his/her interpretation of the relationship between the oral narrative and the projected imagery.

Lantern technology also enabled the manipulation of slides at the moment of exhibition. Each lantern's slide carrier enabled easy transitions from one slide to another, and through the use of multi-lensed lanterns (such as biunial and triunial lanterns) both dissolving views (shifting from lens to lens) and special effects (such as superimposition) could be created. Each time a change of slide occurred, this edit/cut would introduce a new slide that could depict a new event or character within a new space or time or perspective.

Before his first encounter with film in 1896, Smith was active in Brighton, England, as a mesmerist, astronomer, manager of a pleasure garden and a magic lanternist. As a lanternist, he was fully aware of what we can refer to as lantern editing in the service of lantern narratives as well as the photographic skills required to produce lantern slides. His knowledge of this screen practice was invaluable to his work with film from early 1897, as was his awareness of the early development of film in Europe and America. Yet Smith and his contemporaries could not immediately translate their knowledge of the lantern and the manipulation of the projected image to film production and exhibition. This was because film was a new technology, and a new aesthetic needed to be understood and developed. Given this perspective, we can legitimately refer to Smith's work from 1897 to 1900 as his laboratory years as this period was devoted to creating and running a commercial film laboratory and experimenting with the medium.

The first edited films

The early history of the edited film is one that is located within the production of works of both fiction and non-fiction. The majority of films made in Europe and America from 1895 to 1900 were single, unedited shots under 100 feet and around one minute in length. However, there were a number of significant exceptions. The first edited fiction films were produced at the Edison laboratory at West Orange, New Jersey in 1895. In *The Execution of Mary, Queen of Scots*, the most well known Edison example from this year, the edit was used to depict the decapitation of Mary. The sword strikes the neck at the end of shot one and the head falls off the body at the start of shot two. As a 'trick' edit, it was designed to represent plausibly the altered state of this body by attempting to join two shots together seamlessly to thus present continuous action within what appeared to be an uninterrupted recording. The edit, in this case, was designed to be an 'invisible' visual event as the viewer's attention was directed to the decapitation and hopefully not to the visual means of its cinematic representation.

In the next year, Georges Méliès' *The Vanishing Lady* (1896) provided the first European example of this form of 'trick' editing. With this basic device, Méliès would continue to make a significant number of trick films for the rest of the 1890s and into the new century and their construction became increasingly intricate. What is important to clarify, as Tom Gunning and others have established, is that whereas these trick films by Edison and Méliès have been seen as simply the product of stop motion, they did involve careful editing.[2] "Examination of the actual prints of Méliès films," Gunning observes, "reveal that in every case, this stop motion technique was in fact revised through splicing. Variation in hand-cranked camera speed when stopping and starting, as well as refinements possible only at this stage, called for an actual cutting of the film at the beginning and ending of the interrupted action and the subsequent splicing of it together." Gunning argues that this "shows how early film-makers were concerned with issues that traditionally they are thought to have ignored, those of precise continuity of action over a splice. The splices in Méliès' films are managed in order to maintain the flow and rhythm of acting which a mere stopping of the camera could not provide."[3]

All of Smith's key films from 1897 to 1899 reveal this same concern with the creation of elaborate one minute, one scene films which contain a number of separate shots joined together in order to create the illusion of a coherent single-shot with continuous action contained within the same space. Smith's *The X-Rays* (1897) and *Santa Claus* (1898) are excellent examples of this interest. In *The X-Rays* Smith used stop motion to present a comic transition across two shots. An X-Ray cameraman takes a picture of lovers on a bench and they are transformed, in the second shot, into animated skeletons. *Santa Claus* was a far more elaborate illusion because of the use of stop motion and superimposition. Stop motion was first employed to effect a transition, in the children's bedroom, from light to dark. At the beginning of the film, the children are prepared for bed by their nurse in a set with a painted backdrop that depicts a window, fireplace and door. The nurse then carries out the action of turning out the gas. This introduces the second shot in which the painted backdrop is covered in a dark material, perhaps velvet. The actor playing the nurse was instructed to maintain the same position within the frame at the end of the first shot and the start of the second, creating the continuity across the edit. The second instance of stop motion in *Santa Claus* was in the style of Méliès. Having filled the stockings with presents, Santa walks to the middle of the set and vanishes. *Santa Claus* also employed a vision scene, which was designed as a superimposed, circular inset within the right hand side of the frame. As the children sleep in the main image, the vision scene depicts Santa on the roof as he begins to descend down the chimney. This vision of Santa acquires two functions in Smith's narrative. The first is in line with the conventional understanding of the vision scene as it represents the children's dream of Santa's arrival. The second is very filmic as the inset interacts with the main image, producing two planes of simultaneous action within the same frame. In effect, this was an early form of crosscutting.

We can position Smith, like Méliès, as a film pioneer who was seeking difficult and complicated solutions to the problems posed by his narrative concepts. They were not content with working within the constraints of the single, unedited shot, and, as indicated above, Smith at least was very aware of the sophisticated 'editing' which had been developed for the magic lantern. Despite their ingenious representation of visions and transformations through the use of superimposition and stop motion, their films were still contained within standard lengths (Smith at 75 feet and Méliès at 20 metres) and were set within a single space. This would be challenged in 1898 by two fiction films which offered a new sense of editing by telling a story through separate shots depicting action unfolding across different yet related geographical spaces.

The first was the English film-maker Robert Paul's two-shot film *Exhibition* (also known as *Come Along, Do!*). Its first shot depicted an elderly couple sitting outside an art gallery, which they then proceed to enter. The second shot presented the couple in the gallery contemplating the art. This was probably the first time that two shots had been intentionally produced and edited together in order to create a film sequence which represented continuous action across different spaces. Paul's noticeable edit, as opposed to the invisible edit in *Santa Claus*, marked the movement of the characters from one space to another.

The second significant edited film of 1898 was Méliès' *La Lune à un Mètre*. Consisting of three shots and with a length of 60 metres, this film was a more radical departure. Across three scenes, an astronomer falls asleep when viewing the moon and in his dream he is swallowed by the moon and meets Phoebe, the Goddess of the Moon, before waking up. This was an elaborate narrative which was conceived and produced as a three-shot continuous sequence unfolding across roughly three minutes of the astronomer's time within the space of his observatory and his lunar dream space.

La Lune à un Mètre, or *The Astronomer's Dream* as it was entitled in English, was distributed by the Warwick Trading Company (WTC) and exhibited in Britain from late 1898. We can be certain of Smith's awareness of this film because of his and its association with the WTC, and also because of its presence within an exhibition of films by Smith and Méliès at Brighton's Alhambra Theatre in late January 1899.[4] In the next month, February 1899, Smith would conceive and produce *The Kiss in the Tunnel*. Although these two films are very different in terms of their subject matter, they have some conceptual similarity in that they both share a three-part structure and the motif of the journey.

Running in parallel with the evolution of the edited fiction film was the rise of edited non-fiction material.[5] This took the form of linking separate films because of their shared subject matter. Paul produced one of the first examples of this kind of editing with his famous Derby film of 1896. His first catalogue, from late 1896, listed two Derby films. The first depicted the end of the race and the second was described as a "continuation of the above, showing thousands of persons rushing onto the course. (Can be joined to No. 10 [*The Derby*] to form one picture.)"[6] Paul's introduction of the joined film was further developed by him and by other companies in 1897, especially by the series of films on Queen Victoria's Diamond Jubilee. From 1897, film catalogues began to present such series as collections of related views of a particular subject, listing and describing each single-shot film within a suggested order. This created a loose narrative sequence, especially when accompanied during projection by a lecturer's description of the subject matter and the context.

Smith's understanding of this early history of film editing as found within the production and exhibition of fiction and non-fiction films was crucial to his production of *The Kiss in the Tunnel* in early 1899. His close involvement with the WTC in 1899 and 1900 accounts in part for his knowledge of contemporary film practice. In September 1900, the WTC's catalogue referred to Smith as the "Manager of the Brighton Film Works of the Warwick Trading Company."[7] The WTC had been created in 1897, developing out of Maguire and Baucus' Continental Commerce Company – the company that had introduced the kinetoscope to Britain in 1894. From its London base, the WTC's American-born manager Charles Urban produced new British films for the domestic and world markets. He also secured for the WTC its role as the agent in Britain and the United States for films made by Smith and Hepworth and by the French producers Lumière and Méliès. All of these factors provided the WTC with a substantial and unique catalogue of film prints for sale. These commercial assets placed the WTC in an unrivalled position within the emerging British and world film markets.[8] Smith's relationship with the WTC brought him valuable film processing contracts, a very healthy income and an informed context for the production of his own films.

The phantom ride

Before Smith's *The Kiss in the Tunnel* can be examined two related factors need to be introduced: the evolution of the phantom ride and the long film. The origins and nature of the phantom ride in Britain in the late 1890s is important because of this particular history's role in the evolution of film editing. As established, the first films (1893–1897) were all taken from a camera in a fixed position, creating a point-of-view not dissimilar to that found within the histories of Western painting and photography. The phantom ride challenged this mode as its point-of-view was not stationary but moving. To achieve this effect, the film camera was mounted in front of a train engine and its operator positioned the camera so that it faced forward. The operator then began to crank the camera in order to record the changing landscape as the engine moved forward.

The very first phantom ride film was entitled *The Haverstraw Tunnel* and produced by the American Mutoscope Company in the summer of 1897. It made its debut in London in October of that year as part of the American Biograph's programme and its success was instant. *The Era*, the weekly newspaper for the British music hall world, wrote:

> With a very slight stretch of imagination he [the viewer] can fancy himself tearing along at great speed on a cow-catcher, with the landscape simply leaping towards him. He sees the stretch of metals before him, just as if he were travelling with the train, which rushes into the tunnel, seen looming ahead long before the train enters the darkness, from which it emerges into a beautiful country, bathed in sunlight. A more exciting and sensational piece of realism has never been presented to an audience.[9]

In 1898 the British Mutoscope and Biograph Syndicate made and exhibited the first British-made phantom rides to great acclaim: *Conway Castle – Panoramic View of Conway on the L. & N. W. Railway* and *Through Chee Tor Tunnel in Derbyshire – Midland Railway*.

The first phantom ride films of 1897–1898 created an intriguing relationship between the film and the viewer because this was a new visual experience. The majority of viewers would not know the depicted rail journeys, and for all they offered the unfamiliar perspective from the front of the engine, not the familiar side view from a carriage window. The invisibility of the engine and the lack of sounds from it enabled the viewer to become disconnected from the presence of a real train. As essentially a non-narrative experience, these filmed one-minute journeys usually had no clear beginning or end. All of these factors worked to create the illusion of a mysterious, dream-like agency that was carrying the viewer through space and time, hence the name 'phantom ride.' The effect of a phantom ride was also to produce visual pleasure through the viewer's sensual experience of watching the train/the camera as it made its way, at speed, through light and shadow, different landscapes, around bends and into tunnels. The kinaesthetic reactions to such films (watching the film and physically reacting to it) revealed their peculiar and delightful power.

Given the success of Biograph's phantom rides from 1897, it is hardly surprising that the WTC launched its own phantom rides in its 1898 catalogue. In 1898, the WTC produced twelve phantom rides in Devon with the co-operation of the London & South West Railway

Company. Each was given a general title, either *View From an Engine Front* or *View from Back of Train*, and then a specific title, such as *Entering Tavistock*. Following the Paul and Lumière practice of devising film series, they were also grouped together to form particular journeys. For instance *View From an Engine Front – Through Mortehoe* and *View From an Engine Front – Ilfracombe Incline* were made available together as a single continuous length of 250 feet. This was an important innovation in 1898. Thus, the emergence of the longer film became a feature of the WTC's involvement with the genre of the phantom ride.

A number of factors made the long film possible in 1898. The first cameras and projectors could only handle film lengths of around 100 feet. However in 1898, the Prestwich Manufacturing Company of London launched its Cinematographic Camera & Printer Model 4 which could handle a film box for 500 feet, and its Projector Model 3 which was capable of carrying spools for up to 2000 feet.[10] The advent of the larger spool size of 2000 feet for projectors now made it possible for an exhibitor not only to show the longer films but also to join/edit a number of films together, thereby creating a continuous programme of over thirty minutes. The other significant factor in the evolution of the long film was Cecil Hepworth's development of an automatic developing and printing machine for the WTC. It was available from 1898 and designed to process and print "films of any length . . . from single jointless negatives."[11] The arrival of the long film created a more pleasurable and sustained viewing experience, something that the phantom ride could exploit and justify.

In 1899, the WTC capitalised on all of these developments by producing their most ambitious phantom ride, *Dalmeny to Dumfermline, Scotland, via the Firth of Forth Bridge*. This 'epic' work, which is now lost, was described by the WTC as a "panoramic view photographed from the front of a special engine, furnished by courtesy of the North British Ry. Co. The total length is 650 feet. Price £32 10s. Duration of exhibition twelve continuous minutes. All from one negative. This is the longest, most picturesque, and interesting Cinematograph film ever produced."[12] This single-shot, unedited film was very likely made on the WTC's Bioscope Camera, which was designed and manufactured by Alfred Darling of Brighton. It was advertised by the WTC in 1899 as "constructed to take from 50 to 1500 feet of sensitised film, which makes it possible to take a continuous cinematograph picture of events lasting thirty consecutive minutes without re-loading."[13]

This WTC film is connected to Smith's *The Kiss in the Tunnel*. Referred to as *Tunnel Kiss*, it appeared in the 1899 catalogue immediately after the description of the last part of this Scottish film and was presented in these terms: "To further increase the interest, and perhaps add to the humour of these phantom rides, we have pre-arranged a little scene supposed to take place in a compartment in which a lady and gentleman are the only occupants. As the train enters [the tunnel] this couple is supposed to take advantage of the surrounding darkness by giving vent to their pentup feelings, and indulging in a loving kiss or two. The strip can be joined between the black sections representing the passing through a tunnel, and will cause much amusement if exhibited in this manner. *Tunnel Kiss* Length 40 feet."[14] To follow these instructions would add another forty feet and roughly a minute of time to this already very long phantom ride. It would also create an edited sequence, linking the exterior views from the phantom ride to the staged interior of a railway carriage.

As established, Cecil Hepworth's film *View From an Engine Front – Train Leaving Tunnel* represents shots one and three in the Smith/Hepworth film. Hepworth's films of 1899 were the result of his first full year as a producer and his work is well documented in the WTC's 1899 catalogue. It listed around seventy films by Hepworth, of which nine were in the series *View From an Engine Front*. These were new phantom rides which complemented the first series that had been made by the WTC in 1898. All of these Hepworth films were single-shots and varied from 50 to 200 feet in length. It was one of the 75 foot films from this series which was selected to be edited together with Smith's *The Kiss in the Tunnel*. Its special qualities were described in the catalogue as follows: "A highly interesting and sensational picture. A very picturesque tunnel entrance is seen, and presently a London & South Western train emerges rapidly and throws clouds of steam into the air. As it rushes past at high speed, the engine which carries the camera begins to move, and gathering speed, dashes into the tunnel which the passenger train has left. Presently a spot of light is seen in the distance, and this rapidly enlarges until the observer rushes out again into the open country beyond the tunnel, and the picture comes to an end."[15] It is interesting to speculate that the 'tunnel' film was first conceived in order to fill the visual void created by that part of a phantom ride filmed within a tunnel.

The WTC in 1899 was at the forefront of the development of narrative films in Britain. The WTC not only used its 1899 catalogue to launch the long film in the form of the phantom rides and drew attention to how Smith's film could be used to create an edited sequence, but it also presented a new multi-shot narrative film by Méliès, the eleven-part *Dreyfus Court-Martial* (*L'Affaire Dreyfus*). The film was based on key incidents in the arrest and trial of Captain Dreyfus and, at roughly 780 feet and 15 minutes, was one of the longest narrative films ever made up to this point. Its engagement through sets, costumes and actors with an important contemporary news story revealed Méliès' understanding that film now had the ability to create sustained narratives involving a range of places, characters and actions. However this film by Méliès consisted of a set of separate scenes, each consisting of a single tableau-style shot designed to represent a particular stage in the development of the film's narrative. Continuity editing, presenting continuous action across different spaces, played no role in Méliès' work. This development is found in Smith's films.

The Kiss in the Tunnel

Smith's own reference to *The Kiss in the Tunnel* is found in his *Cash Book* in the entry for 11 February 1899. It reads, "New 14 ft cloth + railway carriage, painted in centre – Green, £1 15s."[16] (Green refers to Tom Green who served as Smith's actor and handyman.) The design and production of this back cloth and the selection and organisation of the furniture and props created a credible contemporary representation of the interior of either a first or second class railway compartment. Smith and his wife, Laura, played the couple in their respectable middle class dress. His particular understanding of mise-en-scène and his decision to use a naturalistic acting style produced an effective, realistic depiction of a possible event in a railway compartment. Smith, and the WTC, clearly designed this film to be inserted into a phantom ride. In 1899, this made concrete the purpose of film editing. A shot, as a single unit of meaning, could be combined with other shots in order to create a new entity which could represent, as in this case, continuous action. This innovation marked a significant move away from self-contained, one minute films set within a single space. John Barnes was correct when he stated that "[a]s far as is known, this was the first instance of an edited sequence in the history of the British cinema."[17] However this statement needs some qualification. The WTC and Smith stated their intention for the insertion of *The Kiss in the Tunnel* into an edited sequence that would use a phantom ride. They therefore described how an edited sequence could be constructed. What they did not indicate, however, was which phantom ride should be used. This situation invited the purchaser/exhibitor of 1899 to assume the role of film editor and determine which shots should be selected and combined. Placing the Smith film within other phantom rides would create similar sequences in terms of their three-shot construction yet each phantom ride would bring its own character to the new film sequence and to Smith's shot. The flexible nature of this editing process is very interesting given that we are now so used to the fixed relationship between the Smith and Hepworth films in 'our' version of the film.

The film that we have – the Smith/Hepworth film – requires close analysis and historical contextualisation to trace its meaning. The three-shot film begins with the view from an engine-front. The train is initially stationary and from it 'we' view a tunnel in the distance, from which another train emerges. We then begin to move forwards and at the moment we hit the darkness of the tunnel's entrance, an edit takes place and the next shot – the train interior – is introduced. The objective point-of-view is maintained but we now view a set that is designed to represent the interior of a railway compartment and contains the couple.

This new shot provides us with the ability to enter into a private space and, as voyeurs, we watch without being caught. We see the couple kiss, an action that we can assume is conducted because they are alone and in the darkness of the tunnel. The private space provided them with the licence to act in this fashion. To contemporary observers, their privacy was also assured by the knowledge that this was a carriage without a corridor made up of separate compartments each with its own exterior doors. The couple separates after their gentle kissing and touching and return to their seats on opposite sides of the compartment. The second edit then returns us to the engine-front and the train exits the tunnel and rolling countryside appears in the distance. The pleasures of this film derive from its combination of the familiar gratification of the phantom ride with the illusion of having omnipresence: entering, undetected, the private world of an adult couple and observing their actions. Our right to look is never challenged or questioned as if this film was designed to legitimise this act of looking.

As a linear film sequence, the Smith/Hepworth film makes visual and narrative sense. It unifies an actuality shot (Hepworth's phantom ride) with Smith's fictional scene within what can be interpreted as a continuous time frame. Once the second shot appears, the logic of the sequence is that the couple is on the train from which the phantom ride was filmed in shot one. The moment the train enters the tunnel, the man initiates the kissing and the woman willingly reciprocates. After a short time, their intimacies are concluded and the next edit returns us to the phantom ride and the train's re-emergence into daylight. The logic of the transition from shot two to three is that the couple was aware of the tunnel's short length.

As a whole, the film attempts to create a single, unified geographical and physical space: a train engine and its carriage travelling through a tunnel. We know, however, that it was the product of a phantom ride shot in Devon combined with an acted scene staged close to two hundred miles away in a Hove garden. The film's representation of space, speed and time is one in which we imagine that the duration of the train's journey, which includes the action within the compartment, is defined by the length of the tunnel and the train's velocity. What is fascinating is that this set of relationships is determined largely by one factor: the length of the second shot. The Smith/Hepworth film has literally built a time frame and a geography – a cine-geography – that is completely of its own making. This film is not a trick film in the conventional sense as the edits are very visible, yet it is a carefully conceived and articulated set of illusions. It provides the viewer with a narrative action that is coherent and continuous but this is an artifice defined and determined by a filmic consciousness. This is what makes this film so distinctive within the early history of film editing and relates it to Kuleshov and his theoretical work on the edited film and 'creative geography' in the early 1920s.

There is a second film with a similar title and similar content and structure. *Kiss in the Tunnel* was produced by Riley & Bamforth of Yorkshire (R & B) and it is uncertain as to when this film was made. It could be either 1899 or 1900, and it is likely that its production followed the release of Smith's film by the WTC. The R & B film consists of three separate shots:

a train entering a tunnel, the interior of a railway compartment where a couple kiss, and a train arriving at a station. It differs from the Smith/Hepworth film in that it is not a phantom ride and there is no sense of the shots being related geographically. Shots one and three of the R & B film view the passing train from stationary positions which look at a moving train and they combine with the interior second shot to create a three-shot edited sequence. The R & B concept for the film is transparent. However, when compared with the Smith/Hepworth film, it feels awkward in the way in which the shots have been selected and combined for the sequence. Missing is the lyricism and the momentum found in the Smith/Hepworth film, qualities that reflect a stronger sense of the shots being organised by an editing consciousness that is carefully considering how to construct a film sequence. What is significant here is that the concept of the edited film is beginning to emerge in the work of different producers in different parts of the country at the very same moment.

These two train films were obviously shaped by the railway and its significant place within late Victorian culture. The films reflect this very stratified society through their representation of class. The Smith film is thoroughly bourgeois as signified by the formal and elaborate dress, the range of suitcases, the upholstered compartment and the genteel nature of the couple. In contrast to this 'comfortable' world, the R & B film presents a third class/working class scene through the couple's simple dress and the bare wooden seats within the plain compartment. These films signal very clearly how different producers could adapt the same narrative concept for different exhibitors and audiences. The production context of the Smith film is particularly interesting given the fact that two railway companies, the London & South West Railway Company and the North British Railway Company, had collaborated with the WTC in the production of their phantom rides in 1898 and 1899. This works to re-position Smith's film as an advertisement for the actual and potential pleasures to be experienced on particular trains within the modern and sophisticated service offered by particular British railway companies.

Amidst the many railway narratives found in songs, lantern slides, plays and novels, there was a particular strand which dealt with the connections between railway travel, sexuality and the potential dangers for single women passengers. For instance, a picture postcard from the 1890s in the Barnes Collection at Hove Museum depicts a couple kissing in a tight embrace while seated in a railway compartment. It is entitled "In the Tunnel" and has obvious affinities with the films by Smith and R & B. A more frightening interpretation of the railway journey was found in the short stories "Raped on the Railway" and "A Horrible Fright", both of 1894. The latter involved a woman who has to share a compartment with a criminal during a night-time journey. He says to her: "You are alone in a railway carriage with a man who could strangle you and throw your dead body on the line if he felt the least inclined to do . . . The train is now comfortably on its way, and will not stop for nearly two hours. You see, therefore, that you are completely at my mercy. Your only chance of safety is doing *exactly* what I tell you."[18] In this fictional scenario she is not harmed but the potential for harm gave this story its drama and suspense. To travel to Brighton by train from London has always involved the experience of passing through tunnels and, tragically, this provided the opportunity for sexual assaults. In 1896, for example, a Sussex trial was named the "Railway Outrage".[19] In this case, a man was charged with the attempted murder of one woman and the assault of another, both incidents having taken place on the London to Brighton line and involving single women travellers. Smith's film, like the postcard of the railway kiss, presented consensual pleasure. However, our knowledge of actual train crimes repositions this 'comedy' within a far more serious social and cultural context.

The representation and the display of sexuality was an important feature of early cinema. 'Kissing' films appeared as early as the spring of 1896 with Robert Paul's *The Soldier's Courtship* and Edison's *May Irwin Kiss* or *Kiss*. The latter became very popular and was described in 1900 as follows: "They get ready to Kiss, begin to Kiss, and Kiss and Kiss and Kiss in a way that brings down the house every time."[20] This was probably the film which the 1898 WTC catalogue had advertised as *The Kisses*. Kissing also played a role within the gendered humour of Smith's fiction films. It is the key action in his *Hanging Out the Clothes* of 1897, a film which later acquired the more explicit title *The Kiss Behind the Clothes Line*. In conjunction with *The Kiss in the Tunnel*, these were all 'respectable' films for public consumption but it could be argued that they played on the sexual imagination of contemporary viewers.

Smith and Williamson in 1900

The combination of Smith's single-shot *The Kiss in the Tunnel* with a phantom ride created an edited film of spectacle and narrative which demonstrated a new sense of continuity and simultaneity across three shots. This filmic imagination was radical for the time and Smith used this innovation to develop a series of films in 1900, which along with *The Kiss in the Tunnel* are arguably the most important works of his film career. They are *Grandma's Reading Glass*, *As Seen Through the Telescope*, *The House That Jack Built* and *Let Me Dream Again*.

Grandma's Reading Glass merits particular attention because it offered a new way of entering into a fictional world by dividing a scene into a number of separate shots. It presents two related perspectives: an objective point-of-view of a domestic scene with a grandmother and her grandson and his subjective point-of-view of the objects he views through a magnifying glass. The logic of the film's construction is that we can see what he can see. This film renounced the conventions of the single viewpoint, or theatrical perspective, which had been the dominant model for film production, and replaced it with a shifting point-of-view within a linear narrative composed of alternating medium shots and close-ups.

As film narratives, the above mentioned four films are all clearly insubstantial because of their short length (all between 75 and 100 feet). All they depict are a number of brief actions and as such they are probably better described as narrative fragments. Despite these limitations, the films introduced editing concepts that would be central to the future development of film style. These include the use of close-ups, subjective point-of-view shots, and the use of shot/reverse shot. It makes sense, in this context, to refer to these 1900 films as genuinely experimental. This groundbreaking work taught Smith's contemporaries new ways of creating a film sequence.

Smith's films of 1900 were new and exciting additions to the WTC's catalogue because of their sexualised imagery, sense of spectacle and innovative use of the medium. They had an immediate international impact. In 1902, American Biograph produced its version of *Grandma's Reading Glass* by releasing *Grandpa's Reading Glass*. In 1903, the Edison Company produced *The Gay Shoe Clerk*, which was clearly influenced by Smith's *As Seen Through the Telescope*. In France, the Pathé Company made *La Loupe de Grand-Maman* in 1901, its version of *Grandma's Reading Glass*.

Smith produced very few films of any significance after 1900 but his Hove friend and colleague James Williamson was immediately influenced by these developments in editing. This is best represented by his first edited multi-shot narrative film, *Attack on a China Mission – Bluejackets to the Rescue*. This film of 230 feet was made in the autumn of 1900 and therefore came after Smith's *The Kiss in the Tunnel* and his key films of 1900. It is a chronological arrangement of four shots with an adequately defined sense of simultaneity and consecutive action occurring across the three edit points. The four shots act as an edited sequence without ellipsis and therefore can be interpreted as a real-time narrative drama of uninterrupted action. Unlike Smith's films, *Attack on a China Mission* has a proper, self-contained story with a clear, linear development from introduction to conclusion. Unlike Méliès' contemporary work with its studio-based tableau-style and theatrical nature, Williamson employed a plausible location and naturalistic acting and, like a phantom ride and *Grandma's Reading Glass*, attempted to place the viewer within a fictional world.

Williamson, like Smith, had been a practising magic lanternist before he became a film-maker. His film *Attack on a China Mission – Bluejackets to the Rescue* demonstrated very clearly that the medium of film could now be used to create stories determined by a new and intrinsically filmic sensibility. It can be interpreted, like Smith's work, as representing a transitional moment between the practices of the magic lantern and film. My case study has only addressed a small aspect of the early history of the edited film and drawn attention to 'editing' within the magic lantern and film. This intermedial relationship has been neglected for far too long. It requires proper attention so that we can better understand the origins of continuity editing around 1900.

Notes

1. Lev Kuleshov, "The Banner of Cinematography" (1920), in Lev Kuleshov, *Fifty Years in Films* (Moscow: Raduga, 1987), p. 41.
2. Stop motion (also known as stop action and stop motion substitution) was a procedure which involved placing the camera in a fixed position, filming a scene, stopping the camera, changing the scene and resuming the filming. By working in this manner, stop motion enabled objects and actors to either disappear or reappear or acquire new characteristics.
3. Tom Gunning, "Primitive Cinema: A Frame-up? Or the Trick's on Us", in Thomas Elsaesser with Adam Barker, eds., *Early Cinema: Space, Frame, Narrative* (London: British Film Institute, 1990), pp. 97–98.
4. "The Brighton Alhambra," *Brighton Herald*, 28 January 1899, p. 3.
5. Bottomore's important article outlines the valuable role played by non-fiction films in the development of the edited film in the late 1890s. Stephen Bottomore, "Shots in the Dark: The Real Origins of Film Editing," in Elsaesser ed., *Early Cinema*. John Barnes has charted the development of the edited film within the wider perspective of film production and exhibition from 1894 to 1900. His series of books is now published as *The Beginnings of the Cinema in England*, vols. 1–5 (Exeter: University of Exeter Press, 1998). Barry Salt's article, "Cut and Shuffle," in Christopher Williams, ed., *Cinema: the Beginnings and the Future* (London: University of Westminster Press, 1996), also provides an overview of the early history of the edited fiction film. His more detailed history of film editing is found in *Film Style and Technology: History and Analysis* (London: Starword, 1983).
6. John Barnes, *The Beginnings of the Cinema in England 1894–1901*, vol. 1, p. 248.
7. *Warwick Trading Company Catalogue*, September 1900, p. 72. Museum of Modern Art, New York.
8. Richard Brown, "'England is not big enough . . .' American Rivalry in the Early English Film Business: The Case of Warwick v Urban, 1903," *Film History*, vol. 10, no. 1, 1998, pp. 21–34.
9. *The Era*, 30 October 1897, p. 19, as quoted in Barnes, *The Beginnings of the Cinema in England 1894–1901*, vol. 2, 1996, p. 145.
10. John Barnes, *The Beginnings of the Cinema in England 1894–1901*, vol. 3, pp. 117–121.
11. Barnes, *The Beginnings of the Cinema in England 1894–1901*, vol. 3, p. 148.
12. Barnes, *The Beginnings of the Cinema in England 1894–1901*, vol. 4, pp. 269–271.
13. Ibid, p. 173.
14. Ibid, pp. 270–271.
15. Ibid, p. 207.
16. Smith's unpaginated *Cash Book* is in the collection of the British Film Institute.
17. Barnes, *The Beginnings of the Cinema in England 1894–1901*, vol. 4, 1996, p. 47.
18. L. T. Meade, "A Horrible Fright," *The Strand* (July–December, 1894) pp. 428–429. See Garrett Monaghan's essay for his useful reflections on Smith's film and Victorian rail travel. Garrett Monaghan, "Performing the Passions: Comic Themes in the Films of George Albert Smith," in Alan Burton and

Laraine Porter, eds, *Pimple, Pranks & Pratfalls: British Comedy Before 1930* (Trowbridge: Flicks Books, 2000).

19. "The Railway Outrage," *The Argus* (Brighton), 25 July 1896, p. 3.
20. Charles Musser, *Edison Motion Pictures, 1890–1900: An Annotated Filmography* (Washington DC: Smithsonian Institution Press, 1997), p. 197.

Chapter 4

RICHARD ABEL

THE CINEMA OF ATTRACTIONS
IN FRANCE, 1896–1904

All the visible universe is nothing but a shop of images and signs.

Charles Baudelaire

EARLY FRENCH FILMS WERE PRODUCED and exhibited within a categorical framework already established by the Third Republic's institutions of mass culture. The most important of these were the café-concerts and music halls of the larger urban centers and the fairground theaters that circulated throughout the country, setting up temporary sites of exhibition in cities and towns. Others, however, included screened spectacles (from small-scale magic lantern shows to giant dioramas), mass-produced images printed on paper (from versions of traditional *images Epinal* to illustrated magazines), and even photographs (whether for public or private distribution). Many of these offered a *variety* of subjects to view (and consume), as mass culture equivalents to the display of either consumer goods in the metropolitan department stores (and their catalogs) or postcards at the major tourist sites. The pleasure of such "distractions" or "diversions," Miriam Hansen writes, promised a "modern" form of "short-term but incessant sensorial stimulation" instead of requiring the extended contemplation more characteristic of the traditional arts.[1] As cinema programs became common in the fairs and elsewhere, films also were presented in this variety format, in what seemed to be a discontinuous series of attractions (underscored by constant reel changes) whose selection and order already tended to be maximally inclusive, in terms of not only the subjects offered but also the class, gender, and generation of the spectators addressed. In 1901, for instance, in his Grand Biorama, Charles Sckramson offered three different evening programs per week, mixing actualités, dances, trick films, féeries, and religious films from different sources, including Lumière, Méliès, and R. W. Paul (London). Toward the end of the period, in 1904, Van Langendonck arranged lengthy programs of both live and recorded performances in Le Palais de l'Art Nouveau, the last of which included historical and biblical films, melodramas, comedies and féeries, most of them now supplied by Pathé-Frères.

From the beginning, as evidenced by the Lumière 1897 catalog of film titles or *vues*,[2] French companies also adopted this exhibition model of subject variety—or product differentiation—to determine their production of films in terms of particular *genres*. If some companies tended to specialize in certain genres—Lumière in actualités and travel films, Méliès in trick films and féeries[3]—the largest and most successful corporation, Pathé-Frères, instead quickly moved to encompass the widest spectrum of subjects possible. "For better or worse," an early commentator concluded, "the great merit of the Pathé company is chiefly to have broken new ground and tackled every single genre, whatever the cost." [. . .]

My analysis of early French cinema focuses on its patterns of development within particular film genres accepted by both producers and exhibitors. These include the trick film and féerie, the comic film, the actualité, the historical and biblical film, and the "dramatic and realist" film. Although, by singling out discrete film texts as more or less fixed objects of study, this discussion does violence to the way cinema was experienced by spectators at the time, it recognizes the conditions of their performative practice as cultural forms and thus encourages inquiry into the intertextual web of relations between the cinema and other cultural and social practices in France. Such an approach also emphasizes the differences between French production companies, most notably between Méliès and Pathé, particularly as the latter moved to dominate the industry. What is even more important, this analysis of genre films can pinpoint specifically how, as a mode of representation, the early cinema of attractions, to some extent, actually overlapped with the later narrative cinema. As Tom Gunning has argued, early films are probably best defined as a dialectical interplay of attraction and narrative elements, in which an aesthetics of spectacle or display was generally, but not always, dominant.[4]

Trick films and 'féeries'

Perhaps the most successful genre for French exhibitors during this early period was what they themselves called "transformation views" or "transformation scenes." Generally, these included anything from the short trick film of apparently no more than a single-shot (none lasted more than three minutes) to the longer féerie comprising multiple tableaux. Although none of these films lent themselves to all that much manipulation by exhibitors, they more than made up for this with an amazing display of spectacular feats on the screen, the result of a seemingly miraculous filmmaking process. By 1898, such "transformations" constituted the bulk of Méliès's production; and, with some justification, he claimed the genre as his own and one reason for the cinema's success, even if he would have preferred the term "fantastical scenes."[5] This, of course, did not keep other companies such as Pathé from producing trick films and féeries; but the genre did provide Méliès with some measure of authority within the industry (and some control over the exhibition of his films), at least until Pathé moved into mass production. And it was within the "transformation" genre that Méliès established his own distinctive form of a "cinema of attractions." A film's scenario never amounted to much, he would later insist, because it merely served as a "pretext" for trucs or tricks and striking tableaux.[6] In fact, he claimed that his first task in preparing a film production always was to come up with a series of magical tricks, a central "grand effect," and a final clou of spectacle. Only after constructing the decors and costuming his actors did he actually work out the details of the scenario—using the thread of the story to assemble what was really significant, the trick effects and tableaux of spectacle. As a representative figure of the period, Méliès saw himself, then, not as a storyteller, but rather, and especially in the féeries, as an innovative composer of cinematic revues.

The trick film genre includes the principal films in which Méliès performed as himself— that is, as a celebrated magician. Yet in none, not even in an early one entitled Le Magicien (1898), was he content to simply record any of the illusionist acts he was known for at the Robert-Houdin Théâtre. Instead he invented tricks that displayed the "magical" properties of the cinematic apparatus as well as his own body as spectacle—whether dismembered or transformed.[7] Perhaps the earliest of these properties or cinematic techniques, already visible in *Le Manoir du diable* (1896–1897), was stop motion, which created a series of abrupt appearances, disappearances, or substitutions. In *L'Auberge ensorcelée* (1897), for instance, a traveler systematically "loses" first his clothes and then all of the furniture in a hotel room. At the conclusion of *Illusions fantastiques* (1898), by contrast, a simple box turns into a dove, a boy, then twin boys, and finally huge British and American flags—indirectly providing evidence that the market for Méliès's films quickly extended beyond France. Another technique was reverse motion that, in *Salle à manger fantastique* (1898), allowed a flipped dinner table magically to right itself. A third technique was multiple exposure, which combined rewinding and re-exposing the film stock with the use of black cloth covering certain background areas of the set, resulting in such bizarre marvels as the three singing Méliès heads on a table in *Un Homme de tête* (1898) or the young man's head sticking out of a vase in *Le Chevalier mystère* (1899). This also was coupled with a matte device masking off a specific area of the camera lens, which, in *Le Portait mystérieux* (1899), produced the delightful image of Méliès talking to a life-size portrait duplicate of himself. In film after film, Méliès obsessively repeated himself "like a fetishist," writes Linda Williams, "making the game of presence and absence the very source of . . . the spectator's pleasure, while privileging . . . his own perverse pleasure in the tricks" of that game.[8] [. . .]

Perhaps the most charmingly inventive of these trick films is *Le Mélomane* (1903). Here, against a dark country skyline, crossed by five telegraph wires, in marches Méliès as a band leader carrying a baton and huge G clef, followed by six women and a drummer boy. While the players line up (frame right), Méliès throws the G clef up to hang on the wires (in the far left corner) and, after drawing a face on a large white board, goes to stand under the wires (frame left), taking off his head and tossing it up to be attached to the middle wire. This he repeats five more times, with the help of straight cuts and multiple exposures, so that eventually a half-dozen faces are strung out along the telegraph wires in the upper third of the frame. Then, using his own baton as well as others taken from the waiting women, he turns the faces into half notes and quarter notes in an imaginary two-bar staff of music. After this elaborate preparation comes the real tour de force of the film as the women, now lined up under the wires, display flip cards spelling out each note (solfeggio), and Méliès, standing off to the right, leads them all in a rendition of "God Save the King." Once each line of the song is completed, the face-notes change position on the staff (at Méliès's command), and the women flip their cards to indicate the note changes—suggesting that the cinema audience itself was being asked to join in the celebration, not only of a king (probably the newly crowned Edward VII) but of the magician who could so perfectly synchronize these truc effects. In a final magical twist, after Méliès has led his performers off, each of his face-notes (in a straight cut) turns into a dove that wings away in a white blur. [. . .]

Le Cake-Walk infernal (1903) is interesting not so much for its cinematic trick effects, but for the gendered and ethnic "otherness" of its spectacle. The film's hellish cavern of a stage set, for instance, is thronged with women performing for a satyrlike Satan, doing everything from Rockette-like chorus-line kicks to "oriental" dances. The first centerpiece, however, features a couple in blackface doing the cakewalk as it supposedly should be done; and the second features Satan himself doing it on a cauldron lid, as first his lumpy goat legs and then his arms detach and leap rhythmically around his happily writhing and eventually exploding body. The final tableau brings the entire cast back into the frame with Satan now centered at the top, his command unchallenged and unchecked. This is one of the few moments in Méliès's films when his penchant for the carnivalesque is not reined in by the forces of a social order he seems to have continually sought to evade. Nevertheless, the film remains far from a serious threat, partly because it cannot keep from reproducing, in travesty form, some of the very differences that determine the conventions of that order's representation.

The patriarchal order of power and control which informs Méliès's trick films becomes even more explicit—and also more explicitly called into question—in those predicated on a specifically male vision of the fetishized female body. Perhaps the earliest of these, *Tentation de Saint Antoine* (1898), parodies the saint's story by confronting him, first with a host of loosely clad dancing women and then with one who, in an astonishing cut, replaces Christ and steps down from the huge crucifix before which he kneels in prayer. Later films abandon the shock of this blasphemous transformation for more secular and more conventional deceptions. In *Equilibre impossible* (1902), for instance, before the startled eyes of an old man sketching in a grotto garden, a vase dissolves into a veiled young woman who, with the aid of several others, steps down to dance briefly with him. Costumed now as a circus high-wire artiste, she moves toward the black background and begins a marvelous aerial dance until, as her attendants form a tableau around her, she drifts upward, blowing kisses, and dissolves away—and the old man is pushed offscreen. The spectacle of the fetishized female body is multiplied in *Le Rêve du maître de ballet* (1903). Here, a sleeping ballet master imagines (through a dissolve) that several female dancers in Tyrolean costumes appear in his bedroom. Then, as the room turns into a cavern (through another dissolve), the women are replaced by a dainty, white-clad shepherdess. Once this last figure goes to kiss the ballet master, however, she turns into an ugly matron dressed in black, whom he thrashes mercilessly until another cut abruptly ends the dream—and he falls out of bed pounding on a pillow. [. . .]

In that they constitute a special category of transformation films, Méliès's féeries assume a contextual frame for reading which differs slightly from that of the shorter trick films. For one, they were less ephemeral than the trick films, sometimes playing for months at a single site—as did *Le Voyage dans la lune* at the Olympia musical hall in 1902.[9] For another, although some of their subjects had circulated widely throughout the nineteenth century in simple pictures sold by itinerant peddlers,[10] they were all tied more closely to recent stage spectacles. *La Lune à un mètre*, after all, was closely based on one of Méliès's own miniature fantasy shows first presented at the Théatre-Robert Houdin. *Cendrillon* appeared shortly after Jules Massenet's opera of the same name in Paris, and both were drawn from a popular 1895 pantomime that was being revived on British theatre programs for the New Year's holidays and once had even played at the Robert-Houdin.[11] Similarly, *Rêve de Noël* may have been inspired by an 1897 pantomime produced at the Olympia.[12] And both *Barbe-bleue* and *Le Voyage dans la lune* were based on Jacques Offenbach operettas, with the latter film also drawing on Adolphe Dennery's melodrama adaptation of the original Jules Verne novel as well as a current H. G. Wells story. For that reason, the visual rhythm of the féeries may have been partly determined by musical accompaniment, whether by condensed versions of original scores or by newly written compositions, as was apparently the case with *Le Voyage dans la lune*, at least at the Olympia.[13] And, unlike the trick films, they may have encouraged the use of a *bonisseur* (lecturer), especially in the fairground cinemas either to summarize the story beforehand or else to designate each of the film's unfolding tableaux.

Furthermore, the féeries were marked by a somewhat different mode of representation. Partly because they were constructed of multiple shot-scenes and recorded exclusively in long shot (LS), their elaborate decors acquired an even more privileged role—as tableaux and clous of spectacle—much in the manner of late nineteenth-century French stage productions, on which the popular dioramas had such an impact. [. . .] Méliès himself alluded to the significance of these decors, whose construction consumed more time and money than any other components of his production.[14]

Figure 4.1 Le Voyage dans la lune (1902)

As the longest and most expensive of the early féeries, *Le Voyage dans la lune* constitutes not only a culmination of Méliès's work but also a significant advance.[15] It mixes theatrical and cinematic devices in both old and new ways, it privileges clous of spectacle by means of extended narrative continuity, and, surprisingly, it experiments with dividing up and reconstituting the autonomous shot-scene. Nearly twenty decors provide the principal spectacle material for the film's thirty shots and the raison d'être for its parodic story of a half-dozen scientists who rocket off to the moon, have a series of harrowing encounters with the lunar Selenites, and barely escape to rocket back to public acclaim. The sets range from rather flat spaces of public ceremony (resembling several paintings by Méliès's contemporary, Henri Rousseau) to the "deep space" of the actual rocket launch (out of a huge, telescoping "Big Bertha" cannon) and the rugged lunar surface (with its multiple flyaway flats).[16] The adventuring scientists (who begin as medieval magicians) are all men, of course, with women serving either to help launch the rocket (as a sailor-suited corps de ballet) or to decorate a brief dream of space; the Selenite enemy, half crustacean and half primate in their costumes and behavior (they are played by Folies-Bergère acrobats),[17] seem a neutered composite "other," both biological and colonial. The narrative divides somewhat unevenly into three parts, bookended by a kind of expository prologue and the usual celebratory epilogue. And each of the three evidences a slightly different negotiation between the demands of spectacle "attractions," spatial coherence, and temporal linearity.

The middle section of *Le Voyage dans la lune*, where the scientists actually explore the moon, may break no new ground in its display of trick effects and spectacular decors, yet that hardly detracts from its achievement. The rocket sinks below the lunar surface, for instance, while the earth seems to rise in the far background sky, a "dream" of celestial bodies hovers over the sleeping scientists, ending in a shower of snowflakes, and Selenites keep disappearing in puffs of smoke. The initial section of the rocket launch, however, develops further some of the editing techniques from *Barbe-bleue* and *L'Homme à la tête de caoutchouc*. Three separate decors, for instance, loosely link adjacent spaces, in which the characters repeatedly exit frame left and enter frame right—from the interior of the factory manufacturing the rocket to the exterior rooftop where it is to be launched.[18] The launch itself is represented in two separate shots in which the perspective on the site shifts almost ninety degrees—first looking at the cannon from one side (as the women slide in the rocket) and then looking along the barrel from a point near its base.[19] The "trip to the moon" is condensed into a single tableau, using a matte shot of the enlargening moon, along with cuts to "awaken" the moon's face to the approaching rocket and then to imbed it like a huge shell casing in one eye.[20] And, in this supposedly uninterrupted tableau, what at first seems to be a point-of-view shot (the spectator shares the view of the voyaging scientists) turns into an omniscient view of the crash landing.[21] Finally, the rocket landing is repeated in the following shot, this time from a perspective on the lunar surface, as strict temporal sequentiality is sacrificed for the effect of a doubled spectacle. The third and shortest section, the scientists' return to earth, presents a final, unexpected marvel. Not only does the rocket pass smoothly—by means of repeated descending movements—through four separate spaces (from a cliff on the lunar surface, through space and then the sea surface, to the sea bottom), it does so with amazing speed.[22] Lasting just two and two-and-a-half seconds, respectively, and joined by a cut, the second and third shots of this sequence produce an effect of "rapid montage" that matches, if not surpasses, the earlier comic surprise of the lunar landing.[23] That all these innovations and recapitulated spectacle effects were so successfully structured in the scenario Méliès patched together goes a long way to explaining the worldwide popularity the film so quickly achieved. [. . .]

As perhaps the most significant genres of this early period of filmmaking, the trick film and féerie exemplified several crucial components of the French "cinema of attractions." The shorter trick films presented a series of either marvelous or comic trucs, most of them produced by uniquely cinematic techniques—"invisible" cuts, stop motion, reverse motion, dissolves, multiple exposures, superimpositions, and magnification through close framing. The longer féeries, often in conjunction with such trick effects, displayed for contemplation elaborate, even "deep space" decors in spectacular tableaux, accentuated by either hand-inked or stencil process colors. [. . .] Méliès characteristically mounted energetic, mildly subversive spectacles of "otherness," often in various forms of the carnivalesque, and produced protean displays of metamorphosis, in which procreative power was relocated in a male magician (both before and behind the camera), yet without greatly eroding the boundaries of gender difference. [. . .]

Comic films

From the scant evidence available in surviving catalogs and archive prints, French comic films were not all that numerous before Pathé's move to mass production around 1902. And, even after that date, the genre sometimes overlapped with the trick film, because the latter's cinematic trucs often had a decidedly comic effect—as in Méliès's *L'Homme à la tête de caoutchouc* (1902) or Pathé's *Baignade impossible* (1902). Donald Crafton has shown that Lumière's first comic film, *Arroseur et arrosé* (1895), actually reworked an old joke whose most immediate source was a Christophe comic strip published in *Le Petit Français Illustré* (3 August 1889), and he suggests that such strips provided "a virtually unlimited supply of gags and story material" for early French films.[24] Sadoul, on the other hand, has argued that early comic films were drawn primarily from and sometimes simply recorded short, familiar music hall routines in a single tableau—that is, they put on display a well-known comic's performance of one or more gags—and his thesis, complemented by Crafton's, still makes sense.[25] Certain early Méliès film titles, such as *Chicot, dentiste américain* (1897) and *Guillaume Tell*, with "clowns" (1898), for instance, suggest an origin in variety numbers.[26] Alice Guy's filmography includes titles such as *Saut humidifié de M. Plick* (1900), performed by Plick and Plock, as well as *Les Clowns* (1902) and several others starring a monkey named Jocko.[27] And it should not be forgotten that, from 1896 to 1901, Hatot produced several series of single-shot comic films for Lumière, using circus acrobats, famous clowns such as Footit and Chocolat, and the pantomime artist Bretteau.[28] But it was through Pathé principally that a teeming crowd of nineteenth-century comic stereotypes was imported into French films, along with the music hall's irreverent, knockabout humor.

The earliest of Pathé's comic films presented a simple gag or routine, recorded in LS or full shot (FS), and in the open air against the company's generic painted-flat interior. In *The Artist* (1900), for instance, a bourgeois fellow accidentally knocks over and ruins a painting he is appraising and then unquestioningly buys it from the angry painter. In *Une Dispute* (1900), one man repeatedly slaps and kicks another man (knocking their boaters onto the floor), until the latter seems to agree with his attacker, and they walk off, smiling, arm in arm. Yet this film begins with the boaters already on the floor, after which the two men dissolve in, so that the ensuing argument seems to explain something like a topical riddle or "comic strip" puzzle (the cause coming after the effect). When Zecca took control of Pathé's production, he initially mined the popular acts he knew so well from his own café-concert days—such as those of the Six Daïneuf Sisters, the Omers, the English comic Little Tich, and the clowns Anverino and Antonio.[29] And the performers quickly recognized that the cinema could serve them as a new form of publicity. One of these films, *Rêve et réalité* (1901), predicates its sexist gag on a single dissolve—from an elder man, in medium shot (MS), pouring champagne for and then kissing a lovely young woman to his "awakening" to discover he is in bed with his horse-faced, toothless wife. Another, *Chez le dentiste* (1901), uses an "invisible cut" to produce out of a poor patient's mouth an uprooted tooth the size of his head. A third, *Une Bonne Histoire* (1903), offers evidence of the company's anticlerical politics (it is well to remember that the Pathé family was Protestant)—constructing the incongruous image of a Catholic bishop and priest, reading and chuckling at the republican newspaper, *Le Journal*.

Soon Zecca was exploiting the reputation of famous stage comics, by presenting them in uniquely "intimate" MSs. In *Premier Cigare du collégien* (1903), for instance, Félix Galipaux performs one of his better known music hall routines—that of a young man "enjoying" his first cigar. In *Ma Tante* (1903), Dranem dresses up in "auntie" drag and indulges in a little snuff while sewing, only to have a cat jump on the table and swish its tail in his face; in *Le Mitron* (1904), he appears disguised as a baker blithely plastering dough all over his head and dropping a plug of tobacco into the mixing tub. *La Bonne Purge* (1904), again with Dranem, this time taking some awful medicine, adds the dubious "attraction" of a cut-in close up (CU) of his face and extended tongue reflected in a mirror (actually, a cut-out oval mask) to justify the distasteful remedy. Finally, *Rêve de Dranem* (1904) adds a racist touch to the bedroom gag in *Rêve et réalité*, repeatedly substituting, through cuts, a laughing black woman for the lovely brunette he imagines he is kissing. For reasons that remain unclear, neither of these comics, however, was to become a regular performer for Pathé.

Other Zecca comic films presented slightly more elaborate music hall numbers, even if sometimes still recorded in a single tableau. *Le Chien et la pipe* (1902), for instance, takes place in the interior of a train compartment, where a man and woman, traveling separately, argue over her repositioning of his luggage and his pipe smoking until he simply picks up her little dog and tosses it out the window. A dissolve to a reverse-angle exterior of the train (presumably at journey's end) resolves the conflict when, surprising them both as they descend from the compartment, the dog is there sitting on the station platform, the man's pipe in its mouth, which the woman kindly returns to him. In the painted-flat LS of a Paris street corner, *Ramoneur et patissier* (1903) has a boy who is supposed to be delivering pastries stop to play dice with a policeman, until the latter loses and is replaced by a passing chimney sweep. The loser's consolation, however, is the chance to gobble up a pastry from the basket the first boy has left on a nearby bench. The two boys soon begin arguing over the dice game, and another policeman stops by to laugh at them. The first boy grabs a cream tart and throws it at the sweep, who ducks, and it splatters all over the laughing "intruder." According to this film's premise, conventional authority figures such as policemen are no more than children and easily can be made the butt of their jokes. Finally, *Erreur de porte* (1904) stages a very different kind of railway station gag involving a clownish country bumpkin traveler. In the initial LS tableau, a passing porter points the man, who is suffering intestinal distress, toward a "water closet," but he mistakenly enters a nearby door marked "telephone" instead. A FS of the interior, matchcutting his exit and entrance, shows the traveler now mistaking the wall phone and its pad for a toilet seat, before which he steps up on a stool and drops his pants. The gag then concludes in a cut back to the LS exterior, as a fashionably dressed gentleman enters the telephone booth—once the traveler has exited, with a big grin—only to stumble out with a handkerchief to his nose. This was just the kind of French humor, sensitive to tastes and smells, that prim and proper American reviewers, waving their own figurative handkerchiefs, would later find so excruciatingly unbearable. [. . .]

Diverging paths: from actualités to historical and realist films

The other particularly successful genre for French exhibitors during this early period, whether in the music halls or the fairground cinemas, was the actualité. From the beginning, Lumière produced these films in such profitable numbers that Méliès, Gaumont and Pathé all took to making them as soon as each, in turn, began producing films. The Lumière actualités covered a range of subjects from "current events" to French ceremonies such as the seemingly endless military parades or President Félix Faure's visit to naval bases (late in 1896), and from travelogue footage of foreign countries (including the colonies) to shots of French daily life in either the city streets or around the Lumières' own bourgeois home, such as *Repas de bébé* (1894).[30] The genre's success was due in part to the prior popularity of such topical subjects in photographs and postcards as well as in new illustrated magazines. For actualités participated in the industrial production of images associated with travel and tourism, as Gunning argues, in which "appropriating the world" through a technological extension of seeing had become a thoroughly "modern" source of pleasure.[31] But the genre also depended on the low cost of the films' production and, especially, on the ease with which exhibitors could select and edit their own sequences of such films. In 1897, for instance, an exhibitor could buy from Lumière any combination of at least a dozen different *vues* of a bullfight in Spain, and three years later he could pick and choose from seventeen different shots of the 1900 Paris Exposition.[32] And, because actualités could be recorded and printed the same day, on the very site of a fairground cinema, they served as a novel form of publicity for the more enterprising exhibitors.

The Lumière catalogs distinguished this broad category of actualités from other kinds of films, including what the company labeled *vues historiques* or "historical scenes." These latter films, although never making up more than a miniscule fraction of Lumière's production, covered a wide range of subjects—from *Exécution de Jeanne d'Arc* and *Assassinat du Duc de Guise* to *Mort de Robespierre* and *Entrevue de Napoléon et du Pape*, all directed by Hatot, in 1897.[33] *Mort de Marat* (1897), for instance, condenses into a single, sunlit LS tableau Charlotte Corday's assassination of the Revolutionary leader (trapped in a boot-shaped bathtub) and her immediate arrest—during which several among the crowd flocking into the high-ceilinged room seem to protest her seizure. Pathé's first catalogs, however, conflated actualités and "historical scenes" into a single category for the purposes of distribution. This conflation assumed, at least until sometime shortly before the appearance of Pathé's newsreel, in 1908, that the difference between recording a current public event as it was happening and reconstructing a past (or even present) historical event in a studio was much less significant than Lumière would have it. What did apparently matter, however, was that a representation of the "historical" differed from a representation of the "purely fictive" or imaginary—which meant that referential differences mattered more than differences in modes of representation.[34] Although the indexical link between image and referent was sufficiently established for spectators, the cinema's overwhelming illusion of "reality" as spectacle must have had an effect that exceeded the discriminatory norms of *vraisemblance* then currently operating in the related medium of photography.[35] In other words, the "historical scene" was bound to the actualité within an unbroken continuum uniting historical past and present, each of which could be dissected and displayed as "attractions" of autonomous tableaux. [. . .]

Although classified as a distinct genre in Pathé's catalogs, the "dramatic and realist film" also shared an affinity with the actualité and the historical film during this period. Yet the genre gradually began to diverge from the latter in several ways—"experimenting" with a more continuous narrative line, a more illusionist diegesis, and even a rudimentary character psychology. The earliest of these films, now lost, seems to have been *Mariage de raison* (1900), which, according to the first Pathé catalog, comprised five separate tableaux.[36] Another, *Un Drame au fond de la mer* (1901), however, survives in a nearly complete print, beginning with perhaps the earliest film title card, printed in French, German, and English. As this title scrolls upward, first revealing a painted seascape and then giving the illusion of a descent into the depths, there is a cut (rather than a dissolve) to a LS painted flat of the rocky seafloor, where several dead bodies lay next to the wreck of a sunken ship. What ensues is a terse, cruel tale of simple greed as a deep-sea diver (with deliberately slowed gestures) descends a background rope ladder to find a treasure chest of coins and then is attacked by another diver from behind. In a reworking of the underwater sensation scene from a then current British play, *The White Heather* (1897),[37] the second diver quickly cuts the airhose of the first, who is left to stagger around and collapse, while the murderer grabs the booty and begins to ascend. Unencumbered by moralizing, this short film introduces into the French cinema a *grand guignol* form of melodrama, whose *fait divers* stories of crime and violence or spectacular moments of what, in England, was called the sensation drama[38] would often characterize the genre throughout the prewar period.

The most noteworthy of these early films was *Histoire d'un crime* (1901), which, based on Pathé's own publicity, has sometimes been called Zecca's first really successful film.[39] Again, the subject is a contemporary fait divers involving a violent crime—this time among the "lower classes"—and the surviving print's attached title is given in French, German, and English. Unlike *Un Drame au fond de la mer* or even Méliès's *L'Affaire Dreyfus*, whose episodic tableaux came from topical magazine illustrations, however, *Histoire d'un crime* reconstructs the continuous narrative of a waxworks exhibit first installed in the Musée Grévin in 1899.[40] The film tells the story of an anonymous carpenter, representing his crime of theft and murder, followed by his arrest, conviction, and execution (all within seven LS painted-flat tableaux, linked by dissolves).[41] It also clearly takes its ambivalent attitude of moralizing mixed with fascination from the waxworks exhibit as well as the Paris morgue—confronting the criminal with the murdered man's corpse, for instance, and concluding with the truc spectacle of a beheading by guillotine. Perhaps the most interesting feature of the film, however, occurs in the prison shot-scene, when a series of three "dream" images appears in the upper background area of the frame as the convict sleeps, watched over by a dozing guard at a foreground table. Based on the borrowed theatrical device of the "vision scene" (requiring an enclosed stage built into the set),[42] each of the three images is marked off by a quickly dropped curtain or shutter, yet the pretext for their spectacle effect is a relatively complex narrative strategy. For these dream scenes retell the man's past story sequentially, from the point when he was happily interrupted in his work by his wife and child to the moment when he lost all his money in a café card game. Although this inserted "flashback" story obviously serves as a warning against gambling (which is then trumped by the sensational execution scene), Zecca's attempt, in *Histoire d'un crime*, to narrate two stories simultaneously and to represent the interior life of a character (and a working-class character, at that) makes the film no less anomalous and forward-looking than *L'Affaire Dreyfus* in early French cinema.

Other Pathé "dramatic and realist films" soon followed on the heels of *Histoire d'un crime*. *Victimes de l'alcoolisme* (1902), for instance, reproduces the familiar nineteenth-century "fable" of a worker whose uncontrollable drinking pushes his family into poverty and him into madness. The scenario probably was adapted from Zola's *L'Assommoir*, as Sadoul claims, but it could just as easily have been drawn from any one of several series of popular lithograph prints or their theatrical versions on the music hall or melodrama stage.[43] Each of the film's five LS tableaux constitutes an autonomous shot-scene, illustrating a different stage in the worker's fall from "happiness and prosperity" to "misery" and "madness." At least two things distinguish *Victimes de l'alcoolisme*, however, from *Histoire d'un crime*. First of all, several of the studio decors are much more detailed in their composition. The painted flat of the street corner where the Au Père Colomb bar is located, for instance, depicts a series of sharply defined shops stretching off along a narrow street into the distance. The initial family dining room has not only a window looking out over the city rooftops but a door opening onto a kitchen. Moreover, it includes a good number of "real" props—a sewing machine at which the wife does "put-out" work, a table that she and her mother set with dishes and utensils, and a large gas lamp suspended overhead. Second, each tableau is separated from the others by a straight cut and an intertitle, whose text is printed out in black letters on white strips, like labels roughly pasted on a dark surface.[44] Here, then, is the earliest extant evidence of Pathé's intertitle "innovation," which, within another year—in *Don Quichotte, Le Chat botté, Epopée napoléonienne*, and *La Vie et la Passion de Jésus Christ*—would take the form of a Pathé trademark: terse phrases in large red block letters on a black background.[45] As in those films, a strongly didactic principle governs the interrelation between verbal caption and visual illustration.

Although none of the "dramatic and realist" films Pathé produced during the subsequent two years seems to have survived, the company's catalogs provide some sense of the genre's trajectory. *La Vie d'un joueur* (1903), for instance, presented another warning against gambling (in eight tableaux), apparently this time drawn from a waxworks exhibit at Madame Tussaud's in London.[46] The extremely successful *Roman d'amour* (1904) told the story of a young working-class woman who is seduced by a wealthy client of the dress shop where she works.[47] After a brief life of pleasure, she is abandoned and soon starves; the final LS tableaux focus on her parents' despair, her "terrible atonement," and their reconciliation at her hospital deathbed. Given such descriptions, together with a few surviving publicity stills and posters, these Pathé films seem to have adopted the *fait divers* subjects and tableau style of autonomous shot-scenes in *Histoire d'un crime*, but without the narrative complexity of an inserted "flash-back" story.

The studio decors, however, as in *Victimes de l'alcoolisme*, seemed quite detailed in construction and included "authentic" props, as if the principle of verisimilitude, perhaps emanating from the naturalist theater of Antoine, were beginning to infiltrate the genre's tableaux. Yet the overwhelming moral tone of these early films—preaching the virtues of close family bonds and disciplined work—surely kept them from being "proletarian" works that could serve class ends, as Sadoul once argued.[48] Rather, as the special supplement advertising *Victimes de l'alcoolisme* strongly suggests, they much more likely served to ensure working-class and artisan (as well as petit-bourgeois and white collar) assent to the domestic and public harmony of a bourgeois social order. By 1904–1905, however, certain Pathé films in the genre would not be so reassuring, and the "dramatic and realist film" would play a significant role in the shift from a cinema of *attractions* to a *narrative* cinema.

Notes

1. Hansen, *Babel and Babylon*, 29.
2. The Lumière catalogs are reprinted in Sadoul, *Lumière et Méliès*, 126–145.
3. Méliès produced four kinds of films: actualités, scientific films, mise-en-scène films, and transformation films (trick films and féeries). See Méliès, "Les Vues cinématographiques" (1907), reprinted in English translation in Abel, *French Film Theory and Criticism*, 1: 30–31.
4. Tom Gunning, "Attractions and Narrative Integration," Society for Cinema Studies Conference, Los Angeles, 23 May 1991.
5. See, for instance, the Star Films ads in *Photo-Ciné-Gazette* (*PCG*), beginning on 1 October 1905. Méliès mentions his preference for "fantastical scenes" in "Les Vues cinématographiques."
6. This information as well as the following is drawn from Méliès, "Importance du scénario," *Cinéa-Ciné* 28 (April 1932), reprinted in Sadoul, *Lumière et Méliès*, 220. Méliès is much less insistent on this point, admittedly, in the earlier essay, "Les Vues cinématographiques," 40.
7. The following catalog of cinematic devices is drawn from Frazer, *Artificially Arranged Scenes*, 59–76. See, also, Méliès, "Les Vues cinématographiques," 44–45. [. . .]
8. Williams, "Film Body," 29.
9. Félix Mesguich, *Tours de manivelle: souvenirs d'un chasseur d'images* (1932), quoted in Sadoul, *Histoire générale du cinéma*, 2: 207. *Cendrillon* also did quite well in both French and British music halls. Sadoul, *Histoire générale du cinéma*, 2: 111.
10. Weber, *Peasants into Frenchmen*, 455–456.
11. "New Pieces in Paris," *The Era Almanack* (London, 1900), 80. Frazer, *Artificially Arranged Scenes*, 7, 220. See, also, Vardac, *Stage to Screen*, 152–164; and Katherine Singer Kovács, "Georges Méliès and the Féerie," in Fell, *Film Before Griffith*, 244–257.
12. Sadoul, *Lumière et Méliès*, 171.
13. Mesguich, *Tours de manivelle*, as quoted in Sadoul, *Histoire générale du cinéma*, 2: 207. Musical accompaniment certainly determined the rhythm of later féeries such as *Faust aux enfers* (1903) and *La Damnation de Faust* (1904). See, for instance, Frazer, *Artificially Arranged Scenes*, 133.
14. Méliès, "Les Vues cinématographiques," 40–41.
15. Pierre Jenn's découpage of the film is published in *L'Avant-Scène Cinéma* 334 (November 1984), 29–37. Edison and Lubin were both selling dupes of this film in October 1902. See *New York Clipper* (*NYC*) (4 October 1902), 712; and (11 October 1902), 733. American Mutoscope and Biograph at least advertised their print as a Méliès film. See *NYC* (4 October 1902), 712.
16. Brewster briefly mentions this early representation of "deep space" in "Deep Staging in French Films, 1900–1914," in Elsaesser, *Early Cinema*, 45.
17. Frazer, *Artificially Arranged Scenes*, 97.
18. Salt credits Méliès with realizing "fairly quickly the importance of 'correct' directions of entrances and exits for the smoothness of film continuity." *Film Style and Technology*, 56.
19. Quévrain, "A la redécouverte de Méliès," 163; Jenn, *Georges Méliès cinéaste*, 51.
20. Quévrain, "A la redécouverte de Méliès," 163–164; Jenn, *Georges Méliès cinéaste*, 52–53, 60–61.
21. Quévrain, "A la redécouverte de Méliès," 165.
22. Frazer, *Artificially Arranged Scenes*, 98.

23. André Gaudreault, "'Théatricalité' et 'narrativité' dans l'oeuvre de Georges Méliès," in Malthête-Méliès, *Méliès et la naissance du spectacle cinématographique*, 213–214; Quévrain, "A la redécouverte de Méliès," 164.
24. Crafton, *Emile Cohl*, 249–256.
25. Sadoul, *Histoire générale du cinéma*, 2: 192.
26. Sadoul, *Lumière et Méliès*, 254, 255.
27. Lacassin, "Filmographie d'Alice Guy," in Guy, *Autobiographie d'une pionnière du cinéma* (Paris: Denoël/Gonthier, 1976), 171, 175, 177, 179. [. . .]
28. Sadoul, *Lumière et Méliès*, 136, 137, 139, 140, 142.
29. *Pathé Catalogue (PC)* (Paris, August 1904), 25–30, 74–75. See, also, Sadoul, *Histoire générale du cinéma*, 2: 192.
30. These examples come from the Lumière catalogs reprinted in Sadoul, *Lumière et Méliès*, 126–145.
31. Tom Gunning, "'The World Within Your Reach': Early Cinema and the World Tour," Deuxieme Colloque International de Domitor, Lausanne, 2 July 1992.
32. Sadoul, *Lumière et Méliès*, 138–139, 143. [. . .] For analysis of Pathé trick films, féeries and historical films, see Richard Abel, *The Ciné Goes to Town: French Cinema, 1896–1914* (Berkeley: University of California Press, 1998), 78–86.
33. Sadoul, *Lumière et Méliès*, 137, 140.
34. See, for instance, Francis Doublier's account of using stock actualité footage to produce a four-shot film supposedly about Alfred Dreyfus, for Russian audiences, in 1898, reported in the *New York World Telegram* (23 October 1935), and reprinted, with commentary, in Bottomore, "Dreyfus and Documentary," 290.
35. See, for instance, Roland Barthes's notion of the photograph's principal function as "having been there," in Barthes, *Image, Music, Text*, trans. Stephen Heath (New York: Hill and Wang, 1977), 44.
36. *PC* (Paris, 1900), 26.
37. Michael R. Booth, *English Melodrama* (London: Herbert Jenkins, 1965), 175. [. . .]
38. See, especially, Booth, *English Melodrama*, 165–176.
39. The Pathé catalog supplement for *Alcohol and Its Victims* (May 1902) refers specifically to "the success gained by the STORY OF A CRIME" the previous year.
40. Sadoul, *Histoire générale du cinéma*, 2: 187. Edison's *Execution of Czolgosz, with Panorama of Auburn Prison* (November 1901), by contrast, reenacted the execution of the man who had assassinated President McKinley. Musser, *Before the Nickelodeon*, 187–190.
41. Although the Pathé catalog lists six scenes, the last is divided into two tableaux. As Alan Williams suggests, the only tableau not reproduced from the Musée Grévin is the court trial, probably so as to limit the film's cost. Williams, *Republic of Images*, 46.
42. Vardac, *From Stage to Screen*, 171.
43. Sadoul, *Histoire générale du cinéma*, 2: 188. See, for instance, such British examples as "The Bottle" (1847) and "The Drunkard's Children" (1848). Meisel, *Realizations*, 124–141.
44. The earliest surviving American film to have intertitles is Edison's *The European Rest Cure* (September 1904).
45. See "Very Important Notice," *PC* (London, May 1903), 12; and "Avis Très Important," *PC* (Paris, August 1904), 12.
46. Sadoul, *Histoire générale du cinéma*, 2: 311.
47. See *PC* (London, May–June 1904), 11, as well as the special 1904 supplement for *Annie's Love Story*, the film's title in England. Pathé is reported to have sold one thousand copies of this film. Sadoul, *Histoire générale du cinéma*, 2: 312–313.
48. Sadoul, *Histoire générale du cinéma*, 2: 311. Although Burch resists this temptation to see the system of representation in these films "as an authentically working-class system," he sometimes still tends to conflate the terms *proletarian* and *popular*, resisting the notion that anything like a popular culture was being redefined as a mass culture, certainly by the end of the nineteenth century. Burch, "Film's Institutional Mode of Representation and the Soviet Response," 77.

Bibliography

Abel, Richard. *French Film Theory and Criticism. A History/Anthology, 1907–1939*, 2 volumes (Princeton, NJ: Princeton University Press, 1988).
Bottomore, Stephen. "Dreyfus and Documentary," *Sight and Sound* 53 (Autumn 1984), 290–293.

Burch, Noël. "Film's Institutional Mode of Representation and the Soviet Response," *October* 11 (Winter 1979), 77–96.

Crafton, Donald. *Emile Cohl, Caricature, and Film* (Princeton: Princeton University Press, 1990).

Elsaesser, Thomas. ed., *Early Cinema: Space, Frame, Narrative* (London: British Film Institute, 1990).

Fell, John. ed., *Film Before Griffith* (Berkeley: University of California Press, 1983).

Frazer, John. *Artificially Arranged Scenes: The Films of Georges Méliès* (Boston: G. K. Hall, 1979).

Hansen, Miriam. *Babel and Babylon: Spectatorship in American Silent Film* (Cambridge: Harvard University Press, 1991).

Jenn, Pierre. *Georges Méliès cinéaste* (Paris: Albatros, 1984).

Malthête-Méliès, Madeleine. ed., *Méliès et la naissance du spectacle cinématographique* (Paris: Klincksieck, 1984).

Meisel, Martin. *Realizations: Narrative, Pictorial, and Theatrical Arts in Nineteenth-Century England* (Princeton: Princeton University Press, 1983).

Musser, Charles. *Before the Nickelodeon: Edwin S. Porter and the Edison Manufacturing Company* (Berkeley: University of California Press, 1991).

Quévrain, Anne Marie. "A la redécouverte de Méliès: *Le Voyage a la lune*," *Les Cahiers de la Cinémathèque* 35/36 (1982), 160–165.

Sadoul, Georges. *Lumière et Méliès*, rev. ed., Bernhard Eisenschitz (Paris: Lherminier, 1985).

Sadoul, Georges. *Histoire générale du cinéma, 2: Les Pionniers du Cinéma, 1897–1908* (Paris: Denoël, 1948).

Salt, Barry. *Film Style and Technology: History and Analysis* (London: Starword, 1983).

Vardac, A. Nichols. *Stage to Screen: Theatrical Origins of Early Film: David Garrick to D. W. Griffith* (Cambridge: Harvard University Press, 1949).

Weber, Eugen. *Peasants into Frenchmen: The Modernization of Rural France, 1870–1914* (Stanford: Stanford University Press, 1976).

Williams, Alan. *The Republic of Images: A History of French Filmmaking* (Cambridge: Harvard University Press, 1992).

Williams, Linda. "Film Body: An Implantation of Perversions," *Ciné-Tracts* 12 (1981), 19–35.

PART II

Storytelling and the nickelodeon

INTRODUCTION

LONGER MULTI-SHOT FILMS TELLING STORIES became more prevalent from 1903. They brought with them a shift in the balance in individual films between attractions and the framework of narrative, and also paved the way for replacing the dominant role of the exhibitor in orchestrating filmic meanings and pleasures with the preeminence of the producer. Already by the end of 1903 in the United States more feet of fictional film were being sold (and hence watched) than actuality footage, and by 1907 more fictional than factual films were being produced.[1] Important innovations in the distribution of films also took place from 1903 with the establishment of 'film exchanges' that bought films from manufacturers and rented them out to exhibitors, thus ensuring a steady supply of different films to exhibitors at minimal cost. Variety theatres and travelling exhibitors continued to show moving pictures, which were becoming increasingly popular, but there also developed more permanent exhibition outlets either showing only films or featuring films as their central attraction. This happened first in the United States, where these theatres were called 'nickelodeons', and shortly thereafter in other countries. 'It is not too much to say', Charles Musser has asserted, 'that modern cinema began with the nickelodeons'.[2]

Together these interrelated developments in the mode of representation, distribution and exhibition in the period 1903–07 had profound effects on future cinematic practice and indeed the shape of cinema. How can we best describe and explain these changes? Or, put more precisely: why did longer story films emerge? How can those films be characterized? Why did nickelodeons emerge? Who went to nickelodeons and why? What effects did nickelodeons have on the production of films and their mode of representation? Like before, we will be looking at conditions in the United States, but we will also consider the impact of French films on those conditions.

Legal decisions about patents and copyrights – about controlling the use of motion picture technology and individual films – in the years 1901–02 influenced production practices in the United States and eventually removed an important obstacle for the production of longer story films. In July 1901 Edison won his 1897 patent-infringement suit against the Biograph company, but the appeal in March 1902 went in Biograph's favour in a decision that declared all of Edison's patents as they stood invalid.[3] The decision freed Biograph and indeed the other companies also fighting Edison's patent claims to pursue their motion picture activities, encouraging them to invest further in film production.

Likewise, the settling of legal disputes over copyrighting practices in late 1902 enabled film production companies to claim copyright protection and so to stop other companies illegally copying their films.[4] This cleared the way for new investments and new production practices. Vitagraph began producing longer story films from early 1903. Biograph opened a new indoor film studio in early 1903 and also began to embark on more ambitious projects, particularly the making of longer story films; by June 1904 they were producing one a month.

These legal decisions removed obstacles standing in the way of investment in film studios and in longer story films. But they do not explain why film producers wanted to make more expensive, longer story films and why exhibitors wanted to show them. Let's consider producers first. Artistic innovation is one reason for their interest in longer films, as filmmakers were always trying to find new ways to engage people. An increase in the length of their films allowed them to draw on a wider range of cultural models for their productions. These notably included stories told in other media, which could be used as frameworks for the presentation of filmic attractions. Economic competition between companies also pushed them to produce longer, more elaborate films, using this as one way to differentiate their product.

Longer films were desirable because they enabled producers to sell more feet of film to exhibitors, thus increasing profits as the price depended on a film's length. Some exhibitors presumably found the exhibition of longer films put together by the production company quicker, easier and hence perhaps cheaper than the usual practice of having to organize numerous very short films into a structured programme. No doubt fiction films were also often easier to plan than actualities, the most popular of which often depended, as we have seen, on the vagaries of the news; the shift towards fiction thus meant that production could be increasingly regularized.[5] It may have been the case that the making of longer films was more efficient than the production of a group of shorter films, and that shooting fiction films in a studio was often cheaper than travelling around to produce actualities.

In any case, the popularity of longer story films meant that they outsold actualities. Charles Musser has shown that although actualities continued to be produced in larger numbers until 1907 – as mentioned above – more prints of the longer story films were sold (compare the figures for the Edison Manufacturing Company in the chapter by Musser below).[6] Many of these, it is worth noting, were comic films. Indeed, copyright records suggest that in 1907 about 70 per cent of films produced in America were comedies.[7] Richard Abel's chapter in this section shows that variety theatre managers frequently remarked on the success of longer story films with their patrons. Thus it was audience demand which ultimately motivated film producers, exchanges and exhibitors to produce, buy and show longer story films.

Why, though, were longer story films popular? No simple and easy answer can be given. These films, it seems, were able to involve audiences more deeply, drawing spectators into the story and engaging them in the unfolding events, thus providing a form of entertainment which powerfully combined attractions with the pleasures of narrative. What the pleasures of narrative are in general is, of course, more difficult to define, and has been the subject of much work in film theory and indeed in the disciplines of literary theory, psychology and philosophy.

As Abel shows, most of the successful longer story films were French. Films like Méliès' *A Trip to the Moon* and those made by the increasingly powerful Pathé Freres company were frequently singled out for praise by variety showmen and increasingly dominated exhibition in the United States and indeed worldwide. Pathé had quickly developed into a modern business organization with substantial working capital and during the years 1904–09 established an international network of offices to co-ordinate distribution. Initially many of the French films were simply duped in America, despite strengthened copyright protection, and sold on by American production companies as their own films. However, this became increasingly difficult as Méliès and Pathé established offices in New York City in June 1903 and August 1904 respectively. Biograph began to produce their own longer story films the very month Mélies opened his American office. Lubin quickly followed suit and the Edison Manufacturing Company began to produce longer story films quite regularly from late 1903, including *The Great Train Robbery* in November 1903. Musser's analysis of the film below suggests that it draws on particular American myths and contexts, furthering the national – indeed nationalistic – cinematic practices inaugurated with the Spanish-American war actualities discussed in the previous section. Linked together, Abel and Musser's articles show the importance of French films for the development of American filmmaking and of the American film industry more generally, demonstrating again that this period witnessed a complex and productive interaction between film industries of different countries.

Leaving aside the question of why longer story films emerged, we can begin to direct our attention to the transformations in film form and style wrought by the increased production of such films. Films made up of single-shots, showing actuality scenes or brief fictional skits, dominated the period up until 1902. Longer films were developed by editing shots together. This initially happened at the point of presentation when exhibitors joined distinct films together to create a film programme. However, editing soon moved into the sphere of production, as we have seen, helping to create trick films and the kind of basic multi-shot story films that Frank Gray analysed in the previous section. Editing was also increasingly prominent in actuality production, where filmmakers sought to capture the reality of events and organized various views of these events according to a sequential and/or spatial logic.[8] A hybrid actuality/fiction genre quickly emerged, evident in films like *Rube and Mandy at Coney Island* (Edison, 1903), *A Romance of the Rails* (Edison, 1903) and later *A Policeman's Tour of the World* (Pathé, 1907) that showed fictional characters in films that also functioned as travelogues.[9] The boundaries between actuality and fiction, just as those between attractions and narrative, were fluid and uncertain.

The individual shot was increasingly viewed not as a self-contained unit but as a building block for stories. Industry discourse at the time stressed the need for these stories to be carefully organised and to supply their own internal coherence. A Kleine Film Catalogue from 1904, for example, described the 'perfect film' as follows:

> There should be no lagging in the story; every foot must be an essential part, whose loss would deprive the story of some merit; there should be sequence, each part leading to the next with increasing interest, reaching the most interesting point at the climax, which should end the film.

To achieve these goals filmmakers had to find ways to convey spatio-temporal relations between shots – to convey 'sequence' – in a clear fashion that was intelligible to spectators. Looking backwards from our vantage point after the establishment of rules of filmic storytelling can make that process seem simple, obvious and inevitable – but at the time it was none of those things. How, then, did filmmakers manage to tell stories of increasing length across numerous shots?

One way was to produce films that mimicked the visual conventions of other media, like the magic lantern or comic strips, and told stories already familiar to large audiences. *Uncle Tom's Cabin* (Edison, 1903), for example, consisted of a series of tableaux representing scenes from the very popular novel and play, recognizable to audiences because of their familiarity with the story (a story, incidentally, that Linda Williams will discuss further in her chapter in the section *Feature Films and Cinema Programmes*).[10] Stories developed specifically for the screen were often simple narratives that followed one action in a linear fashion, making the need for audience familiarity with the story or a showman explaining the film unnecessary.

Exemplary here was the chase film, a genre which was particularly common and popular internationally between 1903 and 1905, and which demonstrated that subject matter and narrative organization were interrelated. The film *Personal* (Biograph, 1904), for instance, tells the story of a Frenchman who puts an ad in the personal column of the New York Herald to meet a wife at Grant's Tomb. He is inundated and runs off, chased by a large group of women. Each of the next eight shots begins with the man entering the frame in the distance and running toward and past the camera, and ends with the last of the women exiting in the foreground. The spatial and temporal relations are made extremely clear to the audience, as the film's subject matter, the chase, and the straightforward motivations of the characters help the viewer to follow this simple yet extended narrative.[11] Noël Burch has suggested that the chase 'came into being and proliferated so that continuity could be established'.[12] Like other films of the period, *Personal* balances the presentation of attractions with the stuttering emergence of a fictional narrative discourse, indicating a gradual shift, in the terms of André Gaudreault, from monstration (showing) to narration (telling).[13] It is worth noting that *Personal* was able to engage audiences partly because it lampooned the marriage of impoverished European aristocrats with American women, so again commenting on European–American relations. Furthermore, the chase entailed women clambering over various objects and thus offered spectators a view of women's bodies partially uncovered. The film thus responded to widespread (male) anxieties about the newfound role of women in the public sphere by translating their physical mobility into a concern about sexual propriety. Resolution to the story is reached by the formation of a couple.

Lecturers talking whilst films played could also help explain films to audiences as they unfolded. In some cases this included vocally acting out the parts of the film behind or beside the screen. Likewise, the innovation of intertitles from around 1903, an early example being *Uncle Tom's Cabin*, helped make actions and scenes clearer in a way that internalized the role of the film lecturer.[14] One other way of clarifying actions was to simply repeat them. *Life of an American Fireman* (Edison, 1903), for example, ends with two lengthy shots that show the same action from two vantage points. The first shot shows a fireman coming in a bedroom window to rescue a mother and then returning to rescue her baby. In the second shot, we see both rescues again, from a camera position outside the house.[15] Other films similarly repeated action from different perspectives as one way of clarifying temporal and spatial relations (although for the modern eye this is actually confusing).

Early film's mode of representation evolved, then, partly to intensify visual pleasure and the cinema of attractions and partly to reconfigure the relationship between attractions and narrative. Comedies like *Personal* and many other chase films made up the most popular genre at this time, as we have already seen. The gag, the brief visual joke, lends itself well to a simple and complete narrative form because it has a minimal essential narrative development: a set-up for the gag and a pay-off, usually some minor disaster.[16] Other genres flourished as well. Many of them are visible in *The Great Train Robbery*, as Musser's chapter here shows, for the film incorporates elements of the crime film which had initially been popular in Britain, the train genre we saw emerging in the previous section, the chase film, and actualities.

One of the consequences of this gradual development of an internalized 'filmic narrator' was the marginalization of the exhibitor's role. Since exhibitors no longer had to organize numerous single-shot films into a programme, editorial control and narrative responsibility was increasingly centralized in the production company. This was furthered, Musser has argued, by a process of standardization, which established the reel of film as 'the basic industry commodity'.[17] Previously, companies like Biograph, Vitagraph and Percival Waters' Kinetograph Company rented an entire exhibition service to vaudeville theatres, which included a projector, a motion picture operator and a reel of film. Late in 1903, though, Waters, seeking a competitive advantage to appeal to vaudeville theatres in the East, began simply to rent a reel of film to these vaudeville houses for a lower price. The company was able to do this because the exhibition process had by this time become relatively simple and theatre electricians could be trained to become projectionists. Waters now became a renter or film exchange, while the theatres became the actual exhibitors. Vitagraph and other services quickly followed suit.[18] In this way, the separate roles of producer, distributor and exhibitor began to be more firmly delineated.

Exchanges enabled exhibitors showing films to have a constantly changing supply of films. As a consequence, showmen did not need to move to find new audiences because the same audience could come back again and again to watch new films. This was an important precondition for the establishment of venues showing just films, the so-called 'nickelodeons'. Another precondition was, of course, that production companies released a sufficient number of films for frequent programme changes. Here again, as Abel's analysis shows, Pathé was critically important, for it was in 1904 the one company capable of producing a large enough body of films and hence of sustaining the expansion of film exhibition in the United States.

So what was the scope of this expansion? Variety theatre magnate Harry Davis had run films as part of his variety shows in Pittsburgh and decided in June 1905 to open a small storefront theatre showing just moving pictures. He called it the *Nickelodeon*, joining nickel – 5 cents – with the Greek word for 'concert hall'. The theatre quickly became very popular and nickelodeons, or nickel theatres, spread rapidly, initially in cities in the mid-west and then across the United States. Eileen Bowser has gathered statistics suggesting that the number of nickelodeons in the United States doubled between 1907 and 1908 to around 8000 and it was estimated that by 1910 as many as 26 million Americans visited these theatres every week.[19] Likewise, storefront theatres, or *Ladenkinos*, spread rapidly in Germany. In 1905 there were only 40 cinemas but by 1906 there were 200, by 1908 1,000 and by 1910 2,000.[20] Pathé owned a chain of nearly 200 cinemas in France and Belgium by 1909.[21]

Nickelodeons varied considerably. Often they were small converted storefronts, seating less than 200 so as to be exempt from costly theatre licenses. Typically, the nickelodeon was housed in a long, narrow room, with seating on wooden chairs and a screen hung on the back wall. A piano and drum set were placed to one side of and below the screen. Other nickelodeons however were much bigger, and soon large vaudeville theatres were converted into nickelodeons, some with capacities for well over 1,000 spectators. Exhibition practices were also variable. Programmes lasted between 10 minutes and half an hour or more in length. Generally they ran continuously and audiences would join the programme at any point and stay as long as they liked. Whilst some nickelodeons showed just films many others offered a 'combination show', presenting films together with vaudeville acts and/or illustrated songs. Combination shows were probably dominant throughout most of the United States, though evidence suggests the combination of vaudeville and film was prominent in the Northeast and the combination of illustrated songs and films in the Midwest.[22]

Who went to the nickelodeons? The question is not easy to answer. Film historians have delved ever deeper into various kinds of records to answer this question, working at the same time with various conceptualizations of social identity – particularly in relation to class – and increasingly pondering the methodological and historiographic implications of their practices. Here Ben Singer's essay on nickelodeons in Manhattan is exemplary. Its initial publication also occasioned a vigorous exchange between various scholars. Important to Singer, and to other historians, are the questions: who were the cinema's first audiences, and how heterogeneous were they in their social composition? Did the operators of nickelodeons and converted vaudeville theatres recruit their audiences primarily from the new immigrant populations of the major cities, or did they consciously seek to attract a more affluent, bourgeois audience?

Early writers on American cinema history assumed that audiences at nickelodeons were primarily working class, a group who could now afford the cheap price of attendance. Overall Singer suggests this was not too far off the mark. He carefully delineates the location of nickelodeons in Manhattan, arguing that there is a close correlation between location and audience; because nickelodeons were frequently located in working class and immigrant neighbourhoods they would mainly have attracted audiences from those groups. Singer presents a detailed analysis of various neighbourhoods, utilizing extant primary data and also contemporary historical accounts of New York City.

In arguing that working class immigrant audiences were the primary audience of nickelodeons Singer is explicitly disagreeing with Robert C. Allen who, along with other historians, had previously challenged the traditional account of nickelodeons as principally working class sites of leisure. Movie-going in Manhattan between 1906 and 1912, Allen had written, 'was by no means an exclusive activity of the poor or the immigrant' because the middle class 'embraced the movies much earlier than is generally believed'.[23] Allen returned to this argument in a wide-ranging response to Singer's article. Location is critical to understanding audience composition, Allen notes, but he also suggests that we need to pay attention to the kinds of shows being offered. Here the development of programmes of films interspersed with vaudeville acts in what Richard Abel in his chapter in this section calls 'family vaudeville' from 1905 and the slightly later development of what Allen has called 'small-time vaudeville' from 1907 can be seen as indicative of an appeal to the kind of middle-class audiences who had hitherto attended respectable vaudeville.[24]

Allen's response to Singer suggests the need for further thinking about class formation in America, a point made also by Sumiko Higashi in her contribution to the debate and indeed by Singer in his own response.[25] What are the boundaries between classes and what is the nature of class affiliation in turn-of-the-century America? Historians have recently suggested that this period witnessed the massive expansion of lower middle class groups and a concomitant weakening of the borders between working class and middle class groups. Higashi, Allen and Singer agree that it is the lower middle class segment, made up overwhelmingly of low paid white-collar workers, that was an increasingly important audience for moving pictures in urban areas. There is little agreement, however, about the class affiliation of this segment.

It is worth noting also that important distinctions within class based groupings need to be made and a number of scholars have recently paid attention to the role women played in relation to class distinctions, to differences between various immigrant groups, and also to the distinctive experience of black Americans at the movies.[26] Allen and Singer agree that Manhattan cannot be taken as an exemplary location and that exhibition in small town and rural areas was frequently very different from that in larger cities.[27]

Why does the issue of the audience for the nickelodeon boom in cities generate such controversy?[28] On the one hand it is simply a matter of historians trying their best to provide an accurate and adequate description and explanation of the nickelodeon era. On the other hand, political questions about class and power are involved. Reconfigured in this way, the debate seems to be partly about, in Robert Sklar's words, 'the significance of immigrant and working class audiences, and the possibility of class struggle, in the formation of early cinema' and about the impact of the middle class and its agenda of social control on cinema in America.[29] That is, did the cinema constitute a public sphere for working class audiences – a fact that would, amongst other things, inflect the meaning of films – or was it an agency of social control dominated by the middle class and imposed on the working class? Furthermore, did the experience of moviegoing in the long run have an impact on the class affiliation of those inbetween groups in the lower middle class? Steven Ross, for one, believes it did, arguing that in later years (especially in the 1920s) these groups developed their own sense of middle classness partly at the movies.[30]

What were the more immediate effects of the nickelodeon boom? We will return to this question in the following section, but for now it is worth noting the following consequences. Nickelodeons created a new kind of specialized spectator, the moviegoer, who could now integrate moving pictures into his or her daily life in a way impossible with their exhibition in variety shows.[31] It is no coincidence, Miriam Hansen has noted, that the term 'spectator' becomes common only from 1910.[32]

The nickelodeon boom also precipitated further changes in film production and film form, for the rapid expansion of nickel theatres throughout the United States led to vastly increased demand for new films. The share of overall film output made up of actualities declined dramatically, and fictional narratives became the norm. Earlier innovations in narrative organization were further developed, as individual shots were increasingly linked together to tell original stories that were not predicated on audience foreknowledge. Often these films were more focused on characters and less on physical action. Dramas rather than comedies began to dominate production.[33] Filmmaking became increasingly well-planned, notably with the widespread use of detailed film scenarios, and with the introduction of varied roles for the individuals involved in filmmaking (for example, the role of the cameraman was now separated from that of the director).[34]

Lastly, the perception that nickelodeons were attended by working class and immigrant groups and that films had deleterious effects on these allegedly vulnerable and dangerous audiences led to a flurry of reformist concern about cinema. This in turn had a considerable impact on the shaping of film content, film form and the social function of cinema. We will consider this development in the next section.

Notes

1   Charles Musser, 'The Nickelodeon Era Begins: Establishing the Foundations for Hollywood's Mode of Representation', *Framework*, nos. 22/23 (Autumn 1983); Musser, 'Another Look at the Chaser Theory', *Studies in Visual Communication*, vol. 10, no. 4 (1984), 40; Musser, *The Emergence of Cinema: The American Screen to 1907* (Berkeley: University of California Press, 1990), 337–70, 449–90. Robert Allen's count of the copyrighted films shows that in 1904, 42 per cent were actualities, 45 per cent were comedies, 8 per cent were dramas, and 5 per cent were trick films. Robert C. Allen, *Vaudeville and Film, 1895–1915: A Study in Media Interaction* (New York: Arno Press, 1980), 181.

2   Musser, *The Emergence of Cinema*, 417.

3   Musser, *The Emergence of Cinema*, 305–8. Edison reapplied for modified patents.

4   Immediately following Edison's defeat in the patent case, Sigmund Lubin copied, or duped, films of Prince Henry's visit to the United States that had been made and copyrighted by Edison. Edison sued for copyright infringement. Lubin claimed, though, that Edison's method of copyrighting was inadequate, for rather than submitting each film as a whole for copyright Edison should have submitted each frame because it was a different photograph – a very costly procedure indeed given the amount of frames in each film. Lubin won initially in June 1902 and the decision again discouraged investment in film production, for now films could easily be duped. Later that year, however, the court of appeals found in Edison's favour. This decision had important implications for the definition of film, which could now be seen as analogous to other art forms and as a coherent entity (rather than as a collection of frames), and for the further investment of film producers in longer story films. André Gaudreault, 'The Infringement of Copyright Laws and its Efffects (1900–1906)', in Thomas Elsaesser (ed.), *Early Cinema: Space, Frame, Narrative* (London: British Film Institute, 1990); Musser, *The Emergence of Cinema*, 330–3.

5   Allen, *Vaudeville and Film*, 157–8.

6   Musser, 'The Nickelodeon Era Begins'; Musser, 'Another Look at the Chaser Theory'; Musser, *The Emergence of Cinema*, 337–70, 449–90.

7   Allen, *Vaudeville and Film*, 212.

8   Musser, *The Emergence of Cinema*, 193–296; Stephen Bottomore, 'Shots in the Dark – The Real Origins of Film Editing', in Elsaesser (ed.), *Early Cinema*.

9   Musser, 'The Travel Genre in 1903–1904: Moving Towards Fictional Narrative', in Elsaesser (ed.), *Early Cinema*; Philip Rosen, 'Disjunction and Ideology in a Pre-classical Film: *A Policeman's Tour of the World*', *Wide Angle*, vol. 12, no. 3 (1990); Charlie Keil, 'Steel Engines and Cardboard Rockets: The Status of Fiction and Nonfiction in Early Cinema', *Persistence of Vision*, no. 9 (1991).

10   Musser, *Before the Nickelodeon: Edwin S. Porter and the Edison Manufacturing Company* (Berkeley: University of California Press, 1991), 242; Janet Staiger, *Interpreting Films: Studies in the Historical Reception of Cinema* (Princeton, NJ: Princeton University Press, 1992), ch. 5.

11   Charlie Keil, *Early American Cinema in Transition: Story, Style, and Filmmaking, 1907–1913* (Madison: University of Wisconsin Press, 2001), 47–9.

12   Noël Burch, *Life to Those Shadows*, (trans.) Ben Brewster (London: Ben Brewster, 1990), 149.

13   André Gaudreault, 'Film, Narrative, Narration: The Cinema of the Lumière Brothers', in Elsaesser (ed.), *Early Cinema*.

14   Keil, *Early American Cinema in Transition*, 60–9.

15   André Gaudreault, 'Detours in Film Narrative: The Development of Cross-Cutting', in Elsaesser (ed.), *Early Cinema*.

16   Tom Gunning, 'Crazy Machines in the Garden of Forking Paths: Mischief Gags and the Origins of American Film Comedy', in Kristine Brunovska Karnick and Henry Jenkins (eds), *Classical Hollywood Comedy* (London: Routledge, 1995).

17   Musser, 'The Nickelodeon Era Begins', 257.

18   Musser, *The Emergence of Cinema*, 366–7.

19   Eileen Bowser, *The Transformation of Cinema, 1907–1915* (Berkeley: University of California Press, 1990), 4–6.

20   Joseph Garncarz, 'The Origins of Film Exhibition in Germany', in Tim Bergfelder, Erica Carter and Deniz Göktürk (eds), *The German Cinema Book* (London: British Film Institute, 2002), 117.

21   Richard Abel, 'French Silent Cinema', in Geoffrey Nowell-Smith (ed.), *The Oxford History of World Cinema* (Oxford: Oxford University Press, 1996), 112.

22   Richard Abel, 'Reframing the Vaudeville/Moving Pictures Debate, with Illustrated Songs', in Leonardo Quaresima and Laura Vichi (eds), *The Tenth Muse: Cinema and Other Arts* (Udine: Forum, 2001).

23   Robert C. Allen, 'Motion Picture Exhibition in Manhattan: Beyond the Nickelodeon', *Cinema Journal*, vol. 18, no. 2 (Spring 1979), 3.

24   Robert C. Allen, 'Manhattan Myopia; or, Oh! Iowa!', *Cinema Journal*, vol. 35, no. 3 (Spring 1996), in particular 87–92.

25   Allen, 'Manhattan Myopia', in particular 92–94; Sumiko Higashi, 'Dialogue: Manhattan's Nickelodeons' and Ben Singer, 'New York, Just Like I Picture It . . .', both *Cinema Journal*, vol. 35, no. 3 (Spring 1996).

26   Lee Grieveson, ' "A kind of recreative school for the whole family": making cinema respectable, 1907–1909', *Screen*, vol. 42, no. 1 (Spring 2001); Judith Thissen, 'Jewish Immigrant Audiences in New York City, 1905–1914'; Giorgio Bertellini, 'Italian Imageries, Historical Feature Films and the Fabrication of Italy's Spectators in Early 1900s New York'; Alison Griffiths and James Latham, 'Film and Ethnic Identity in Harlem, 1896–1915', all in Melvyn Stokes and Richard Maltby (eds), *American Movie Audiences: From the Turn of the Century to the Early Sound Era* (London: British Film Institute, 1999); Mary Carbine, ' "The Finest Outside the Loop": Motion Picture Exhibition in Chicago's Black Metropolis, 1905–1928', *Camera Obscura*, no. 23 (May 1990); Gregory Waller, 'Another Audience: Black Moviegoing, 1907–1916', *Cinema Journal*, vol. 31, no. 2 (1992).

27   Gregory Waller, *Main Street Amusements: Movies and Commercial Entertainment in a Southern City, 1896–1930* (Washington: Smithsonian Institution Press, 1995); Kathryn H. Fuller, *At the Picture Show: Small-Town Audiences and the Creation of Movie Fan Culture* (Washington: Smithsonian Institution Press, 1996).

28   For further discussion of the nature of audiences in the nickelodeon era and the historical debates about them, see Lee Grieveson, 'Audiences: Issues and Debates', in Richard Abel (ed.), *Encyclopaedia of Early Cinema* (New York: Routledge, 2004).

29   Robert Sklar, '*Oh! Althusser!*: Historiography and the Rise of Cinema Studies', *Radical History Review*, vol. 41 (1988), 24.

30   Steven J. Ross, *Working Class Hollywood: Silent Film and the Shaping of Class in America* (Princeton, NJ: Princeton University Press, 1998).

31   Musser, *The Emergence of Cinema*, 430–2.

32   Miriam Hansen, *Babel and Babylon: Spectatorship and American Silent Film* (Cambridge, Mass: Harvard University Press, 1991), 84–5.

33   See Peter Krämer, 'The Fall and Rise of Slapstick Films: Physical Comedy in American Cinema, 1907–1913', in Leonardo Quaresima, Alessandra Raengo and Laura Vichi (eds), *The Birth of Film Genres* (Udine: Forum, 1999).

34   David Bordwell, Janet Staiger and Kristin Thompson, *The Classical Hollywood Cinema: Film Style and Mode of Production to 1960* (London: Routledge, 1985), in particular 113–27; Charles Musser, 'Pre-Classical American Cinema: Its Changing Modes of Film Production', in Richard Abel (ed.), *Silent Film* (New Brunswick, NJ: Rutgers University Press, 1996).

Chapter 5

CHARLES MUSSER

MOVING TOWARDS FICTIONAL NARRATIVES
Story films become the dominant product, 1903–1904

T HE SHIFT IN FILM PRODUCTION from actualities and short comedies to story films has been a topic of long-standing interest and some debate within the field of film studies. Indeed, we must begin by engaging this subject on the most basic level, with the simple issue of chronology. Did the rise to dominance of the story film precede the boom in specialized storefront motion picture theaters (which we can date from mid-1905 to 1906), coincide with this phenomena, or follow in the boom's wake? The answer to this question will obviously have serious implications for our larger historical understanding, since we want to know not only when but how film practice was transformed in this way. For film and cultural historians, the timing of this change inevitably has profound implications for our larger under-standing of cinema practice – for instance, the reorganization of productive forces in areas of distribution and exhibition, of which the nickelodeon boom is in some way indicative. The ripple effect that comes from different chronological orderings affects the contours of film history in a most serious way. More generally, different datings of this shift inevitably produce different understandings regarding the very nature of historical causality (at least within a local-ized time and place). Furthermore, we might extend these issues still further, to include not only the dynamics that transformed forces of production, but the relationship between changing subject matter and various aspects of film form. That is, the historiographic stakes underlying the solution to this simple question of chronology are both broad and deep.

Given its centrality in the American film industry, the Edison Manufacturing Company provides an effective way to explore this historiographic nexus within the United States. Not only was the Edison Company a central force in the American film industry between 1894 and 1909, but its many extant films and surviving business records allow for detailed analysis. Moreover, like other leading companies in this period, Edison was a multifaceted entity. While we tend to focus our attention on Edison productions themselves, we cannot forget that Edison was also distributing copies of films made by the leading European producers (pirating might be a less polite but more precise term for these activities). To take a broad view, one might argue that the rise of story films began as early as 1899 (if not earlier) and was fully completed by late 1907 to early 1908, by which time Edison-licensed production companies had a regular, weekly release schedule that was filled almost entirely by fiction story films. The challenge within this decade-long period, therefore, is to locate the pivotal moment(s) when a decisive shift to story films occurred. The shift from nonfiction and short comedies to story films within the United States was a development occurring on different levels and Edison production was by no means always in the forefront. Its commitment to story films occurred in fits and starts in the first few years of the 20th century. Although it is tempting to see *The Great Train Robbery* (December 1903) as a decisive turning point in this process, it was not until the later part of 1904 that Edison personnel consistently focused the bulk of their own production efforts in this area. Between January 1903 and October 1904 output of staged/acted films remained irregular, as the Edison Company sought to avoid undue negative costs and was thwarted by legal and personnel problems. Ambitious, commercially successful story films were made, yet they were usually followed by much more modest productions, if not an outright hiatus in filmmaking.

Disruptions

One strong indication of the Edison Company's increasing commitment to fiction filmmaking was the opening of its glass-enclosed roof-top studio on 41 East 21st St, New York City, in late January 1901. Nonetheless, a series of legal battles and injunctions between 1901 and April 1903 left the American industry in shambles. Uncertainties for many would-be American producers on one hand and lack of competition for the Edison Company on the other discouraged investment in plant and negatives. Thomas A. Edison's court victory against the American Mutoscope & Biograph Company on July 15, 1901, which sustained his motion picture patents, gave his company an apparent monopoly in the United States. Although Biograph won its appeal of this decision in March 1902, it remained a weakened competitor during the following year. The subjects and representational practices for its large-format service were increasingly antiquated. A typical program from Biograph during the first week of April 1903 relied on a miscellaneous collection of short actualities with a few trick films and comedies thrown in for relief. In contrast, Vitagraph had recognized the value of "headline attractions all of which are long subjects lasting from 10 to 20 minutes each."[1] This enabled Vitagraph to take over the Keith circuit from Biograph during the first week of April. Afterwards one trade journal observed that the new Vitagraph program was "the best series of films seen here in many weeks."[2] George Spoor's Chicago-based exhibition service made a similar shift toward story films in mid-1903, a key element in the reviving popularity of vaudeville film programs.[3]

Edison, Vitagraph, Lubin, Spoor, and Selig – all relied heavily on European imports. Like Edison, many took local, inexpensive films that could not be provided by European producers. To a remarkable degree, Edison's competition with its rivals revolved around the rapidity with which newly released European story films could be brought to the United States, duped, and sold. The original prints that Edison acquired for these purposes were then purchased by Percival C. Waters' Kinetograph Company, while dupes were marketed to other exhibitors. An urgent telegram from the manager of the Edison Manufacturing Company, William Gilmore, to European Sales Manager James White in England underscored the importance of this business practice:

> Vitagraph Co. getting foreign films ahead of us. They have received poachers, deserters, falling chimney and others at least ten days ahead of us. This very embarrassing. Unless can have your assurance that arrangements can be made for immediate shipments will send someone to take charge this end of the business.[4]

Edison executives had adopted a business strategy that largely ignored the production capabilities of its film department. By duping foreign films on a massive scale, the department could limit its investment primarily to the cost of negative stock.

The easy money Edison and other American producers had been making from dupes was threatened in March 1903, when Gaston Méliès arrived in the United States to represent his brother Georges. In June he opened a New York office and factory to print and distribute Méliès' "Star" films and to secure the economic benefits for their creator. His first catalog chided American manufacturers, announcing

> GEORGE MELIES, proprietor and manager of the Théâtre Robert-Houdin, Paris, is the originator of the class of cinematograph films which are made from artificially arranged scenes, the creation of which has given new life to the trade at a time when it was dying out. He conceived the idea of portraying comical, magical and mystical views, and his creations have been imitated without success ever since.[5]

He also announced, "we are prepared and determined energetically to pursue all counterfeiters and pirates. We will not speak twice, we will act." Star films were then considered "the acme of life motion photography,"[6] and Georges Méliès was using a double camera to take two negatives of each subject, shipping one to New York. Henceforth, these were copyrighted, putting an end to the duping of future Star films.[7] Edison and other American companies found different makes to dupe, but they now had to face competition in the domestic market from the world's foremost manufacturer.

Méliès' entry into the American market and the resolution of various court cases encouraged US film companies to produce more ambitious films with American locales and subject matter. If Edison films such as *Appointment by Telephone* (May 1902), *Jack and the Beanstalk* (June 1902), and *Life of an American Fireman* (January 1903) were part of nonspecific urban/industrial genres found in all major producing countries, American story films made in the second half of 1903 tended to be more nationalistic. Biograph's dramatic headliners *Kit Carson* (1903) and *The Pioneers* (1903) as well as Edison's *Uncle Tom's Cabin* (July 1903), *Rube and Mandy at Coney Island* (August 1903), and *The Great Train Robbery* (December 1903) all used American myths and entertainments as a source.[8] Certainly this made sense, since less nation-specific pictures could be acquired from overseas.

The Great Train Robbery

Many of the important Porter/Edison films made in 1903–1904 not only participated in the shift from actuality to fiction, this shift was inscribed in the films' form: systems of editing, genres, methods of constructing viewing positions, depiction of landscapes. This complex marking is particularly evident with *The Great Train Robbery*. In late October 1903, Porter began working with a young actor, Max Aronson. Earlier that month, the thespian had toured with Mary Emerson's road company of *His Majesty and the Maid*.[9] The engagement did not work out, and he returned to New York in need of employment. After changing his name to George M. Anderson, Aronson found work at the Edison studio, thinking up gags (*Buster's Joke on Papa*, shot October 23) and appearing in pictures (*What Happened in the Tunnel*, photographed on October 30 and 31). Porter continued to collaborate with Anderson on numerous subjects over the next several months, including *The Great Train Robbery*.

The Great Train Robbery was photographed at Edison's New York studio and in New Jersey at Essex County Park (the bandits cross a stream at Thistle Mill Ford in the South Mountain Reservation) and along the Lackawanna railway during November 1903. Justus D. Barnes played the head bandit; Anderson the slain passenger, the tenderfoot dancing to gunshots, and one of the robbers; and Walter Cameron the sheriff. Many of the extras were Edison employees.

Most of the Kinetograph Department's staff contributed to the picture: J. Blair Smith was one of the photographers and Anderson may have assisted with the direction.[10]

The film was first announced to the public in early November 1903 as a "highly sensationalized Headliner" that would be ready for distribution early that month.[11] Since the Edison Manufacturing Company urged exhibitors to order in advance and the film was not ready until early December, the delay probably explains why the Kinetograph Department submitted a rough cut of the film for copyright purposes. It avoided distribution snags once the release prints were available. The paper print version of the film, copyrighted by the Library of Congress, is longer than the final release print by about fifteen feet. Over the years, surviving copies of the film have been duped and offered for sale. Although a few have suffered extensive alteration, most have their integrity fundamentally intact. One of the most interesting versions was hand tinted.[12]

The Great Train Robbery had its debut at Huber's Museum, where Waters' Kinetograph Company had an exhibition contract. The following week it was shown at eleven theaters in and around New York City – including the Eden Musee.[13] Its commercial success was unprecedented and so remarkable that contemporary critics still tend to account for the picture's historical significance largely in terms of its commercial success and its impact on future fictional narratives. Kenneth Macgowan attributes this success to the fact that *The Great Train Robbery* was "the first important western."[14] William Everson and George Fenin find it important because "it was the first dramatically creative American film, which was also to set the pattern – of crime, pursuit and retribution – for the Western film as a genre."[15] Robert Sklar, viewing the film in broader terms, accounts for much of the film's lasting popularity. He points out that Porter was "the first to unite motion picture spectacle with myth and stories about America that were shared by people throughout the world."[16] Little more has been said about Porter's representational strategies since Lewis Jacobs praised the headliner for its "excellent editing."[17] Noël Burch, André Gaudreault, and David Levy are among the few who have discussed the film's cinematic strategies with any historical specificity; their useful analyses, however, can be pushed further.[18] *The Great Train Robbery* is a remarkable film not simply because it was commercially successful or incorporated American myths into the repertoire of screen entertainment, but because it incorporates so many trends, genres, and strategies fundamental to cinematic practice at that time.

Porter's film meticulously documents a process, applying what Neil Harris calls "an operational aesthetic" to the depiction of a crime.[19] With unusual detail, it traces the exact steps of a train robbery and the means by which the bandits are tracked down and killed. The film's narrative structure, as Gaudreault notes, utilizes temporal repetition within an overall narrative progression. The robbery of the mail car (scene 3) and the fight on the tender (scene 4) occur simultaneously according to the catalog description, even though they are shown successively. This returning to an earlier moment in time to pick up another aspect of the narrative recurs again in a more extreme form, as the telegraph operator regains consciousness and alerts the posse, which departs in pursuit of the bandits. These two scenes (10 and 11) trace a second line of action, which apparently unfolds concurrently with the robbery and getaway (scenes 2 through 9), although Porter's temporal construction remains imprecise and open to interpretation by the showman's spiel or by audiences through their subjective understanding. These two separate lines of action are reunited within a brief chase scene (shot 12) and yield a resolution in the final shoot-out (shot 13).

The issue of narrative clarity and efficiency is raised by *The Great Train Robbery*. At one point, three separate actions are shown that occur more or less simultaneously in scenes 3, 4, and 10. How were audiences, even those that understood the use of temporal repetition and overlap in narrative cinema, to know that scenes 3 and 4 happened simultaneously, but not scenes 1 and 2? How were they to determine the relationships between shots 1–9 and 10–11 until they had seen shot 12? There are no intertitles, and much depended on audience familiarity with other forms of popular culture where the same basic story was articulated. Scott Marble's play *The Great Train Robbery*, Wild West shows, and newspaper accounts of train holdups were more than sources of inspiration: they facilitated audience understanding by providing a necessary frame of reference. While *The Great Train Robbery* demonstrated that the screen could tell an elaborate, gripping story, it also defined the limits of a certain kind of narrative construction. The common belief that *The Great Train Robbery* was an isolated breakthrough is inaccurate. While Porter was making his now famous film, Biograph produced *The Escaped Lunatic*, a hit comedy in which a group of wardens chase an inmate who has escaped from a mental institution.[20] On the very day that Thomas A. Edison copyrighted his celebrated picture, Biograph copyrighted a 290 foot subject made by British Gaumont, *Runaway Match*, involving an elaborate car chase between an eloping couple and the girl's parents. Eleven days later the film was offered for sale as *An Elopement a la Mode*.[21]

A Daring Daylight Burglary, which the Edison Company had duped and marketed in late June, was particularly influential in creating the framework within which Porter produced *The Great Train Robbery*,[22] even though American popular culture provided the specific subject matter. Edison's 1901 *Stage Coach Hold-up*, a film adaptation of Buffalo Bill's "Hold-up of the Deadwood Stage," served as yet another source. The title and initial idea for the film were suggested, however, by Scott Marble's melodrama. *The New York Clipper* provides a story synopsis:

> A shipment of $50,000 in gold is to be made from the office of the Wells Fargo Express Co. at Kansas City, Mo., and this fact becomes known to a gang of train robbers through their secret agent who is a clerk in the employ of the company. The conspirators, learning the time when the gold is expected to arrive, plan to substitute boxes filled with lead for those which contain the precious metal. The shipment is delayed, and the lead filled boxes are thereby discovered to be dummies. This discovery leads to an innocent man being accused of the crime. Act 2 is laid in Broncho Joe's mountain saloon in Texas, where the train robbers receive accurate information regarding the gold shipment and await its arrival. The train is finally held-up at a lonely mountain station and the car blown open. The last act occurs in the robber's retreat in the Red River cañon. To this place the thieves are traced by United States marshals and troops, and a pitched battle occurs in which Cowboys and Indians also participate.[23]

The play premiered on September 20, 1896, at the Alhambra Theater in Chicago, and soon came to the New York area, where it was well received.[24] Periodically revived thereafter, the melodrama played at Manhattan's New Star Theater in February 1902. Porter could have easily seen it on several occasions.

The Great Train Robbery was advertised as a reenactment film "posed and acted in faithful duplication of the genuine 'Hold-ups' made famous by various outlaw bands in the far West."[25] News stories of train holdups, like the ones appearing in September 1903, may have encouraged a more authentic detailing of events. Eastern holdups, also evoked in Edison ads, took place in Pennsylvania on the Reading Railroad in late November – after the film was completed. A telegraph operator was murdered and several stations held up by "a desperate gang of outlaws who are believed to have their rendezvous somewhere in the lonely mountain passes along the Shamokin Division."[26] It was hoped that such incidents would make the film of timely interest.

The Great Train Robbery continued to be indebted to at least one aspect of the newspapers, the feuilletons in Sunday editions, with their highly romanticized, but supposedly true, stories of contemporary interest. [. . .]

As David Levy has pointed out, it was within the genre of reenactment films that Porter exploited procedures that heighten the realism and believability of the image.[27] *Execution of Czolgosz* and *Capture of the Biddle Brothers* provided Porter with an approach to filming the robbery, chase, and shoot-out. In *Execution of Czolgosz* he had intensified the illusion of authenticity by integrating actuality and reenactment, scenery and drama. In *The Great Train Robbery* he took this a step further, using mattes to introduce exteriors into studio scenes. On location, Porter used his camera as if he were filming a news event over which he had no control. In scenes 2, 7, and 8 the camera is forced to follow action that threatens to move outside the frame. For scene 7 the camera has to move unevenly down and over to the left. Since camera mounts were designed either to pan or tilt, this move is somewhat shaky. This "dirty" image only adds to the film's realism. The notion of a scene being played on an outdoor stage was undermined. Biograph described the desired effect when advertising *The Escaped Lunatic*: "Fortunately there were a number of . . . cameras situated around the country . . . and this most astonishing episode was completely covered in moving pictures."[28]

The chase

The chase became a popular form of screen narrative in 1903; *The Great Train Robbery* and Biograph's *The Escaped Lunatic* were the first American productions to reveal its impact. The chase appeared early in cinema history: an Irish cop chases a "Chinaman" through a revolving set in *Chinese Laundry Scene* (1894), and a mad dash lasting a split second ends G. A. Smith's *The Miller and the Sweep* (1898). James Williamson's *Stop Thief!* (1901) isolated the provocation, the chase, and the resolution in three different camera setups. These remained isolated occurrences. Porter's *Jack and the Beanstalk* (1902), for instance, ignored the dramatic potential of the chase as the giant climbs down the beanstalk after Jack. According to American catalogs and trade journals from the early nickelodeon era, the two English imports *A Daring Daylight Burglary* (Sheffield Photo, 1903) and *Desperate Poaching Affray* (Haggar, 1903) initiated the craze.[29] The chase provided a new kind of subject matter, a new narrative framework that would be elaborated and refined in succeeding years until one-reel pictures such as Griffith's *The Girl and Her Trust* (1912) and Mack Sennett's comedies had seemingly exhausted its possibilities within their alloted one thousand feet.

Although the chase is implied throughout most of *The Great Train Robbery*, it only becomes explicit for a single-shot (scene 12). *The Escaped Lunatic*, in contrast, makes the chase the dominant element of the film, as it would be for subsequent Biograph subjects such as *Personal* (June 1904) and *The Lost Child* (October 1904). As used by Biograph, the chase encouraged a simplification of story line and a linear progression of narrative that made the need for a familiar story or a showman's narration unnecessary. These chase films locate the redundancy within the films themselves as pursuers and pursued engage repeatedly, with only slight variation, in the same activity. Rather than having a lecture explain images in a parallel fashion, rather than having the viewer's familiarity with a story provide the basis for an understanding, chase films created a self-sufficient narrative in which the viewer's appreciation was based chiefly on the experience of information presented within the film. This had, of course, been true for certain types of films since the 1890s, most particularly short comedies, trick films and some actualities. The chase, however, greatly expanded the domain and the means by which this relationship between audience and screen subject could operate.

While *The Escaped Lunatic* and its English predecessors pointed the way to a more modern form of storytelling by presenting a self-sufficient narrative, they did not inaugurate a full-scale transformation of the representational system, which was necessary before this modern viewer/screen relationship became the dominant mode of reception. Although historians usually place *The Great Train Robbery* at the cutting edge of cinema, noting correctly that it was often the first film to play in an opening nickelodeon, Porter's work can already be seen as moving at a tangent to cinema's forward thrust. Porter's initial use of the chase was not to create a simple, easily understood narrative but to incorporate it within a popular and more complex story.

The railway subgenre: spectator as passenger

To be fully appreciated, *The Great Train Robbery* must be situated within the travel program's railway subgenre. The railroad and the screen have had a special relationship, symbolized by the Lumières' famous *Train Entering a Station* (1895) and half a dozen other films. Both affected our perception of space and time in somewhat analogous ways. Describing the shift from animal-powered transportation to the railroad, Wolfgang Schivelbusch has remarked: "As the natural irregularities of the terrain that were perceptible on the old roads are replaced by the sharp linearity of the railroad, the traveler feels that he has lost contact with the landscape, experiencing this most directly when going through a tunnel. Early descriptions of journeys on the railroad note that the railroad and the landscape through which it runs are in two separate worlds."[30] The traveler's world is mediated by the railroad, not only by the compartment window with its frame but by telegraph wires, which intercede between the passenger and the landscape. The sensation of separation that the traveler feels on viewing the rapidly passing landscape has much in common with the theatrical experience of the spectator. It is not surprising, therefore, that an important subgenre of the travelogue centered on the train. This equation of train window with the screen's rectangle found its ultimate expression with Hale's Tours.

In the 1890s illustrated lectures, often known as "lantern journeys," featured railroads as the best way to reach and view American scenery. These frequently created a spatially coherent world with views of the train passing through the countryside, of the traveler/lecturer in the train, of scenery that could be seen out the window or from the front of the train, and finally of small incidents on sidings or at railway stations. The railroad, which carried its passengers through the countryside, was ideally suited for moving the narrative forward through time and space. John Stoddard and other lecturers presented these journeys as alternatives to travel for those who lacked the time, money, or fortitude for such undertakings.[31] Offering personal accounts of their adventures, these professional voyagers were figures with whom audiences could identify and from whom they could derive vicarious experience and pleasure. Audience identification with showman Burton Holmes took place on three levels: with the traveler shown by the camera to be within the narrative – a subject of the camera; with the showman as the cameraman – the producer of images of a certain quality; and, finally, as a speaker at the podium – with a certain voice and narrational perspective. The point-of-view shot out the window or from the front of a train was privileged in such a system because it conflated camera, character, and narration.

The introduction of moving pictures reinforced the parallels between train travel and projected image. "According to Newton," observes Schivelbusch, "'size, shape, quantity and motion' are the only qualities that can be objectively perceived in the physical world. Indeed, those become the only qualities that the railroad traveler is now able to observe in the landscape he travels through. Smells, sounds, not to mention the synesthetic perceptions that were part of travel in Goethe's time, simply disappear."[32] This new mode of perception, which is initially disorienting, then pleasurable, is recreated as the moving pictures, taken by a camera from a moving train, are projected onto the screen.

The epiphany of going through a tunnel likewise found a prominence in this subgenre that matched its significance in train travel. An early review of such a film begins by contrasting the resulting effect to an earlier moving picture novelty derived from pre-cinema lantern shows – the onrushing express:

> The spectator was not an outsider watching from safety the rush of the cars. He was a passenger on a phantom train ride that whirled him through space at nearly a mile a minute. There was no smoke, no glimpse of shuddering frame or crushing wheels. There was nothing to indicate motion save that shining vista of tracks that was eaten up irresistibly, rapidly, and the disappearing panorama of banks and fences.
>
> The train was invisible and yet the landscape swept by remorselessly, and far away the bright day became a spot of darkness. That was the mouth of the tunnel, and toward it the spectator was hurled as if a fate was behind him. The spot of blackness became a canopy of gloom. The darkness closed around and the spectator was being flung through that cavern with the demoniac energy behind him. The shadows, the rush of the invisible force and the uncertainty of the issues made one instinctively hold his breath as when on the edge of a crisis that might become a catastrophe.[33]

As this novelty wore off, phantom rides became incorporated into the travel narrative, enabling the showman to literalize the traveler's movement through time and space.

The railway subgenre soon incorporated short scenes for comic relief. G. A. Smith made a one-shot film of a couple kissing in a railway carriage – a gag that had comic strip antecedents. He suggested that showmen insert *Kiss in the Tunnel* into the middle of a phantom ride, after the train had entered the tunnel. Comedy and scenery were contained within the same fictional world. Ferdinand Zecca's *Flirt en chemin de fer* (1901) was intended for the same use, but rather than require the entrance of the train into a dark tunnel, Zecca matted in a window view of passing countryside. A Lubin film, *Love in a Railroad Train* (1902), depicts a male traveler's unsuccessful attempts to sneak a kiss from a woman passenger. When they emerge from the tunnel, it turns out that he is kissing her baby's bottom.[34] Porter combined a variation on Lubin's gag with Zecca's use of a matte to make *What Happened in the Tunnel*. A forward young lover (G. M. Anderson) tries to kiss the woman sitting in front of him when the train goes into the tunnel but ends up kissing her black-faced maid instead. The two women, who anticipate his attempt and switch places, have a laugh at his expense. The substitution of a black maid for a baby's bottom suggests the casual use of demeaning racial stereotypes in this period. *What Happened in the Tunnel* (1903) was the last film Porter made before *The Great Train Robbery*: its matte shot served as an experiment for similar efforts (scenes 1 and 3 of the headliner).

A Romance of the Rail, filmed in August but not copyrighted until October 3, 1903, elaborated on the comic interlude. To counter its image as a coal carrier, the Lackawanna Railroad, known as "The Road of Anthracite," developed an advertising campaign in which passenger Phoebe Snow, dressed in white, rode the rails and praised the line's cleanliness in such slogans as:

Says Phoebe Snow, about to go
Upon a trip to Buffalo:

"My gown stays white from morn till night
Upon the Road of Anthracite."[35]

A Romance of the Rail lightheartedly spoofs not only the slogans but the advertisements' photographic illustrations. Like *Rube and Mandy at Coney Island*, the film combines scenery and comic
relief. The narrative is clearly paramount as Phoebe Snow meets her male counterpart (also
dressed in white) for the first time at a railway station. They fall in love and marry in the
course of a brief ride, spoofing romantic associations with train travel. Scenery is pushed into
the background, except in the fourth shot, where the camera framing gives equal emphasis to
the scenery and the couple, who are, like the spectator, watching the scenery. Although *Romance
of the Rail* has a beginning, middle, and end, it lacks strict closure since exhibitors often inserted
the film into a program of railway panoramas. The ratio and relative importance of scenery to
story were left to their discretion.

Audiences for these films continued to assume the vicarious role of passenger. One moment
they would be looking at the scenery from the train; at another they would be looking at the
antics of fellow passengers. Hale's Tours made this convention explicit by using a simulated
railway carriage as a movie theater, with the audience sitting in the passenger seats and the
screen replacing the view from the front or rear window. This theater/carriage came complete
with train clatter and the appropriate swaying. The superrealism of the exhibition strategy was
adumbrated by bits of action along the sidings and in the train, which contradicted the suggestion of a fixed point of view. Coherence was sacrificed in favor of variety and a good show.
Whether *What Happened in the Tunnel* or *A Romance of the Rail* were used in the first Hale's
Tour Car at Electric Park in Kansas City during the summer of 1905 is not known, but such
use would seem logical.[36] When Hale's Tours became a popular craze in 1906, however, these
films were advertised again in the trades as "Humorous Railway Scenes" with this purpose
specifically in mind.[37]

The Great Train Robbery brought the railway subgenre to new heights. During the first eight
scenes, the train is kept in almost constant view: seen through the window, as a fight unfolds
on the tender, from the inside of the mail car, by the water tower, or along the tracks as
the cab is disconnected and the passengers are relieved of their money. Although the film
was initially shown as a headliner in vaudeville theaters with its integrity intact, it was also
introduced by railway panoramas in Hale's Tours-type situations. The spectators start out as
railway passengers watching the passing countryside, but they are abruptly assaulted by a close-
up of the outlaw Barnes firing his six-shooter directly into their midst. (This shot was shown
either at the beginning or end of the film. In a Hale's Tours situation it would seem more
effective at the beginning, in a vaudeville situation at the end as an apotheosis.) The viewers,
having assumed the role of passengers, are held up. The close-up of the outlaw Barnes reiter-
ates the spectators' point of view, brings them into the subsequent narrative, and intensifies
their identification with the bandits' victims. Since this shot is abstracted from the narrative
and the "realistic" exteriors of earlier scenes, the title that the Edison catalog assigned to this
shot – "Realism" – might at first appear singularly inappropriate.[38] Yet the heightening of realism
in twentieth-century cinema has been associated not only with a move toward greater naturalism but with a process of identification and emotional involvement with the drama. It is this
second aspect of realism that the close-up intensifies.

The process of viewer identification with the passengers in a Hale's Tour presentation of
The Great Train Robbery was overdetermined: introductory railway panoramas, reinforced by
the simulated railway carriage and the close-up of Barnes, turned viewers into passengers.
These strategies of viewer identification coincided with the viewer's social predisposition to

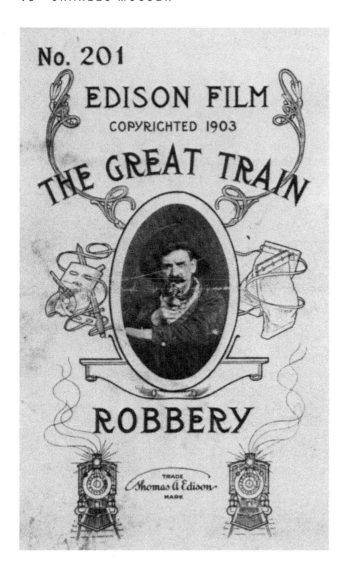

Figure 5.1
The Great Train Robbery
(1903)

side with responsible members of society being victimized by lawless elements. The second portion of the film, however, breaks with the railway subgenre and this overdetermination and becomes a chase. The presence of the passengers is forgotten. Music or simulated gunshots, rather than railway clatter, became the appropriate sound effects. The breakdown of the viewer-as-passenger strategy, always just below the surface of the railway genre, was complete by the end of the film. Within *The Great Train Robbery* itself, Porter and his collaborators inscribed the shift from actuality to story film.

Comedy, dupes, and story production

Although *The Great Train Robbery* caused Edison film sales to surge in December 1903, such "headliners" were still considered only one dimension of Porter's production responsibilities. Indeed, during the spring and summer of 1904, the Kinetograph Department avoided production of narrative "features," just when such activities were increasing at other studios. Duping

Table 1 Edison film production, March–July 1904

Subject type	Number in category	Negative feet	Print feet	Print to neg. ratio[a]
Actualities	40 (82%)	5,045 (68%)	42,915 (38%)	8.5
Staged/fiction	9 (18%)	2,335 (32%)	69,560 (62%)	29.8
Total	49	7,380	112,475	15.2

[a] Includes only sales of prints for the 1904 business year (March 1, 1904, to February 29, 1905).

foreign subjects not covered by copyright continued to be viewed as a less expensive and surer way to provide customers with dramatic headliners. When, as sometimes happened, an American competitor put out a popular film protected by copyright, Porter was asked to imitate it. Whatever the reasons – objective business analyzes of costs and sales, changes in management, disorganization, complacency, or Porter's lack of a collaborator – the Kinetograph Department became inordinately derivative. [. . .]

The composition and distribution of Edison productions for the March–July 1904 period can be analysed using a surviving survey of Edison film sales during the years 1904–6. The data are given in table 1. Two features (*The Buster Brown Series* and *Skirmishes Between Russian and Japanese Advance Guards*) sold 45,595 feet struck from 1,275 feet of negative, for a print/negative ratio of 35.8 to one. These two films, listed in the staged/fiction category, were 4% of all the listed subjects and 17% of the negative footage but accounted for over 40% of total film sales. This statistical analysis would be significantly altered if information about dupes was available. Such a revised analysis would reinforce what is already clear from the table: staged/fiction "headliners" were the most popular (and potentially profitable) types of productions.

One might argue that the Russo-Japanese films were "news based" and "re-enactments" and from the perspective of audience tastes should be analyzed differently from *The Buster Brown Series* and other fiction films. Although this has some truth to it, from the perspective of film production, these films were made very much like fiction films. In terms of representational techniques, they had much in common with fiction as well. Certainly the mix of genres and styles among Edison films in the first half of 1904 must be acknowledged, though a strong case can still be made for the dominance of staged and fiction films by this period. Not only were continuing sales of *The Great Train Robbery* robust but Edison print sales were greatly increased by its sale of "dupes" or pirated copies of Pathé and other European fiction films. Although a naïve or superficial reading of Edison sales catalogs might suggest otherwise, Edison production was not at the forefront of the shift to fiction. Of the thirty-four pictures listed in Edison's January 1904 catalog, nineteen were dupes. In the September 1904 catalog, thirty-six of fifty-two were dupes.

By the summer of 1904, the Edison Company had abdicated its position as America's foremost motion picture producer to the American Mutoscope & Biograph Company. Biograph had recognized the importance of fiction headliners and had begun regular "feature" production by mid-1904. With Wallace McCutcheon acting as producer, Biograph's staff made *Personal* in June, *The Moonshiner* in July, *The Widow and the Only Man* in August, *The Hero of Liao Yang* in September, and *The Lost Child* and *The Suburbanite* in October. [. . .] In August and September the Edison Company remade two of Biograph's biggest hits: *Personal*, which was re-titled *How a French Nobleman Got a Wife Through the New York Herald Personal Columns* (photographed August

Table 2 Edison film production, August 1904–February 1905

Subject type	Number in category	Negative feet	Print feet	Print to neg. ratio
Actualities	8 (38%)	1,525 (16%)	7,610 (3%)	5.0
Staged/acted	13 (62%)	7,790 (84%)	214,705 (97%)	27.6
Total	21	9,315	222,315	23.9

1904) and *The Escaped Lunatic*, which became *Maniac Chase* (September 1904). Culminating with these two features, the Kinetograph Department's legal piracy destroyed Biograph's structure of exhibition and sales. It was precisely the two-tiered structure of exhibition and sales adhered to by Biograph, of initial distribution on Biograph's circuit and subsequent sales to non-Biograph exhibitors, that made these remakes so profitable for Edison.

By mid October 1904 Edison's policy of duping and remaking the films of his competitors was no longer profitable. Pathé had opened a New York City office and was supplying the American market before the British. Edison's company had to take the risk of investing in original productions, and its output for the second half of its 1904 business year reflected the demand for "feature" story films and acknowledged increasing competition from Biograph and Pathé. Edison sales records for the August 1904–February 1905 period yield the statistics in table 2. The commercial importance of staged/acted films is obvious (even exaggerated in this instance, since there were no major news films to boost actuality sales). Feature acted films had become the Kinetograph Department's principal source of income. A statistical analysis for the 1904–6 period shows a steady relationship between actuality and fiction films in terms of negative production and prints sold (see table 3).

Film historians have tried to pinpoint the moment when narrative acted "features" of approximately 500 to 1,000 feet in length began to dominate the cinema. Robert C. Allen has located the shift in 1907 and ties it to the need for greater control over the rate of production. He argues that "the spurt in narrative film production cannot be attributed to a sudden drop in public interest in the documentary film."[39] Allen and others have relied on raw quantitative data of titles copyrighted to reach this conclusion. This methodological approach has a fundamental weakness, which tables 1–3 demonstrate. Quantification by subject titles offers little insight (or more accurately skewed insight) into what spectators are likely to be watching. Furthermore, during 1905 and 1906, the bulk of print sales for actualities came from three major news events: Roosevelt's inauguration, the Russo-Japanese Peace Conference, and the San Francisco earthquake. In many cases, no prints of an actuality subject were sold. Except for a few comparatively rare events of national import, the public had generally lost interest in nonfiction subjects.[40]

From the summer of 1904 onward, the Edison Manufacturing Company made acted headliners in substantial quantities and these consistently outsold actualities. (This was true at the American Mutoscope & Biograph Company as well.) Excepting occasional "hits," actuality material continued to be manufactured primarily because 1) local news footage was desired by vaudeville houses renting films from the Kinetograph Company and it was considered expedient to accommodate them; and 2) such films were so inexpensive to make that a small profit could be gained on a local subject if two or more prints were sold.

This analysis of the shift from actualities, short comedies and trick films to longer story films has important implications for how we understand the history of cinema in the era before

Table 3 Edison film production, 1904–1906

Subject type	Number in category	Negative feet	Print feet	Print to neg. ratio
March 1904–February 1905				
Actualities	48 (69%)	6,570 (39%)	50,525 (15%)	7.7
Staged/acted	22 (31%)	10,125 (61%)	284,265 (85%)	27.6
Total	70	16,695	334,790	20.0
March 1905–December 1905				
Actualities	21 (48%)	6,940 (36%)	60,580 (14%)	8.7
Staged/acted	22 (52%)	12,382 (64%)	365,060 (86%)	29.5
Total	43	19,322	425,640	22.0
February 1906–February 1907				
Actualities	49 (80%)	7,715 (47%)	118,438 (14%)	15.4
Staged/acted	12 (20%)	8,750 (53%)	741,490 (86%)	84.7
Total	61	16,465	859,928	52.2

Griffith (what I once liked to call "early cinema"). In the 1904–1907 period, there was a place for actualities – primarily local views and films of important news events – but it was a modest one, accounting for only about 15% of Edison's total film sales on a per-foot basis. Moreover, this amount of nonfiction material was higher than at some other companies, notably Méliès, Pathé, and Vitagraph. With 85% of Edison-originating film sales consisting of fiction "story" films, filmmaking resources at Edison and other companies were concentrated in this area. If audiences had been interested in nonfiction more than fiction, it would have been easy for Edison and other companies (particularly smaller firms unable to invest in studio infrastructure) to provide it. The move to fiction was a response to audience demand, not a conspiracy among studios eager to regularize production. In the 1910s, in fact, the studios did regularize nonfiction production, with the release of weekly, semi-weekly and even briefly daily newsreels. If there had been a strong appetite for this in 1907 (or even earlier), it could have been and I believe would have been accommodated. This was also because nonfiction subjects were less expensive to produce than fiction in 1905–1906 as it is still today.

The shift to acted "features" was not, as Robert Allen has suggested, a result of the nickelodeon era but a precondition for it. There needed to be a sufficient output as well as a sufficient reservoir of older films to support the nickelodeons with their rapid turnover of subject matter. Storefront theaters had been around since the beginning of cinema, but it was only in late 1905 and 1906 that they became the nickelodeons of film history fame. It was more than just the shift to story films that made this possible. The rapid adoption of the three-blade shutter on projectors in late 1903–1904 made viewing more pleasurable. It strikes me as not entirely coincidental that the dominance of story films in 1903–1904 coincided with the diffusion of the three-blade shutter. Fiction has much to do with visual pleasure while nonfiction is part of the discourse of sobriety, as Bill Nichols has pointed out.[41] (An increase in viewing pleasure undoubtedly sparked an increase in the amount of viewing per moviegoer as well as the number of interested viewers.) Significantly, story films also became the dominant industry product in 1903–1904 just as the rental of films was replacing the letting of an exhibition service to the theaters. If films could be rented to vaudeville theaters they could also be easily rented to exhibitors showing films in storefronts.

It is reasonable then to ask why the nickelodeon boom did not begin a year earlier. The answer to that question would include the success of Sunday concerts in major cities such as New York and of travelling showmen. The expansion of established methods of distribution and exhibition could accommodate increased demand for movies, at least for a time. Moreover, to provide these nickelodeons with enough product, the shift to story films had to be accompanied by sufficient quantitative increase in their overall rate of output. In this respect, the increased rate of fiction film production among European producers (particularly Pathé) and the Vitagraph Company's emergence as a leading producer of story films in the second half of 1905 were as important as the increased rate of production at Edison and Biograph during late 1904–1905.

The nickelodeons, which dominated exhibition in the US after 1906, certainly pushed Edison and other production companies to emphasize the production of longer fiction films. During the summer of 1906, Porter shot a few films of sporting events such as *The Vanderbilt Cup* and *Harvard–Yale Boat Race*. Such subjects sold between three and eight copies. On July 31 he filmed *Auto Climbing Contest* in New Hampshire at the request of the Keith vaudeville organization. According to Edison executive Alex T. Moore, these subjects were money losers that were made only to please important customers.[42] Robert K. Bonine continued to make actualities, primarily travel films such as those he took in Hawaii; their production was subsidized by transportation companies and similar organizations. The ten to fourteen actualities Bonine shot at the Panama Canal in March 1907 were the last he made for the Edison Company.[43] He left Edison employ in May, explaining:

> You can't imagine the great demand there has been for moving picture films within the past year, due of course to the great number of cheap picture shows springing up all over the country, but the demand is all for "comedy" or, in other words, anything of a subject nature, and it was the demand for this class of work that kept the place so busy and held my Hawaiian subjects back so long.[44]

After Bonine's fourteen Panama Canal films (copyrighted by Thomas A. Edison April 12 1907), Edison production was devoted virtually exclusively to story films. Of the nineteen

Table 4 Edison film production, March 1907–February 1908[a]

Subject type	Number in category	Negative feet	Print feet	Print to neg. ratio
Actualities[b]	15 (44%)	1,855 (11%)	n.a. (3%) est.	n.a.
Staged/acted	19 (56%)	15,640 (89%)	n.a. (97%) est.	n.a.
Total	34	17,495	n.a.	n.a.

[a] Based on copyright records and files, Edison National Historic Site. Staged/acted films from *Lost in the Alps* (March/April 1907) to *Animated Snowballs* (February 1908).
[b] Does not include "approximately 20 motion pictures" made at the Walkover Shoe Company, taken by Robert K. Bonine for the George Keith Company.

films that he subsequently copyrighted, between *Lost in the Alps* (April 1907) and *Animated Snowballs* (February 1908), all were staged/fiction films. We don't know the amount of print footage sold in each category, but the amount of negative footage was already 89%. Some additional nonfiction films may have been produced but they were not considered worth copyrighting and, with the exception of some films of the Walkover Shoe Company that were made as industrials and not apparently for general release, not worth reporting in the press. Assuming the print ratio of nonfiction to fiction (1 to 5), this meant that 97% of the footage sold by the Edison Company was from material that was acted/staged (see table 4). By the following year it would be 100%. Nonetheless, this merely completed a process that had undergone its decisive phase some four to five years earlier. This shift, however, is not only apparent in the statistical evidence. For those willing to engage in close readings of individual films, it can be discovered in the representational fabric of the pictures as well.

Notes

This essay is drawn from and reworks sections of Chapter 8 of *Before the Nickelodeon: Edwin S. Porter and the Edison Manufacturing Company* (Berkeley: University of California Press, 1991).

1. *New York Clipper*, 21 and 28 March 1903, pp. 108 and 132.
2. *Clipper*, 11 April 1903, p. 168.
3. Charles Musser, *The Emergence of Cinema* (New York: Scribners, 1990), pp. 337–8.
4. Quoted in letter, Gilmore to White, 3 December 1903, Edison National Historic Site, West Orange, New Jersey.
5. Gaston Méliès, *Complete Catalogue of Genuine and Original Star Films* (New York, 1903), p. 5.
6. *Clipper*, 12 September 1903, p. 680, a review of Méliès' *La Royaume des fées* (*Fairyland*) shown at Keith's Union Square Theater.
7. Balshofer indicates that Lubin, at least, continued to dupe Méliès productions into 1905–6. Fred Balshofer and Arthur C. Miller, *One Reel a Week* (Berkeley: University of California Press, 1967), pp. 5–9.
8. Robert Sklar, *Movie-Made America: A Social History of American Movies* (New York: Random House, 1975), p. 26.
9. "Engagements," *New York Dramatic Mirror (NYDM)*, 3 October 1903, p. 9.
10. For Anderson's claim to joint direction, see "2 Survive Great Train Robbery," *New York Herald Tribune*, 9 October 1961, p. 13, cited in David Levy, "Edwin S. Porter and the Origins of the American Narrative Film," (PhD diss., McGill University, 1983), p. 29. For Cameron, see *Theatre News*, 22 September 1938, p. 2. For Smith, see *Moving Picture News*, 2 April 1910, p. 11. Barnes and Anderson can be identified by pictures. Terry Ramsaye (who gave Barnes the wrong first name) adds Frank Hanaway as a bandit and Mae Murray as a dancer in the dance hall scene. Ramsaye, *The Million and One Nights: A History of the Motion Pictures Through 1925* (New York: Simon & Schuster, 1926) pp. 417–18.
11. *Clipper*, 7 November 1903, p. 896.
12. This copy is made available through the Museum of Modern Art, courtesy of David Shepard.
13. *Mail and Express*, 22 December 1903, p. 6; *Clipper*, 6 January 1904, p. 113.
14. Kenneth Macgowan, *Behind the Screen: the History and Techniques of the Motion Picture* (New York: Delacorte Press, 1965), p. 114.
15. George N. Fenin and William K. Everson, *The Western: From Silents to Cinerama* (New York: Bonanza Books, 1962), p. 47.
16. Sklar, *Movie-Made America*, p. 338.
17. Lewis Jacobs, *Rise of the American Film: A Critical History* (New York: Harcourt and Brace, 1939), p. 43.
18. André Gaudreault, "Detours in Film Narrative: The Development of Cross-Cutting," *Cinema Journal* 19 (Fall 1979), pp. 39–59; David Levy, "Reconstituted Newsreels, Re-enactments and the American Narrative Film," in Roger Holman (ed.), *Cinema 1900–1906: An Analytical Study* (Brussels: FIAF, 1982), pp. 243–60.
19. Neil Harris, *Humbug: The Art of P. T. Barnum* (Boston: Little, Brown, 1973), pp. 72–89.
20. American Mutoscope & Biograph Company, production records, Biograph Collection, Museum of Modern Art, New York City.

21. *Clipper*, 12 December 1903, p. 1016.
22. George C. Pratt, *Spellbound in Darkness: A History of the Silent Film* (Greenwich, Conn.: New York Graphic Society, 1973), pp. 38–39.
23. *Clipper*, 24 October 1896, p. 544. William Martinetti brought *The Great Train Robbery* play to Porter's attention (Ramsaye, *Million and One Nights*, p. 416).
24. *Brooklyn Eagle*, 13 October 1896, p. 11.
25. *Clipper*, 12 December 1903, p. 1016.
26. "Outlaws Rob Station," *New York Tribune*, 23 November 1903, p. 1.
27. David Levy, "The Fake Train Robbery," in Holman (ed.), *Cinema 1900–1906: An Analytic Study* (Brussels: FIAF, 1982).
28. Biograph Bulletin no. 33, 10 October 1904, reproduced in Kemp Niver, *Biograph Bulletins* (Los Angeles: Locare Research Group, 1971), p. 132.
29. Kleine Optical Company, *Complete Illustrated Catalog of Moving Picture Machines, Stereopticons, Slides, Films* (Chicago, November 1905), p. 207.
30. Wolfgang Schivelbusch, *The Railway Journey: Trains and Travel in the 19th Century* (New York: Urizen Books, 1980), pp. 25–27.
31. John L. Stoddard, *John L. Stoddard Lectures* (10 vols.; Boston: Balch Brothers Co., 1907).
32. Schivelbusch, *Railway Journey*, p. 59.
33. *Mail and Express*, 21 September 1897, p. 2.
34. Sigmund Lubin, *Complete Lubin Films*, January 1903, p. 34. This basic gag had newspaper antecedents. See "A Tunnel Mystery," *New York Journal*, 31 March 1898, p. 12.
35. Advertisement, *New York Herald*, 24 January 1904, magazine section, p. 16.
36. *Kansas City Star*, 28 May 1905, p. 7B. See Raymond Fielding, "Hale's Tours: Ultra-Realism in the Pre-1910 Motion Picture," in John Fell (ed.), *Film Before Griffith* (Berkeley: University of California Press, 1983), pp. 116–30.
37. *Clipper*, 28 April 1906, p. 287.
38. The important function of this shot has been misunderstood by historians since Lewis Jacobs, who saw it as an extraneous trick, unconnected to the film's narrative.
39. Robert Allen, *Vaudeville and Film: A Study in Media Interaction* (New York: Arno Press, 1980), p. 217; see also Robert Allen, "Film History: The Narrow Discourse," in Ben Lawton and Janet Staiger (eds), *Film: Historical-Theoretical Speculations: The 1977 Film Studies Annual (Part Two)* (Pleasantville, NY: Redgrave Publishing Co., 1977), pp. 9–17.
40. The case of the Edison Company in 1906 shows the fallacy of statistical analyses that simply rely on copyright data. Thomas Edison copyrighted forty films in 1906; twenty-nine of these were actuality films taken by Robert K. Bonine in Hawaii. Bonine's films were from 75 to 770 feet in length, totaling 3,700 feet of negative. In contrast, ten fictional films by Porter were copyrighted during the 1906 calendar year varying in length from 60 to 1000 feet and totaling 6,815 feet (all but one was a "feature"). In 1906 one Porter film, *Dream of a Rarebit Fiend*, sold 192 copies or 90,240 feet, while all of Bonine's Hawaii films only sold 29,060 feet. *Dream of a Rarebit Fiend* had three times the commercial value of the twenty-nine Bonine films.
41. Bill Nichols, *Representing Reality: Issues and Concepts in Documentary* (Bloomington: Indiana University Press, 1991).
42. Alex T. Moore, deposition, 13 May 1912, White and Schermerhorn v. Waters. Waters, however, claimed that Bonine rather than Porter took these films.
43. Edison Copyright files only list ten Panama Canal films as submitted for copyright but these probably include five different scenes of *Making the Dirt Fly* that were listed as separate copyrights by the Copyright Office of the Library of Congress. See Elias Savada, compiler, *The American Film Institute Catalog of Motion Pictures Produced in the United States: Film Beginnings, 1893–1910, A Work in Progress* (Metuchen, NJ: Scarecrow Press, 1995), pp. 644–5.
44. *Film Index*, 16 July 1907, p. 8.

Chapter 6

RICHARD ABEL

PATHÉ GOES TO TOWN
French films create a market for the nickelodeon, 1903–1906

FOR CHARLES MUSSER, the "key preconditions for the nickelodeon era" were the development of story films and rental exchanges between 1903 and 1905.[1] For Robert Allen it was "the rapid development of a type of inexpensive vaudeville, variously called 'ten-cent,' 'nickel,' or 'family' vaudeville."[2] These preconditions obviously were important, but a crucial component of all three has long been overlooked: the quantity and quality of Pathé films on the American market. Pathé's well-crafted, well-packaged films, I would argue, promoted the new product category of moving pictures in the United States to a degree unmatched by any others. During the years leading up to the nickelodeon boom, and even during its initial months, the trademark spectators associated over and over with moving pictures was the Pathé red rooster. Indeed, the Pathé trademark became almost synonymous with the movies and the ever-renewed satisfaction of "going to the show." Put simply, Pathé's presence on the American market provided the single most significant condition of emergence for the nickelodeon.

In order to reconstruct the stages (or exhibition sites) on which French films played during this period, and to gauge their impact, I draw not only on the extensive research of Musser, Allen, and others but also on several strands of public and private discourse then in circulation. First, there are catalogs and trade press ads of production companies (from Edison and Biograph to Méliès and Pathé), as well as exhibition services, sales agents, and rental exchanges (from Vitagraph and Kleine Optical to National Film Renting), all of them promoting films (and various apparatuses) on the American market.[3] Second, in the trade press, notably *Billboard* and *New York Clipper* (both long committed to promoting live performance), and in certain daily newspapers, there are scattered reports, expressing varying degrees of enthusiasm, about different exhibition sites throughout the country. Third, and most specifically, there are privately circulated managers' reports on weekly programs presented in a half dozen "high-class" vaudeville houses operated by the Keith circuit, from Boston and Washington in the East to Detroit and Cleveland in the Midwest.[4] These strands of discourse turn out to be unusually heterogeneous. Accordingly, I want to examine the disjunctions within this discourse on how French films were figured at the same time that I use that figuring to recover their shifting significance, season by season, from 1903 to 1906. These were the years (modifying Musser's schema slightly) of the cinema's "transition to story films," its "saturation" of a wide range of exhibition venues—with vaudeville houses, according to Fred C. Aiken, easily being the most important—and the initial "proliferation of specialized storefront moving-picture theaters."[5]

The Pathé "red rooster" as a vaudeville feature attraction

It might seem poetic justice to argue that *A Trip to the Moon* single-handedly created a stable market for cinema exhibition and for the "staged" story film in this country. Unfortunately, the argument simply won't fly, even if Méliès's film clearly enjoyed an unusual popularity with vaudeville audiences for at least a year.[6] Along with his earlier fairy plays, *A Trip to the Moon* provided a potential, if expensive, model for the staged story film, although it still used the story primarily as a pretext for spectacle attractions. It also emblematized the difference between one kind of travel views in time and space and another, as if projecting the cinema itself into the future. Indeed, as Musser discovered, Edwin S. Porter studied Méliès's film in order to make his own *Life of an American Fireman*, which Edison released in January 1903.[7] What one can argue is that *A Trip to the Moon* fueled the transition to story films and the concomitant expansion of the American cinema market that accelerated during the 1903–1904 season. Yet, by then, Méliès's films offered just one of several models for the story films that would soon be popular. Others came from manufacturers like Edison, Biograph, Warwick, Hepworth, Haggar & Sons, British Gaumont, and especially from the largest French producer, Pathé-Frères. Recovering Pathé's role, compared to American and English producers in this period of transition and expansion, however, is not easy. For there are discrepancies in the trajectory of cinema's emergence as a viable form of mass culture, depending on which strands of public and private discourse one chooses to privilege.

The evidence for a continually expanding cinema market between the summers of 1903 and 1904 is compelling. According to trade press reports, exhibition increased only moderately that fall—most notably in Denver, where no less than four vaudeville houses now included moving pictures in their programs.[8] Over the winter and spring, however, another forty houses began listing them, with the biggest increases occurring in the Northeast (in and around Boston, for instance), throughout the upper Midwest, and along the West Coast; everywhere family vaudeville houses, with their shorter, more frequent programs, were competing with larger high-class vaudeville theaters. It was then, too, that Archie Shepard went from doing "black top" shows to booking circuit tours of commercial theaters throughout New England, presenting two-hour shows (with Sunday concerts) that were especially popular with working-class audiences. By the summer of 1904, the number of exhibition sites was double what it had been the year before, with moving pictures firmly established not only in amusement parks throughout the Northeast and Midwest but also in vaudeville houses from San Antonio to Oakland.[9] In late 1903, Percival Waters (New York) and Miles Brothers (San Francisco) initiated a system of renting films to their customers.[10] Within months, ads for new selling agents and rental exchanges suddenly appeared, most of them based in Chicago, like Eugene Cline & Co. or George Spoor's new Film Rental Bureau—already suggesting the significance of the Midwest market.[11] [. . .]

That many more new film subjects were available is clear from the trade press and newspapers, but which ones contributed most to the market's expansion? All kinds of films still attracted notices. Throughout the year, travel views and actualités (or fictional reenactments) could be found as headliners—from the "moving pictures of India" at the Lyric Theater in Los Angeles to views of catastrophes like the "Baltimore Fire" at the Orpheum in Brooklyn or the "Iroquois Theater Fire" at the Gem Theatre in Sioux City.[12] The outbreak of war between Russia and Japan certainly sustained this interest—witness Biograph's *Battle of Yalu*, featured at Keith's in Boston in early April, and the scattered references to battle scenes on land and sea throughout the summer. Méliès's *féerie* films also continued to serve as special attractions, especially, but not exclusively, for children. That fall, for instance, Talley screened *Fairyland* for over a month at the Lyric Theater in Los Angeles, while the Keith Theatre in Providence placed it prominently in the middle of its bill.[13] The next spring, the Bijou Theatre in Duluth used *The Damnation of Faust* as one of its first features; the Lyric Theater in Portland did likewise with *Robinson Crusoe*; and several houses offered reprises of earlier films.[14] But Méliès-like fairy plays, such as Hepworth's *Alice in Wonderland* (shown in Boston and Buffalo during the Christmas season), received nearly as much attention. The newest story films were the "sensational chase pictures" from England, such as British Gaumont's *The Poachers*, cited at Keith's in Providence in early January.[15] But there were others from Edison and Biograph, ranging from condensed versions of melodramas like *Uncle Tom's Cabin*, cited at the Orpheum in Brooklyn, to traditional comic sketches like *Rube and Mandy at Coney Island* or "episodes" in the life of *Kit Carson*, cited at Keith's in Boston, and later at Keith's in Providence, as well as at Cleveland's Theatre in Chicago.[16]

The most famous of these new subjects, of course, was *The Great Train Robbery*, released by Edison in December 1903.[17] Our assumption of its popularity in some twenty vaudeville houses from New York to Chicago in late December, however, comes not from trade press reports but from two ads run by Edison and Kleine Optical in the *Clipper*.[18] Otherwise, the trade press itself mentioned the film rarely: once in December, at the Orpheum in Brooklyn, once in February, at the Park Theatre in Youngstown, and once again two months later at Keeney's Theatre in Brooklyn. The earliest newspaper citations also appeared in February, when, according to Musser, Edison's film "reportedly scored the biggest moving picture hit ever made in Rochester."[19] More frequent references to *The Great Train Robbery* occurred that summer, not only in amusement parks but also in vaudeville houses from Detroit to Duluth. Repeated ads by Edison, Kleine Optical, Lubin, and others throughout the spring and summer also testified to the film's impact; and in June, Kleine Optical claimed that the film was "the most popular subject" it had ever sold.[20] Yet *The Great Train Robbery* alone cannot account for the cinema market's expansion any more than *A Trip to the Moon* could the year before.[21] Many more new subjects, and subjects of sufficient quality and variety, had to be available for purchase, rental, and exhibition. And that, I would argue, is what Pathé was able to supply, given its relatively high production capacity. The problem is that not once during this entire year did trade press reports on exhibition refer to a Pathé title, even though Pathé films were known to be in circulation as early as the summer of 1902 (and as deep into the provinces as Des Moines).[22] The initial silence over *The Great Train Robbery*'s popularity—due perhaps to the *Clipper*'s and *Billboard*'s investment in live performance—was even greater over Pathé's films.

When one looks at the catalogs and trade press ads of American producers, rental exchanges, and exhibition services, however, Pathé story films suddenly become quite visible, whether in "original" or duped versions. Certain Pathé titles already had been cropping up (their maker unidentified, of course) the year before. Both Edison and Lubin, for instance, offered copies of Pathé's fairy play, *Ali Baba and the Forty Thieves*, while Edison also sold copies of *The Story of a Crime* and *The Gambler's Crime*.[23] By spring 1903, when Vitagraph began advertising its exhibition service in earnest, it too was offering Pathé films, and not only travel views of Algiers and the Alps.[24] Within six months, and with the addition of *Sleeping Beauty*, as well as a new comic fantasy, *Don Quixote*, Pathé story films constituted nearly a quarter of the titles the company featured as "spectaculars" in its new catalog addressed to vaudeville managers.[25] All of them "headliners" running fifteen to twenty minutes in length, they now equaled the Méliès titles in number, making French films, arguably, the most important on Vitagraph's programs. Further evidence of Pathé's growing presence appears in weekly *Clipper* ads, in which Edison, Biograph, and even Méliès substantially increased the number of new subjects they were offering for sale. Although some of that increase resulted from Edison's and Biograph's own slightly higher levels of production, even more was the result of imports from English producers, most of them short comic subjects or chase films sold during the summer and fall.[26] In the winter and spring, however, it was the longer Pathé films (still not identified as such) that came to the fore, especially in Edison's ads. In early November, for instance, Edison offered Pathé's *Life of Napoleon* (in its full two-reel format, as well as in separate scenes) along with *The Great Train Robbery*.[27] In January, its featured films were Pathé's *William Tell* and the "spectacular" *Puss-in-Boots*; in February, the principal new subject was Pathé's *Marie Antoinette*.[28]

All the titles released by Edison, of course, were dupes. Yet Pathé's own prints, with their red block-letter titles and red rooster trademark, seem to have been not only in circulation but highly valued.[29] One indication was an April 1904 ad from Harbach & Co. (in New York), the first firm to single out "original 'Pathé-Frères' films" for sale.[30] The most telling sign, however, comes from the weekly managers' reports of the Keith vaudeville theaters,[31] all of which attest to the popularity of *Fairyland* (which played three weeks at one theater in Philadelphia), *The Poachers* (which played two theaters, consecutively, also in Philadelphia), and *The Great Train Robbery*. But they also call attention to and highly praise Pathé's longer films. In September, for instance, *Sleeping Beauty* played on one of the first programs at the Empire in Cleveland. In October, *The Rise and Fall of Napoleon* was featured at Chase's Theatre in Washington; a month later the same two-reel film scored a hit in Cleveland. And it was this particular Pathé historical series, as Musser has shown, that both Lyman Howe and Edwin Hadley made the "featured subject" of their "high-class moving pictures" tours that fall and winter, capping a decade-long American fascination with Napoleon as the epitome of the heroic individual.[32] [. . .] Yet it was not until August 1904, when Kleine Optical confirmed that such "feature films were in great demand," that Pathé, along with Edison and Biograph, at last was acknowledged publicly as a leader in their production.[33]

Pathé stakes a claim of dominance

Recognizing the demand for its films on the American market, the French company finally opened a sales office in New York late that summer. The initial ads placed by Pathé Cinematograph, like those of Méliès the year before, drew attention to the "worldwide reputation" of its films, "which have been copied and duped by unscrupulous concerns"—an unmistakable indictment of Edison and Lubin.[34] Not only did Pathé promise to sell only "original films," but it offered most of them at a lower price than the dupes then on the market.[35] Moreover, its September list of two dozen titles still available, along with eight new "novelties," covered every kind of story film then being produced and included many already featured by its American competitors.[36] The earliest surviving Kleine Optical catalog, from October 1904, also called attention to the popularity of Pathé films over the course of the previous year, in a warning to exhibitors about the inferior quality of duped films. Explicitly naming "Pathé-Frères, of Paris" as "victims of this practice to a greater extent than any other manufacturer," Kleine Optical listed ten Pathé story films (as well as three from Méliès) "among the [most] successful films . . . duplicated in America"—from older titles such as *Napoleon* and *Marie Antoinette* to new ones such as *Indians and Cowboys* and *The Strike*.[37] . . . And in advising exhibitors to purchase at least one feature film per program, Kleine Optical gave as examples Pathé's *Christopher Columbus* and Edison's *Great Train Robbery*.[38]

Firmly established in New York and Chicago, through its sales agent Kleine Optical, Pathé Cinematograph was well positioned to take advantage of the continuing upsurge in exhibition during the 1904–1905 vaudeville season, especially as "ten-cent" or "family" houses continued to proliferate.[39] That fall, the trade press reported that moving pictures for the first time had become a regular vaudeville feature in several major cities—for instance, the Maryland Theatre (now part of Keith's circuit) in Baltimore, the Star Theatre in Atlanta, the new Hopkins Theatre (seating twenty-two hundred people) in Louisville, the Grand and Crystal Theatres in Milwaukee, and a new Orpheum in Minneapolis.[40] They became part of even more vaudeville houses in New York City and the region around Boston; it was in the latter area that Vitagraph again took over complete programs for several days in October and, along with Shepard's Moving Pictures, became a fixture on the "Sunday concerts" in certain "legitimate" theaters.[41] That winter, George Spoor's Film Rental Bureau and kinodrome service (featuring "foreign and American" films) expanded northward into family vaudeville houses in Duluth and Winnipeg, westward into others in Des Moines and Dubuque, and southward into several in Saint Joseph and Evansville.[42] In the New York area, the Colonial, Alhambra, Amphion, and Atlantic Garden theaters all introduced moving pictures onto their vaudeville programs. At the same time, on the West Coast, several new family vaudeville houses began showing films in Seattle and Portland, and others reported screening them in Vancouver and Fresno. [. . .]

Yet again, trade press reports provided little evidence that specific Pathé films spurred the cinema market's expansion. Instead, they continued to celebrate *The Great Train Robbery*, which served to kick off moving picture shows in new family vaudeville houses like the Star in Pittsburgh and the Bijou in Des Moines.[43] In terms of new subjects, they quickly picked up on the popularity of Biograph's comic chase film, *Personal!*, which played for four weeks that August at Keith's in New York and then was followed by others such as *The Lost Child*, *The Chicken Thief*, *The Suburbanite*, and *Tom, Tom, the Piper's Son*, as well as Edison variants like *The Escaped Lunatic*. The trade press also took notice of the crime films trying to imitate *The Great Train Robbery*'s success—from Lubin's *Bold Bank Robbery* and *The Counterfeiters* to Biograph's *The Moonshiners* and Edison's own *Capture of the "Yegg" Bank Burglars*.[44] Otherwise, the only new Méliès film to receive attention was *The Impossible Voyage*, whose citings were scattered from Milwaukee, Des Moines, and Fort Worth to Lowell, Massachusetts.[45] The references to Pathé films were just as slim: *The Strike* at the Crown Theatre in Fort Worth, *The Passion Play* at the Opera House in Lowell, *A Drama in the Air* at the Star Theatre in Saint Louis, and *The Incendiary* at the Des Moines Bijou (all but one of them family houses). In other words, according to trade press reports, the American films of Biograph, Edison, and even Lubin would seem to have been far more popular than the French films of either Méliès or Pathé.

Yet the local newspapers in at least two widely separate cities suggest something very different. From June through November, in Cedar Rapids (Iowa), Selig Polyscope supplied French films almost exclusively to the Auditorium (a family house), including *Faust and Marguerite* and *Fairyland* (each twice), as well as Pathé's *Forsaken* or *Annie's Love Story*, a rare reference to this allegedly popular title.[46] In December the Polyscope service shifted to another family house, the new People's Theatre, and its opening attraction, Pathé's *Passion Play*, ran for nearly a month.[47] In Portland (Oregon), French films were even more prominent. During the summer of 1904, the Lyric "specialized" in Pathé films from *Sleeping Beauty* and *Christopher Columbus* to *Annie's Love Story*, the only film to be held over for an extra week.[48] The following December, the Bijou Theater drew special attention to Pathé's *The Strike* during its Christmas week program.[49] At the same time, the Grand Theater advertised *The Impossible Voyage* as "the latest Parisian film" and then rebooked the Méliès film in January for a repeat performance.[50] At the end of December, it promoted Pathé's *Life of Louis XIV* exactly the same way; six months later, this "Parisian film story" returned to the Star Theater, which only once before had advertised its concluding act as an "imported film."[51] Throughout the winter and spring of 1905, along with Biograph's comic chase films, the Grand consistently booked Pathé titles from *From*

Christiana to North Cape and *Hop o' My Thumb* to *The Bewitched Lover* and *The Incendiary*.[52] In Portland, billing a closing act as "the latest Parisian film" seems to have meant more to family vaudeville audiences than simply calling it the "latest Biograph film" or "latest Edison film."[53]

That difference is no less telling when one looks at the Keith managers' reports.[54] As before, these reports parallel the trade press in noting the popularity of American comic chase films and crime subjects, and they initially give greater attention to Biograph titles: *The Lost Child*, for instance, ran for four weeks in New York, and *The Moonshiners* played for two weeks in Pittsburgh (at the Grand Opera House, now part of Keith's circuit).[55] They also indicate that English titles (even if no longer new) sometimes served to fill out (but never headline) the film programs. Méliès's *The Impossible Voyage* came in for high praise: it was held over for an extra week at Christmas in Boston (and later in Philadelphia) as "one of the laughing hits of the show," and it was described as the "best picture of that kind" in Providence.[56] References to Pathé films, however, are extensive and cover a wide range of genres. In January 1905, for instance, the Providence manager called the fairy play *Puss-in-Boots* "very good for children," as did those in Pittsburgh, New York, Philadelphia, and Boston three months later, referring to *Hop o' My Thumb*. Throughout the previous fall, one of the first titles Pathé advertised, *Nest Robbers*, was judged a "very good" comedy in Pittsburgh, Cleveland, and Boston; another early title, *A Drama in the Air*, first called a "good novelty" in New York and Cleveland, later ran as "the principal picture" in Pittsburgh.[57] In Boston, in January, audiences watched the "beautiful" historical film *Life of Louis XIV* "with deep interest"; in May, they gave the "well carried out" chase film *The Incendiary* "considerable applause at the finish." There, too, in December, the "melodramatic" feature *The Strike* (one of the few films representing labor unrest) was "watched with deep interest," ending in applause. And the words "watched with deep interest" were used for no other films shown on the Keith circuit throughout the 1904–1905 season.

Production company catalogs and trade press ads, as well as rental exchange ads, also suggest that, through Pathé Cinematograph, the French company was becoming the principal supplier of new subjects on the American market. In September 1904 both Edison and Eugene Cline, for instance, featured either new Pathé dupes or "originals," with the latter promoting *The Strike* as a "sensational film," one of the "greatest headliners since *The Train Robbery*."[58] In October a Lubin ad in the *Clipper* listed a half dozen Pathé titles, including *Puss-in-Boots*, as his company's own product.[59] This duping was so extensive that, in a December *Billboard* ad., J. A. Berst, the company's New York manager, could turn the practice to Pathé's advantage, declaring that "the best advertising for our films is the fact that so many concerns dupe them."[60] Meanwhile, Lubin kept exploiting the French company, publishing a catalog the next spring that not only listed seventy-five Pathé titles (out of a total of ninety) as its own but also actually reproduced the page layout of Pathé's new English-language catalog.[61] In May, Pathé finally sought to discredit the publicity from this "well known house in Philadelphia," and protect itself further, by printing "Pathé Frères Paris 1905" along the perforation edge of each copy it sold.[62] More important, the New York office now claimed to be able to offer its sales agents (Kleine Optical and the Miles Brothers), exchanges like National Film Renting or the newly organized Chicago Film Exchange, and exhibitors like Vitagraph and Spoor's kinodrome service "something new every week."[63] If the public, in *Billboard*'s words, now had "grown to expect a wonderful creation each week,"[64] Pathé's ads promised to fulfill that expectation, with every possible kind of story film.

Clearly, no American company could make such a claim in 1905. Edison had thwarted Biograph's production surge by raiding some of its key personnel that spring, yet its own production schedule actually decreased slightly (Porter made only fifteen story films over the course of the next year) as the company invested its resources instead in the manufacture of projectors and other related equipment.[65] Vitagraph also began producing its own films that summer in order to fill a projected fall schedule of biweekly releases, but its output (along with the increases at Lubin) did little more than compensate for the production declines at Biograph and Edison, as well as Crescent and Selig. Besides, none of the American companies had more than a single studio available for shooting interior scenes; both Edison and Vitagraph started construction on new studios in late 1905, but neither would be ready until the following summer or fall. By contrast, Pathé had three studio facilities on the outskirts of Paris (two of which had double stages), where "director units" headed by Ferdinand Zecca, Lucien Nonguet, Gaston Velle, Georges Hatot, and Albert Capellani all would be able to work more or less simultaneously.[66] As the French company shifted into a factory system of production, its extensive laboratories geared up to print an average of forty thousand feet of positive film stock per day (primarily story subjects), a good percentage of which now was being shipped to the United States.[67]

Pathé fuels the early nickelodeon boom

That summer in Pittsburgh, a real estate developer and impresario named Harry Davis opened the Nickelodeon, a storefront theater with a continuous program of moving pictures.[68] The idea for such a theater was hardly new, and many of those who had experimented with the venue were associated with the amusement parlor or penny arcade.[69] The association was apt, as David Nasaw writes, for, by 1903–1904, "visiting an arcade was almost like window shopping."[70] One of the best known was T. L. Talley in Los Angeles, with his Electric Theatre, in 1902 and again in 1903.[71] Some later would even become major figures in the industry. Adolph Zukor, for instance, claimed to have converted the second floor over his Fourteenth Street Arcade (on Union Square, New York) into the Crystal Hall, in 1904.[72] [. . .] Others who had experimented with storefront theaters, however, were traveling showmen, like J. W. Wilson, who operated one in Houston, between February and April 1905, and Frank Montgomery, who briefly opened an "Edison's Family Theatre" in Fort Worth.[73] The Nickelodeon also originated in an amusement arcade (attached to the Avenue Theatre), part of which Davis used to project moving pictures to standing spectators.[74] When a fire destroyed both the theater and the arcade that June, Musser writes, Davis simply "moved his motion-picture show to a larger storefront," one of his commercial properties nearby: within weeks, it was "an instant hit."

Throughout the fall, Davis and other entrepreneurs opened more storefront theaters in Pittsburgh (one report, undoubtedly exaggerated, claimed there were twenty by December), and similar theaters began appearing in Philadelphia—at least one of which, the Bijou Dream, was financed by Davis.[75] By November, either Davis or his associate John Harris had entered the Chicago market, where Eugene Cline may have been operating a "promotional" storefront adjacent to the New American Theatre; by Christmas, on State Street, Aaron Jones was turning one of his downtown arcades into a moving picture show, and Gustav Hollenberg was about to open the Chicago Theatre.[76] About the same time, in New York, Loew was converting his Twenty-third Street arcade into a People's nickelodeon; he was soon followed by Zukor (after a short investment in Hale's Tours), J. Austin Fynes with his first Nicolet "miniature playhouse" on West 125th Street, and William Fox with a "nickelette" in Brooklyn.[77] [. . .] In parallel with this trend, Miles Brothers announced that its offices would offer film program changes not just weekly, which had long been standard in vaudeville houses, but semiweekly— probably to service the small theaters in or near such amusement parks as Coney Island's Steeplechase or Luna Park and Chicago's White City, some of which already were featuring only films.[78] That the first nickelodeons emerged in the region of the country from Pittsburgh

Figure 6.1 Chicago Theatre, on State Street between Harrison and Polk (Chicago), January 1906

and Philadelphia west to Chicago strangely coincides with a relative lack of prior trade press reports on moving picture programs in vaudeville houses there, almost as if there had been an attempt to suppress or deny their growing appeal.

By the opening of the 1905–1906 vaudeville season, according to Kleine Optical and National Film Renting ads in both *Billboard* and the *Clipper*, nearly every theater in the country (in hundreds of downtown shopping districts), from Keith's "high-class" house in Boston (seating twenty-seven hundred) to the Bijou "family" house in Des Moines (seating five hundred), was showing moving pictures.[79] Moreover, many of those in eastern urban centers were presenting regular Sunday concerts exclusively given over to films: in New York alone, Shepard now was supplying nearly two dozen theaters.[80] Anticipating the "exceptional" demand for features or "headliners"[81] in vaudeville houses, amusement parks, and now nickelodeons, Kleine Optical substantially upped its orders from Pathé Cinematograph, from June through September, making the French company the principal supplier of the films it sold on the American market—among them the 1903–1904 *Passion Play*, which it strongly recommended over all others.[82] And on the strength of Pathé's unusual production capacity, Kleine Optical now claimed to be the industry's largest sales agent, not only in the Midwest but across the country as a whole.[83]

Throughout the summer and fall, Pathé titles became more and more prominent on the Keith vaudeville circuit and elsewhere.[84] *The Moon Lover*, the comic fantasy of a drunk's "trip to the moon," first played at Keith's New York house in late May and was still circulating as a "very good comedy" at the Providence house in early November. *The Life of a Miner*, or *The Great Mine Disaster*, a loose adaptation of Zola's *Germinal*, was a major hit from June through August. In New York it was described as "rather serious" but "very good"; in Boston it "won considerable applause from the balconies" (that is, from working-class audiences); and in Des Moines it was one of only five titles singled out in ads that summer and concluded the season at Ingersoll Park.[85] In July the Philadelphia house found *Two Young Tramps* an excellent color film; six weeks later, it was an opening feature at the Boston Theatre in Lowell.[86] In August, the New York house called the sports feature *The Great Steeplechase* "the greatest racing picture . . . ever"; two months later, the Temple Theatre in Detroit found it "beautiful, exciting, a masterpiece."[87] And managers everywhere agreed that the industrial "feature" *Scenes at Creusot's Steel Foundry* was "excellent." Throughout August and September, Pathé titles clearly dominated programs on the Keith circuit. Over the Labor Day weekend, for instance, the Boston house showed nothing but Pathé films; for consecutive weeks, both the New York and the Philadelphia houses made Pathé titles their principal features, among them, *The Wonderful Album*, which served as an apt and timely advertisement.

That Pathé films maintained their prominence within the Keith vaudeville circuit throughout the 1905–1906 season is clear from the weekly managers' reports, especially from New York and Boston.[88] That they enjoyed a similar prominence on family vaudeville and nickelodeon programs is less obvious. One reason is that, during this period, the trade press offered fewer and fewer references to individual film titles playing at specific exhibition sites. In the *Clipper*, for instance, only the Boston and People's Theatres in Lowell now consistently listed the films on their weekly programs—and People's kept Pathé's *The Deserter* for a rare second week in February 1906.[89] Instead, what interested the trade press—and that interest seemed grudging, given its long-standing commitment to live performance—was the phenomenal growth of moving pictures and moviegoing generally within the entertainment industry. For nickelodeons represented a different kind of amusement: they catered to a drop-in audience through programs of films and illustrated songs that could last anywhere from fifteen to thirty minutes each but ran continuously from noon (or even earlier) to late at night.[90] In the spring of 1906, for instance, *Billboard* may have been the first to acknowledge the nickelodeon's phenomenal growth, as well as its potential value, in a regular column entitled "Moving Picture Shows."[91] [. . .]

For references to specific film titles, again one can turn to certain local newspapers. Here, ads for the Bijou Theater in Des Moines provide some measure of the French company's continuing penetration of the family vaudeville market. Two weekly programs in December 1905, for instance, were composed almost exclusively of Pathé films, and at least one Pathé title was included on nearly every program for the next five months.[92] In Portland, Pathé's dominance now extended to the Star as well as the Grand, leaving few program slots open for the films of Edison and Vitagraph or for Méliès *féeries* such as *Arabian Nights*.[93] The Grand singled out Pathé's *French Coal Miners* as a "Great Film" but attributed it to Edison (which indicates the company still was duping its competitor's films), and it described *Christian Martyrs* as "special," "sensational."[94] Repeatedly, Pathé titles such as *French Coal Miners*, *The Moon Lover*, and *Young Tramps* would appear at the Grand one week and then return months later at the Star.[95] Yet, by the end of the year, there were enough Pathé subjects available that the Star could feature such films as *Modern Brigandage*, *The Hen with the Golden Eggs*, and *The Deserter*.[96] Whether or not similar references can be gleaned from local newspaper ads in other cities during this period ought to be the subject of further research.

The question of Pathé's prominence on family vaudeville and nickelodeon programs is crucial, however, because those were the sites of the cinema's real expansion. As early as

December 1905, *Billboard* suggested that the "great impetus" for the new industry's "remark-able leaps and bounds" over the previous year came from the "popular [or 'ten-cent'] vaudeville circuits.[97] For the first time, circuits for such houses appeared beyond the West Coast, as in the Consolidated Vaudeville Managers Association, whose theaters were named Bijou or Crystal.[98] *Variety* seems to have taken a special interest in the growth of family vaudeville (and generally ignored moving pictures); by March 1906, it was predicting that the country would be "thoroughly vaudevillized very soon."[99] By that time, however, the nickelodeon had become a fad (especially for a mixed class of shoppers, offwork employees, and neighbor-hood residents, many of them women and children) and was beginning to compete with family vaudeville.[100] At least two dozen storefront theaters were operating in Pittsburgh; there were another dozen or more in Philadelphia.[101] Others were cropping up in New York (on the Bowery, lower Sixth Avenue, 14th Street, and 125th Street) and in Chicago (on State and North Clark Streets, as well as on Halstead and Milwaukee Avenues, with Carl Laemmle's White Front Theatre among them).[102] Partly fueled by Harry Davis—whose Bijou Dreams now stretched from New York and Buffalo to Cleveland and Detroit—nickelodeons, theator-iums, and electric theaters now could be found from cities like Birmingham, Louisville, and Des Moines (where the Bijou turned into the Nickeldom) to small towns like Charleroi, Pennsylvania, and Pine Bluff, Arkansas.[103] As Shepard, with the financial backing of Philadelphia developer Felix Isman, began leasing theaters for permanent picture shows, Keith opened nickelodeons near several of his Rhode Island theaters.[104] By the summer of 1906, there were ten nickelodeons around the boardwalk area of Atlantic City and at least thirty on Coney Island.[105]

That Pathé could and did supply a major portion of the films used on family vaudeville and nickelodeon programs admittedly has to be inferred, but the cumulative weight of infer-ences, I think, is persuasive. For one thing, along with "biograph," "vitagraph," and "kineto-graph," the term "cinematograph" (now associated with Pathé's American offices) was appearing more frequently as a generic label for the film programs shown in vaudeville houses and amuse-ment parks.[106] For another, rental exchanges like Miles Brothers and Eugene Cline, as well as sales agents like Kleine Optical, all of whom drew attention to their distribution of Pathé films (Eugene Cline, for instance, had an extensive list of the company's titles), generally were linked to the family vaudeville circuits and earliest nickelodeons.[107] In fact, in late December 1905, Pathé itself became the first to address ads specifically to these new "moving picture men."[108] By then, of course, there was a sufficient backlog of older films, both American and foreign, so that storefront theaters could fill their programs, at least initially, with already popular titles, especially for spectators who may not have seen them before. Yet once they began to compete with one another (and with vaudeville houses) for customers—a moment which George Kleine later dated as December 1905—the nickelodeons too had to have a ready supply of new subjects.[109] And Pathé clearly was the principal supplier of new subjects throughout 1905–1906. Moreover, while Edison, Vitagraph, and Biograph tended to produce a limited number of rela-tively lengthy "headliner" films, Pathé could offer a wide range of film lengths, from one hundred to more than one thousand feet, and in a variety of genres.[110] Such a production strategy was perfectly suited to nickelodeons, which demanded variety, novelty, and increas-ingly frequent changes in their programs. And it was endorsed by the Mueller Brothers, who were running four moving picture shows on Coney Island in May 1906: their clientele, who loved melodramas and comedies, clearly preferred Pathé films.[111]

Finally, there is evidence that Pathé itself developed several strategies to solidify its domi-nant position on the American market, especially among the new storefront theaters. In early September 1905, it established a second sales agency in Chicago, which *Billboard* now claimed as "the leading film market in the world."[112] That fall, Pathé's ads began stressing the superior quality of its films: not only were they "photographically finer . . . and steadier than any other films," but because they were "imported from Paris" they were all "good subjects" simply because the company could not "afford to pay heavy duty on doubtful sellers."[113] By November, Pathé Cinematograph was so entrenched on the American market that, along with Kleine Optical, Vitagraph, Biograph, and Méliès (but, significantly, not Edison), it would participate in the first attempt to organize "the leading manufacturers of films," the Moving Picture Protective League of America.[114] By March, well before a court decision seemed to further weaken Edison's control over moving picture patents, Pathé was selling its own projector, the "New 1906 Model Exposition Machine," shipped direct from its Paris factories (which now had a production capacity of two hundred projectors, cameras, and other apparatuses per month).[115] Within another month, now in partnership with Vitagraph, the French company would finance the first trade weekly devoted almost exclusively to exhibitors in the new moving picture industry, *Views and Films Index* (whose readers allegedly reached several thousand within weeks).[116] And it was then that the Grand Theater, in Portland, began advising audiences they could always find "the latest Pathé films" on its weekly programs.[117] By the summer of 1906, "the air [was] full of moving picture exhibitions,"[118] largely because Pathé was releasing from three to six subjects per week, its production of positive film stock having doubled over the previous nine months to eighty thousand feet per day.[119] According to *Billboard*, the French company was close to having advance orders, on average, of seventy-five prints of each new film title it placed on the American market.[120]

If, as Musser writes, echoing the words of Fred Aiken, the "nickelodeon boom" in the United States constituted a "radical change" or "revolution in exhibition on an unprecedented scale,"[121] it was due in no small part to Pathé-Frères and its capacity, by 1905–1906, to produce and deliver a variety of films of high quality, en masse and on a regular, relatively predictable basis. By fulfilling the basic economic imperatives of standardization and differentiation, by orchestrating both "the effect of stability and the effect of novelty," the French company almost single-handedly assured the viability of a new kind of cheap amusement. It assured nickelodeons of precisely what Edward Bok, the editor of *Ladies' Home Journal*, considered essential to the success of the new mass magazine or modern store: "wares [that are] constantly fresh and varied to attract the eye and hold the patronage of its customers."[122] In other words, the "foreign bodies" of Pathé films, which American film historians so long have overlooked, once played perhaps the determining role in the emergence of our own cinema.

Notes

1. Charles Musser, *Before the Nickelodeon: Edwin S. Porter and the Edison Manufacturing Company* (Berkeley: University of California Press, 1991), 284.
2. Robert Allen, *Vaudeville and Film, 1895–1915: A Study of Media Interaction* (New York: Arno Press, 1980), 203–205.
3. These catalogs are collected in Charles Musser, *Thomas A. Edison Papers: A Guide to Motion Picture Catalogs by American Producers and Distributors, 1894–1908: A Microfilm Edition* (Frederick, MD: University Publications of America, 1985).
4. These managers' reports can be found in the Keith-Albee Collection at the University of Iowa Library (KA). See M. Alison Kibler, "The Keith/Albee Collection: The Vaudeville Industry, 1894–1935," *Books at Iowa* (April 1992), 7–23.
5. Charles Musser, *The Emergence of Cinema to 1907*, vol. 1 of *History of the American Cinema* (New York: Scribner's, 1991), 297–417. See, also, Allen, *Vaudeville and Film*, 218; Fred C. Aiken, "Ethics of Film Renting Worthy of Deep Study," *Show World* (SW) (27 June 1908), 24.

6. When the Orpheum reopened in Los Angeles, in the fall of 1903, it featured *A Trip to the Moon* on its initial program—see "Amusements," *Los Angeles Times* (*LAT*) (7 September 1903), 1.

7. Musser, *The Emergence of Cinema*, 325. See, also, Martin Sopocy, "French and British Influences in Porter's *American Fireman*," *Film History* 1.2 (1987), 137–148. [. . .]

8. "Denver," *Billboard* (*Bill*) (19 September 1903), 6, and (5 December 1903), 10.

9. *New York Clipper* (*NYC*) (25 June 1904), 407; *NYC* (30 July 1904), 527; *NYC* (13 August 1904), 571.

10. Musser, *The Emergence of Cinema*, 367. See, also, "Notes from Miles Brothers," *Bill* (27 June 1908), 31; "Kinematography in the United States," *Moving Picture World* (*MPW*) (11 July 1914), 175; and Lewis Jacobs, *The Rise of the American Film: A Critical History* (New York: Harcourt, Brace, 1939), 52–53.

11. See the first Eugene Cline ad in *NYC* (27 February 1904), 15; and the first Film Rental Bureau ad in *NYC* (7 May 1904), 263. Within months, the latter was emphasizing its "superior weekly service"—see the Film Rental Bureau ad in *NYC* (9 July 1904), 458.

12. Unless otherwise cited, the primary sources for this and the following paragraphs are vaudeville listings (by state and/or city) in *New York Clipper* and *Billboard*. "Amusements," *LAT* (23 September 1903), 1. [. . .]

13. "Amusements," *LAT* (4 October 1903), 1, and (1 November 1903), I.1. See, also, the Keith Programme for 9 November 1903—Providence Clipping Book 1903–1904, KA.

14. See the Lyric Theater ad in *Ore* (22 May 1904), 19. *Robinson Crusoe*, however, was advertised as an Edison moving picture.

15. See, for instance, the *Pawtucket Gazette* article on the Keith Theatre program (1 January 1904)—Clipping Book 1903–1904, KA. [. . .]

16. See the *Providence News* article on the Keith Theatre program (15 March 1904)—Clipping Book 1903–1904, KA; and "Chicago," *Bill* (2 April 1904), 4.

17. Edison first advertised the film in *NYC* (7 November 1903), 896.

18. See the Kleine Optical ad in *NYC* (26 December 1903), 1067; and the Edison ad in *NYC* (9 January 1904), 1113.

19. Musser, *The Emergence of Cinema*, 366. See, also, the *Providence News* article on the Keith Theatre program (6 February 1904)—Clipping Book 1903–1904, KA.

20. See the Kleine Optical ads in *NYC* (18 June 1904), 400, and (3 September 1904), 647; and the Kinetograph ad in *NYC* (20 August 1904), 584. Edison and Lubin claimed to offer "original" versions of the film in side-by-side ads in *NYC* (23 July 1904), 508. [. . .]

21. For one of the earliest "histories," which credits Méliès and Edison with "stirring up" interest in story films, see "Picture Stories," *Views and Films Index* (*VFI*) (21 September 1907), 3.

22. Pathé's *Aladdin and His Lamp* (a 230 meter film released in 1901) was shown along with *The Destruction of Mt. Pelée* (perhaps also Pathé's version) as part of Selig Polyscope's program at the Ingersoll Park theater the last week of July—see the Ingersoll Park ad in *Iowa State Register and Leader* (22 July 1902), 2.

23. See the Edison catalogs of September 1902 and May 1903; the Edison ad in *NYC* (1 November 1902), 808; and the Lubin ad in *NYC* (28 February 1903), 36.

24. See the American Vitagraph ad in *NYC* (21 March 1903), 108.

25. See the American Vitagraph Catalog (ca. fall 1903), 3–6. *Don Quixote* was first announced in a special Pathé-Frères supplement, London, August 1903.

26. See, for instance, the Edison ad for Urban Trading's *Daylight Burglary* in *NYC* (20 June 1903), 408; and the Biograph ads in *NYC* (10 October 1903), 796, (31 October 1903), 872, (21 November 1903), 944, (28 November 1903), 968, and (12 December 1903), 1016.

27. See the Edison ad in *NYC* (7 November 1903), 896. The film also appeared in Edison's January 1904 catalog, entitled *The Rise and Fall of Napoleon the Great*.

28. See the Edison ads in *NYC* (2 January 1904), 1077, and (16 January 1904), 1136.

29. Pathé-Frères first referred to its trademark red titles in its London catalog, May 1903. According to later catalogs that year, both *Don Quixote* and *Puss-in-Boots*, for instance, were available in hand-colored versions.

30. See the Harbach & Co. ad in *NYC* (16 April 1904), 188.

31. Unless otherwise cited, the primary sources for this paragraph are the 1903–1904 Keith Managers' Reports, KA.

32. Charles Musser with Carol Nelson, *High-Class Moving Pictures: Lyman H. Howe and the Forgotten Era of Traveling Exhibition, 1880–1920* (Princeton: Princeton University Press, 1991), 134–142. [. . .]

33. See the Kleine Optical ad in *NYC* (6 August 1904), 546.

34. See the Pathé Cinematograph ads in *NYC* (27 August 1904), 613, and (3 September 1904), 644. The first of these was positioned opposite a Lubin ad; the second was positioned just below an Edison ad.

35. "What Does It Mean?" *MPW* (26 October 1907), 535.

36. See the Pathé Cinematograph ad in *NYC* (24 September 1904), 718.

37. Kleine Optical Company, "Copied Films," *Complete Illustrated Catalogue of Moving Picture Machines, Stereopticons, Slides, Views* (October 1904), 2–3. [. . .]

38. George C. Pratt excerpts this section from Kleine Optical's catalog, but only to focus on the success of *Great Train Robbery*, and Pathé is not identified as the maker of *Christopher Columbus*—Pratt, ed., *Spellbound in Darkness: A History of the Silent Film* (Greenwich, Conn.: New York Graphic Society, 1973), 36–37. Kleine himself pointed out that Kleine Optical had ordered fifteen prints of *The Great Train Robbery* that summer, in an 18 August 1904 letter to W. E. Gilmore—see Box 18: Edison Manufacturing Company, George Kleine Collection, Manuscripts Division, Library of Congress (GK).

39. Small traveling exhibitors such as Bert Cook and Fannie Harris also relied on Pathé's entrance into the American market for new supplies of moving pictures—see Kathryn Fuller, *At the Picture Show: Small Town Audiences and the Creation of Movie Fan Culture* (Washington, D.C.: Smithsonian Institution Press, 1996), 10–12. This upsurge in moving picture exhibition may also have been facilitated by the move to consolidate vaudeville houses into circuits—see, for instance, "Vaudeville," *Bill* (26 March 1904), 3; "Big Vaudeville Combine," *Bill* (25 June 1904), 2; the Keith circuit ad in *NYC* (25 February 1905), 30; the Western Vaudeville Association ad in *NYC* (11 March 1905), 78; and the Affiliated Western Vaudeville ad in *NYC* (15 April 1905), 207.

40. Unless otherwise cited, the primary sources for this and the following paragraphs are vaudeville listings (by state and/or city) in *New York Clipper* and *Billboard*.

41. Vitagraph took over the Colonial Theatre in Lawrence, 24–26 October, and then the Bijou Theatre in Fall River, 27–29 October—"Massachusetts," *NYC* (29 October 1904), 831, and (5 November 1904), 855.

42. See, also, the Film Rental Bureau ad in *NYC* (20 August 1904), 600.

43. See, also, "The Theatres," *Des Moines Register and Leader* (*DMRL*) (27 November 1904), 2.6.

44. See, also, the Bijou ad in *DMRL* (23 January 1905), 5.

45. See, also, the Bijou ad in *DMRL* (1 January 1905), 3.3. [. . .]

46. See the Auditorium ads in *Cedar Rapids Daily Republican* (12 July 1904), 8, (2 October 1904), 10, (6 November 1904), 11, and (20 November 1904), 10. *The Great Train Robbery* was shown the week of 13 November, but it received less publicity than *A Trip to the Moon*, the week of 14 August. *Annie's Love Story* or *Roman d'amour* was said to have sold one thousand copies worldwide—see Georges Sadoul, *Histoire générale du cinéma, II: Les Pionniers du cinéma, 1897–1908* (Paris: Denoël, 1948), 312–313.

47. See the People's Theatre ads in *Cedar Rapids Daily Republican* (18 December 1904), 8, (8 January 1905), 8, and (15 January 1905), 6.

48. See the Lyric Theater ads in *Oregonian* (Portland) (*Ore*) (24 July 1904), 19, and (31 July 1904), 19. The only reference to *The Great Train Robbery* was during that same week of 31 July, when it played at the Star Theater.

49. See the Bijou Theater ads in *Ore* (20 December 1904), 14, and (26 December 1904), 8.

50. See the Grand Theater ads in *Ore* (25 December 1904), 19, and (15 January 1905), 19.

51. See the Grand Theater ad in *Ore* (1 January 1905), 19; and the Star Theater ads in *Ore* (5 March 1905), 19, and (18 June 1905), 29.

52. See, for instance, the Grand Theater ads in *Ore* (18 December 1904), 19, (22 January 1905), 19, (5 February 1905), 19, (26 February 1905), 19, (19 March 1905), 19, and (16 April 1905), 19.

53. The Grand used these latter phrases only twice in its ads in *Ore* (14 May 1905), 27, and (21 May 1905), 29. The only other moving picture "brand" mentioned was Lubin's *The Counterfeiters*, by the Star Theater, in its ad in *Ore* (14 May 1905), 27.

54. Unless otherwise cited, the primary sources for this paragraph are the 1904–1905 Keith Managers' Reports, KA.

55. The Grand Opera House in Pittsburgh (managed by Harry Davis) came under Keith's control in September 1904 and immediately began showing moving pictures.

56. Several Méliès trick films also came in for praise: *The Clockmaker's Dream*, *The Black Imp*, and *The Crystal Cabinet*.

57. Other Pathé comic subjects and trick films receiving good notices included *Fantastic Fishing*, *August the Monkey*, *Fireworks*, *The Bewitched Lover*, and *The Clown's Revenge*. The managers' reports from Cleveland are particularly interesting because not once does *New York Clipper* refer to films being shown there.

58. See the Edison Films Catalog Supplement no. 222 (September 1904), and the Eugene Cline & Co. ad in *Bill* (24 September 1904), 40.

59. See the Lubin ad in *NYC* (22 October 1904), 824.

60. See the Pathé ad in *Bill* (31 December 1904), 32.

61. See *Lubin's Films*, May 1905. Fred Balshofer says that when he first came to work for Lubin, in 1905, all he did was make "duplicates of pictures that had been produced in France, by the Méliès company and Pathé-Frères"—see Fred Balshofer and Arthur Miller, *One Reel a Week* (Berkeley: University of California Press, 1967), 5–6.

62. See the Pathé ads in *NYC* (13 May 1905), 316, and (20 May 1905), 336. This coincided with congressional legislation, in 1905, establishing "trademark registration as prima facie evidence of ownership," which Pathé apparently could not take advantage of until the American branch office's incorporation in 1907—see Susan Strasser, *Satisfaction Guaranteed: The Making of the American Mass Market* (New York: Pantheon, 1989), 45.

63. See, for instance, the Pathé ad in *NYC* (6 May 1905), 290; and the Chicago Film Exchange ad in *Bill* (1 July 1905), 47.

64. "Pat-Chats," *Bill* (15 July 1905), 3.

65. Musser, *The Emergence of Cinema*, 386–393, 458.

66. For further information on Pathé-Frères in France, see Richard Abel, *The Ciné Goes to Town: French Cinema, 1896–1914* (Berkeley: University of California Press, 1994), 20–22.

67. This figure comes from the Pathé ad in *Phono-Ciné-Gazette*, 13 (1 October 1905), 209.

68. The Nickelodeon was credited with opening in 1903, in the special exhibition issue of *Moving Picture World* (15 July 1916), 405. This is a good example of why *Moving Picture World* itself warned readers that, in many of the issue's stories, showmen probably were "shooting the bull."

69. For a good summary of the amusement parlor or penny arcade at the turn of the century, see David Nasaw, *Going Out: The Rise and Fall of Public Amusements* (New York: Basic Books, 1994), 155–160. See, also, Robert Grau, *The Theatre of Science: A Volume of Progress and Achievement in the Motion Picture Industry* (New York: Benjamin Blom, 1914), 16–19. [. . .]

70. Nasaw, *Going Out*, 158.

71. For information on other earlier storefront theaters, see Musser, *The Emergence of Cinema*, 299–303.

72. See Will Irwin, *The House That Shadows Built* (Garden City, N.Y.: Doubleday, Doran, 1928), 3–8, 90–97; Adolph Zukor, *The Public Is Never Wrong* (New York: Putnam's, 1953), 36–40; and Neal Gabler, *An Empire of Their Own: How the Jews Invented Hollywood* (New York: Doubleday, 1988), 17–18, 22.

73. For information on Wilson's theater, at 205 San Jacinto, Houston, see "Texas," *NYC* (25 February 1905), 24, and (29 April 1905), 263. Montgomery's theater in Fort Worth is cited prominently in Grau, *The Theatre of Science*, 293.

74. Musser, *The Emergence of Cinema*, 418–420. [. . .]

75. "Philadelphia: Gossip of the Week," *Bill* (21 October 1905), 3; "Philadelphia Pencilings," *Bill* (18 November 1905), 6; "Pat-Chats: Adopting the Pittsburgh Idea," *Bill* (2 December 1905), 3; and "Philadelphia," *Bill* (20 January 1906), 7. A later report suggested there were perhaps a dozen in Pittsburgh by January 1906—"To Our Readers," *VFI* (30 June 1906), 3. According to ads in the *Philadelphia Public Ledger*, Lubin was showing films regularly at his Auditorium theater by September 1902—see Linda Woal, "When a Dime Could Buy a Dream: Siegmund Lubin and the Birth of Motion Picture Exhibition," *Film History* 6.2 (Summer 1994), 161. See, also, Musser, *The Emergence of Cinema*, 421–422.

76. See, for instance, "Chicago," *Bill* (28 October 1905), 12; K. S. Hover, "Police Supervision in Chicago," *Nickelodeon* (*Nick*) (January 1909), 11; "Chicago Reports Many Variations in Picture Shows," *MPW* (15 July 1916), 413–414; and Musser, *The Emergence of Cinema*, 423.

77. "J. Austin Fynes Enterprises," *NYC* (17 March 1906), 108; Robert Grau, "Fortunes in the Moving Picture Field," *Overland Monthly* (April 1911), 396; Grau, *The Theatre of Science*, 18–21; William Fox, "Reminiscences and Observations," in Joseph Kennedy (ed.), *The Story of the Films* (Chicago: A. W. Shaw, 1927), 309–310; Bosley Crowther, *The Lion's Share* (New York: Garland, 1985), 26–27; and Gabler, *An Empire of Their Own*, 65–66.

78. See the Miles Brothers ads in *NYC* (27 May 1905), 368, and (15 July 1905), 540, and in *Bill* (5 August 1905), 48. Miles Brothers, for instance, had Paul Howse of White City testify in support of its service in *Bill* (9 August 1905), 48. [. . .]

79. See the Kleine Optical ads in *NYC* (9 September 1905), 723, and *Bill* (16 September 1905), 13, and the National Film Renting ad in Bill (9 September 1905), 48.

80. Musser, *The Emergence of Cinema*, 374.

81. See the Kleine Optical ad in *NYC* (30 September 1905), 824.

82. Kleine Optical purchased $2,350 of material from Pathé in June, $5,292 in July, $2,345 in August, and $3,635 in September; only once during those months did it purchase more from Biograph, $3,802 in September—see Musser, *Before the Nickelodeon*, 482. See, also, Kleine Optical's *Complete Illustrated Catalog* (November 1905), 272.

83. Kleine Optical first began to assert its leading position in an ad in *Bill* (28 January 1905), 40.

84. At least two Méliès titles also received notice, Faust and Marguerite at the Metropolitan in Duluth and *The Automobile Chase* at the Aerial Garden in New York—see "Minnesota," *NYC* (1 July 1905), 483, and "New York City," *NYC* (8 July 1905), 504. Unless otherwise cited, the primary sources for this paragraph are the 1905–1906 Keith Managers' Reports, KA.

85. See, also, the Ingersoll Park ad in *DMRL* (27 August 1905), 2.6. The film also played at the Bijou in Duluth the first week of July—"Minnesota," *NYC* (8 July 1905), 508.

86. See, also, "Massachusetts," *NYC* (16 September 1905), 751.

87. The film also played at the Globe Theatre in Saint Louis in early October—"Missouri," *NYC* (7 October 1905), 831.

88. See, for instance, the 9 October 1905 program at Keith's Theatre in Boston, which featured four Pathé films out of a total of five, or the 5 February 1906 program at Keith's Theatre in New York, which featured four Pathé films—*The Prince of Wales at Lanori*, *Victims of the Storm*, *The Deserter*, and *The Fancy Garden Party*—all of which then were shown two weeks later at Keith's in Philadelphia—KA.

89. "Massachusetts," *NYC* (10 February 1906), 1303, and (17 February 1906), 1331. The only titles the *NYC* repeatedly called attention to, perhaps in a move to stigmatize the cinema's appeal, were Lubin's and Houseman's competing films of the Britt-Nelson fight.

90. One of the earliest descriptions of nickelodeon programs appears in "Our Head Office Boy Wants to Be a Reporter," *VFI* (25 April 1906), 10–11.

91. *Billboard*'s "Moving Picture Shows" column first appeared in the 7 April 1906 issue; it was appearing almost weekly by May. [. . .]

92. See the Bijou ads in *DMRL* (10 December 1905), 2.2, and (31 December 1905), 3.11.

93. See the Grand ad in *Ore* (30 July 1905), 29.

94. See the Grand ads in *Ore* (2 July 1905), 29, and (23 July 1905), 29.

95. See the Grand and Star ads in *Ore* (6 August 1905), 29, (20 August 1905), 29, (17 September 1905), 29, (8 October 1905), 29, and (22 October 1905), 29.

96. See the Star ads in *Ore* (26 November 1905), 29, (17 December 1905), 29, and (7 January 1906), 29.

97. "Pat-Chats: The Film Industry," *Bill* (30 December 1905), 7.

98. The "Family Theatres" of the Consolidated Vaudeville Managers Association were all located in Illinois, Michigan, Indiana, Ohio, and Wisconsin—see the association's ad in *NYC* (25 November 1905), 1032. [. . .]

99. "Nickel Vaudeville," *Variety (Var)* (17 March 1906), 4. For the trade weekly's initial distinction between "high-class" and "family" vaudeville, see *Variety* (30 December 1905), 6. That the "high-class" vaudeville circuits were in the process of establishing a giant combine that linked Keith's, Proctor's, Poli's, and the Western Orpheum theaters all together, with Keith as the central booking agent, may also have encouraged the development of both "family" vaudeville and moving picture theaters—see, for instance, "Keith and Proctor Unite," *New York Dramatic Mirror (NYDM)* (19 May 1906), 18; "Poli Joins the Merger," *NYDM* (26 May 1906), 18; and "The Big Merger Completed," *NYDM* (23 June 1906), 16.

100. George Kleine identified April 1906 as an important date in the emerging industry: because of the nickelodeons, film subjects began to acquire a much shortened "shelf life"—George Kleine, "Optical Projection in the Past Half Century," *SW* (27 June 1908), 15.

101. "Fire at the Circle Theatre," *Bill* (10 February 1906), 14; and "News," *VFI* (30 June 1906), 6.

102. See, for instance, "J. Austin Fynes Enterprises," *NYC* (17 March 1906), 108; "Nickel Theatre Pays Well," *Chicago Tribune* (8 April 1906), 3; "A General Outlook: Moving Pictures in Manhattan," *VFI* (12 May 1906), 4; and "Carl Laemmle Made Start in Chicago Storefront," *MPW* (15 July 1916), 420. [. . .]

103. "Louisville," *Bill* (7 April 1906), 12; "Miscellaneous," *Bill* (6 May 1906), 30; "Special Correspondence from Important Points" and "The Moving Picture Shows," *Bill* (12 May 1906), 8, 9, and 37; "Davis a Ten-Center," *Var* (31 May 1906), 13; and "Moving Picture Shows," *Bill* (29 December 1906), 41. [. . .]

104. Musser, *The Emergence of Cinema*, 425–427. [. . .]
105. "To Our Readers," *VFI* (30 June 1906), 3; and "Atlantic City," *Bill* (21 July 1906), 7. At least four new rental exchanges, all based in Chicago, began advertising in *Billboard* from April through June 1906: the American Film Company, the Inter-Ocean Film Exchange, the United States Film Exchange, and the Temple Film Company.
106. See, for instance, such family vaudeville houses as the Empire (Los Angeles), the Dewey (Oakland), the Dreamland (Decatur), the Electric Theatre (Waterloo), and the Zoo (Toledo), as reported in *New York Clipper* and *Billboard* throughout 1905. By October 1905, Davis also was using "cinemato-graph" to designate his film programs at the Grand in Pittsburgh—see "Pennsylvania," *NYC* (28 October 1905), 921.
107. See, for instance, the Kleine Optical ad in *NYC* (30 September 1905), 824; and the Miles Brothers ad in *Bill* (4 November 1905), 38. There were more than 200 Pathé titles listed in the Eugene Cline Catalog (Chicago, 1906), 19–20. Kleine Optical also singled out its Pathé films of "foreign" views for Hale's Tours, which the company originally had serviced at Electric Park in Kansas City in 1905—see the Kleine Optical ad in *Bill* (17 March 1906), 47.
108. See, for instance, the Pathé ads in *NYC* (30 December 1905), 1156; and in *Bill* (6 January 1906), 34.
109. Kleine, "Optical Projection in the Past Half Century," *SW* (27 June 1908), 15.
110. Throughout February 1906, according to its ads in *Billboard*, Pathé released two subjects per week.
111. "The Pictures: From the Standpoint of One Who Shows Them," *VFI* (19 May 1906), 6. The Muellers reported 200 moving picture machines then in operation at Coney Island, a figure that probably included those in penny arcades.
112. "Pat-Chats," *Bill* (1 July 1905), 3, and (15 July 1905), 3. Even Edison implicitly acknowledged the city's importance by listing its Chicago dealers first (they constituted fully one-third of the total) in an ad in *NYC* (9 December 1905), 1088.
113. See, for instance, the Pathé ads in *NYC* (30 September 1905), 828, (14 October 1905), 869, and (28 October 1905), 930.
114. "Moving Picture Makers Organize," *NYC* (23 December 1905), 1118.
115. See, for instance, the Pathé ads in *Phono-Ciné-Gazette* (1 October 1905), 209; and in *Bill* (10 March 1906), 40. [. . .]
116. "To Our Readers," *VFI* (9 June 1906), 3. [. . .]
117. See the Grand Theater ad in *Ore* (8 April 1906), 29.
118. "Editorial," *VFI* (28 July 1906), 3.
119. Throughout May and June, Pathé ads in *Views and Films Index* listed three to six new subjects per week. See, also, the Pathé ad in *VFI* (4 August 1906), 11. All this suggests that a relatively reliable distrib-ution system was in place by 1906 and that exhibitors now had advance notice each week of what film titles would be available and when. [. . .]
120. "Moving Pictures," *Bill* (13 October 1906), 21. This figure is for initial orders delivered from Paris, not for additional orders that may have been requested later for the more popular titles. If certain Edison films seem to have sold even more prints (the 1906 *Train Wreckers*, for instance, sold 157), that is because its figures were cumulative, covering one or more years—see Musser, *Before the Nickelodeon*, 317.
121. Musser, *Before the Nickelodeon*, 328. See, also, "Theatres and the Pictures: An Attitude Explained," *VFI* (7 September 1907), 3.
122. See *The Americanization of Edward Bok: The Autobiography of a Dutch Boy Fifty Years After* (New York: Scribner's, 1921)—quoted in Richard Ohmann, *Selling Culture: Magazines, Markets, and Class at the Turn of the Century* (London: Verso, 1996), 229. [. . .]

Chapter 7

BEN SINGER

MANHATTAN NICKELODEONS
New data on audiences and exhibitors

T HE NICKELODEON BOOM IN MANHATTAN was an extraordinary phenomenon. At the close of 1905 movies were still a relatively marginal amusement, filling brief slots at the end of vaudeville shows or running on Sundays in melodrama theaters that aimed to evade New York's blue laws against live performance. Two years later, nickelodeons had revolutionized urban recreation and altered the commercial landscape of Manhattan. Well over 300 small storefront movie theaters, known as "nickelodeons," and converted larger theaters screened movies full-time by 1908.

Early exhibition in Manhattan holds special interest for film history, not because it was necessarily the most extensive or important (although it may well have been, since New York City was the nation's commercial and cultural capital, as well as the center of the pre-Hollywood film industry) or because it was particularly representative of the emergence of cinema elsewhere in the country (recent historians have stressed different patterns of development in different cities and towns),[1] but rather because Manhattan's nickelodeon boom so often has functioned as historical shorthand for the rise of the movies in general. For most people, even those of us who know better, the image of cramped, dingy nickelodeons in Manhattan's Lower East Side ghetto stands as a symbol for the cinema's emergence in America. This synecdoche stems largely from the superficiality of traditional survey histories and perhaps, more generally, from the ideological convenience of the notion that the birth of mass entertainment in America took place at the gateway of the promised land, welling up "from below," from the lives of new immigrants and working people.

Because Manhattan's nickelodeon boom has played such a prominent role in shaping our conception of early film history, as well as American social history, it is crucial that we derive an accurate picture of that phenomenon. How big was the nickelodeon boom in Manhattan? What was the make-up of the nickelodeon's audience in terms of both class and ethnic composition? In what kinds of neighborhoods were nickelodeons located, and what explains their distribution? Who were the exhibitors? How stable was the nickelodeon business? These questions have remained unresolved for a surprisingly long time.

The issue of early cinema's class composition and orientation has been especially pivotal in recent historical work. Whereas traditional film histories (Jacobs, Hampton, Ramsaye, etc.)[2] framed early cinema as a lower-class amusement patronized predominantly by immigrants and workers (at least until after World War One), revisionist historians in the late seventies stressed the importance of middle-class audiences throughout the nickelodeon era and teens. The revisionist argument maintained that the middle class was at the cinema from virtually the very start, or at least the middle class managed to appropriate and "uplift" the cinema to suit its own tastes and objectives as soon as it realized how big the cinema actually was. Along with works by Russell Merritt and Lary May, Robert C. Allen's 1979 essay "Motion Picture Exhibition in Manhattan, 1906–1912: Beyond the Nickelodeon" deserves special recognition, in this context, as a key revisionist intervention.[3] More recently, several important works on early cinema (Burch, Stead, Hansen, and Uricchio and Pearson, among others) have absorbed aspects of this class scenario into their historical narratives, suggesting that the revisionist argument has evolved from a maverick position to a comfortable paradigm.[4]

The scholarly acceptance of the revisionist argument is due, at least in part, to its clear, if unstated, compatibility with familiar models of social power. On the one hand, the revisionist focus on the middle class's importance in the cultural arena fits the concept that America, the great melting pot, transformed itself in the early part of this century into a mass culture, consolidated under common middle-class tastes and values. On the other hand, the implication that the middle class "colonized" the cinema early on supports influential Marxist models of bourgeois domination and social control.[5] In addition to their theoretical appropriateness, revisionist histories were persuasive because they represented a new kind of film history committed to innovative empirical research. With their use of primary materials such as fire insurance maps, business directories, government documents, and daily newspapers, they seemed inherently more credible than the traditional survey histories, which tended not to bother about such things as supporting evidence or footnotes.

Primarily, however, the revisionist class argument has gained acceptance simply by default; that is, by virtue of the fact that little new evidence has surfaced to fuel debate about early cinema's social milieu. This essay aims to reopen the discussion. In several ways, my findings prompt one to reconsider the thrust of the revisionist argument. When one returns to the materials the revisionist histories draw on and takes advantage of more detailed historical data, significant problems and limitations in the revisionist research emerge. Reexamining early exhibition in Manhattan reminds us that recent film history – ostensibly historiographically aware history emphasizing primary research – cannot be taken at face value any more than the "old-fashioned" history it replaces.[6]

How big a boom?

The first step in examining early audiences and exhibitors is to determine the number and locations of movie theaters. Recently discovered evidence suggests that nickelodeons were far more abundant in Manhattan than scholars have assumed. Roberta Pearson and William Uricchio have found a handwritten memo from New York's police commissioner to Mayor McClellan dated December 11, 1908 (a couple of weeks before the mayor's famous Christmas Eve closing of every nickelodeon in the city), that enumerates the number of movie theaters in Manhattan and the other boroughs.[7] For Manhattan, the memo counts 194 "common shows" (ordinary nickelodeons), 93 "concert moving pictures" (vaudeville theaters that had switched over to mixed bills or to movies altogether), and 28 "theaters with moving pictures" (theaters that interspersed runs of plays and films, or theaters that had switched over to movies altogether but whose more expensive theatrical license had yet to expire). In total, the memo counts 315 theaters in Manhattan.[8]

This number is significantly larger than the figure of 123 movie theaters cited in Robert C. Allen's article. Allen's primary source for locating nickelodeons was the 1908 edition of

Trow's Business Directory of Greater New York. This directory is an extraordinary historical resource, and Allen deserves credit for unearthing it in the context of film history. But in light of the police commissioner's memo, it appears that *Trow's 1908* listed only about two-fifths of the movie theaters operating in Manhattan in 1908. A number of factors might account for the incompleteness of the *Trow's* listing. Perhaps a respectable business directory like *Trow's* was reluctant to list hole-in-the-wall, fly-by-night ghetto theaters. A more likely explanation is that the 1908 edition probably documented an earlier, smaller-scale phase of the nickelodeon boom in New York. There was apparently a lag between the time the listings were compiled and the time they were published. *Trow's 1908* was probably prepared in mid-1907 and released later that year.[9]

Unfortunately, one cannot simply turn to the police commissioner's memo as the basis for research into the early theaters, since the memo lists no addresses, theater names, or other information – just a single sum next to each type of theater. One can compile a fairly comprehensive record of Manhattan nickelodeons in 1908, however, by supplementing the *Trow's 1908* listings with the directory's 1909 listings and then also including information found in ledgers of building permits maintained by the New York Bureau of Buildings.[10] In addition, trade journal articles and books from the period contain scattered information on theater locations. Using all these sources, I have been able to locate 221 movie theaters. This number is still only about 70 percent of the 315 theaters counted in the police commissioner's memo. Moreover, unlike the police commissioner's count (which one presumes was up-to-date as of the time it was compiled), my enumeration does not give us a snapshot of exhibition at any one point in time. The data I use reflect listings of theaters made over a two-year period, and, as I will discuss later, many of the theaters recorded in the early part of that period had gone out of business by the time others opened up.[11] I will assume, however, that my expanded list provides a reasonably faithful representation of the exhibition situation between mid-1907 and mid-1909. The information we have on the 221 theaters constitutes a rich basis for a more accurate historical analysis of early movie theaters and their audiences. (Figure 7.1 gives an overview of theater locations.)[12]

A middle-class audience?

[. . .] At the heart of the image of nickelodeons in traditional histories is an assertion about class: movies were a proletarian amusement; proper middle-class types stayed away, at least until after World War One. A passage from Lewis Jacobs's 1939 survey *The Rise of the American Film* exemplifies the traditional scenario: "Concentrated largely in poorer shopping districts and slum neighborhoods, nickelodeons were disdained by the well-to-do. But the workmen and their families who patronized the movies did not mind the crowded, unsanitary, and hazardous accommodations most of the nickelodeons offered."[13] How accurate is this historical sketch? Descriptions such as this one prompt Robert C. Allen to contend that the "accounts of early motion picture exhibition contained in secondary sources are grossly inadequate." Allen argues that neither were nickelodeons and larger theaters (often overlooked in traditional film histories) concentrated primarily in ghetto neighborhoods, nor did they cater solely to a proletarian audience. Movies, he suggests, attracted a middle-class audience throughout the nickelodeon era and early teens.

Allen bases his argument largely on research into the location of early movie theaters in Manhattan (as well as research on the role of vaudeville in early exhibition). Using *Trow's 1908*, Allen finds that, contrary to the impression generally given by traditional histories, the majority of nickelodeons were located outside the Lower East Side ghetto, many in putatively middle-

Figure 7.1
Map of Manhattan
nickelodeons, 1907–1909

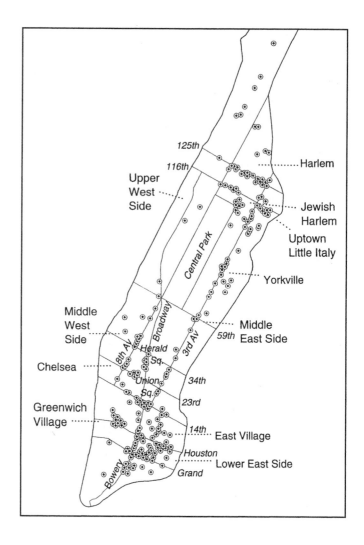

class neighborhoods or in traditional entertainment districts that presumably served a variety of social types. "In terms of social class," he argues, "more nickelodeons were located in or near middle-class neighborhoods than in the Lower East Side ghetto."[14]

In one respect, Allen's statement is correct: theaters in the Lower East Side and Union Square area, while by far the thickest concentration, constituted only about 40 percent of Manhattan's total number of movie theaters. Allen's research is more centrally interested in the remaining 60 percent, however, since he believes these call into question the traditional characterization of the nickelodeon's working-class and immigrant foundation. Allen maintains that "nickelodeons were not just located in working-class neighborhoods. They seemed to be clustered in middle-class sectors, as well as *certain* poor neighborhoods."[15]

The key areas in question are four uptown neighborhoods: Little Italy, Jewish Harlem, the Upper East Side (or Yorkville), and Harlem proper. Allen implies that these neighborhoods were middle class and, by implication, that the nickelodeons found there were frequented by middle-class patrons. Unfortunately, Allen may have been a bit hasty in characterizing as middle class immigrant neighborhoods whose class compositions in 1908 were ambiguous at best. For example, solely on the basis of a brief 1899 description of the picturesque qualities of uptown

Manhattan's Little Italy (an area roughly bounded by Third Avenue and the East River between 100th and 120th Streets), Allen suggests that this area was "much more affluent than the immigrant ghettoes of Lower Manhattan." The quotation, from E. Idell Zeisloft's monumental book *The New Metropolis*, describes Little Italy as "one of the most flourishing and picturesque Italian colonies in New York . . . The tenements that line these streets are not much to look at in themselves, but the quaintly furnished rooms in them . . . the gay lines of wash, the small shops and street scenes make up a picture that never loses interest . . . These are the peaceful Italians from the north of Italy, and the stiletto is rarely brought into play here."[16] While Zeisloft found the neighborhood colorful, quaint, and unthreatening, there is nothing in the description to establish Little Italy as a middle-class area. The passage is typical of a bourgeois touristic interest in the "old world charm" of immigrant community life.[17] But elsewhere in the book Zeisloft takes a different stance, stating that Little Italy's "tremendous population is increasing every year, and promising to engulf the neat dwellings and drive out the better population . . . Reformers and philanthropists regard this growing colony with dismay . . . This uptown foreign colony bids fair to present extreme difficulties in the near future."[18] Other descriptions and statistics are even more decisive in portraying the area as an out-and-out slum. Harlem historian Gilbert Osofsky, for example, writes:

> In the less attractive areas of Harlem on the periphery of the middle-class community lived people by-passed by Harlem's late nineteenth-century affluence. Italians crowded in "common tenements" . . . In the 1890's the poverty of "Harlem's Little Italy" seemed a glaring incongruity in a neighborhood known as the home of "the great middle-class population" . . . Italians were the first New Immigrant group to come to Harlem and a source of embarrassment and displeasure to the richer people who lived nearby. The smells that emanated from their "vile tenements," one critic said in 1894, "annoyed their brownstone neighbors" . . . "Here can be found the refuse of Italy making a poor living on the refuse from Harlem ashbarrels," a caustic reporter commented.[19]

Thomas Kessner's *The Golden Door: Italian and Jewish Immigrant Mobility in New York City 1880–1915* gives information about uptown Little Italy's class profile. Drawing on federal census data, Kessner found that in 1905 over 85 percent of members of Italian households in the neighborhood worked in blue-collar jobs. One person in seven worked in a low white-collar occupation (such as small shopkeeper or salesperson), and only one person in one hundred held a high white-collar professional or business position.[20] Uptown Little Italy was also very densely populated, containing as many as 637 people per acre. The enclave was, in fact, considerably more crowded than any part of Lower Manhattan's Italian sections.[21] These findings hardly convey the image of a middle-class community. The class composition of moviegoers in uptown Little Italy was probably very similar to that generally assumed for nickelodeons in the downtown ghetto.

The characterization of Jewish Harlem as a middle-class neighborhood is more understandable, since in the 1890s many of the more affluent Russian Jews did in fact leave the Lower East Side and settle in this area surrounding the northeast corner of Central Park, between 98th and 118th Streets. But the neighborhood's class profile changed so rapidly during the next decade that by the time nickelodeons sprouted there, it was probably no longer thought of as a middle-class area. Jeffrey S. Gurock, in his scholarly history of Jewish Harlem, notes the influx of poorer Jews from the Lower East Side and the simultaneous exodus of the middle class:

Once-ideal or acceptable residential areas were almost overnight beset with problems common to all heavily populated areas, and lost much of their glamour. Such was the case with [the area] that had attracted most of Harlem's early more affluent Russian-Jewish settlers. It was inundated by thousands of poorer Jewish settlers; they settled in the new tenements built on previously vacant lands or which replaced the small private dwellings that had dotted Fifth and Madison Avenues' landscape. By 1910, this once moderately populated section of uptown contained population densities in excess of 480 and 560 persons per acre. As the neighborhood began to be weighed down by overcrowding, East Harlem's white-collar class began leaving for new, better accommodations . . . And their old neighborhood was quickly proletarianized. The basic shift both in general neighborhood composition and in the Russian-Jewish economic profile was well under way as early as 1905.[22]

Gurock's sample of census data reveals that working-class residents outnumbered middle-class residents in 1905, and one can assume the blue-collar proportion continued to grow rapidly thereafter as the middle class fled to better neighborhoods. Its population was made up mainly of tailors and various kinds of garment workers (by far the largest occupations among the Jewish residents), cigar makers, upholsterers, carpenters, masons, small shopkeepers, clerks, salespeople, and peddlers. Very few residents held professional or high white-collar positions (about one household head in ten in the blocks near Central Park; about one in fifty in the blocks farther away from the park).[23] Statistics do, however, show a relatively high number of low white-collar workers – somewhere between one-quarter to two-fifths of Jewish Harlem's household heads were classified as such in 1905. The presence of these low white-collar workers might lead one to infer that Jewish Harlem had a degree of affluence approaching middle-class status. But two points contradict such an assessment. First, Jewish Harlem's occupational/class breakdown evidently was not very different from that of the Lower East Side ghetto,[24] and second, most of these low white-collar positions were socioeconomically closer to high blue-collar jobs than to high white-collar professions. Most clerks, bookkeepers, small merchants, cashiers, dealers, and peddlers (which, strangely enough, are listed as low white collar in the standard occupational classification) earned roughly the same (and often less) than their neighbors in skilled blue-collar trades (such as textile workers, carpenters, and masons) or even than those in semiskilled jobs (like teamsters, longshoremen, and janitors).[25] Although perhaps not a bona fide ghetto, Jewish Harlem could be described as a predominantly working-class neighborhood, with some lower middle-class pockets.

The third ostensibly middle-class area Allen discusses is Yorkville, an area between Third Avenue and the river roughly between 69th and 94th Streets.[26] The only evidence Allen gives to suggest this area was middle class is a single-line secondary-source quotation stating that "many of the residents were small merchants or tradesmen."[27] Considering that the same could be said of the Lower East Side ghetto, this description is not enough to establish Yorkville as a middle-class neighborhood. Zeisloft's The New Metropolis, which gives an almost street-by-street account of the city, reveals a rather mixed and unstable class profile for the area, at least in 1899. Third Avenue, bustling with small shops, restaurants, and pubs in the shadow of the elevated railway, he describes as "several degrees above the slums, with many prosperous businessmen and much gaiety." But Second Avenue, also under an elevated railway, was "a characterless street of insignificant shops, and the homes of mechanics and laborers," while First Avenue was "from start to finish, an avenue of the poor [primarily] German and Hebrew working people." As for the cross streets, respectable tenements and apartments prevailed between 69th and 72nd Streets. But the next nine blocks, between 73rd and 81st Streets, contained "tenements, varying from poor to good," with those near Third Avenue "having a general likeness to the downtown slums." The tenements on the next three blocks "could not be called slums and are yet commonplace." 89th Street all the way to 103rd Street was comprised of "tenements of the poorest class."[28] If Zeisloft's descriptions were still accurate in 1910 (as we have seen, a neighborhood could change a lot in ten years), it seems fair to call Yorkville a mixed-class area, predominated by the working class but also containing a fairly significant lower-middle-class minority.[29] [. . .]

The fourth uptown neighborhood Allen points to is Harlem proper. Harlem's main artery, 125th Street, was, as a contemporaneous travel guide noted, "the busiest business and theatrical center in Manhattan, north of Central Park."[30] Seventeen nickelodeons and larger theaters showing mixed bills of vaudeville and movies crowded along 125th Street between Third and Eighth Avenues. Most of these theaters were between Third and Lenox, a strip in which, according to the guidebook, "most of the shops are small and a large proportion of the dealers, and also of the purchasers, are Hebrews." In 1910, Harlem was a neighborhood in transition. In the 1880s and 1890s it was widely recognized as a genteel middle-class neighborhood offering a balance between suburban openness and urban convenience. Many middle-class families – largely native-born Americans, along with Irish, Germans, and German Jews – still lived there in 1910 (although they would not remain there long).[31] But already by 1899, Zeisloft noted the emergence of "cheap tenements," particularly below 125th Street, and bemoaned that "there is little left to remind one of old Harlem." "Eventually," he predicted, "this region will be given over to the poor."[32] The neighborhood's transformation was hastened when the speculative real estate fever that seized Harlem between 1900 and about 1905 (catalyzed by the planning of subway lines) suddenly went bust. Developers realized too late that Harlem was overbuilt, that the rents they sought were too high, and that the demand for middle-class houses and apartments was simply insufficient to fill all the vacancies. The recession of 1907–8 made matters worse. Forced to compete for tenants, landlords reduced rents and accepted working-class and immigrant tenants. In addition to the expansion of the Italian and Russian Jewish population below 125th Street, an African-American center grew rapidly a few blocks above it. Already by 1913, white businessmen and residents were declaring, "Harlem has been devastated as a result of the steady influx of Negroes"; "The best of Harlem is gone"; "We are approaching a crisis: it is a question of whether the white man will rule Harlem or the negro."[33]

Harlem in the nickelodeon-boom years was a socioeconomically mixed neighborhood, comprised of a residual middle-class and an emergent working-class population. The nickelodeons along 125th Street thus raise a methodological question about our ability to infer the composition of nickelodeon audiences from the composition of the population at large. While it seems reasonable to assume some degree of correspondence between the kind of neighborhood a nickelodeon inhabited and the kind of patrons it drew, it is hard to know how close such correlations actually were. [. . .] The composition of movie audiences may not always have exactly mirrored the composition of the outside neighborhood. This uncertainty is particularly pertinent in business and entertainment centers like Times Square, 23rd Street, and Union Square – and 125th Street – where the population was relatively transient and socially heterogeneous. It is difficult in such cases to know whether the middle class ventured into the nickelodeons with any regularity.

This review of the socioeconomic character of uptown neighborhoods suggests that Allen may have misconstrued the nickelodeon's social context. While his initial point is worth underscoring – traditional histories were misleading in suggesting that movie exhibition was simply a phenomenon of the Lower East Side ghetto – the broader implication that many theaters were located in middle-class areas may be equally misleading.

Why were nickelodeons where they were?

A range of factors shaped the distribution of nickelodeons in Manhattan: neighborhood class, population density, ethnic concentration, municipal codes and regulations, transportation patterns, the availability of commercial space, rent rates, and so on. These factors, among others, combined in different ways in different neighborhoods to create conditions that either fostered or discouraged the opening of nickelodeons.

Although a multidimensional approach is needed, population density appears to be the best predictor of nickelodeon distribution. Nickelodeons invariably clustered in the densest areas of the city – densest either in terms of residential concentration or volume of pedestrian traffic. The constant stream of potential customers in commercial districts like Union Square, Herald Square, 23rd Street, and 125th Street obviously accounts for the abundance of nickelodeons and larger movie theaters found there. As for neighborhood nickelodeons (by far the majority of movie theaters in Manhattan), they were almost always located in neighborhoods with high residential densities (at least 300 persons per acre) spread over a substantial number of blocks (at least fifteen or twenty). The greater the density and the wider the area, the greater the number of nickelodeons. Areas that did not meet these minimum requirements (the Upper West Side, for example) contained only a few nickelodeons here and there. [. . .] Market forces appear to have found a level of nickelodeon saturation that was commercially sustainable under the demographic and logistical conditions of these neighborhoods.[34]

Two neighborhoods had significantly fewer nickelodeons relative to their populations. The middle part of the East Side contained 7 nickelodeons scattered along Third Avenue, translating into 1 for every 13,000 people. The neighborhood just north – the Yorkville area (between 69th and 94th Streets) – contained quite a few nickelodeons along Third and Second Avenues (at least 14), but this number was relatively low in light of the area's large and dense population. The ratio translates to 1 nickelodeon for every 13,500 people.

The discrepancy between these East Side neighborhoods and the others in Manhattan indicates that population density was not the only factor determining the location of nickelodeons. Social class may be crucial in explaining why the East Side had relatively few nickelodeons per capita. As I mentioned earlier, Yorkville was a socially mixed neighborhood and as such it may well have had a greater proportion of lower-middle- or middle-class individuals than those areas with greater concentrations of nickelodeons. Perhaps there were fewer nickelodeons there because these classes tended to steer clear of them, viewing them as a somewhat unsavory lower-class haunt. Such a hypothesis would obviously run counter to the revisionist emphasis on the nickelodeon's multiclass appeal.

Who went to the movies? Ethnic composition and variation in movie-going

We know very little about the ethnic composition of early audiences, although the generalization that "new" immigrants from Eastern and Southern Europe comprised a large proportion of moviegoers is common. Two basic questions need to be explored: Who formed the primary audience for nickelodeons? And were there significant differences in movie attendance among different ethnic groups, that is, did the values, attitudes, and other social and cultural circumstances relating to ethnic identity influence how different ethnic groups responded to the nickelodeon?

Since, as far as I know, there are no survey data on the ethnic composition of New York movie audiences in the nickelodeon era, another approach to the issue is necessary. Presumably, as with the question of class composition, one could gain insight into the ethnic makeup of movie audiences (at least at neighborhood nickelodeons) by determining the ethnic makeup of the areas in which nickelodeons were located. Although neighborhood ethnic composition may not automatically have translated into movie-audience composition, it is probably fair to assume a relatively close connection in most cases. [. . .]

Historians working on New York City around 1910 are fortunate because a progressive philanthropist named Walter Laidlaw paid for a team of thirteen clerks to spend a year rearranging and recounting the federal census data into aggregates covering about eight city blocks each. *Statistical Sources for Demographic Studies of Greater New York*, published in 1913 by the New York Federation of Churches, divides Manhattan into 224 tracts and gives the population of over 35 different immigrant groups for each, along with figures for "Native Whites of Native Parentage" and "Negroes." (This extraordinary source also provides statistics on sex, population density, literacy, education, and voter registration, among other things.)[35] With this detailed picture of Manhattan's ethnic landscape, one can infer the ethnic breakdown of moviegoing in Manhattan as a whole, as well as in specific neighborhoods.

The majority of nickelodeons were in overwhelmingly Jewish areas (the Lower East Side and East Harlem), so one can assume that Jews constituted the largest sector of Manhattan's nickelodeon audience. This fact probably had much less to do with any inherently greater receptivity among Jews than with the commercial logic of putting nickelodeons in thickly populated areas. These areas were the two largest and most densely populated residential neighborhoods in the city. But Jews by no means had a monopoly on moviegoing. As I will discuss shortly, many nickelodeons catered to Italian customers, both in Lower Manhattan and in Uptown Little Italy. Moreover, both the Middle West Side and the East Side contained a diversity of ethnic groups and so too, presumably, did the nickelodeons located there.

An examination of the East Side's ethnic makeup brings into focus the second question posed above, concerning whether certain ethnic groups were significantly more or less receptive to early movie exhibition than others. To what extent did the ethnic character of the East Side (both Yorkville and the Middle East Side) account for the fact that proportionately fewer nickelodeons were located there? Is it possible that ethnicity helps explain why the East Side had a relatively low number of nickelodeons per capita?

The East Side's ethnic composition was very different from the main areas where nickelodeons were clustered. For one thing, it was much less homogeneous. The nickelodeon-rich Jewish and Italian neighborhoods tended to be extremely homogeneous (as high as 90 to 95 percent), whereas in the East Side no one ethnic group constituted more than 20 percent of the population. Furthermore, a very different assortment of ethnic groups lived in the East Side. The area was composed of a mix of Germans (20 percent), Irish (18 percent), Austrians (probably from Bohemia, now part of the Czech Republic) (13 percent), and Americans ("Native Whites of Native Parents") (12 percent). Italians, Hungarians, and Russians (probably Russian Jews) each constituted about 6 or 7 percent.[36] One is tempted to conclude, therefore, that the ethnic groups on the East Side were somewhat less avid moviegoers than the Jews and Italians in Lower Manhattan and East Harlem. But such a conclusion is hardly clear cut, since one still wonders whether the area's class profile, rather than its ethnic makeup, was primarily responsible for its relatively low number of nickelodeons.

This question might be answered by comparing the populations of the East Side and Middle West Side. The residential core of the Middle West Side had many more nickelodeons per capita than the East Side. But its ethnic mix resembled the East Side's in certain respects. Like the East Side, the Middle West Side was comprised largely of Irish (26 percent), Americans (18 percent), and Germans (13 percent). Since these ethnic groups inhabited both areas, the difference in the number of nickelodeons per capita between the two areas probably resulted more directly from the fact that the Middle West Side (which contained the notorious "Hell's Kitchen" section, as well as a number of predominantly African-American blocks) was a much poorer neighborhood than the East Side. This comparison points to class, rather than ethnicity, as the key factor.

The issue is still open to argument, however, since the Middle West Side's population was not simply a carbon copy of the East Side. One of every three inhabitants of the East Side was German or Austrian/Bohemian, whereas in the Middle West Side fewer than one in seven was. Perhaps the "upright" German immigrant community found the nickelodeon unappealing, particularly in light of its association with newer and poorer immigrants such as the Italians and East European Jews. On the other hand, according to Zeisloft, the "frightfully clannish" Bohemians "refuse to mingle with any but their own . . . [and are] almost untouched by the [Americanizing] influences that are refining most of the other foreign colonies."[37] Perhaps they stayed away from nickelodeons due to an antiassimilationist cultural attitude. These hypotheses remain speculative at this point. It may be prudent simply to conclude that while there is no overwhelming evidence of ethnic variation in moviegoing, differences in ethnic identity may have had at least *some* influence on the distribution of nickelodeons in Manhattan. The topic needs further research.[38] [. . .]

Who got into the nickelodeon business? The ethnicity of exhibitors

The mythology of early cinema has traditionally emphasized the prominence of Jews as exhibitors, in part because a number of Hollywood moguls (such as William Fox, Adolph Zukor, and Marcus Loew) began as small-time nickelodeon owners in New York City. As far as I know, however, no study has tried to substantiate this notion with statistics on the ethnic makeup of exhibitors. The information in *Trow's* 1908 and 1909 directories gives us a clearer picture of the ethnic makeup of New York exhibitors. While the *Trow's* listings do not, of course, overtly specify the ethnicity of exhibitors, they do list most of them by name. Using standard genealogical reference tools, one is able to determine ethnic descent with reasonable accuracy.[39]

The results confirm that the large majority of early exhibitors in Manhattan were indeed Jewish. Of the 189 exhibitors listed by name in *Trow's*, Jews accounted for 112, or 60 percent. Italians follow with 18 percent of the named exhibitors, individuals of English/American descent 14 percent, and Irish 7 percent. A handful of exhibitors of French, German, and Scandinavian descent make up the remaining 2 or 3 percent.[40] These numbers differ in interesting ways from the ethnic breakdown of Manhattan's population at large, in which Jews comprised only about 25 percent; English and "Native Whites of Native Parentage" constituted about 17 percent; Italians and Irish 13 percent each; and Germans 10 percent.[41] We thus see that Jews became exhibitors in disproportionately large numbers. Italians and English/Americans got into the exhibition business in numbers that roughly reflected their relative proportion of the total population (Italians a bit more, English/Americans a bit less). Irish were under-represented among exhibitors; and Germans were not at all inclined toward nickelodeon entrepreneurship.

The large majority of exhibitors appear to have been small-time businessmen (and a few women)[42] running only one theater. But signs of consolidation were already apparent before 1910. About one-fifth of Manhattan's movie theaters belonged to small- to medium-sized chains. Several of the early theater moguls are well known: William Fox owned eight theaters; Marcus Loew owned eight as well (most under the People's Vaudeville name); Adolph Zukor owned six (most named Automatic Vaudeville); F. S. Proctor owned four (most named Bijou Dream). But others have been totally forgotten: J. Valensi owned five theaters; the partnership of McCarn and Weissman owned five; and Morris Boom owned four. A few other exhibitors, such as Lawrence Bolognino, Tomasi Cassesi, Stephen Scherer, and Adolph Weiss, each operated two or three nickelodeons.[43] [. . .]

How volatile was the nickelodeon business?

While the phrase "nickelodeon boom" conveys a sense of unmitigated commercial expansion, the nickelodeon business was in fact extremely risky and unstable. For the 1907 to 1910 period (and probably later as well), the phrase "nickelodeon bust" would better apply to the experience of many fledgling exhibitors. The notion that anyone with the wherewithal to rent a store, a projector, and some chairs could capitalize on the movie craze is mistaken, at least regarding Manhattan. Scores of exhibitors went out of business every year, while at the same time dozens of others ventured into the game. The nickelodeon business was in a state of constant upheaval during these years.

In June 1908, the trade journal *Moving Picture World* began noting the large number of nickelodeon failures in Manhattan:

> Each week brings to light a list of moving picture places that have passed into the hands of the sheriff . . . Poor locations, bad management and a score or more of other contingencies develop in the picture line with the same frequency that they do in any commercial business. In many cases, failures are due to a bad start. Too many people imagine that all they need is sufficient money to fit up a place and pay the first week's expenses. They count upon the receipts to do the rest. The men who win out on this policy are few.[44]

In September of that year, *Moving Picture World* estimated that in just three months over 100 nickelodeons had gone out of business in New York. The journal suggested that most of these failures were suffered by "people who rushed into the business, selecting poor locations where the audiences were not to be had."[45] These conditions were still being noted eight months later, in May 1909: "A number of picture places in Greater New York are steadily falling by the wayside," the journal observed. The writer pointed to increasingly stringent building and fire department regulations as a major cause, but he also stated that "a good many people who were in the game solely for the coin have justly been driven back to their peanut and lemonade stands."[46] One wonders what motives for getting into the game other than "the coin" the writer had in mind; in any case, he appears to have been stressing the high failure rate among small-timers drawn to movie exhibition as a get-rich-quick scheme.

The *Trow's* data reveal a clear picture of the nickelodeon business's extraordinary instability. By comparing the addresses listed in the 1908 and 1909 editions, one can determine the number of exhibitor failures, start-ups, and turnovers. Of the 117 exhibitors listed in *Trow's* 1908, only 52 (44 percent) were also listed a year later. Unless other reasons explain why certain exhibitors were not relisted, it appears that more than *half* of all nickelodeons open in mid to late 1907 had gone out of business by mid to late 1908 (when the 1909 listing was probably compiled). Interestingly, only a handful of theaters appear to have changed hands from one owner to another. The vast majority (93 percent) of the nickelodeons that went out of business in 1908 appear to have gone under for good, rather than reopening under new management. This may suggest the bare-bones quality of the failing nickelodeons: perhaps so few continued as movie theaters because they really were not theaters in any real sense of the word – just storefront rooms with folding chairs.

At the same time that so many nickelodeons were closing, scores of new nickelodeons were continually opening and a number of preexisting theaters were converted into movie houses. *Trow's* 1909 directory contains seventy-one locations that were not in the previous year's listing. Thus, even with the disappearance of half the 1907–8 nickelodeons, the total number of movie theaters in Manhattan had increased by about 10 percent by 1908–9.

Conclusions

The evidence brought to light in this essay gives us a picture of the commercial, socioeconomic, and ethnic dimensions of early exhibition in Manhattan different from those conveyed in previous histories. (1) Census data on the composition of Manhattan neighborhoods call into question the revisionist argument about the importance of middle-class audiences in the nickelodeon era and early teens. While traditional survey histories were indeed "grossly inadequate" due to their superficiality, their emphasis on the immigrant and working-class foundation of early exhibition may not have been as far off the mark as revisionist historians maintain. (2) Demographic data on Manhattan's population and more detailed (but still not complete) information on the locations of nickelodeons suggest that population density and social class were major factors determining the concentration of early movie theaters. Ethnic identity was also a factor, but it is still unclear how much influence it exerted. Although the majority of nickelodeons were located in areas inhabited mainly by Jews (due mainly to population density), there is only limited evidence to suggest any significant variation in moviegoing among different ethnic groups. [. . .] (3) There was, however, significant ethnic variation in patterns of nickelodeon entrepreneurship. Jews became exhibitors in disproportionately high numbers, and Germans steered clear of the business. (4) A comparison of theater addresses in listings from 1908 and 1909 indicates that, contrary to the popular conception, the nickelodeon era was an extremely unstable period for exhibitors: there was an almost fifty-fifty chance that a nickelodeon operating at the end of 1907 would be out of business a year later.

Until further research is undertaken, we have no way of knowing how closely other American cities paralleled the commercial, socioeconomic, and ethnic patterns of the Manhattan nickelodeon boom. What is apparent from this case study, however, is that future research must delve deeper into demographic data and commercial records than have previous generations of film history.

Notes

This essay has been abbreviated from the *Cinema Journal* original. The original essay also included six neighbourhood-level maps showing nickelodeon locations.

1. Robert C. Allen and Douglas Gomery, *Film History: Theory and Practice* (New York: McGraw-Hill, 1985), 202–7; Charles Musser, *The Emergence of Cinema* (New York: Charles Scribner's Sons, 1990), chap. 13; Gregory Waller, *Main Street Amusements: Movies and Commercial Entertainment in Lexington, Kentucky, 1896–1930* (Washington, DC: Smithsonian Institution Press, 1995).

2. Lewis Jacobs, *The Rise of the American Film* (New York: Harcourt Brace, 1939); Benjamin Hampton, *A History of the Movies* (New York: Covici, Friede Publishers, 1931), reprinted as *History of the American Film Industry: From Its Beginnings to 1931* (New York: 1970); Terry Ramsaye, *A Million and One Nights: A History of the Motion Picture through 1925* (New York: Simon and Schuster, 1926).

3. Russell Merritt, "Nickelodeon Theaters 1905–1914: Building an Audience for the Movies," in Tino Balio, ed., *The American Film Industry* (Madison: University of Wisconsin Press, 1976, rev. ed. 1985); Lary May, *Screening Out the Past: The Birth of Mass Culture and the Motion Picture Industry* (New York: Oxford University Press, 1980); Robert C. Allen, "Motion Picture Exhibition in Manhattan, 1906–1912: Beyond the Nickelodeon," *Cinema Journal* 18, no. 2 (spring 1979): 2–15, reprinted in John Fell, ed., *Film before Griffith* (Berkeley: University of California Press, 1983). Allen recapitulates the main points of his essay in Allen and Comery, *Film History*, 203–5.

4. Noël Burch, "Business Is Business: An Invisible Audience," in *Life to Those Shadows* (Berkeley: University of California Press, 1990); Peter Stead, *Film and the Working Class: The Feature Film in British and American Society* (London: Routledge, 1989), chaps. 1 and 2; Miriam Hansen, *Babel and Babylon: Spectatorship in American Silent Film* (Cambridge: Harvard University Press, 1991), chap. 2; William Uricchio and Roberta Pearson, *Reframing Culture: The Case of the Vitagraph Quality Films* (Princeton: Princeton University Press, 1993); Anton Kaes, "Mass Culture and Modernity: Notes toward a Social History of Early American and German Cinema," in Frank Trommler and Joseph McVeigh, eds, *America and the Germans: An Assessment of a Three-Hundred-Year History* (Philadelphia: University of Pennsylvania Press, 1985), Vol. 2: 317–31. All of these works appear to accept the revisionist argument about class more or less as a given. Uricchio and Pearson, however, base their discussion primarily on their own research on a body of "uplift" films.

5. Robert Sklar makes this observation in "*Oh! Althusser!*: Historiography and the Rise of Cinema Studies," in Sklar and Musser, eds, *Resisting Images: Essays on Cinema and History* (Philadelphia: Temple University Press, 1990).

6. My critique of revisionist film history emphasizes Robert C. Allen's work on early exhibition in Manhattan. I should stress that I single it out as a target of criticism simply because of its importance as the only prior serious work on this topic. Allen's study was a pioneering effort in empirical film history and has inspired a generation of scholars to dig deeper into primary historical documents. My study could not have been written without Allen's initial contribution.

7. George B. McClellan Jr Papers, Container 4 (1908), Manuscript Division, Library of Congress. I would like to thank Pearson and Uricchio for sharing this item of evidence with me. Their forthcoming book on the municipal regulation of movie exhibition in New York will illuminate mechanisms of social control from both empirical and theoretical perspectives.

8. The police commissioner's count of common shows is more or less corroborated by a municipal audit I have found indicating that the Bureau of Licenses issued or renewed 238 common-show licenses in 1908 for nickelodeons in Manhattan and the Bronx (grouped together in this report). It seems reasonable to assume that at least 194 of these common-show nickelodeons were in Manhattan proper. Commissioners of Accounts of New York City, "A Report on the Bureau of Licenses, an Audit of Receipts for the Period from July 1, 1907, to Dec 31, 1908" (New York: December 22, 1909), 37. The report lists issues and renewals of common-show licenses for all boroughs, broken down into three six-month periods. It is in the New York City Municipal Archives. Throughout this essay, I use the word "nickelodeon" to refer to any movie theater, including large theaters that converted from stage shows to movies. It could be objected that this general usage of "nickelodeon" obscures the distinction between cheap storefronts and grander venues. In the 1907 to 1909 period (and perhaps beyond), however, most of the larger theaters that switched, such as the 14th Street Theater or the Grand Opera House, were playing popular melodrama and had already lost any refinement they once might have had. The difference in theater size would probably not have pointed to significant differences in the audiences or qualities of the show.

9. In support of the publication-lag hypothesis, one notes that the 1907 edition of *Trow's* lists only a handful of exhibitors, although the nickelodeon boom was already in full swing by then. I've also found that most of the nickelodeons cited in trade journal articles or city records from 1908 don't show up in *Trow's* until the 1909 edition.

10. Bureau of Buildings, Annual Ledgers for Alterations and New Buildings. Located in the New York City Municipal Archive. These city records, for both alterations and new construction, indicate the kind of buildings involved (moving picture theaters are named as such), addresses, owners, architects, dimensions, durations, and costs of the construction activity.

11. If the police commissioner had counted all nickelodeons that had ever operated in Manhattan between 1907 and the end of 1908, instead of just those that existed the week he made his report, the count would have been significantly higher than the 315 his memo records. One assumes that the police commissioner had relatively accurate information on the number of nickelodeons actually in operation in mid-December 1908; however, his memo gives no indication of how he made his count. If he relied on records of the Bureau of Licenses (now, sadly, destroyed), which probably would not have been kept up to date about nickelodeon closings, the information might not have been so accurate.

12. Space limitations unfortunately prevent me from including full information on the 1907 to 1909 theaters. I have created a database table including theater names, addresses, cross-streets, exhibitor names, exhibitor ethnicity, and source of documentation. [. . .]

13. Jacobs, *The Rise of the American Film*, 56.

14. Allen, in Allen and Gomery, *Film History*, 202.

15. Ibid., 204.

16. E. Idell Zeisloft, *The New Metropolis* (New York: D. Appleton and Co., 1899), quoted in Grace Mayer, *Once upon a City* (New York: Macmillan, 1958), 138, and by Allen, "Motion Picture Exhibition in Manhattan," 167.

17. Compare, for example, the opening paragraph of Emily Wayland Dinwiddie, "Some Aspects of Italian Housing and Social Conditions in Philadelphia." Before turning to a discussion of the neighborhood's congestion and poverty, Dinwiddie writes, "Philadelphia's 'Little Italy' is one of the most picturesque sections of the city. For about thirty-five blocks the Italians are closely packed together. One can walk the streets for considerable distances without hearing a word of English. The black-eyed children rolling and tumbling together, the gaily colored dresses of the women and the crowds of street vendors all give the neighborhood a wholly foreign appearance." *Charities*, May 7, 1904, 48.

18. Zeisloft, *The New Metropolis*, 528.

19. Gilbert Osofsky, *Harlem, the Making of a Ghetto: Negro New York, 1890–1930* (New York: Harper and Row, 1963), 82.

20. Thomas Kessner, *The Golden Door: Italian and Jewish Immigrant Mobility in New York City 1880–1915* (New York: Oxford University Press, 1977). Census statistics, 124, table 24. Little Italy corresponds to Assembly District 32. A map indicating assembly district boundaries in Manhattan is included in Edward Ewing Pratt, *Industrial Causes of Congestion of Population in New York City* (New York: Columbia University, 1911), 29. Throughout this paper, I assume that statistics about an area's occupational breakdown can tell us about the class composition of its population. This seems logical, given the primacy of economic factors in determining class. But I should stress that social class is a function of numerous factors having to do not only with jobs and income but also with education, values, and living conditions (which branches off into other issues such as family size and structure, religious practices, etc.), and, more generally, social stratification derives not only from class but also from social status and social power (as Max Weber argued). The basic dimensions of social stratification are discussed in Daniel Rossides, *The American Class System: An Introduction to Stratification Analysis* (Lanham, MD: University Press of America, 1976), 18–29. Criteria for evaluating the social status of particular occupations are discussed briefly, with useful references, in Stephan Thernstrom, *The Other Bostonians: Poverty and Progress in the American Metropolis, 1880–1970* (Cambridge: Harvard University Press, 1973), 293.

21. Walter Laidlaw, ed., *Statistical Sources for Demographic Studies of Greater New York, 1910* (New York: New York Federation of Churches, 1913).

22. Jeffrey S. Gurock, *When Harlem Was Jewish, 1870–1930* (New York: Columbia University Press, 1979), 50.

23. Ibid., 175, table A.5; 177, table A.9.

24. Thomas Kessner's census sample of Russian Jewish households shows that the uptown neighborhood did have a somewhat higher proportion of skilled laborers (relative to semiskilled) than the downtown area, but neither had any unskilled laborers to speak of, and, interestingly enough, parts of the Lower East Side actually had a higher proportion of Jews in white-collar positions. Kessner, *The Golden Door*, 184, table 25.

25. For information on the incomes of different occupations in this period, both by total family income and earnings of father, see Robert Coit Chapin, *The Standard of Living among Workingmen's Families in New York City* (New York: Russell Sage Foundation, 1909), 46–7, 49–52, tables 3, 4, and 6. The standard socioeconomic grouping of occupations into five classes derives from census statistician Alba M. Edwards, "A Social Economic Grouping of the Gainful Workers of the United States," *Journal of the American Statistical Association* 27 (1933): 377–87. A detailed list of occupations within different classes is found in Thernstrom, *The Other Bostonians*, appendix B, 289–92.

26. Allen locates Yorkville as being between 74th and 89th Streets. Statistics on population density and ethnic makeup suggest that by 1910 the neighborhood stretched from 69th Street to 94th Street, at which point it began to give way to Jewish Harlem and Little Italy. This slightly broader definition of Yorkville better corresponds to the location of the theaters I have found in this area.

27. Allen, "Motion Picture Exhibition in Manhattan," 167, quoting Thomas M. Henderson, *Tammany Hall and the New Immigrants* (New York: Arno Press, 1976), 17–19.

28. Zeisloft, *The New Metropolis*, 612, 633–35.

29. Germans and Irish were the largest ethnic groups in Yorkville. A paragraph on the class composition of these groups in other cities at the turn of the century has been omitted.

30. *Rider's New York City, a Guide-Book for Travelers* (New York: Henry Holt and Co., 1916), 340.

31. Laidlaw, ed., *Statistical Sources.*

32. Zeisloft, *The New Metropolis*, 636.

33. Osofsky, *Harlem, the Making of a Ghetto*, 87–123. Quotations on 107 and 121.

34. A paragraph and long footnote analyzing the consistent ratio of residents to nickelodeons among the key neighborhoods has been omitted.

35. Laidlaw, ed., *Statistical Sources.* Something of a demographics zealot, Laidlaw was frustrated that the Census Bureau presented its population data in units that were too big to be of value to social workers and planners interested in issues such as neighborhood population densities. For Manhattan, the book summarizes census data into 224 tracts of about 43 acres each – a big improvement over the government Census Abstracts, which cluster the data only in terms of assembly districts, of which there were 29 in Manhattan, of widely varying sizes. Laidlaw's recategorization, in other words, provides seven times more specificity to a demographic picture of New York in 1910. *Statistical Sources* is included, along with similar sources for later censuses, in a ten-reel microfilm series: Benjamin Bowser *et al.*, eds., *Census Data with Maps for Small Areas of New York City, 1910–1960* (Ithaca: Cornell University Libraries, 1979; distributed by Research Publication, Woodbridge, Conn.). A separate microfilm copy is at the New York Public Library, and the original hard copy is at the Library of Congress. Laidlaw also compiled a volume based on the 1920 census.

36. The remaining 15 percent or so was made up of various other ethnic groups (English, Scandinavian, etc.), none of which comprised more than 1 or 2 percent of the population. My assumption about the "Austrian" population is based on Zeisloft's description of the area (*The New Metropolis*, 527). Unfortunately, it is impossible to tell, using Laidlaw's census data or other descriptions, what proportion of Germans were German Jews.

37. Ibid, 526.

38. A long section challenging "The Italian Thesis" – an argument concerning ethnic variation in nickelodeon attendance – has been omitted.

39. Patrick Hanks and Flavia Hodges, *A Dictionary of Surnames* (Oxford: Oxford University Press, 1988); Elsdon C. Smith, *New Dictionary of American Family Names* (New York: Harper and Row, 1973); Heinrich W. Guggenheimer and Eva H. Guggenheimer, *Jewish Family Names and Their Origins: An Etymological Dictionary* (Ktav Publishing House, 1992); George F. Jones, *German-American Names* (Baltimore: Genealogical Publishing Co., 1990).

40. In cases where a theater was owned by two people, I figured both names into the percentages. In cases where the same person owned more than one theater, I calculated using two methods: first, by counting each person only once, and second, by recounting the owners. I found that the ethnic breakdown percentages were virtually the same using either method. Along with the 187 theaters listed by personal name, 16 theaters were listed only by corporate names (e.g. Pastime Amusement Co.) that give no clue about owners' ethnicity, and 16 other theaters lack any information whatsoever about ownership.

41. This ethnic breakdown is adapted from Laidlaw, ed., *Statistical Sources*, summary page. Since the census enumerated people by country of origin rather than ethnicity, it is difficult to determine an exact number for the Jewish population, which was recorded under such nationalities as Russian, German, Hungarian, Austrian (Galician Jews), and Romanian. My estimate is based on analyses in Erich Rosenthal, "The Equivalence of United States Census Data for Persons of Russian Stock or Descent with American Jews: An Evaluation," *Demography* 12, no. 2 (May 1975): 275–90, and Simon Kuznets, "Immigration of Russian Jews, Background and Structure," *Perspectives in American History* 9 (1975): 35–126. Two excellent primary sources provide statistical and historical data on Jewish immigration: Samuel Joseph, "Jewish Immigration to the United States, from 1881 to 1910" (PhD dissertation, Columbia University, 1914); and Edmund J. James *et al.*, *The Immigrant Jew in America* (New York: B. F. Buck and Co., 1906).

42. *Trow's* 1908 list of exhibitors shows Minnie Stafford at 687 9th Street, between 47th and 48th Streets, and Caroline Sirignano at 196 Grand Street, in the Lower East Side (however, I am unsure whether Caroline might not have been a man's name). The 1909 edition shows Catherine McCormack as owner of the Arena theater on First Avenue between 75th and 76th Streets and Louise Meyer as an exhibitor at 249 Third Avenue, in Chelsea.

43. I am using the term "owner" to denote owner of the business. Many of the actual theaters were leased from other property owners.

44. "Failures of Nickelodeons," *Moving Picture World*, June 13, 1908, 1908 [*sic*].

45. "Greater New York Notes," *Moving Picture World*, September 19, 1908, 214.

46. "Observations by Our Man about Town," *Moving Picture World*, May 8, 1909, 589.

PART III

Cinema and reform

INTRODUCTION

LATE IN 1906 IN THE UNITED STATES and Germany, and shortly thereafter in various other Western countries, journalists and social reformers began investigating the audiences drawn to the new nickelodeons and *Ladenkinos* (German storefront theatres), asking questions about the social composition of the audience and of the pleasures and dangers of movie-going. Working class groups were frequently identified as central to the audience in large cities, drawn by the low-cost of admission that made cinema the first modern mass medium providing commercial entertainment accessible to almost everyone on a regular basis. Women, children and, in the United States at least, immigrants were also frequently singled out as important groups amongst the cinema audience.

Here, for example, is the description of an audience at a nickelodeon in Chicago in early 1907 from the *Chicago Tribune*: 'The children in this place were mostly the children of the poor. They were of the families of foreign laborers and formed the early stage of that dangerous second generation which is finding such a place in the criminals of the city'.[1] Linking immigrants to children and the poor, the *Tribune*'s description of the audience was fuelled by anxiety about the effects of moviegoing and movies on groups who were seen as both vulnerable and potentially dangerous. Widespread rhetoric on the deleterious effects of cinema on the social body spread quickly from early 1907. Cinema was causing what one critic described as 'moral malaria'.[2]

Various interventions followed these discourses, including those aimed at regulating the space of exhibition and the establishment of censor boards to regulate film content. The film industry in turn responded in various ways, seeking in broad terms to make movies respectable to middle class groups both to avoid attacks from these groups and to appeal to them so as to increase their attendance (without, it was hoped, alienating the working class). The strategies of reformers and of the industry interacted in various ways to shape film content and form and to define the social role of cinema, that is the way cinema could and indeed should function in society.[3] Let's break this down into four separate questions: why were élite groups anxious about cinema? What did they do as a consequence of this? How did the film industry respond? And what were the outcomes of this interaction between reformers and the film industry? Like before, our main focus will be on the United States, though we will also reference scholarship on regulation in the United Kingdom and Germany.

Various reasons for élite anxiety about cinema can be deduced from reform rhetoric and ensuing practices, which were, it seems, underpinned by concerns about the maintenance of public order in the face of fundamental social transformations associated with modernity (industrialization, urbanization, immigration, internationalization). Labour organization and unrest and widespread concerns about imminent social and political breakdown pervaded the period. In Chicago, for example, industrial action between 1904 and 1906, coupled with what one contemporary commentator called a 'wave of crime', no doubt informed the concern of the *Tribune* and others about nickelodeons in the city.[4] Cinema was regarded with suspicion as a gathering place of disaffected and impressionable groups, like those children of foreign labourers singled out for comment in the article quoted earlier. Children were often the focus of anxieties because they constituted what one commentator called 'the entire raw material of future citizenship'.[5] Concern was expressed about the possibility that movies could influence children to commit criminal or immoral acts. Nickelodeons, the *Tribune* argued, 'minister to the lowest passions of childhood. They make schools of crime where murders, robberies and holdups are illustrated. The outlaw life they portray in their cheap plays lends to the encouragement of wickedness. They manufacture criminals to the city streets'.[6] Such anxieties about children and the nickelodeons tapped into prevalent discourses about juvenile delinquency, which emerged in the late nineteenth century.[7]

Anxieties about immigrant groups were central to these debates, as is suggested by the *Tribune*'s description of the audience as children of foreign labourers and by widespread rhetoric about the foreign basis of juvenile delinquency. Children were often cast in a synechdochal relationship to an audience and population that threatened disorder in terms mainly of class and ethnicity. Regulatory concerns were expressed about immigrant audiences and about the formation of national identity, linking anxieties about the cinema with broader nativist concerns about the social and cultural values of immigrants.

Likewise, commentators often singled out foreign films for condemnation, principally those of 'Parisian design', as the *Tribune* phrased it.[8] The target here was probably predominantly the Pathé company, for, as Richard Abel has told us, Pathé dominated the American market and their films had helped create and support the nickelodeon boom.[9] Concerns were expressed about the morality of these films and about their effect in particular on immigrant groups, whose morality was in any case suspect by the standards of white Anglo-Saxon Protestant élite groups. It is worth noting that regulatory debates in Germany were often also tied together with anxieties about the effects of foreign films on national identity, notably a fear that the international process of capitalism, in particular the circulation of American goods and entertainment, were destroying German tastes and culture.[10]

Nickelodeons and moving pictures emerged as a focus of regulatory concerns in both the United States and Germany also because they symbolized broader shifts in the topography of public and private spaces which were characteristic of the turn-of-the-century period, especially with regards to the changing social role of women.[11] Historians have shown how the expansion of a heterosocial leisure sphere and 'culture of consumption' and 'abundance' in the early years of the twentieth century, effectively altered women's – and particularly working women's – participation both in the world of commercialized amusements and in the broader public sphere.[12] The redefined relationship between the public and the private spheres and the emergence of a mass cultural public sphere presaged an apparent breakdown of social and moral order. This was usually figured in terms of sexual immorality by commentators steeped in the patriarchal Victorian ideology of separate spheres. Ill-lit nickelodeons, many suggested, were ideal 'recruiting stations of vice' or 'breeding places of vice', where 'mashers' and 'vicious men and boys ... take liberties with very young girls'.[13] Equally troublesome were the films themselves, for they seemed to project new ideas about sexuality and were consequently seen as particularly damaging to girls and young women. Extending their voyeuristic freedom and 'optical omnipotence' to survey sights of the public world hitherto unavailable to them, such films were linked to delinquency which for young women was invariably coded in terms of sexual immorality.[14] Cinema was a problematic space and site of fantasy, a 'place of darkness, physical and moral'.[15]

What strategies did élite groups develop, then, to regulate cinema? Legal regulation before 1907 had been carried out in the main via the imposition of pre-existing licensing laws, often those used to control various travelling side-shows and carnivals.[16] Zoning regulations, 'blue laws' (Sunday closing laws), and fire code regulations were central in this period but these did not directly attend to the content of moving pictures or to the concerns over the social functioning of cinema after the proliferation of nickelodeons and the association of cinema with a mass public. Local investigations into the spread of nickelodeons from 1906 and their effects on audiences led to calls for stricter governmental regulation of cinema.

A more specific regulatory arena emerged late in 1907 with the formation of a Police Censor Board in Chicago in part as a response to the crusade against nickelodeons in the city mounted by various reform and religious groups and by the *Tribune* from late 1906. Exhibitors and film exchanges in Chicago now had to apply for a screening permit for each film and then provide a copy of the film for examination by the police board of censors. The board would not issue a license if the film was found to be 'immoral, obscene or indecent', consistent with widely held beliefs about the centrality of morality to public order.[17] Now regulation concentrated in the main on the cultural control of cinema, on what could be shown and on how cinema should function in the social body rather than the political control of who could show moving pictures and when and where they could be shown. This constituted an important shift from a regulatory focus on buildings and spaces to the focus both on the social function of cinema and on representations and effects which has dominated policy discussions of cinema ever since.

Late in 1908 a legal case sought to work out the constitutionality of the police censor board and, by implication, the constitutionality of other censor boards directed at moving pictures. Lawyers working for an exhibitor called Jake Block argued that the censorship ordinance unconstitutionally discriminated against the exhibitors of moving pictures, making a distinction between moving pictures and other forms of commercialized amusements. In particular they argued that the ordinance drew an unfair distinction between cinema and the theatre, for whilst films were disallowed 'certain plays and dramas were being performed in certain playhouses in the city of Chicago of which the pictures were reproductions of parts'.[18]

Early in 1909 Chief Justice James H. Cartwright dismissed these claims in the Illinois Supreme Court. It was the purpose of the law, Justice Cartwright asserted, 'to secure decency and morality in the moving picture business, and that purpose falls within the police power'.[19] Even though the ordinance focused solely on moving pictures, Cartwright noted, it did not necessarily license other immoral representations and, furthermore, there is something specific to the regulation of moving pictures – the audience. 'On account of the low price of admissions', Cartwright claimed, nickel theatres are frequented and patronized by a large number of children, as well as by those of limited means who do not attend the productions of plays and dramas given in the regular theatres. The audiences include those classes whose age, education and situation in life especially entitle them to protection against the evil influence of obscene and immoral representations.[20]

He concluded that exhibition of the pictures 'would necessarily be attended with evil effects upon youthful spectators'. Important precedents were set here, paving the way for the proliferation of municipal and state censor boards from this moment on.[21] Thus, discourses about the effects of moving pictures on vulnerable and dangerous audiences had concrete effects on regulatory practices.

The Mayor of New York City, George McClellan, had called a public hearing late in 1908 to debate the legality and propriety of the Sunday opening of nickelodeons and a host of questions about the safety and morality of nickelodeons and moving pictures. The following day, Mayor McClellan ordered all the nickelodeons in the city closed pending further investigation, vowing that future licenses would not allow Sunday opening.[22] This was the most extreme measure of regulation in the pre-classical era, striking the industry at the core in the most profitable market in the country. New York exhibitors responded quickly by banding together and gaining a temporary injunction against McClellan's actions.[23] They approached the People's Institute, a civic reform group, about the prospect of setting up a Censorship Board in New York City and the People's Institute readily agreed.[24]

The Institute had been a strong advocate of progressive civic reform, encouraging an active and informed electorate by holding frequent 'People's Forums' at which citizens could debate and vote on pressing issues of the day. It also sponsored a thrice-weekly lecture series on topics ranging from personal hygiene to engineering and literature. Members of the Institute believed that cinema could be used as a positive 'counterattraction', drawing audiences away from institutions like the saloon and burlesque and functioning as a force for social good.[25] 'Here is a new social force', a prominent member of the Institute wrote, 'perhaps the beginning of a true theatre of the people, and an instrument whose power can only be realized when social workers begin to use it'.[26]

Censorship of moving pictures as opposed to the regulation of cinema space defined the problem of cinema as a problem of films and placed the onus of responsibility on film producers. It was initially unclear whether the producers would agree to cooperate with the Censorship Board, though in the event they readily acquiesced in order to avoid being locked out of the market in New York City.[27] Various production companies had banded together in the legal superstructure of the Motion Picture Patents Company (MPPC) just before the McClellan hearings, bonded now by adherence to Edison's and Biograph's patents (this ended, for the time being, the constant patent litigation problems we have discussed in the previous two sections).[28] The Motion Picture Patents Company was incorporated on 9 September 1908, and was officially launched on 18 December 1908, just six days before the McClellan hearings. Various manufacturers agreed to transfer their patents to a holding company, which then licensed them to manufacture films under the patents it now held; the MPPC also licensed exhibitors. Thus it was able to organize and regulate all sectors of the motion picture industry. This arrangement established monopoly power by organizing corporations into a mutually profitable cartel that would work also as a barrier to entry for other producers.

Censorship could be turned to the advantage of these film producers, both in terms of deflecting concerns about monopolistic practices and in terms of providing another barrier to entry to non-mainstream production companies. MPPC members immediately sought to co-opt the moral authority of the Board, supplying a screening room and a stipend for expenses and proclaiming in public statements that the MPPC had started the Board and that the Board 'will put the moving picture show on a level with the very finest and highest types of theatrical entertainment'.[29] Likewise, the MPPC adopted the slogan, 'Moral, Educational and Amusing'.[30] It is worth noting also that the MPPC claimed that one of its goals was to 'eliminate the cheap and inferior foreign films which have been forced upon the market, and to so educate the public taste that only high class and attractive films will be accepted as reaching the American standard'.[31] Regulatory and commercial practices coalesced, working to marginalize non-American film producers in the American market. Though Pathé was included in the MPPC its earlier economic dominance was increasingly reined in by the terms of the agreements joining the companies together.

Largely staffed by 'progressive' reformers, overwhelmingly middle class women, the New York Board of Censorship met for the first time in April 1909; it was renamed the National Board of Censorship in May 1909. It can be seen as a concrete example of the interaction between reform groups and the film industry. Early statements of the standards of the Board focused on 'obscenity' and on 'crime-for-crime's sake'.[32] '[C]rime for its own sake we condemn', secretary of the Board John Collier wrote in June 1909, 'pictures whose chief appeal is to morbid appetite we condemn, bad taste where it becomes vulgarity we condemn. We condemn anything that seems dangerously suggestive in its tendencies'.[33] Yet the Board focused in the main less on content as such and more on the organization of content. '[B]arring indecency, barring ghoulishness', Collier continued, 'there is hardly any incident in life or drama that may not be so treated', for the Board would evaluate whether 'the sum total of effect, the unified effect, is positive and harmless' and thus base its 'decisions on the general effect a picture will have on an audience'.[34] Similar statements can be found in the Board's first articulation of its policy and standards of censorship in October 1909, which again pointed out that scenes glorifying crime and vice would be objected to but that '[t]his does not imply the cutting out of any representation of a crime for such might be incidental to an entirely proper and desirable story'.[35]

Here, as Tom Gunning argues in his chapter in this section, censorship and the Board played a productive role in shaping film form, pushing filmmakers to be conscious of moral norms and to integrate potentially risqué content within an overall moral framework. Gunning's essay shows that the emergence of a particular configuration of narrative from 1909 was closely tied with regulatory pressures (and was not linked solely to the 'genius' of D. W. Griffith, as earlier historians had often suggested). Economic and regulatory concerns dovetailed again, for it was crucial for film producers to appeal to avoid offence and to appeal to wide and diverse audiences. Likewise, Roberta Pearson and William Uricchio's essay considers the production of a number of 'quality' films based on Shakespeare plays (focusing on *Julius Caesar* [Vitagraph 1908]), arguing that the films were linked to the industry's efforts to represent itself as respectable and also to efforts to attract an affluent middle class audience. Similar efforts to produce 'art films' took place simultaneously in France and Italy.[36] Pearson and Uricchio are careful, though, to show how widespread knowledge of Shakespeare was, suggesting then that the films were an ideal way for the film industry to extend its audience base but also to keep their working class and immigrant audiences. Pearson and

Uricchio consider evidence from the production companies and from social and cultural history to delineate the competing interests at play in the production and reception of these films.

Even though the National Board was staffed by eminent social figures and estimates suggested it passed on 85–90 per cent of films circulating in the United States, this did not mean that the film industry was now immune from criticism and this did not stop the establishment of further State regulation. Immediately after the Board was established the African-American boxer Jack Johnson won the world heavyweight title against a white boxer. Johnson's fights and films were highly controversial, for the image of a black man defeating a white man was seen to undercut prevailing notions of racial hierarchy and white supremacy. In 1912 the federal government passed the Sims Act to prevent the interstate transportation of fight films, directly aimed at Johnson's films. Lee Grieveson's chapter demonstrates that the ramifications of this act, the first federal intervention into cinema, were considerable, for it defined films as 'commerce' and so placed them within the jurisdiction of the federal government. This suggested that cinema was distinct from the press and could not claim constitutional guarantees of free speech. In this case federal regulation of cinema was clearly propelled by racist anxiety. Related xenophobia was evident with the passage of the Tariff Act in 1913 regulating the importation of foreign films.

As with the Johnson fight films, the white slave films like *Traffic in Souls* (1913) that emerged in late 1913 and the controversy over the D. W. Griffith directed, racist, civil war epic *The Birth of a Nation* (1915) also caused the Board considerable problems (and we will consider these films further in the following section).[37] In 1914 and 1916 debates were held in the House of Congress about the possibility of establishing a federal film censor board. In the debates, the New York Board was strongly criticized for being too closely tied to the industry, for not reviewing all films, and for reviewing the ones they did with only the metropolitan standards of New York City in mind.[38] Even though no federal censor board was ultimately created, ongoing anxiety about the power and effect of moving pictures on audiences, alongside the New York Board's perceived failures, led some state governments to establish their own censorship boards. Pennsylvania led the way in 1911, though the Board did not start functioning until 1914; Ohio, Kansas and Maryland all set up state boards between 1913 and 1916.[39] The Boards all took aim at prohibiting 'sacrilegious, obscene, indecent, or immoral' films.[40] Concerns were frequently expressed about sexuality and the representation of political corruption or industrial unrest. Attention was directed towards particular images and stories but also, more generally, towards a delimitation of the public role cinema might take.

The activities of state censor boards soon led to a definitive statement on the nature of cinema at the federal level. Late in 1913 the interstate film exchange Mutual challenged the legality of the Ohio board and, in separate cases, of other local and state boards.[41] Mutual argued that the boards were unconstitutional and, in particular when the case reached the Supreme Court in early 1915, that the laws contravened the constitutional guarantees of free speech. The Justices denied this argument, though, arguing that cinema was not akin to the press and could not be included in those guarantees. Cinema was, the Justices claimed, a 'business pure and simple' and, furthermore, had a unique 'capacity for evil'.[42] Legal prior restraint was acceptable, then, and state intervention was necessary; the movies became the only medium of communication in the history of the United States to be subject to official censorship.

The decision was perhaps the most important one ever rendered in relation to cinema in the United States, for it helped shape what cinema would become. Not conceived of as akin to the press and as capable of engaging with pressing social problems, the film industry would have to establish Hollywood as a place of 'harmless entertainment' to circumvent regulatory concern. Other countries' film industries were similarly constructed, often, like in Britain, through more direct State intervention (many European countries did not have the tradition of free speech protection central to the Constitution of the United States).[43]

It is important to note that industry and State interests frequently coalesced in these developments, because money was to be made first and foremost from the demand of mass audiences for entertainment. The marginalization of the interest of some groups to use cinema for other purposes – for example labour agitation – was of great political importance, yet had little economic significance for the film industry. Hence one answer to the question posed earlier about the results of the interaction between regulatory forces and the film industry, is this: it lead to the formation of a classical cinema that sought to avoid offence and provide harmless entertainment to diverse audiences.

Certainly this conception of the social function of cinema could change and indeed did so briefly with the entry of the United States into the First World War in April 1917, when cinema was used for propaganda purposes by the State.[44] Yet this was short-lived and the pre-war conception of cinema quickly re-asserted itself after the end of the conflict.[45] Regulatory concerns about cinema continued, including in the immediate post-war period the establishment of three state censor boards between 1919 and 1922 and the enactment of federal regulations banning interstate transport of all 'obscene' films (logically extending the precepts of the Sims Act).[46] One of the main functions of the film industry's new and lasting self-regulatory body, the Motion Pictures Producers and Distributors of America (MPPDA), set up in 1922, was to police the social function of mainstream cinema so as to deflect external criticism of the industry and mute further State involvement.

It is in the context of these concerns about, and interventions into, the public role of cinema that key transformations in film formats, exhibition sites and industrial organization took place. We will deal with these in the next two sections, concentrating first on the rise of multiple-reel feature films and balanced cinema programmes in the 1910s, and then exploring the fairly stable, yet also highly responsive industrial and aesthetic system which had been established in the United States by the 1920s and has come to be known as 'classical Hollywood cinema'.

Notes

1 *Chicago Tribune* (15 April 1907), 1.
2 Reverend John Wesley Hill, *New York Times* (28 December 1908), quoted in William Uricchio and Roberta E. Pearson, *Reframing Culture: The Case of the Vitagraph Quality Films* (Princeton, NJ: Princeton University Press, 1993), 30.
3 For a fuller account of this process, see Lee Grieveson, *Policing Cinema: Movies and Censorship in Early Twentieth Century America* (Berkeley: University of California Press, 2004).
4 George Kibbe Turner, 'The City of Chicago: A Study of the Great Immoralities', *McClure's* (April 1907), 580; Sydney L. Harring, *Policing a Class Society: The Experience of American Cities, 1865–1915* (New Brunswick, NJ: Rutgers University Press, 1983), 228–33.
5 Maude McDougall, 'The Mission of the Movies: The Theatre with an Audience of Five Million', *The Designer* (January 1913), 160, quoted in Uricchio and Pearson, *Reframing Culture*, 29.
6 *Chicago Tribune* (10 April 1907), 10.
7 Anthony M. Platt, *The Child Savers: The Invention of Delinquency* (Chicago: The University of Chicago Press, 1969); Steven L. Schlossman, *Love and the American Delinquent: The Theory and Practice of 'Progressive' Juvenile Justice* (Chicago: The University of Chicago Press, 1977). On the connection between discourses about child audiences and juvenile delinquency, see Lee Grieveson, 'Why the Audience Mattered

in Chicago in 1907', in Melvyn Stokes and Richard Maltby (eds), *American Movie Audiences From the Turn of the Century to the Early Sound Era* (London: British Film Institute, 1999).

8   *Chicago Tribune* (13 April 1907), 3.
9   Richard Abel, *The Red Rooster Scare: Making Cinema American, 1900–1910* (Berkeley: University of California Press, 1999), 87–101, 118–39.
10 Anton Kaes, 'The Debate About Cinema: Charting a Controversy (1909–1929)', *New German Critique* no. 40 (Winter 1982); Karen J. Kenkel, 'The Nationalisation of the Mass Spectator in Early German Film', in John Fullerton (ed.), *Celebrating 1895: The Centenary of Cinema* (Sydney: John Libbey, 1998); Scott Curtis, 'The Taste of a Nation: Training the Senses and Sensibility of Cinema Audiences in Imperial Germany', *Film History*, vol. 6, no. 4 (1994).
11 Miriam Hansen, 'Early Cinema – Whose Public Sphere', *New German Critique*, no. 29 (1983).
12 William Leach, *Land of Desire: Merchants, Power, and the Rise of a New American Culture* (New York: Pantheon Books, 1993); Kathy Peiss, *Cheap Amusements: Working Women and Leisure in Turn-of-the-Century New York* (Philadelphia: Temple University Press, 1986), 139–62; Lauren Rabinovitz, *For the Love of Pleasure: Women, Movies, and Culture in Turn-of-the-Century Chicago* (New Brunswick, NJ: Rutgers University Press, 1998), 68–102.
13 Dr. Anna Howard Shaw, quoted in *Moving Picture World* (12 March 1910), 370–1; The Chicago Vice Commission, *The Social Evil in Chicago* (Chicago: Chicago Vice Commission, 1911), 247–8.
14 Shelley Stamp, *Movie-Struck Girls: Women and Motion Picture Culture After the Nickelodeon* (Princeton, NJ: Princeton University Press, 2000), 99; on girls and delinquency, see, for example, *The Social Evil in Chicago*, 174–5; Mary E. Odem, *Delinquent Daughters: Protecting and Policing Adolescent Female Sexuality in the United States, 1885–1920* (Chapel Hill: University of North Carolina Press, 1995).
15 Michael David, *The Exploitation of Pleasure* (New York: Russell Sage Foundation, 1911), 34.
16 Daniel Czitrom, 'The Politics of Performance: Theater Licensing and the Origins of Movie Censorship in New York', in Francis Couvares (ed.), *Movie Censorship and American Culture* (Washington: Smithsonian Institution Press, 1995).
17 *Proceedings of the City Council of the City of Chicago* (4 November 1907), 3052.
18 *Block v. City of Chicago*, 87 N.E. 1011, 239 Ill. 251 (1909), 1013.
19 Ibid., 1013.
20 Ibid., 1013.
21 The Board became a model for other cities. See *Moving Picture World* (21 September 1907), 454; and *Moving Picture World* (14 December 1907), 665. On the legal significance of the Board for later municipal and state boards, see Edward De Grazia and Roger K. Newman, *Banned Films: Movies, Censors and the First Amendment* (New York: R. R. Bowker, 1982), 8–10, 177–80.
22 *New York Times* (25 December 1908), 1.
23 *New York Daily Tribune* (26 December 1908), 1 and 3; *New York Herald* (27 December 1908), 5; *New York Herald* (30 December), 3.
24 Charles Mathew Feldman, *The National Board of Censorship (Review) of Motion Pictures, 1909–1922* (New York: Arno Press, 1977), 2–33.
25 Uricchio and Pearson, *Reframing Culture*, 33–40.
26 John Collier, 'Cheap Amusements', *Charities and the Commons*, vol. 20 (11 April 1908), 74–5, quoted in Uricchio and Pearson, *Reframing Culture*, 38.
27 *Moving Picture World* (20 March 1909), 335.
28 See Robert Anderson, 'The Motion Picture Patents Company: A Revaluation', in Tino Balio (ed.), *The American Film Industry* (Madison, Wis.: University of Wisconsin Press, 1985), 142; Eileen Bowser, *The Transformation of Cinema, 1907–1915* (Berkeley: University of California Press, 1990), 29.
29 *Nickelodeon* (April 1909), 92.
30 Tom Gunning, *D. W. Griffith and the Origins of American Narrative Film: The Early Years at Biograph* (Urbana: University of Illinois Press, 1991), 145.
31 Announcement to Exhibitors from Motion Pictures Patents Company, 1 February 1909, cited in Nancy Rosenbloom, 'Progressive Reform, Censorship, and the Motion Picture Industry, 1909–1917', in Larry Bennett and Ronald Edsforth (eds), *Popular Culture and Political Change in Modern America* (Buffalo: State University of New York Press, 1991), 46. See also Gunning, *D. W. Griffith and the Origins of American Narrative Film*, 146–7; and Abel, *The Red Rooster Scare*, 87–94.
32 Circular Letter, John Collier to Manufacturers of Motion Pictures, 15 March 1909, cited in Czitrom, 'The Politics of Performance', 34.
33 John Collier, *Moving Picture World* (12 June 1909), 797.

34 Collier, *Moving Picture World* (12 June 1909), 797; Lewis E. Palmer, 'The World in Motion', *Survey* (5 June 1909), 363.
35 *Moving Picture World* (23 October 1909), 524–5.
36 Richard Abel, 'French Silent Cinema', in Geoffrey Nowell-Smith (ed.), *The Oxford History of World Cinema* (Oxford: Oxford University Press, 1996), 113; Paolo Cherchi Usai, 'Italy: Spectacle and Melodrama', ibid., 124–6.
37 Lee Grieveson, 'Policing the cinema: *Traffic in Souls* at Ellis Island, 1913', *Screen*, vol. 38, no. 2 (Summer 1997); Shelley Stamp, 'Moral Coercion, or the Board of Censorship Ponders the Vice Question', in Matthew Bernstein (ed.), *Regulating Hollywood: Censorship and Control in the Studio Era* (New Brunswick, NJ: Rutgers University Press, 1999); Nickieann Fleener-Marzec, *D. W. Griffith's 'The Birth of a Nation': Controversy, Suppression, and the First Amendment as it Applies to Filmic Expression, 1915–1973* (New York: Arno Press, 1980).
38 'Extracts from Hearings Before the Committee on Education, House of Representatives 63rd Congress, Second Session, on Bills to Establish a Federal Motion Picture Commission' (Washington, DC, 1914), 4–6.
39 Lee Grieveson, *Policing Cinema*.
40 *Journal of the House of Representatives of the Commonwealth of Pennsylvania*, Part IV (1911), 3905–6.
41 *Mutual Film Co. v. Industrial Commission of Ohio* et al., 215 Federal Reporter (September–October 1914); *Mutual Film Corporation v. City of Chicago*, 224 F. 101 (USCCA Ill. 1915); *Buffalo Branch, Mutual Film Corporation v. Breitinger*, 250 Pa. 225 (1915); *Mutual Film Corp. of Missouri v. Hodges*, 236 US 230 (1915); John Wertheimer, 'Mutual Film Reviewed: The Movies, Censorship, and Free Speech in Progressive America', *The American Journal of Legal History*, vol. 37 (1993).
42 *Mutual Film Corporation v. Industrial Commission of Ohio*, 236 US 230 (1915), 244.
43 See Annette Kuhn, *Cinema, Censorship, Sexuality, 1909–1925* (London: Routledge, 1988).
44 Leslie Midkiff DeBauche, *Reel Patriotism: The Movies and World War I* (Madison: University of Wisconsin Press, 1997).
45 Grieveson, *Policing Cinema*, chapter 7.
46 Ruth A. Inglis, *Freedom of the Movies* (Chicago: University of Chicago Press, 1947), in particular 62–73.

Chapter 8

TOM GUNNING

FROM THE OPIUM DEN TO THE THEATRE OF MORALITY

Moral discourse and the film process in early American cinema

I HAVE IN MIND TWO FILMS, products of the same production company, filmed and released some six years apart. However, that six year gap represents a profound fissure in American film history, so that each film belongs to a radically different conception of style, narrative, characterisation and – most important to my essay – moral attitude.

The first film is entitled *The Heathen Chinee and the Sunday School Teachers*. It was shot on 17 December 1903 by a cameraman named Weed at the Biograph studio in New York. Its director, if it had one other than its cameraman, is not recorded. It consists of four shots, a fairly long film for Biograph in this period. The first shot shows the set of a laundry manned by Chinese men with long queues. A Caucasian woman customer enters and adjusts her stocking, revealing her legs. The laundry men do not react and she leaves, apparently disappointed. Two other women enter – the eponymous sunday school teachers. They distribute tracts to the Chinese who respond happily, waving goodbye as the women depart. The next shot presents the interior of the sunday school, with various pupils seated on chairs. The Chinese enter and are greeted by the teachers. They sit together and sing hymns, holding hands in an increasingly intimate manner as the shot ends. The third shot brings us to an opium den. The teachers enter, wearing veils, escorted by the laundrymen. They are given pipes and lie down together on low divans to smoke them. This idyll is interrupted by a police raid. The fourth and final shot shows a jail cell, the Chinamen behind bars. The school teachers enter, bearing gifts of candy and flowers for the prisoners. After the teachers depart, waving affectionately to their Chinese friends, their gifts are snatched away by the prison guard.

The second film is *The Drunkard's Reformation*, filmed by Biograph on 25 and 27 February and 1 March 1909. Its cameraman was Billy Bitzer and its director was D. W. Griffith. It is more than three times the earlier film in length, and consists of 32 shots. Since a detailed description would be too lengthy, I will give a synopsis of the film's plot. A young husband neglects his wife and daughter by spending time in a tavern. Returning home late one evening he is violent and makes a scene. Later his daughter persuades him to take her to the theatre, where they see a dramatisation of Zola's *L'Assommoir* (The Dive). The young man sees on stage the degradation of a man (like himself married and with a daughter) through alcoholism. The play ends with the stage drunkard's death during a fit of *delirium tremens*. The husband is overwhelmed by the play and, returning home, vows never to drink again. The last shot of the film shows his family, now united in love and temperance, basking in the light of the parlour hearth.

The six years that divide these films witness the foundation of a new style in American narrative film through the encoding of a series of narrative devices that are evident in *The Drunkard's Reformation* (parallel editing, shot-counter-shot, implied POV, an emotional use of lighting, increased closeness of the camera for characterisation, etc.) and a series of ideological themes that accompany them (the drama of the family, the subjectivity of characters, the idea of reformation). But what I wish to focus on is the centrality of the 'moral lesson' in this later film, contrasted to the anti-genteel attitude of *The Heathen Chinee*, which does not seem to condemn either the promiscuity and drug-taking of the female missionaries, or the racist corruption of the guard. It is my proposal that part of the transformation of American cinema from its earliest period to the era we associate with the founding of narrative codes (roughly 1908–1913) lies in its increased relation to morality, its conscious movement into a realm of moral discourse. I want to outline the group of forces that contributed to this transformation, certainly one with far-reaching effects on the filmmaking process. [. . .]

If, as I have maintained elsewhere,[1] the period of 1908–1909 represents a particularly important juncture in American film history, the first context for this must be economic. The formation of The Motion Picture Patents Company (MPPC) at the end of 1908 was a move to consolidate the film industry on an economic basis and to raise the social status of film as a form of entertainment. Seeking to establish motion pictures as the entertainment of "all classes" rather than the "theater of the working class man" (as it had been called since the nickelodeon explosion of 1905), the MPPC undertook a campaign to attract a middle class audience. In early 1909, MPPC advertisements appealed to sterling middle class virtues by characterising their products as "Moral, Educational and Cleanly Amusing".[2] If the films released by the MPPC could be certified as inoffensive to middle class morality it would be an important step towards achieving the Film Trust's announced intention "to encourage in all possible ways the commendation and support of the moving picture business by the better class of the community".[3] For the MPPC, acceptance of film as an entertainment form by the middle class meant economic stability and the possibility of higher admission prices (and therefore higher rentals).

The need to establish a moral pedigree for film during this period is indicated by the action taken by Mayor McClellan of New York City, in December of 1908, revoking all licenses for nickleodeons in the metropolitan area and ordering them closed. The mayor's action came as a result of a hearing he had called in which a series of clergymen and reform leaders had testified to the immoral influence of film shows, particularly on children. Although testimony was given on immoral aspects of the films themselves – such as depictions of horse racing and gambling, prize fights, train robberies, as well as "lovemaking, etc."[4] – emphasis was placed on film theatres as breeding places of immorality. The darkened theatres were pictured as locales of sexual misconduct and places where children went wrong: girls seduced, and boys led into lives of crime.[5] Basing his action on such testimony the mayor announced he was acting "with the firm conviction I am averting a public calamity".[6]

The immediate reaction of the film industry was to unite and take the mayor's decision to court, where it was found that the wholesale revocation of licenses was illegal. Although they scored a definite victory against the anti-film forces with this decision, exhibitors and the production companies of the MPPC took the criticisms offered at the mayor's hearing seriously. The agitation against the film industry had been growing since the enormous increase in nickel theatres that had begun about 1905. It is one example of the panic experienced by the guardians of genteel culture when faced by the forms of mass entertainment that had appeared in the United States at the beginning of the century. The movies became the locus of a number of social anxieties which included the sexual behaviour of children, the uneasy integration of immigrants into American life and business (many New York exhibitors seem to have been immigrants – or at least this was indicated by contemporaneous newspaper accounts[7]), and the existence of a form of entertainment that seemed to be evolving outside the restraints of dominant culture (and of which *The Heathen Chinee and the Sunday School Teachers* must stand as an emblem).

It was precisely this anxious image of film that the newly formed MPPC wished to dispell. At the McClellan hearing, J. Stuart Blackton of the Vitagraph Company testified that at the recent founding of the MPPC, all production companies had pledged to halt production of "indecent or suggestive films".[8] Although denying most of the criticisms presented at the hearing, the motion picture men were anxious to establish film as a medium inoffensive to public morality and an integral part of dominant culture. The lawyer representing motion picture interests at the hearing, Gustavus Rogers, even suggested that the mayor appoint a police censor to review all films shown in New York and eliminate any that would be offensive to public standards.[9]

One witness at the McClellan hearing testified that films could be a positive force in city life and were in need only of supervision, not eradication. Stating that there were many things in New York City more rotten than motion pictures, he was loudly applauded by the exhibitors, who drew a rebuke from the mayor.[10] This witness was Charles Sprague Smith, the director of The People's Institute, a liberal reform organisation dealing particularly with the problems of the working class. In early 1908, the Institute had undertaken a study of the amusements a working man could afford, and found the nickleodeon superior to other forms of cheap entertainment.[11] Wishing to solidify their legal victory over the mayor with a step that would guarantee the morality of the motion picture, The New York Exhibitors Association asked The People's Institute to set up a board to review all the films shown in New York.

The Board of Censorship was formed in March of 1909. As a censor, it had no legal powers. Production companies submitted their films to it and abided by its suggestions on a voluntary basis. Although an independent organisation, it was soon embraced by the MPPC, who realised that submitting their films to the Board would give tangible evidence of the moral purity of their product. This official recognition by the MPPC allowed the organisation to take the name The National Board of Censorship (in the 1910s this was changed to The National Board of Review, which survives to this day). The Board recognised its close relation with the film industry, emphasising its awareness that it was dealing with a business. Officially it characterised itself as a means of "internal trade regulation".[12]

The sort of moral pressure the Board exerted on the film industry was considerably different from that called for by the clergy at the McClellan hearing. Its primary aim seemed to be film's integration into the dominant culture, as called for by the MPPC's economic policy. The Board refused to publish a list of absolutely forbidden subjects, stating that motion pictures should have the freedom of expression accorded to other forms of culture. The Board made it a principle to judge each film as a narrative whole:

> . . . if the incident is essential to the plot of the story and the development of the character of the play, it is often permissible if not necessary to show some scenes which are in themselves open to criticism but which have sufficient value in the play to make it obligatory upon the Board to pass them to avoid arbitrarily and irrationally limiting the possibilities of photoplay development.[13]

The Board's reports on screenings of films from its first year of operation have been preserved at the Edison National Historical Site Archives in West Orange, New Jersey. They show that the Board not only suppressed the release of some films, but was involved in cuts and alterations (mainly in intertitles) of some that they passed. The report from 10 May 1909 is typical and worth quoting at length:

> One picture was condemned in toto as follows: Pathe: *La Parapluie d'Anatole*. This picture, while a farce, deals throughout with corrupt people in corrupt relationships and closes with a sign (the two horns) familiar to the vulgar as a sign of adultery. One picture was passed providing changes be made as follows: *Le Boucher de Moudon*, Pathe. This picture is the height of the gruesome throughout and many of those who support the Censorship among the public would expect that it is to be condemned in toto. The Committee, however, after discussing the picture on two separate days is willing to approve it with these changes:
>
> 1 – Cut out letter from son to mother, "I am condemned, etc." Either substitute a title such as "remorse" or leave no title here. That is, a certain moral lesson is given to the picture if we believe that remorse for the deed works upon the mother, this interpretation is negatived [sic] by the epistle in question.
>
> 2 – There are two versions – the first wherein the woman sees the recollection of the scene of murder, the second where she remembers the secreting of the victim's body under the hay. Cut out the first of these, representing the murder.
>
> 3 – In the prison scene immediately before the mother's confession is brought in, a morbid scene is shown depicting the cutting of the man's shirt preparatory to the guillotine. Eliminate this; it is not generic to the plot and is gratuitously gruesome in a tale too gruesome already. That is, cut out a few feet where the jailers are slicing the man's clothing . . .
>
> "Two Memories" Biograph. The Committee recognized at once that the reveling, the champagne bottles etc. were not presented for their own sake but to heighten dramatic effect through contrast. The picture takes itself seriously and will be so taken by most of the public. The Committee still believes that a dramatic contrast fully as satisfactory might have been obtained without employing a device as shocking to many, but this is a matter of debate, and there was divergence of opinion in the Committee. The severe intent of the picture and the fact that it is an earnest effort at dramatic method proper to the moving picture carried it with the Committee in spite of the doubtful point. This picture is approved.[14]

It is evident that the Board was not only engaged in eliminating objectionable material from films, but in reinforcing a conception of film narrative as a form of moral discourse, a form that had a responsibility to present "moral lessons." The Board clearly saw itself as part of a general 'uplift' of the photoplay, which yoked developments in the "dramatic method proper to moving pictures" to the gaining of a moral voice. The sort of transformations in narrative style which we associate with the work of D. W. Griffith at Biograph (and which are evident in *The Drunkard's Reformation*) were wedded to film's accreditation as a form of moral discourse. Certainly the Board cannot be naively seen as the sole cause of this transformation (*The Drunkard's Reformation* was actually filmed just before the Board was set up – but after the McClellan hearing and the MPPC's pledge to produce moral, inoffensive films). Rather, the Board itself is a manifestation of a new attitude toward film's position in society, motivated largely by the new economic policy of the MPPC and its desire for middle class respectability.

My initial comparison has problematic aspects. Alongside a film like *The Heathen Chinee*, there were many films made before 1908 with moral or religious messages, such as Biograph's *The Downward Path* or the numerous versions of the Passion Play. However, I would argue that the moral rhetoric of such films is limited because of the lack of the possibility of expressing the elements of characterisation called for by the sort of moral lesson offered by *The Drunkard's Reformation*. The codes of shot-counter-shot and parallel editing (allowing the "dramatic contrast" which the Board of Censorship realised was in fact a *moral* contrast) were lacking in these early films, and limited the sort of moral argument they could present.[15] At the same time my comparison should not be read as a claim that before 1908, American film existed in a utopian environment free from repression. Even in *The Heathen Chinee* the signs of repression are clear; not everything we desire to see is shown. The issue is the forms and meanings that such repression takes at different stages in film history.

The fact remains that a film like *The Heathen Chinee* could not have been released in the United States in 1909. Although film comedies could continue to introduce a number of socially disreputable themes, or poke fun at organised religion (as the early films of Chaplin demonstrate), the presentation of hypocritical missionaries, drug-taking, and implied miscegenation in this 1903 film could not have passed The National Board of Censorship. The genre of the erotic film which had flourished in America from 1900 to about 1907[16] totally disappeared – or was radically transformed – after 1909. The Biograph Company discontinued production of Mutoscopes in 1909, a primary outlet for erotic films (and possibly the intended mode of exhibition for *The Heathen Chinee*).

Zecca's *L'Histoire d'un Crime* is a good example of an early film in which a moral theme is present without a clear articulation of a moral rhetoric within the narrative codes of the film. The direct progression from brutal crime to its dire punishment clearly is based on a sort of moral argument. However, the ideology that condemns the original act of murder by the thief and approves the final act of murder by the State is not embodied in the film itself; Zecca relied on its presence in his audience. Griffith in *The Drunkard's Reformation* makes a similar assumption about his audience undoubtedly, but the form of his narrative works to reaffirm that ideology and even to introject it into his audience. In its "earnest effort at the dramatic method proper to the motion picture", *The Drunkard's Reformation* moves from the presentation of moral themes to a filmic rhetoric that seeks to convince its audience of the value of morality (and, as we shall see, of the value of motion pictures).

It is important in this context to realise that the transformation in film style represented by Griffith's early Biograph films is, in part, a response to a crisis in film form. With inflated aesthetic and social ambitions (of the sort typified, but not limited to, the Films d'Art), films in the years 1907–1908 had turned increasingly to adaptations of established stage pieces and works of literature. However, it was discovered that in attempting this more narratively complex material, filmmakers were risking incomprehensibility. Here, for instance, is the review from the trade journal *The Moving Picture World* of Edison's 1908 version of a famous stage play, Friedrich Halm's *Son of the Wilderness, Ingomar the Barbarian*:

> The scenery, the actors, the photography, and the general execution left little to be desired – in fact it is a splendid film, but it was not received by the audience with anything like the appreciation it merited. As one intelligent and elderly gentleman remarked in our hearing – "what is it all about? Very fine, but what does it mean?"[17]

This review is typical of the period, which frequently complains that in trying to bring material from literary sources to the screen, films had lost narrative clarity.

The same review offers one solution for this crisis:

> If the lecturer of the theater had simply read the synopsis of the play, such as the Edison Company send out with all films, the audience would have understood each scene and left the show with a desire to come again.

The "film lecturer" is a little emphasised aspect of early film history in the United States, but with important relations to the development of film narrative. Derived from the fairground barker and, particularly, the magic lantern reader, the film lecturer seems to have been of special import during the first decade of film exhibition. Providing a spoken commentary to accompany films as they were projected (based frequently on material contained in catalogue descriptions or production company bulletins), the lecturer had a major role in defining the film experience for early audiences. But with the rise of more sophisticated films at the end of the nickleodeon period, the lecturer had a new role: to interpret the more narratively complex action in stage and literary adaptations which the lack of dialogue and cultural reference left obscure to film audiences.

If the film lecturer was a proposed solution to the crisis in narrative comprehensibility, it was a relatively short lived one. Although trade journals continue to argue for the use of a lecturer (less frequently, however) into 1913, the phenomenon seems to disappear as the feature film era is firmly established. The cultural reasons why film lecturers would find themselves at odds with the complete narrative development of film (while existing in Japan through the silent era) are well laid out in Noël Burch's *To the Distant Observer*.[18] In any case, by 1914, film in the United States is understood as a narrative form which is comprehensible without any aid from beyond the screen (other than the considerable role of musical accompaniment; but this is clearly of a different order than a spoken commentary, underlining meanings present on the screen, rather than supplying them). This comprehensibility is accomplished by the development of legible film codes which were capable of conveying the moral and psychological material contained in the older narrative sources they were now putting to use. It is this transformation in film style that Griffith's work at Biograph represents. It is interesting to read a review from another trade journal of Biograph's version of the same play attempted by Edison, *Ingomar the Barbarian*, this time directed by Griffith:

> It is a fine example of what can be done in adapting stage drama for motion picture purposes when there is an intelligent recognition of the limitations of motion photography. Portions of the stage story which could only be interpreted adequately by spoken words are eliminated or re-arranged so that the picture reads to the spectator like a printed book.[19]

An important part of this new narrative legibility is the creation of a moral rhetoric through the new filmic codes that would allow audiences to understand the film's evaluation of different sorts of behaviour. *The Drunkard's Reformation* is perhaps Griffith's most emblematic film of moral rhetoric. It is a film that not only represents a theme of conventional morality – a theme already treated in a number of films of the pre-Griffith cinema, such as Zecca's *Victimes de l'Alcoolisme* and Biograph's *Ten Nights in A Barroom* – but endows it with the moral rhetoric in filmic form that was not present in the earlier films. But perhaps most revealing is this film's self-referential structure, embedding its moral discourse within an exploration of the role of the spectator, and the edifying effect of spectacles upon an audience. Lest anyone think that this claim of self-referentiality is a contemporary imposition on a primitive work, I refer to a bulletin issued by Biograph in early 1909 to promote the film:

> The whole construction of the picture is most novel, showing as it does, a play within a play. It is sort of triangular in motive, that is to say, the play depicts to the leading actor in the picture the calamitous result of drink, while the whole presents to the spectator the most powerful temperance lesson ever propounded.[20]

This film, then, was shot barely two months after the McClellan hearing, and in the midst of the MPPC's announced policy of moral and inoffensive films. It was released shortly after the formation of the Board of Censorship. Clearly the Biograph Company and Griffith are not only presenting a film with a moral lesson, but a film one of whose lessons is that film can be moral; that watching an edifying drama can have a transforming effect on the spectator. *The Drunkard's Reformation* is not only instructing its audience of the dangers of drink, but of the redeeming possibilities of motion pictures through the act of being a spectator.

Let us examine, a little more closely, the moral rhetoric of this film. We may begin with the simplest example – the use of the recently solidified code of parallel editing to present a moral contrast. We cut from shot 2 which presents the wife and daughter patiently waiting in the family parlour to shot 3 which reveals the husband neglecting his family by spending his time with two cronies in a bar. The parallel edit defines the temporal relation between the two events (and the establishment of a coherent and consistent temporality between shots was one of the tasks performed by the narrative transformation which Griffith represents), a relation accentuated by the wife's reference to the clock in both shot 3 and shot 5 (following the shot of the husband in the bar). The temporal relation underpins a moral contrast which turns, as so much of Griffith's moral rhetoric does, on attitudes towards family life. The actions of wife and child preparing for and anxiously awaiting the father's return show their desire to maintain the family unit. The husband by his delay at the bar maintains the separation of the elements indicated by the parallel editing. This separation portrayed by the editing of the first few shots visualises the narrative tension which the process of the film will resolve.

It is the witnessing of the temperance play that will allow this resolution and the re-establishment of family harmony. During this sequence the separation of the family is maintained, since the wife stays at home. At the end of shot 7, when father and daughter depart for the theatre, the wife first collapses on the table, then kneels in prayer. When father and child return after the play she is still leaning upon the table, hands grasped before her. The events at the play, though occurring without the presence of the mother, are in this way presented as the answer to her prayer.

Griffith's very first film, *The Adventures of Dollie*, also involved the rupturing and then resolution of family unity. However the difference in the narrative form of these two films is made clear by the different form both the rupture and the resolution takes in *The Drunkard's Reformation*. In *Dollie* both rupture and resolution are purely physical – the girl's abduction from her family by gypsies and her return via the floating barrel. In *The Drunkard's Reformation* the resolution comes from the modification of the character's behaviour, rather than the tangible return of a lost object. *The Drunkard's Reformation* is, in this sense, one of the first psychological films. The radical alternation which allows the resolution of the narrative comes, not through physical action, but through a psychological response, a drama of reformation.

The actual process of reformation is conveyed by another code of alternation through editing, a sort of prefiguration of shot-counter-shot with an indication of point of view.

Although the pattern of shots differs from the later classical form of point of view shot (primarily in terms of shot size; although father and daughter are foregrounded in this shot, they share the spectator position with a dozen other figures), the pattern of alternation is clearly designed to indicate a shift from spectator to spectator along the line of sight. The zone between the two realms, the line upon which the alternation turns, is strongly marked at the bottom of each frame, with the rope-like barrier that marks the limit of the stage visible in shots of the performance, and the music stands of the orchestra visible at the bottom of shots of the audience.

Although this sort of alternation between stage and spectators had been used in several films before *The Drunkard's Reformation*, I know of no film in which it plays a similar narrative role of providing the incident that resolves the narrative. Nor do I know of an earlier film in which it plays the same psychological role of portraying the moral reformation of a major character.

This pattern of alternation consists of some 24 shots in a film of 33 shots in all. It interlaces the unfolding of the action of the temperance play performed on stage with the stages of the spectator/husband's involvement – from amusement to boredom to the growing horror of recognition and the final realisation. In the early part of the alternation the cuts to the husband come after completed actions or scenes, generally on exits. Beginning with the cut from shot 15 to 16, the editing pattern starts to interrupt action unfolding on stage to cut to the husband's reaction. This first occurs as the stage father embraces his daughter. We cut to the spectator/husband as he nudges his own daughter and makes a gesture that mirrors the basic structure of the sequence; he points from the stage family to his daughter and himself, making a gesture of analogy.

The next cut between stage and audience makes an even stronger use of the interruption of action. In shot 17 the stage husband is joined by some companions who invite him to drink. He refuses at first, but they continue to try to persuade him. The moment of the stage husband's fatal decision to take a drink is articulated by this cut to the husband which forestalls the moment of decision. The cut also therefore interpellates the husband into the stage character's dilemma, as he recognises it as the image of his own life: shot 18 returns to the stage as the husband decides to take a drink. At two other points in the film, both at moments of violence by the stage drunkard against his wife, the cuts interrupt the action to show the spectator's horrified reaction. In the last shot but one of the husband (shot 30, missing in the Library of Congress paper print), he watches the drama leaning forward on his seat with his hand outstretched to the bottom of the stage, as if the separation of the two zones has been bridged by the intensity of his identification.

This "triangular" film is worthy of study in the archeology of what Christian Metz has called the "secondary identification" of audience with characters. Here the issue of identification is literally mimed out by an actor within the film, an identification made possible through the editing pattern which is founded on a primary identification of the view of the camera with the act of watching. Yet whatever the underlying psychological dynamics of this sequence may be, they are regulated by the economics of a moral lesson delivered through the process of recognition.

The narrative reaches resolution with the young husband's return home after the play. This second homecoming operates in paradigmatic opposition with the first homecoming from the bar. Whereas the first homecoming was marked by his brutal handling of objects associated with family unity (smashing a plate, throwing down his slippers), now he returns home and throws down the bottle of wine. We see that he is a changed man, and we have watched the process of that change carefully developed through editing codes.

Griffith does not end the film with this simple act of resolution, but adds another shot somewhere outside the narrative, which, like the apotheosis of earlier films, marks the harmony gained by the resolution of the narrative tension. The famous use of lighting in this last shot shows the way Griffith transformed elements of earlier cinema into the signifiers of narrative structure and moral rhetoric. This directional lighting from a parlour hearth had appeared in previous films, such as Edwin Porter's *The Seven Ages*. However, in Porter's film it serves a decorative rather than a narrative purpose, beautifully conveying the mood of an old couple by their fireside. For Griffith it depicts the closure of narrative. The glowing hearth serves as a cultural symbol for family harmony regained – with the nuclear family, dispersed across the unfolding of the narrative, now reunited and absorbed into an image of security, never to be broached again.

The light that pours from the right of the frame carries a number of associations which are seized and determined by the narrative order of the film to buttress its moral rhetoric. It represents, first of all, the hearth – the frequent nineteenth century metonym for family order (as exemplified by Dicken's "The Cricket on the Hearth", a story Griffith adapted to the screen some six weeks after *The Drunkard's Reformation*) with its associations of warmth and comfort. The directional light with its highlights and shadows also gives a pictorial ordering to the shot; rendering it, in this sense, into a *tableau*. But whereas in Porter's film this pictorial value was an end in itself, in Griffith's it takes on the narrative significance of order regained and stabilised. Finally, the light in this shot (as more explicitly in other 1909 Biograph films – such as *The Baby's Shoe* and *The Slave*) also carries the metaphorical significance of illumination: the family basks in the glow of the self-knowledge which the young husband received in his role as spectator.

The daughter sits in this glow and reads her book, the hearth providing the light necessary for instruction. Could we perhaps see here a reference to the screen as a source of light? The cinema, condemned by reformers as a realm of darkness, reveals itself (defines itself) as a source of light, a means of illumination and instruction.

Notes

1. Tom Gunning, "Weaving a Narrative: Style and Economic Background in Griffith's Biograph Films", *Quarterly Review of Film Study* (Winter 1981).
2. *The New York Clipper*, Vol. 5 (1909), p. 233.
3. The Motion Picture Patents Company, "Announcement to the Exhibitors", January 1909.
4. Accounts of such testimony can be found in *The New York Times* (24 December 1908), p. 4; *The Brooklyn Eagle* (26 December 1908), p. 4; and *The New York American* (24 December 1908), p. 2.
5. See the *New York Daily Tribune* (24 December 1908), p. 4; and *The New York World* (27 December 1908).
6. *The Film Index* (2 January 1909), p. 5.
7. See the *New York Daily Tribune* (26 December 1908), p. 1.
8. *New York Tribune* (24 December 1908), p. 4.
9. *New York Herald* (24 December 1908), p. 7.
10. *The Film Index* (2 January 1909), p. 5.
11. See John Collier, "Cheap Amusements", *Charities and the Commons* (11 April 1908).
12. "The Standards of The National Board of Censorship" pamphlet, n.d. (*c.* 1911), p. 3.
13. ibid.
14. "Report of The Board of Censorship on films shown May 10, 1909", on file at the Edison National Historical Site, West Orange, New Jersey. For the sake of clarity I have corrected a number of typographical errors that appear in the original.
15. A comparison with Zecca's *Victimes de l'Alcoolisme* from 1902 may be illuminating, but it is beyond the scope of this paper.
16. See John Hagan, "L'Erotisme des premiers temps", *Les Cahiers de la Cinémathèque* (Winter 1979).

17. *The Moving Picture World* vol. 3 (1909), p. 231.
18. Noël Burch, *To The Distant Observer: Form and Meaning in the Japanese Cinema*, Berkeley, University of California Press, 1978, pp. 75–80.
19. *The New York Dramatic Mirror* (24 October 1908), p. 8.
20. Reproduced in Eileen Bowser (ed.), *The Biograph Bulletins 1908–1912*, New York, Farrar Straus & Giroux, 1973, p. 77.

Chapter 9

ROBERTA E. PEARSON AND

WILLIAM URICCHIO[1]

HOW MANY TIMES SHALL CAESAR
BLEED IN SPORT

Shakespeare and the cultural debate about
moving pictures

I. Cheap amusements and cultural crisis

IN DECEMBER OF 1908 the *New York Daily Tribune* editorialized about the need for social control of the new moving picture medium. 'The moving picture business is a new business, in the hands of inexperienced persons, conducted in places at best ill designed for the safety of audiences, subject to very little publicity and to every temptation to degenerate into a source of corruption.'[2] The *Tribune*'s editorial commended New York City Mayor McClellan for revoking the licences of the city's over five hundred nickelodeons two days earlier. Though New York's producers and exhibitors quickly sought legal remedy and the moving picture shows reopened, the debate and the events around the nickelodeon closings highlight the pressures facing the American film industry during the crucial transitional years of 1907 to 1913. During this period, the film industry struggled to enter the mainstream of American culture, striving to disassociate itself from kindred cheap amusements, such as saloons and vaudeville, and to ally with an emerging cultural consensus. [. . .]

In this essay, we wish to re-examine one aspect of this transitional moment in relation to the larger culture. Focusing on Shakespearean film production between 1908 and 1913 in the context of Shakespeare's broader cultural circulation, we address one of the primary conditions of production and reception for these films. We do this by adducing evidence commonly associated with cultural rather than film history, though we still maintain an emphasis upon film texts and the film industry. Where possible, we illustrate our argument with one play, *Julius Caesar*, and the filmed version made by the Vitagraph Company in 1908.

Cheap amusements such as penny arcades, dance halls, saloons and vaudeville, in short, any venue for the congregation of the 'lower orders', were connected in the public mind with the problems of rapid urbanization and rising immigration so prominent in the turn-of-the-century United States. The spectre of immigrants and laborers liberated from the regimentation of the workplace and congregating freely to revel in 'crude,' 'vicious' and 'lascivious' entertainments struck fear into the hearts of many 'respectable' Americans. Indeed, in New York City as well as several other major urban centres, the problem of cheap amusements had

attracted the attention of civic reform groups, resulting in at least fourteen major investigations between 1908 and 1914.[3] These investigations often resulted in recommendations for
public and/or private regulation, and can be seen as part of a broader movement to impose
social control on both immigrants and the working classes, partially through the formation of
an emerging cultural consensus.[4]

The relatively new store front moving picture shows represented the most rapidly growing
and, to some, the most dangerous of the unregulated cheap amusements pandering to the
masses in their leisure time. The Vice Commission of Chicago reported that:

> Among the recreational conditions directly tributary to the increase of the victims of
> vice, are the privately managed amusement parks; dance halls, . . . candy, ice cream
> and fruit stores used as pleasure resorts; immoral shows, theatre plays and moving
> pictures; saloons where music, vaudeville performances, and other recreational attrac-
> tions are accessory to the drink habit; drug stores, where gambling devices and the
> selling of cocaine and other drugs are accessories.[5]

Film content uncontrolled by private or public interests and ill-regulated dark, crowded,
potential fire-trap storefront moving picture shows frequented by immigrants and the working
classes generated intense opposition from religious organizations and other civic activists. In
1909, *The Nickelodeon* reprinted an article from *Moving Picture News* which reflected the industry's
awareness of its precarious status.

> The motion pictures have made little headway with the intelligent classes. . . . They
> still remain the cheap amusement of the uncultured classes. The deplorable selection
> of subjects has aroused the feelings of all the newspapers, churches, schools, etc.,
> against motion pictures, to such a point that parents refuse permission to their chil-
> dren to see motion pictures even in churches and school rooms. If the manufacturers
> had catered a little more to the wants of decent audiences, instead of allowing them-
> selves to be guided by the greedy exhibitors, we would see many cinematograph shows
> in our best districts; we would see motion pictures as an established feature in all of
> the churches; . . . we would see them popular in schools, etc.[6]

The most vocal protests against the moving picture shows occurred in New York City,
the urban centre with the largest concentration of nickelodeons. An array of civic groups,
ranging from the Interdenominational Committee for the Suppression of Sunday Vaudeville to
the Society for the Prevention of Cruelty to Children, began to demand government intervention. Responding to this pressure, and concerned as well about the dangerous physical
conditions of the nickelodeons, Mayor McClellan convened hearings on the moving picture
shows. Opponents and proponents of the moving picture fought to define its cultural function.
The New York Herald reported that 'Clergymen and officers of societies to prevent crime . . .
condemned the nickel theatre as a moral sinkhole and physical deathtrap, and . . . those interested in the business . . . defended them as places necessary for the amusement of the poor
and for their moral and educational uplifting.'[7]

'Public spirited' citizens denounced the nickelodeons as dens of iniquity harbouring criminal elements from pickpockets to prostitutes. The atmosphere also was said to encourage
lascivious behaviour on the part of even the more respectable clientele. 'The darkened rooms,
combined with the influence of pictures projected on the screens, have given opportunities for
a new form of degeneracy.'[8] The Mayor, having listened to the testimony, revoked the current

licences of all New York nickelodeons, offering reinstatement contingent upon demonstrated compliance with the building code and upon the exhibitor's pledge to observe the Sunday blue laws.

The nickelodeon owners quickly responded to this threat to their livelihoods, forming the Moving Picture Association of New York and obtaining a legal injunction countermanding McClellan's revocation. While the exhibitors sought and obtained legal remedy, the film producers developed more long-ranging strategies for transforming the new medium from despised cheap amusement to widely accepted mass entertainment. During the hearings, J. Stuart Blackton, co-founder of the Vitagraph Company of America '. . . explained to the Mayor how the very recent merging of interests would facilitate better control over the moral atmosphere of the productions.'[9] Only a week before the nickelodeon closings, the most powerful elements of the film industry, headed by the Edison and Biograph Studios, had formed the Motion Picture Patents Company (MPPC), a trust intended to regulate distribution and exhibition and to respond to increasing pressures on the film industry from public and private critics.[10]

The formation of the MPPC signalled the film industry's implementation of strategies for dealing with the incipient crisis on several fronts. The MPPC strove to gain public support, instituting a short-lived attempt at site regulation and supporting a long-lasting scheme of self-imposed censorship which involved the creation of the National Board of Censorship. This Board would ensure that films would be 'Moral, Educational and Cleanly Amusing', serving both to attract a more desirable patronage and to uplift the current clientele.[11]

Though not clearly mandated by the MPPC, making films 'moral, educational and cleanly amusing' entailed transformations of subject matter and signifying practices as well as the omission of offensive material. During 1908–09, film manufacturers increasingly drew material from such respectable sources as Shakespeare, Dickens, and Tennyson. At the same time, their narrative structures came increasingly to resemble that of the socially acceptable 'realist' novel and play, rather than that of the declassé melodrama. Some film scholars have seen these adaptations as part of a ploy to attract a more 'middle class' audience.[12]

The film industry, perhaps already feeling public pressure, had been pursuing this last strategy prior to both the formation of the MPPC and the 1908 nickelodeon closings. On December 1, 1908, the Vitagraph Company had released its *Julius Caesar*. Surprisingly, given its eminently respectable derivation, the critics of the nickelodeon denounced this film as emblematic of the evils of the moving picture. A clergyman claimed that a moving picture 'show was immoral' because of the representation of 'an actual scene in *Julius Caesar*'. Apparently, the Mayor agreed.[13] J. Stuart Blackton served as the motion picture industry's spokesman at McClellan's hearings. He defended his film from further charges of immorality predicated upon Julius Caesar's wearing of 'a short skirt; Mr. Blackton showed the costume is historically accurate, and that the Vitagraph Company could not regulate the skirts of the noble Romans of long ago'.[14]

The Roman Emperor continued to haunt the proceedings. On Christmas Day, several hundred of New York City's exhibitors met to organize their defense. Many referred ironically to the censorship of *Julius Caesar*, unable to believe that anyone could possibly find filmed Shakespeare immoral or objectionable. The 'morality joke' became a running gag as 'they cheered the great Julius time and again and altogether had a merry Christmas time of it.' They pointed to *Julius Caesar* as a primary example of film's contribution to culture. 'Several of the orators appealed to the shade of *Julius Caesar* to acclaim the moving picture as an artistic triumph of the century, a triumph which no devotee of the liberal arts could ignore and every true artist must celebrate.' The exhibitors also referenced the film's theatrical antecedents, as if to gain respectability through this alliance. 'The shades of old William Shakespeare, of Booth and of Barrett, of Davenport and several others were called upon to witness "this blasphemous libel upon their royal selves and of the character they set forth".'[15] Indeed, the players in the Vitagraph film were alleged to have been garbed in the very costumes worn by their theatrical predecessors.

The defaming of *Caesar* remained a cause *célèbre* among the moving picture folk well after the brouhaha surrounding the nickelodeon closings had subsided. The film trade press responded to attacks on the film, *The Nickelodeon* implying that even the moving pictures' uneducated and immigrant clientele knew Shakespeare well enough to resent censorship of the film. An article quoted 'an Italian.' 'The Romans – they killed Julius Caesar. Then show it – all of it. Why not? It took place. For what is the censorship board – to give us skimmed milk and spoil art? In Rome they wore the *toga virilis* to the knee. Now they show it long and clumsy. For why? Would they put corsets on the "Venus of Milo"? Bah.'[16] The Chicago police had actually demanded the excision of the film's assassination scene. Three years later Blackton still voiced his disgust. 'They cut out the killing of Julius Caesar. Ye Gods! Imagine a couple of brawny policemen walking on the stage of a New York theatre and (not) politely ordering E. H. Sothern to "cut out the murder part, cull".'[17]

Despite *Caesar's* contentious reception, the industry persisted in its Shakespeare strategy. From 1908 to 1913, American film companies produced at least thirty-six 15 minute Shakespearean films, while importing a great many more foreign Shakespeare productions. Among the plays most frequently filmed were: *King Lear, Hamlet, Macbeth, The Merchant of Venice, Romeo and Juliet* and *A Midsummer Night's Dream*. Additionally, films such as a *Comedy of Errors* (Solax, 1913) used Shakespearean titles, while other films such as a *Village King Lear* (Gaumont, 1911) presented versions of the plays in contemporary settings. Variant American titles, along these lines, included: *A Modern Portia* (Lubin, 1912); *Taming Mrs. Shrew* (Rex, 1912); and *A Galloping Romeo* (Selig, 1913).[18] Many of these films emphasized their Shakespearean connections, as did *Indian Romeo and Juliet* (Vitagraph, 1912): 'It is far more Shakespearean than Shakespeare.'[19]

In the face of initial discouragement, why did the film industry persist in its Shakespearean adaptations? Clearly, as the members of the industry themselves indicated, the negative reception of the Vitagraph *Julius Caesar* conflicted with the generally valorized position of Shakespeare in late nineteenth and early twentieth century American culture.[20] But this assertion alone cannot fully explain either the film industry's production of Shakespearean films or the probable reception of those films among a wide spectrum of viewers. While we may never know with certainty why certain cultural authorities objected to the Vitagraph film, examination of the film industry's discourse concerning its Shakespearean adaptations can at least begin to illuminate the conditions of production for these films.

II. Shakespeare and film

The industry had several good reasons to produce these particular films at this historical juncture. First, in the wake of the 1907 *Ben Hur* copyright decision, studios were acutely aware of material in the public domain, and knew that Shakespeare was not only respectable but free. Secondly, as we will demonstrate, Shakespeare may have been far more accessible to a diverse spectrum of viewers than may be apparent from a late twentieth century perspective. Thirdly, Shakespeare provided as many thrills – duels, illicit romances, murders – as the rankest cheap melodrama. And fourthly, if critics accused filmmakers of excessive depiction of duels, etc., the industry could feign outraged innocence and wrap itself in the Bard's cultural respectability.

Yet trade press utterances and publicity copy never mentioned any of these motivations, focusing rather upon the uplifting qualities of Shakespeare while at the same time assuring exhibitors that this uplifting fare would not drive away their present clientele.

Shakespeare has formed a part of the literary canon for so long that we take for granted the equation of his works with cultural respectability. Yet examination of the similar utterances of turn-of-the-century cultural arbiters as diverse as Andrew Carnegie and immigrant uplift associations reveals greater complexity. In 1903, Carnegie, funder of countless libraries and museums, addressed the New York City immigrant aid society, The Educational Alliance, to which he also contributed. He stressed the assimilationist possibilities of the playwright's works, an emphasis particularly appropriate in light of the Alliance's efforts to Americanize the thousands of Eastern European Jewish immigrants pouring into New York City. 'But, ladies and gentlemen, language makes race. You give me a man who speaks English and reads Shakespeare. . . . You give me that man, or that young woman, and I don't care where he was born, or what country he comes from. . . .'[21] Carnegie was not alone in his assessment of Shakespeare's Americanizing potential. In 1886, Thomas D. Weld advanced reasons for the inclusion of Shakespeare in school curricula, one of which was a thinly veiled nativist stance. 'Nothing would so withstand the rush into our language of vapid, foreign dilutions as a baptism into Shakespeare's terse, crisp, sinewy Saxon.'[22]

Progressive groups such as the Educational Alliance and the People's Institute, a civic reform and educational organization, believed that productions of Shakespeare's works had many beneficial effects: they would keep people from cheap amusements, teach them moral lessons, and generally improve them; in short, the productions had '. . . educational and inspirational value. . . .'[23] Thomas Davidson, who lectured at the Educational Alliance, remarked on the moral lessons Shakespeare teaches. 'How we hate hypocrisy after reading *Measure for Measure*; reckless ambition, after reading *Macbeth*; indecision, after reading *Hamlet*, and so on!'[24]

Many studios, such as the Vitagraph Company, which accounted for the bulk of the American Shakespearean productions, specifically referenced the films' high cultural associations and benefits, echoing the sentiments of civic reformers and uplifters. The Biograph Company claimed that its *Taming of the Shrew* (1908) would provide 'an object lesson – "See ourselves as others see us".'[25] In reviewing the Vitagraph Company's *Twelfth Night* (1910), *The Moving Picture World* said,

> It elevates and improves the literary taste and appreciation of the greatest mass of the people, performing in this way a service which cannot be measured in material terms. Such work is the nature of an educational service which is deserving of the heartiest support of all who are working for the improvement of humanity.[26]

The industry also expected that viewers would be able to engage with the films on various levels, suggesting different receptions for different segments of the audience. Both studio publicity and the trade press implied that some viewers came to the nickelodeon with detailed knowledge of the Bard and his plays and enjoyed the films through narrative engagement. The same sources also implied that other viewers enjoyed these films either through engagement with their spectacular elements, or through narrative comprehension gained from lectures or extremely simplified plots. *The Vitagraph Bulletin* emphasized the dual appeal of *A Midsummer Night's Dream* (1910). 'Students of the great dramatist's works will thoroughly enjoy the careful pictorial presentation of the many scenes, while the whole play is so clearly portrayed that it will not fail to delight the spectator who is not familiar with the works of Shakespeare.'[27] [. . .] Reviewing Vitagraph's *Anthony and Cleopatra* (1908), *The New York Dramatic Mirror* referenced both clarity and spectacle. Comparing it to the favourably received *Richard III* (1908), the reviewer said, 'It is clearer in telling the story, and even more elaborate in the spectacular features. The costumes and scenic effects are of the finest . . .'[28]

The industry seems to have assumed that the more affluent and better educated viewers whom it wished to attract with Shakespeare would engage with the narratives while the spectacular elements would appeal to the nickelodeon's old clientele. But what were the conditions of reception?

III. Shakespeare's cultural circulation

Shakespearean texts had far-reaching manifestations, encompassing everything from relatively inexpensive editions of the complete works, to inclusion in school curricula, to ephemera such as advertising cards, to various theatrical productions. We believe that knowledge of these 'intertexts' and their circulation more fully illuminates conditions of production and reception for *Julius Caesar* and other filmed Shakespeare than does film-industry discourse alone. This wider array of evidence permits discussion of how Shakespearean texts functioned in the culture. While these texts originated from specific institutions (school curricula and textbooks, advertising, etc.), they circulated among a broad class spectrum, creating the conditions for a multiplicity of modes of engagement with Shakespeare and the Shakespearean films. In other words, delineating the general cultural circulation of 'Shakespeare' permits speculation about the range of possible negotiations of *Julius Caesar*.[29] [. . .]

To adumbrate the incredible pervasiveness of Shakespearean images and phrases in late nineteenth and early twentieth century America, we look first at one of the most important of Shakespeare's manifestations – public school curricula. We then briefly discuss a selection of Shakespearean ephemera. Finally, we look at the Shakespearean activities of New York City institutions involved in 'uplifting' the city's immigrants and wage-earners.

Exposure to Shakespeare in public schools, for a certain age cohort, would have been systematic and widespread, since attendance through the eighth grade was legally mandated in most locations. Such exposure may also have constituted the clearest instance of the Bard's role in the formation of cultural consensus, particularly in New York City's public schools, whose resources at the time were devoted almost entirely to 'Americanizing' the children of the newly arrived immigrants. A common culture was represented in the excerpts from key scenes and key speeches which constituted much of the Shakespeare covered in the classroom.

New York City curricula guides mandated Shakespeare at every level, beginning with the memorization of Ariel's Song 'Where the Bee Sucks' in Grade 2B. In Grade 8B students read 'This was the Noblest Roman of Them All.' Eighth grade curricula also included the reading of Lambs' *Tales from Shakespeare*, *The Merchant of Venice* and *Julius Caesar*. The *New McGuffey Fifth Reader*, widely adopted in public schools, included both 'Under the Greenwood Tree' from *As You Like It* and 'Antony's Oration over Caesar's Dead Body'.

The above tells us that students memorized and read Shakespeare, but does not tell us how they were taught or what they might have learned. Though intended for college students, the outline for study for *Julius Caesar* in the journal *Education* gives some notion of how educators taught this play. The outline for study suggests three readings of the play: the first for narrative comprehension, the second for dramatic qualities and the third for broader cultural resonance. Included in the outline for the third reading is a list of 'the most striking scenes of the drama': 'Caesar and his train; the thunderstorm; the midnight meeting; Brutus and Portia; Portia on the Ides of March; the assassination; over Caesar's body; the tent scene; the parley; the ghost of Caesar appears to Brutus.'[30]

While teachers may have wished to incorporate their students into the cultural consensus, contemporary comments indicate that, as one would expect, reception was incredibly diverse. What might students actually have learned? Not much, asserted a *Harper's Weekly* column. 'Nearly everyone in the educated class who was questioned had read one or two plays, usually at school, but nearly all held mistaken ideas about what they had read, and had a most superficial knowledge of the construction of the plays, the significance of the characters, and the points of preeminent excellence.'[31] A short piece in *The Atlantic Monthly*, put together from 'several examination papers lately presented at an academy in Pennsylvania' confirmed this impression. 'Then Caesar reached the Senate safe, but Cascada stabbed him deep and Brutus gave him the most kindest cutting, which made the tyran yell, Eat, too, Brutus?'[32] Apparently both teachers' lessons and students' reception simply centred on key phrases, scenes and speeches.

Meanwhile, the pervasive Shakespearean cultural ephemera both reflected and reinforced Shakespeare's central place in the dominant culture and attested to wide-spread familiarity with his work, even if income, reading habits, consumption patterns, etc. meant varying exposures to it. Relatively inexpensive versions of Shakespeare proliferated. Shakespearean references even surfaced in the popular penny press directed at working class readers. For example, in 1889 *The New York World* issued a complementary city guide. A short piece, 'The National Game', listed twenty seven Shakespearean quotes meant to 'convince one that the game [baseball] is of remote origin'. Among these: 'A hit, a palpable hit.' (*Hamlet*) and 'Let me be umpire in this.' (*Henry VI*).[33]

Other Shakespearean ephemera, most with a strong visual component, abounded: stereographs; sculpture; illustrated calendars with 'quotes of the month'; writing tablets, again with quotes and illustrations; and card games. Here we will just give examples of advertising specifically related to *Julius Caesar*. N. K. Fairbanks and Company, Lard Refiners, issued a series of tradecards (circa 1880–90) featuring 'familiar quotations' from the Bard. One shows a pig in a rendering vat. The quote under him reads 'Let me have those (sic) about me that are fat, sleek headed chaps (sic), and such as sleep o'nights.'[34] A tradecard for Libby, McNeill and Libby's Cooked Corned Beef shows caricatures of a plump toga-clad Caesar and Brutus conversing about a slim Cassius lurking in the background. Caesar complains 'Yon Cassius has a lean and hungry look, . . . would he were fatter.' Brutus suggests feeding Cassius the advertiser's product. A card for Barker and Company Coal shows Brutus and Cassius in Roman military costume with the caption, 'Away, slight man' – a verbatim quotation. [. . .]

The slight misquotings and elisions on the trade cards perhaps reflect the way in which such 'familiar quotations' became common parlance. The illustrations suggest one means by which visual representations of Shakespearean characters became fairly standardized. Both trade cards featuring the play's characters show them in the proper attire for the quoted scenes, the images both reflecting and reinforcing a sense of the appropriate iconography. Yet the caricatured and parodistic nature of the images in combination with their hucksterish purpose make clear that Shakespeare was no sacred cow. This use of Shakespearean scenes and phrases also attests to widespread recognition that may have transcended class barriers. Products such as lard and corned beef were probably not sold simply to the 'respectable' middle classes.

While school curricula and cultural ephemera potentially crossed class boundaries and served many functions for recipients, 'uplift' institutions, primarily located in New York City's tenement districts, specifically directed Shakespeare at the immigrant and working classes associated with the nickelodeon and other cheap amusements. Organizations such as settlement houses, the YMCA, the Ethical Culture Society, the New York City Department of Education's Bureau of Lectures, the Educational Alliance, and the People's Institute, all sponsored lectures, classes, clubs and theatrical productions, many centred around Shakespeare's plays and characters.

Obviously, Shakespeare, the 'greatest' poet of the English language, proved powerfully attractive to those seeking to acculturate the non-English speaking immigrant as well as the illiterate working man. James Hamilton, Head Worker of the University Settlement, wrote to the People's Institute supporting its plans for a People's Theatre and mentioning the recent Shakespearean productions at the Educational Alliance.[35]

> No intellectual tonic could be finer or more stimulating. A good percentage of the audiences have not long been masters of the English Language. They have scarcely crossed the threshold of our literature. What a grand and inspiring entrance was here provided for them – the best English Literature ever cast in dramatic form . . .[36]

The hegemonic implications of this Shakespearean fare did not go unnoticed. A reporter for the *Boston American* criticized the uplifters' efforts, declaring that 'wage-earners' should not have Shakespeare forced down their throats but should rather do their own thinking and select their own entertainments. 'Why should theatrical benevolence always take the form of Shakespeare? Apparently because Shakespeare is safe, and is supposed to be good for the blood.'[37]

One should not assume, however, that cultural arbiters such as the People's Institute were forcing Shakespeare upon the 'lower orders'. Indeed, the Educational Alliance asserted that its lower East Side clientele already had a taste for Shakespeare for which the Alliance's activities catered.

> There is no necessity on the East Side to *create* a taste for the fine and elevated in literature. The taste is there. All that is necessary is to guide its development. The classes in Shakespeare and in English literature can well serve as the barometer of the literary atmosphere permeating such part of the lives of the working people of the community as is not taken up with earning their daily bread.[38]

[. . .] Certainly, the prevalence of Shakespeare in New York City's Yiddish and Italian theatres further attests to the playwright's widespread popularity.

Consistent with their hegemonic intent, as well as attempting to appeal to the evident interests of the community, the People's Institute sponsored a series of ongoing Shakespearean recitals at the Cooper Union, supplementing the Bard's inclusion in their lecture series. By 1905, these recitals had become so popular that 500 to 1000 people were turned away each night during the Christmas week performances.[39] *The New York Evening Mail* described an audience at what became the traditional Christmas recital:

> Their attention was close, their eyes eager, their faces full of intelligent appreciation. There was no clapping of applauding hands because someone else did so. There was no someone else to them save the characters portrayed by the man on the platform before them. The applause, given with appreciation quite as much for the literary passages as for the emotional dramatic climaxes, burst like waves on the shore from all parts at once.[40]

In May, 1904, the Ben Greet Company gave three performances at the Cooper Union under the auspices of the People's Institute, performing the *Merchant of Venice* twice and *Twelfth Night* once.[41] The performances, including a special matinee for school children, sold out and generated favourable publicity for the People's Institute. The Greet Company continued to give numerous performances under the auspices of both the People's Institute and the Educational Alliance. The evident success meeting the Shakespearean offerings of such institutions as the People's Institute seems to attest to Shakespeare's cross-class appeal. This popular response may have substantiated the film industry's perceptions of its Shakespearean films as appreciated by 'the greatest mass of the people.' [. . .]

Of course, the Shakespearean films constituted part of the circulation of Shakespearean texts, and may actually have had greater potential for elevation and improvement than even the People's Institute, since filmed Shakespeare may have reached those to whom the free or inexpensive offerings of New York's uplift educational institutions remained inaccessible. Theatre historian and critic Montrose Moses, writing in *The Theatre*, stated that people too poor to afford even discounted theatrical admissions sought uplifting culture at the nickelodeons. 'In numbers measuring over two hundred thousand throughout New York City, this kinetoscopic clientele is composed of people who cannot afford to go to the theatre, even though such an organization as the People's Institute strive (sic) to reduce for them the theatre prices along Broadway.'[42]

Moses went on to discuss a lower East Side nickelodeon specializing in Shakespearean films, indicating that some amongst the immigrant population did indeed attend and enjoy these films. The proprietor was 'anxious to make of his five cent theatre an educational center among the children and grown people of the lower East Side, and to judge by the manner in which the crowd are flocking through the gaily painted entrance, and by the overflow left standing on the sidewalk waiting for the next performance there is no doubt that [he] is meeting with success.'[43]

IV. Conditions of production and reception for *Julius Caesar*

The non-film evidence we have presented concerning Shakespeare's cultural circulation permits us to contextualize and thus complicate the film industry's discourse on several levels. While a late twentieth century perspective might lead one to associate Shakespearean subjects simply with 'high culture' or 'respectability', we have seen that Shakespeare was in fact culturally pervasive during this period. Certainly, Shakespeare's inclusion in school curricula supports the respectability argument, but the eager embrace of Shakespeare by people 'below Fourteenth Street' suggests other sorts of popular appropriation. If high-priced Shakespeare at the standard theatres relied heavily upon spectacular elements, the presentations to which the 'masses' were exposed foregrounded the verse rather than the staging, reversing the conclusion one might draw from industry discourse alone.

We can further explore the issue of audience reception by specific reference to *Julius Caesar*. The film, shot on painted theatrical sets in the standard tableau style of the period, is a compression of Shakespearean text: the fifteen shots omit six of the play's seventeen scenes. Vitagraph's publicity release described the film as follows:

> Scene 1 – Street in Rome. Casca and Trebonius upbraid the citizens for praising Caesar. Scene 2 – The Forum. A soothsayer bids Caesar 'beware the Ides of March.' Scene 3 – Mark Antony wins the race and 'thrice he offers Caesar a crown.' Scene 4 – Cassius tempts Brutus to join the conspiracy against Caesar. Scene 5 – Brutus' garden. Meeting

of the conspirators. Scene 6 – Caesar's palace. Calphurnia tells Caesar of her dream and begs him not to go to the senate. The conspirators enter, laugh at his fears, urge and get his consent to go. Scene 7 – Street near Capitol. The soothsayer again warns Caesar. Scene 8 – The Capitol. The assassination of Caesar. Scene 9 – The Forum. Brutus addresses the mob. Antony enters with Caesar's body. Scene 10 – Brutus' camp near Sardis. Cassius upbraids Brutus. Scene 11 – Brutus' tent – quarrel – Caesar's ghost. Scene 12 – Plains of Phillipi. Armies of Mark Antony and Octavius Caesar, and Brutus and Cassius. Scene 13 – The Battle. 'Caesar, thou art revenged even with the sword that killeth thee.' Scene 14 – Brutus slays himself. 'Caesar, now be still. I killed not thee with half so good a will.' Scene 15 – Brutus' funeral pyre. 'This was the noblest Roman of them all.'[44]

Late twentieth century viewers might find this fifteen shot, 15 minute film a somewhat inadequate realization of Shakespeare's lengthy and complex original text. Yet, the film is consistent with the key phrase, key scene, key image approach to Shakespeare that we have discovered in much of the cultural ephemera of the period. The film contains four direct quotes and a paraphrase of some of the play's best known lines, foregrounded by the Vitagraph publicity. Just as the film features key phrases, it features key scenes. Above we mentioned the college study outline which enumerated the 'most striking scenes of the drama'. Of the ten scenes listed, eight appear in the Vitagraph film. The scenes omitted both from this list and the film deal with Mark Antony and his co-rulers, perhaps indicating a culturally prevalent narrative simplification. Architecture and costuming accord with the images circulated on Shakespearean ephemera, such as the trade cards we have described. The film thus fits the culturally prevalent 'reductionist' approach to Shakespeare we have sketched out, and contemporary viewers, Shakespearean scholars perhaps exempted, would have found the Vitagraph film perfectly consonant with their previous exposure to the play.

If the key scene, key phrase treatment of Vitagraph's *Julius Caesar* accorded with the Shakespeare who circulated across class boundaries, such was not the case with the film's staging, which employed the spectacle of the higher-priced theatre rather than the stark presentations of, for example, the Ben Greet Company. The film's action takes place in front of sets painted to resemble Roman architecture. Stephen Bush, in *The Moving Picture World*, compared Vitagraph's 'excellent' representation of the Forum to the famous painting by Gerome.[45] The on-screen depiction of off-stage action further illustrates Vitagraph's incorporation of spectacle. In the play, during Act I, scene ii, Mark Antony thrice offers Caesar the crown offstage, while onstage, Brutus and Cassius listen. The film's third shot, preceded by the intertitle 'Mark Antony three times offers Caesar the crown,' shows Caesar seated in a grandstand, surrounded by a crowd of extras. While he watches the race which Shakespeare's Casca only describes, Antony presents the crown to him. Indeed, we suspect that the producers emulated the elaborate staging and costumes of the theatre as closely as possible precisely to appeal to an audience which at this time primarily attended the theatre rather than the nickelodeon. The referencing of the stage tradition through claims about the theatrical antecedents of the Vitagraph Company's costumes supports this conclusion.

What, then, can we conclude about the reception of *Julius Caesar* and other Shakespeare films? As we suggested above, even if the film industry chose Shakespearean subjects for their hegemonic function, the period's parodic forms, such as advertising cards, indicate that Shakespeare could be taken lightly. While cultural arbiters and educators may have played up the Bard's uplifting and even Americanizing potential, lard and corned beef manufacturers circulated 'vernacular' Shakespeares which counted on an easy familiarity with the 'great' works. Hence, response to filmed Shakespeare would have depended to some extent upon a viewer's previous exposure to specific intertexts, as would readings of the films' representational strategies. The minimalist rendering of the text would have surprised neither the nickelodeon's current patrons nor more affluent viewers that *Julius Caesar* and other Shakespeare films may have attracted. But the film's representation of spectacle may have been read differently by viewers from different social formations. Viewers accustomed to the spectacular staging of the high-priced theatre would have found much in the Vitagraph production that was familiar. But how might those viewers accustomed to recitals and minimal staging have responded to the spectacular elements of the Vitagraph film? Was their visual pleasure affected by the absence of the familiar verbal text?

Our evidence allows us to draw three broad conclusions about the conditions of reception for *Julius Caesar* in particular and Shakespearean films generally: 1) Shakespeare would have had a range of possible associations, ranging from the hegemonic to the parodic; 2) most viewers would not have found the 'reductionist' interpretation of the text surprising; 3) some viewers would have expected and appreciated the spectacle, while others may have found it an unexpected bonus, but missed a fuller narrative engagement.[46]

But the shade of Julius Caesar haunts us still. None of the intertexts we have adduced would suggest anything in the slightest degree immoral or objectionable about this play. Why then the complaints from Chicago officials and the New York clergy? Francis V. F. Oliver, the

Figure 9.1 The contentious assassination scene from *Julius Caesar* (Vitagraph, 1908) (Courtesy of the Academy of Motion Picture Arts and Sciences)

chief of the New York City Bureau of Licenses, which regulated the nickelodeons, uttered a very revealing statement about the play and the filmed version. 'Scenes of crime and depravity on the stage, which are witnessed by the most respectable people in the land, seem to be too violent and harmful in their effects upon the minds of the young to be permitted in show houses. . . . Brutus must not murder Caesar in the presence of our children.'[47]

Mr. Oliver's opinion concerning the relative harmfulness of theatrical and filmic depictions of depravity provides an insight which may begin to answer our question. We have asserted that the film industry, at least discursively, sought to ally itself with cultural arbiters whose efforts at social control took the form of establishing a cultural consensus. The film industry attempted to forge this alliance through the selection and, in most cases, the reverent treatment of culturally valorized texts, which accounts for the abundance of Shakespeare films. But compliance with the concept of appropriate culture advocated by the industry's adversaries apparently required more than the selection of valorized texts and the correct discourse concerning them.

Most Shakespearean texts and intertexts circulated in venues which carefully structured reception and sought to restrict textual polysemy. The standard theatre had mechanisms for controlling both audiences and interpretations. The price regulated audience composition, and certainly prohibited the attendance of unaccompanied children, while newspaper reviews policed content and provided interpretive guidelines. In the wake of the nickelodeon closings, the *New York Daily Tribune* argued that the theatre required no censorship, but that the moving picture certainly did. 'Public safety on the moral side is, moreover, no better provided for, there being practically no supervision of the character of the [moving picture] shows given, and the need of censorship being very different from that in the case of theatres, where the press keeps the public informed of what is being presented.'[48] School curricula and textbooks attempted to contain polysemic texts, as teachers' manuals and other instructors' aids favoured some interpretations over others. Film on the other hand escaped such control mechanisms, the exhibitors not regulating audience composition or attempting to structure reception, while the daily programme changes precluded popular press reviews.[49]

Our essay has demonstrated the importance of non-filmic discourse for an understanding of the conditions of production and reception of early cinema. Admittedly, *Julius Caesar* was an anomaly, as the outraged protests of the exhibitors as well as the lack of similar complaints directed against other Shakespearean adaptations indicate. But the case of this film in no way invalidates the utility of the intertextual method this essay has proposed. We would argue that augmenting film-specific evidence (the films themselves and the industry's own discourse) with intertextual evidence more fully illuminates the conditions of cinematic production and reception.

Notes

1   The order of the authors' names was decided by a coin toss. The authors collaborated to such an extent that they could not themselves distinguish their 'individual' contributions to the article.
2   'Moving Picture Shows', *The New York Daily Tribune*, Dec. 26, 1908.
3   Alan Havig, 'The Commercial Amusement Audience in Early 20th-Century American Cities', *The Journal of American Culture*, 5 (Spring 1982), pp. 1–19.
4   On the subject of cheap amusements, see, for example, the work of Lewis Erenberg, John Kasson, Kathy Peiss, Roy Rosenweig and Robert Sklar.
5   The Vice Commission of Chicago, *The Social Evil in Chicago: A Study of Existing Conditions* (Chicago: Gunthorp-Warren Printing Company, 1911), p. 230.
6   'Scientific and Educational Pictures', *The Nickelodeon*, Dec. 1909, p. 168.

7   'See in Cheap Shows Peril to Children', *New York Herald*, Dec. 24, 1908.

8   R. Fellowes Jenkins of the Society for the Prevention of Cruelty to Children, quoted in *The New York Daily Tribune*, Dec. 26, 1908.

9   'Crucial Hour for the New York Shows', *The Film Index*, Jan. 2, 1909, p. 5.

10   For detailed accounts of the Motion Picture Patents Company see Tom Gunning, 'D. W. Griffith and the Narrator-System' (PhD Diss., New York University, 1986), and Robert Anderson, 'The Motion Picture Patents Company' (PhD Diss., University of Wisconsin, 1983).

11   Motion Picture Patents Company, 'Advertisement', quoted in Gunning, p. 447.

12   See Russell Merritt, 'Nickelodeon Theaters, 1905–1914: Building an audience for the Movies' in Tino Balio ed., *The American Film Industry* (Madison: University of Wisconsin Press, 1976), pp. 83–102.

13   'Picture-Show Men Organize to Fight', *The New York Times*, Dec. 26, 1908.

14   'Crucial Hour'.

15   'Show Men Will Fight', *The New York Daily Tribune*, Dec. 26, 1908. The exhibitors referred to several nineteenth century actors well known for their enactments of various roles in the play: Edwin Booth, Lawrence Barrett and Edward Loomis Davenport.

16   *The Nickelodeon*, Sept. 1909, p. 71.

17   *The Nickelodeon*, Jan. 7, 1911, p. 12.

18   Robert Hamilton Ball, *Shakespeare on Silent Film: A Strange Eventful History* (London: George Allen & Unwin, 1968). [. . .]

19   *Vitagraph Life Portrayals*, Jan. 17–Feb. 1, 1912, p. 21.

20   For more on Shakespeare's position in late nineteenth century America, see Lawrence Levine, *Highbrow, Lowbrow: The Emergence of Cultural Hierarchy in America* (Cambridge: Harvard University Press, 1988).

21   *Eleventh Annual Report of the President and Board of Directors* (New York: Educational Alliance, 1903), p. 82.

22   Theodore D. Weld, 'Shakespeare in the Class-room', *Shakespeariana*, 3 (1886), pp. 437–8.

23   Charles Sprague Smith, 'A Theatre for the People and the Public Schools', *Charities*, Feb. 4, 1905, p. 5.

24   Thomas Davidson, *The Education of the Wage-Earners: A Contribution Toward the Solution of the Educational Problem of Democracy* (New York: Ginn and Company, 1904), p. 80.

25   Eileen Bowser (ed.), *Biograph Bulletins*, 1908–12 (New York: Octagon Books, 1973), p. 35.

26   *The Moving Picture World*, Feb. 19, 1910, p. 257.

27   *The Vitagraph Bulletin*, Dec. 1–15, 1909.

28   *The New York Dramatic Mirror*, Nov. 14, 1908, p. 10.

29   We are aware that such an approach potentially establishes an infinite regress of negotiations. We would argue, however, that exposures to a particular topic within the broader fabric of the supravening cultural context help to delimit and structure patterns of reception. This approach attempts to address the tension between, on the one hand, the infinite interpretative possibilities of the individual subject and, on the other, the determinism of social construction, by exploring the resonant variations of a particular figure's cultural presence and the patterns of its social circulation.

30   Maude Kingsley. 'Outline Study of Shakespeare's *Julius Caesar*', *Education*, 22:4 (1901), p. 229.

31   'Is Shakespeare Read?', *Harper's Weekly*, 51:2615 (1907), p. 152.

32   'A School Comment on Shakespeare's *Julius Caesar*'. *The Atlantic Monthly*, 96:3 (1905), p. 431.

33   *Cyclopedia of Useful Information and Complete Handbook of New York City* (New York: New York World, 1889), p. 48.

34   Meat, Food. Green Boxes. Bella C. Landauer Collection, The New York Historical Society.

35   The Educational Alliance, funded by wealthy German-Jews, ran a settlement house and immigrant aid society in the heart of the lower East Side. The Alliance offered its members a variety of Shakespearean fare: lectures, recitals, plays, classes and clubs. The Alliance's members responded so favourably that 'hundreds are turned away from performances, because of lack of room' (Minutes of Meeting of the Advisory League, April 19, 1906, Papers of the Educational Alliance, RG 312 #14, YIVO).

36   Letter from James Hamilton, Head Worker, University Settlement Society, to Michael M. Davis, Secretary, People's Institute, Nov. 23, 1905. Box 16, People's Institute Records, the Rare Books and Manuscripts Division, The New York Public Library. (Hereafter, PIR, RBMD/NYPL.)

37   'Dramatic Soup Kitchen', *The American* (Boston), March 18, 1906. Box 37, PIR, RMBD/NYPL.

38   *Eleventh Annual Report*, p. 44.

39   *Ninth Annual Report of the Managing Director to the Corporation of the People's Institute*, Oct. 1906, n.p., Box 1, PIR, RBMD/NYPL.

40   'Shakespeare on the East Side', *The New York Evening Mail*, Jan. 7, 1905, Box 37, PIR, RBMD/NYPL.
41   *Seventh Annual Report of the Managing Director to the Corporation of the People's Institute*, 1904, p. 8, Box 1, PIR, RBMD/NYPL.
42   Montrose J. Moses, 'Where They Perform Shakespeare for Five Cents', *The Theatre Magazine*, Oct. 1908, p. 265.
43   Ibid., p. 264.
44   'Julius Caesar, An Historical Tragedy', *The Film Index*, Dec. 5, 1908, p. 9.
45   *The Moving Picture World*, Dec. 5, 1908, p. 447.
46   While our examination of culturally pervasive Shakespearean intertexts permits us generally to characterize the conditions of reception, characterizing the particular reception of actual historical viewers falls outside the realm of historical investigation: we would not presume to 'reconstruct' an actual historical viewer's negotiation of a particular text, which would have depended not only on his/her exposure to a variety of intertexts but upon an intersecting web of social determinants (age, race, ethnicity, gender, etc.) as well.
47   *The Film Index*, Nov. 12, 1910. p. 1.
48   'Moving Picture Shows', *New York Daily Tribune*, Dec. 26, 1908.
49   Except in those cases where films were accompanied by lectures, of course.

Chapter 10

LEE GRIEVESON

FIGHTING FILMS
Race, morality, and the governing of
cinema, 1912–1915

TWO EVENTS (OR ACCOUNTS OF EVENTS) involving the African American
boxer Jack Johnson, taken together, tell us something about the curious historical inter-
twining of disciplinary regimes aimed both at producing subjugated racialized bodies and
suppressing moving pictures. Johnson's challenge, in his professional and personal life,[1] to a
"color line" hitherto assumed to be stable and secure provoked reaction from (among others)
the national policing organization, the Bureau of Investigation.[2] Surveying Johnson's movements, the bureau pushed for a charge of "white slavery," the transportation of a white woman
across state lines for "immoral purposes," though there was considerable difficulty in fitting
Johnson's actions in his relationship with white women to the terms of the "White Slave Traffic
Act."[3] Convicted in May 1913, Johnson was sentenced to a year and a day in the Illinois State
Penitentiary. Discipline, Michel Foucault's work has suggested, "fixes, . . . arrests or regulates
movement."[4] A governmental reinvigoration of the disciplinary structures of white supremacy
worked through a policing of Johnson's mobility, closely linked to a policing of the "mobility"
of sexuality to cross racial borders.[5] [. . .]

Johnson's mobility was not, however, limited to the movement of his body but extended
outward, to the movement of filmic representations of that body fighting. A further apparatus
of security would emerge to arrest the movement of those representations, drawing on the
policing of Johnson himself to fashion a regulation of both moving pictures of Johnson and a
broader policing of the emerging institution of cinema. A concern with disciplining the movement of a particular black body through social space, closely linked to the restoration of a
moral social order, became enmeshed with the regulation of moving pictures. Johnson
would emerge as a crucial pivot around which governmental intervention into the regulation
and definition of "cinema" would swivel.

Consider in this context a second curious event centered around Johnson and the policing
of national borders. Following his exile from the United States after the white slavery conviction,[6] Johnson fought a number of times in Europe and South America. Although these fights
were filmed, they were not seen in the United States because of a 1912 act banning the interstate transportation of fight films. In 1915, however, Johnson fought Jess Willard in Havana
and lost his title, his punishment in the ring able at last to function as specular assurance of
the negation of the threat Johnson had posed to the existing structures of racism. "The Great
White Hope" had fashioned a closure to a narrative that had run across individual fights, and

fight films, since 1908. There was much demand to see the film. The *Chicago Post* suggested that "it may be necessary to rejigger the interstate law that forbids the transportation of fight pictures from one state to another."[7] Perhaps on this understanding, the producer, Lawrence Weber, attempted to import the film through Newark, New Jersey, "past the frowning watch-fulness," in the words of W. Stephen Bush, "of Uncle Sam."[8] The film was confiscated by port authorities, and although Weber went on to challenge the constitutionality of the 1912 act, he was defeated in a federal district court and in the U.S. Supreme Court.[9] Another plan was, it seems, set in play.

The negatives of the film had been developed and printed in Toronto and were to be exported from there to the South American and European markets. A scheme was devised whereby those pictures could be transported across the border of North America without contravening the terms of the 1912 act: the film was to be projected from the Canadian side of the border and recorded on film in the United States, across a border measuring just a few centimeters. On April 15, 1916, more than a year after the actual fight, a group carried the negatives to a rendezvous point at the international boundary stone one mile north of the Delaware and Hudson railway stations at Rouses Point. A tent was set up over the stone with its northern stakes pegged into Canada and its southern stakes pegged into the United States. A customs official observed the proceedings. The rephotographing apparently took five days.[10] The images of the fight—of Johnson's defeat and of Willard's knockout blow—crossed the now permeable border in patterns of light.

Weber's conceptual move was impressive, repositioning the ban on interstate commerce as referring only to the actual filmic material—the celluloid itself—and thus freeing the images from their embodiment on/as film; however, this plan ran aground on the ultimate intransi-gence of the panoptical customs authorities. A federal statute for unlawful importation of a fight film was issued. Weber again challenged this in the federal district court, although the judge's verdict reversed his attempt to separate images from celluloid. The *Moving Picture World* reported: "The argument that this process did not amount to bringing in the picture from Canada is met, Judge Hand said, by the unquestioned fact that a pictorial image, though not a physical object, was in Canada and is now in New York and that its presence here was caused by the traveling of rays of light."[11] The policing of the national border could extend to a disci-plining of the movement of rays of light, one example of how modern "state sovereignty," as Benedict Anderson observes, "is fully, flatly, and evenly operative over each square centimeter of a legally demarcated community."[12] The attempt to discipline Johnson's movements had shifted to an effort to control the movement of celluloid and rays of light.

Taken together, the curious similarities in the events sketched here suggest that a policing of Johnson's movements shifted to an equally intensive policing of the movement of pictures of Johnson fighting. Regulation aimed at the content and effect of moving pictures—the subver-sion of racial hierarchies and the capability of Johnson's fight films to disaggregate fixed national communities and problematize the maintenance of cultural identity—was achieved through the disciplining of movement. This regulation is, however, explicable only in reference to the wider structures and more general aims of a particular interventionist system. Moving pictures are inscribed into a broader "regulatory space," one element among other regulatory issues subject to public decisions and government intervention. The term "regulatory space" is used here, then, to refer to a broad arena of regulation, including measures directed at the economic sphere—particularly the control of the flow of commerce and of large corporations—and other measures directed at, for example, the control of sexual morality, the "traffic" in "white slaves," structures of white supremacy, the dissemination of "immoral" representations, and so on.[13] A genealogy of this critical interlinking of regulatory projects necessitates a series of border crossings of my own, as I move from a discussion of the agitation over Johnson's fight films, to debates about white slavery and Johnson's inscription within that, to wider debates about the social functioning of cinema.

Regulation is, of course, virtually a defining feature of social organization, which almost inevitably involves the presence of rules and the attempt to enforce them. In this sense, one may approach regulation as the design of rules, the creation of institutions responsible for their implementation, and the clarification of the exact rule in a particular circumstance.[14] To take the examples of the two curious events introduced above, this is apparent in the similar design of acts to ban the movement of "immorality" across state lines, its policing via federal government power invested in customs officials, port authorities, and the courts, and the clarification of this power in federal district courts and in the Supreme Court. The principle of constitutional democracy means that the range and forms of regulation are deeply influenced by the historically and geographically specific conception of the scope and purpose of law. In the United States, in the absence of a strong tradition of public administration, judicial processes filled what Morton Keller terms "the void of governance."[15] Accordingly, this analysis will track the parameters of this regulatory space through four government acts and sundry legal decisions utilizing those acts: the 1910 Mann Act, banning the transportation of women across state lines for immoral purposes (the regulation of the movement of people); the 1912 Sims Act, banning the interstate transportation of boxing films (the regulation of the movement of moving pictures); the 1915 decision in the federal government's antitrust suit against the Motion Picture Patents Company (the regulation of a corporation distributing films across the nation); and the 1915 Supreme Court decision on the validity of state censorship of motion pictures (upholding a localized regulation of the content and movement of moving pictures). [. . .]

Debates about the social functioning of cinema were effectively over what cinema was used for—broadly speaking, its educational potential or its basis as "pure" entertainment. As the term *regulatory space* suggests, one may conceive of this debate in relation to processes of inclusion and exclusion, to the drawing of boundaries around objects and spaces. The central question here, in relation to the object "cinema," thus became: Is cinema similar to the press and hence protected by First Amendment rights? Or is cinema simply a type of "commerce," distinct from the press (and "literature") and hence governable in a way that the press or literature is not? This question, which emerged most forcefully over the Johnson fight films and was contested until the 1915 Supreme Court decision brought a (temporary) end to the debate, is central to the definition and institutionalization of cinema during a period when it was still juridically malleable. The debates about cinema and the legally based conception of the governance of cinema are crucial transformative moments in a genealogy of the construction and reification of something we now call "classical Hollywood cinema." [. . .]

Sims and Sherman: acts and charges, 1912

Though prizefighting had been banned in most states of the United States by 1896, the exhibition of moving pictures of fights that took place at various marginal locations—on the Mexican border, on barges on the Mississippi, in Nevada—was tacitly accepted after a bill aimed at banning the interstate transportation of fight films failed to pass in the House of Representatives in 1897.[16] Though banned in actuality, images of fights could be seen; some representations managed to circumvent the law. But this tacit acceptance would not extend to images of Johnson beating white opponents: after films of his 1908 world championship victory arrived in the United States from Australia in March 1909, a new round of suppression developed. It intensified when Johnson beat Jim Jeffries, the retired undefeated heavyweight champion, on July 4, 1910. The fight was a national event, widely discussed before it took place and widely reported. Johnson's victory resulted in some rioting, mainly in the South by whites who were dissatisfied with the result;[17] his victory on Independence Day problematized discourses intent on unifying the nation and resulted in a resurgence of localism.[18]

The fight had been filmed by members of the Motion Picture Patents Company (MPPC) and was to be nationally distributed.[19] The United Society for Christian Endeavour immediately called for a ban on the film and suggested in a message to every governor in the United States that the exhibition of the film would "multipl[y] many times fold" the race riots that followed the fight.[20] The fear of what the Woman's Christian Temperance Union more generally termed an "ungovernable response" to prizefight films was here racially inflected, linked closely to a concern over the effects of the representation of a powerful and assertive black masculinity on a disempowered black population.[21] Many governors and other local officials responded favorably to the call to ban the film. For example, the chairman of the Atlanta Police Board, treating the film as if it were equivalent to Johnson's physical presence, asserted: "We don't want Jack Johnson down in this part of the country. If he is wise he will not come to Atlanta."[22] The policing of the movement of black bodies through social space had shifted onto an emergent policing of the movement of motion pictures. The film was not exhibited across the South or in most major American cities.[23]

Johnson did not fight again for the world title until 1912, against the next "Great White Hope," Jim Flynn. The fight was to be held in New Mexico on July 4 and again was to be filmed.[24] In light of the debates over the 1910 fight and concern that the fight would be widely distributed, Representative Seaborn A. Rodenberry of Georgia and Senator Furnifold Simmons of North Carolina introduced bills, in May and June 1912, calling for the prohibition of the interstate transportation of fight films. Representative Rodenberry's motivation was clear. Referring to Johnson as "an African biped beast," he asserted that "no man descended from the old Saxon race can look upon that kind of contest without abhorrence and disgust."[25] On July 1, in the House of Representatives, Thetus Sims of Tennessee attempted to pass the bill even though a quorum was not present. Sims described it as a bill "to prevent the shipping through the mails and in interstate commerce of moving picture films of prizefights, especially the one between a negro and a white man to be held in New Mexico on the 4th of July."[26]

The bill would suppress the movement of prizefight films, not their exhibition, which, theoretically, could take place if the films were produced and exhibited in one state. Regulation therefore concentrated on the disciplining of movement.[27] Congress moved swiftly after Johnson's victory to pass the act on July 31. As Al-tony Gilmore suggests, Johnson, "at least on film, had proven vulnerable to the 'white hopes' of Congress."[28] The federal government intervened directly in constructing the boundaries of what could legitimately be seen, an intervention evidently aimed at bigger cultural and political game. [. . .]

The 1912 Sims Act is a crucial but unexplored moment in the history of the federal government's intervention into the policing of cinema. The House Committee on Interstate and Foreign Commerce stated that "this bill simply protects the more advanced States which have forbidden pugilism as brutal and brutalizing against having prizefights brought into their borders by way of moving-picture shows, which are only a little less harmful than the degrading sport which they describe."[29]

"Advanced" states had their moral borders problematized by the mobility of moving pictures "describing" immoral events, and the federal government acted to protect the morality of states.[30] The Sims Act effectively defined moving pictures as commerce and thus brought them within the orbit of federal government intervention. This intervention was clearly linked to a moral concern over the effect both of prizefights in general and the effect of images of Johnson's victories in particular. Moving pictures moved into the orbit of federal governance in relation to movement and morality; the films of Johnson boxing entered the statute book as problems of traffic.

The legal issue was more complex and was debated, here and there, at the time. Is a representation of an illegal event in itself illegal? An editorial in the *Nickelodeon* in 1910 reported that the chief of police of Chicago declared that "no pictures or representations in any form of acts illegal in the state of Illinois" would be permitted. The order was aimed explicitly at the Johnson-Jeffries fight but, as the journal pointed out, "it is scarcely a step further to declare the printed description of illegal acts to be illegal in itself."[31] For the journal, and for the defenders of the film industry, this became the central point: the press had been running reports on the fight, so why couldn't the fight be documented on film? The issue came to center on a discussion of the relation of cinema to the press: was cinema, but not the press, to be conceived of as "commerce"? And further, if the fight pictures were commerce, does that mean that the federal government has the right to regulate moving pictures more generally? These debates must be seen as a crucial site for a discursive battle over the definition of cinema and its social functioning, important in the broader discursive construction of cinema as an entertaining aesthetic medium distinct from the press and the "political." That this construction emerged most forcefully over a concern to police images of an assertive black masculinity suggests that a racial politics of exclusion was integral to the discourse of cinema.

The *Moving Picture World* asserted that "there was never a time when the general interests of the moving picture business were more at stake than during the period immediately following the Johnson-Jeffries fight."[32] They called consistently for the inclusion of moving pictures into the category of "the press" from the time of the 1910 fight onward. The pressure intensified with the debate over the Sims Act in 1912:

> If "public morality" upon which alone the enactment of such bills could be defended, is injured through moving pictures, why is it not equally injured through pictorial representations of a prize fight in the newspapers? . . . The roots of this evil of discriminating against the moving pictures must be attacked by enfranchising the motion picture and placing it on an equal footing with the newspapers before the law.[33]

In a discussion of the history of the freedom of the press two months later (seen as "one of the most valued traditions of the race"), the paper imagined "the day when the same express privilege of freedom now bestowed upon the newspapers will be extended to the motion picture." The paper called on the government to amend the First Amendment to read: "No law shall be passed to abridge the liberty of the press *or of the cinematograph*."[34] Without this recognition of the fundamental similarity between the press and the cinema, the cinema would become subject to further measures of censorship. "While we have not a word to say in favor of prize fights," the paper editorialized, "we cannot help pointing out once more that, under the theory of this bill, Congress would have the right to bar from the benefits of interstate commerce any film which, in its argument, might be objectionable."[35]

In the words of Frederick Howe, the film industry was quick to question "the *ultimate* effect of the assumption by the State of the right of regulating this important avenue of expression," fearing that the Sims Act would open the floodgates to other measures of censorship, with "the Congress of the United States . . . becom[ing] a censor in the old historic sense of the word, i.e., an inspector and supervisor of public morality."[36] Indeed, in 1915 the *Moving Picture World* published comments by Postmaster General Albert S. Burleson suggesting that the 1912 Sims Act "could be extended to include other objectionable films. . . . I think it is very probable that the Government's complete control in the field of interstate commerce would be adequate to debar from interstate commerce films held to menace public morals."[37] Burleson, who as postmaster general had executive power to ban objectionable mail, was drawing clear links between the federal government's power to regulate the mails and to regulate interstate commerce. These attempts to stop what Burleson termed the "traffic in films of obviously indecent character" via an extension of section 211 of the U.S. Penal Code, which banned from the mails publications containing "obscene, lewd, lascivious, filthy or indecent matter," culminated in the 1920 revision of this section to include moving pictures passing through the mails or in interstate commerce. [. . .]

When Lawrence Weber attempted to import moving pictures of Johnson's defeat by Jess Willard into the United States in 1915, Weber's lawyer, ex-senator Towne, argued: "We most emphatically deny that these films are articles of commerce. . . . It has been declared again and again that theatrical exhibitions, operas, plays, and the like are not articles of commerce."[38] Other "amusements" were not defined as commerce, a fact that was further established by the Supreme Court in 1922.[39] Towne also questioned what exactly the article of commerce was— that is, if Weber was not actually selling the films but merely transporting them to exhibit them, the commercial transaction was the exhibition context, not the interstate shipping of the films. The federal government had no jurisdiction over policing that, which fell under the police powers of the states. Justice Thomas G. Haight dismissed Towne's arguments and asserted that moving pictures were "articles of commerce whose exclusion from entry by Congress was no different in legal character than sponges gathered at a certain season of the year . . . imitations of coins . . . diseased cattle . . . lottery tickets," and other articles whose similar exclusion by Congress had been upheld by the courts.[40]

This definition of moving pictures as commerce was extended in a decision rendered on the federal government's antitrust suit against the Motion Picture Patents Company. By invoking the Sherman Anti-Trust Act of 1890, which forbids "every contract, combination, in the form of trust or otherwise, or conspiracy in the restraint of trade,"[41] the government exerted its power to regulate interstate commerce across state lines to control not only actual commerce but also to control those industries manufacturing products that were to move in interstate commerce.

The MPPC was a monopolistic patents pooling structure set up in late 1908 that consisted of nine of the major film production companies that would dominate the industry in America from 1909 to 1914. By utilizing strategies of consolidation and structures of exclusion familiar from other big businesses at the turn of the century, the MPPC ended a period of disorganization within the film industry and tapped into the emerging national domestic market. The MPPC's dominance was extended after the formation of a national distribution arm linked to the MPPC, the General Film Company, in April 1910.[42] On August 15, 1912, just over two weeks after the enactment of the Sims Act, the federal government filed suit against the MPPC, charging it with operating as a trust that utilized unfair business practices.[43] The trust question was central to progressive redefinitions of governance, which in this sense was effectively centered on the question of where corporate autonomy should end and government regulation begin.[44] Part of the attention generated around trusts (particularly the role of the MPPC) reflected a concern that the increasingly national economy was overpowering a local specificity, in particular, local morality. As we shall see, debates about the immorality of oligopolistic film corporations were central to the establishment of the legality of state censorship in 1915.

The trial against the MPPC began in January 1913. The MPPC, among various strategies, argued that motion pictures "are not articles of commerce like lumber, cheese, beef or

turpentine. They are works of fine art and of a literary and dramatic essence."[45] If this definition was accepted, moving pictures would not be subject to interstate trade regulations, and
the MPPC would not be liable to prosecution under the terms of the Sherman Act.[46]

This was not to be the case, however, as the policing of the Johnson fight films had already
suggested. The decision was announced in October 1915. The district judge agreed with the
government that the MPPC had violated the Sherman Act, and he ordered the company
dissolved. In explaining his decision, the judge pointed out that the motion picture business
was commerce and thus subject to interstate and business regulation.

By 1915, moving pictures were generally conceptualized as articles of commerce, as Justice
Haight's upholding of the Sims Act had suggested in May of that year. But, as we have seen,
there is a logical difficulty with this definition since it evolved in close conjunction with a
concern over what motion pictures signify (in particular, the subversion of racial hierarchies).
In a strange twist, the linking of film with cheese, turpentine, beef, and so on was facilitated
by the ability of moving pictures to function as signs.

These decisions and the emergence of this regulatory space narrowed the legal definition
of moving pictures. This in turn circumscribed the social functioning of cinema—what
cinema could be and what it could not be, what should be included in the category of cinema
and what should be excluded. In effect, the argument went, motion pictures should avoid
documenting potentially controversial real-life issues and events—such as the Jack Johnson
fights—because they were seemingly not inscribed into the constitutional guarantees of free
speech. Moving pictures should be fictional, entertaining, "harmless," and apolitical.

The marginalization of nonfictional filmmaking was already a tendency within the film
industry, partly because pressures toward the clear adumbration of morality leaned toward
the production of fictional narrative films and partly because fictional narrative films had
become increasingly profitable. The regulatory space centered on boxing films reinforced
these tendencies and made this process of marginalization central to the definition of mainstream cinema. This technology of exclusion was central to the reification of classical Hollywood
cinema.

The governing of cinema through the 1912 Sims Act and the decision in the antitrust suit
brought against the MPPC were thus closely linked to an attempt to police immorality, an
interest that had important ramifications for the definition and institutionalization of the cinema.
As the Sims Act suggested, this attempt was linked to a regulation of the movement of images
of "immoral" black "others" (because notions of morality were delimited by concepts of race),
a regulation that shifted from images to bodies when Johnson was inscribed into the broader
crisis of mobility and governance visible in the moral panic over white slavery.

Jack Johnson and white slavery, 1913

The moral panic over "white slavery" emerged most prominently in the United States in 1907
after the publication of the first of George Kibbe Turner's three influential articles on the
topic.[47] According to Turner, the abduction of white women into prostitution was carried out
by various "racial others." Almost invariably coded in terms of race, these "white slavers" became
threatening symbols of the dangerous and immoral sexuality of other races and nations.

Turner's brand of nativism influenced later formulations of the problem of white slavery,
which developed alongside an increasingly racist strain in nativist thought that proliferated from
about 1906 on and that encompassed notions of "race suicide" and the development of the
eugenics movement in the 1910s.[48] The importance of regulating sexuality, clearly visible in
debates about white slavery, was part of a concern with regulating relations between racial

groups so as to maintain a "color line" to reinforce racial hierarchies and maintain the strength and "purity" of the nation. Notions of morality were integral to this discourse, as indeed they were to concepts of race and nation more generally.[49] [. . .]

The prosecution of Jack Johnson as a white slaver in 1912, a few months after the banning of his fight films from movement within the nation, crystallized concerns over race, sexual immorality, and nationalism that were important to Progressive reform in general and to the construction of the white slavery scare in particular. In tracing out aspects of that construction here and of Johnson's inscription within it, this account will sketch in related aspects of the regulatory space around morality, race, mobility, and nationalism that was so crucial to the definition and governing of cinema.

At a 1902 international conference on white slavery a treaty was signed calling for a "supervision . . . [of] stations, ports of embarkation," and international journeys to monitor and legislate against the "traffic in women."[50] The U.S. delegates, who were at that time unconvinced that white slavery was actually a threat in the United States, were unable to fully ratify the treaty with the other European countries in 1904 because it called for enforcement by national police, and the United States had no such institution. President Theodore Roosevelt had been using the detectives of the Post Office department or those of the Secret Service of the Treasury freely for varied criminal investigations but was encountering opposition to this practice. After Congress adjourned, however, Roosevelt and Attorney General Charles Bonaparte established the very detective force that Congress had refused to authorize, naming it the Bureau of Investigation (this became the Federal Bureau of Investigation in 1935).[51] On June 15, 1908, Roosevelt proclaimed the treaty in effect, partly as a response to the rising tide of concern about white slavery. The transnational surveillance of borders set in play by the 1902 treaty was central to the establishment of a national policing institution; the regulation of sexuality, racial hierarchies, and the sanctity of the nation fed directly into the construction of a state-controlled agency of surveillance that would bring order to society in part through an ordered knowledge of its component populations and population movement.

This policing of borders was closely associated with the surveillance of racial others in relation to the perceived importation of immorality. Immigration acts of 1903 and 1907 had intensified a policing of the nation's space, which was seen as increasingly important because of the influx of non-Protestant Southern European immigrants. The 1907 act set up an immigration commission to report on the effect of immigration on economic conditions, education, vice, crime, insanity, and so on. Part of that report, entitled "The Importation of Women for Immoral Purposes," was published in 1909. Explicitly asserting that immigration had increased "offenses against chastity," the report went on: "The vilest practices are brought here from continental Europe, and beyond doubt there have come from imported women and their men the most bestial refinements of depravity. The toleration with which continental races look upon these evils is spreading in this country."[52] [. . .]

To counter the immoral traffic in women, the report called for a strengthening of state intervention and increased cooperation between states. This clearly led to the creation of a federal law to regulate interstate "commerce" in women. Theodore Roosevelt wrote: "The Federal government must in ever increasing measure proceed against the degraded promoters of this commercialism, for their activities are inter-State, and the Nation can often deal with them more effectively than the States."[53] Influenced by the report, Representative James Mann, Republican chairman of the House Committee on Interstate and Foreign Commerce, introduced a commerce bill making it a felony under the U.S. criminal code to knowingly transport any girl or woman in interstate or foreign commerce for the purposes of debauchery or any other immoral purposes. Mann, who had previously used the expanding power of the commerce clause to enact railroad rate regulation and the Pure Food and Drug Act, used large parts of the Immigration Commission report to fashion a narrative of innocent white women abducted into sexual slavery primarily by immigrants. Different discourses of purification were merged here.

On December 8, President Taft lent support to the legislation, which came to be known as the Mann Act, in his annual message to Congress. The principles of this act are indeed familiar: the utilization of the commerce clause enabled the federal government to intervene directly in the policing of morality. It is an important precursor to the 1912 Sims Act, directed at preventing the movement of "immoral" moving pictures.

Though the debate in the House concentrated on immigration as the cause of the perceived breakdown in immorality increasingly visible in urban spaces, there was comment about the dangers of an internal other: African American men.[54] An external racism, directed against foreigners, fused with an internal racism, directed against a population regarded as a minority within the national space. The black male was, as Robyn Wiegman has shown, denied full admittance to the patriarchal province of the masculine through the social scripting of blackness as innate depravity.[55] In this way, the white slavery scare fused with the myth of the black man as rapist. This link became clearer in late 1912 when Johnson was tried under the Mann Act. Briefly, the mother of a white woman who worked for Johnson—and/or was linked romantically with him—accused Johnson of abducting her daughter. On October 18, 1912, Johnson was arrested. There was considerable outrage. The Texas *Beaumont Journal* asserted that "the obnoxious stunts being featured by Jack Johnson are not only worthy of but demand an overgrown dose of Southern 'hospitality'"; the *Fort Worth Citizen Star* commented, "We bet we know one person that isn't singing 'I Wish I Was in Dixie.'"[56] As Randy Roberts's account makes clear, the Bureau of Investigation decided to press for a Mann Act conviction immediately.[57] The bureau, which owed its existence to the moral panic over white slavery, had its power steadily increased when Congress consistently assigned it investigations under the commerce clause of the Constitution. For the bureau, the Mann Act had been a "bureaucratic bonanza" (as late as 1938, J. Edgar Hoover suggested that the act would enable the bureau to attack "the problem of vice in modern civilization").[58] There were problems, however, in prosecuting Johnson as a white slaver: the act was aimed at commercial transportation, and, as such, abduction did not fall within its parameters. Moreover, the daughter, Lucille Cameron, had traveled by herself to Chicago, had been a prostitute for some time, and would not testify against Johnson, her future husband. Nevertheless, given Johnson's libertine lifestyle and frequent movement across state and national borders, the bureau reasoned that he might well have been guilty of transporting another woman across state lines for immoral purposes. Assistant District Attorney Harry Parkin told the bureau to "endeavour to secure evidence as to illegal transportation by Johnson of any other woman for an immoral purpose."[59] The bureau actively pursued Johnson, submitting his past to an exhaustive inquiry, finally succeeding in finding another white woman who had had a relationship with Johnson and in the process traveled across state lines to meet him.[60] Johnson became a white slaver because of his relationships with white women. The framework of discipline and the strategy of policing effectively controlled and limited black male sexuality.

A grand jury was convened on November 7, 1912, to consider Johnson's charges, and he was subsequently indicted and arrested. Tried in May 1913, he was quickly convicted. [. . .] Johnson, the son of a former slave, had become a *white* slaver, with that term clearly functioning as a displacement of an entirely different configuration of slavery (and of the racial sexual abuse under that). This government intervention functioned in a way similar to the performative and specular structure of lynching as Wiegman has theorized it: "as a disciplinary activity that communalizes white power while territorializing the black body and its movement through social space."[61] Discipline replaced the physical punishment that Johnson seemed to avoid every time he entered the boxing ring. [. . .]

Miscegenation bills were introduced after Johnson's conviction in half of the twenty states that still permitted interracial marriages. Johnson's Mann Act conviction was, as this legislative activity suggests, effectively a conviction of miscegenation, which had, since the demise of slavery, functioned as the ultimate sanction of the American system of white supremacy.[62] Representative Rodenberry, so central to the passage of the Sims Act, angrily observed that "in Chicago, white girls are made slaves of an African brute," further asserting that intermarriage was "abhorrent and repugnant to the very principles of a pure Saxon government" and "destructive of moral supremacy."[63] [. . .]

Johnson's conviction was clearly linked to broader concerns around the sanctity and *purity* of the race and nation addressed by Rodenberry. As an icon of immorality, Johnson—and constructions of Johnson—would help define what was moral and acceptable behavior. His challenge to government authority and morality led directly to his exile and was enmeshed with the banishment of fight films from the screens of the United States. This convergence was explicitly referenced by Justice Haight when he banned the films of the Johnson-Willard fight from entering the United States in 1915. Haight pointed out a case in which a man had sent for a woman from a different state and had been held to have violated the Mann Act though no prostitution had taken place.[64] The case was, of course, that of the government versus Johnson. A racial politics of exclusion, central to the emergence of the Mann Act and at the core of a discourse of the nation, was implicated in the discourse of cinema. It is toward the further elaboration of that discourse that I now turn.

The Supreme Court on cinema, 1915

[. . .] The film industry's attempt to circumvent government intervention into the cinema through the establishment of the National Board of Censorship in 1909 was never entirely successful. The board lost the battle to regulate cinema for the nation as states began to construct their own moral borders. This was influenced both by concern over fight films and by the furor over a number of films representing aspects of white slavery, including *Traffic in Souls* (1913), *The Inside of the White Slave Traffic* (1913), *The House of Bondage* (1914), *Smashing the Vice Trust* (1914), and *Is Any Girl Safe?* (1916).[65] In a special debate on *Traffic in Souls,* Orrin Cocks, a member of the General Committee of the National Board of Censorship, "felt that we must not look at this picture in [*sic*] the point of view of people living in the big cities. The majority of the people in the United States hesitate to speak of these things and they would not like this picture."[66] Part of the concern was clearly directed at the difficulty of a national distribution of films supplanting local morality.

The introduction of feature films from 1912 on more generally produced difficulties in this area. The process of marketing big features necessitated the development of a new distribution system that would eventually swallow up the old film exchanges.[67] Often feature films were distributed on a states' rights basis, whereby the right to exploit the film in a state or states was sold to an entrepreneur. These films frequently slipped below the gaze of the National Board of Censorship. *Motography* noted in June 1912: "Feature films, not released through the regular channels but sold on the states rights plans, have introduced a new problem in censorship. Until they appear on the screen they are seen by no one but their manufacturers, the states rights dealers and the buyers—all inefficient censors because of their nearness to the subject."[68] Furthermore, feature films were, at least initially, primarily foreign made;

the agitation over films morally compromising the locality and the nation was thus enmeshed with a national and racial politics of exclusion.[69]

Ohio established a state censorship board in 1913, Kansas in 1914, Maryland in 1916, and so on. The 1913 Ohio statute is instructive here, since it became central to the momentous 1915 Supreme Court decision on the cinema. The statute was dependent on the police power abrogated to states. The police power may effectively be defined as the right (and duty) of the states to protect the health, morals, and safety of their citizens. It was, Morton Keller notes, implemented with special vigor when public health and morals appeared to be at stake and was thus effectively the rationale for most state economic regulation.[70] The police power was thus central to the emergence of state censorship, likened in one article in the *Literary Digest* to "State Board[s] of Health to protect us from the moral pestilence which lurks in the attractive, seductive motion pictures."[71] Utilizing the police power, the state of Ohio proposed to license every film in the state, after viewing it, if it was of a "moral, educational or amusing and harmless character."[72]

This statute was challenged by the Mutual Film Corporation. Mutual was an interstate film exchange conglomerate that purchased films from producers and rented them out to exhibitors across the nation. There were thirty or so exchanges operating at the time, most of which distributed films in more than one state. Mutual claimed that the Ohio statute was unconstitutional because it was an unfair burden on interstate commerce and because it failed to set precise standards. Mutual also claimed that the Ohio statute violated the free speech guarantees of the Ohio Constitution and the First Amendment in the Bill of Rights. Section 11, Article I of the Ohio Constitution stated that "every citizen may freely speak, write and publish his sentiments on all subjects, being responsible for the abuse of the right; and no law shall be passed to restrain or abridge the liberty of speech, or of the press."[73]

During the course of the legal proceedings, Mutual's defense came to be constructed almost entirely around the defense of free speech.[74] In this, Mutual claimed that moving pictures depict "the same events which are described in words and by photographs in newspapers, weekly periodicals, magazines and other publications, of which photographs are promptly secured a few days after the events which they depict happen."[75] This claim, which certainly echoed some of the claims made for the protection of the Johnson fight pictures prior to the passage of the Sims Act, would enable moving pictures to be more than simply moral or amusing or harmless entertainment. They could be instructive in a way that was not delimited by a restrictive definition of the moral.

For the justices, though, the Ohio statute was a reasonable exercise of state police power. Moving pictures had a "capacity for evil" and could be restrained prior to the due process of law because of that potentiality. This triumph of police power over private economic interest prompted one legal observer to label this decision a "great forward step in government regulation of business and social conditions."[76] The duty of the state of Ohio to protect its citizens from immorality, to construct impenetrable moral borders, meant that it could police the movement and the content of moving pictures. The police power of the states thus complemented the national powers to regulate commerce.

Furthermore, the Supreme Court denied Mutual's definition of moving pictures. For the justices, "film was a business pure and simple, originated and conducted for profit, like other spectacles, not to be regarded . . . as part of the press of the country, or as organs of public opinion."[77] A border between moving pictures and the press was firmly established. This was, in many ways, the logical extension of the definition of moving pictures as commerce implicit in the Sims Act, only now *all* films were defined and regulated as commerce. This decision, tracked through a broader context from the Sims Act to the government's antitrust suit against the MPPC, stands as a crucial moment in the definition of the social functioning of cinema. Not protected by free speech guarantees and capable of evil, moving pictures would have to offer harmless entertainment or they could be regulated, in varying ways, by federal and state government power.

The Supreme Court decision of 1915 was announced at the same time as D. W. Griffith's racist epic *The Birth of a Nation* was being extensively debated throughout the country. Griffith emerged as one of the sternest critics of the Supreme Court decision, publishing a pamphlet in 1916 entitled *The Rise and Fall of Free Speech* in which he claimed that "the moving pictures are simply the pictorial press."[78] Ironically, the call for the rights of cinema under the constitutional guarantees of free speech, which if not begun over the image of Jack Johnson was certainly intensified by it, culminated in Griffith's call for the exclusion of African Americans from social participation. In a film so often seen as fundamental to the birth of a classical Hollywood cinema, Griffith's narrative of sexually rapacious black men incapable of government authority and laying claims to white women leads to a finale in which, as Donald Bogle writes, "a group of good upright Southern white males . . . wearing sheets and hoods . . . [defends] white womanhood, white honour, and white glory . . . restor[ing] to the South everything it has lost, including its white supremacy. Thus we have the birth of a nation."[79] A new political entity, America, results from the expulsion or segregation of African Americans; for Griffith, the Ku Klux Klan embodied the complete coincidence of racial identity with national identity.[80]

The film was complexly linked to debates on Johnson and has even been seen as a response to Johnson's fight victories.[81] The film, Richard Maltby suggests, superseded Johnson's defeat in the boxing ring: "The Great White Hope longed for in saloons across the country finally appeared in 1915: not Jess Willard, who defeated Johnson in Havana in July, but Henry B. Walthall, D. W. Griffith's Little Colonel."[82] One should note that the reverse of this also occurred: in Chicago, a group of African Americans responded to the local debut of *The Birth of a Nation* by putting on a tent-show revival of the 1910 Johnson–Jeffries fight.[83]

The 1915 Supreme Court decision defining cinema and upholding the legitimacy of state police power to patrol its moral borders had the additional effect of reviving attempts to enforce federal government censorship of the cinema. A bill was introduced in 1916 to establish a federal motion picture commission that would comprise five commissioners appointed by the president to "license every film submitted to it and intended for entrance into interstate commerce, unless that it finds that such a film is obscene, indecent, immoral, or depicts a bull fight or a prize fight."[84] The supporters of the bill claimed this was not the same as censorship because they were advocating the "licensing" of films, which merely utilized the federal authority to license interstate commerce. As with the Sims Act, a film could technically be produced and exhibited in one state and be subject to licensing only when it was distributed. Of course, as the industry always pointed out, the national structure of production and distribution meant that all films would effectively have to be licensed.[85] The bill had actually been debated in 1914 and defeated, but the Supreme Court decision reintroduced the possibility of federal censorship.

Johnson made a reappearance during the discussion, a fact not too surprising given his role in these debates in defining and governing motion pictures. Crafts, superintendent of the International Reform Bureau, referred to the banning of the importation of the Johnson-Willard fight in 1915 and 1916: "It would have been worthwhile to have lived if only to save the country from being flooded with pictures of a negro indicted for white slavery and a white man voluntarily standing on the same brutal level, which, but for that, would have been shown all over the country as a brace of heroes."[86] Worthy of the life's work of this eminent reformer, the banning of images of the white slaver Johnson clearly functioned as a highly emotive issue by which Crafts imagined governmental legislation could be enacted. For Crafts and others, the federal government alone was capable of reinforcing moral authority on a dangerously fragmented nation. Crafts, who also spoke of a need to "rescue the motion pictures from the hands of the Devil and 500 un-Christian Jews,"[87] was speaking in the context of the efforts to import the Johnson-Willard fight via Newark and Rouses Point. As we have seen, one of the legal strategies of the producer, Lawrence Weber, was to argue that prizefight films were not articles of commerce. Defeated in the federal district court, Weber appealed to the Supreme Court. Declining even to hear the state's rebuttal of Weber's case, the Court cited the Mutual precedent and rejected the "fictitious assumption" of Weber's claim.[88] The circle of regulatory efforts had turned: the Mutual decision, which had been buttressed by the Sims Act, could come now to justify the constitutionality of the Sims Act (which, as noted above, had also been buttressed by the Mann Act). [. . .]

Conclusion

[. . .] The monitoring of moral standards in motion pictures took many forms: self-regulatory efforts to "uplift" the industry, municipal and state attempts to censor the content of moving pictures, and federal and state attempts to police the movement of movies. The Johnson fight films became part of this emerging and fragmentary regulatory space, highly visible—because of Johnson's visibility—contested signs over which battles about the definition and governing of cinema were fought. The ramifications of these battles were unforeseen and coincidental, though nevertheless of fundamental importance to the definition, delimitation, and—I would say—*production* of "cinema."

The battle over the Johnson fight films and over cinema was fought largely over the definition of film. This debate emerged most forcefully from 1910 on and was central to the three moments of legislation I have concentrated on here: the Sims Act, which defined moving pictures of prizefights as commerce and banned them from movement within the national space; the 1915 decision on the Motion Picture Patents Company, which regulated the largest production-distribution combine and in the process defined moving pictures as commerce like lumber, cheese, and turpentine and not like literature; and the 1915 Supreme Court decision, which emerged from Mutual's attempt to transcend the moral boundary of the state of Ohio and which defined moving pictures as a business distinct from the press. Through these decisions, the cinema would come to be shaped in specific ways. It would not function like the press, it was not like literature, and it thus had to become "entertaining" and "morally instructive" but fundamentally "harmless" and "amusing." This definition would be central to the emergence and reification of classical Hollywood cinema and, incidentally, to the production and marginalization of a space for films manifesting a different sense of the possible social function of cinema. In the midst of these decisions and debates was the figure of Johnson, and through the border crossings of my own analysis I hope to have shown how those decisions and their effects on the definition and governing of cinema were linked to the broader issues that proliferated around the figure of Johnson.

Notes

1. Famous not only for being heavyweight boxing champion of the world but for flaunting social conventions in his marriages to three white women and his associations with other white mistresses and prostitutes, Johnson rapidly became an extraordinary nexus where debates about racial hierarchies, racial

identities, and immorality were combined, contested, and revised. Gail Bederman begins her book *Manliness and Civilization: A Cultural History of Gender and Race in the United States, 1880–1917* (Chicago: University of Chicago Press, 1995) with a brief discussion of "the Jack Johnson controversy" to exemplify the way ideas about white supremacy produced a racially based ideology of male power (see in particular 1–10). For more general work on Johnson, see Al-tony Gilmore, *Bad Nigger!: The Life and Times of Jack Johnson* (Port Washington, N.Y.: Kennikat Press, 1975); Randy Roberts, *Papa Jack: Jack Johnson and the Era of White Hopes* (London: Robson Books, 1986); Finis Farr, *Black Champion: The Life and Times of Jack Johnson* (London: Macmillan, 1964); and Lerone Bennett, Jr., "Jack Johnson and the Great White Hope," *Ebony* (April 1994): 86–98. Johnson would figure also as an important precursor to Black Power rhetoric in the 1960s and 1970s, particularly after the reprinting of his autobiography in 1969 and the filming of his life story, *The Great White Hope* (1970). [. . .]

2. "The problem of the Twentieth Century," W. E. B. DuBois wrote, "is the problem of the color line." Dubois, *The Soul of Black Folk* (1903), quoted in Cornel West, *Race Matters* (Boston: Beacon Press, 1993), x. DuBois argued that injustices against black people and white society's insistence on the centrality of racial segregation as a principle of governance wrought the nation's gravest social difficulties.

3. The initial case against Johnson, such as it existed at all, centered on a charge of abduction and not the commercial transportation that the White Slave Traffic Act was directed against. Randy Roberts's account makes clear that the Bureau of Investigation decided to press for a white slave traffic violation immediately, indicative of the extent to which Johnson was perceived as an undesirable participant in the body politic. Roberts, *Papa Jack*, 138–54.

4. Michel Foucault, *Discipline and Punish: The Birth of the Prison*, trans. Alan Sheridan (New York: Vintage, 1979), 219.

5. I am using the term "race" as it figured in the politics of industrializing America. It refers to people of color and to white people we commonly refer to today as "ethnics."

6. Johnson escaped from the United States while on bail after his conviction for white slavery. The narrative of this escape, as related in his autobiography, is worthy of a Hollywood fiction: masquerading as a member of an all-black baseball team and utilizing one of the predicates of racism, that "black men all look the same," Johnson boarded a train for Canada, where the team was due to play. Though trailed by members of the bureau, Johnson was not arrested because the White Slave Traffic Act was not covered under the extradition treaty between the two countries. Further, because Johnson had bought a ticket from Canada to Europe, he could not be deported from Canada as an "undesirable immigrant" (he was officially classified as an "alien" passing through). Sailing for Europe, Johnson joined the transatlantic traffic in exiled African Americans; he entitled this chapter in his autobiography simply "Exile." Jack Johnson, *Jack Johnson in the Ring and Out* (Chicago: National Sports Publishing, 1927), 60–61. Randy Roberts challenges this narrative in his biography of Johnson. Roberts quotes bureau chief DeWoody's earlier prophetic memorandum: "I believe we all agree . . . on the advantage to the country if Johnson were to be exiled from it." For Roberts, Johnson was simply allowed, even encouraged, to leave. Roberts, *Papa Jack*, 166.

7. *Chicago Post*, April 6, 1915, quoted in Gilmore, *Bad Nigger!*, 139. [. . .]

8. W. Stephen Bush, "Arguments on Fight Films," *Moving Picture World*, May 15, 1915, 1049. On this understanding of the banning of prizefight films as an attempt to defend the borders of national space, see also "Uncle Sam Bans Prize Fight Films," *Moving Picture World*, April 17, 1915, 366.

9. See the details in Edward De Grazia and Roger K. Newman, *Banned Films: Movie Censors and the First Amendment* (New York: Bowker, 1982), 185.

10. For details, see Terry Ramsaye, *A Million and One Nights: A History of the Motion Picture* (London: Cass and Co., 1926), 695; *Motography*, April 29, 1916, 983; *Moving Picture World*, September 16, 1916, 1808.

11. Judge Augustus N. Hand, quoted in *Moving Picture World*, September 16, 1916, 1808. *Motography* also noted that "in any event the films could only be permitted to be shown in New York State as the same law which prohibits them from being brought in or sent to the United States prohibits their transportation in interstate commerce in the United States." *Motography*, April 29, 1916, 983. There is some suggestion that Weber intended to repeat this rephotographing of the film at each state border.

12. Benedict Anderson, *Imagined Communities: Reflections on the Origin and Spread of Nationalism* (London: Verso, 1983), 26.

13. For a discussion of the term "regulatory space," primarily from an economic standpoint, see Leigh Hancher and Michael Moran, "Organizing Regulatory Space," in Leigh Hancher and Michael Moran, eds., *Capitalism, Culture, and Economic Regulation* (Oxford: Clarendon Press, 1989).

14. Ibid., 271.

15. Morton Keller, *Affairs of State: Public Life in Late Nineteenth-Century America* (Cambridge: Harvard University Press, 1977), 409. On the links between government and the judiciary, see also Robert Harrison, "The 'Weakened Spring of Government' Revisited: The Growth of Federal Power in the Late Nineteenth Century" in Rhodri Jeffreys-Jones and Bruce Collins, eds., *The Growth of Federal Power in American History* (Edinburgh: Scottish Academic Press, 1983); and Hancher and Moran, "Organizing Regulatory Space."

16. A House bill was drafted to ensure that "no picture or description of any prize fight . . . shall be transmitted." There was considerable reform impetus for the passage of this act. Some of the House members argued that it was "right to establish a censorship of the press in the interest of public morals," but others argued that this legislation would necessitate the establishment of a government censorship board. Too broadly written, the act failed. See Dan Streible, "A History of the Boxing Film, 1894–1915: Social Control and Social Reform in the Progressive Era," *Film History* 3, no. 3 (1989), 238–40.

17. On July 6 and 7, 1910, the *New York Times* ran more than thirty reports on the effect of the films and the growing attempts to ban them. See also the account of the disorder resulting from the fight in Roberts, *Papa Jack,* 108–14.

18. As John Bodnar has shown, at least since the end of the Civil War "public memory" (e.g., commemorative and patriotic activity) had become increasingly nationalized. Bodnar argues also that this became increasingly linked to strategies of representation, with cultural production becoming central to the promotion of loyalty to the nation. Fourth of July celebrations and other festivals were thus conceived as demonstrating the unity of the nation rather than the development of competing local interests. Bodnar, *Remaking America: Public Memory, Commemoration, and Patriotism in the Twentieth Century* (Princeton: Princeton University Press, 1992). [. . .] The fight was held in Nevada, and there was a flurry of criticism of the state for allowing it to take place within its borders. For many reformers, the state's geographic liminality translated into a kind of moral marginality that suggested that it should be placed outside the nation. The Chicago Baptist minister Reverend M. P. Boynton argued that "there should be some way by which our nation could recall the charter of a state that has become a desert and a moral menace. Nevada has no right to remain a part of our nation." Quoted in Roberts, *Papa Jack,* 96.

19. On the Motion Picture Patents Company, see below and Eileen Bowser, *The Transformation of Cinema, 1907–1915* (Berkeley: University of California Press, 1990), 21–36. The Johnson-Jeffries fight cost the MPPC the considerable sum of $200,000. This was shared among the members, though J. Stuart Blackton of Vitagraph seemingly had control of the filming. There also were cameras from Selig and Essanay, and it seems that the Vitagraph pictures were to be exhibited in the East and the others in the West. For details, see *Variety*, July 23, 1910, 6.

20. Quoted in Gilmore, *Bad Nigger!*, 76. There were, it seems, historical precedents for a bill that banned images that might incite racial panic. In 1906 the Kentucky State Legislature passed a law making it illegal to present "any play that is based upon antagonism between master and slave, or that excites racial prejudice." The law was aimed at preventing productions of *Uncle Tom's Cabin*, particularly versions of the play that were overtly critical of the institution of slavery (most likely the abolitionist Aiken-Howard production). For details, see Linda Williams, "Versions of Uncle Tom: Race and Gender in American Melodrama," in Colin MacCabe and Duncan Petrie, eds., *New Scholarship from BFI Research* (London: BFI, 1996), 123, and Gregory A. Waller, *Main Street Amusements: Movies and Commercial Entertainment in a Southern City, 1896–1930* (Washington, DC: Smithsonian Institution Press, 1995), 45. [. . .]

21. The Woman's Christian Temperance Union, quoted in Alison M. Parker, "Mothering the Movies: Women Reformers and Popular Culture," in Francis Couvares, ed., *Movie Censorship and American Culture* (Washington, DC: Smithsonian Institute Press, 1996), 81. [. . .]

22. Quoted in John Dittmer, *Black Georgia in the Progressive Era, 1900–1920* (Chicago: University of Illinois Press, 1977), 72. The mayor of Atlanta initiated an ordinance prohibiting the film.

23. See the details in Gilmore, *Bad Nigger!*, 75–90. [. . .]

24. New Mexico had only just been admitted to the Union and did not have antifight laws. Again, there was a flurry of criticism of the state for allowing the fight to take place.

25. Rodenberry quoted in Streible, "A History of the Boxing Film," 247. For details of the bill at this stage, see W. Stephen Bush, "Indirect Federal Censorship," *Moving Picture World*, June 29, 1912, 1206.

26. Sims, quoted in Streible, "A History of the Boxing Film," 247.

27. On these legal parameters, see De Grazia and Newman, *Banned Films*, 185. There was, of course, a long history of the regulation of objects moving in the mails, often carried out via the regulation of "obscenity." This was, Terence Munby suggests, possibly the first problem in public morals to claim the attention of the national government. The banning of the movement of obscene materials through the mails was

initiated in 1842 but only enforced coherently after moral reformer Anthony Comstock proposed a revision in 1873 that effectively broadened the customs statute to include books, pamphlets, and pictorial matter. In 1876, post office censorship was specifically authorized through the alteration of the statute to declare all obscene matter "nonmailable" and prohibit its delivery. This was aided in time by the growth of federal powers under the commerce clause. For details, see Terence J. Munby *Censorship: Government and Obscenity* (Baltimore: Helicon Press, 1963), 75–76, and P. R. Macmillan, *Censorship and Public Morality* (Aldershot: Gower Publishing, 1983), 363–64. [. . .]

28. Gilmore, *Bad Nigger!*, 90.

29. Quoted in *Moving Picture World*, June 29, 1912, 1206.

30. Through a process of "divestment," the federal government would give up its powers to regulate commerce to the states where particular states sought to prohibit certain goods. For details, see John H. Ferguson and Dean E. McHenry, *The American Federal Government* (London: McGraw-Hill, 1947), 139–40.

31. "That Chicago Police Order," *Nickelodeon*, August 1, 1910, 48.

32. *Moving Picture World*, July 23, 1910, 190.

33. *Moving Picture World*, June 29, 1912, 1206. [. . .]

34. *Moving Picture World*, August 10, 1912, 520.

35. Ibid. There is a discernible shift in *Moving Picture World*'s attitude toward fight films from 1910 to 1912. In 1910 the journal consistently defended them, but by 1912 it maintained a more complicated stance, clearly trying to distance itself from the furor but not wanting to allow this controversy to develop into more general censorship measures.

36. Frederick Howe, quoted in W. P. Lawson, "The Movies: Their Importance and Supervision," a series of articles appearing in *Harper's Weekly* and reprinted by the National Board of Censorship, February 1915, 19. Howe was director of the board from 1910 to 1915. *Moving Picture World*, June 29, 1912, 1206.

37. "The Postmaster General on Moving Pictures," *Moving Picture World*, September 18, 1915, 1969.

38. Towne, quoted in *Moving Picture World*, May 15, 1915, 1049.

39. This emerged in relation to a charge brought against the National League of Baseball that it had conspired to monopolize the baseball business and thus violated the Sherman Anti-Trust Act. The Supreme Court ruled that the league did not come within the scope of the act because its primary purpose was that of providing a local exhibition. The interstate transportation of players and supplies was incidental to the principal purpose of providing local entertainment. Amusements were not then interstate commerce. For details on this case, see Ferguson and McHenry, *The American Federal Government*, 361. Moving pictures, which too may have claimed to have been providing local entertainment, were defined as commerce. Towne cited the example of baseball players and football players to the judge but was interrupted when the judge pointed out examples of how Congress could regulate interstate commerce. See *Moving Picture World*, May 15, 1915, 1049.

40. Judge Haight, quoted in De Grazia and Newman, *Banned Films*, 185.

41. A copy of the Sherman Anti-Trust Act is reprinted in Leon Fink, ed., *Major Problems in the Gilded Age and the Progressive Era* (Lexington, Mass.: Heath, 1993), 46–47. Along with the 1887 Interstate Commerce Act, the Sherman Anti-Trust Act was a prototype for the structure of supervision of the industrial sphere that came into being in the twentieth century. See Keller, *Affairs of State*, 409–38, and on the Sherman Act in particular, 436–37.

42. Prior to the formation of the MPPC and the General Film Company, films from, for example, New York or Chicago production companies might have reached only a limited locale. The MPPC standardized production, which was then translated into a system of distribution. The creation of the MPPC thus marked a moment when the film industry became a truly national industry. See Bowser, *The Transformation of Cinema*, 21–36, and on the General Film Company, 81–85.

43. Specifically, the government charged that the MPPC had garnered 70 to 80 percent of the film business, that the licensing procedures for moving picture theaters determined which theaters could be open, and that the General Film Company had acquired a distribution monopoly that had prevented all but a small amount of import competition. See Janet Staiger, "Combination and Litigation: Structures of U.S. Film Distribution, 1896–1917," in Thomas Elsaesser, ed., *Early Cinema: Space-Frame-Narrative* (London: BFI, 1990), 199–202.

44. The government's suit was part of a broader government intervention into the oligopolistic power of large corporations involving the nature of government and business power, a struggle over the shape and rule of law and government, and the relations between the state and the social body. See Martin

J. Sklar, *The Corporate Reconstruction of American Capitalism, 1890–1916: The Market, the Law, and Politics* (Cambridge: Cambridge University Press, 1988), in particular 86–173.

45. Quoted in Staiger, "Combination and Litigation," 200. See also the details of the court proceedings in *Film History* 1, no. 3 (1987): 187–289.

46. On the protection of literature from customs powers, see Munby, *Censorship*, 80–81.

47. Two of these, "The City of Chicago: A Study of the Great Immoralities" and "The Daughters of the Poor," are collected in Arthur and Lila Weinberg, eds., *The Muckrakers* (New York: Capricorn, 1964).

48. See John Higham, *Strangers in the Land: Patterns of American Nativism, 1860–1925* (New Brunswick, N.J.: Rutgers University Press, 1988), 143–58. For an incisive discussion of the white slavery scare, see Richard Maltby, "The Social Evil, the Moral Order and the Melodramatic Imagination, 1890–1915," in Jacky Bratton, Jim Cook, and Christine Gledhill, eds., *Melodrama: Stage, Picture, Screen* (London: BFI, 1994).

49. On the links between the discourse of nationalism and "respectability," see George Mosse, *Nationalism and Sexuality: Middle-Class Morality and Sexual Norms in Modern Europe* (Madison: University of Wisconsin Press, 1985), and Andrew Parker *et al.*, eds, *Nationalisms and Sexualities* (London: Routledge, 1992). On the ways in which the concept of race has delimited structures of moral evaluation, see David Theo Goldberg, *Racist Culture* (London: Blackwell, 1993).

50. A copy of this treaty is published in Francesco Cordasco and Thomas Monroe Pitkin, *The White Slave Trade and the Immigrants: A Chapter in American Social History* (Detroit: Blaine Ethridge, 1981), 85–86.

51. For details, see Fred J. Cook's account in *The FBI Nobody Knows* (New York: Macmillan, 1964), 49–70.

52. A copy of this report is published in Cordasco and Pitkin, *White Slave Trade*, 58–84. This passage, 80.

53. Theodore Roosevelt, *An Autobiography* (New York: Macmillan, 1913), 216.

54. See the account of the house debate in Frederick K. Grittner, *White Slavery: Myth, Ideology, and American Law* (New York: Garland Publishing, 1990), 92–96.

55. Robyn Wiegman, "Feminism, 'The Boyz,' and Other Matters Regarding the Male," in Steven Cohan and Ina Rae Hark, eds., *Screening the Male: Exploring Masculinities in Hollywood Cinema* (London: Routledge, 1993), 174.

56. *Beaumont Journal*, quoted in Roberts, *Papa Jack*, 146; *Fort Worth Citizen Star*, quoted in Gilmore, *Bad Nigger!*, 96.

57. Roberts, *Papa Jack*, 138–54.

58. J. Edgar Hoover, quoted in Cook, *The FBI Nobody Knows*, 58.

59. Quoted in Roberts, *Papa Jack*, 148.

60. A memorandum from the Bureau of Investigation, dated October 1912 and titled "In re. Jack Johnson— Probable Violation White Slave Traffic Act," is available on microfiche in the Schomberg Center for Research in Black Culture, New York City. The memo calls for a quick investigation of the Lucille Cameron case and references other women whom Johnson might have "procured." My thanks to the center for access to this document.

61. Robyn Wiegman, *American Anatomies: Theorizing Race and Gender* (Durham, N.C.: Duke University Press, 1995), 13.

62. See Peggy Pascoe, "Miscegenation Law, Court Cases, and Ideologies of 'Race' in Twentieth-Century America," *Journal of American History* 83, no. 1 (June 1996): 44–69. Miscegenation would consistently be banned from the screen by censorship dictates. This was made explicit in 1927 by the MPPDA, which formulated a "Don'ts and Be Carefuls" list for producers. Among the list of topics to avoid were both white slavery and miscegenation. See Arthur F. McClure, "Censor the Movies! Early Attempts to Regulate the Content of Motion Pictures in America, 1907–1936," in Arthur F. McClure, ed., *The Movies: An American Idiom* (Crawbury, N.J.: Associated University Press, 1971), 132–33.

63. Rodenberry, quoted in Finis Farr, *Black Champion*, 164.

64. *Moving Picture World*, May 15, 1915, 1049.

65. Richard Koszarski notes that the increasing public support for federal censorship of moving pictures during these years was influenced by concern over fight films and white slave films. *An Evening's Entertainment: The Age of the Silent Feature Picture, 1915–1928* (Berkeley: University of California Press, 1990), 198. [. . .]

66. Orrin Cocks, in "Record of the Meeting Held at the Universal Film Company, 1600 Broadway, on October 27, 1913, to View the Seven Reel Production, *Traffic in Souls*," Controversial Film Files, Box 107, National Board of Review of Motion Pictures Collection, Rare Books and Manuscripts Division, New York Public Library.

67. Because the distribution system prior to 1912 was centered on the rapid distribution of a number of one-reel films, it was ill equipped to distribute features. The emergence of features thus necessitated a series of changes in the distribution system. See Bowser, *Transformation of Cinema*, 191–215.
68. "New Problems in Censorship," *Motography*, June 1912, 76. Johnson's boxing films were sold on a states' rights basis. *Moving Picture World* invoked this as a positive aspect of the films, because the films would thus be exhibited at a higher price than was average for the exhibition of films. The journal noted, "The children whom the daily press so sensationally defends, or pretends to, will not see the pictures at all, and the audience will be composed of people who are competent to discriminate between right and wrong." *Moving Picture World,* July 23, 1910, 191. Fight films, and filmed passion plays, were in fact important to the development of feature films playing in "higher-class" venues. These films demonstrated the commercial viability of longer films and provided something of a template for this development, as the two genres both had clear narrative trajectories but also incorporated moments of spectacle within that.
69. On the more general attempts to equate foreign films with immorality, see Richard Abel, "The Perils of Pathé, or the Americanization of the American Cinema," in Leo Charney and Vanessa R. Schwartz, eds., *Cinema and the Invention of Modern Life* (Berkeley: University of California Press, 1995).
70. Keller, *Affairs of State*, 409–38.
71. Quoted in Arthur McClure, "Censor the Movies!," 142.
72. For details, see Garth S. Jowett, "'A Capacity For Evil': The 1915 Supreme Court Mutual Decision," *Historical Journal of Film, Radio and Television* 9, no. 1 (March 1989): 59–78.
73. See "Mutual Film Corp. v. Industrial Commission of Ohio, United States Supreme Court," in Gerald Mast, ed., *The Movies in Our Midst: Documents in the Cultural History of Film in America* (Chicago: Chicago University Press, 1982), 139. [. . .]
74. See John Wertheimer, "Mutual Film Reviewed: The Movies, Censorship, and Free Speech in Progressive America," *American Journal of Legal History* 37, no. 2 (April 1993): 158–89. [. . .]
75. In Mast, ed., *Movies in Our Midst*, 137.
76. Quoted in Wertheimer, "Mutual Film Reviewed," 186.
77. Quoted in Jowett, "'A Capacity for Evil,'" 68.
78. D. W Griffith, *The Rise and Fall of Free Speech*, in Mast, ed., *Movies in Our Midst*, 132.
79. Bogle, *Blacks in American Films and Television*, 1988, quoted in Robyn Wiegman, "The Anatomy of Lynching," in John C. Fout and Maura Shaw Tantillo, eds, *American Sexual Politics: Sex, Gender, and Race since the Civil War* (Chicago: University of Chicago Press, 1994), 232.
80. See Michael Rogin, "'The Sword Became a Flashing Vision': D. W. Griffith's *The Birth of a Nation*," *Representations* 9 (Winter 1985): 150–95.
81. For this suggestion, see Charlene Regester, "Black Films, White Censors: Oscar Micheaux Confronts Censorship in New York, Virginia, and Chicago," in Francis Couvares, ed., *Movie Censorship and American Culture.* For African American links between *The Birth of a Nation* and Johnson, see Streible, "A History," 409.
82. Maltby, "Social Evil," 226.
83. See Dan Streible, "Race and the Reception of Jack Johnson Fight Films," in Daniel Bernardi, ed., *The Birth of Whiteness: Race and the Emergence of U.S. Cinema* (New Brunswick, NJ: Rutgers University Press, 1996), 193. This did not contravene the Sims Act because the films already existed in Chicago. The Sims Act was never intended to suppress exhibition, only movement.
84. Quoted in Jowett, "'Capacity for Evil,'" 71.
85. Some members of the industry flirted with this idea of a federal licensing board, which would have potentially enabled a national standard to be applied to films. See Koszarski, *Evening's Entertainment*, 201–3, and Arthur McClure, "Censor the Movies!," 136. The National Board of Censorship vigorously argued that states would not give up their own police powers, and this argument prevailed within the industry.
86. Crafts, quoted in Jowett, "'Capacity for Evil'," 72.
87. Crafts, quoted in Francis G. Couvares, "Hollywood, Main Street, and the Church: Trying to Censor the Movies before the Production Code," in Couvares, ed., *Movie Censorship*, 133.
88. Quoted in Streible, "A History," 416.

PART IV

Feature films and cinema programmes

INTRODUCTION

LONGER MULTI-SHOT FILMS REACHING up to a thousand feet in length, lasting around 15 minutes and constituting one reel of film, had, as we have seen, become prevalent from 1903. At this time, the term 'feature' was often applied to significant films like *La Voyage dans la Lune* (*A Trip to the Moon*, Méliès, 1902) and *The Great Train Robbery* (Edison, 1903), borrowing from the variety theatre tradition that labelled headlining acts 'features'. Films singled out as 'features' also included those dealing with controversial subject matter, for example *The Unwritten Law: A Thrilling Drama Based on the Thaw-White Scandal* (Lubin, 1907) which dealt with a sexual scandal dominating the news at the time.[1] Later, the demand for films fuelled by the nickelodeon boom in the United States and the policies of the MPPC from late 1908 supported a system of production, distribution and exhibition predicated on the rapid manufacture and turnover of films of one-reel length, and of shorter, 'split-reel' films which could be put together on a reel of film. Variety principles still dominated the film programme, which was made up of a number of separate and often varied films – actualities and a range of fictional genres – frequently interspersed with live acts or illustrated songs.

Before 1910, then, the American film industry had developed an efficient and popular practice based on the single reel standard. Manufacturers produced one-reel and split-reel films in large numbers; exchanges distributed them rapidly to nickelodeons, charging differently depending on how new the films were; and nickelodeons ran short programmes usually of about three reels of film that changed daily, enabling them to have a rapid turnover of audiences and to attract audiences back on a regular basis.

In the early 1910s, though, important changes took place despite the reservations of many invested in the established system. In effect, the industry moved from the single-reel standard to a system centred on the production of large numbers of multi-reel films lasting anywhere from 40 minutes to 3 hours. Now the term 'feature' was reserved for films of more than one reel. Why did this shift from the successful one-reel system to the dominance of multi-reelers take place? What effects did this have on film form and style, and on film production and exhibition? Our answers here and in the chapters that follow focus initially on the United States, though we will also refer to developments in Europe because of their important influence on the American situation. In addition to questions of industrial development and aesthetics, we will consider the social and political issues worked through by some of the films produced between 1912 and 1915, particularly in relation to gender and race.

Length had imposed obvious limitations for filmmakers, causing some of them to propose longer films to allow for greater elaboration of character and story. D. W. Griffith, for example, made a two-reel film of Tennyson's poem *Enoch Arden* (Biograph, 1911), though the film was released one reel at a time which is indicative of the rigid nature of the one-reel system. Griffith would leave Biograph in 1913 amidst concerns about the company's reluctance to produce multi-reel films. Commentators in the trade press too noted that the standardization of the one-reel length could lead to an artificial compression of the story. Here, for example, is an editorial from the *Moving Picture World* in January 1911:

> It would seem that the time has come when the length of the film should in no way have anything to do with the subject matter; there is too much evidence of 'cutting off' to the detriment of continuity of the pictures and this slaughtering of the subject only increases the ambiguity of the whole ... Clear, well sustained plots, carried to a full and finished ending, leaving with the audience a feeling of satisfaction and completeness, are demanded.[2]

Certain filmmakers and commentators in the trade press, then, proposed the lengthening of films so that they could adequately tell different kinds of stories.

Claims made for film as a form of art comparable in some respects to the legitimate theatre were also important in the shift to multi-reel films. Griffith, a former stage actor and dramatist, played an important role here, but rhetoric concerning the artistic potential of film and its connections to legitimate theatre was extremely widespread in the trade press of the period. Linking internal pressures on film form with the external pressures of regulatory concern, the conception of film as an art like theatre worked to assuage anxiety about cinema by raising its cultural status. Vitagraph was a particularly important production company in this respect, as Roberta Pearson and William Uricchio showed in the previous section. Highlighting increased length as an outward sign of legitimacy, Vitagraph produced a number of multi-reel 'quality' films of well-known historical and biblical events and of literary classics like *Life of Napoleon* (1909, two reels), *Life of George Washington* (1909, two reels), *Les Miserables* (1909, four reels), *Life of Moses* (1909, five reels) *Uncle Tom's Cabin* (1910, three reels), *A Tale of Two Cities* (1911, three reels) and *Pickwick Papers* (1913, two reels). Like Griffith's *Enoch Arden*, however, the Vitagraph quality films were released one reel at a time and were only shown together in special exhibitions after their initial release. We can call these films, Ben Brewster suggests in his essay here, 'nickelodeon multi-reelers'. Often these films reverted to the tableau style characteristic of films from earlier periods.

The development of film serials from late 1912 was one important response to the limitations of the single reel standard. Although the films were released one reel at a time, they began to establish close links between reels through the development of an overarching narrative which involved the continuing adventures of a central character. Each episode was self-contained but frequently – and by 1915 almost always – culminated with a suspenseful 'cliffhanger' ending (so-called because characters often ended up suspended from cliffs or buildings). Hence there was a high level of continuity from one reel to the next, pushing at the borders of the one-reel tradition and developing textual strategies that would become important for the construction of multi-reel features. *What Happened to Mary* (Edison, 1912), released in twelve monthly 'chapters' beginning in July 1912, was the first American serial with a storyline connecting separate instalments.[3]

A number of American serials such as *The Perils of Pauline* (Pathé, 1914), *The Adventures of Kathlyn* (Selig, 1914) and *The Hazards of Helen* (Kalem, 1914) featured a female central character who, Shelley Stamp observes in her chapter in this section, demonstrated toughness, bravery, agility and intelligence in facing a series of dangerous challenges. These qualities were mirrored in the publicity surrounding the films and their powerful and extremely popular female stars. Even so, the agency of the serial heroines was circumscribed in the films and, to a lesser extent, in accompanying fan magazine articles, Stamp argues. After all, the films told alarmist tales about the often explicitly sexualized threats which independent females acting in the public sphere would have to confront, and about the inevitability of marriage, which might offer safety. Looked at in this way, the representation of serial heroines can be seen as an important nego-tiation of broader transformations in the social role of women and in the public debates about this role. Indeed, as Stamp suggests, the actresses playing serial heroines and the substantial star discourse that surrounded them were important examples of these transformations. Like other stars, serial queens were public personalities, conducting their lives and doing their work in full view of the press, exerting power at their workplace and displaying their accumulated wealth at home. Within the film industry such prominence and influence was not restricted to female stars, as women also had important roles as screenwriters and film directors.[4]

Returning to the question of film length, it is important to note that commercial benefits could be derived from exhibiting multi-reel films in a unified presentation, rather than breaking them up into separate instalments. The subject matter of these films, their increased cultural status and especially their affiliation with the legitimate theatre was capable of drawing in a better paying crowd. Longer feature films could be shown in larger venues, notably legitimate theatres where they replaced the live performance of a play, at prices ranging from 25 cents to $2; these films provided audiences with an experience comparable to an evening's enter-tainment at the theatre. An important role was played here by a series of European historical epics that perfectly married cultural status with commercial benefits. Prominent among these were Italian imports which made up over half of the multi-reel films distributed in the United States in the early 1910s.[5] *Italian Cavalry Ride* (1909), a two-reel film, was released in 1909 and was a commercial success outside the regular distribution system. Later, *La Caduta Di Troia* (*The Fall of Troy*, Itala, 1910), *La Gerusalemme Liberata* (*The Crusaders*, Cines, 1911), *L'Inferno* (*Dante's Inferno*, Milano Films, 1911), *Life of Dante* (Ambrosia, 1912), *Gilultimi Giorna di Pompei* (*The Last Days of Pompeii*, Ambrosia, 1913), *Quo Vadis* (Cines, 1913) and *Cabiria* (Itala Film, 1914) were big successes. *Quo Vadis* was probably the most successful film of 1913. Like some of the other Italian epics, it was shown as a 'roadshow' attraction, which means that it was exhibited in legitimate theatres as the equivalent of a famous theatrical touring company, with special sound effects and orchestral music. *Cabiria* in particular was very influential for stylistic developments in the period. Long tracking shots, complex camera movements, and staging in depth characterized the film, providing further evidence of the artistic potential of cinema.[6]

Various other European countries produced significant multi-reel feature films as well, Ben Brewster suggests here, partly because these countries were not constrained by the one-reel system dominant in the United States and also perhaps because the greater influence of cultural élites fostered a more widespread conception of film as art. Hence important films from Denmark like *The Four Devils* (Nordisk, 1911) and *Dodespringet til Hest fra Cirkus-Kuplen* (*Death Jump on Horseback from the Circus Dome*, Nordisk, 1912) and from Sweden like *Ingeborg Holm* (Svenska, 1913) and *Terje Vigen* (*A Man There Was*, Svenska, 1916) were widely seen, commercially successful, and, like the Italian feature films, stylistically influential.[7] Kristin Thompson considers film style in her wide-ranging chapter in this section, tracing how filmmakers in Europe, India, South America and the United States developed the expressive potential of cinema through the 1910s. Her analysis shows that developments in staging, set design, lighting, camera movement, and editing created a new expressive repertoire of filmmaking which lent atmosphere, meaning, and suspense to films and worked to deepen the spectator's emotional involvement.

As in earlier years, European films again had a significant impact on American production. The case of the Famous Players company, and its president Adolph Zukor, is instructive. In the summer of 1912 Zukor imported the four-reel French film *Queen Elizabeth*, starring the legendary stage actress Sarah Bernhardt, and exhibited it at prestigious legitimate theatres accompanied by a specially composed score. Encouraged by the commercial success of the film, Zukor made a number of films starring well-known and respected theatrical actors and often based on literary classics, adopting the slogan 'Famous Players in Famous Plays'. Late in 1912 Famous Players produced *The Count of Monte Cristo*, starring matinée idol James O'Neill, and followed this with *The Prisoner of Zenda* (February 1913, with James Hackett who had starred in the theatrical production), and *Tess of the D'Urbervilles* (September, with theatre star Minne Maddern Fiske). Zukor's promise to release '30 Famous Features a Year' in late 1913 was a significant development, because it combined the one-reel system of regular production with the multi-reel format which hitherto had been associated with special events. His next production, *In the Bishop's Carriage* (September), starred Mary Pickford, who had initially been an actress at the Biograph Company but had left to star in well-known theatrical entrepreneur David Belasco's *A Good Little Devil* on Broadway in 1913. Her role as a star for Famous Players signalled a further integration of the film and theatre worlds and of the previously separate spheres of one-reelers and multi-reelers. Pickford went on to become one of the most popular stars of the silent era.[8]

Famous Players and other independent production companies like Universal, operating outside the MPPC, were increasingly turning to the production of feature films and soon gained dominance over the production houses associated with the Patents Company. The legal dissolution of the MPPC in 1915, on charges of unfair restraint of trade filed initially in 1912, came after the Company was already struggling commercially.[9]

As Zukor's slogan and strategies suggested, the rise of the multi-reel feature film coincided with a redefined relationship between the cinema and theatre industries. Legitimate theatres began to exhibit films in ever greater numbers. Late in 1913, for example, leading theatrical impresarios Klaw and Erlanger began showing films in the New Amsterdam Theatre in New York City, their most prestigious house, in the afternoons and on Sunday nights. The Shubert brothers similarly decided to replace the Sunday night band concerts at their Hippodrome Theater in the city with moving pictures. Why would theatrical entrepreneurs be interested in this? Aside from the popularity of films, and anxieties about the fading popularity of theatre, the central reason would seem to be an economic one – it was simply cheaper to rent films than pay live performers.

Important agreements were also reached between a number of theatre and film producers. Klaw and Erlanger combined forces in 1913 with Biograph to produce film adaptations of the plays for which they controlled the rights; these adaptations were to be exhibited in legitimate theatres. Later in 1913 the Jesse L. Lasky Feature Motion Picture Company was formed, headed by Lasky who had been a producer of extravagant vaudeville acts and featuring among its most prominent employees the former playwright and member of a well-known theatrical family Cecil B. DeMille. The World Film Company was established in 1914 mainly to adapt plays owned by the Shuberts and others.[10]

Another important example of the interaction between the film and theatrical industries came late in 1913 when the Shubert brothers helped finance the film *Traffic in Souls* (Universal, 1913) and formed the Shubert Feature Film Booking Company to book films for their large chain of theatres.[11] *Traffic in Souls* turned out to be considerably different from nickelodeon multi-reelers, European epics, and early American theatrical and literary adaptations in terms of subject matter, cultural status and narrative construction. Telling a sensational story about the abduction of a young woman into 'white slavery', or forced prostitution, and her subsequent rescue by her older sister and the police, the film seemed to borrow from the serial films and their representation of female imperilment and empowerment rather than from high cultural sources. It was, as Ben Brewster notes in his chapter in this section, the first American feature not based on a well-known novel, play or historical event. Here then the feature film merged with a tradition of sensational melodrama, concentrating on action and sensation, rather than participating in the gentrification efforts of the film industry. Brewster's analysis shows also that the film utilized alternation, which had been central to the one-reel tradition exemplified by Griffith's Biograph films, to develop a form of filmic storytelling which was distinct from the tableau-like construction of the nickelodeon multi-reelers and the long takes, deep staging and general staginess of early European and American feature films. The film became an important model for later productions, and to some extent it prefigured what would become standard classical Hollywood narrational practices.

Traffic in Souls stands as an important film in the development of filmic storytelling. It also was, as we discussed in the previous section, important in relation to debates about censorship. The film was viewed a number of times by the National Board of Censorship, who ultimately passed it with a few minor cuts. Later white slave films, cashing in on the popularity of *Traffic in Souls*, were often banned, regarded by the Board and others as unsuitable entertainment for a mass audience. Lee Grieveson has argued that the debates about *Traffic in Souls* and other white slave films developed important distinctions about the social functioning of cinema and its engagement with pressing social and political problems.[12] *Traffic in Souls* has been the subject of other scholarly work focusing on the film's representation of white slavery and women, and on its negotiation of the terrain of modernity.[13]

Like *Traffic in Souls*, *The Birth of a Nation* (Epoch, 1915) was of central importance for the development of the multi-reel feature film in terms of its form and style, its intertextual heritage and its economic success. The film was quickly hailed as an artistic masterpiece, and subsequently seen by many scholars as a crucial step towards the classical Hollywood cinema. Griffith, the film's director, utilized the strategies he had perfected while working on one-reel films at Biograph to tell an epic story, shifting from large scale scenes to intimate details and, in the later parts of the film, building up tension with a characteristic ride to the rescue. Griffith was skilled in 'creating and prolonging suspense', *Moving Picture World* noted, 'to the agonizing point'.[14] *Variety*, *Moving Picture World*, and other trade journals praised the film highly, noting that it was the first film that could charge $2 for admission and be widely sold out.[15] Standard feature films at the time could usually be seen for between 10 and 25 cents. *The Birth of a Nation* was indeed phenomenally successful. Exhibited with a specially commissioned score in legitimate theatres as a roadshow attraction and then distributed more widely through the selling of states rights, the film grossed an estimated 60 million dollars at the box office, making it, after adjustments for inflation, one of the most successful films of all time.[16] It was the first film shown at the White House in Washington DC.

It was also one of the most controversial films ever made, even more so than *Traffic in Souls*, for it told a story about the heroic role of the Ku Klux Klan in the aftermath of the American Civil War and presented a racist account of history. *The Birth of a Nation* made a strong case for the necessity of racial hierarchies separating white and black people; such thinking was certainly commonplace at the time but it was also strongly contested. *Variety*, *Moving Picture World*, and the National Board of Censorship effectively downplayed the film's racism by prioritizing its aesthetic brilliance, a strategy that Clyde Taylor has suggested has underpinned much of the subsequent scholarship on the film.[17] Already in 1915, there were groups contesting this separation of the aesthetic from the political, most notably predominantly black organizations like the National Association for the Advancement of Colored People (NAACP) which protested against the film's racism and its rewriting of history.[18] Indeed, some black protesters tried to counter the film's influence by producing their own films. One of the curious ironies of *The Birth of a Nation* is the role it played in spurring on politically motivated black film production, for the film made clear to many the power of images to shape the way people saw themselves and others. The sense of purpose, community spirit and collective action instilled in African Americans as a result of their organized challenge to the film did 'result in their winning one crucial battle', Anna Everett observes: 'the battle over the right of a subjugated people to self-definition and expression'.[19] Important recent work by film historians has been directed at discussing this black film production.[20]

Linda Williams discusses *The Birth of a Nation* in her essay in this section by concentrating on the way the film articulated what she sees as a new kind of racial melodrama predicated on the denigration of black males and the representation of suffering white women. Williams argues that the film was directly descended from the tradition of stage melodrama, characterized mainly by its combination of pathos and action.[21] Her account points to the centrality of melodrama to the formation of classical Hollywood cinema, an issue we will pursue further in the following section. Questions of race were at the heart of the melodramatic tradition in the United States, and, firmly situated within this tradition, *The Birth of a Nation* infuses the multi-reel format with distinctly American themes and problems, linking feelings about race to notions of a national identity and overtly celebrating white supremacy.

In the wake of the success of films like *Traffic in Souls* and *The Birth of a Nation*, increasing numbers of legitimate theatres were converted into movie theatres. This marked an important shift in the mediascape as legitimate theatre came to be perceived as part of a minority élite culture and moving pictures as a mass medium capable of attracting a middlebrow audience.[22] Construction of purpose-built cinemas gathered pace also. Often these were so-called 'movie palaces', complete with large and distinctive facades, vast ornate lobbies, armies of uniformed ushers and in some cases fully staffed nurseries. Important also was the orchestra accompanying films and the frequent presence of an organist, who played a solo before the feature film began.[23] Polls conducted in the 1920s revealed that audiences often chose the theatre they attended because of the quality of its music.[24]

While multi-reel feature films were inextricably connected to the emergence and appeal of movie palaces, they were seen as only one element of a programme that included music, sometimes live acts, and usually a number of one- or two-reel films. Variety and legitimate traditions effectively merged in such programmes, providing different kinds of pleasures to a diverse mass audience. Comedies, animated films, and serials were important components of the support programme preceding the feature film. Well known exhibitor T. J. West wrote in 1914: 'As far as the "make-up" of an ideal programme is concerned, the best possible selection of pictures for an average audience is, to my mind, one which has variety as its keynote. It should include dramas, comedies, scenic, educational and scientific subjects'.[25] Weekly newsreels were established from around 1911 and provided an important component of non-fiction to the film programme.

Charles Maland's chapter here focuses on the star of what were probably the most popular short films of the 1910s, Charles Chaplin. Chaplin was a British music hall performer who became a film performer at the Keystone studio in 1913, bringing with him performance traditions associated with the variety theatre. His early films included violent humour and a lot of vulgarity, especially in his character's treatment of women, with which Chaplin clearly deviated from the romantic norms of most feature films. Maland traces Chaplin's rapid rise to superstardom as well as the forceful criticisms he was subjected to. Chaplin responded, Maland's analysis shows, by slowly changing his performance style and persona, bringing them more in line with genteel norms and, at the same time, increasingly presenting himself as an artist. Chaplin gradually developed forms of characterization – fully rounded and marked by pathos – that were in line with the norms of the emerging classicism in American cinema and that demonstrated a further merging of variety and legitimate traditions.[26] We will consider this process further in the next section in relation to the career of Buster Keaton.

By about 1915, then, the future shape of films, of movie theatres and their programmes, of film companies and indeed of the film industry as a whole was becoming clear. Large numbers of nickelodeons still existed, showing programmes of short films, but the trend was towards the production of multi-reel feature films exhibited in large theatres as the main attraction of a varied programme. Legitimate theatre, rather than variety theatre, became the dominant model for cinema, though, as we have seen, various traditions were merged in movie theatre programmes that included elements of live performance and shorts films together with the feature. The demands of making longer feature films encouraged the development of new narrative and expressive norms.[27] To produce these films a more carefully organized production process was necessary, which crucially depended on the introduction of continuity scripts serving as detailed blueprints to be used by all production personnel, and the rise of the central producer system, involving greater division of labour between production personnel, a more layered hierarchy and greater power for company executives.[28]

Most of the large studios which dominated feature film production were located in and around Los Angeles, in particular in a suburb called Hollywood which gave the industry the name it would be known under from then on.[29] Increasingly Hollywood became defined less as an industry than as a space of fantasy and entertainment, closely associated with the film stars who lived in the vicinity of the studios and who were gaining ever more prominence in American public life. We will consider Hollywood's internal organization, its aesthetics and its role in American culture in more detail in the next section, moving from the transitional period of the 1910s into the classicism of the 1920s.

Notes

1   For a discussion of the film, see Lee Grieveson, 'The Thaw-White Scandal, *The Unwritten Law*, and the Scandal of Cinema', in Adrienne McClean and David Cook (eds), *Headline Hollywood: Perspectives on Scandal and Cinema* (Brunswick, NJ: Rutgers University Press, 2000).

2   *Moving Picture World* (7 January 1911), 14–15, quoted in Eileen Bowser, *The Transformation of Cinema, 1907–1915* (Berkeley: University of California Press, 1990), 198. Charlie Keil has shown that the trade press in the period constituted an important feedback mechanism for the industry and actively helped shape formal developments. Charlie Keil, *Early American Cinema in Transition: Story, Style, and Filmmaking, 1907–1913* (Madison: University of Wisconsin Press, 2001), 27–9.

3   It is worth noting that serials began earlier in some European countries. In France, for example, the regular production of detective series began in 1908 and continued through the production of the well-known *Zigomar* (Éclair, 1911) and *Fantomas* (Gamount, 1913). For a discussion of these films, see the special issue of *The Velvet Light Trap*, no. 37 (1996), especially Richard Abel, 'The Thrills of the *Grande Peur*: Crime Series and Serials in the Belle Epoche'; David Bordwell, '*La Nouvelle Mission de Feuillade*; or, What was Mise en Scene?'; and Tom Gunning, 'A Tale of Two Prologues: Actors and Roles, Detectives and Disguises in Fantômas'. On American serials, see Ben Singer, *Melodrama and Modernity: Early Sensational Cinema and Its Contexts* (New York: Columbia University Press, 2001), 221–88.

4   For more see, for example, Cari Beauchamp, *Without Lying Down: Frances Marion and the Powerful Women of Early Hollywood* (New York, Scribner, 1997); Anne Morey, '"Would You be Ashamed to Let Them See What You Have Written?": The Gendering of Photoplaywrights, 1913–1923,' *Tulsa Studies in Women's Literature*, vol. 17, no. 1 (1998); Jennifer Bean and Diane Negra (eds), *A Feminist Reader in Early Cinema* (Durham, NC: Duke University Press, 2003).

5   Charles Musser, 'On "Extras," Mary Pickford, and the Red-Light Film: Filmmaking in the United States', *Griffithiana*, no. 50 (1991), 149.

6   For a discussion of Italian cinema in this period, see Paolo Cherchi Usai, 'Italy: Spectacle and Melodrama', in Geoffrey Nowell-Smith (ed.), *The Oxford History of World Cinema* (Oxford: Oxford University Press, 1996); also see the essays collected in the special issue of *Film History*, vol. 12, no. 3 (2000), edited by Giorgio Bertellini.

7   See John Fullerton and Jan Olsson (eds), *Nordic Explorations: Film Before 1930* (Sydney: John Libbey, 1999).

8   Tino Balio, 'Stars in Business: The Founding of United Artists', in Tino Balio (ed.), *The American Film Industry* (Madison: University of Wisconsin Press, rev. ed. 1985), in particular 157–63; Lee Grieveson, 'Stars and Audiences in Early American Cinema', *Screening the Past* (Winter 2002); and Gaylyn Studlar, 'Oh, "Doll Divine": Mary Pickford, Masquerade, and the Pedophilic Gaze', *Camera Obscura*, no. 48 (2001).

9   Janet Staiger, 'Combination and Litigation: Structures of US Film Distribution, 1896–1917', in Thomas Elsaesser (ed.), *Early Cinema: Space, Frame, Narrative* (London: British Film Institute, 1990), 199–204.

10 Roberta Pearson, 'The Menace of the Movies: Theatre and Cinema in the Transitional Period', in Charlie Keil and Shelley Stamp (eds), *American Cinema's Transitional Era* (Berkeley: University of California Press, 2004); Bowser, *The Transformation of Cinema*, 225–7.

11 Kevin Lewis, 'A World across from Broadway: The Shuberts and the Movies', *Film History*, vol. 1 (1987).

12 Lee Grieveson, 'Policing the cinema: *Traffic in Souls* at Ellis Island, 1913', *Screen*, vol. 38, no. 2 (Summer 1997).

13 Kevin Brownlow, *Behind the Mask of Innocence* (New York: Alfred A. Knopf, 1990), 71–80; Shelley Stamp, 'Wages and Sin: *Traffic in Souls* and the White Slavery Scare', *Persistence of Vision*, vol. 9 (1991); Janet Staiger, *Bad Women: Regulating Sexuality in Early American Cinema* (Minneapolis: University of Minnesota Press, 1995), 116–46; Shelley Stamp, *Movie-Struck Girls: Women and Motion Picture Culture After the Nickelodeon* (Princeton, NJ; Princeton University Press, 2000), 41–101; Tom Gunning, 'From the Kaleidoscope to the X-Ray: Urban Spectatorship, Poe, Benjamin, and *Traffic in Souls* (1913)', *Wide Angle*, vol. 19, no. 4 (October 1997); and Kristen Whissel, 'Regulating Mobility: Technology, Modernity, and Feature-Length Narrativity in *Traffic in Souls*', *Camera Obscura*, no. 49 (2002).

14 *Moving Picture World* (13 March 1915), 1587.

15 *Variety* (12 March 1915); *Moving Picture World* (13 March 1915), 1586–1587.

16 Richard Schickel, *D. W. Griffith* (London: Pavilion, 1984), 281.

17 Clyde Taylor, 'The Re-Birth of the Aesthetic in Cinema', in Daniel Bernardi (ed.), *The Birth of Whiteness: Race and the Emergence of U.S. Cinema* (New Brunswick, NJ: Rutgers University Press, 1996).

18 Nickieann Fleener-Marzec, *D. W. Griffith's 'The Birth of a Nation': Controversy, Suppression, and the First Amendment as it Applies to Filmic Expression, 1915–1973* (New York: Arno Press, 1980); Anna Everett, *Returning the Gaze: A Genealogy of Black Film Criticism, 1909–1949* (Durham, NC: Duke University Press, 2001), 70–106; Lee Grieveson, 'Not Harmless Entertainment: State Censorship and Cinema in the Transitional Era', in Keil and Stamp (eds), *American Cinema's Transitional Era.*

19 Everett, *Returning the Gaze*, 102.

20 See, for example, Charles Musser, 'To Redream the Dreams of White Playwrights: Reappropriation and Resistance in Oscar Micheaux's *Body and Soul*', *The Yale Journal of Criticism*, vol. 12, no. 2 (1999); Pearl Bowser and Louise Spence, *Writing Himself Into History: Oscar Micheaux, His Silent Films, and His Audiences* (New Brunswick, NJ: Rutgers University Press, 2000); Jane M. Gaines, *Fire and Desire: Mixed-Race Movies in the Silent Era* (Chicago: University of Chicago Press, 2001); Pearl Bowser, Jane Gaines and Charles Musser (eds), *Oscar Micheaux and His Circle: African-American Filmmakers and Race Cinema in the Silent Era* (Bloomington: Indiana University Press, 2001).

21 For more on this definition, see Linda Williams 'Melodrama Revised', in Nick Browne (ed.), *Refiguring American Film Genres: History and Theory* (Berkeley: University of California Press, 1998).

22 Pearson, 'The Menace of the Movies'.

23 Richard Koszarski, *An Evening's Entertainment: The Age of the Silent Feature Picture, 1915–1928* (Berkeley: University of California Press, 1990), 41–8.

24 Koszarski, *An Evening's Entertainment*, 30–1.

25 Letter from T. J. West, 'What the Public Wants', *The Bioscope* (26 February 1915), 955, quoted in Stephen Bottomore, 'Rediscovering Early Non-Fiction Film', *Film History*, vol. 13 (2001), 164.

26 See Peter Krämer, 'Vitagraph, Slapstick and Early Cinema', *Screen*, vol. 29, no. 2 (Spring 1988).

27 Keil, *Early American Cinema in Transition*, 45–82.

28 David Bordwell, Janet Staiger and Kristin Thompson, *The Classical Hollywood Cinema: Film Style and Mode of Production to 1960* (London: Routledge, 1985), 121–54.

29 Bowser, *The Transformation of Cinema, 1907–1915*, in particular 159–65.

Chapter 11

CHARLES J. MALAND

A STAR IS BORN
American culture and the dynamics of Charlie
Chaplin's star image, 1913–1916

BETWEEN DECEMBER 1913, when Charles Spencer Chaplin first stepped on the Keystone Studios lot, and mid-1916, when he completed his final film for his second company, Essanay, Chaplin—buoyed by his comic persona Charlie—became one of Hollywood's first huge movie stars. During that brief but intense period, Charlie's *star image*—fashioned by Chaplin himself, by his movies, by certain ideological and signifying practices within the film industry, by the press, and by representatives of other social institutions—became firmly established in the public mind. That star image, which would also evolve in fascinating ways for the rest of Chaplin's life, consists of the complex and shifting set of meanings, attitudes, and mental pictures associated in the public mind with Chaplin—both the real person and Charlie, the persona he played in his films. It is generated through the interplay of filmmaker and culture. On the one hand, Chaplin, through his actions, words, and films, played a large role in generating the star image. On the other, American society generally and the film industry more specifically—through the activities of reviewers, editorialists, moralists and censorship groups, fan magazines, intellectuals, and press publicists—also helped to make Chaplin a star and to shape the way that star was perceived.[1] This essay examines the dynamic process through which Chaplin's star image was first established from his arrival at Keystone through his departure from Essanay Studios in 1916.

The rough-edged diamond: Charlie at Keystone

On 12 May 1913 Alf Reeves, manager of a Fred Karno music-hall company touring in America, received a telegram at the Nixon Theater in Philadelphia:

> IS THERE A MAN NAMED CHAFFIN IN YOUR COMPANY OR SOMETHING LIKE THAT STOP IF SO WILL HE COMMUNICATE WITH KESSEL AND BAUMAN 24 LONGACRE BUILDING BROADWAY NEW YORK

Reeves, suspecting that the telegram must be referring to one of his featured players, Charles Chaplin, showed it to him. When Chaplin learned that the Longacre Building primarily housed legal offices, he surmised that he had inherited some money and immediately arranged a trip to New York City. But he soon learned otherwise. Adam Kessell, Jr., and Charles O. Bauman were owners of the New York Motion Pictures Company. The telegram had been sent by Mack Sennett, head of one of their subsidiaries—a film production company in Los Angeles called Keystone. Sennett had seen Chaplin perform in 1911 at the American Music Hall and thought that Chaplin might do as a replacement for Ford Sterling, a leading Keystone comedian who was threatening to leave. Although Chaplin had no previous experience in film, he was lured to accept the offer by a princely salary: $150 weekly for three months, raised to $175 for the rest of the year. Before joining Keystone, however, Chaplin had to complete his Karno tour. After his last performance, in Kansas City on November 28, an eager yet anxious Chaplin parted with his Karno associates and took a train to California. Little did he know that within two years he would be one of the most famous people in the United States.[2]

Chaplin's timing was fortunate because in the previous several years, the film industry, groping toward the star system that would later dominate it, had begun to market films by featuring particular actors. Thanks partly to the stability created by the Motion Picture Patents Company (the "Trust") after its foundation in 1908, the industry was able, in the words of one scholar, "to turn investment away from patent litigation and into product development." Actors soon received attention as one way to differentiate and sell films. (I use the term "actors" to refer to both men and women.) As early as February 1910, an author in *Nickelodeon* noted that movie audiences were demanding a "better acquaintance with those they see upon the screen," and by 1912—the year before Chaplin's arrival on the Keystone lot—a "star system" was beginning to establish itself. It provided a way for one company to differentiate its product from that of other companies.[3]

But Chaplin did not become a full-fledged star immediately. In fact, it would probably be more accurate to say that although he gained a considerable following among moviegoers during his year at Keystone, he did not actually become a star until after he signed with Essanay in early 1915.

The construction of the star image did begin at Keystone, however, primarily as a result of the films themselves rather than promotion of them or publicity and commentary about them. Chaplin appeared in thirty-five films for Keystone in 1914. The first, *Making a Living*, was released on February 2; the last, *His Prehistoric Past*, on December 7. Although most of the films were one-reelers (about ten minutes long), several were only about five minutes, and one, *Tillie's Punctured Romance*, featuring Marie Dressler, took up six reels. Chaplin appeared in his "tramp" or "Charlie" costume very early—in his second film, *Kid Auto Races at Venice*.[4] By his twelfth film, *Caught in a Cabaret*, he had finally persuaded Sennett to let him co-direct (with Mabel Normand, his costar). Chaplin went on to direct or co-direct (with Normand, four more times) twenty of his last twenty-three films at Keystone. The year was a frenetic, educational one for Chaplin. He learned moviemaking by doing.

A look at some characteristics of the Keystone films, particularly of the persona Chaplin played, indicates the kind of star image that Chaplin began to develop during his year there. That image was shaped in part by the studio in which Chaplin worked; Sennett's studio was famous for its iconoclastic nose-thumbing at propriety and its frantic Keystone cop chases. Chaplin himself, accustomed to the more polished acting and pantomime of the English music hall, felt uneasy with the hectic, broad Keystone style (*My Autobiography*, pp. 147–50, hereafter MA). Even though he began to differentiate himself through the creation of a character and to achieve some level of independence by directing his own films, Chaplin still created a persona that was tempered by the Keystone stamp.

Generalizing about Chaplin's persona at Keystone is nearly impossible, largely because he was much less conscious of the character he played (and less able to control that persona, given his position as Sennett's employee) than he became in later years. Although viewers today associate Chaplin's screen persona with a distinct outfit and props—derby and cane, tight-fitting coat and baggy pants, floppy shoes—this costume was not his trademark during the early Keystone days. In his first film Chaplin played a dandy; he wore a top hat, a double-breasted overcoat, black gloves, spats, and a goatee. Even after he began directing himself, Chaplin's costume varied. The top hat appeared again, for example, in *Mabel's Married Life* (his nineteenth Keystone film). Sometimes his occupation in a film determined his clothing: coatless, Chaplin wore a waiter's apron over his vest in *Caught in a Cabaret*. As the Keystone year passed, however, the costume became more conventional. By his final Keystone, the Charlie persona must have been widely known to a growing audience, for in that film—*His Prehistoric Past*—Charlie wore his derby and big shoes with his caveman's skins, suggesting that the derby and shoes were already trademark enough.

Much has been written about the essential appeal of Charlie's costume and character, and these discussions often revolve around conceptions of contrast that Chaplin, in his autobiography, recalled using when trying to describe his new character to Sennett after piecing together the costume: "You know this fellow is many-sided, a tramp, a gentleman, a poet, a dreamer, a lonely fellow, always hopeful of romance and adventure. He would have you believe he is a scientist, a musician, a duke, a polo player. However, he is not above picking up cigarette butts or robbing a baby of its candy. And, of course, if the situation warrants it, he will kick a lady in the rear—but only in extreme anger" (MA, 144). In writing this passage Chaplin was either disingenuous or forgetful, because such a multifaceted and complex conception of Charlie's character was not apparent during the Keystone year. In fact, it would be relatively accurate to say that Chaplin's description would fit his Keystone persona pretty well if the first half were deleted and the second half—about picking up cigarette butts, stealing candy from babies, and kicking ladies—were emphasized.

The Charlie persona that emerged from the Keystone films was often mean, crude, and brutish. Examples from the films abound. In *Between Showers*, for example, Charlie pokes Ford Sterling in the backside with an umbrella and thumbs his nose to a cop. In *A Film Johnnie* he gets ejected from a movie theater for disruptive behavior, and in *Mabel and the Wee*, he sticks a pin in Mabel's thigh and her boyfriend's buttocks. As a waiter in *Caught in a Cabaret*, he dusts off some food with a dirty rag, then drops the food on the floor, steps on it, puts it back on the plate, and serves it. As a dentist's odd-job man in *Laughing Gas*, he hits a man on the mouth with a brick, causing the man to spit out a mouthful of teeth. In the same film he poses as a dentist and clambers onto a woman in the chair: when she resists, he pulls the woman's nose with a forceps and kisses her. Though the Keystone films also contain a number of graceful and clever comic touches that would become a Chaplin trademark, the humor in these films is generally broad and sometimes bawdy slapstick. The gentle and tender character apparent in later Chaplin films—*City Lights*, for example—is at this point nowhere to be found.

Given this screen persona, what evidence exists in the trade press that Chaplin was becoming familiar in the film industry? *Moving Picture World* reviewed at least seventeen of Chaplin's Keystones, and its varying levels of awareness of Chaplin suggest the degree to which he was becoming known while at Keystone. Without naming him specifically, the magazine noted his performance in its review of Chaplin's first Keystone, *Making a Living*: "The clever player who takes the role of the nervy and very shifty sharper in this picture is a comedian of the first water, who acts like one of nature's own naturals."[5] There were no references to Chaplin in March or April. In a May issue, however, a review of *Caught in a Cabaret* stated, "Charles Chaplin was the leading funmaker" (9 May 1914: 821). This allusion would suggest that Chaplin's name was becoming familiar, but that may not have been true: in a number of later reviews, Chaplin's name was misspelled. In June he was called "Charles Chapman"

(27 June 1914: 65), in an August review he was "Chaplain" (29 August 1914: 1242), and in the September 19 and 25 issues, the spelling reverts to "Chapman." By October, *Moving Picture World* had finally learned to spell Chaplin's name correctly (17 October 1914: 932). Even then, however, reviews suggest that he was not as established and settled a performer as Mabel Normand or Mack Swain. Note the review of *His Musical Career*: "Chas Chaplin and Ambrose disport themselves in this number as a pair of piano movers" (14 November 1914: 932). Ambrose was the name of the character Mack Swain played in the Keystone films at that time; reviewers and apparently audiences regularly referred to Ambrose and to Mabel, but Chaplin had not yet become known as Charlie or the tramp or the little fellow, at least not until near the end of his year at Keystone.

Figure 11.1
Motion Picture Magazine,
November 1915

A similar indication that Chaplin's popularity began to grow near the end of this year comes from *Motion Picture Magazine*. The periodical featured a regular section called "Green Room Jottings," which consisted of one- or two-sentence references to people, primarily actors, in the movie business. The first reference to Chaplin appeared in the August 1914 "Jottings," in which readers learned that "Charles Chaplin (Keystone) has been an 'actor man' for sixteen years, yet he is now only twenty-four years young."[6] That same issue contained a rather bizarre caricature of Chaplin on a page with nine other people, including Ford Sterling, John Barrymore, and—the largest in size—V. A. Potel, the "Funny Man at G. M. Anderson's Essanay Camp" (p. 131). The Chaplin sketch showed him with brawny shoulders, barrel chest, bulging biceps, and tiny waist and legs, a bulldog at his side. To George Edwards, the artist, Chaplin seemed to suggest a young athlete or acrobat. Mustache, derby, and cane played no part in his star image here.

In its October 1914 issue *Motion Picture Magazine* announced the results of its "Great Player Contest," in which over eleven million ballots had ostensibly been cast by readers before the cutoff date of August 20. Earl Williams, Clara K. Young, and Mary Pickford topped the list of the one hundred leading vote getters. Mabel Normand, in fortieth place, was the highest-ranking Keystone star; the name of Charles Chaplin did not appear (p. 128). In the December issue another caricature of Chaplin appeared, this time in baggy pants, tight coat, and top hat, and carrying a cane (p. 130); in addition there was a full-page collage containing five pictures of Chaplin's face in closeup. This was significantly more attention than he had received in the August issue.

The January 1915 issue provided a stark contrast to the "Great Player Contest" of the previous October, for in it, the results of the "Great Cast Contest" were announced (p. 126). The contest featured twelve categories, including leading man, leading woman, old man, old woman, villain, and so on. In the male comedian category, Charles Chaplin came out on top, accumulating 10,390 votes and edging out John Bunny, in second place with 9,510 votes. Even more striking, perhaps, is the fact that only Mary Maurice, who won the "old woman" category, received more votes than Chaplin did. Since voting took place during the third week in November, it is apparent that by the last months of the Keystone period, Chaplin's films had become very popular. The "Great Cast Contest" was also held the following year, and by November of 1915, Chaplin had garnered 1.9 million votes, with Ford Sterling a distant second at 1.4 million (p. 124). Even if we are skeptical of the numbers and the voting procedures, the fact remains that by late 1914, readers of the magazine were learning about Chaplin in terms that were full of praise.

These two magazines give us a good general picture of how Chaplin's reputation began to grow during 1914, but it is important to make a distinction here between Charlie and Chaplin. Evidence suggests that Chaplin's screen persona did become popular with viewers by the end of the Keystone period. But Chaplin himself had not yet become a star: there was little discussion in the press of the man who was responsible for the creation of the character. Recalling in 1916 his experiences near the end of his Keystone contract, Chaplin wrote: "It was odd, walking up and down the streets, eating in cafes, hearing Charlie Chaplin talked about, seeing Charlie Chaplin on every hand and never being recognized as Charlie Chaplin. I had a feeling that all the world was cross-eyed, or that I was a disembodied spirit. But that did not last long."[7] Up to the end of the Keystone period, then, the star image of "Charlie Chaplin" revolved almost entirely around a character on the movie screen.

One does not really become a star until the publicists and journalists focus on, and the audience gets interested in, the personality of the actor behind the mask, and it seems likely that Sennett and Keystone, realizing how popular Chaplin was becoming and how high his salary demands might go when it was time to renew his contract, were careful not to exploit the private life of the performer. Despite their efforts, when Chaplin's contract ran out at the end of 1914, other studios became interested in signing him up. Nineteen-fifteen was to be the year in which Chaplin would be come a bona fide movie star.

"Chaplinitis": Charlie at Essanay

As Chaplin's Keystone contract neared its end, Mack Sennett had to decide what he and his associates would be willing to pay to keep Chaplin on. Sennett knew that audiences around the United States were lining up to see the Charlie films, but Chaplin did, too. Chaplin himself remembered asking Sennett to increase his salary to $1,000 per week, a request Sennett denied, protesting that even *he* did not make that much money (MA, 159). After Chaplin and Keystone failed to come to terms, Chaplin signed a one-year contract with Essanay on 2 January 1915. The terms included a $10,000 bonus for signing and $1,250 per week. The first of three large and increasingly publicized contracts for Chaplin, it ushered in a remarkable twelve months for the actor—the year of what one writer called a national case of "Chaplinitis."[8]

Chaplin's stardom grew during the Essanay period partly because the persona he had begun to create the year before became in 1915 part of a widespread craze. Of course, Chaplin's Essanay films (thirteen released in 1915), all of which featured Charlie, contributed to the enthusiasm. (The new dimensions added to the persona during this period will be discussed in the following section.) In addition, however, the Charlie persona was proliferating throughout American culture. Manifestations of this included advertisers' use of Chaplin's character to sell toys and other paraphernalia, as well as cartoons about Chaplin.

Throughout 1915 and particularly in the last half of the year, Chaplin's name or Charlie's picture was used to sell all sorts of products. *Motion Picture Magazine* ran a picture of Charlie in its July issue to help advertise its August issue, which concluded its article on Chaplin (171). The July issue also offered a free portrait of Chaplin in his Charlie costume to anyone who ordered a back issue of the magazine (177). The September issue contained an advertisement by the Kirkham Company headed "Charlie Chaplin's Surprise—the Funniest Novelty Ever" (159). Although it was not entirely clear exactly what the novelty was, for ten cents a Chaplin fan could find out. By the October issue, the Fisher Novelty Company was offering a "Charlie Chaplin Squirt Ring" for fifteen cents; a picture of Charlie with Derby and mustache topped the ring (164). By the December issue, the Nuidea Company was advertising a "Charlie Chaplin Outfit," consisting of a Charlie Chaplin mustache, an imitation gold tooth, a $1,000 bankroll of stage money, and a medallion coin with a "life-like image" of Charlie on it—all for only a dime plus two cents postage (158). The fact that entrepreneurs were appropriating the Charlie persona to merchandise their wares stresses how popular that persona had become.

Cartoons were another manifestation of the national case of Chaplinitis. These were the first in a long line of cartoons, editorial and otherwise, that attested over the years to Chaplin's star status and reflected the press's various reactions to him. At least as early as April 1915, there appeared a regular comic strip entitled "Charlie Chaplin's Comic Capers."[9] More important for the purposes of this discussion are the single-frame cartoons alluding to Charlie. Sketches of Charlie—and also of Chaplin—began to be printed regularly in the fan magazines after the first few months of 1915. One of the most important and interesting appeared in *Motion Picture Magazine* (June 1915: 152). Headed "Charles Chaplin, Essanay Mirth Provoker," it presented a mini-biography of Chaplin himself, distinguishing between the filmic persona and the man behind the mustache. It slotted Chaplin in the typical rags-to-riches category so central to the American success myth: "from a penniless immigrant stranded in New York—to a small-time comedy acrobat—to the highest paid movie actor—is the story of Chaplin's rapid rise to success." Small matter that the description bore little relation to reality; it made good copy and—along with a number of other cartoons—began to factor Chaplin the man into the calculus of the Chaplin star image.

If Chaplin's star image was spread by films, advertisements, and cartoons, it was also extended in 1915 by articles about the man himself, a topic not discussed during the Keystone period. As the author of "Chaplinitis" put it, after Chaplin signed the Essanay contract, "the world went mad. From New York to San Francisco, from Maine to California, came the staccato tapping of the telegraph key. 'Who is this man Chaplin? What are his ambitions? What's his theory of humor? Is he married, or single? How does he like American life? Does he eat eggs for breakfast? Is he conceited?' The newspapers wanted to know; the country demanded information."[10] The country's appetite for learning more about the funny little man in the movies was for a time insatiable.

What picture of Chaplin the man emerged from these 1915 profiles? Richard Dyer has suggested that the American success myth, which holds that the society is so open that anyone can rise to the top,[11] is frequently associated with stars: they become symbols of the myth. If closely examined, the 1915 articles on Chaplin together draw a portrait of the man entirely consistent with Dyer's observation.

Chaplin's humble beginnings and his personal quality of humility are stressed. "Unknown a few months ago," one article stated, Chaplin "is now said to be the highest salaried funny man in the film world." He has, continued the article, a "violet-like reluctance" to talk about himself. "There's nothing worth while talking about," it quotes Chaplin. "I am no one—just a plain fellow." A second essay called him "a little Englishman, quiet, unassuming." Yet another article reinforced that view: "Personally he is said to be extremely modest, retiring, declining to assume he has accomplished much worth making a fuss about."[12]

This humility, according to one article, was "one of the best things that can be said about anybody and one of the real proofs of greatness." The essay also associated Chaplin with extraordinary talent or ability. The author of "Chaplinitis" was one of the first writers to call Chaplin a "genius" at his work, although as time passed that term came to be regularly associated with Chaplin's star image. "Once in every century," the article intoned, "a man is born who is able to color and influence his world." In the twentieth century, "Charles Chaplin is doing it with pantomime and personality." The genius and greatness attributed to Chaplin, according to one of the articles, were "proof that talent will come to the top despite adverse circumstances."[13]

Thanks to the national bout of "Chaplinitis," a Chaplin star image, combining the persona created in the films with the man who created it, was firmly anchored in the United States by the end of 1915. The man was portrayed as humble and unassuming, yet imbued with greatness. The persona, while immensely popular, was nevertheless in a state of flux. If the crude and mischievous persona from the Keystone era had helped to initiate Chaplin's stardom, it also met with resistance in certain sectors of American culture.

The genteel tradition and the "vulgar" Charlie

Not everyone was caught up in the Chaplin craze. In fact, a significant minority found Chaplin's films a social menace. As we have noted, the character Chaplin played in his Keystone films was often abrasive and crude, however funny. Such a character was a common target of genteel critics, particularly given Chaplin's mass popularity. A 1914 review of *The Property Man* in *Moving Picture World* indicates the dilemma some observers faced: "Some of the funniest things in the picture are vulgar," wrote the critic. "They are too vulgar to describe; but are too funny to pass for vulgarity when only seen."[14]

Although this commentator was generous enough to allow that Chaplin was funny despite his vulgarity—it would be difficult for a movie reviewer to react otherwise—more genteel observers were not so tolerant. One attack on Chaplin by a custodian of culture appeared in a 1915 letter to the editor of the *New Orleans American*.[15] The purpose of the letter, in its author's words, was "to justify the stand taken by so many of the better class and better educated people in New Orleans, who find that the [Chaplin] films are not worth going to see." Why were the films unworthy? The writer pulled no punches: because of the "grotesque and vulgar antics of that product of the slums of Whitecastle." Instead of debasing public taste by presenting the low comedy of Chaplin and his ilk, the author urged, theater owners should present more inspiring programs: travel films, filmed opera, and adaptations of classic novels, poems, and plays.

Others, including religious leaders, joined in the anti-Chaplin chorus. A headline in the *Detroit News* indicates the form such criticism often took: "Low Grade Persons Only Like Charlie Chaplin and Mary Pickford, Says Pastor."[16] The article gave an account of the denunciations of these two movie stars by a prominent Detroit minister. Reactions like this one give an idea of the threat that moralists believed Chaplin's Keystone persona posed to genteel moral standards.

How did Chaplin respond to these criticisms? "The New Charlie Chaplin," a 1916 article in *Motion Picture Magazine*, suggests not only that Chaplin was aware of these challenges to his popularity but also that he was consciously beginning to shift and mold his star image in response to them.[17] The article is J. B. Hirsch's account of a meeting between Chaplin and W. W. Barrett, a member of the executive staff of the National Board of Censorship. According to the article, Barrett visited Chaplin not only because the National Board was concerned about some questionable aspects of Chaplin's movies but also because its members believed that there were "great possibilities in the comedian's future work, both as a helpful influence in the community and as a factor in the artistic development of the Motion Picture" (115). In the essay Chaplin defended himself against charges of vulgarity: "It is because of my music-hall training and experiences that . . . work into my acting little threads of vulgarisms." Linking his humor to a venerable tradition, Chaplin added, "This Elizabethan style of humor, this crude form of farce and slapstick comedy . . . was due entirely to my early environment, and I am now trying to steer clear from this sort of humor and adapt myself to a more subtle and finer shade of acting" (115). The essay portrays Chaplin as apparently contrite, or at least as being careful not to antagonize a group that could limit his popularity.

This "new Charlie Chaplin," wrote Hirsch, has "burst the tawdry chrysalis of the . . . English Music-hall manner" in favor of "a new fame, to be built on the basis of a more delicate art that will not countenance the broad sallies his old technique demanded" (115). The essay recounts one of the first recorded instances of Chaplin's conflicts with pressure groups in America, conflicts that were to become more frequent as his career progressed. In this early example, Chaplin bowed to the pressure group and assured it that he would evolve as an artist in directions that would prove suitable to the National Board of Censorship and to the American public. At a time when the middle classes were beginning to attend movies in ever-increasing numbers, the Chaplin described in the article was thinking about altering the character of his movies to make them more palatable to this larger audience.[18]

Hirsch's piece is also notable because it shows how Chaplin's star image was changing after he had been in the limelight for over a year. The picture of Chaplin that accompanies the article—"as he appears in real life," according to the caption—portrays a youthful-looking, handsome man wearing a dinner jacket and bow tie and gazing seriously at the viewer. The text reinforces the image. Barrett found Chaplin to be quite different from his screen persona: "a neat and stylishly dressed young man; as charming and affable a boy . . . as anyone would wish to meet." In a list of features that corresponds in several ways to the list of qualities Richard Dyer associates with stardom, Hirsch describes Chaplin as a "hard worker, who writes, acts, produces and manages; an unusually intelligent man, modest, not in the least affected by his great popularity, and very keen, businesslike and thrifty—not at all like the usual actor of the 'get-rich-quick' variety." (Chaplin's thriftiness, even stinginess in certain respects, did not fit the star pattern of conspicuous consumption; it nonetheless was consistent with the Ben Franklin/Horatio Alger tradition and a quality often associated with his star image throughout his career.) Finally, Barrett saw in Chaplin an ambitious artist: "He has shaped for himself the slogan 'Art for Art's sake,' and he has dreams of unmeasured possibilities for the future of the films—all from an artistic point of view" (115).

This new view of Chaplin as the unaffected yet serious artist appeared in another 1916 article, "The Real Charlie Chaplin," by Stanley W. Todd.[19] Todd claimed that those interested in knowing Chaplin rather than Charlie are "certain to encounter some surprises" (41). According to Todd, Chaplin's friends knew him as "a serious-minded young fellow whose accession to affluence has not spoiled his democracy or ambitions." Chaplin also constantly sought to improve himself, telling Todd that "no man or woman should be satisfied with having won a fortune or fame in one line of work. I expect to be at it fifty years from now" (44). This affirmation of hard work was a cardinal virtue of turn-of-the-century genteel culture, as was another of Chaplin's qualities imputed by Todd's article: interest in high culture and the fine arts. Todd told his readers that Chaplin had read Shakespeare "from beginning to end" and was familiar with "the works of George Eliot and other noted writers" (44). Chaplin, who had little formal education, was already compensating for that lack by talking with the press about his intellectual aspirations, and the press dutifully reported them.

These articles portray a star concerned about cleaning up his image and presenting a picture of his private life that would make him acceptable even to genteel Americans. The potentially damaging clash between American gentility and the "vulgar" persona created by Chaplin was partly averted when the man behind the persona began to present himself as a hard-working, serious, aspiring artist. But there was another significant element in this new view of Chaplin: the films he made during the Essanay period from early 1915 to early 1916. How did they portray Charlie in this period when the American gentility was attacking the vulgarity of Chaplin's films?

Romance and pathos: the "refining" of Charlie

The Essanay films contributed to this "new" star image. Chaplin made fourteen films at Essanay: the first in the company's Chicago studios; the next five in G. M. Anderson's ill-equipped Niles studios, near San Francisco; and the remainder in Hollywood. The first seven were released within three months; thereafter, Chaplin slowed his work pace and made about one film a month. Although no neat progression from film to film is apparent, Chaplin clearly did try out new ideas, some of which broadened the appeal of his films, during the period.

At first, however, Chaplin seemed to be repeating himself. As Theodore Huff points out, a number of the Essanays resemble the Keystones. *A Night Out* treats the comic misadventures of two drunks in much the same way as *The Rounders* had. *In the Park* and *By the Sea* both show the flirtatious and slightly lecherous Charlie being chased by a policeman, as did a number of the Keystone films, including *Twenty Minutes of Love*. *The Champion* is a boxing story similar to that in *The Knockout*, although *The Champion* was more successful at the box office, while both *Work* and *Shanghaied* continue the slapstick comedy prominent in Keystone movies. Reaching back even earlier than the Keystone films, *A Night in the Show* draws from an old Karno sketch entitled "A Night in the English Music Hall."

Despite these continuities, Chaplin also changed during the Essanay period. The most significant alteration was in the portrayal of Charlie's relationships with the heroines of the films. During the Keystone period, Charlie was most often at odds with women, at least in part because of the feisty screen persona of Mabel Normand, who often appeared opposite Chaplin. A fairly typical example is *Getting Acquainted*, in which Charlie, unhappily married to a demanding wife, flirts with the wife of another man until a policeman breaks up the affair.

Beginning with his second Essanay film, however, Chaplin was paired with a new actress, Edna Purviance, who was to remain his leading lady through his first United Artists film, *A Woman of Paris* (1923). For several reasons, the heroines in Chaplin's films began to change, as did Charlie's relationships with them. First, Purviance's appearance and demeanor—more youthful, passive, rounded, delicate, and innocent than Normand's—prompted a shift toward a gentler interaction between Charlie and the heroine. Second, Chaplin and Purviance themselves began to develop a relationship outside of work almost immediately after she began to act in his films. Chaplin tells in his autobiography that after they had moved to Los Angeles (immediately after making *The Tramp*), they dined nearly every night at the Los Angeles Athletic Club, where Chaplin had rented an apartment (MA, 204). As would often happen during his career, Chaplin's feelings for other people worked themselves into the characterizations and narratives of his films. Third, Chaplin's awareness of criticism from genteel quarters also encouraged him to think about altering his films to broaden their appeal; one way to accomplish this was to idealize the heroine and involve Charlie in a romance with her. Fourth, the switch from one- to two-reel films gave Chaplin the opportunity to develop Charlie's relationship with another character more fully. Finally, as film historians have shown, signifying practices in the film industry were changing. In the movement from primitive to classical cinema (or from a cinema of attractions to a cinema of narrative integration) in the early 1910s, the goals and desires of central characters began to structure film narratives. One of the most common of these desires was for a romantic relationship.[20]

The shift in Chaplin's portrayal of women and of Charlie during the Essanay period occurred gradually. In several of the early Essanay films, the portrayal of women is indistinguishable from that in the Keystones. Women are either objects of Charlie's lust, targets of his antics or inconsequential to the narrative. In *A Night Out*, for example, Edna's husband discovers her in bed with a drunken, sleeping Charlie. Though Charlie does give Edna a discreet kiss at the end of *The Champion*, her role is not important in the film. Charlie's involvement with women in both *In the Park* and *By the Sea* consists almost entirely of his attempts to pursue the wives or sweethearts of other men. And Edna's part as the maid in *Work* is relatively unimportant. In these films Charlie is often as irreverent and "vulgar" as he was at Keystone. *Variety*'s review of *Work*, Chaplin's eighth Essanay, was similar to the kind of criticism he often received in his Keystone days: "The Essanay release of the Charlie Chaplin picture for this week is *Work*, in two reels. It is the usual Chaplin work of late, mussy, messy and dirty." Charging that "the Censor Board is passing matter in the Chaplin films that could not possibly get by in other pictures," the reviewer joined the genteel chorus of Chaplin critics.[21]

By the time *Work* was released, however, Chaplin had already begun displaying an emergent gentility and greater attention to characterization in his work, although sometimes these were only brief moments in otherwise knockabout films. In *A Jitney Elopement*, for example, Chaplin used an iris out (a circular lab transition effect that closes down to emphasize a detail) when Charlie sniffs a flower under Edna's window, just after we learn that Edna is being made to marry someone else against her wishes. The use of the flower and the attempt at pathos both foreshadowed aspects of Chaplin's work that would later recur often, most notably in the final shots of *City Lights*. The moment provided one of the first examples of Charlie's stretching to do something different and more serious in his work, although it was not at all sustained in this particular film.

Chaplin's next film, *The Tramp*, concentrated more on trying to achieve pathos. It, along with *The Bank*, represented Chaplin's most careful attempts to move in directions that would make his films more acceptable to genteel audiences. The two films share several elements. First, Charlie still exhibits some of the cruelty and "vulgarity" he had become known for during the Keystone period, usually while working with other men. Second, Charlie becomes romantically attracted to the Edna Purviance character. Third, after Charlie's feelings become known, the audience learns that Edna already has a suitor—larger, more handsome, or of a higher social class than Charlie. Fourth, Charlie becomes caught between social groups and opts to side with Edna. Finally, Charlie's hopes are dashed when he learns that his relationship with Edna will not succeed, and he thus evokes pathos.

The sympathy both films elicit, as well as the romanticizing of women in them, gives them a more gentle quality, more breadth of feeling, than the Keystone films. Largely because of this shifting treatment of women and Charlie's relationship to them, Chaplin's films began to appeal to a broader audience.

In addition to romance and pathos, *The Tramp* and *The Bank* contain yet another similarity that reinforced a value dear to the cultural traditions that had been rejecting Chaplin as "vulgar." In both films Charlie feels deeply discouraged and shakes off that discouragement with an energetic resilience. The final shots of both show Charlie walking in long shot away from the camera, which emphasizes the depth of the frame and Charlie's isolation; he then springs forward with a sprightly step, straightening and walking off as if renewed. Though it is difficult to describe the movement adequately, its effect is clear: Charlie will not let his disappointment overwhelm him. He will move on with as much vitality and inventiveness as before, accepting a contingent universe in which suffering is a part of life. This determination to go on in spite of the odds, in spite of travail and disappointment, was a cardinal value of genteel culture. Even if Charlie did not always act with propriety, this quality endeared him to respectable audiences as much as did any other.

Thus, elements of Chaplin's films during the Essanay period made them more palatable to his genteel opposition. The films show a learning filmmaker cautiously moving in directions that deepened his work and broadened his audience appeal. Chaplin seems to have been conscious of the new directions he was taking and concerned about whether the experiment was working. When a journalist left Chaplin after a day on the set, Chaplin called after him: "Say, did you see *The Tramp*? I know I took an awful chance. But did it get across?"[22] For an increasing number of viewers, it did.

Chaplin also showed an increasing tendency to include other "serious" elements in these films, the most prominent of which was a clear depiction of class conflict and difference. In *Work* the class differences between Charlie and Edna on the one hand and the owners of the home on the other are particularly clear, just as in *The Bank*. Charlie and the other janitor stand in contrast to the bank owners and other wealthy bank patrons. *Police*, the final Essanay film, contains an interesting satire on reformers: in it, the do-gooder tries to move Charlie toward righteousness and ends up stealing his watch. The same film interestingly shows Charlie caught between the law and the lawless, as he would be again in later films, including *The Pilgrim* (1923) and *Modern Times* (1936). John McCabe tells us that during the final months of his

Essanay contract Chaplin began working on a film called *Life* (never finished) that would draw on his own painful childhood experiences and "show the tragicomic world of flophouses, grimy alleys, and living 'on the beg.'"[23]

Thus Chaplin's star image had grown and begun to shift significantly by the time he left Essanay in 1916. Beginning more as a slapstick and—from the perspective of genteel critics— "vulgar" comedian, shaped by the dominant knockabout aesthetic of Sennett's Keystone Studio, Chaplin began to change as his films became more popular, as he gained more press attention, and as he began to be attacked by critics for that "vulgarity" during the Essanay period. By the time he left Essanay, however, Chaplin's star image was composed of a softer, more romantic Charlie and the hard-working, ambitious, and modest young filmmaker who aspired to high art. A new, more serious Chaplin was emerging, one who in 1916 asked film writer Terry Ramsaye to refer to him as "Charles" rather than "Charlie."[24] In the space of barely more than two years, the young music-hall comedian had been vaulted to fame and fortune in Hollywood. He had also faced the genteel moralists of America, responding to their challenge by making films that, in certain ways, were more palatable to them.

Apparently he overcame this challenge with flying colors: on 25 February 1916 Chaplin agreed to a contract with the Mutual Film Corporation that gave the comedian $10,000 a week, plus a $150,000 signing bonus, to make twelve two-reel comedies.[25] While fulfilling that contract, he built his own movie studio in 1918 and became in 1919 a founding member of United Artists with D. W. Griffith, Douglas Fairbanks, and Mary Pickford. If his studio and United Artists provided the structure that enabled Chaplin to become one of the chief icons of the cinema, it's important to remember that the foundation of that structure, Chaplin's star image, was first firmly established during those two frenetic, creative years at Keystone and Essanay.

Notes

1   For a broad discussion of the dynamics of stars, see Richard Dyer, *Stars* (London: British Film Institute, 1979). For a more specific exploration of how Chaplin's star image evolved through his career in the United States, see my *Chaplin and American Culture: The Evolution of a Star Image* (Princeton: Princeton University Press, 1986), from which this chapter is adapted. Dyer usefully notes that the star image emerges from the interplay among four sets of media texts: the films themselves; studio promotion material; publicity ("what the press finds out" about stars); and criticism and commentary about the stars and their films. See Dyer, pp. 69–72. A filmmaker like Chaplin, through his films and his various public and private actions, helps shape the star image, but he can't control it entirely.

2   The account of Chaplin's entry into the movies comes from Chaplin's *My Autobiography* (New York: Simon and Schuster, 1964), 137–39; the date of his departure from the Karno company is found in Theodore Huff, *Charlie Chaplin* (1951; reprinted New York: Pyramid, 1964), 3, and corroborated by John McCabe, *Charlie Chaplin* (Garden City, New York: Doubleday, 1978), 46–7. David Robinson, in *Chaplin: His Life and His Art* (New York: McGraw-Hill, 1985), 102–07, also treats Chaplin's introduction to the movies and reprints a part of his first contract. These three, along with Kenneth S. Lynn's *Charlie Chaplin and His Times* (New York: Simon & Schuster, 1997), are presently the most reliable of the Chaplin biographies in English and can be supplemented by Georges Sadoul, *Vie de Charlot* (Paris: Lherminier, 1978). Hereafter, Chaplin's autobiography will be cited as MA and the Robinson biography as CHLA.

3   On the emergence of the star system, see Janet Staiger, "Seeing Stars," *Velvet Light Trap*, no. 20 (Summer 1983): 13; David Bordwell, Kristin Thompson, and Janet Staiger, *The Classical Hollywood Cinema: Film Style and Mode of Production to 1960* (New York: Columbia University Press, 1985), ch. 9, esp. 101–02; and Richard deCordova, *Picture Personalities: The Emergence of the Star System in America* (Urbana: University of Illinois Press, 1990).

4   Though the persona portrayed by Chaplin in so many films has been called a number of different names— the tramp, the little tramp, the little fellow, and others—in this essay I will refer to the persona as "Charlie."

5   *Moving Picture World* 19 (17 February 1914): 678. The subsequent references in this paragraph come from volumes 19–22 of the same periodical. Dates and page numbers are cited parenthetically in the text.

6   *Motion Picture Magazine* 13: 7 (August 1914): 126. The subsequent references in the next few paragraphs come from the same volume. Issues and page numbers are cited in the text.

7   Charles Spencer Chaplin, *Charlie Chaplin's Own Story*, ed. Harry Geduld (1916; reprinted Bloomington: Indiana University Press, 1985), 140. This book, actually written by a journalist named Rose Lee Wilder after interviews with Chaplin in 1915, was published by Bobbs-Merrill in Indianapolis but never released. See CHLA for further information on the book.

8   Charles J. McGuirk, "Chaplinitis," *Motion Picture Magazine* 9: 6–7 (July and August 1915): 85–9 and 121–24. The quotation is from Part I, p. 87.

9   An example of the comic strip appears in Chaplin, *My Life in Pictures* (New York: Grosset and Dunlap, 1975), p. 16. The Chaplin files in the Robinson Locke Collection (RLC), Volume 110, housed in the Billy Rose Collection at the Lincoln Center Library for Performing Arts contains one such cartoon from the 5 April 1915 issue of the *Cleveland Leader*.

10 McGuirk, Part 1, p. 87.

11 Dyer, *Stars*, pp. 48–9.

12 E. V. Whitcomb, "Charlie Chaplin," *Photoplay* 7 (February 1915): 35–37; "A Real Film ABC," *Moving Picture World* (6 February 1915), both in RLC, vol. 110. The point here is not whether Chaplin actually was humble—and evidence suggests that his pride did grow with age and accomplishment—but that he was being presented as humble by the press.

13 The quotations come from the articles by Whitcomb, McGuirk, and "A Real Film ABC." See also, in RLC, vol. 110: Victor Eubank, "The Funniest Man on the Screen," *Motion Picture Magazine* (March 1915); and "Charlie Chaplin, Cheerful Comedian," *Picture-Play Weekly* 1:3 (24 April 1915): 1.

14 Review of *The Property Man* in *Moving Picture World* 21 (15 August 1914): 961.

15 9 September 1915, RLC, vol. 110.

16 13 April 1916, RLC, vol. 110.

17 J. B. Hirsch, "The New Charlie Chaplin," *Motion Picture Magazine* 10: 12 (January 1916): 115–17.

18 By 1910 the film industry was trying to broaden its audience by appealing to more respectable and middle-class viewers. For a detailed discussion of one company's attempts, see William Uricchio and Roberta Pearson, *Reframing Culture: The Case of the Vitagraph Quality Films* (Princeton: Princeton University Press, 1993).

19 *Motion Picture Classic* 3 (September 1916): 41–4.

20 See CHC, 177–83.

21 Quoted in Gerald E. McDonald *et al.*, *The Films of Charlie Chaplin* (New York: Bonanza, 1965), 99.

22 "Chaplinitis," part 1, p. 89.

23 *Charlie Chaplin*, p. 78. Apparently, Chaplin also shot footage during the early 1920s for another film dealing with the flophouses he saw in his childhood. Kevin Brownlow's fascinating compilation film, *The Unknown Chaplin*, includes some of that footage.

24 This request is reported in the *Toledo Blade*, 10 March 1916, RLC, vol. 110.

25 The Chaplin/Mutual contract negotiations are discussed in Robert Grau, "The More People Laughed at the Idea of Chaplin's Salary, the More They Had to Pay," *Motion Picture Magazine* (May 1916), RLC, vol. 110; and Terry Ramsaye, *A Million and One Nights* (1926; reprinted NY: Simon and Schuster, 1964), 731–36.

Chapter 12

SHELLEY STAMP

AN AWFUL STRUGGLE BETWEEN LOVE AND AMBITION
Serial heroines, serial stars and their female fans

A REFLEXIVE PROLOGUE to Pathé's 1917 serial, *The Mystery of the Double Cross*, acknowledges the pivotal role that female audiences played in sustaining interest amongst the various inter-textual discourses surrounding serials. Actress Mollie King is shown "at home" in the opening scene receiving a letter from the studio inviting her to star in the drama. Excited about playing the part of heroine Phillipa Brewster, King sits down to read the novel from which the film is to be drawn. King's shoulders begin to quiver as reaction shots register her growing interest in the tale. "I'd love to play that!" she exclaims in an intertitle. As King flips through the book, inserts show us pages containing photos of the characters and the famed "double cross," as if her imagination has brought them to life on film. King herself soon appears on the pages of the book in a split-screen matte shot. Still engrossed in the book, King rises from her chair and walks towards the camera, filling up both the book page and the right-hand portion of the frame. The image then dissolves from a shot of King, head buried in book, to King, now glamorously dressed as Phillipa. After a cut the matte shot is replaced by a full-screen image of Phillipa, no longer confined to the pages of the book, who then looks directly into the camera inviting viewers to "come with me through my adventure and try to solve the Mystery of the Double Cross."

By playing upon an awareness of how King's private life might inflect her portrayal of the heroine, the prologue emphasizes an interplay between screen character and celebrity persona that was central to the evolving star system, at the same time as it acknowledges an inter-textual mode of film viewing essential to early motion picture fan culture. Interestingly, King herself is depicted as an avid consumer of serialized stories, shown absorbed in a plot she will subsequently enact for viewers. King's role as glamorous Hollywood actress, as adventurous screen heroine, and as serial aficionado are collapsed together in a gesture that re-casts the fan's typically passive consumption as active engagement. Encouraged to connect together various versions of the story available in print tie-ins and on screen, asked to sustain their engagement over multiple installments, and invited to enhance their enjoyment by fostering an interest in the star's private life, fans become the central catalyst in any serial narrative. Finally, by continually pointing outside itself—to the star's life, to other versions of the tale available in print, and to the audience watching—*The Mystery of the Double Cross*'s prologue foregrounds just how dramatically serials fostered a female audience by stepping outside classical norms.

Figure 12.1
Molly King poster
(1917)

If serial viewing offered women novel, even radical, forms of viewing pleasure, stories enacted on the screen furnished far more cautionary delights and reveal more than a little ambivalence about their famously modern heroines. Serials catered to their large female fan base with engaging portraits of plucky young women beset by harrowing adventures and blessed with unrivaled strength and bravado. Pauline Marvin (played by Pearl White), focus of the *Perils of Pauline* (1914) series named in her honor, was the antithesis "of the old-time melo-drama heroine," according to one observer, a meek creature who "would perish ignominiously if faced by half the perils that surround her more advanced sister of the screen."[1] Like so many other female leads, Pauline manifests athletic talents and a taste for adventure that belie outmoded notions of demur "lady-like" behavior and stay-at-home femininity. These young women lead independent lives, noticeably freed from familial obligations, marital bonds, and motherhood. Still, however much they promoted a kind of modern femininity clearly tailored to appeal to their cadre of female fans, serials' woman-oriented plots offered alarmist tales in which independence is always circumscribed by the shadow of danger, the determinacy of familial ties, and the inevitability of marriage. In fact, formulaic serial plots repeatedly, even obsessively, staged the same cautionary tale in thinly disguised repetitions from episode to episode, and serial to serial, as plotlines quickly came to resemble one another.

At the beginning of many serials, a heroine's seeming independence is conspicuously marked by the loss of a parent or guardian: Pauline Marvin's beloved guardian dies in the first episode of *The Perils of Pauline*; Kathlyn Hare's father is kidnapped at the outset of *The Adventures of Kathlyn* (1914), prompting her to set out in search of him; and Elaine Dodge's father is murdered in the initial chapter of *Exploits of Elaine* (1915), with much of the ensuing mystery embroiled in the search for his killer. Each woman's story begins then with her release from familial bonds, figured in each instance as paternal authority. Pauline's autonomy is especially marked. Not only are her natural parents no longer living, her legal guardian dies in the opening installment, and she refuses a marriage proposal from her guardian's son Harry, forsaking the one chance she might have for "normal" domesticity.[2] Hoping that Harry will care for Pauline after his death, guardian Stanford Marvin had urged her to accept his son's proposal, but she declines, choosing instead to strike out on a bold path of independence. Postponing marriage will allow her to travel the world and establish her name as an adventure writer, an ambition she has long cherished. "It may be that I shall consent to marry Harry some day," Pauline tells a dying Mr. Marvin, "but you know my adventurous spirit and my desire to live and realize the greatest thrills so that I can describe them in a romance of adventures." The old man reluctantly agrees to the plan, saying, "Live your life. Write your romance. And, if you love Harry, marry him." When Harry presses the issue further, Pauline insists, "No Harry, I wish to be absolutely free for a year." Despite Harry's continued attentions, the couple makes no definite plans to wed. Hence Pauline's "perils" are initiated not only by the death of her beneficent patriarch Stanford Marvin, but also by her marked refusal of a conventional feminine role, and her willful insistence on seeking adventure outside of marriage. "Pauline has an awful struggle between love and ambition," Pathé announced in its promotion of the series, immediately posing the terms in opposition.[3]

Like Pauline, virtually all early serial heroines are cut adrift from conventional family relationships. Although a parent's death or an infant's kidnapping often provide the dramatic pretext for a heroine's independence, her circumstances strongly echo the economic and social autonomy increasingly experienced by many women living away from their families for the first time while working in urban centers. Indeed, many serials stage the heroine's "liberation" from home and family in early installments as a necessary prelude to her exploits, implying that *only* women who renounced familial and marital obligations could pursue such unconventional endeavors. At the same time, by explicitly enacting the heroine's escape from paternal control, serials drew attention to the constraints under which many women still lived, bound by the dictates of marriage and domesticity.

Despite their initial break from home life, however, heroines' lives are inevitably circumscribed by familial ties in the end, since heredity and lineage come to assume central importance in virtually all of the plots, and marriage, though initially forsaken, usually marks the conclusion of a heroine's escapades. Complex tales of hidden ancestry and cryptic inheritance schemes, favored in so many serials—where characters remain ignorant of genealogical ties that will ultimately determine their fate, a family fortune to which they are entitled, or a forgotten royal title—express the attenuated relationships that heroines have with their families. Moreover, it is this lineage which usually causes complications in many plots: heroines often find they cannot claim their inheritance, for instance, either because they are unable to prove their lineage or because they cannot wrest the estate from the hands of a villain. Pauline spends most of her "perils" fighting off the designs of her guardian's secretary, plotting to kill her so that he can retain control of her estate. Kalem's *Ventures of Marguerite* (1915) series features a similarly orphaned heiress struggling to retain control of her fortune, as do Thanhouser's two serials, *The Million Dollar Mystery* (1914) and *Zudora* (1915). In the first story, Florence Hargeaves searches for a fortune hidden by her father; and in the subsequent tale, the heroine's guardian conceals the fact that she will inherit the rights to the profitable Zudora mine upon her eighteenth birthday.[4] In short, women who declare themselves freed from familial obligations usually find their fates complicated by hidden details of their ancestry. Only by claiming their lineage or their inheritance can heroines free themselves from danger.

Even as serial heroines strike out on their own, then, kinship plots reassert the primacy of familial bonds in these women's lives. Those who considered themselves freed from domestic obligations find they are entirely circumscribed by them in the end: seemingly orphaned women discover living parents; impoverished women inherit ancestral fortunes; and ordinary women unearth surprising royal bloodlines. That so many ordinary women find extraordinary hidden aspects of their lives suggests that serial plots provided rich fantasy terrain for many viewers. Fantasies of freedom and entitlement would have held particular appeal for single, working women otherwise lacking this element of their lives, as Nan Enstad suggests.[5]

Pleasing though these fantasies of independence might have been for contemporary viewers, they were invariably laced with peril, for even as the absence of family ties frees serial heroines to enjoy lives of adventure, it usually also places them in grave danger. Serials demonstrate, rather paradoxically then, that if pioneering feminine norms are only possible outside of marriage and paternal authority, life beyond the safe confines of one's home remained hazardous for most women. Like white slave narratives, serials evoke the peculiar mixture of liberation and trepidation many young women might have experienced when living away from home for the first time. In both cases, new freedoms increasingly open to women were circumscribed within an aura of danger, often explicitly sexualized.[6]

Nowhere is this contradiction more pronounced than in *The Perils of Pauline*, for, ironically, it is Pauline's refusal to wed, not her taste for adventure, that repeatedly places her in jeopardy. Had she married, control of her substantial inheritance would have passed from her guardian Stanford Marvin to his son Harry, her fiancé. Since she declines to do so, her finances remain in the hands of Mr. Marvin's secretary, Owen, who obsessively and repeatedly plots the young woman's demise in the hope of keeping the fortune for himself. By the end of the first installment the intricacies of Pauline's inheritance have been spelled out and it is obvious she will have no authority over her money until she marries: "it is clearly to her interest to elope with almost anyone," *Moving Picture World* concluded.[7] Still Pauline declines Harry's proposal for the foreseeable future so that she can pursue her writing career unencumbered. Her willfulness draws marked attention to the constraints under which she is asked to live, for viewers are made acutely aware that Pauline does not—and will not—manage her own finances, that her assets pass, quite pointedly, through a succession of male hands—from her grandfather, to her guardian Mr. Marvin, to his executor Owen, then ultimately to a future husband. By refusing to take cover under marriage after her guardian's death, Pauline marks out a distinctly feminist stance. But Pauline's attempts to exert some influence over her fate are undercut by the perils of such a choice: unmarried she remains a persistent target of Owen's murderous intentions.

When villains are not plotting to kill or kidnap heroines in order to hijack their assets, they are often times scheming to coerce the women into wedlock, hoping to gain a more legitimate foothold. If Pauline Marvin escapes marriage at the outset of the narrative, leaving her free to pursue her adventures, many other heroines must foil attempts to force them into unseemly unions with scoundrels who are greedily eyeing their fortunes. While Pauline is imperiled when she forsakes marriage, other heroines are threatened *by* marriage: Marguerite fends of her chauffeur's matrimonial designs in *The Ventures of Marguerite*; Phillipa Brewster is nearly blackmailed into marrying dastardly Bridgey Bentley, "gangster and society pet," in *The Mystery of the Double Cross*; and Kathlyn Hare, visiting the land of Allah in search of her father, is chosen to be the country's next queen and almost forced to marry a nefarious consort who has been selected for her, an outcome which leaves the heroine "stricken with terror," according to Selig's published herald.[8] Just as the wedding is about to take place, the first installment ends, leaving viewers in suspense about whether or not Kathlyn will elude the bounds of matrimony. The second installment resumes with the wedding about to go forward, but, as the herald explains, Kathlyn "conserves all her powers of resistance to this proceeding," and manages to postpone the ceremony for at least a week.[9]

Even as women dodge suspect nuptials with scheming villains, many of the plots drive toward marriage nonetheless, for matrimony still signals closure at the end of most heroines' endeavors. By the end of *The Adventures of Kathlyn*, the heroine's narrow escape from wedlock in early installments has been replaced by her inevitable union with sweetheart Bruce, an American hunter. In the final moments of the last episode she and her father set sail back to California, "where Kathlyn's marriage to Bruce is assured," according to Selig's herald.[10] Indeed, marketing campaigns often stressed the romantic component of their tales in equal measure with their adventurousness: *The Exploits of Elaine* was a "thrilling story of romance, mystery and adventure," while *The Mystery of the Double Cross* was billed as "the feature serial of perils and love."[11] The drive toward marriage allowed serial narratives, with their otherwise unorthodox plotting, to enforce some measure of closure in the end. A perpetually suspended romance plot was touted as the main continuing thread in the *Hazards of Helen* (1914) series which otherwise stressed the integrity of its individual installments. "The only connecting link" between episodes of the heroine's adventures, the *New York Dramatic Mirror* explained, "will be Helen's love affairs, which will progress through each installment and not be finally settled until the final reel."[12] Significantly, the absence of marriage at the conclusion of *What Happened to Mary?* (1912) became the pretext for the serial's sequel which asked, *Who Will Marry Mary?* (1913), as if a fundamental question had been left unanswered. The final installment of Mary's first exploits serialized in *The Ladies' World* portrayed the young woman lying in bed fantasizing about how she would spend her newly-discovered inheritance, but ended with her pondering "I wonder, oh, indeed I do wonder, Who Will Marry Mary?"[13]

Again Pauline's situation is instructive, for despite her initial retreat from matrimony, her adventures are always circumscribed by her engagement to Harry Marvin. Even though she initially side-steps the young man's proposal, even wielding a tennis racket to fend off his kisses in the opening installment, he remains at her side throughout a series of risky undertakings, often stepping into the breach just as things get rough. By introducing their betrothal at the outset, the series plants the seeds of the couple's union from the beginning; it is really only a matter of time before Pauline will agree to marry her persistent beau, for the couple's wedding becomes the inevitable conclusion to her "perils." A circular plot structure bounded by betrothal and marriage draws attention to the traditional expectations circumscribing Pauline's narrative,

a pattern doubled further within individual installments, many of which stage Pauline's departure from the Marvin home, the dangerous adventures that ensue, then her eventual return to
the security of this household. An identical camera set-up showing Pauline safely at home with
Harry is repeated at the beginning of several episodes. These establishing shots tend to be the
only interior shots of each chapter and certainly the only ones at the Marvin home: in earlier
installments we see Pauline sitting at the desk where her beloved guardian once worked; in
later episodes she sits in the living room. With each repetition the sense of security and familiarity associated with these surroundings amplifies. Tempted away from this cocoon by some
exploit or other, Pauline is inevitably reunited there with Harry in the end.

Each installment offers a double-edged pleasure then, allowing audiences to revel in
Pauline's spectacular escapades, while also enjoying the comfort of seeing her back in Harry's
arms in the final moments, a circular trajectory that mirrors the ultimate goal of the series as
it propels the couple toward marriage. For there is no question that matrimony signals the
termination of Pauline's exertions. *Moving Picture World*'s review of the twentieth and final
installment announced, with some regret, that "Pauline has had the last of her perils, and her
adventures that have entertained us so long are now ended—she is going to marry Harry and
settle down."[14] Pauline herself declares at the end of the concluding episode, "I have once and
forever finished with this life of adventure. I am quite prepared to marry you, Harry, and we
shall be happy at last." The narrative thus allows us to enjoy the pleasures—and perils—of
Pauline's autonomy, while also clearly circumscribing it within a temporary time frame, doubly
enacted at the close of each installment and the termination of the serial itself. Thus, Pauline's
independence, like that of so many other serial protagonists, is carefully abridged: their
autonomy places the young heroines in immediate danger; familial ties which they seem to
have abandoned reassert themselves in the form of mysteries about lineage and inheritance;
and although several heroines plainly decline marriage, their adventures are often framed with
a betrothal or chronicled along with a budding romance that ends in matrimony. While the
women appear to live beyond the strictures of domestic femininity, in fact their exploits are
heavily circumscribed by the parameters of familial life.

This same paradox may be seen in the physical daring of serial heroines, for while they
appear to be strong capable women fending off extraordinary dangers, in fact individual episodes
often stage the heroine's disempowerment. Pauline Marvin is, again, a case in point, for
although she willfully embarks on daring pursuits like speed racing, yachting, and flying, it is
not these activities *per se* that place her in danger or elicit her exceptional feats. Rather, it is
Owen's persistent attempts to sabotage these escapades that repeatedly highlight Pauline's
inability to control the mechanisms she experiments with. In the sixth episode, for instance,
Owen prompts Pauline's curiosity by showing her an advertisement for an upcoming air balloon
demonstration, then accompanies her to the park where he persuades her to climb in the basket,
only to set the device loose, sending her afloat without a pilot. With Owen capitalizing upon
Pauline's bravado, her boyfriend Harry tries to reign in her taste for adventure but is usually
unable to prevent her from becoming embroiled in some form of derring do. "Harry, as
Pauline's self-appointed protector, is kept very busy," *Moving Picture World*'s critic observed.[15]

In fact, hero and villain often work in concert to frustrate Pauline's adventures. Unable
to persuade her to adopt the more staid lifestyle he prefers, Harry thinks nothing of foiling
her plans, sometimes forging an unwitting alliance with Owen as he does so. This is especially
evident when Harry thwarts Pauline's attempt to fly in an airplane test in the series' second
installment. After Owen and Hicks have convinced a pilot to take Pauline along on a flight that
they plan to sabotage, Harry arrives and offers the man money *not* to take his fiancée up in the
airplane. When this proves unsuccessful, and he remains unable to dissuade Pauline from her

flight plans, Harry disables her car in the hopes of delaying her arrival at the air field long enough to prevent her from boarding the plane. Acting just as Owen does, Harry seeks to control Pauline's actions through covert means, not because he is aware of Owen's ploy; he remains as ignorant of the secretary's ruse as Pauline does. Harry simply disapproves of his sweetheart's adventuresome spirit. Given the nature of Owen's villainy, Harry's cautious attitude proves well-founded. But in the absence of any knowledge of Owen's designs, Harry's actions appear needlessly restrictive and foreshadow the strictures Pauline will experience once married. Curiously then, it is the villain who encourages Pauline's taste for the unexpected while her fiancé attempts to restrain it.

Owen's insidious plotting is registered in compositions and editing strategies that stress his command over each situation while simultaneously underscoring Pauline's naïveté. He is, for instance, repeatedly shown lurking in the background eavesdropping on Pauline's plans. Even as she announces her intentions to be "free" in the opening installment, we are aware of the danger she faces, for Owen is visible hovering in the rear of several shots. "His face, at times, reflects gleams of wickedness which freeze the blood and make the observer shudder," one ad claimed.[16] When Pauline pens a telegram announcing her plans to visit a relative's ranch, Owen listens as Harry dictates it over the telephone; when Pauline decides to enter an automobile race in the fifteenth episode, Owen watches as she receives her entry form, then plots to sabotage the vehicle. By placing both participants in the frame at once these compositions stress Pauline's lack of awareness and her failure to see Owen lurking in plain sight, while trumpeting Owen's command of the frame's visual and aural field. Patterns of cross-cutting juxtapose scenes of the young woman, unaware of any imminent danger, with scenes of Owen and his henchmen plotting her demise, further underscoring Pauline's vulnerability while offering viewers a position of narrative omnipotence aligned with Owen's masterful deceit. Here, and throughout the series, viewers know far more about Pauline's plight than she herself does. She is forever ignorant of Owen's death plots which always seem to take place just out of her sightline, but in full view of the audience. Owen's domination is rendered especially vividly in a sequence that shows him glancing out of frame to watch as his accomplice Hicks throws Pauline over his shoulder and kidnaps her. Poor Harry can only watch in the foreground as Hicks disappears with his beloved into background space. Owen's command over the situation, exercised from afar and by proxy, is contrasted with Harry's relative impotence despite his proximity to the action.

In addition to stressing her lack of control over narrative and visual space, Pauline's perils repeatedly stage her entrapment in close quarters or in mechanisms over which she has little mastery. Fascinated by all manner of modern conveyance like automobiles, airplanes, and sea vessels, Pauline is not always shown to be in command of these devices. Instead, they usually serve to imprison her, to *restrict* her movement in episodes where she finds herself prisoner in machines gone haywire: an air balloon let loose over the Palisades; an abandoned structure used as target practice by the Navy; a submarine capsule submerged underwater; a boat that has sprung a leak; and a malfunctioning speedster—scenarios where her imprisonment is often doubly inscribed in images of her body bound and gagged. Pauline's ingenuity and athletic agility usually allow her to devise a means of escape, however: she shimmies down the air balloon's rope; she forces herself into a torpedo tube and is ejected from the sinking submarine; she sends her dog for help when fired upon by the navy. Perhaps her most spectacular escape occurs in episode fourteen, when she and Harry swim up the chimney of a flooded building and onto the roof, then rappel themselves on a wire suspended across a canal. Still, Pauline's physical prowess, however impressive in these episodes, is exercised almost solely to free herself from Owen's traps; rarely does she initiate athletic feats for any other reason.

Indeed, Pauline's adventures might be said to offer a reflexive treatment of restraint and entrapment, showing how the heiress, already imperiled by her decision not to marry, is further endangered by men who seek to restrict her freedom exactly as she exercises it.

The passive victimization that Pauline and others endure at the hands of villains who seek nothing less than their destruction was not a feature of all serials, however. In *What Happened to Mary?* and *The Hazards of Helen* heroines engage in risky ventures of their own initiation, exercising control over narrative space at every turn. Unlike Pauline Marvin, constantly subject to labyrinthine death plots orchestrated by Owen, or Elaine Dodge, forever at the mercy of schemes perpetrated by the Clutching Hand, Mary herself initiates the adventure, volunteering her skills to a stranger in need, taking calculated risks for another's benefit. Much like Mary Dangerfield, Helen is a woman of strength and independence rare amongst serial heroines. Her willingness to take on adventure, her absence of male companions, and most significantly, her control of cinema's spatial and optical field all set her apart from other female leads. Yet Helen's story runs counter to the pattern of most serials, where women are persistently endangered outside their traditional sphere in unvaried scenarios of imprisonment and rescue. Although serials engaged in radical narrative experiments, by offering multiple texts with varied points of entry, such a novel approach was not often repeated at the story level. On the contrary, continuing, inter-textual narratives only served to reproduce and reinscribe cautionary lessons about the dangers of female independence.

Yet, for a complete understanding of the template serial heroines offered viewers we must look beyond the screen exploits of Pauline and her compatriots towards the substantial star discourse that circulated around the actresses who played these women on screen. Of all the extra-textual renditions that surrounded serials—the myriad tie-ins, prize schemes, souvenirs, and contests—none is more important to understanding the address to female fans than the elaborate discourse that circulated on "serial queens," some of the earliest movie stars. In profiles of these women's private lives and professional careers models of modern femininity emerge that off-set the more staid, even alarmist, depictions of female independence within the films themselves.

An enormous fan culture surrounded movie serials in the mid-1910s, fueled by continuing stories that encouraged viewers to extend curiosity beyond the confines of individual texts and product tie-ins that facilitated prolonged and varied enjoyment of the material. Much of the attention focused on so-called "serial queens" like Pearl White, Kathlyn Williams, and Helen Holmes, actresses who appeared repeatedly in the serial dramas. Details of their private lives— their homes, their romances, their backgrounds, their beauty routines—circulated alongside contests and tie-ins in which their characters' exploits were variously inscribed. But profiles of stars' offscreen pastimes stood alone among the multiple discourses that surrounded serials, because they furnished a sustained extratextual engagement for viewers by tracing a parallel narrative to the sensational lives of heroines on the screen. Fans could measure the hyperbolic exploits of characters like Pauline Marvin and Kathlyn Hare against the "real" lives of motion picture players.

Actresses like Pearl White were among the earliest of Hollywood celebrities, for serial fan culture dovetailed neatly with the early evolution of the movie star system.[17] Of all early film genres, serials were particularly well-suited to the development of celebrity culture: their continuing stories promoted prolonged audience fascination with a single heroine and star, and the use of multiple tie-ins invited a heterogeneous, extradiegetic mode of audience consumption tailor-made for the cult of personality. Because plots so often centered on one young woman's exploits, fans who saw actresses play that same character week after week could not be blamed for conflating the two personalities, especially given how often heroine and actress shared the same name: Mary Fuller, Kathlyn Williams, Helen Holmes, Marguerite Courtot, and Ruth Roland were only some of the early stars for whom serials were named, or who adopted the name of their screen character. The serial format itself, where the exploits of a single heroine, already aligned with the star, were repeated at regular intervals, only fueled such close interest and identification. Enjoyment of motion picture stars was already serialized to some degree, since fans eagerly followed performers like Mary Pickford or Clara Kimball Young from picture to picture; serialized releases merely institutionalized this process, guaranteeing fans' future sightings of the star in a consistent, stable persona. Viewers accustomed to seeing beloved players in a variety of roles could now watch for the same actress in a continuing part. And precisely because plot details were circulated and repeated in so many forms—on the screen, in print tie-ins, in story contests—viewers were free to contemplate other elements of the texts, namely their stars, a point Gaylyn Studlar stresses in her examination of 1920s fan culture.[18]

If serial plot lines register marked ambivalence about women's independence and physical prowess, this was rarely in evidence in fan discourse, for actresses' astonishing athletic accomplishments became one of the central features of celebrity profiles. Fans were repeatedly told that players performed their own stunts, that tremendous skill and stamina were required to execute these maneuvers, and that many stars braved incalculable dangers while filming. The fact that audiences could plainly see the peril many actresses faced added a decided level of anxiety to the viewing experience. Describing an installment of *The Hazards of Helen* where a stunt featuring actress Helen Gibson nearly went wrong, *Moving Picture World* declared, "it is a tense moment to the person watching the picture and able to see clearly the girl's danger."[19] Indeed, the mettle performers summoned before the camera rivaled that of the heroines they played on film. "All over the world [Pearl White's] name has become a synonym for courage and daring," *American Magazine* reported. To her "leaps over cliffs, and dives off decks of ocean liners, are as prosaic and uneventful as her morning grapefruit."[20] So hazardous were the stunts performed by Mollie King in Pathé's *Mystery of the Double Cross* series that no insurance company would assume the risk.[21] Helen Gibson, dubbed "the most daring actress in pictures," ultimately issued a challenge to other performers, vowing to prevent Kalem from promoting her in this fashion "if any other player will attempt the feats shown in 'The Girl Who Dared'."[22] When the inevitable injuries were sustained, they were always carefully detailed in fan publications, for stars bore real traces of bravery—scars and permanent injuries—that their characters did not.[23] "Death is ever lurking for these daring performers," *Moving Picture World* concluded.[24]

The women's bravado extended beyond their performances on the set, for even after cameras were turned off, fans were told, many actresses pursued high-octane adventure. Well before she appeared for Pathé as Pauline Marvin and Elaine Dodge, Pearl White's publicity trumpeted her love of exploits more frequently associated with men. "For recreation I like beefsteak and aviation," the actress announced in a piece celebrating her devotion to those most modern indices of speed and velocity, the automobile and the airplane, machines also favored by Kathlyn Williams. White had "none of the usual qualms or fears about taking risks," one publication explained, for she favored "the excitable and thrilling recreations, and prefers speeding over the country road in a six-cylinder 'gas wagon' to occupying a box at grand opera." White's rival at Universal, Grace Cunard, was described as "the perfect devotee of motoring" for whom no speed was great enough. Kalem's Ruth Roland, star of several serials, also pursued pastimes not always associated with motion picture beauties. "An expert with the rifle and shotgun," whose rooms were decorated with "boxing gloves and fencing foils," Roland was said to be "equally proficient with rod and line."[25] In most cases an actress's bravery and athleticism was traced to her childhood, such as in stories that stressed Helen Holmes' background in a family of railroad workers, for instance, or Williams' early life on a Montana ranch, an upbringing which, she said, gave her "that indefinable 'something' which allowed me to mix with wild beasts without much danger."[26] The women's accomplishments, in other words, were not skills honed for motion picture cameras, but deep-seated character traits.

Evidence that serial players carried a taste for sensationalism into their private lives blurred boundaries between their screen characters and their celebrity "personas" in a way that was elemental to the early movie star system, since the star was said to summon the same skills on set (and at home) as her character was shown to embody on the screen. Stories celebrating the women's physical prowess downplayed cinematic illusion, insisting, quite forcefully, upon the authenticity of diegetic action sequences. Knowing that actresses performed many stunts themselves, and that they continued such risky undertakings on their own time, only enhanced the "hazards" and "exploits" on film: the women's exertions were real, not trickery achieved for gullible audiences; their courage was genuine, not mimicked for the camera. So central was this conceit that fans came to rely on the authenticity of screen stunts. Writing to *Photo-Play Journal*, fan Helen Tarbox confessed, "most of all, [Pearl White's] dare devil acting is what I admire."[27] Hence the acute disappointment expressed by viewers robbed of this pleasure: "I pay my money to see the star and not their double," one admirer complained to *Photoplay*.[28]

Proficient stunt work and ardent professionalism was also matched by the dynamic role many stars assumed behind the camera as they sought artistic control over their productions. Indeed, movie actresses struggling to assert themselves in a male-dominated industry became vivid symbols of emergent womanhood in fan discourse, as potent, perhaps, as images of Helen Holmes leaping between moving railroad cars. It was Holmes herself who took over much of the production of the *Hazards* series when husband and director J. P. MacGowan was hospitalized in early 1915, writing scripts, directing episodes, and assuming a leading role in the management of Kalem studios.[29] Nor was Holmes unique in this regard. Grace Cunard boasted of the creative role she played in serials where she appeared with Francis Ford, claiming "I write almost every scenario which is used by Mr. Ford and myself. I play the feminine lead in some of them, and I direct some of them besides!"[30] Mary Fuller also wrote many of her own films. Several stars were outspoken in their belief that women ought to assume a much more central role in film production. Women's creative influence would be the only means of ensuring a greater diversity of female characters on the screen, since players would only get strong, active roles if they wrote them themselves, Holmes declared. "And the reason is odd: nearly all scenario-writers and authors for the films are men; and men usually won't provide for a girl things to do that they wouldn't do themselves. So if I want really thrilly action, I ask permission to write it in myself."[31] Following Holmes' lead, Kathlyn Williams argued that women were ideally suited to direct motion pictures because they were naturally "more artistic than men" and their eye for detail was well-suited to the screen's visual canvas. "I believe that women would make as big a success directing as men, if given the right chance and opportunity," she maintained.[32] While trumpeting the women's directorial achievements, publicity materials often could not help but draw parallels between the courage of fictional serial heroines and that of women in the film industry. When *The Leopard's Foundling* (1914), a film written and directed by Williams, was released two weeks after the final installment of *The Adventures of Kathlyn*, ads described how it had been "written, directed and acted by 'Kathlyn' herself," as if the screen heroine, back from fighting lions in the Land of Allah, had made her own motion picture.[33]

GEORGE · EDWARDS.
KATHLYN WILLIAMS IS FOND OF ANIMALS, BUT ALL CAMERA-MEN ARE NOT

Figure 12.2 Kathlyn Williams cartoon, August 1916

In the same breath with which they cheered the daring and bravado of serial queens, however, many celebrity profiles were also careful to set the stars' rugged personas against more conventional portraits of womanhood, to contrast visions of strength and tenacity with a softer femininity evident only after cameras had stopped filming. "When one meets [Pearl White] face to face, she is refreshing in her simplicity and womanly charm," *Motion Picture Classic* reported. "At home the moving picture star, who will dare anything to make her last picture the greatest, reads and plays and cooks and eats and primps like any other girl."[34] *Photoplay*'s interviewer confessed to having been taken aback upon meeting Kathlyn Williams for the first time: "So closely associated has she been of late with deeds of daring and dangerous exploits that one expects to find a dashing, mannish woman arrayed in more or less masculine attire." He professes it "disconcerting" to meet instead "a decidedly womanly lady." Williams was "sweet and girlish and fetching" off camera, another reporter confessed.[35]

Certainly these stories reassured fans that stars retained their femininity even while performing feats of cinematic daring. But they also insistently marked the unaccustomed juxtaposition of feminine delicacy with might and brawn. Athleticism and beauty, perpetually twinned aspects of the serial queen persona, were almost always presented in paradoxical opposition, as many commentators noted the unlikely intersection of fragile feminine anatomy with such rough handling. One writer expressed his astonishment that Helen Holmes' "dainty figure" was "concerned chiefly with tossing itself around the tops of speeding freight trains or over yawning chasms on a horse's back" in the *Hazards of Helen* series. "You'd think a pretty girl like Helen would be afraid of spoiling her looks," Holmes' husband claimed, "but nothing worries her."[36] Indeed, many sobriquets drew attention to the uncharacteristic conjunction of femininity and physical action: Holmes was dubbed a "charming dare-devil," White became "A Pearl in the Rough."[37] "Very few men, not to mention women, would risk themselves to undertake many of the feats accomplished by Kathlyn Williams," one profile declared noting the actress possessed traits "unusual to her sex."[38] Williams was depicted in tears as she stood between two lip-smacking lions in one *Motion Picture Magazine* cartoon, crying not because she feared the beasts, but because her two cameramen had fled in terror—only she remained brave enough to face the animals. The puzzling amalgam of traditionally masculine fortitude and arresting feminine beauty was manifest most strikingly in a *Sunset* magazine portrait of the star:

> Make, in your mind, a composite picture of Roosevelt in Africa, Daniel in the lions' den, Toomai of the Elephants, Lincoln Beachey and the most daredevilish jacky in the American navy, and if it comes out all pink and white and pretty, with a row of matched pearls for teeth, big blue eyes and a mass of spun-gold hair, you will have a true portrait of Kathlyn Williams, the nerviest "movie" lady in the land.[39]

Even as commentators struggled to reconcile the serial queens' femininity with their taste for action, Helen Holmes insisted that strength was one of the key attributes of modern femininity, appealing again to the ethic of professionalism. Performing stunts was simply "one of the demands upon a leading woman in pictures that must be met," Holmes maintained, adding that actresses ought to carry them out without "losing sympathy or that air of femininity of which we are all so proud. But by that I do not mean the frail side of woman. I mean the heroic side, deeds of valor, based upon the highest ideals."[40]

Alongside celebrations of their career highlights, accounts of actresses' domestic habits circulated widely in fan publications, furnishing details about romance, home life, and children. If at first fan culture concentrated on the professional resumés of motion picture players, celebrities' personal lives became an increasing target of interest among movie fans in the early 1910s, as the star system grew to encompass a much broader discussion of family life. Details about intimate attachments between actresses and beloveds, husbands and wives, parents and children all became fodder for the public gaze.[41] Features on stars' homes and home-lives, which quickly became central components of their publicity in the mid-teens, took on additional resonance in the case of serial queens because of the marked absence of domestic life in their screen stories. Were the resolutely independent exploits of fictional heroines echoed in the "real" lives of serial stars as well? Could celluloid fantasies of feminine athleticism and autonomy find parallels offscreen? One might assume that celebrations of female stars' domestic talents undermined, or at least qualified, the vigor they displayed on the screen. Yet, far from eroding the actresses' strength, publicity items on their home lives often showed them able to combine independence, physical prowess, and cunning with more expected feminine pastimes in ways that were not presented within serial plots which tended to counterpose adventure and domesticity. Fan culture showed actresses embracing new feminine roles at home, eking out more egalitarian relationships with men, integrating motherhood with work, and redefining the home front. Details that emerged in these write-ups thus played an important role in suggesting ways that the hyperbolic feminism of screen heroines might be extended into more prosaic, if no less revolutionary, goals. Though less spectacular, perhaps, than leaping onto speeding locomotives, small domestic revolutions in the lives of film personalities helped sketch the contours of modern womanhood for serial fans.

Some actresses explicitly rejected orthodox home life, sounding much like characters they played on film. Professing her dislike of housework, Kathlyn Williams declared a much greater fondness for baseball, fencing, and motoring. "Frankly, I am not domestic," Pearl White confessed at the height of her success, brushing aside conventional expectations.[42] White, who remained single during the early years of her fame, also promoted novel ideas about how contemporary men and women might interact, advocating new "companionate" relationships between the sexes. A complaint from the New York State Federation of Women's Clubs that "films are exerting a degenerating influence upon the young" by encouraging women to be "pals" with men prompted a strong rebuttal from the actress. Women no longer wanted to be placed on pedestals, White insisted, claiming "we don't want to be marble; besides, there would not be enough pedestals to go around, anyway." Instead, she offered a model of partnership between the sexes based on friendship and equality. "Why not give our men the same comradeship that many of them never find outside of their clubs?" she asked.[43]

If White advocated a life that "Pauline" herself might have endorsed, other stars, many married with children, offered a more nuanced counterbalance to the resolutely independent characters they played on the screen. Although marriage signified the end of so many heroines' celluloid adventures, this was not always the case, and fan publications attentive to stars' love lives often demonstrated how marital domesticity did not interfere with the women's professional careers. An announcement of Kathlyn Williams' wedding in 1913 informed fans that the actress "did not allow her marriage to interrupt her picture work, for the day following the ceremony found her busy at work," giving no indication that a strenuous working life threatened blissful matrimony.[44] An article on Helen Holmes' marriage to J. P. MacGowan, called "How Helen Holmes Became Mrs. Mack and a Picture Star," insisted in its very title that the roles of wife and working woman were compatible, if nonetheless separate. The actress's professional identity ("Helen Holmes") is clearly distinguished from her domestic role as "Mrs. Mack."[45] Some items eager to reconcile seemingly incongruous aspects of the women's lives suggested that the stars channeled their formidable talents into household chores off the set, insisting rather forcefully upon the synchronicity of domestic science and fearless professionalism: "Kathlyn Williams can bake cherry pies and many other kinds of pies after she comes in from the lion's cage," boasted a feature that included the actress's recipe for lemon custard pie.[46] *Motion Picture Magazine* supplemented a rather conventional tour of the star's home, in "Kathlyn Williams, Builder," with commentary explaining how she designed and built much of the structure herself.[47]

Helen Holmes' adopted infant daughter provided unique opportunities to feature the performer in intimate circumstances not normally associated with the fictional "Helen," but also to demonstrate how Holmes broke new ground in her maternal role. Holmes lies on the ground, wrench in hand, grease smearing her face in a photo showing her repairing her stunt car, while infant daughter Dorothy sits inside an empty tire beside her. Mother and daughter pose within the tire frame in another shot parodying familiar oval-framed serial queen glamour shots.[48] Asked how she planned to rear her daughter, Holmes replied, "She will be dressed in a pair of overalls and play with a monkey wrench . . . and in time you'll see her tied to a driving rod—while the locomotive speeds on its way," as if young "Dot" embodied the promise of womanhood that "Helen" and Holmes herself only pointed toward. Yet always careful to balance these statements with indications of Holmes' womanly virtues, an accompanying story told of two-year old Dot's debut in a river-crossing stunt with her mother, reporting that the normally fearless Holmes grew nervous while filming the scene. Orthodox maternal traits, like fear for the safety of one's off-spring, were held in balance with less customary feats of maternal daring, like forging a river, toddler in hand.[49]

Like star profiles that lauded an actress's delicate femininity offscreen, stories of maternal love and pie-baking might have reassured audiences that serial stars still cherished lady-like pastimes in their time off. Yet, these stories also served a substantial function in reconciling conventional spheres of femininity, like marriage and motherhood, with much more updated incarnations of womanly strength and autonomy, thus furnishing crucial road maps for female fans who might be trying to reconfigure their own lives beyond the customary strictures of family life. Office workers, retail clerks, and factory laborers, the likely fan base for these films, might have looked to the serials queens' offscreen lives for fresh ideas about woman-hood that they could emulate in small, but meaningful ways.

Thus screen narratives which too-frequently offered marriage as the conclusion to a heroine's adventures were explicitly countered by the attention paid to stars' private lives in fan publications. Stories that emphasized how actresses combined marriage and work, moth-erhood and professionalism, pie-baking and lion-taming resisted the opposition of strength and femininity, so often structurally reinforced in serial plot lines. Only outside the bounds of the text proper could "heroines" like Pearl White and Kathlyn Williams lead truly modern lives. As Gaylyn Studlar stresses in relation to 1920s fan magazines, the circulation of extratextual, biographical information in a fan culture chiefly addressed to women shifted the female gaze toward an invisible, extratextual realm hidden from the screen. Celebrity profiles encouraged reading strategies that "diversified the possibilities of women's looking, as well as their intel-lectual and emotional response."[50]

Even though "love and ambition," marriage and independence, are posed as irreconcilable opposites in virtually every serial, audiences' growing knowledge of actresses' personal and professional lives drew attention to the novel ways in which many stars approached marriage, motherhood, and work in their offscreen experiences. If scenarios of imprisonment and rescue outweighed daring action sequences in most serial plots, and tangled familial inheritance plots quashed most heroines' ostensible liberation from family ties, celebrity profiles allowed fans to glimpse the small-scale gender "revolutions" lived by movie actresses. Indeed, fan discourse became a vital conduit between the sensational embodiments of modern womanhood viewers saw on film and the more pedestrian, but no less significant, changes in the everyday lives of many of their fans. Serial queens re-wrote feminine norms within a burgeoning fan culture where the integration of onscreen and offscreen lives became the norm. Even if heroines like Pauline and Elaine were repeatedly victimized on screen, fan magazines celebrated the profes-sional accomplishments and private pastimes of their "lost twin sister," Pearl White, offering a telling counterbalance to images that circulated at the cinema. Serials must always be read against the intertextual field in which they circulated, for such extratextual discourse is funda-mental to understanding their address to female audiences encouraged to translate breath-taking screen exploits into characteristics of strong femininity that they might introduce into their own lives.

Notes

1. "The Real Perils of Pearl White," *Literary Digest*, 5 December 1914, 1147.
2. There are considerable discrepancies between the original episodes of *The Perils of Pauline* and those that survive in Blackhawk editions, released by Grapevine Video. Surviving prints are not based on the orig-inal 35mm 1914 release version of *The Perils of Pauline*, but on a 28mm version that Pathé re-cut and re-released after the initial run. The original twenty installments were pared down to nine episodes, some of which integrate material from two or three of the original chapters; other material is left out entirely. See *Blackhawk Bulletin*, July 1974, 63. While I have relied on these surviving versions for visual descriptions of the action, I have attempted to reconstruct the original episode demarcations, based on plot summaries available from reviews and written commentaries published in 1914. When describing plot details I have endeavored to cite the original episode number. Similarly, although I will quote from inter-titles, I cannot vouch for their historical accuracy. Inter-titles in surviving prints appear to be English re-translations of French translations of the original, and therefore potentially quite different from those American audiences saw in 1914. Most notably, Stanford Marvin's secretary is referred to as "Koerner" in surviving prints, whereas all contemporary sources list his name as "Owen," the name by which I will also refer to him.
3. *Moving Picture World*, 28 March 1914, 1698.
4. *Moving Picture World*, 4 July 1914, 47; and *Moving Picture World*, 14 Nov 1914, 912.

5. Nan Enstad, "Dressed For Adventure: Working Women and Silent Movie Serials in the 1910s," *Feminist Studies* 21, no. 1 (1995), 76.
6. Ben Singer makes a similar point in "Female Power in the Serial-Queen Melodrama: The Etiology of an Anomaly," *Camera Obscura* 22 (1990): 122–23.
7. *Moving Picture World*, 4 April 1914, 38.
8. *Adventures of Kathlyn*, Herald no. 1, "The Unwelcome Throne." Folder 560, Selig Collection, Margaret Herrick Library, Academy of Motion Picture Arts and Sciences, Los Angeles. (Hereafter, MHL).
9. *Adventures of Kathlyn*, Herald no. 2, "The Court of Death," MHL.
10. *Adventures of Kathlyn*, Herald no. 13, "The Two Ordeals," MHL.
11. *San Francisco Examiner*, 4 Jan 1915, 10; and *Photoplay*, May 1914, 131.
12. *New York Dramatic Mirror*, 2 September 1914, 26.
13. *The Ladies' World*, July 1913, 36.
14. *Moving Picture World*, 26 December 1914, 1846.
15. *Moving Picture World*, 25 April 1914, 572.
16. *San Francisco Examiner*, 22 March 1914, Editorial and Dramatic Section, 4.
17. Pearl White was, according to Anthony Slide, among the very earliest motion picture players to receive mention in the trade press, warranting an article in *Moving Picture World* in December 1910, long before her association with serials. Slide, "The Evolution of the Film Star," *Films in Review* 25 (1974): 591–94. Quoted in Janet Staiger, "Seeing Stars," *Velvet Light Trap* 20 (1983): 11.
18. Gaylyn Studlar, "The Perils of Pleasure? Fan Magazine Discourse as Women's Commodified Culture in the 1920s," *Wide Angle* 13, no. 1 (1991): 28.
19. *Moving Picture World*, 11 March 1916, 1668. Traditional histories of the serials also recount the dangers actresses faced while filming. See Kalton C. Lahue, *Continued Next Week: A History of the Motion Picture Serial* (Norman: University of Oklahoma Press, 1964), 11–15, 17–18.
20. Mary B. Mullet, "The Heroine of a Thousand Dangerous Stunts," *American Magazine*, September 1921, 32. See also, Pearl White, "Putting It Over," *Motion Picture Magazine*, February 1917, 61–62; and Frank V. Bruner, "What Sort of Fellow is Pearl White?," *Photo-Play Journal*, February 1919, n.p., vol. 306, Robinson Locke Scrapbook Collection, Billy Rose Theater Archive, New York Public Library for the Performing Arts. (Hereafter RLSBC.)
21. *Moving Picture World*, 6 January 1917, 65.
22. *Moving Picture World*, 1 January 1916, 46; *Moving Picture World*, 15 January 1916, 405; and *Moving Picture World*, 11 March 1916, 1668.
23. Unidentified press clipping, March 1916, Helen Holmes file, MHL; *New York Dramatic Mirror*, 6 May 1914, n.p., vol. 331, RLSBC; and Bertha H. Smith, "A Nervy Movie Lady," *Sunset* 32 (June 1914): 1325.
24. *Moving Picture World*, 16 January 1915, 382.
25. *Moving Pictures Stories*, 21 February 1913, 31; *Montgomery Journal*, 10 May 1913, n.p., vol. 331, RLSBC; *Moving Picture World*, 19 February 1916, 1115; Richard Willis, "Kathlyn the Intrepid," *Photoplay Magazine*, April 1914, 45; *Moving Picture World*, 23 August 1913, 832; and *Moving Picture World*, 11 July 1914, 263.
26. Kathlyn Williams, "Kathlyn's Own Story," *Photoplay Magazine*, April 1914, 39.
27. *Photo-Play Journal*, May 1917, n.p., vol. 331, RLSBC.
28. *Photoplay*, December 1917, n.p., envelope 737, vol. 1, Robinson Locke Collection, Billy Rose Theater Archive, New York Public Library for the Performing Arts. (Hereafter RLC.)
29. *Moving Picture World*, 16 January 1915, 382.
30. *Motion Picture Magazine*, May 1915, 119; and *Moving Picture World*, 19 February 1916, 1115.
31. Brian Duryea, "The Necessity of Thrills," *Green Book*, April 1916, 741–743, envelope 737, vol. 1, RLC.
32. "Some Confessions by Kathlyn Williams," *Movie Pictorial*, 4 July 1914, n.p., vol. 308, RLSBC; and Willis, "Kathlyn the Intrepid," 45.
33. *Moving Picture World*, 13 June 1914, 1559.
34. Hector Ames, "The Champion Heroine of Movie Perils, Exploits, Plots and Conspiracies," *Motion Picture Classic*, June 1916, n.p., vol. 306, RLSBC; and *Moving Picture Stories*, 4 July 1913, 31.
35. Willis, "Kathlyn the Intrepid," 43; and *Moving Picture World*, 13 June 1914, 1517.
36. Unidentified newspaper clipping, 19 December 1915, n.p., vol. 308, RLSBC; and "Photo-Player Puts Pep in Perilous Pictures," *State Journal* (Madison, Wisc.), 24 May 1915, n.p., envelope 737, vol. 1, RLC.
37. "A Charming Dare-Devil," *Pictures and the Picturegoer*, 13 March 1915, 504–505; and Frederick James Smith, "A Pearl in the Rough," *Motion Picture Classic*, February 1919, n.p., vol. 306, RLSBC.

38. "Kathlyn Williams, The Jungle Actress," *Picture-Play Weekly*, 17 April 1915, 1–4, vol. 308, RLSBC.

39. Smith, "A Nervy Movie Lady," 1323.

40. "Action is the Spice of Life, Says Miss Holmes," *New York Telegraph*, 21 Nov 1915, n.p., envelope 737, vol. 1, RLC.

41. Richard deCordova, *Picture Personalities: The Emergence of the Star System in America* (Urbana: University of Illinois Press, 1990).

42. Willis, "Kathlyn the Intrepid," 45; and Ames, "The Champion Heroine of Movie Perils, Exploits, Plots and Conspiracies."

43. *New York Tribune*, 7 December 1919, n.p., vol. 331, RLSBC.

44. *Moving Picture Stories*, 11 April 1913, 14.

45. Pearl Gaddis, "How Helen Holmes Became Mrs. Mack and a Picture Star," *Motion Picture Magazine*, March 1917, 102–106.

46. "Can She Bake A Cherry Pie, Billy Boy?," *Photoplay*, February 1915, n.p., envelope 2603, RLC.

47. Hector Ames, "Kathlyn Williams, Builder," *Motion Picture Magazine*, July 1916, 89. Also see Roberta Courtlandt, "At Home With Helen," *Motion Picture Classic*, August 1917, n.p., vol. 308, RLSBC.

48. "Film Play Work Hard on Tires," *Los Angeles Examiner*, n.d., n.p., envelope 737, vol. 1, RLC.

49. "The Mother Love that Spoiled a Movie Thriller," unidentified newspaper clipping, 1917, envelope 737, vol. 1, RLC.

50. Studlar, "The Perils of Pleasure?" 28.

Chapter 13

BEN BREWSTER

TRAFFIC IN SOULS (1913)
An experiment in feature-length narrative construction

*T*RAFFIC IN SOULS WAS PREMIERED at Joe Weber's Theater on Broadway and 29th Street, New York City, on 24 November 1913. It has at least two claims to fame. First, its sensational subject matter linked it and a number of other more or less contemporaneous films with a moral panic that eventually resulted in the inclusion of the "white slave trade" (the entrapment of young women into prostitution) in the list of topics explicitly barred under the Hays Office's Production Code.[1] Second, and more important for this study, it is a relatively early American-produced feature length film, apparently, in fact, the first released on Broadway not based on a famous novel or play.[2] It is also the first film of more than three reels produced by the Independent Motion Picture Company, whose president Carl Laemmle was at this time, and for some time to come, publicly committed against the feature film.[3] Terry Ramsaye, whose source seems to be the film's editor, Jack Cohn, reported that it was made secretly in Imp's studios against Laemmle's wishes. I. G. Edmonds already expressed skepticism about this claim, and it has been effectively refuted by Kevin Brownlow: the film was a project of its producer and scriptwriter Walter MacNamara openly made at Imp for Universal; by the time of the premiere, a third interest was owned by the proprietors of Joe Weber's Theater, the Shubert brothers, but it is not clear if they were involved in the production from its inception.[4] However it remains the case that this film was twice as long as any previously made by its production company and (as far as I know) by anyone involved in its production. This essay is concerned with the way the filmmakers responded to the problems implicit in this jump in length.

A six-reel movie cannot be called unprecedented, of course, as by the time of the premiere films as long and longer were being regularly screened in the U.S. These were, however, predominantly European productions, and, as we shall see, *Traffic in Souls* in many ways rejects the models of narrative construction these productions offered. Although almost all the production companies active in America between 1910 and 1915 made some two- or three-reel pictures for hire to their normal licensed or independent outlets, feature cinema in the teens is not a simple outgrowth from one-reel cinema. The enormous growth in the production of short films in the years after 1906 occurred to feed the nickelodeon or shop-front theater. Nickelodeons were small and charged low seat prices; to make a profit (and they were very profitable) every seat had to be sold many times over each day, and each patron had to be attracted back to the theater as often as possible. Hence programs were short—a half-hour or hour—and frequently changed, often every day. Coalitions of producers attempted to control this market by insisting that exchanges and theaters book films exclusively from their coalition; in return they had to guarantee a constant supply of new, high-quality films. Such a system effectively tied all parties to the thousand-foot reel unit: exhibitors needed a standard-length module to construct their programs and had no room in them for anything longer than the two-reeler or rare and special three-reeler; producers, committed to extremely demanding schedules of production for their regular program of short films, did not have the immediate capacity to develop regular feature production alongside short film production, nor would their internal organization allow them to switch entirely into the feature form.

Nevertheless, there was a market for feature-length films in the U.S., because a film with sufficient drawing power could he handled like a stage production, a single print being booked into a circuit of large theaters, usually within a limited territory, for relatively long runs. In Europe, where more open film markets prevailed,[5] producers could manage more easily to produce a mix of shorts and features, and as the native oligopoly strangled their access to the American short-film market, European producers switched to features to exploit this niche. The enormous success in the American market of some European titles encouraged speculative investment in spectacular features. In many ways 1913 is *the* high point in the history of European cinema, with films like *Quo Vadis?*, *Ingeborg Holm*, *Ma l'amor mio non muore*, *L'Enfant de Paris*, *Der Student von Prag*, and, as culmination, *Cabiria*, released early in 1914.[6] Once this market was proven, American producers of features emerged, and the established companies geared themselves up to produce occasional feature-length films. *Traffic in Souls* is a relatively early example of the latter trend. Not until 1914 did any American producer embark on a regular program of feature production.

Most of the earlier European features were adaptations from prestigious literary works: for example, *La Divina Commedia di Dante Alighieri: Inferno* (U.S.: *Dante's Inferno*, 5 reels), *Les Misérables* (12 reels), *Quo Vadis?* (8 reels), and two Italian versions of *The Last Days of Pompeii* (*Gli ultimi giorni di Pompeii*, 8 reels, and *Jone, overro gli ultimi giorni di Pompeii*, 8 reels). Modern and original subjects eventually joined these, but the literary origins mark these films, too. They are generally slow cut, they are staged in depth in large, ornate sets, and they rely heavily on intertitles. Thus, *Cabiria* (13 reels), an original story set in the Punic Wars, has, in current prints, an average shot length (ASL) of 20.2 feet and 148 titles in 519 shoots. *Le Roman d'un mousse* (7 reels), an original story set in the present day, has an ASL of 19.8 feet and 111 titles for its 315 shots.[7] *Traffic in Souls* is markedly *unlike* this. It is an original story set in contemporary New York; it is shallow-staged and fast cut (ASL 7.9 feet); and it has relatively few intertitles (99 in 740 shots).

As I have said, by 1913 American producers of short films included in their programs regular releases in two or three reels, as well as one-reelers proper. These grew out of an earlier practice where a literary or biblical classic was made as a series of single reels released over a number of weeks, for example Vitagraph's adaptation of *Les Misérables* in four parts, released between September and November 1909, and its *Life of Moses* in five parts, released from December 1909 to February 1910. On 26, 29, and 30 July 1910, i.e., in the three Vitagraph slots in a week's (Motion Picture Patents Company) Licensed program, Vitagraph released three reels of *Uncle Tom's Cabin,* and it seems some exhibitors waited until the Saturday to be able to screen all three parts together.[8] On 19 December 1911, Vitagraph released a three-reel version of *Vanity Fair* on a single day. By the following year, two- or three-reel films released on one day were a frequent, and for the larger companies a regular occurrence, and many of them were original contemporary subjects rather than adapted costume subjects. Most production companies with the capacity to produce more than one reel a week were devoting some of that capacity to multiple-reel subjects by 1913.

Not surprisingly, multiple-reel series released over a period were divided into reel-long, partly self-contained sections. Thus, *Uncle Tom's Cabin* has one reel for the Shelby plantation, one for the St. Clair plantation, and one for the Legree plantation; the only character to appear in more than one reel is Uncle Tom himself, apart from a brief reappearance of young Shelby and the spirit of Little Eva at the end of the third reel. In this it differs notably from the stage versions of the novel, all of which, despite division into acts, attempt to give the story more unity by expanding the roles of the slave trader Haley, his associate Marks, and the plantation owner Legree so there is some continuity in the villains to match that of the hero, a tightening in which they are followed by the Edison 1,100–foot film version of 1903.[9] The simultaneously released multiple-reels, even when original stories, follow the Vitagraph *Uncle Tom's Cabin* in retaining a relative independence of their individual reels. Epes Winthrop Sargent advised prospective screenwriters that "as a rule in writing a two-reel script you make a definite break between the two parts, winding up the first with a minor climax, as is generally done at the end of each chapter in a novel."[10] *The Strength of Men* (two reels) establishes its two strong men and their rivalry for the hand of Marie, later duplicated in rival claims for an Alaskan gold strike. The first reel ends when the two men have reached the recorder's office together and he has sent out an agent to check the claims, which are eighty miles away. The next reel begins with the agent's return to the office, and the recorder's decision to declare both claims null, forcing the claimants to race each other back to the site to stake a new claim, the race and its aftermath providing the material of the second reel. The two prints I have seen, a British one in the National Film Archive and the Nederlands Filmmuseum's Dutch print from the Desmet Collection, differ slightly in their articulation of the break, the former ending the first reel with a fade-out from a cutaway to Marie, the latter placing this shot, complete with fade-out, at the beginning of the second reel after a title translating as "A vision of the girl he loves," but both prints leave a suspenseful ellipse at the reel end.

The prints of those European features I have been able to study closely have such murky histories it is hard to be confident where the original reel breaks were. *Cabiria,* current prints of which derive from a sonorized reissue, has a rough, though not perfect, correspondence between the "episodes" into which the narrative is divided and the reels.[11] *Le Roman d'un mousse* was originally released in France in two parts. The National Film Archive's print (copied from one in the collection of the Cinémathèque Royale de Belge, apparently a contemporary Belgian release print) has cue marks for a seven-reel division, reel lengths in the surviving print varying from 780 to 1,010 feet, and the bipartition being marked by a distributor's title announcing a short pause ("La suite dans un instant") at the end of reel four. Most of the reel breaks coincide with a major temporal ellipsis and the end of a coherent segment of the narrative. Between reels two and three, and reels four and five, however, there is no ellipsis and immediate continuity of the action; in fact, the break would be a room-to-room cut were it not for the reel-end and beginning titles. Nevertheless, these breaks are not exceptions. Reel two ends with the marriage of the widowed Comtesse de Ker Armor to the Marquis de Luscky and their departure on their honeymoon, entrusting the Comtesse's son Charles-Henri to a sinister tutor who is to accompany him on a study tour of Brittany. In the last shot of the reel, Charles-Henri and his tutor, Werb, survey St. Malo from the balcony of their hotel room, then exit back toward the room. The first shot of reel three shows the inside of the room; they enter, Werb sets Charles-Henri a composition, then leaves to arrange his kidnapping. At the end of reel four, the Marquis returns home in the small hours having left poisoned water for his wife to drink. Seeing her inert form in her bedroom, he has a fit of the horrors, staggers out into the hall, drinks convulsively from what, unbeknownst to him, is the poisoned carafe, and dies. In the first shot of the next reel, his wife, unscathed, is wakened in her bedroom by his death throes; she goes into the hall, is found next to his dead body and subsequently charged with his murder. Thus in both cases, although there is no temporal or spatial ellipsis at the reel break, it corresponds to the end of one narrative move and the beginning of another. These breaks are like the one in *The Strength of Men,* providing both a strong delimitation into reels and a powerful hook leading on to the next reel.

Such a suspense-laden pause at the reel end obviously allows for a reel change in a venue with only a single projector. The smaller nickelodeons did not (and often, given the necessarily restricted size of their projection booths, could not) have multiple projectors. In 1911, most of the letters from projectionists cited in F. H. Richardson's column on projection matters in the *Moving Picture World* refer to their writer's "machine" in the singular. However, almost all the new or refurbished theaters described in the column or elsewhere in the magazine that same year seem to have two, and by 1912 theaters so equipped must have predominated among what were already classified as first-run houses in cities of any size. But this does not imply that continuous projection of multiple-reel films was the norm. The principal reason for having more than one projector was to cover for possible machine failure,[12] and reel changes were handled in a variety of ways. Some houses interspersed reels and live acts or song slides.[13] Some showed a slide announcing the next film between reels.[14] Some adopted the lantern-slide practice of dissolving the end of one reel into the beginning of the next.[15] Some even used 2,000 foot reels.[16] Some switched current directly from one projector's arc to the other's, and could declutch and reclutch a single motor from one projector to the other at the throw of a lever, giving a pause of about one second between the two reels.[17] Richardson himself argued strongly that there should be a pause of at least half a minute, with the house lights up or down, between two subjects, even when these were on a single reel.[18] None of this discussion, however, distinguishes between one-reel and multiple-reel films, which suggests the latter were screened continuously or discontinuously according to whether the theater screened the set of one-reel films in its programs continuously or discontinuously.

In 1913, exhibition practice with longer features was similarly varied. On Broadway, *Quo Vadis?* was presented in three parts with intervals, like a stage play (which does not, of course, preclude a brief pause between the reels in a single part, like a curtain between scenes in a play).[19] *Cleopatra* (5 reels) was screened continuously: "There is no wait between the parts, immediately after the interscriptive [intertitle] announces the end of one part another interscriptive is flashed upon the screen announcing the part following."[20] The reviewer implied this was exceptional; at the end of the year, it was becoming more standard, but still evoked protest: "The possession of two machines and the chance to rush the programme through and get rid of those patrons whose dimes are already in the till, leads many an exhibitor to danger by showing a four and five reel film without a break. . . . Two reels, and even three may be shown continuously without danger [to the spectator's eyes], but when you see, as I did on Broadway last week, a six-reel melodrama without a pause in the whole unfolding of the film, then I defy any man to have more than a feeling of weariness at the close."[21] By August 1914, a trade paper editorial was arguing that unless it consists of more than six reels, a film should be screened continuously, but noted that "in even some of our best theatres in this city" (New York), exhibitors still broke multiple-reel films into parts.[22]

Given this variety of practice, it is not surprising that screenwriting manuals continued to describe the narratives of features as a series of one-reel units. As late as 1919, in *The Photoplay Synopsis,* A. Van Buren Powell wrote of five-reel features as follows: "The actual length of film to a reel is elastic enough to allow of a few feet more or a very few feet less on a reel, so as to permit the proper continuity of scenes and to allow an important but minor crisis of the plot to occur in the final section of each such division."[23] There are hints, however, of the emergence of a filmmaking practice that was much less respectful of the reel end. Louis Reeves Harrison remarked on the fact that shooting ratios are much higher on some five-reel films than others, and attributed it partly to the fact that the lower-ratio films are made with "the scenes . . . timed in advance so that the end of each 'act,' or reel, contained an element of suspense, due to consideration being given to the fact that all exhibitors are not provided with two projectors. . . . Each act of a thousand feet was so well timed that little more than that amount of film was used, perhaps an excess of a few hundred feet in all."[24] He called this the "old" method. The other he regarded simply as wasteful, but it might rather result from conceiving the narrative as a single unit, and thus having a much less precise sense of the distribution of the action over the length of the movie, with the result that more leeway had to be allowed for adjustments in the final cut.[25]

The National Film Archive has no information about the provenance of its print of *Traffic in Souls* beyond the name of the donor and a stock date of around 1918. The print's main title includes the words "Owned by J. D. Tippet, 37 Oxford St., London." Tippet was the manager of Trans-Atlantic Films, Universal's London subsidiary and this was its address. Although it looks rather dupy, I see no reason to doubt that it is a direct copy of the film as originally released in Britain.[26] It seems virtually complete (longer than the surviving American print in the Library of Congress), and in its original order. Reels two, three, and four have introductory titles announcing Part Two, etc., but reels five and six do not. Narrative and dialogue titles are sequentially numbered, and the sequence is nearly complete and correctly ordered if the appropriate numbers are assigned to the opening title, the introductory titles to reels two, three, and four, and to all inserts (letters, newspapers, etc.). There are a few extra titles (numbered, e.g., 77a), and a few places where the sequence is deviated from; these probably result from changes in the final stage of assembly of the print, perhaps from changes made for the British print, which has more titles than the Library of Congress's American one. These reorderings notwithstanding, there are no gaps in the numbered sequence. It is particularly interesting, then, that there are no such gaps for the beginnings of reels five and six. I assume, therefore, that they never had introductory titles. An explanation for this might be that the intended pattern of projection was to run the first three reels with a reel-change pause, but then to run the last three continuously.

However, none of the reel breaks, including the first three, coincide with a narrative pause. The first significant such pause occurs at shot 330, forty-two shots into reel three, the next at shot 436, thirty-five shots into reel four; thereafter, the extreme continuity of the narrative is relaxed until the beginning of the climactic raid on the brothel at shot 600, fifteen shots short of the end of reel five.

Ignoring the physical reel-breaks, however, the film does show what might be a relic of a reel-based construction. It can be divided into three parts, a prologue, a main section, and an epilogue. The epilogue is relatively short (shots 710–40), whereas the prologue ends at shot 330, near the beginning of reel three. This prologue is like a separate two-reeler: it introduces the heroine and her policeman boyfriend, then presents a quasi-documentary of the white slavers' organization and methods, then the boyfriend's detection and successful arrest of one division of the white slavers. This is grafted onto the main narrative by two doublings: the heroine has a less reliable younger sister; and we are shown two of the white slavers' brothels.[27] During the prologue there are a number of cutaways to show the pimp at the first brothel reconnoitering and making an assignation with the younger sister, and immediately after the heroine's boyfriend has been congratulated for the elimination of the second brothel, this first pimp abducts the younger sister and imprisons her in the first brothel, setting off the main narrative. This narrative is much less documentary-oriented than the prologue, crime and detection occurring within the heroine's family (the heroine herself discovers the slavers' headquarters, collects the incriminating evidence using an adapted dictaphone invented by her invalid father, and joins her boyfriend in the race to rescue her sister from the brothel before it is too late). This prologue/story structure is reminiscent of the two reels of *The Strength of Men,* indeed, the prologue constitutes a much more complete story of its own than the latter's first reel. In fact, Walter MacNamara had already used such a two-part structure in his script for an Imp two-reeler that seems (from plot summaries—I know of no surviving print) to have been a dry run for *Traffic in Souls.* In *The Rise of Officer 174*, the eponymous hero detects and arrests a notorious art thief, and in the first reel is promoted to detective; in the second, the underworld appeals to the "man higher up" to get the Officer off their backs, but the Officer's girlfriend, who happens to be a stenographer in the front organization of the "man higher up," overhears him plotting against the Officer and records the plot on a dictaphone, thus bringing about his arrest. The *Moving Picture World* critic remarked on the double plot: "We would have shortened the scenes leading up to the first incident somewhat, as it really makes the film tell two complete stories."[28]

However, *Traffic in Souls* goes to some length to weaken the junction between its prologue and main story: not only does this junction not coincide with a reel-break, there is also no ellipsis in the narrative. There is, in fact, no detectable temporal ellipsis in the film from the beginning to shot 436, which has a fade-out after an alternation showing the end of the day for the head of the slavers, the imprisoned sister, and the heroine and her father. This is about fifty-five minutes into the film at sixteen frames per second; a day has passed from breakfast to bedtime, so there has obviously been a lot of compression, but the action has been continuous.

The rest of the film is not quite such a *perpetuum mobile,* but it is still (until the epilogue) reduced to the least possible story time. The day after the action of the prologue and the kidnapping, the heroine loses her job, is reemployed in the head slaver's front organization, discovers the activity it is fronting, and informs her boyfriend in her lunch hour. That night the pair plant the dictaphone in the office. Next day, she records the incriminating transactions, takes the evidence to the police, and the raid is launched on the brothel. Her sister is rescued, and the whole gang arrested. Thus the entire action is restricted to three days. The constant deployment of alternating editing, between the heroine, the police, the sister as victim, and the gang, with the last divided into a whole series of locations and activities (the chief's home, his office, his assistant's office downstairs, the brothels, and a series of New York street locations), similarly serve to homogenize and unify the film.

I want to say more about this homogeneity, but before doing so, I should like to consider two other aspects of the narrative of *Traffic in Souls:* first, its handling of coincidence, and second, its deployment of an epilogue.

Coincidence was one of the main sins of film narrative denounced in screen-writing manuals both in the one-reel period[29] and in the classical feature cinema of the 1920s and later.[30] *Traffic in Souls* clearly relies on some major coincidences: on the day her sister is kidnapped, the heroine loses her job and is reemployed by the head of the gang responsible for the kidnapping.[31] However, as the Chinese adage has it, "no coincidences, no stories."[32] The manualists recognized that what was at stake was not so much the absence of coincidences as their motivation, and the appeal to empirical causality in such motivation usually rationalizes all sorts of other kinds of foreshadowing—sufficiently foreshadowed, a coincidence, however empirically unlikely, becomes acceptable. In *The Photoplay Synopsis*, Powell divides coincidences into "condoned" minor ones and condemned major ones, the difference amounting almost entirely to the latter's lack of motivation. Discussing the scenario that constitutes his model throughout the book, he remarks: "Such a [minor] coincidence is the arrival of the villain at the cave when Marion is with her father; but we can remove the coincidental quality to a great degree by having the villain 'planted' as using his car till the gasoline is all gone, which occurs in such fashion that he is near, not at, the cave; and the fact that he is attracted to the cave by seeing the dog takes away the coincidental quality still more, for it would be a major coincidence, indeed, to have the villain go into the cave at that time merely because the plot demands it."[33]

One-reel films, however, lacked the time even for very elementary foreshadowing, and, whatever the manuals said, unsupported coincidence abounded. In *Just Gold*, three brothers prospecting for gold split up and go off in different directions in search of a strike. One starts a mine, and the other two then coincidentally run across it, not knowing whose it is, and kill or are killed to win it, with the result that all three die. The film offers no explanation for the coincidental meeting, but it did not worry the makers, nor, as far as one can tell, contemporary audiences; nor does it worry me.

Early feature filmmakers occasionally resort to such bare coincidence, with less success. When the Earl of Kerhill needs to be removed from the scene in the first film version of *The Squaw Man,* there is a sudden cutaway from the American West to the Swiss Alps: the Earl is a member of a climbing party, falls from a crag and dies. The effect is fairly risible, but could have been made much less so if his Alpinism had been established in the first, English-set, part of the film. Interestingly, although the Earl dies in a mountaineering accident in the print I have seen (the Library of Congress's) and Sumiko Higashi's summary of the video copy at Brigham Young University has the same incident, contemporary plot summaries have the Earl dying in a polo accident, far more probably given the initial establishment of his aristocratic and military background.[34] The comparison with *Just Gold* is perhaps unfair to the makers of *The Squaw Man*, insofar as secondary, path-clearing coincidence is more problematic than central— "fatal"—coincidence. Although no contemporary manual I know of makes the distinction, the point would seem to be that the central coincidence immediately produces its desirable effect—an ironic meeting, a "scene"—the pleasure of which stills any worries about the plot mechanisms involved, whereas the pleasure made possible by the path-clearing coincidence is deferred, leaving the critical faculties in full force. The chance arrival of Lord and Lady Kerhill at a railroad station in remotest Wyoming just in time to be near-witnesses to the shooting of Cash Hawkins is far less probable than the Earl's death, even as motivated in the surviving prints, but it is far less a "plot-hinderer," to use the term by which Van Buren Powell condemns coincidence. The coincidence mentioned in *Just Gold* is clearly a central one. However, the path-clearing kind is also common in the one-reel film. It is frequently necessary that a male suitor rejected by his sweetheart's father for lack of wealth acquire such wealth to make a resolution possible. In many films (e.g., *Coronets and Hearts* and *Just a Shabby Doll*), the hero goes out West, sets out prospecting, picks up a rock—behold! gold; in the next scene he is back in New York in an expensive coat.

Traffic in Souls, in contrast to all these examples, is very careful to foreshadow its crucial plot incidents. Indeed, one of the main functions of the constant alternation is to produce anticipatory cutaways. We see the pimp setting about the seduction of the sister throughout the prologue. The wife of the gang leader (who is ignorant of her husband's criminal life) is seen during the prologue as a customer at the candy shop where the heroine and her sister work. After the sister is kidnapped, the news gets into the papers (we see the reporter acquiring the story in anticipation of this incident), and the heroine is sacked by the shop because of the

notoriety. Meanwhile the cause of the vacancy in the gang leader's office has also been established. We see his assistant flirting with the stenographer; on the crucial day, the leader's wife
catches the assistant kissing the stenographer, insists she be sacked, then goes to the candy shop
where she finds her innocent protegée also losing her job, so procures her the position in her
husband's office. Thus, a whole series of incidents preceding this central coincidence clear a
way for it. This is eminently the way later feature cinema dealt with this problem.

Second, the epilogue. The film's story proper ends at shot 709, with the sister rescued
and restored to her father's arms, the pimp shot dead in the raid on the brothel, and the gang
leader arrested, his guilt established by the dictaphone cylinders. This ends the third day of
the story. But a further thirty shots precede "THE END": a long track across the malefactors
in their cells awaiting trial; a sequence showing the gang leader's release on bail and return to
his home to find his wife dead of heart failure and his daughter insane from grief and shame;
a shot of a newspaper in a trash can, an insert enabling the audience to read of the leader's
subsequent suicide; and a sequence in which the heroine's boyfriend asks for leave to go
on his honeymoon, concluding with a final joke between the heroine, her boyfriend and the
police chief.

This kind of epilogue, and especially the joke ending to the thriller, has become such a
cliché that it is worth emphasizing how few precedents it had in 1913. One- or two-reelers
almost never had epilogues, though the captured villains tipping their hats to the heroine who
has outbluffed them, followed by the hero and heroine's embrace, at the end of *The Lonedale
Operator* might be counted an exception. More commonly they had endings that are reminiscent of and probably ultimately derive from the "emblematic ending" of the primitive cinema:
the final shot outside the narrative concatenation that serves as an epitome of the film, and is
also often in a closer framing.[35] An example is the medium shot of the protagonists in convict
garb in jail at the end of *Bold Bank Robbery*. In one-reel narrative films, the end is usually more
firmly diegetically linked to the rest of the story, and in the teens the closer framing is often
abandoned, but the action closes with a static scene grouping the principal characters in a
tableau, a pose summarizing the narrative "point," the stasis usually naturalistically motivated.
For example, *A Friendly Marriage* ends in its standard medium-long-shot framing, with Lord
Towne presenting his successful novel on a cushion to his wife, the gift symbolizing the future
source of the couple's livelihood and hence his assumption of the proper place of the husband
in the marriage. *Traffic in Souls* in fact has a shot even more like the primitive emblematic shot
than this: the track past the cells containing the arrested members of the gang (shot 711), very
reminiscent of the final shot of *Bold Bank Robbery*, and marked out not so much by the closer
shot-scale as by the track—a very rare device before *Cabiria*. But this is not the end of the
film. It is noteworthy that the reviewer in the *New York Dramatic Mirror* saw the further ending
as "an anticlimax that might well be shortened," an instance of the padding more conservative
commentators at this time claimed to characterize the feature film.[36]

Perhaps more interesting, though, is the fact that this kind of epilogue is not common in
contemporary drama, either. More popular traditional melodrama ended with a tableau rather
like the end of the one-reeler, though the stasis could be markedly unmotivated, a true tableau
vivant, while traditional opera ended with a final ensemble or chorus, usually moralizing on
the action in a similar way; and naturalistic drama and veristic opera favored very abrupt
endings, ringing down the curtain at the high point of the last act (e.g., the suicides that close
Rosmersholm and *La Tosca*). Indeed, the importance of the epilogue to the feature film first struck
me at a viewing of the film version of *Carmen Jones*. Bizet's score ends so soon after José/Joe
has killed Carmen that the film is forced into what is a very abrupt ending by feature-film standards. In the operatic case, the point seems to be to maximize applause, and this may explain

the prevalence of epilogues in feature cinema, for it seems always to have been true that audiences are reluctant to applaud anything but artists present *in propria persona*—applauding films has always been the exception. Nevertheless, the epilogue in *Traffic in Souls* seems too assured not to be derived from a well-established precedent, and I would like to know what it is.

Thus, in certain respects *Traffic in Souls* is highly anticipatory of the feature cinema of the post-war period, most notably in its careful foreshadowing and its assured deployment of an epilogue. Moreover, it achieves this anticipation without building on the two obvious models for the construction of a long film available to its makers: the European feature, and the two- and three-reelers produced as part of their regular programs by the established American short-film producers, whether licensed or independent. The first of these possible models seems almost consciously defied, while, if the latter can be detected in the relation between the prologue and the main story, the gap between the two has been sealed as far as possible, both in the physical organization of the film into reels, and in the insistence on temporal continuity across it in the narrative. *Traffic in Souls* seems to represent, as it were, the miraculous birth of an entirely new kind of cinema. But in one respect, at least, the film differs markedly from the classical feature.

Classical films are usually clearly divisible into a fairly large number of major segments (several times the number of reels). These are usually scenes or ordinary sequences in Metz's sense, but more rarely they may be alternating sequences or other types.[37] The main actions of the narrative take place in these segments, and they are linked by strong punctuations occasionally amounting to transitional segments (in the later 1920s these would often be montage sequences). It would be very difficult to segment *Traffic in Souls* in this way. It has virtually only one kind of segment, the alternating sequence, and the whole of the first day, the first fifty-five minutes of the film, could be described as a single such segment. The temporal restriction of the film is itself uncharacteristic of feature cinema, at least until the spate of "experimental" mainstream films of the 1940s.

However, both of these characteristics—the lack of segmentation and the temporal restriction—are found in one-reel films of the teens. *In Peril of the Sea*, directed by George Loane Tucker the same year, has some of *Traffic in Souls*'s characteristics, most notably the low ASL (7.4 feet), the paucity of intertitles (13 in 121 shots), and the use of alternating editing; it lacks the temporal restriction, however, having three sections separated by indefinite but long temporal ellipses. The Biograph one-reeler *Fate* is closer. Its ASL is 8.4 feet and it has 14 titles in 120 shots. All its action takes place on a single morning, the only possible ellipses being omissions of the time it takes the characters to move between the four neighboring locations among which it alternates: two cabins in the woods, a village with its saloon, and a schoolhouse. The opening consists of an establishing alternation between the home of the villains and that of the heroes, the middle brings the two groups together in conflict, and then, as is frequently the case with Biograph movies, a suspenseful climactic alternation turns around the threatened explosion of an infernal machine. This kind of one-reel movie seems to have been the model for the makers of *Traffic in Souls*.

The implications of this choice of models will perhaps be made clearer by a digression. From 1912 to 1915, multiple diegesis becomes relatively common in both European and American one-reel films. By films with multiple diegesis I mean those in which a character narrates (or remembers, or dreams) part of the story. In *Nozze d'oro* a grandfather tells his granddaughter how he met her grandmother; the events narrated are separated from the primary diegetic time by fifty years, but themselves only occupy a few months, and most occur on one day. In several American examples, by contrast, the events narrated themselves involve the passage of many years. In *The Passer By* the narrator tells how he declined from a prosperous businessman to a down-and-out; in *Just a Shabby Doll*, a father tells his daughter of his childhood friendship with, unsuccessful courtship of, separation from, and eventual reunion with her mother; in *The Man That Might Have Been*, a shoe clerk whose wife dies in childbirth imagines the life story of the child if it had lived.

Now to enact such stories in a quarter of an hour requires enormous ellipsis. *A Friendly Marriage*, while not covering the time span of these multiple-diegesis films, does have to bridge comparable geographical and social gulfs, and thus illustrates the difficulties attendant on a more straightforward narration of such plots. It tells the story of the daughter of a poor Californian gold prospector who becomes a rich heiress, travels to New York and then London, marries an impoverished English aristocrat for his title, wins his love and finally his support when her gold mines fail, all in the course of a single reel. Most scenes consist of only one shot, with perhaps an insert, and very few locations are repeated, with the result that almost every scene needs an introductory title (the film has 21 titles and 6 letter inserts for its 33 picture shots). In a sense these titles fill in the gaps, but to avoid anticipatory redundancy they are often themselves quite elliptical (for example, the betrothal scene is followed by the title "Lady Towne," introducing a shot of the heroine and her bridegroom signing the register). The result is an extreme exposure of narrative causality. For me, this makes *A Friendly Marriage* one of the masterpieces of one-reel cinema, but it has also led to its dismissal by a modern critic as "a perfect example of the limitations of the rigid one-reel format that hogtied early film-makers—a convoluted and complex narrative reduced to a series of tableaux that only come to make sense with the lengthy subtitles that precede them. It is a poor film and must have seemed so even in 1911."[38] Without conceding Birchard's final point, it can be admitted that it is much easier to cover and motivate the kind of gaps found in such plots by recurrent returns to a narrator telling the story. Hence multiple diegesis became the preferred way of telling long-time-period stories in one-reel films. This had, in fact, already been recognized by a commentator before the earliest of my examples of a multiple-diegesis film. In one of the first articles on screenwriting in the *Moving Picture World*, in January 1911, George Rockhill Craw discussed the Vitagraph film *The Three Cherry Pits*, in which a Napoleonic veteran vindicates his honor against three young men who insult him, the vengeance being motivated in a prelude that shows the Emperor awarding him a medal: "The prelude would have been best used as a retrospective vision of the Colonel's, after he had returned home from the garden where the insults took place. A chasm of forty years between a prelude and an introduction, is a long jump for an audience to span, and the illusion would have been best conserved by showing what happened in the past after the audience is familiar with and interested in the old Colonel, rather than before it is aware of his existence."[39]

American feature films from the end of the teens to *Citizen Kane*, by contrast, rarely resort to multiple diegesis.[40] They deal with the ellipses involved in long-time-period stories by locating them in the transitions between their major segments. The characteristic rhythm of the feature film, often described with respiratory metaphors,[41] alternates moments of tension, where screen time tends to approach diegetic time, and moments of relaxation, with much greater ellipsis and also more marked style and narration. These moments of relaxation can accommodate large ellipses more or less as well as small ones, while the markedness of the narration falls short of that of the introduction of an explicit narrator as required by the multiple-diegesis film. The more exposed device continued to be favored by European film-makers anxious to differentiate their films from the American mainstream—hence the proliferation of diegetic levels in a film like *Körkarlen*—but was avoided in classical American cinema, in favor of simpler narratives. Kristin Thompson has argued that the significance of the move to feature-length films in the development of the classical narrative cinema is, broadly speaking, that longer films required more complex narration.[42] Without invalidating the general thesis, this discussion of multiple diegesis indicates an area where, on the contrary, longer films allowed simpler narration.

The alternative for the one-reel film was to choose more temporally (and geographically and socially) compact stories. Such stories, if filmed in the style of *A Friendly Marriage*, might present the opposite danger of a tedious uniformity, but alternating editing provided a means of elaborating the films of such stories (scene dissection, the principal resort in the same case for most classical feature films, remains rare even into the middle teens). The most elaborated of such compact story films were Biograph subjects of the kind I have argued provided the principal model for *Traffic in Souls*.[43] It is as if, wishing to insist on the unique unity of their feature-length film, and hence rejecting the "halfway house" of the nickelodeon multiple-reeler with its strongly demarcated reels, the filmmakers decided to extend the temporally most compact and unified kind of one-reel narrative to feature length.

Thus, *Traffic in Souls* is not, perhaps, the miracle it might at first seem. On the other hand, it is not one point in a steady transition from the one-reeler to the feature. Its transitional character lies rather in the way it cobbles together available devices from one-reel cinema and elsewhere to construct something qualitatively new.

Notes

1. The fifth of the topics warned against in the list known as the "Don'ts and Be Carefuls" issued by the Motion Picture Producers and Distributors' Association in 1927 was "white slavery." See Garth Jowett, *Film: the Democratic Art* (Boston: Little, Brown and Co., 1976), 467. For an account of the problems *Traffic in Souls* and the other films in the "white slavery" cycle presented for American censorship, see Kevin Brownlow, *Behind the Mask of Innocence* (New York: Alfred A. Knopf, 1990), 70–85. The Second Annual Report of the British Board of Film Censors already included dealing with "the white slave traffic" as a ground for refusal of a certificate in 1914. See James C. Robertson, *The British Board of Film Censors: Film Censorship in Britain, 1896–1950* (London: Croom Helm, 1985), 10.
2. George Blaisdell, "Irish History on the Screen," *The Moving Picture World* (hereafter *MPW*) 21, no. 9 (29 August 1914): 1245. The claim is made in connection with an essentially promotional interview with Walter MacNamara and should be treated with some skepticism.
3. See the quotations from Universal's newsletter given in I. G. Edmonds, *Big U: Universal in the Silent Days* (South Brunswick and New York: A. S. Barnes, 1977), 33–4; and Carl Laemmle, "Doom of Long Features Predicted," *MPW* 21, no. 2 (11 July 1914): 185.
4. See Terry Ramsaye, *A Million and One Nights* (New York: Simon and Schuster, 1926), chapter 61; Edmonds, *Big U,* 33–6; Kevin Brownlow, "Traffic in Souls," *Griffithiana* 32–33 (Sept. 1988): 227–36; Jack Lodge, "First of the Immortals: The Career of George Loane Tucker," *Griffithiana* 37 (Dec.1990): 36–68; and a letter of 10 May 1915 from an unnamed lawyer representing "the Shubert interests" to Carl Laemmle in the Aitken Papers (Wisconsin Center for Film and Theater Research), Box 11.
5. European exhibitors seem, in particular, to have been much less tied to the 1,000–foot module. Both *Le Courrier de Lyon* and *Notre Dame de Paris* were released in Britain in two parts, despite the fact that their total lengths were, respectively, 2,580 and 2,672 feet (see *The Bioscope*, no. 238 [4 May 1911]: 185–87, and no. 258 [21 Sept. 1911]: 635–37). I do not know if this was achieved by using spools of larger capacity than 1,000 feet, or by dividing the film into four short reels. The surviving English prints in the National Film Archive only show evidence of a single reel division about half-way through. In the U.S., both films were released as three-reelers, but the summaries given in the *MPW* (10, no. 11 [16 Dec. 1911]: 884–85; and 12, no. 9 [1 June 1912]: 860) give little indication as to how the narrative was distributed among the reels.
6. Total exposed footage imported into the U.S. (almost all of which would have come from Europe) peaked early in 1914. See Kristin Thompson, *Exporting Entertainment: America in the World Film Market 1907–34* (London: British Film Institute, 1985), 24–7, 224.
7. The statistics are taken from the National Film Archive print discussed below; as a bilingual Belgian print (the French and Flemish texts are printed on the same title cards, but in some cases the length

requires two titles where one would have been enough for one of the languages alone) it probably has more titles than the original French prints.

8. "Spectator's Comments," *The New York Dramatic Mirror* (hereafter *NYDM*) 65, no. 1676 (1 Feb. 1911): 29.

9. See the play text by George Aiken in *American Melodrama* (New York: Performing Arts Journal Publications, 1983).

10. *MPW* 12, no. 12 (22 June 1912): 1125; cf. 11, no. 8 (24 Feb. 1912): 669. On both occasions, Sargent notes that the Bison Company is an exception: "The Bison Company, however, seems to want a continuous script, preferring to make the division itself." See also his *Technique of the Photoplay*, 2d ed. (New York: Moving Picture World, 1913), 121–24.

11. See Paolo Cherchi Usai, *"Cabiria,* an Incomplete Masterpiece: The Quest for the Original 1914 Version," *Film History* 2, no. 2 (June-July 1988): 155–65.

12. *MPW* 9, no. 3 (29 July 1911): 208.

13. *MPW* 10, no. 9 (2 Dec. 1911): 723; 13, no. 4 (27 July 1912): 348.

14. *MPW* 14, no. 11(14 Dec. 1912): 1076.

15. *MPW* 12, no. 12 (22 June 1912): 1129; 18, no. 7 (15 Nov. 1913): 732.

16. *MPW* 14, no. 12 (21 Dec. 1912): 1188.

17. *MPW* 17, no. 7 (16 Aug. 1913): 741; 17, no. 11 (13 Sept. 1913): 1172; 17, no. 12 (20 Sept. 1913): 1282; 18, no. 11(13 Dec. 1913): 1275. The difficulty with this was the time it took to form a proper crater in a new carbon resulting in a poor picture at the opening of the new reel.

18. *MPW* 12, no. 12 (22 June 1912): 1129; 13, no. 10 (7 Sept 1912): 980.

19. *MPW* 16, no. 5 (3 May 1913): 467; 16, no. 10 (7 June 1913): 1029; 16, no. 13 (28 June 1913): 1366.

20. *MPW* 15, no. 5 (2 Feb. 1913): 477.

21. "The Film Man," "Comment and Suggestion," *NYDM* 70, no. 1825 (12 Dec. 1913): 28. The film referred to here may well, given the dates, have been *Traffic in Souls,* which would certainly qualify as a "melodrama" by contemporary definitions of that term. See Ben Singer, "Female Power in the Serial-Queen Melodrama: The Etiology of an Anomaly," *Camera Obscura,* no. 22 (Jan. 1990): 91–129. The film's popularity caused Weber's Theater to raise the number of shows per day from three to four, *MPW* 18, no. 10 (6 Dec. 1913): 1157. With nearly 100 minutes' worth of film for each show, there would indeed have been pressure to minimize the amount of time in which nothing was on the screen.

22. "Facts and Comments," *MPW* 21, no. 7 (15 Aug. 1914): 931.

23. A. Van Buren Powell, *The Photoplay Synopsis* (Springfield, Mass.: Home Correspondence School, 1919), 51–2.

24. "Production without Method," *MPW* 20, no. 4 (25 April 1914): 489.

25. It should perhaps also be pointed out that "instantaneous changeover" at this time probably meant something rather different from what it means today. When projection manuals begin to discuss changeover, at the end of the War, they make no mention of cues marked on the film. American manuals refer vaguely to "the proper time, when the end of reel No. 1 is reached" (James R. Cameron, *Motion Picture Projection* [New York: Technical Book Co., 1922], 737), or "when the time comes to swing over to [the second] machine" ([F. H.] *Richardson's Handbook of Projection for Theater Managers and Motion Picture Projectionists,* 4th ed. [New York: Chalmers Publishing Co., 1922], 496). British writers are more specific, but even so, Colin Bennett in the 1923 edition of his *Guide to Kinematography (Projection Section)* (London: Pitman), 100, describes the changeover cue as "the film incident and sub-title which precedes by five or ten seconds the part ending," while W. S. Ibbetson *(Kinema Operator's Hand Book, Theory and Practice* [London: E & F. N. Spon, 1921], 130) advises changing "as soon as white spacing shows, or the film leaves the upper case," advice still being repeated in R. V. Johnson's *Modern Picture Theatre Electrical Equipment and Projection* (London: The Technical Press, 1927), 122: "The operators . . . will watch carefully for the four feet of white spacing which is on the end of the film." Nevertheless, a correspondence in the *Kinematograph and Lantern Weekly* (14, no. 343 [20 Nov. 1913]: 3; no. 344 [27 Nov. 1913]: 6; no. 347 [18 Dec. 1913]: 3) reveals that there *was* a practice—a practice all but one of the correspondents deplored—of "cutting out bits of film (usually diamond shape) about three or four yards from the end of each reel" among British projectionists at the time. I suspect, however, that the cues mentioned above in the National Film Archive's print of *Le Roman d'un mousse* date from long after its first release. While on the subject, it should also be pointed out that the "count-down" leaders standard on modern prints were unknown in the silent period. Each reel was laced up with the first frame of the first shot or title in the gate, and apparently not wound back, so a few feet would always be lost as the projector accelerated to the speed at which its safety shutter opened. It seems clear that silent changeovers were never as precise as the sound cinema came to require.

26. The pattern of the British release is, nevertheless, puzzling, at least to me. In August 1914, George Blaisdell claimed (*MPW* 21, no. 9 [29 Aug. 1914]: 1245) that by then the film had completed a four-month run at the Free Trade Hall in Manchester. However, the principal British trade papers, the *Bioscope* and the *Kinematograph and Lantern Weekly*, neither summarize nor review it, and editorial comment is restricted to a reply by the latter's columnist "Stroller" to an exhibitor's inquiry reassuring him as to the film's propriety (15, no. 369 [21 May 1914]: 1). I was inclined to discount Blaisdell's claim until, in the Manchester trade paper *Pictures and Pleasures*, I found a full review (no. 18 [16 March 1914]: 4) and confirmation that it played the larger auditorium in the Free Trade Hall for at least five weeks (no. 24 [27 April 1914]: 1). A study of local reports in the principal papers reveals its subsequent sale as an exclusive to regional distributors and a series of play dates at provincial theaters until the spring of 1915; however, it seems never to have played in the West End. None of these references links the film to Imp, Universal, or Trans-Atlantic. I infer that Universal and/or Tippet himself were reluctant to associate their companies' names with a film they expected to have censorship problems, and did not submit it to the British Board of Film Censors (which has no record of ever having considered it for certification), thereby radically restricting its distribution possibilities.

27. The parallel here is so arbitrarily introduced and so close—the sets representing the hallways of the two brothels are virtually identical—that it has confused the titlers, who present both of the pimps in charge of them as "The Cadet." This is, in fact, not quite a name or nickname for, as Kevin Brownlow has noted ("Traffic in Souls": 227), "cadet" is contemporary slang for a pimp, but it is still an inappropriately repeated definite description.

28. See *MPW* 16, no. 5 (3 May 1913): 512; no. 6 (10 May 1913): 597.

29. "Above all things avoid coincidence. Coincidence is the make-shift of a writer who cannot make the characters of his plot work out the story," Eustace Hall Ball, *The Art of the Photoplay*, 2nd edn (New York: G. W. Dillingham and Co., 1913), 35–6.

30. "The third [in a list] of the undesirable plot-hinderers is the matter of coincidence," Powell, *The Photoplay Synopsis,* 143.

31. This reliance on coincidence was noted by Robert Allen in one of the first discussions of *Traffic in Souls* since Ramsaye's in the 1920s: "Traffic in Souls," *Sight and Sound* 44, no. 1 (Winter 1974–75): 50–2. See also Clive Hirschhorn *The Universal Story: The Complete History of the Studio and Its 2,641 Films* (New York: Crown Publishers, Inc., 1983), 16. Contemporary reviewers do not seem to have found it so obvious. No early commentary I have read makes such a criticism; on the contrary George Blaisdell describes its action as unfolding "coherently" in *MPW* 18, no. 8 (22 Nov. 1913): 849, and the *NYDM* reviewer remarks: "With all the sensational action throughout the six reels, there is nothing to stagger our credulity." 70, no. 1822 (19 Nov. 1913): 33.

32. "The Oil Peddler Courts the Courtesan," translated by Lorraine S. Y. Lieu, Y. W. Ma and Joseph S. M. Llau, in Ma and Llau, eds., *Traditional Chinese Stories, Themes and Variations* (New York: Columbia University Press, 1978), 179.

33. Powell, *The Photoplay Synopsis*, 144.

34. See Sumiko Higashi, *Cecil B. DeMille: A Guide to References and Resources* (Boston: G. K. Hall, 1985), 43; and *MPW* 19, no. 6 (7 Feb. 1914): 730. I infer that the scenario called for the polo game, and was subsequently used by the publicity department for the summary it sent to the trade papers, but Apfel and DeMille seized the chance to film the mountaineering accident while on location for other scenes in the film so it appeared in all prints. Such discrepancies between published summaries and surviving prints are not uncommon in films of this period.

35. See Noël Burch, *Life to Those Shadows* (London: British Film Institute, 1990), 193–96.

36. "Feature Films . . . The *Traffic in Souls*," *NYDM* 70, no. 1822 (19 Nov. 1913): 33.

37. Cf. Christian Metz, "Problèmes de dénotation dans le film de fiction" in *Essais sur la signification au cinéma,* tome 1 (Paris: Editions Klincksieck, 1971), 111–46; and Raymond Bellour, "To Analyse, to Segment," *Quarterly Review of Film Studies* 1, no. 3 (August 1976): 331–45.

38. Robert Birchard reviewing the *Before Hollywood* package of films in *Film History* 1, no. 4 (1987): 397. The intertitles, by the way, are strikingly short. Many consist of only one or two words, and the longest of ten; the longest letter insert of only nineteen.

39. "The Technique of the Picture Play—Structure (Second Article)," *MPW* 8, no. 4 (28 Jan. 1911): 180. I am grateful to Barry Salt for drawing this passage to my attention.

40. See David Bordwell, Janet Staiger, and Kristin Thompson, *The Classical Hollywood Cinema, Film Style and Mode of Production to 1960* (London: Routledge and Kegan Paul, 1985), 42. In her *Flashbacks in Film: Memory and History* (London: Routledge, 1989), 106, Maureen Turim argues that the flashback was

common throughout the silent period, then became rarer in the first decade of sound. However her "flashback" is more extensive than my "multiple diegesis;" in particular, it includes brief memory flashes.

41. For example, by Burch, *Life to Those Shadows,* 270.
42. See Bordwell, Staiger and Thompson, *The Classical Hollywood Cinema,* part three: "The Formulation of the Classical Style, 1909–28," esp. 167–73.
43. For an account of the genealogy of these two types of one-reel narrative, see Barry Salt, "L'Espace d'à côté" in *Les Premiers ans du cinéma français,* ed. Pierre Guibbert (Perpignan: Institut Jean Vigo, 1985), 198–203.

Filmography

This filmography gives extended credits for *Traffic in Souls* and brief credits for the other films mentioned in this study. Abbreviations are as follows:

au.	author
d.	director
dist.	distributor
ed.	editor
l.p.	leading players (character names in parentheses)
p.	producer
p.c.	production company
ph.	photographer
r.d.	release date
sc.	scriptwriter

Traffic in Souls; U.S.; p.c. Independent Motion Picture Co. (Imp); dist. Universal Film Mfg. Co.; p. Walter MacNamara; d. George Loane Tucker; sc. Walter MacNamara and George Loane Tucker; ph. Henry Alden Leach; ed. Jack Colin; l.p. Jane Gail (Mary Barton), Ethel Grandin (her sister Lorna), William Turner (their father Isaac Barton), Matt Moore (policeman Larry Burke), William Welsh (William Trubus, the "Man Higher Up"), Mrs. Hudson Lyston (his wife), Irene Wallace (their daughter Alice), William Cavanaugh (Bill Bradshaw, pimp, abductor of Lorna Barton), Arthur Hunter (another pimp), Howard Crampton (the "Go-Between"), William Burbidge ("Respectable" Smith), Laura Huntley (country girl), William Powers (Swedish girls' brother); premiere: 24 November 1913, Joe Weber's Theater, Broadway and 29th Street, New York City; 6 reels (National Film Archive print, 5,895 feet).

Bold Bank Robbery; U.S.; p.c. Lubin Mfg. Co.; U.S. copyright 25 July 1904; 600 feet (Library of Congress Paper Print, 16mm, 227 feet—equivalent to 568 feet of 35mm).

Cabiria—visione storica del terzo secolo A.C.; Italy; p.c. Itala Film, Turin; d. Giovanni Pastrone; au. Giovanni Pastrone; titles Gabriele D'Annunzio (originally credited as director and scriptwriter also); premiere: 18 April 1914, Teatro Vittorio Emanuele, Turin, and Teatro Lirico, Milan; 14 reels (National Film Archive print, 8,345 feet).

Carmen Jones; U.S.; p.c. Twentieth-Century Fox; d. Otto Preminger; story and lyrics Oscar Hammerstein II, based on the opera *Carmen* by Bizet, itself based on a story by Prosper Mérimée; sc. Harry Kleiner; r.d. 5 October 1954; 107 minutes.

Citizen Kane; U.S.; p.c. Mercury Productions; dist. RKO-Radio-Pictures; d. Orson Welles; sc. Herman Mankiewicz and Orson Welles; premiere 9 April 1941, New York and Los Angeles; 119 minutes.

Cleopatra; U.S.; p.c. Helen Gardner Picture Players; d. Charles L. Gaskill; Sc. Charles L. Gaskill from the play by Victorien Sardou; premiere (or preview?): 13 November 1912, New York City; 5 reels (George Eastman House print, 16mm, 2,084 feet—equivalent to 5,210 feet of 35mm).

Coronets and Hearts; U.S.; p.c. Vitagraph Co. of America; d. William Humphrey; au. Eliza G. Harral; r.d. 3 September 1912; 1,000 feet (National Film Archive print, 898 feet).

Le Courrier de Lyon (U.K.: *The Courier of Lyons*; U.S.: *The Orleans Coach*); France; p.c. Pathé Frères; d. Albert Capellani; from the play by Paul Siraudin, Delacour and Eugène Lemoine-Moreau; r.d. March 1911; U.K. version 2,580 feet (National Film Archive print, 2,151 feet).

La Divina Commedia di Dante Alighieri: Inferno (U.S.: *Dante's Inferno*); Italy; p.c. Milano Film; d. Francesco Bertolini and Adolfo Padovan; private view 2 March 1911, Teatro Mercadante, Naples; 5 reels, c. 4,265 feet.

L'Enfant de Paris (U.K. and U.S.: *In the Clutch of the Apaches*); France; p.c. Gaumont; d. Léonce Perret; r.d. September 1913, 7,875 feet (Cinémathèque Française print).

A Friendly Marriage; U.S.; p.c. Vitagraph Co. of America; d. Van Dyke Brooke (?); r.d. 5 September 1911; 1,000 feet (National Film Archive print, 848 feet; Library of Congress print 1,013 feet).

Ingeborg Holm (U.K.: *Margaret Day*); Sweden; p.c. Svenska Biografteatren; d. Victor Sjöström; sc. Nils Krok, from his play; premiere: 3 November 1913, Röda Kvarn i Regina, Stockholm; length at censorship (20 October 1913) 6,581 feet; length after cuts 6,480 feet (Swedish Film Institute print).

In Peril of the Sea; U.S.; p.c. Independent Motion Picture Co.; d. George Loane Tucker; au. Jack Byrne; r.d. 29 September 1913; 1 reel (National Film Archive print, 890 feet).

Jone, overro gli ultimi giorni di Pompeii; Italy; p.c. Pasquali and Co., Turin; d. Enrico Vidali; sc. from the novel *The Last Days of Pompeii* by Edward Bulwer-Lytton; premiere: August 1913; 8 reels (National Film Archive print, 3,851 feet).

Just a Shabby Doll; U.S.; p.c. Thanhouser Film Company; r.d. 11 March 1913; 1 reel (National Film Archive print, 869 feet).

Just Gold; U.S.; p.c. Biograph Company; d. D. W. Griffith; au. D. W. Griffith; r.d. 24 May 1913; 999 feet (Museum of Modern Art print).

Körkarlen (U.K.: *Thy Soul Shall Bear Witness*, U.S.: *The Stroke of Midnight*; also known as *The Phantom Carriage*); Sweden; p.c. Svensk Filmindustri; d. Victor Sjöström; sc. Victor Sjöström, from the novel by Selma Lagerlof; premiere: Röda Kvarn, Stockholm, 1 January 1921, length at censorship (15 December 1920) 6,975 feet (National Film Archive print 5,878 feet).

The Life of Moses; U.S.; p.c. Vitagraph Co. of America; au Rev. Madison C. Peters; part 1: r.d. 4 December 1909, 981 feet, part 2: *Forty Years in the Land of Midian*, r.d. 1 January 1910, 868 feet (National Film Archive print 1,127 feet including interpolations from a Pathé film), part 3: *The Plagues of Egypt and the Deliverance of the Hebrews*, r.d. 25 January 1910, 976 feet (Library of Congress print, 664 feet); part 4: *The Victory of Israel*, r.d. 12 February 1910, 955 feet (Library of Congress print, 608 feet); part 5: *The Promised Land*, r.d. 19 February 1910, 990 feet.

The Lonedale Operator; U.S.; p.c. The Biograph Company; d. D. W. Griffith; au. Mack Sennett; r.d. 23 March 1911; 998 feet (National Film Archive print, 962 feet).

Ma l'amor mio non muore (U.S.: *Love Everlasting*); Italy; p.c. Gloria Films, Turin; d. Mario Caserini; sc. E. Bonetti and S. Monleone; r.d. 1913; 6 reels (Museum of Modern Art Circulating Library print, 16mm, 1,856 feet—equivalent to 4,640 feet of 35mm).

The Man That Might Have Been; U.S.; p.c. Vitagraph Company of America; d. William Humphrey; au. Rupert Hughes; r.d. 3 December 1914; 1,000 feet (National Film Archive print, 987 feet).

Les Misérables; U.S.; p.c. Vitagraph Co. of America; part 1: *The Galley Slave—From Victor Hugo's Famous Novel Les Misérables*, r.d. 4 September 1909, 885 feet; part 2: *Fantine; or, A Mother's Love*, r.d. 25 September 1909, 997 feet; part 3: *Cosette*, r.d. 16 October 1909, 987 feet; part 4: *Jean Valjean*, r.d. 27 November 1909, 990 feet.

Les Misérables; France; p.c. SCAGL; d. Albert Capellani; four parts, r.d. 30 November to 21 December 1912; c. 15,750 feet.

Notre Dame de Paris; p.c. SCAGL; d. Albert Capellani; sc. Michel Carré from the novel by Victor Hugo; r.d. 1911; U.K. version, 2,672 feet (National Film Archive print, 2,081 feet).

Nozze d'oro; Italy; p.c. Ambrosio and Co.; d. Luigi Maggi; au. Arrigo Frusta; premiere: October 1911, Turin; 2 reels (National Film Archive print, 1,232 feet).

The Passer By; U.S.; p.c. Thomas A. Edison, Inc.; d. Oscar Apfel; au. Marion Brooks; r.d. 21 June 1912; 1,000 feet (National Film Archive print, 1,028 feet; Library of Congress print, 1,001 feet).

Quo Vadis?; Italy; p.c. Cinès; d. Enrico Guazzoni; sc. from the novel by Henrik Senkiewicz; premiere: 1 March 1913, Teatro Costanzi, Rome; 8 reels, c. 7,381 feet (National Film Archive print, 5,613 feet; Museum of Modern Art Circulating Library print, 16mm, 2,961 feet—equivalent to 7,403 feet of 35mm).

The Rise of Officer 174; U.S.; p.c. Independent Motion Picture Co.; au. Walter MacNamara; r.d. 1 May 1913; 2 reels.

Le Roman d'un mousse, (U.K. and U.S.: *The Curse of Greed*); France; p.c. Gaumont; d. Léonce Perret; two parts, r.d. January 1914; 7,875 feet (National Film Archive print, 6,228 feet).

The Squaw Man; U.S.; p.c. Jesse J. Lasky Feature Play Co.; d. Oscar C. Apfel and Cecil B. DeMille; sc. from the play by Edwin Milton Royle; r.d. 3 February 1914; 6 reels (Library of Congress print).

The Strength of Men; U.S.; p.c. Vitagraph Co. of America; d. Ralph Ince(?); au. James Oliver Curwood; r.d. 19 March 1913; 2,000 feet (National Film Archive print 1,249 feet; Nederlands Filmmuseum print 1,334 feet).

Der Student von Prag (U.K.: *The Student of Prague*, U.S.: *A Bargain with Satan*); Germany; p.c. Deutsche Bioscop GmbH, Berlin; d. Stellan Rye; sc. Hanns Heinz Ewers (originally credited as director also); premiere: 22 August 1913, Mozartssaal, Berlin; 5 reels, length at censorship (16 June 1913) 5,046 feet.

The Three Cherry Pits; U.S.; p.c. Vitagraph Co. of America; r.d. 23 August 1910; 995 feet (National Film Archive print 762 feet).

Gli ultimi giorni di Pompeii; Italy; p.c. Ambrosio and Co., Turin; d. Mario Caserini; sc. Arrigo Frusta, from the novel *The Last Days of Pompeii* by Edward Bulwer-Lytton; premiere: August 1913; 8 reels.

Uncle Tom's Cabin; U.S.; p.c. Vitagraph Co. of America; au. Harriet Beecher Stowe; part 1: r.d. 27 July 1910, 935 feet; part 2: r.d. 29 July 1910, 1,000 feet; part 3: r.d. 30 July 1910, 1 reel (National Film Archive print, three parts, 2,108 feet).

Uncle Tom's Cabin; or, *Slavery Days*; U.S.; p.c. Thomas A. Edison; d. Edwin S. Porter; U.S. copyright 30 July 1903; 1,100 feet (National Film Archive print, 1,056 feet).

Vanity Fair; U.S.; p.c. Vitagraph Co. of America; d. Charles Kent; au. William Makepeace Thackeray; r.d. 19 December 1911; 3,000 feet (George Eastman House print, 16mm, 1,109 feet—equivalent to 2,773 feet of 35mm).

Chapter 14

LINDA WILLIAMS

RACE, MELODRAMA, AND
THE BIRTH OF A NATION
(1915)

The white women of the South are in a state of siege. . . . Some lurking demon who has watched for the opportunity seizes her; she is choked or beaten into insensibility and ravished, her body prostituted, her purity destroyed, her chastity taken from her . . . Shall men . . . demand for [the demon] the right to have a fair trial and be punished in the regular course of justice? So far as I am concerned he has put himself outside the pale of the law, human and divine. . . . Civilization peels off us . . . and we revert to the impulse . . . to "kill! kill! kill!"

—South Carolina senator Ben Tillman, 1907

Some people were crying. You could hear people saying God. . . . You had the worse feeling in the world. You just felt like you were not counted. You were out of existence. I just felt like . . . I wished somebody could not see me so I could kill them. I just felt like killing all the white people in the world.

—William Walker (on recalling viewing *The Birth of a Nation*)

IN JULY 1914, CARPENTERS WORKING on a large vacant lot between Sunset and Hollywood Boulevards began to construct the main street of Piedmont, South Carolina, for the primary set of D. W. Griffith's new film, then titled *The Clansman*. According to Karl Brown, Griffith's assistant camera operator, force of habit instilled by years of backstage training caused the carpenters building the street to include hinges on scenery so it could be easily "folded up and shipped to any op'ry house in the country" (Brown 1973, 64). These unnecessary hinges on stationary film sets for an antebellum southern town are a dramatic reminder of the importance of the melodramatic stage tradition to the developing medium of film and of the crucial architecture of *Uncle Tom's Cabin* within this tradition. Brown explains in his memoirs:

There was no question as to what the town should look like or how it should be dressed. I doubt if there was a man on that work crew who hadn't been out with a "Tom" show, as the *Uncle Tom's Cabin* shows were called. There were Tom shows scattered all over the country by tens and dozens. It was not so much a show as an institution, a part of the American scene for the past sixty-odd years. . . . Stage crews had been constructing Tom shows for so long that there wasn't a detail of the Civil War period, inside or out, that they hadn't built, up to and including wobbly ice for Eliza to flee across, one jump ahead of the bloodhounds, which were usually Great Danes.

(Brown 1973, 63)

Brown's anecdote encapsulates the strange confluence of the most popular and influential play of the nineteenth century with the most popular and influential film of the early twentieth century. To evoke an antebellum southern town (which for Brown condenses, in the wake of the influence of the very film he had photographed, into a more general "Civil War period") was automatically to conjure up the conventional architecture of *Uncle Tom's Cabin*. These two works, premiering in theaters over a half-century apart, were the unparalleled hits of their respective centuries and the pioneers of their respective media. [. . .]

Woodrow Wilson's famous, though apparently apocryphal, statement—"It is like writing history with lighting"—has been the best remembered description of the film, conveying the thunderstruck impression of most audiences who became immediately convinced of its historical "truth".[1] What is often not recognized in this remark is the fact that the "truth" recognized here—the "southern view of slavery and Reconstruction"—had been previously disparaged. What *The Birth of a Nation* did, as a film, was to convert an Uncle Tom-style sympathy for the sufferings of a black man to an anti-Tom antipathy for the black male sexual threat to white women. [. . .]

Uncle Tom's Cabin had deployed melos, pathos, and action to draw northerners who had previously been uninvolved in the debate over slavery into its orbit, making the "good nigger" into a familiar and friendly icon, for whom whites had sympathy. Now, sixty years later, on the fiftieth anniversary of the end of the Civil War, *The Birth of a Nation* solidified North and South into a new national feeling of racial antipathy, making the black man into an object of white fear and loathing. We can see, then, that each work in its time succeeded in moving unprecedentedly large numbers of the American public to feel implicated in the trials and tribulations of groups whose virtue forged through suffering had not previously been recognized by the mass audience: African-American slaves in *Uncle Tom's Cabin* and white women in *The Birth of a Nation*. [. . .] Let us begin, then, by trying to understand how Stowe's Tom story of racial sympathy became Griffith's anti-Tom story of racial hatred.

Thomas Dixon's anti-Tom novels

When Thomas Dixon, Jr., gave up his popular ministry to write a series of novels about the Reconstruction period, he followed a familiar antebellum, anti-Tom, novelistic tradition. His inspiration to write came in 1901 at a performance of a Tom play. Infuriated by what he saw as the injustice of the play's attitude toward the South, he vowed to tell what he considered to be its true story. The result of his first attempt, published the next year, was a sprawling 469–page historical novel entitled *The Leopard's Spots: A Romance of the White Man's Burden 1865–1900*. It would be followed in 1905 by the more tightly focused *The Clansman: A Historical Romance*. Both of these novels would then be combined into Dixon's 1905 play, *The Clansman*, which in turn became the basis of Griffith's 1915 film. [. . .]

Without actually idealizing the "good old days" of slavery—which he has several staunch southern characters in *The Leopard's Spots* admit were an economic and social mistake—Dixon nevertheless wants his readers to long for a time when blacks knew their place and did not need to suffer the agonies of lynching, for political and social equality inevitably leads in Dixon's novels to the black male claim to the white woman as a mate. As one character puts it, "The beginning of Negro equality . . . is the beginning of the end of this nation's life" (244). "Mongrelization" of the races is Dixon's greatest fear. The burning question of the novel is posed repeatedly and italicized for emphasis: "*Can you hold in a Democracy, a nation inside a nation of two hostile races?* We must do this or become mulatto, and that is death" (Dixon 1903, 244).[2]

Such, then, are the explicitly racial, explicitly anti-Tom politics of Dixon's first novel, as it directly attempts to refute Stowe's romantic racialism with a new twentieth-century demonic racism. Dixon attempts to dismantle this structure by turning the "good nigger" bad by sexualizing his relations with white womanhood and by having him assault the "holy of holies"—the white female virgin. [. . .] Thus Stowe's antebellum, feminized "good Negro" is sexualized and demonized into the postbellum, hyper-masculine rapist who can only be stopped by lynching. Stowe describes Uncle Tom in the novel as "a large, broad-chested, powerfully-made man, of a full glossy black, and a face whose truly African features were characterized by an expression of grave and steady good sense, united with much kindliness and benevolence" (1983, 18). Stowe's Tom is certainly not feminine in his physical features—"large, broad-chested," "glossy black"—but his masculine physicality leaves the details of his "truly African features" quite vague, tempered by feminine qualities of soul—kindliness, benevolence, dignity, humility, and so on.[3]

Compare Dixon's description from his second novel, *The Clansman*, of another uncle, Uncle Alec:

> His head was small and seemed mashed on the sides until it bulged into a double lobe behind. Even his ears, which he had pierced and hung with red earbobs, seemed to have been crushed flat to the side of his head. His kinked hair was wrapped in little hard rolls close to the skull and bound tightly with dirty thread. His receding fore-head was high and indicated cunning intelligence. His nose was broad and crushed flat against his face. His jaws were strong and angular, mouth wide, and lips thick, curling back from rows of solid teeth set obliquely in their blue gums . . . His thin spindle-shanks supported an oblong, protruding stomach, resembling an elderly monkey's, which seemed so heavy it swayed his back to carry it.
>
> (Dixon 1905, 249)

In contrast to Stowe's generality, Dixon offers specifics, assuming that villainous qualities of soul emanate from "angular jaw," "thick lips," "cunning fore-head," and "spindle-shanks." To Stowe the feminine soul transcends the masculine body. To Dixon there is no spiritual transcendence for the Negro who is all animal, even when, like Uncle Alec, he *isn't* lusting after white women. Thus it is not simply that Stowe feminizes the black man, while Dixon hypermasculinizes him; it is also that Stowe deemphasizes the corporeal for the spiritual, while Dixon sees blackness as an excess of the corporeal that harks back to the jungle and retards civilization. [. . .]

Insistently, Dixon counters the myth of the gentle, familiar, melodic, and rhythmical "good nigger" with a new myth of the rapacious "bad nigger." Citizenship had transformed the black man from a piece of property into the potential owner of property, including the property of women. As Robyn Wiegman explains, the black man's threat to white masculine power thus "arises not simply from a perceived racial difference, but from the potential for masculine sameness" (1995, 90). It was this possibility of sameness that the rape myth disavowed. Its peculiar logic was to exaggerate the very quality of masculinity that granted black men the vote.

Excessive, hypermasculine corporeality disqualified him from manhood, reducing him to the status of beast. Dixon's predatory beast is forever baring his fangs and claws. [. . .]

The Clansman: An Historical Romance of the Ku Klux Klan (1905) stages the pathos of the white women endangered by black men in a key scene showing the brutal rape of Marion Lenoir, by the former slave Gus. Gus's punishment by lynching can be read in gendered terms as a castration that returns the hypermasculine body to its prior feminized state.[4] Dixon, however, gives very little physical detail, either of Gus's attack or of the Clan's lynching of Gus. He concentrates, instead, on an almost obsessive deployment of evidence of the crime. [. . .] The crowning piece of evidence, and high point of the melodrama in the chapter entitled "The Fiery Cross," is the moment Dr. Cameron hypnotizes Gus to induce him to reenact the crime by the torchlight of the cave with hooded Clansmen as jury.

> Gus rose to his feet and started across the cave as if to spring on the shivering figure of the girl, the clansmen with muttered groans, sobs and curses falling back as he advanced. He still wore his full Captain's uniform, its heavy epaulets flashing their gold in the unearthly light, his beastly jaws half covering the gold braid on the collar. His thick lips were drawn in an ugly leer and his sinister bead-eyes gleamed like a gorilla's. A single fierce leap and the black claws clutched the air slowly as if sinking into the soft white throat.
>
> (Dixon 1905, 323)

These various strategies of evidence all boil down to detailed descriptions of the black male body—of Gus's jaw and lips as imprinted on the mother's retina, the indexical imprint of his oversized foot, and his whole racialized and sexualized body as he physically reenacts the crime. The very absence of hard evidence of the act itself becomes the occasion for a ritualized enumeration of the features of the black body that are themselves considered incriminating. These features come to stand in for the unmentionable details of the crime itself.[5] [. . .]

Dixon's description of Gus's punishment is remarkably reticent. After the "trial," when the hysterical Clansmen are ready to rip Gus to pieces, Dr. Cameron is seized instead by "a sudden inspiration." Taking a silver cup, he mixes the blood of the raped virgin with river water and ties together two sticks in the form of a cross. Back inside the cave he adapts "the old Scottish rite of the Fiery Cross" to a new form of worship, proclaiming that the liquid "red stain of the life of a Southern woman" represents a "priceless sacrifice on the altar of outraged civilization." At this point Ben Cameron removes his hood and pronounces Gus's sentence of execution. How he dies, we do not learn. Thus, in Dixon's novel, the animal passion of the Clansmen is sublimated into the ritual celebration of the southern woman's "priceless sacrifice."

Dixon builds white male solidarity around the ritual celebration of the white woman's bloody "sacrifice," rather than around the bloody sacrifice of the black male scapegoat. As Jacquelyn Dowd Hall notes, the constant threat of rape was not simply a rationalization used to obscure the real function of keeping black men in their place, it was also a way to keep white women in their place. The "fear of rape, like the threat of lynching, served to keep a subordinate group in a state of anxiety and fear" (Hall 1993, 153). Thus, it is in a very real sense that the white woman is sacrificed "on the altar of outraged civilization." White men need her to be sacrificed to keep both blacks *and* women in their place. This sacrifice, ultimately, was Dixon's most successful revenge on Mrs. Stowe. [. . .]

Dixon's two novels were instant popular successes.[6] They invited extravagant praise and condemnation along predictable sectional lines (Cook 1968, 73). In 1905 Dixon combined the two novels in the play *The Clansman*. Produced by the aptly titled "Southern Amusement Company," the play swept triumphantly through the South, garnering enthusiastic reviews and sometimes generating controversy among those southerners who subscribed to more liberal racial views.[7] Dixon exacerbated the controversy by giving curtain speeches to make sure audiences got his point.[8] The play's tour continued to sell out throughout the Midwest and the West, where it was more controversial but still successful. On the strength of these successes, a second company was put together for New York City that premiered January 8, 1906, at the Liberty Theatre—where *The Birth of a Nation* would receive its New York premiere nine years later. Here was Dixon's chance to "teach the North" its lesson about white southern suffering. To the surprise of many, it sold out there as well (Cook 1968, 145–46).[9]

Thus Dixon capitalized on the notoriety of his play to preach the anti-Tom message that had impelled him to write fiction and drama in the first place.[10] Five years after he had seen the Tom show whose love for the antebellum Negro had changed the racial sentiments of the North, Dixon had made a significant assault on those sentiments. However, his radical racial views excoriating Negroes still represented the extreme fringe of southern politics. Though the tour of his play beyond the South represented a measure of success, conservative racial views, which simply wanted to maintain the Negro's inferior position, were still much more dominant in the South. Liberals supporting uplift represented another minority. As melodrama, however, Dixon's ideas had an emotional viability and power that his speeches and sermons did not. [. . .]

The Birth of a Nation

[. . .] The idea of a spirit of national re-birth forged through the expulsion of racial scapegoats is deeply embedded in Dixon's work.[11] [. . .] Nevertheless, it was Griffith's film, and not Dixon's novel and play, that achieved the "moving picture" felt by many whites to heal national divisions. For it was not until Griffith's much grander ride "to save a nation" managed a much more effective form of racial exclusion than Dixon's lurid race hatred that audiences most deeply felt a sense of national rebirth in the empowering of the film's white hero.

Griffith's own explanation for the film's effect—that his "ride to the rescue" transcended that of ordinary melodramatic rescues—points to the important phenomenon of "multiple rescue operations" discussed by Michael Rogin. Rogin quotes Griffith's statement in his autobiography that upon reading Dixon's novel he skipped quickly through the book until he got to the Clan's ride: "We had all sorts of runs-to-the-rescue in pictures and horse operas. . . . Now I could see a chance to do this ride-to-the-rescue on a grand scale. Instead of saving one little Nell of the Plains, this ride would be to save a nation" (Rogin 1984, 191; Hart 1972, 88–89). The power of the grand climax of the film, to which many critics of the time refer, has been understood by Rogin as the effect of a new spatial-temporal organization made possible by the dynamization of cinematic editing.[12]

Most importantly, Rogin argues that the multiple rescues enacted by the ride of the Clan reenacted and reversed the Civil War battles that Griffith added to the first half of his film. Where blue and grey intermingle and become almost indistinguishable in the Civil War charges in the first half, the white robes of the Clan stand out against black masses in the second. Clansmen on horseback tower over black men on foot. "Civil War close-ups show suffering; Clan close-ups show movement and power" (Rogin 1984, 222). Thus, the extreme pathos of the defeat of the South, which Dixon did not represent, resonates powerfully against the extreme action of the climax in which the Clan rescues everyone in sight. The extremes of pathos, typified by sufferings on the battlefield and in the famous painfully slow homecoming in which Ben Cameron registers the full measure of southern defeat in the soot-daubed cotton ("southern ermine") of his little sister's dress, are balanced by the extreme action of the Clan's vengeance on Gus and rescues that exceed Dixon's rescue of Phil (in the novel) or Elsie (in the play).

In these exciting climaxes Griffith, unlike Dixon, sets up two endangered groups, both in need of rescue. Northerner Elsie Stoneman is caught in the clutches of Silas Lynch in his house in town while a mixed northern and southern group composed of Dr. Cameron, his wife, daughter, the Cameron family's two former slaves, and Phil Stoneman are trapped in a rural cabin with two Union veterans. This cabin is surrounded by attacking black troops. Since this second endangered group differs considerably from its source in Dixon, it is worth examining.

As Negro "misrule" grows, Dr. Cameron is arrested for possession of a Clan costume— for which the penalty is death. After arrest he is taunted and humiliated in the slave quarters (a title reads, "The master paraded before his former slaves"). Two of his former slaves, Mammy and Jake, sympathetic "good" slaves borrowed from the Tom tradition and eschewed by Dixon, pretend to join the black mockers in order to position themselves to rescue the doctor. Jake jokes with the white captain, asking him "Is I yo equal cap'n—jes like any white man?" just before knocking him out. Mammy, at the same time, pretends friendliness to two black soldiers, putting her ample arms around them and then crushing them to the ground with the weight of her body. Thus Griffith, unlike Dixon, comically heroicized his "faithful souls"—by which he means the types of Negroes who, like Uncle Tom, remained faithful and selfless in the service of kind masters[13]—by involving them in the rescue. The comic vein of these heroics, however, employing the obese (blackface) Mammy's body weight and an outlandish claim to equality, under-cuts their seriousness. Nor are they very effective, since this preliminary rescue party led by "faithful souls" fails when a wheel falls off their wagon, causing all to seek refuge in a nearby Union Veterans' cabin. This failed rescue thus permits Griffith to maneuver this interracial group of whites and blacks, northerners and southerners, into a rural cabin where they will eventually be rescued by the Clan. Thereafter, the film cuts rapidly between Lynch's sexual threat to Elsie, the discovery of that threat by "white spies" disguised as blacks, the endangered extended "family" fighting off the black troops, and the Clan riding first to the rescue of Elsie, then to the family in the cabin.

Michael Rogin brilliantly argues that this rescue of the family from the cabin is not just from any cabin but a "Lincoln log cabin" whose refuge ironically democratizes and merges, as the famous intertitle puts it, "former enemies of North and South . . . reunited again in common defense of their Aryan birthright." Rogin thus shows us the national unity that Griffith's rescue accomplishes and that Dixon's didn't. For if Dixon had radically shifted Stowe's sectionally divisive narrative of escape and bondage to romance and rescue, Griffith's innovative rescue of the cabin by the Clan radically shifts the meaning of what is rescued. The cabin wraps the former slave owners in the mantle of humble beginnings and reconciles former enemies (in the first part of the scene "Auld Lang Syne" is played). For while it is "former master" Dr. Cameron who is actually rescued, his location in the rural cabin—and his association with the humble Union Veterans frying bacon over their hearth—dissociates him from the once grand Cameron Hall and the institution of slavery. Griffith could easily have had the doctor take refuge in his own home and had the black troops surround it. During the first half of the film he had done just that when he showed the Cameron parents and daughters besieged in the house, while "black guerrilla" troops raided the town. However, this later variation of rescue replaces the iconography of the grand plantation with the humble home of the cabin, which the reenergized doctor defends vigorously with his North and South, rich and poor, black and white comrades. Griffith, unlike Dixon, thus makes his audience feel

Stowe-like emotions of democratic inclusion even while rooting for the "common" defense of an exclusive "Aryan birthright."

But perhaps the real reason Griffith can get away with such contradictory gestures of white supremacy and democracy is that the association of this cabin is not limited to Abraham Lincoln. Its emotional and iconographic resonance extends further back than Lincoln, to the iconographically prior cabin of Tom himself.[14] Nostalgia for a democratic and humble "space of innocence," so central to all melodrama, was located in the icon of Tom's cabin. [. . .] The cabin, seen on the cover of volume one of the novel's first edition, also figured in the first act of most stage productions of the play. After the Civil War, travelling Tom shows would frequently include a mobile cabin as part of their parade through the streets of each new town. As the American *locus classicus* of honest and humble beginnings, the cabin has now become in Griffith's film as important a mantle of virtue for the former masters as it once had been for the former slaves. Symbolizing variously the elusive lost home of slaves, the poor but honest home of the free white man, it now attempts to spread its mantle of homey virtue over the sins of the former masters. [. . .]

Griffith's "good Negro" appears to have made it possible for his activation of greater race hatred as well—both in the sexual attacks on white women and in the Clan's punishment of Gus. For even though in Dixon's novel Gus actually rapes the Cameron family friend, Marion Lenoir, we have seen that Dixon substituted detailed descriptions of the horror of the lascivious black male body for descriptions of the horror of the act of rape. In his stage version, however, he was less willing to show the black beast in physical contact with the white woman and so changed the crime to Gus's pursuit of Flora Cameron (no longer Marion), culminating in her jump off a cliff to save herself from the proverbial "fate worse than death." In both the case of rape (in the novel) and attempted rape (in the play), he has Gus narrate the scenes while in a hypnotic state and thus avoids any direct depiction.

Griffith, of course, directly depicts the Gus/Flora episode in the form of a prolonged chase, with Ben Cameron arriving too late for the rescue. However, his adaptation does not include any instances of actual black/white sexual aggression. To modern audiences used to all kinds of sexual attack, the sequence seems tame and Flora's jump a trifle premature.[15] But Griffith's other scene of sexual attack in the Elsie/Lynch episode is without parallel in Dixon, or in the history of film, for its depiction of black lust.[16] Indeed, Dixon's novel has no scene depicting Lynch's sexual assault—Lynch does not even ask for Elsie's hand. Although his play includes a scene in which Lynch asks both Elsie and then her father for her hand, it does not depict Lynch forcing his attentions upon her. In Griffith's film, however, Lynch begins the scene already, as an intertitle puts it, "drunk with wine and power." His strikingly lascivious sexual overtures to Elsie are drawn out over a long scene frequently intercut with the assembling of the Clans. In the first instance, after his initial proposal has been rudely repulsed, Lynch (played by the large and, here, swarthy George Siegman) kneels beside the seated Elsie and presses the hem of her white blouse to his lips. Elsie withdraws in horror to the door, which she finds locked. In the second instance Lynch, now seated in a chair and smiling at her, thrusts his hips forward and rubs his thighs insinuatingly. If there was any doubt as to the sexual nature of his gesture, Elsie's widening eyes and scream of horror make it clear. It is at this point that Griffith first cuts to two Clansmen on horseback. The ride of the Clan thus appears entirely activated by this assault on a white woman. The scene continues, punctuated by frequent, brief cross-cutting with the gathering of the Clans, Lynch grabbing Elsie and pushing her to the center of the room. He shakes a fist and pounds his chest, explaining the forced marriage; then he chases her further around the room until she finally faints into his arms and is held close to his body before being restrained in a chair.

Figure 14.1 Elsie faints in Lynch's arms (*The Birth of a Nation*, 1915)

The last twenty minutes of the film build sexual threat upon sexual threat. The besieged "family" in the cabin is depicted in a melodramatic tableau showing Margaret Cameron kneeling at her father's feet as he holds the butt of a rifle over her head. In a parallel shot the young daughter of the Union Veteran embraces Mrs. Cameron. Over her head her father holds a rifle as well. In the next room of the cabin, already invaded by the black troops, a soldier leers over a white handkerchief left by one of the women. The melodramatic tableaux of two white fathers holding empty guns poised to bludgeon their daughters before permitting them to fall to the encroaching hordes, are reminiscent of Elsie's imminent danger of forced marriage to Lynch and Flora's solution of preferring death to the touch of the black man. Griffith thus multiplies the sexual threat to white women and with it the need for white counterviolence. [. . .]

In each of the multiple rescues carried out in the last third of the film, black men are quite literally wiped from the screen by what poet Vachel Lindsay once called the "white Anglo Saxon Niagara" of the Clan.[17] Indeed, the ride of the Clan is repeatedly figured as a flushing of blackness from the screen. Chaos and disorder represented as dark bodies in riot are swept aside by the Clan. This pattern is repeated with each new rescue, in which nearly all-black frames are suddenly flooded with white. When Elsie is rescued the shot begins with the white-robed Elsie, partly hidden behind her dark-clad father, surrounded by the black-clad Lynch and his dark-clothed black henchmen. When the white-robed Clansmen enter, they push the dark-clad Lynch and Stoneman to the side. Lynch cowers to the left and Stoneman is now mostly hidden behind Elsie's white gown.

A most striking moment of black exclusion also occurs in a scene that an intertitle calls "Disarming the blacks." Griffith shows a group of black soldiers on foot in their dark Union uniforms surrounded on both sides by white-robed Clansmen on foot and horseback. The dark soldiers drop their guns and rapidly exit both front and rear of the frame, leaving an empty white middle that now blends with the white Clansmen on both sides. The culminating shot effectively "parades" the racial cleansing that the multiple rescues have accomplished in what an intertitle of some prints calls the "Parade of the Clansmen." Elsie and the group rescued from the cabin are surrounded on both sides by the white-robed and hooded Clansmen. Since Elsie is still in her white gown and the rescued men are mostly without jackets, the effect is again of a flood of white almost completely filling the screen. Not surprisingly, neither Mammy nor Jake—nor any other "faithful souls"—are anywhere to be seen. [. . .]

Griffith's film achieves its power to the extent that it does not appear to be an exhortation to race hatred, but a natural process of heroic rescue that, in the process, just "happens" to wash the screen "clean." [. . .] Members of the black audience understood what the film was saying and returned the sentiment. William Walker, a black man who saw the film in a black theater in 1916, recalls as quoted in the epigraph, "Some people were crying. You could hear people saying God . . . You had the worse feeling in the world. You just felt like you were not counted. You were out of existence." Walker does not explain how the film accomplished his sense of eradication, of being "out of existence," but I would submit that it had more to do with the visceral experience of the logic of black disappearance than specific instances of white-on-black violence or even of more explicit depictions of black men attacking white

Figure 14.2 Dark chaos swept aside by the "white Niagara" of the Clan (*The Birth of a Nation*, 1915)

women. Walker seems to have recognized that what he had seen spelled the end of his very representation in any but the most servile or villainous roles in the new medium being born. Indeed, his further reaction extends the logic of his having been made invisible: "I just felt like . . . I wished somebody could not see me so I could kill them. I just felt like killing all the white people in the world."[18]

Griffith's film, which would be used as a recruiting tool by the Clan later in the decade, sparked a vigorous campaign by the National Association for the Advancement of Colored People to have it banned. Though the campaign ultimately did not succeed, the film was in fact banned in eighteen states and numerous cities and the campaign did bring about some cuts. However, for every mayor who banned the film out of respect for blacks or a desire to keep the peace, there were, as Jane Gaines tells us, others who did so for its depiction of interracial sex (Gaines 2000). One thing is clear, however: Griffith's film was more incendiary, more racially hateful in its consequences, more likely to produce the phenomenon of race riot (which more often than not meant whites attacking blacks) than Dixon's novels and play. But the reason may not only lie in the greater lust of his Lynch or the greater violence of missing sequences. At a deeper level its effectiveness as race hatred, its ability to make William Walker impotently despair of ever being counted and to resolve that the only possibly effective reaction would be, like Senator Ben Tillman, to "kill! kill! kill!" in turn lies in Griffith's greater willingness to deploy the familiar features of the Tom material. For it was Griffith, not Dixon, who ultimately created the most effective counter to the Tom story. He did so by refunctioning the enormous emotional appeal of the antebellum story of the old South into a new kind of racial melodrama. [. . .]

Notes

1. According to Kevin Brownlow, what Wilson actually said was, "I congratulate you on an excellent production" (1992, documentary film, *D. W. Griffith, Father of Film*).
2. Interestingly, however, when abundant evidence of a prior racial mixing by white men and black women slaves is brought up in the novel, Dixon's spokespersons are unconcerned. This particular mongrelization is simply the "result of the surviving polygamous and lawless instincts of the white male" (Dixon 1903, 336). Thus Dixon minimizes the scandal of the infusion of white male blood (and semen) into black women while maximizing the horror of the infusion of black blood (and semen) into white women. The mix of "blood" thus only threatens white racial integrity. The black woman has no racial or sexual integrity to violate. As for the white woman: "The South must guard with flaming sword every avenue of approach to this holy of holies" (Dixon 1903, 336).
3. Robyn Wiegman (1995, 198) argues that Tom is released from the confines of his black masculine body in order to be "ushered into Stowe's humanizing agencies of the feminine." [. . .] On the stage there was no release from corporeal presence, and this was at least one reason for the advanced age of a great many stage Uncle Toms.
4. As Robyn Wiegman argues, to the white supremacist male the threat of masculine sameness posited by the enfranchising of the black man was "so terrifying that only the reassertion of a gendered difference can provide the necessary disavowal" (Wiegman 1995, 90).
5. Jacquelyn Dowd Hall observes that rumors and descriptions of interracial rape became a kind of "acceptable folk pornography" in the heyday of southern lynching (1993, 150). On the evidence of Dixon's novel, it would seem that this folk pornography was much more titillating to viewers in its evocations of the lascivious black male than any picture of his contact with the white woman.
6. *The Leopard's Spots* sold over a hundred thousand copies within a few months; *The Clansman* sold more than a million within a few months. Both books established the fortunes of the publishing house that would become Doubleday (Cook 1968, 112; Williamson 1984, 172). Neither book rivaled the success of *Uncle Tom's Cabin* but, as we shall see, the combined novels' "leap" into the new medium of film would accomplish the challenge to Stowe that Dixon had so fervently desired.

7. Reviews in the South were often wildly enthusiastic. However, one Chattanooga editor called it a "riot breeder . . . designed to excite rage and race hatred" and Dixon's own father, upon seeing the play in Shelby, North Carolina, found it "too hard on the Negro" (Cook 1968, 103, 149).

8. In one speech he said the following: "My object is to teach the north, the young north, what it has never known—the awful suffering of the white man during the dreadful reconstruction period. I believe that Almighty God anointed the white men of the south by their suffering during that time immediately after the Civil War to demonstrate to the world that the white man shall be supreme" (Cook 1968, 140).

9. Reviews in the North were decidedly mixed. In his autobiography, D. W. Griffith called the play "a terrible frost." In fact, it did respectable business. It so happened that the New York run of *The Clansman* coincided with a mass fund-raiser for Booker T. Washington's Tuskegee Institute, held at Carnegie Hall. Newspapers reportedly made much of the melodramatic opposition between the crowds gathered to cheer the negrophobic play and the crowds at Carnegie Hall gathered to support the uplift of Negroes. Dixon sent Washington a note offering to donate ten thousand dollars to the institute if Washington would declare at the meeting that he did not seek social equality and that his school was opposed to racial amalgamation. Washington declined to answer and Dixon continued his attack in a speech the following week: "We must remove the negro or we will have to fight him. He will not continue to submit to the injustice with which we treat him in the North and South. The negro makes a magnificent fighting animal. . . . When the negro smashes into your drawing room . . . his flat nostrils dilated, his yellow eyes and teeth gleaming, you will make good on your protestations of absolute equality or he will know the reason why" (Cook 1968, 147).

10. Indeed, when a shark attack killed the leading man when the company was swimming at a beach in North Carolina, Dixon eagerly took over the role of Ben Cameron with some success.

11. Variations of the phrase occur repeatedly in his novels. For example, the "ark of the covenant of American ideals rests [in] the South . . . From these poverty stricken homes, with their old fashioned, perhaps medieval ideas, will come forth the fierce athletic sons and sweet-voiced daughters in whom the nation will find a new birth!" (Dixon 1903, 337).

12. Rogin writes: "By cutting back and forth, Griffith juxtaposed events separated in time (the flashback) and space (the cutback) and collapsed the distinctions between images in the head and events in the world. By speeding up, reversing, and stopping time, he brought the past into the present. . . . By juxtaposing events widely separated in space, he overcame barriers of distance (barriers overcome in the film plot by the ride to the rescue). Griffith created an art of simultaneities and juxtapositions rather than traditions and continuities" (Rogin 1984, 199).

13. Griffith had already sketched the pathos side of this updating of the Tom-like "faithful soul" portrait in his Biograph two-reeler, *His Trust* and *His Trust Fulfilled* (1911). The two-part film tells the story of a (blackface) slave who pledges his trust to protect the family of a master who goes off to fight the Civil War. Faithful to his trust, he cares for the mother and daughter, giving the daughter a ride on his back like a horse and caring for their every need. When the father is killed and Union soldiers burn and loot the house, he risks his life to save first the daughter and then the father's sword. He then offers his "little cabin" as their home, sleeping on its doorstep like a guard dog. In the film's second part, "emancipation" shows all the slaves but George running away. When the daughter's mother dies, George becomes her only protector, sacrificing all his "savings" to place her in a nice home, paying a lawyer who pretends the money comes from the girl's estate. When George offers to shake the lawyer's hand, the lawyer refuses, making the exchange of money replace the handshake. Later, when the daughter wants to go away to school, George gives "the last of his savings." Now in rags, George is tempted to steal from the lawyer for the girl. Thinking better of it, he is nevertheless caught and chastised by the lawyer. When the girl finally marries, George, still in rags, and not a guest at the wedding, congratulates her, hobbles home to his cabin, and strokes the white father's sword. His only reward for a life of sacrifice is the arrival of the lawyer at his cabin who now offers the hand that was earlier refused. George smiles.

14. The abolitionist senator Charles Sumner, portrayed visiting Austin Stoneman in Griffith's film, once said that without *Uncle Tom's Cabin* there would have been no Lincoln in the White House (Whicher 1963, 563; Hanne 1994, 77).

15. It is possible that this, too, is the result of cuts made in the film after its release. Seymour Stern asserts that a scene showing "the actual rape of *Flora* by *Gus*, on the rock" was eliminated, along with scenes of Negro rapists whisking white women into doorways and back alleys of Piedmont. Eliminated also, according to Stern, was the indirectly depicted castration of Gus, an epilogue featuring Lincoln's statement opposing racial equality, and images of the deportation of masses of Negroes from New York

Harbor to the jungles of Africa. In all, Stern claims that the film was cut from 1,544 shots in the first Liberty Theater run to the 1,375 shots of the 12½ reels in the present version (Stern 1965, 66). I am inclined to doubt that Griffith ever showed an "actual rape" on the rock, though he may have intimated this rape by indirect means.

16. Critics have understandably made much of actor Walter Long's portrayal of Gus, citing his unnatural hunched-over, bestial walk and run and his frothing lips caused by swilling hydrogen peroxide, during his pursuit of Flora (see Rogin 1984, Taylor 1991, Robinson 1997). Despite the bestial pose, however, there is nothing in the scene as now played that insinuates his sexual intentions toward Flora. The Lynch/Elsie scene, on the other hand, is remarkably lascivious.

17. Lindsay (1915, 152–53) writes that "white leader, Col. Ben Cameron . . . enters not as an individual, but as representing the white Anglo Saxon Niagara. . . . The wrath of the Southern against the blacks and their Northern organizers has been piled up through many previous scenes. As a result this rescue is a real climax, something photoplays that trace strictly personal hatreds cannot achieve."

18. Walker says this as an old man in an on-camera interview in Kevin Brownlow and David Gill's 1992 documentary, *D. W. Griffith, the Father of Film*. We do not know what precise version of the film Walker saw.

Bibliography

Karl Brown, *Adventures with D. W. Griffith* (London: Martin Secker and Warburg, 1973).

Raymond Allen Cook, *Fire from the Flint: The Amazing Careers of Thomas Dixon* (Winston-Salem, NC: John F. Blair, 1968).

Thomas Dixon, Jr, *The Leopard's Spots: A Romance of the White Man's Burden* (New York: Doubleday, 1903).

Thomas Dixon, Jr, *The Clansman: An Historical Romance of the Ku Klux Klan*, 1905 (repr., Lexington: University Press of Kentucky, 1970).

Jacquelyn Dowd Hall, *Revolt against Chivalry: Jesse Daniel Ames and the Women's Campaign against Lynching* (New York: Columbia University Press, 1993).

Jane Gaines, *Fire and Desire: Mixed Race Movies in the Silent Era* (Chicago: University of Chicago Press, 2000).

Michael Hanne, *The Power of the Story: Fiction and Political Change* (Providence: Berghahn Books, 1994).

Thomas Hart ed., *The Man Who Invented Hollywood: The Autobiography of D. W. Griffith* (Louisville: Touchstone Publishing, 1972).

Vachel Lindsay, *The Art of the Moving Picture* (New York: Macmillan, 1915).

Cedric J. Robinson, "In the Year 1915: D. W. Griffith and the Whitening of America," *Social Identities: Journal for the Study of Race, Nation and Culture* 3:2 (1997).

Michael Rogin, " 'The Sword Became a Flashing Vision': D.W. Griffith's *Birth of a Nation*," 1984, in *Ronald Reagan, the Movie, and Other Episodes in Political Demonology* (Berkeley: University of California Press, 1987).

Seymour Stern, "Griffith I: *The Birth of a Nation*," *Film Culture* 36 (Spring–Summer, 1965).

Harriet Beecher Stowe, *Uncle Tom's Cabin; or, Life Among the Lowly*, ed. Ann Douglas. 1852. (repr., New York: Penguin American Library, 1983).

Clyde Taylor, "The Re-Birth of the Aesthetic in Cinema," *Wide Angle* 13:3–4 (July–October 1991).

George Whicher, "Literature and Conflict," in Robert Spiller ed., *The Literary History of the United States* (London: Macmillan, 1963).

Robyn Wiegman, *American Anatomies: Theorizing Race and Gender* (Durham, NC: Duke University Press, 1995).

Joel Williamson, *The Crucible of Race: Black–White Relations in the American South Since Emancipation* (New York: Oxford University Press, 1984).

Chapter 15

KRISTIN THOMPSON

THE INTERNATIONAL EXPLORATION
OF CINEMATIC EXPRESSIVITY

IT HAS COMMONLY BEEN ASSUMED that during the 1910s, cinematic techniques developed in the directions of clarity and expressivity. This change occurred mainly in the USA, Italy, and Scandinavia. In most histories, the notions of clarity and expressivity are combined. Here I would like to distinguish between these two concepts and try to suggest how and when expressivity rose to be a common goal of filmmakers.

I am assuming that many techniques of early cinema were introduced in order to assure narrative clarity. A cut-in could reveal a vital detail of a scene that would not be visible in the more distant establishing view. Cutting back and forth between two or more spaces implied strongly that the separate actions were occurring simultaneously. Eyeline matches showed that nearby spaces were visible to the characters. Shot/reverse shots established that people were face to face. As we are now well aware, by 1917, these techniques were firmly in place in the Hollywood filmmaking establishment. Indeed, the influence of these techniques quickly spread around much of the globe.

I suspect that by around 1912, enough of these techniques were in place that many filmmakers were able to tell stories clearly. At about this time, some directors went further, exploring the expressive possibilities of the medium.

I am using the term 'expressivity' broadly and simply here, to mean those functions of cinematic devices that go beyond presenting basic narrative information and add some quality to the scene that would not be strictly necessary to our comprehension of it. In many cases such expressive devices were included in order to deepen the spectator's emotional involvement in the action. Increased suspense during a chase, deeper sympathy for a character in distress, awe over the sudden revelation of a spectacular setting – such tactics could push the spectator beyond comprehension to fascination.

Traditional historians have typically assumed that the growing sophistication of the cinema in this period lay in its move from a theatre-based art form to a more independent, 'cinematic' art. For years, this led to an emphasis on those techniques which most seemed to separate cinema from the stage – primarily editing and camera movement. Those films which employed distant framings, a static camera, painted sets, and/or long takes were considered to be backward. Thus, D. W. Griffith became the hero of the tale of editing's evolution, *Cabiria* was the landmark film for popularizing camera movement, and the Swedes were valued for taking the camera out into nature.

Figures 15.1–15.5 Ingeborg Holm

In fact, the exploration of expressivity encompassed a great many techniques, including long takes, distant framings, and the static camera. These devices may have superficially seemed the same as techniques used in earlier films, but they gained functions in the 1910s that made them part of the new expressive repertoire of filmmaking.

One example should clarify what I mean by expressivity. In many cases, the most celebrated stylistic innovations of the early cinema were designed to make objects, characters, gestures, and other aspects of the mise-en-scène more clearly visible. These included closer framings and cut-ins. Yet by the early teens, some films actually contain devices designed to make the action *less* visible. Victor Sjöström's 1913 masterpiece *Ingeborg Holm* contains a deceptively simple shot that uses such a tactic. The heroine has been reduced to poverty and is living with her family in a poorhouse. Her son is leaving with his new foster mother, and Ingeborg goes into the yard before the door to see him off. The action is staged in depth in a single take, without a cut-in to any of the characters; Ingeborg's back remains turned to the camera during most of the shot; no camera movements or intertitles are employed. The boy repeatedly turns to embrace her, unable to tear himself away, while the guard at the rear opens the gate for the pair (Fig. 15.1). Finally, Ingeborg ducks inside the door of the poorhouse while the boy is not looking (Fig. 15.2). Turning back, he sees that she is gone (Fig. 15.3) and resignedly turns to go (Fig. 15.4). Once they have gone and the gate is closed, Ingeborg re-emerges; the guard moves to catch her as she begins to faint (Fig. 15.5).

It is easy to imagine how this scene would have been staged only a few years earlier. The poorhouse would probably have been a painted drop or flats, seen straight-on facing the door. It would have occupied most of the back wall, with the gate visible, also frontally, at the side and a painted cityscape or landscape glimpsed beyond it. The characters would have emerged from the door toward the front, and the action would have moved back and forth in a shallow space, with their faces visible.

Despite its lack of 'progressive' techniques, the shot in *Ingeborg Holm* uses deep staging and setting in a way which distinguishes it considerably from earlier usage. Logically, it would seem that hiding a central character's facial expressions would detract from narrative clarity. Yet by putting Ingeborg's back to us, Sjöström displays an awareness that a de-emphasis on her facial expression could actually enhance our sense of her anguish and the poignancy of the moment. Similarly, the facade of the poorhouse is less clearly visible than it would be if filmed straight-on. The perspective of the set as filmed, however, emphasizes the gateway as the backdrop of the action and also allows the pair to exit quickly to the left outside the gate, placing the emphasis in the final portion of the shot on Ingeborg's breakdown. The oblique, off-center view of the doorway also makes it a more startling moment when Ingeborg suddenly ducks inside. Clearly, Sjöström has felt confident enough of his story-telling abilities to exchange a certain amount of redundant clarity for enhanced expressivity.

Similar explorations of the expressive possibilities of the cinema were going on in many countries simultaneously during the 1910s. I think that relatively few of these explorations involved direct influence. Similar impulses to use depth or to move the camera or to shoot into mirrors seem to have surfaced independently within different national cinemas.

It is particularly significant that this process was occurring largely during the First World War. Although in the key early years, especially 1913 and 1914, films were still circulating freely, by the middle of the war some markets were largely cut off. In particular, Scandinavia, Germany, and Russia had far less access to French and Italian films, which had dominated world markets before the war. By 1916, Hollywood films were becoming dominant in many parts of the world, such as South America, Australasia, the United Kingdom, and some parts of Western Europe. As domestic industries developed, distinctive styles were able to flourish briefly. A vivid demonstration of one such distinctive national style can be seen in 1910s Russian films. The characteristic slowly paced melodramatic plots, the emphasis on virtuosic acting, and the tragic endings all indicate a cinema in which expressivity far outstrips simple narrative clarity. The war, coming just at a time when continuity guidelines were becoming well established, discouraged the sort of international uniformity that might otherwise have developed. Instead, the disruptions in the international circulation of films at this crucial time probably encouraged the astonishing variety that characterizes the 1910s cinema.

The international spread of continuity devices

Before examining the great variety of expressive techniques explored in 1910s cinema, I shall briefly show that basic guidelines for narrative clarity were indeed picked up widely by film-makers around the world. That familiarity with standard storytelling devices may well have been what allowed venturesome film-makers to manipulate techniques for expressive purposes.

Given how few films of the silent era survive from most of the period's small producing countries, it is difficult to make firm generalizations about stylistic influences. Still, enough examples do exist to suggest that many film-makers around the globe quickly absorbed the lessons of early continuity practice and used them to create clear narratives.

In 1913, the earliest Indian fiction feature film made by an Indian director was released. Only about half of D.G. Phalke's *Raja Harishandra* survives, but it displays a distinct knowledge of continuity. Indeed, it is comparable stylistically to films made contemporaneously in the USA by some independent firms. It uses consistent screen direction, as when the king walks rightward through the forest and, in a cut to a contiguous space, arrives at the hut of the villainous sage. In a scene where the king stands talking with his wife, the framing follows the convention of the nine-foot line or *plan americain*.

Shot/reverse shot seems also to have spread quickly, though not all film-makers grasped it completely at first. An Argentinian film of 1917, *Ul Ultimo Malon* ('The Last Indian Attack', directed by Alcides Greca) contains an editing pattern that I have not encountered in any other film. The scene, an argument between a father and daughter, begins with an establishing long shot of the pair and a dialogue intertitle returning to the long shot. A cut moves to a close three-quarter view of the father, looking left. We might expect a balancing view of the daughter, but instead the next shot returns to the establishing view. Yet the next shot provides us with the expected three-quarter frontal view of the daughter, facing right. Without the intervening long shot, the two close views would create a standard shot/reverse shot. After the close view of the daughter, there is another re-establishing long shot. It is perhaps relevant that American films began to be widely distributed in Argentina in 1916. This may be a rare case where we can see a filmmaker in an undeveloped country who has only partially adapted a convention of mainstream cinema. Possibly, the director of *Ul Ultimo Malon* had seen films with shot/reverse shot and wished to use this device without understanding that the close shots could be edited together without re-establishing shots in between.

Other somewhat unorthodox uses of shot/reverse shot are evident in the late 1910s. In a 1918 Hungarian film directed by Sándor (later Alexander) Korda, *Az Aranyember* ('Man of Gold'), there are a few attempts at shot/reverse shot. In one scene, three characters are visible in medium-long shot (Fig. 15.6). The woman at the left is only partially visible, but she appears prominently at the right in the next shot, which is essentially only a lateral cut to the left with a move closer to the figures (Fig. 15.7). In a later scene, however, *Az Aranyember* contains a shot/reverse shot cut with conventional framing.

Surprisingly, in at least one case shot/reverse shot had an impact in Russia very quickly. The Russian retrospective at the Pordenone festival of 1989 showed us a cinema that was largely untouched by Hollywood influences. Yet Lev Kuleshov was able to use contemporary continuity techniques with great skill in his 1918 film *Proekt Inzhenera Praita* ('Engineer Prite's Project'). One of the fragments that survive contains a scene that would do credit to a Hollywood director of the same date.[1] A woman drops an object from a first-floor window; an establishing shot on the sidewalk below shows two men, including Prite, noticing it; a cut-in shows Prite picking the object up; there is a match on action as he straightens up and looks toward the woman; a perfectly executed reverse shot shows her looking down at him. Some

Figures 15.6–15.7 Az Aranyember

intertitles are missing at this point, but the scene continues in continuity style as she comes down to meet the two men.

Such continuity techniques spread through the dissemination of Hollywood films. Similarly, the fact that certain countries were cut off from the American supply during the war helps explain why distinctive stylistic practices arose.

Mise-en-scène

● *Acting*   In *The Classical Hollywood Cinema*, I argued that the early pantomime style of film acting was quite efficient at telegraphing a good deal of narrative information in a short time. With the advent of feature films, film-makers quickly realized that it would be possible to linger over actors' reactions in closer framings. This lingering would not necessarily convey any new narrative information; instead, it added an emotional charge to the scene. By the mid-1910s, a key moment in the story would be allotted a virtuosic bit of acting, often with its own beginning, middle, and end. In *Weisse Rosen* ('White Roses', 1916, Urban Gad) the Asta Nielsen character receives a letter from her lover in which he wrongly accuses her of being a thief. She reads it (Fig. 15.8), reacts in disbelief (Fig. 15.9), reads it again, crumples it, then reads it a third time before slowly slumping down, despairing (Fig. 15.10). A similar three-part reaction occurs in *The Birth of a Nation* as the Little Sister, played by Mae Marsh, trims her dress with cotton in imitation of ermine. At first she is pleased, then loses her smile as she realizes what a poor imitation it is, and finally seems near tears.

As the example from *Ingeborg Holm* indicated, film-makers also realized that withholding such explicit depictions of emotion could also be effective. The homecoming scene in *The Birth of a Nation*, in which the Little Colonel leans into the doorway to embrace his off-screen mother, is only the most famous case where a highly emotional scene is partially blocked in order to heighten its impact. Numerous other films of the era use similar techniques. In Paul von Woringen's 1913 film, *Die Landstrasse* ('The Country Road'), an escaped convict has committed a murder, but a passing tramp has been arrested and falsely convicted. The trial scene ends as the court-room empties and we see the convict, his back to the camera. He moves to speak with a lawyer, but the lack of information about his reaction leads to greater suspense on the part of the audience. Also in 1915, Cecil B. DeMille's *The Warrens of Virginia* shows Blanche Sweet from behind as she strikes on the door of a room where, it is

Figures 15.8–15.10   Weisse Rosen

implied, her lover may be trying to shoot himself. The action begins in long shot as she pounds (Fig. 15.11). The film's first cut-in moves straight in, still showing her from behind (Fig. 15.12), and the camera tilts down as she slides to her knees in despair (Fig. 15.13). Here cut-in and tilt seem to offer us new narrative information, but in fact we can see little more than if the action had continued in long shot. Clearly the camera does not move around to show, say, a profile view that would reveal her expression because DeMille felt that the understatement would intensify the gesture's affect.

Film-makers also occasionally strove for the opposite effect, emphasizing facial expression by having actors move toward the camera while staring into the lens. The earliest case I know of occurs in *The Musketeers of Pig Alley* (1912, D.W. Griffith), where the Snapper Kid moves into looming close-up. The effect goes far beyond the demands of narrative clarity; it functions to create a sense of menace. Most if not all of the other examples I have found use the technique for the same purpose. Early in Phillips Smalley's *Suspense* (1913), the heroine looks from an upper window and sees a tramp on her doorstep. Here his threatening glance into the lens is motivated as her point of view. Later, however, he moves up the stairs and toward the lens, while the wife hides in a nearby room. Now the menace seems directed at us without showing us anything she can see. The effect is perhaps comparable to the novelty medium shot of a cowboy firing a gun at the camera in *The Great Train Robbery* (1903, Edwin S. Porter), but by now the startling threat has been made part of the diegesis.

Figures 15.11–15.13 The Warrens of Virginia

Not surprisingly, then, we find characters staring into the lens in shot/reverse-shot situations during fights. In John Ford's *Straight Shooting* (1917), the hero's glance off camera right leads to a reverse close view of his opponent looking straight out. In Maurice Tourneur's *The Last of the Mohicans* (released in 1920), a knife duel between two Indians is handled with each of them staring into the lens.

● *Mirrors* Perhaps one of the most conspicuous ways in which film-makers sought to strengthen the impact of scenes was by shooting into mirrors. In A.W. Sandberg's 1917 Danish film, *Klovnen* ('Clowns'), the hero is onstage with a large mirror that reflects an unseen curtain. The curtain rises to reveal his lover embracing another man (Fig. 15.14), at which point he smashes the mirror. Here the space of the scene is perhaps a trifle convoluted, but the revelation is dramatized by the centered mirror.

An extraordinarily complex use of a mirror occurs in Gad's *Weisse Rosen*. In one shot we see the heroine Thilda standing by a mirror, then placing a bouquet of roses on the table beneath it as she joins some friends.[2] A cutaway shows two detectives searching Thilda's room for a diamond they think she has stolen. A return to the mirror shows the real thief, Kenley, slipping the jewel case into her bouquet; we glimpse Thilda in the mirror, her back turned so that she cannot see this gesture. Kenley leaves the shot, and people mill about; we then see Thilda and Kenley moving leftward in the mirror, and they soon enter the shot from the right.

Kenley hands Thilda the bouquet, and they exit in opposite directions. Almost immediately the two detectives enter, and they split up to follow Kenley and Thilda. One could hardly ask for a better example of a scene in which narrative clarity is sacrificed in order to engage the viewer's attention more forcefully.

Films of this era found a great variety of ways to use mirrors. In Erich von Stroheim's *Blind Husbands* (1919), the heroine's view of her sleeping husband in a mirror leads to a rack focus to her face and triggers a fantasy of a romantic lover. Yermoliev's *L'Anoissante Aventure* (1919) contains a disorienting shot which apparently begins as a straightforward image of the hero and heroine, then seems to slide vertiginously as the side of a mirror appears, revealing a group of filmmakers using a shiny reflector while on location.[3] Mirrors, with their reversal of relations among objects, provided an obvious way of undercutting spectators' understanding of scenes.

● *Lighting*   Changes in lighting practice during the 1910s have been studied quite extensively. The focus has been on the shift from general, flat lighting – mainly dependent on sunlight – to highly selective 'effects' lighting based on artificial light. Intuitively, one might expect this to have been a gradual process. Filmmakers might have started with flat lighting, then gradually adopted more selective techniques. They might then have worked up to the stark low-key lighting characteristic of 'Lasky light' as exemplified by *The Cheat* (1915, Hector Turnbull).

Instead, many film-makers quickly hit upon an occasional alternative to flat frontal lighting: stark backlit silhouettes. Many of the most striking films of the 1910s create silhouettes using available light, whether indoors or in the open air. In most cases, such lighting seems to function generally to enhance the emotional impact of the scene.

Thomas H. Ince's *The Indian Massacre* (1912), ends with a dramatic view of an Indian mother mourning her baby (Fig. 15.15). Films of 1913 and 1914 are full of such shots. *Atlantis* (August Blom, 1913) places its hero against a bright seascape in the shipboard scene. Léonce Perret's early features *L'Enfant de Paris* (1913) and *Roman d'un Mouse* ('Tale of a Cabin Boy', 1914) contain several famous examples of silhouette lighting against doors and windows. In Benjamin Christensen's *Det Hemmelighedsfulde X* ('The Mysterious X', 1913), some scenes contain dramatic silhouette effects (Fig. 15.16). The same is true of his *Haevens Nat* ('Night of Revenge', 1916). In the USA, Maurice Tourneur increasingly used silhouette effects in his films, as in this shot from *The Last of the Mohicans* (Fig. 15.17).

By the middle of the decade, however, film-makers were creating somewhat comparable silhouette shots in the studio using artificial light. Forest Holger-Madsen's 1915 Danish film, *Evangeliedmandens* ('The Evangelist'), contains a complex set with a detailed miniature cityscape model outside the window.[4] Careful backlighting creates several striking silhouette compositions. In the same year, DeMille's *The Cheat* used stark backlighting as a motif. In one scene, the heroine and villain listen through a Japanese paper screen as the lights go on in the next room, and the shadows of two figures appear on the screen. Later, the shooting of the villain is handled with a stark spotlight picking him out against a screen[5]; a cut to the other side of the screen reveals his shadow; the heroine's husband enters and reacts in shock as he realizes that the villain has been wounded. Such silhouette views using artificial light continued to be used in the next few years, as in this dramatic scene from John Collins' *The Girl without a Soul* (1917, Fig. 15.18).

During the same period, 'effects' lighting, where the light comes from a source within the scene, was also being introduced. The scene from *The Girl without a Soul* suggests that all the light comes from the single lamp visible at the rear. The main motivation for such lighting

Figure 15.14 Klovnen

Figure 15.15 The Indian Massacre

Figure 15.16 Det Hemmelighedsfulde X

Figure 15.17 The Last of the Mohicans

Figure 15.18 The Girl without a Soul

Figure 15.19 Homunculus

seems to be realism. In many cases, however, the stark silhouette composition seems to have stood out as something more extreme than mere effects lighting. Silhouettes retained their expressive impact despite the development of other forms of selective illumination.

● *Sets and Staging*   During the 1910s, set design was of course becoming more elaborate. The move toward features permitted higher budgets for individual films. Several sets from Nordisk's epic production *Atlantis* serve a straightforward narrative purpose of portraying the home of the protagonist, a sculptor; it also, however, shows evidence of a concern with pictorial beauty that is almost distracting in relation to the ongoing action.[6] Some filmmakers of this era consistently used elaborate sets that contribute little to narrative clarity but add considerable compositional interest; these include Georg af Klercker in Sweden, Evgenii Bauer in Russia, and Maurice Tourneur in the USA.

With the advent of longer narratives, some film-makers also increasingly tried to create parallelisms that would link scenes that might be widely separated temporarily. Echoes within the settings provided a simple way of doing this. For example, von Woringen's *Die Landstrasse* consistently compared the escaped convict who commits a murder and the tramp who is accused of the crime. The two wander about the same village, but are almost never seen in the same space until the film's end. Yet motifs of setting and staging connect them. Shortly after his escape, the convict pauses in a forest to eat something; considerably later there is an extraordinary long take in which the tramp, having bought a loaf and stolen some meat, walks slowly from the background in a similar setting, then sits in the foreground and eats his meal. I should note that there is no particular reason in the plot why the film should visually compare the two men, who are actually quite different. The parallelisms, however, emphasize the irony of the mistaken accusation of the tramp.

● *Depth*   There had been many cases of staging in depth before 1912.[7] These were used mainly for moving characters from one space to another and for situations where the action demands it, as when a character in a foreground room eavesdrops on others in a room beyond. By 1912, however, depth shots seemed to be used occasionally for more expressive purposes, and in situations where it would have been possible to stage the scene in other ways.

A motif of deep staging could serve to create parallels across a film. Victor Sjöström's 1912 short feature, *Trädgardmästeren* (released in the USA as 'The Broken Spring Rose'), uses several striking stagings to stress the moments when the heroine is reunited with or must part from the young man she loves: the early scene of his return sets up this motif as the heroine stands with her back to the camera by the dock[8]; later, the couple bid each other goodbye as the young man's father stands by that same dock in the background; in the next shot she waves as the ferry departs; the motif culminates near the end, as the heroine herself returns to her home, and the camera again places her in the foreground, but this time on the ferry approaching the dock.

These examples all take place outdoors. One of the most common uses of deep staging, however, places a character in the foreground of a set, looking at someone in the background. A typical example would be a shot from *Dodspring til hest fra Circus-kuplen* (1912, Eduard Schnedler-Sørensen).[9] Similarly, the looking character could be placed in the distant background, as in this shot from *Homunculus* (Fig. 15.19, 1916, Otto Rippert). Such depth shots look quite dramatic to us today, but they are so common in the early to mid-1910s that I suspect they originally functioned to convey the same information that the eyeline match was soon to fulfill more frequently. That is, filmmakers who needed to show clearly that one character was watching another but who did not yet know about glance-object editing could employ this sort of depth staging.

During the 1910s, however, many filmmakers began to use this device of deep staging in a new way, placing a curtain in the foreground which the character or someone else pulls aside. Here I suspect the purpose is more to create a dramatic revelation of a new space than simply to show that a character is looking at something else. In *Fabiola*, a 1917 Italian film (Enrico Guazzoni), the villain moves into the foreground (Fig. 15.20) and furtively parts the curtains to spy on the heroine (Fig. 15.21). By this point in film history, the eyeline match technique was presumably becoming known among filmmakers internationally. Yet here the depth shot remains as a sort of flourish for the presentation of a new set.

This function is quite clearly present in *Madame Dubarry* (1919, Ernst Lubitsch). Early in the film, scenes take place in the millinery shop, in the streets, or in modest apartments. Here the heroine goes for the first time to dine with a wealthy man. She pauses expectantly by a curtain (Fig. 15.22), which is then drawn aside by an unseen hand, revealing the first of the film's many rich interiors (Fig. 15.23). The fact that the man she has come to visit is not yet present in the room reinforces the notion that here staging in depth functions primarily to create spectacle.

Depth staging could also be used for other purposes. To give one brief example, the most famous shot from *Terje Vigen* ('A Man There Was', 1916, Victor Sjöström) juxtaposes the protagonist with the sea seen through a window as a storm is brewing. Here depth serves a poetic purpose, as part of a metaphorical linking of the tempestuous sea with Vigen's desire for revenge.

Camera movement

I shall say relatively little about camera movement, since this subject has been quite extensively researched. There had been earlier uses of expressive camera movement, as when in 1909 Griffith began and ended his Biograph short *The Country Doctor* with panning movements across a landscape. But *Cabiria* popularized camera movement in 1914 by using slow tracking movements that ordinarily did not follow characters but instead served to show off the deep, impressive sets. We might note that at least one other director of the same era was employing such tracking movements. Evgenii Bauer's *Ditya Bol'Shogo Goroda* ('Child of the Big City', released in early 1914, at about the same time as *cabiria*) tracks the camera slowly forward through the relatively large cabaret set (Fig. 15.24), dividing its attention between the heroine, at the right, and the stage beyond (Fig. 15.25).

Griffith used camera movement for a narrational comment on the action when in *The Birth of a Nation* he tilts down, while introducing the Cameron patriarch, to the puppies sprawled at his feet. He then emphasizes Cameron's kindliness by cutting in to a closer view of the animals. In *Intolerance*, he underlines the Dear One's shock after her husband's death sentence with a short track-in as she walks slowly toward the camera, until she is slightly out of focus and a slow fade-out begins.

Christensen's *Haevens Nat* provides a rare example of camera movement being used for shock effect. He frames a young woman in a house at night, reacting in terror to something she sees off right front; as she struggles to open the door, the camera pulls back, seemingly directly through the closed French doors and continues to draw away from her; the intruder suddenly appears as a silhouette, breaking in and rushing forward to seize her.[10] Such uses of expressive camera movement would be developed considerably by the French Impressionists and German film-makers in the 1920s.

Figures 15.20–15.21 Fabiola

Figures 15.22–15.23 Madame Dubarry

Figures 15.24–15.25 Ditya Bol'Shogo Goroda

Editing

Continuity editing emerged during the 1910s as a system for creating coherent narrative space and time. Surprisingly quickly, however, filmmakers discovered ways of using editing for authorial comment, for enhancing suspense, for creating parallelism, and even for disorienting the viewer for various purposes.

The ordinary cut-in had begun as a means for commenting on the action. In *Intolerance*, for example, the introduction of the French court includes a detail shot of a small attendant hiding a yawn, hinting at the court's stultifying pomp. *Intolerance* is famous as having emphasized the affecting detail, as when a general view of the Dear One collapsing after her child is taken away leads to a close view of the baby's bootie.

Another editing device that shows up occasionally in mid-1910s cinema is the expressive graphic match. In the scene of the gangster's death in *Intolerance*, Griffith cuts from the Boy, hunched on the floor, to the Dear One, in a similar posture. Presumably this cut functions partly to show why neither sees who fires the shot, but it also enhances the emotional tone of the scene by stressing their mutual helplessness. In *Terje Vigen*, Sjöström edits together a medium shot of several soldiers rowing (Fig. 15.26) and one of Vigen rowing as he tries to escape them (Fig. 15.27). The low framing and direction and rhythm of the gestures creates a graphic match that I think functions to add to the suspense.

The shot/reverse shot editing pattern became common practice during the 1910s. Quickly filmmakers found ways of enhancing the expressivity even of this staple device. For example, two scenes from very different sorts of films use shot/reverse shot to heighten the romantic overtones of their respective scenes. In *Oberg-Ejvind Och Hans Hustru* ('The Outlaw and His Wife', 1917), Sjöström presents the first meeting of Berg-Ejvind and Halla in an unusually extended series of shot/reverse shots. The fugitive Berg-Ejvind has just been hired as a servant on Halla's estate and carries a large trunk into a loft. Halla, seated at her desk, turns and sees him for the first time. These two will soon fall in love and flee together, and Sjöström dramatizes their meeting by lingering over it. A depth shot shows Berg-Ejvind in the loft, with Halla just visible below; a cut-in shows Halla turning and registering surprise at seeing the stranger; in reverse shot, he stares back at her. Despite the fact that there is neither dialogue nor significant movement, the next cut returns us to a shot of Halla continuing to stare; the next shot returns to the original depth framing but again simply shows the two staring at each other; finally, in a new reverse depth shot, Berg-Ejvind explains that he has been ordered to store the trunk in the loft.

A different approach occurs in Tourneur's *The Last of the Mohicans*. In this film the romantic attraction between Cora and Uncas is conveyed largely through their intense gazes at each other in shot/reverse shot. Tourneur shoots a scene between the two in a cave with each staring almost directly into the lens; each also has one arm up touching the roof of the cave (Figs. 15.28 and 15.29). This off-balance echo subtly compares them and underscores the romance.

● *The Long Take*   As I have suggested, traditional histories of the 1910s favor editing and camera movement. Long, static shots are seldom discussed as examples of 'progressive' style. Yet, as we saw with the example from *Ingeborg Holm*, the long take could be expressive. After all, there would have been no reason why film-makers of this era would feel compelled to use editing or camera movement to display their sophistication. They presumably felt free to explore all the possible techniques of the new art form.

Die Landstrasse provides a good example of a film which earlier historians might have dismissed as static and theatrical. We have seen how it uses nearly actionless shots to create

Figures 15.26–15.27 Terje Vigen

Figures 15.28–15.29 The Last of the Mohicans

Figures 15.30–15.31 Die Landstrasse

parallels between the convict and the tramp as they sit eating. The scene of the testimony concerning the murder and the questioning and arrest of the tramp takes place in a long take, as we watch the tramp react to the accusations (Figs. 15.30 and 15.31). Later, the climactic deathbed confession by the convict again occurs in a lengthy shot as the tramp again listens and responds.[11]

The opening scene of the German film *Der Student von Prag* ('The Student of Prague', 1913, Stellan Rye) consists of a single long take, staged in depth with reframing camera movements and interrupted by several expository intertitles. Balduin enters and sits dejectedly in the foreground, waving his friends away. His depression is emphasized as Lyduschka appears in the background and dances, watched by all the students except Balduin. Soon Scapinelli's coach pulls up in the middle ground, and he sits with Balduin; the pair are spied upon by Lyduschka, in the far left rear. She comes forward and watches worriedly as Balduin and Scapinelli strike their bargain. The camera pans right as the pair leave, still watched by the apprehensive Lyduschka. Again this seems to me a case that could be dismissed as primitive. Yet it could also be described as a complexly staged scene that sets up the basic narrative situation and uses depth and unexpected appearances from off-screen to heighten the impact of the action.

Even *The Birth of a Nation*, ordinarily considered important primarily for its virtuosic editing and camera movements, creates some of its most affecting moments in intricately staged static long takes. For example, the Cameron family's reaction to news of a son's death begins with all four characters clustered in the foreground. The older sister stares left, then turns her back to the camera as the Little Sister moves forward; at the same time, the mother moves to the sofa and collapses on it. The others then move to cluster around her. Exactly the same framing is used later in this set for a similar shot: as her parents and sister watch, the Little Sister gives away her last good dress to help the Southern cause; Cameron chides her for doing so; the others turn and move away, the older sister to the sofa, the parents out left rear while we focus on the Little Sister's wistful expression; finally, she cheers up a bit and moves to display her dress to her sister before the two embrace on the sofa. I would argue that, far from being mundane, old-fashioned handlings of these scenes, such static takes effectively concentrate on the emotions of the whole family. Moreover, by making the scenes so similar, a nostalgic echo is created that enhances the emotional impact of the family's declining fortunes.

Conclusions

These examples are, I hope, enough to give some sense of the breadth and variety of techniques explored during the 1910s for their expressive possibilities. We tend to think of the 1920s as the period in which an 'art cinema' arose in the form of avant-garde stylistic movements like German Expressionism, French Impressionism, and Soviet Montage. Yet I would suggest that the period from approximately 1913 to 1919 saw the creation of the basis of what would later come to be seen as artistic cinema.

At the war's end, films began again to circulate more freely internationally. Some observers recognized that national approaches to cinema had emerged during the past few years. Louis Delluc was perhaps one of the earliest to comment on this phenomenon. When *The Outlaw and His Wife* appeared in France in 1919, he praised it highly and commented:

> We know what the factory of American beauty has produced. Charlie Chaplin sums up six years of creative activity with his genius. But are the Americans alone? Soon you will get to see how carefully and attentively the Russians, Norwegians [sic], and

Germans have been working. Here is one instance of this worldwide effort, in which France still comes in last: *The Outlaw and His Wife*.[12]

The premiere of *Das Cabinet des Dr. Caligari* in Paris in late 1921 revealed the new German movement. During the 1920s, histories of national cinemas appeared, including two book-length studies of Soviet film and special issues of journals which contained individual essays on Scandinavian, French, German, Soviet, American, and Italian cinema.

One thing that fascinates us in the films made in the era before 1913 is the struggle to create means of ensuring narrative clarity. For the period from 1913 to the end of the 1910s, the main fascination that films hold for us may well be the search for enhanced expressive means. The 1920s then become the decade in which modernism entered the cinema, expanding the new art form's possibilities in even bolder directions.

References

The original presentation of this paper involved a great many slides of frames from films of the 1910s. The editors of this volume have allowed me a generous sampling of those illustrations. In cutting, I deleted virtually all images from films that are available in the USA in either 16mm or video. I have also added references directing the reader to publications that reproduce frame enlargements from the examples used here. I am grateful to the following people and film sources: Gabrielle Claes and the Cinémathèque Royale de Belgique, BFI Distribution, the National Film and Television Archive, Donald Crafton and the Wisconsin Center for Film and Theater Research, Mark-Paul Meyer and the Nederlands Filmmuseum, and Jan-Christopher Horak, Paolo Cherchi Usai, and the International Museum of Photography at George Eastman House.

Notes

1 For illustrations of this scene, see David Bordwell and Kristin Thompson, *Film History: An Introduction*, New York: McGraw-Hill, 1994, p. 130.
2 For an illustration of the opening shot of this scene, see *Film History*, p. 58.
3 For illustrations of three stages of this shot, see Kristin Thompson, 'The Ermolieff Group in Paris: Exile, Impressionism, Internationalism', *Griffithiana* 35/36, October 1989, p. 48, Figs. 4–6.
4 *Film History*, Fig. 3.15, p. 64.
5 Ibid., Fig. 3.38, p. 73.
6 Ibid., Fig. 3.14, p. 63.
7 Ben Brewster, 'Deep Staging in French Films 1900–1914', Thomas Elsaesser (ed.), *Early Cinema: Space, Frame, Narrative*, London: BFI Publishing, 1990, pp. 45–55, and the early chapters of Barry Salt's *Film Style & Technology: History & Analysis*, London: Starword, 1983.
8 Three frame enlargements illustrate stages of this scene in John Fullerton, 'Spatial and articulation in pre-classical Swedish film', *Early Cinema*, p. 383.
9 See *Film History*, Fig. 2.8, p. 30.
10 For illustrations of two stages of this shot, see *Film History*, Figs. 3.17 and 3.18, p. 64.
11 *Film History*, Fig. 3.2, p. 57.
12 Louis Delluc, 'Cinema: *The Outlaw and His Wife*', Richard Abel, *French Film Theory and Criticism 1907–1939*, vol. 1, Princeton, NJ: Princeton University Press, 1988, p. 188.

PART V

Classical Hollywood cinema

INTRODUCTION

L ATE IN 1925 A FRENCH REVIEWER of Chaplin's film *Pay Day* (First National, 1922) described it as representative of a 'cinematic classicism'. Likewise, French film-maker Jean Renoir spoke in 1926 of Chaplin and others as contributors to a 'classical cinema' of the future, 'where the smallest detail takes its place of importance in the overall psychological scheme of the film'.[1] Later, this sense of American cinema as in some way 'classical' became central to the work of the influential French critic André Bazin. 'The American cinema is a classical art', Bazin wrote in 1957, 'but why not then admire in it what is most admirable, i.e. not only the talent of this or that film-maker, but the genius of the system, the richness of its ever vigorous tradition'.[2] 'Classical' was used by these European writers watching Hollywood films to highlight their adherence to a certain form and style dominated by a particular narrative organization and by rules of composition that produced unity, balance, and order in the resulting art-work. Leading on from Bazin's conception of the 'genius' of the Hollywood 'system', other scholars began to address 'classical Hollywood cinema' as a particular film aesthetic associated with the industrial conditions of filmmaking that could be found in the major American studios from the late teens onward.[3]

What are classical Hollywood films like, then? And how was film production organized in classical Hollywood cinema? In their justly influential book *The Classical Hollywood Cinema: Film Style and Mode of Production to 1960*, David Bordwell, Janet Staiger and Kristin Thompson delineate what they call a 'mode of film practice' dominant in Hollywood from around 1917 onwards. A mode of film practice, they write, 'consists of a set of widely held stylistic norms sustained by and sustaining an integral mode of film production. Those norms constitute a determinate set of assumptions about how a movie should behave, about what stories it properly tells and how it should tell them, about the range and functions of film technique, and about the activities of the spectator'.[4] Central to classical storytelling is 'a specific sort of narrative causality [that] operates as the dominant, making temporal and spatial systems vehicles for it'.[5] The classical feature film is characterized by the overriding objective of telling a particular kind of story, focusing on goal-oriented characters who set in motion a series of causally linked events in which they confront and overcome, or less often are overcome by, counter-forces to the achievement of their goals. In either case, the ending closes the issue definitively, by resolving, usually happily but sometimes tragically, all tensions between the characters and their surroundings that were set up at the beginning.

A range of cinematic techniques for telling such stories both clearly and expressively were developed by filmmakers both in the US and in Europe throughout the 1910s, as we saw in the last section, particularly in Kristin Thompson's contribution, which also pointed out that by the late 1910s Hollywood had integrated these techniques into a highly efficient aesthetic system. Inextricably linked to Hollywood's classical aesthetic was an equally efficient mode of film production. According to Bordwell, Staiger and Thompson a mode of film production comprises 'a characteristic ensemble of economic aims, a specific division of labor, and particular ways of conceiving and executing the work of filmmaking'.[6] In Hollywood's case, the application of many of the principles of factory production to filmmaking was crucial. These principles included the following:

- Centralization of the work place. All work processes were physically united within the production plant (the studio), which comprised the buildings for various departments, the stages for the shooting of interiors and the standing sets and back-lots for the shooting of exteriors. Virtually all studios were located in and around Los Angeles.
- Separation of the conception from the execution of work. The former was the domain of management, the latter that of the labour force. The ultimate decisions concerning the choice of stories and their particular translation into films lay not with the technicians and artists working in the studios, but principally with the head offices of film companies in New York and with studio heads and individual producers heading separate units within the studios.
- Detailed preplanning and standardization of work processes. The work of technical and creative personnel was based on continuity scripts, which provided a blueprint for the finished product. The execution of the script's specifications followed established work routines, which had been conveyed to employees, including directors, during their apprenticeship in the studio.
- Detailed division of labour. The overall process of production was broken down into discrete segments which specialized workers were assigned to, executing certain standardized work patterns (like on an assembly line).[7]

Thus, Los Angeles based production subsidiaries of New York based film corporations adopted an industrial mode of production to the making of large numbers of feature films, whereby the films' classical style and the organization of their production were mutually reinforcing. This resulted in the efficient production of films of a certain, guaranteed quality but also, of course, in the narrowing down of the range of formal and stylistic options available in mainstream filmmaking. A more detailed description of the Hollywood mode of production constitutes the first part of Kristin Thompson's essay in the next section, which then compares it with the organization of film production in three European countries.

How did the corporate organizations of classical Hollywood cinema ensure that they made a profit? Let's start with the structure of the film industry. Following on from previous, unsuccessful attempts to monopolize American cinema (most notably through the MPPC), the American film industry organized itself in the 1920s in the form of an oligopoly, which means that a small number of very large companies controlled the market, financing the bulk of film production and collecting the majority of box office revenues. Vertical integration was central to this. Companies that were vertically integrated combined a large theatre chain with a world-wide distribution network and a production plant in Los Angeles. Vertical integration ensured that there was a steady supply of product for the weekly change of programme in the company's theatres, and that there was a guaranteed outlet for the company's weekly output of films.

Leading the way were Famous Players and First National. In 1917 Adolph Zukor, head of Famous Players, merged twelve producers and the distributor Paramount to form the Famous Players-Lasky Corporation.[8] Zukor's commercial strategy to tie together production and distri-bution was predicated on the enormous popularity of a number of film stars contracted to the company, including Mary Pickford, Gloria Swanson and Rudolph Valentino (the latter two discussed in the following chapters by Sumiko Higashi and Gaylyn Studlar).[9] Famous Players capitalized on the popularity of stars by 'block booking' its yearly output of 50 to 100 feature films, which meant that theatre owners who wanted to show the profitable films of, for example, Pickford also had to take pictures featuring less well known players. Exhibitors understandably resented this. In 1917, in an attempt to challenge the power of Famous Players, a group of local theatre chains formed its own distribution company, First National, and moved into film production, most notably by signing Chaplin.[10] First National was now verti-cally integrated, and in response Zukor began buying theatres until in 1925 he merged Paramount, as his company was now called, with Balaban and Katz, a Chicago-based theatre chain controlling many of the biggest auditoriums in the Midwest. The result was a huge production-distribution-exhibition combine whose main asset was the world's largest theatre chain.[11] Other companies also achieved vertical integration in the period, including Loew's Inc., the parent company of MGM and, later in the 1920s, Warner Bros., which took over First National.

Vertically integrated companies did not own the majority of theatres. In the mid-1920s, for example, Paramount owned roughly 500 theatres, while MGM had about 200. Yet the theatres they owned included most of the big first-run movie palaces in cities, with seating capacities in the thousands and higher admission prices than regular cinemas. Late in the 1920s about three-quarters of all box office receipts in the US came from these large theatres.[12] The vertically integrated companies cooperated by exhibiting each other's films. In conjunction with the practice of block-booking forced upon independent exhibitors, this left little room in theatre schedules for the screening of releases by independent production companies, which therefore lacked attractive exhibition outlets for their products.

In order to keep their output inoffensive and thus potentially appealing to everyone, the major film companies were willing to comply with a system of self-regulation. A series of scan-dals involving film stars in the early 1920s highlighted the need for effective public relations.[13] Furthermore, ongoing anxieties about State intervention via censorship boards and anti-trust legislation encouraged cooperation between the major studios. As a consequence, in 1922 the industry formed a new trade organization, called the Motion Picture Producers and Distributors of America (MPPDA). Its president Will Hays was given the task to coordinate the industry's efforts to improve its public image. Hays sought to persuade the studios that the movies they produced had to be inoffensive both to cultural and legislative leaders and to audiences. Ruth Vasey's essay in this section shows how the MPPDA pursued these goals. In particular, Vasey explores the ways in which the MPPDA and Hollywood began to respond to the international market. The commercial imperative to appeal to as broad a world audience as possible, she argues, contributed to a form of filmmaking that submerged any elements that might be polit-ically contentious, and so narrowed down the field of representation. This created films of considerable ambiguity which could be, and indeed were, understood quite differently by different audiences. The MPPDA thus intensified the conception of Hollywood cinema as harm-less entertainment which had emerged from the regulatory debates and legal decisions considered in the section *Cinema and Reform*.

Vasey's analysis shows classical Hollywood cinema to be responsive to social and cultural pressures wherever they impinged on its profitability. This differs in important ways from the account given by Bordwell, Staiger and Thompson, who conclude that, although economic factors have played a crucial part in the development of the classical style in the 1910s, it is the maintenance of this style which has guided Hollywood's operations ever since. Against this dominance of style, Vasey's analysis highlights the external pressures on the Hollywood system and foregrounds the fact that Hollywood movies are determined, in the last instance, by their existence as commercial products and so operate according to the principles of what Richard Maltby has called Hollywood's 'commercial aesthetic'.[14] In short, this perspective suggests that Hollywood's principal aim has always been to make money by entertaining audiences, enter-tainment being perhaps best understood as the carefully orchestrated provision of intense sensual and emotional stimulation in a safe environment; for Hollywood, film form and style are ulti-mately in the service of such stimulation and not ends in themselves.

As the various contributions to this section show, narrative was certainly an important means for engaging audiences, but if these audiences could successfully be stimulated outside the framework of narrative, there was no reason why Hollywood would refrain from doing so (and in this respect at least, classical Hollywood is not so different from the earlier cinema of attractions).[15] The regular presence of newsreels and travelogues, and the enormous appeal of musical shorts and feature-length musical revues during the introduction of synchronized sound in the late 1920s are useful reminders of Hollywood's fundamental formal and stylistic flexibility.

At the same time, it is important to recognize that the narratives of classical feature films, in addition to involving audiences in their characters and chains of cause and effect, also served as a framework for the presentation of diverse attractions. For example, Cecil B. DeMille's films of the 1920s, Sumiko Higashi shows, displayed the spectacle of consumer extravagance just as the films starring Rudolph Valentino, according to Gaylyn Studlar's analysis, highlighted star performance and exotic locations as sources of filmic pleasure. Movie marketing was often aimed precisely at emphasizing the range of diverse attractions and pleasures offered by a film. The elaborate pressbook produced by the distributor to accompany a film's release, for example, typically included material on the stars, on fashion, and on the themes of the film so as to open it up to diverse interests, tastes and forms of pleasurable engagement.

One way scholars have addressed the diversity of pleasures embedded in the classical feature film is to link it to the tradition of melodrama in popular theatre and literature, which fore-grounded the presentation of sensational action, violence, thrills, awesome sights, physical spectacle and heightened emotional states.[16] Linda Williams explored this connection in her analysis of *The Birth of a Nation* in the previous section, and Rick Altman has characterized classical Hollywood features more generally as 'an amalgam of deformed, embedded melo-dramatic material and carefully elaborated narrative classicism'.[17] Of course, the feature film was in turn just one item – albeit the concluding and most important item – on a movie theatre's programme, which can be understood, we argued in the introduction to the last section, as an amalgamation of the traditions of variety and legitimate theatre, of the cinema of attractions and classical Hollywood storytelling. That moviegoers did indeed engage with the programme as a whole, and not just with its final segment, is indicated by polls taken in the 1920s which found that 68 per cent of the audience went to the movies for the overall 'event', while only 10 per cent went specifically to see the featured movie.[18]

It is reasonable to assume that audiences had different expectations for, and gained different pleasures from, the various aspects of the programme. Features and short films both contrasted with, and complemented each other. Whereas feature films invited the audience to forget about the reality of the cinema auditorium and immerse themselves in the fictional world on the screen, short films (especially cartoons) sometimes confronted the audience with the technological basis of filmic entertainment and their presence in a theatre – an effect reminiscent of earlier trick films and even of the initial display of film projection as a tech-nological marvel. Whereas features invited audiences into a fictional universe, newsreels and travelogues, like early actualities, provided documentary views of the world. Furthermore, slapstick shorts of the 1910s and 1920s were often remarkably similar to the comedies of earlier periods and tended to deviate from classical norms in being concerned primarily with comic routines and spectacle rather than the careful delineation of their stories, and with the uniqueness of the physical capacities of performers rather than the psychological states of fully rounded characters. More generally, whereas feature films demanded a certain amount of delayed gratification (the full emotional pay-off coming at the end), many short films concen-trated on the immediate satisfaction provided by a series of interesting views, gags or, in the early sound period, musical numbers. Still, the overall structure of the movie theatre programme clearly implied a hierarchy. The serious and legitimate part of the film programme was presented as the main item in relation to which everything else could be seen as a mere sideshow. This presentation worked in conjunction with an extensive discourse, in publicity and reviews as well as in the narratives and iconography of the films themselves, about the respectability, artistry and positive moral influence of the filmic medium, so as to provide a cover for the basic pleasures it provided.[19]

The sheer entertainment value of cinema and the loftier claims made on its behalf were not always easily reconciled. For example, the popularity of some performers in short films led to a redefinition of their style, as we saw in Charles Maland's account of Chaplin, and their entry into feature films that could be described as 'classical', as our opening quotations in this introduction suggested. Peter Krämer's chapter considers the process of making slapstick more respectable in his essay here, focusing on Buster Keaton and his starring role in the feature film *The Saphead* (Metro, 1920). Like Chaplin, Keaton entered the movies from variety theatre and his feature films in the 1920s, Krämer suggests, are a rich site for considering both the negotiation of different performance traditions and the contradictory sets of demands made on the work of the great comedians of the silent era. Krämer's analysis further suggests the diver-sity of entertainments on offer in classical Hollywood cinema, showing that many feature films can perhaps best be understood as hybrid constructions merging the traditions of legitimate theatre, variety performance, cinematic attractions and classical Hollywood storytelling.

Like Krämer, Gaylyn Studlar's chapter focuses on an important star of the 1920s, Rudolph Valentino, whose films incorporated a physically oriented performance tradition – in this case dance – into the narrative framework of Hollywood features. Valentino became extraordinarily popular, particularly amongst women audiences, functioning in some respects as a site of spec-tacle and pleasure for audiences that existed to one side of the narrative drive of the films.

Such pleasure was also promoted outside the films in the publicity discourses that surrounded Valentino and other stars, notably in fan magazines. More important to Studlar's analysis of Valentino, though, is the way in which the films of Valentino and the extra-filmic discourse surrounding him were connected to the period's key social concerns about gender, sexuality and ethnicity. In the context of a growing cultural preoccupation with apparent changes in female sexual and social identity and their effects on masculinity, the Italian born Valentino was presented as a threat to traditional sexual relations and standards of masculinity because of the connotations of sexual ambiguity, social marginality and ethnic/racial otherness connected to his star image. Valentino's positioning as an object of erotic contemplation for women was deeply controversial, even more so, Studlar suggests, because this gaze was directed at a 'foreign body'.

Lastly here, Sumiko Higashi's chapter shifts attention to the representation of women in the context of broader discourses and practices of consumption in the post-war era, the so-called Jazz Age. Looking closely at a number of DeMille's films from the late teens/early 1920s, Higashi shows how they constructed the potentially radical 'new woman' as a sexual playmate and as a commodity and so validated consumption rather than sexual or political equality. Cinema, Higashi shows, served the purposes of consumer capitalism and potentially had considerable effects on American and world society as a whole.

Later in the 1920s the innovation of synchronized sound brought an end to the so-called 'silent era', temporarily introducing a fundamental transformation of film production and exhibition, of film form and style. The history of the emergence of sound cinema, briefly retold, can function as a useful conclusion to our discussion of classical Hollywood cinema. Initially introduced partly as a way of bypassing the high costs of live prologues and of the orchestras accompanying the film programme, the first sound films were short musical numbers that featured opera and vaudeville performers and quickly thereafter short newsreels detailing major news events.[20] As in the very early years of cinema, these films can be considered in the context of an aesthetic of attractions and of a sense of cinema as a visual newspaper, harking back to an earlier moment in film history – when the technology itself could be considered an attraction – at the same time as pointing towards future developments. Here the addition of the microphone to the camera finally realized Edison's original technological aim as stated in his first motion picture caveat of 1888, namely to do 'for the Eye what the phonograph does for the Ear'.[21]

Starting with *Don Juan* (Warners, 1926), Vitaphone programmes included both a feature film with a synchronized sound track of music and some sound effects, and a series of musical shorts. The aesthetics of feature films were not initially changed. The well-known *The Jazz Singer* (Warners, 1927) combined classical storytelling with musical display by including short sequences of Al Jolson singing within a traditional melodramatic story (interestingly dealing with race, tradition and modernity) which was accompanied by a pre-recorded orchestral score.[22] Music based features quickly became very prominent. Yet while revue films strung together a series of variety attractions, other films, following the model of *The Jazz Singer*, more clearly situated these attractions in a narrative context, bringing sound technology and its possibilities in line with classical storytelling.[23] Hence the basic stability of Hollywood's classical style and its industrial mode of production was not seriously challenged by sound. Hollywood's commercial aesthetic assured their stability precisely because American cinema audiences, despite their initial enthusiasm for sound, had long become habituated to classical feature films as the centrepiece of their evening's entertainment.

As we will see in the next section, American audiences were not alone in their attachment to feature films, and the US was not unique in its development of a commercially oriented and complexly organized film industry. However, by extending the systematic analysis of film style and mode of production to European cinemas between the mid-1910s and late 1920s, we will also identify differences between classical Hollywood cinema and European films and film industries.

Notes

1 A. Haut-Pré, 'Les Moving Pictures Américaines', *Ciné-Revue* (11 September 1925), 10; Marcel Zahar and Daniel Burret, 'Une Visite a Jean Renoir', *Cinéa-Ciné Pour Tous* (15 April 1926), 15, cited in David Bordwell, Janet Staiger and Kristin Thompson, *The Classical Hollywood Cinema: Film Style and Mode of Production to 1960* (London: Routledge, 1985), 3.
2 André Bazin, 'On the *Politique des Auteurs*' (1957), in Jim Hillier (ed.), *Cahiers du Cinéma, I: The 1950s: Neo-Realism, Hollywood, New Wave* (London: Routlege and Kegan Paul, 1985), 257–8.
3 Thomas Schatz, *The Genius of the System: Hollywood Filmmaking in the Studio Era* (London: Simon and Schuster, 1989); Bordwell, Staiger and Thompson, *The Classical Hollywood Cinema*. See also Peter Krämer's discussion of changing conceptualizations of classical cinema in 'Post-classical Hollywood', in John Hill and Pamela Church Gibson (eds), *The Oxford Guide to Film Studies* (Oxford: Oxford University Press, 1998).
4 Bordwell, Staiger and Thompson, *The Classical Hollywood Cinema*, xiv.
5 Ibid., 12.
6 Ibid., xiv.
7 Ibid., in particular 128–54. See also Schatz, *The Genius of the System*, 15–68; Richard Koszarski, *An Evening's Entertainment: The Age of the Silent Feature Picture, 1915–1928* (Berkeley: University of California Press, 1994), 63–94.
8 Douglas Gomery, *The Studio System* (London: Macmillan, 1986), 26–8.
9 On the rise of the star system in Hollywood see, in particular, Richard deCordova, *Picture Personalities: The Emergence of the Star System in America* (Urbana: University of Illinois Press, 1990); Lee Grieveson, 'Stars and Audiences in Early American Cinema', *Screening the Past* (Winter 2002). On the star system in France, see Ginette Vincendeau, *Stars and Stardom in French Cinema* (London: Continuum, 2000), 1–58.
10 Charles J. Maland, *Chaplin and American Culture* (Princeton, NJ: Princeton University Press, 1992), 32–3.
11 Douglas Gomery, *Shared Pleasures: A History of Movie Presentation in the United States* (London: British Film Institute, 1992), 34–56.
12 Ibid.
13 On these scandals see Richard deCordova, *Picture Personalities: The Emergence of the Star System in America* (Urbana: University of Illinois Press 1990); Adrienne L. Mclean and David A. Cook, *Headline Hollywood: A Century of Film Scandal* (New Brunswick, NJ: Rutgers University Press, 2001).
14 Richard Maltby, *Hollywood Cinema: An Introduction* (Oxford: Blackwell, 1995), in particular 6–9.
15 See here also Peter Krämer, ' "Clean, Dependable Slapstick": Comic Violence and the Emergence of Classical Hollywood Cinema', in J. David Slocum (ed.), *Violence and American Cinema* (New York: Routledge, 2001).
16 See, for example, Rick Altman, 'Dickens, Griffith, and Film Theory Today' and Christine Gledhill, 'Between Melodrama and Realism: Anthony Asquith's *Underground* and King Vidor's *The Crowd*', both in Jane Gaines (ed.), *Classical Hollywood Narrative: The Paradigm Wars* (Durham, NC: Duke University Press, 1992); Linda Williams, 'Melodrama Revised', in Nick Browne (ed.), *Refiguring American Film Genres: History and Theory* (Berkeley: University of California Press, 1998); Elizabeth Cowie, 'Classical Hollywood Cinema and Classical Narrative', in Steve Neale and Murray Smith (eds), *Contemporary Hollywood Cinema* (London: Routledge, 1997); Ben Singer, *Melodrama and Modernity: Early Sensational Cinema and Its Contexts* (New York: Columbia University Press, 2001).
17 Altman, 'Dickens, Griffith, and Film Theory Today', 41.
18 Maltby, *Hollywood Cinema*, 36.
19 Kramer, ' "Clean, Dependable Slapstick"', 111.

20 Don Crafton, *The Talkies: American Cinema's Transition to Sound, 1926–1934* (Berkeley: University of California Press, 1999).

21 Thomas Edison, 'Motion Picture Caveat I', October 1888, reprinted in Gordon Hendricks, *The Edison Motion Picture Myth* (Berkeley: University of California Press, 1961), 158.

22 Charles Wolfe, 'Vitaphone Shorts and *The Jazz Singer*', *Wide Angle*, vol. 12, no. 3 (July 1990); also see Michael Rogin, *Blackface/White Noise: Jewish Immigrants in the Hollywood Melting Pot* (Berkeley: University of California Press, 1996).

23 Henry Jenkins, *What Made Pistachio Nuts: Early Sound Comedy and the Vaudeville Aesthetic* (New York: Columbia University Press, 1992); Bordwell, Staiger, Thompson, *The Classical Hollywood Cinema*, in particular 298–308.

Chapter 16

PETER KRÄMER

THE MAKING OF A COMIC STAR
Buster Keaton and *The Saphead* (1920)

IN 1920, AFTER THREE YEARS of supporting roles in Roscoe Arbuckle's short films, Buster Keaton appeared in *The Saphead*. The film is distinguished by the comedian's first feature film appearance, and by his last ever smile on screen. When Bertie, the saphead of the title, is confronted by his sister Rose with a newspaper article about his presence at a gambling club raided by the police the night before, a proud smile appears on his face. Bertie is happy about the bad reputation he is acquiring, because that, an advice book tells him, is the best way to impress the 'Modern Girl'. Anyone familiar with Keaton's work in the 1920s will appreciate the outstanding quality of Bertie's smile. Throughout the decade, and indeed during his later career, Keaton, on screen and off, was known as 'The Great Stone Face'.[1] What is the significance, then, of Keaton's smile in *The Saphead*? What does it reveal about Keaton's changing performance strategies, and about the historical moment at which Keaton made the transition from slapstick shorts to feature-length comic dramas and from supporting roles to starring roles?

Promoting Keaton: Joseph M. Schenck, Comique and *The Saphead*

Keaton entered the film industry after a long and distinguished career in vaudeville as the youngest member of the famous family act 'The Three Keatons'.[2] In spring 1917 Keaton started work at the new Comique studio in New York, a joint operation of vaudeville and film entrepreneur Joseph M. Schenck and former Keystone star Roscoe Arbuckle. Keaton appeared in fifteen of the twenty-one two-reelers that Arbuckle made for Comique.[3] Due to his military service, which brought him to France during the last months of World War I, Keaton missed several productions between the autumn of 1918 and April 1919. Afterwards only three more Arbuckle/Keaton films were produced (the last of which, *The Garage*, was released in January 1920). In December 1919, Arbuckle started to make feature films at the Famous Players studio, and Keaton became the star attraction of Comique. However, at this point, Keaton was mostly seen in the trade press, fan magazines and newspaper reviews as an adjunct to Roscoe Arbuckle rather than as a performer and personality in his own right. Keaton's performance showed more restraint than that of his fellow comedians, and in particular contrasted sharply with that of his main rival at Comique, Arbuckle's brother-in-law Al St. John, who was known for his facial agility. Yet, Keaton did engage in a fair amount of mugging (exaggerated smiling, laughing and crying directed at the camera). Both in terms of his public recognition and his acting style, then, Keaton in 1919 was far removed from the status and the distinctive identity he acquired in 1920.

Schenck bought Chaplin's former Lone Star studio in Los Angeles for the Keaton team, which included several people taken over from the Arbuckle group. The studio ran into problems soon after its opening in January 1920. During the first four months, only one two-reeler, *The High Sign*, was made at Comique (whereas Arbuckle had taken about six weeks for each of his shorts). When finally completed, the film was shelved because it did not satisfy Keaton's expectations for his first star vehicle, on which much of the success of the Keaton series of two-reelers depended.

The opportunity to appear in a full-length comedy arose in this context. Metro intended to make a film version of the stage hit *The New Henrietta* (a successful 1913 revival of Bronson Howard's classic *The Henrietta*), bringing in playwright and stage director Winchell Smith and producer John Golden, the men responsible for the revival. The film was to reunite the two stars of the 1913 production, William H. Crane and Douglas Fairbanks. Fairbanks' first film, *The Lamb* (1915), had been loosely based around the character of Bertie Van Alstyne, and was followed by a string of successes which by 1920 had made Fairbanks one of the top film stars.[4] With Fairbanks tied up at United Artists, a substitute was needed. Keaton was chosen because of close links between Schenck and Metro. In January 1920, Metro had been taken over by Loew's, which was run by Joseph Schenck's brother Nicholas. While the film went into production in the spring of 1920, Metro was negotiating with Comique about the distribution of Keaton two-reelers. The film, being based on a stage hit and co-starring a Broadway legend, was going to be a prestige production with considerable popular appeal. Casting Keaton gave Joseph Schenck the perfect vehicle to launch his latest star and Metro the opportunity to advertise their new comedy series.[5]

Metro had assigned its chief scenarist, June Mathis, to the task of adapting the play for the screen. The first two scripts, still using the stage title *The Henrietta,* had been written in March and April before Keaton joined the production team.[6] Keaton's involvement led to fundamental changes in the script. These resulted in a shift in emphasis away from the stage original and Crane, and towards Keaton and his distinctive interpretation of the role of Bertie Van Alstyne, signaled by the film's new title, *The Saphead*.

On the same day (1 June 1920) that Comique contracted with Metro for the distribution of eight Keaton two-reelers, the distributor issued a press release to film magazines and daily newspapers across the country, focussing attention on their new star attraction and his simultaneous launch in full-length comic drama and slapstick two-reelers.[7] As the first sustained publicity effort for Keaton as an independent comic star, the Metro publicity sheet explicitly placed Keaton at the intersection of two performance traditions. His 'chief claim to fame hitherto has been his ability to hurl custard pies and perform pat (sic) falls' in Roscoe Arbuckle's comedies and, before that, on the vaudeville stage. His twenty years of experience in physical comedy would now be complemented by the 'high comedy characterization' of Bertie 'the lamb' in *The Saphead*, 'being co-starred with William H. Crane at the head of a noteworthy cast.' His appearance in the film version of a Broadway comedy was not a final departure from low comedy, but a temporary separation, after which he would return to the kind of comedy he was known for with 'a series of laughing two-reelers' for Metro. After his promotion from the ranks of supporting players, Keaton would combine the comic spectacle of stage and screen slapstick with the rounded characterization of legitimate comedy. Metro's Keaton would be a respectable slapstick comedian associated with the comedy tradition of Broadway, an actor as well as a clown. Keaton's own brand of two-reel slapstick comedy would draw, it was implied, on this tradition of quality, by injecting seriousness and depth into his acrobatics, and, most importantly, by leaving room for 'moments of stabilizing gravity'.

The meanings of restraint: slapstick, legitimate acting and the production of *The Saphead*

Originally referring to two flat pieces of wood joined together at one end, used to produce a loud slapping noise creating the impression of someone having been dealt a hard blow on stage, the term 'slapstick' came to cover various forms of violent comedy. To transform acts of willful maliciousness and intense pain into comedy, performers had to signal clearly that their actions were mere make-believe and constituted highly accomplished athletic routines. The actions' excess, their fantastic exaggeration, as well as performers' self-conscious address of the audience, were the most obvious indicators of their professional and ritualistic nature.[8]

Keaton had gained recognition for his ability to take spectacular falls and engage in acrobatic fights, first with his father on the vaudeville stage, then with Arbuckle and Al St. John in their Comique shorts. However, Keaton's performance skills were much more wide-ranging. On the variety stage he had performed monologues, parodies, impersonations and songs; the melodramas he appeared in as a child, and also Arbuckle's two-reelers, had demanded a fair amount of straight acting. Unlike slapstick, such acting was not supposed to draw attention to its physicality and athletic accomplishment. Instead, it sought to transparently project a fictional character, evoking an interior, psychological realm of desires and ambitions, as well as external character conflicts. Without acknowledging the audience, the reality of the performer's body was subsumed into the fictional character. To achieve this aim, the overall trend both in the legitimate theatre and, since about 1909, in dramatic films had been to deemphasize the performer's actual physical presence and activity; the actors restrained their movements so as to focus attention on subtle gestures and facial expressions that derived significance from their complex narrative context. Classical devices such as intertitles, close-ups and eyeline matches, for example, were used to convey mental processes and establish social relations. Thus they replaced, to some extent, the performer's actual physical activity. In particular, immobile faces shown in close shots served as blank screens onto which thoughts and emotions could be projected.[9] In addition to concern about looks at the camera which destroyed the illusion of a self-contained fictional world, a key issue in discourses about screen acting throughout the teens and early twenties was the need for actors, especially those coming from the stage, to restrain their performance.[10]

Typically working in short film production where the rules and norms of dramatic features did not apply, slapstick comedians systematically transgressed both of the above stipulations. They frequently and self-consciously directed their performance to the camera, and they constantly drew attention to their bodies through exaggerated stunts, contorted faces and overanimated gestures. This performance style aimed for an immediate impact on the audience, either laughter or breathless amazement. Yet, their films usually also included quieter sections, where the dramatic situation was established or audience sympathy was evoked. Thus slapstick comedies shifted back and forth between delayed gratification and immediate emotional release, restrained and excessive physical activity, one seen as the norm, the other as its amusing and/or astonishing transgression.

When Keaton made *The Saphead*, the balance between these two performance modalities shifted in favour of legitimate acting. The film's stage origin, its complex narrative, the presence of William H. Crane and, most importantly, the objectives of Metro's promotional campaign encouraged him to make restraint the centrepiece of his impersonation of Bertie Van

Alstyne. Interestingly, against the explicit prescription of the script, Keaton decided to take the notion of restraint beyond the level of illusionistic acting, until his avoidance of facial expressions drew attention to itself as the clearest and most striking mark of his physical presence as a performer. Keaton's performance stood out both in those scenes where he engaged in traditional slapstick tumbling, that is an excess of activity, and in those where he acted straight, that is with an excess of restraint. In both cases, Crane, who represented the traditions and highest achievements of legitimate acting in stage comedies, served Keaton as a perfect foil.

After twenty-four years as a comedian on the legitimate stage, forty-two-year-old William H. Crane had found the role that he would be associated with for the rest of his life: Nicholas Van Alstyne, 'the lion of Wall Street', in Bronson Howard's *The Henrietta*. Opening at the Union Square Theater in New York in 1887, the play had been such a success that even twenty-five years later it was considered a property valuable enough for a major revival. Winchell Smith and Victor Mapes's updated version, *The New Henrietta*, co-starred Crane with Douglas Fairbanks, at the time one of the leading young comedians on Broadway. During the 1913–14 season, the play enjoyed a long run at the Knickerbocker Theatre in New York, and in the following year it went on the road.[11] In December 1915, Crane announced his retirement from the stage after the end of the *New Henrietta* tour, which was still going strong. In future, he would 'act only on special occasions'.[12] A few months later, the *New York Sun* reported that Crane, 'stage dean', had been honored at a special dinner, attended by 'stars of all professions', and recognized by a note from president Woodrow Wilson.[13] Critics emphasized his exalted position in the theatrical profession, while noting the refinement of his comedy: He was 'one comedian who did his training in the library in place of in the gymnasium'. Both as an actor and a producer, he was said to have been involved only in plays that were 'sane, and, to his eternal credit, sanitary'.[14]

Crane represented a tradition of quality that was explicitly set against the verbally and physically aggressive performance of musical comedy and vaudeville. However, when Crane came out of retirement in the 1917–18 season, he appeared in a vaudeville playlet, which brought him closer to low-brow comic traditions. Apart from his limited role, the sheer presence of the legendary star was expected to appeal to audiences. This thought must have also occured to Winchell Smith and John Golden, who, in 1920, wanted the seventy-five-year-old Crane for their film adaptation of *The New Henrietta*. Crane had already appeared in a film version of his stage hit *David Harum* in 1915, but he was not prepared for the radical turn this particular adaptation would take.[15] 'And they made Berty, the Lamb, a slapstick character', he complained in a newspaper interview in 1925: 'Mr. Keaton was never suited for the role and the result was terrible'.[16]

The original play highlighted Nicholas Van Alstyne's romance with one Mrs. Opdyke. This romance, which spans most of the play, is a counterpart to Bertie's relationship with Nick's ward Agnes. The play places Nick at the centre of his own love story and carefully intertwines the romances of father and son, as well as the themes of love and business. The first film script, dated March 1920, retains the play's dual focus.[17] Nick's romance foregrounds his subjectivity, his desire for love and companionship. Given the pressures of his work on Wall Street, Nick is unable to properly guide his children. His daughter Rose has married a crook, whom Nick mistakenly grants his power of attorney; his interference with the romance of his son and his ward delays their happiness. Yet Mrs. Opdyke, whose insight into people's characters and emotions enables her to tell right from wrong, helps him to recognize and rectify his mistakes. His business is saved and the family unit reconstituted. In the classic theatrical tradition of New Comedy, the play ends with the reconciliation of father and son, and with two weddings.[18]

The narrative was reorganized once Keaton became involved, to foreground his part. Contrary to what one might expect, this was not done by adding slapstick material. The spectacular scenes of Bertie being violently initiated into the stock exchange fraternity by having his hat knocked off and being pushed around, and his subsequent acrobatically executed purchase of shares, which may seem typically Keaton, are extensively described in the script. They were possibly derived from Douglas Fairbanks's performance in the 1913 revival.[19] Otherwise, Keaton's physical stunts are limited to two brief and isolated instances of comic tumbling, in which Bertie's confrontation with his angry father causes him to slide down the stairs on his backside, and to jump off a windowsill. The transformation of the script into a Keaton vehicle was mainly achieved through drastic cuts in Crane's part which subordinated Nick's previously dominant storyline to that of his son. With the removal of Mrs. Opdyke from the film, Nick's activities lost their driving force and over-arching goal, his storyline now lacking cohesion, and disintegrating into a series of largely disconnected scenes. Nick became a mere blocking figure. In the light of Crane's old age and his perceived status as a bulwark against vulgar comedy, one could see the generational conflict between the two main characters as enacting a cultural conflict between the two performers playing them. The film's shift of narrative focus from father to son thus mirrored and facilitated the transfer of comic stardom from a master of the old school to the representative of a new generation. On both levels, the improved status of the younger man was finally validated by the handshake of his elder.

The centrality of Bertie's (and thus Keaton's) shortcomings, ambitions, misfortunes and final triumph is already signaled by the film's title. The original title introduced and foregrounded the narrative complexities associated with the name Henrietta and its multiple referents in the story.[20] *The Saphead*, however, makes Bertie the focus of attention, and in introducing his comic stupidity, it poses a problem for the narrative to resolve. Calling Bertie a saphead builds expectations that he will overcome his shortcomings. Plot complications constitute an obstacle course which will allow, and indeed force, the ignorant, passive fool to encounter the world at large and act in it. In the process, Bertie gains, if not knowledge and insight, then at least tangible success and an improved social standing. In the end, Bertie's new status is confirmed by his grateful father, and symbolized most effectively by the marriage to Agnes and the fathering of twins.

Bertie is first introduced by an intertitle as 'his father's hope and pride', which, right from the start, foregrounds the social pressures eventually forcing him to transcend his comfortably passive existence. Agnes is first mentioned as 'the girl Bertie loved. He had confided this to his sister and his valet – but had never mentioned it to her'. Bertie's failure to communicate his love reflects his painful awareness that he lacks those qualities that define contemporary manhood. An advice book on courtship, *How To Win The Modern Girl*, tells him: 'The Modern Girl has no use for the old-fashioned man. She prefers sports to saints. Few girls now-a-days can resist a dashing, gambling, drinking devil'. While the opposition is couched in moral terms (saint vs. devil), what separates Bertie from the ideal of masculinity is decisive action. Accepting this ideal, Bertie starts playing the role of the good sport, forever in pursuit of a bad reputation, which leads him into the world of nightclubs and gambling dens obviously alien to him. He wins at roulette, yet never even understands that he is playing for money. Initially, his role-playing backfires. Agnes cries when she first learns of his nightclubbing, clearly preferring the idiotic saint to the dashing devil. Only after Bertie has unknowingly revealed his love does Agnes fully understand his behaviour. Yet, he fails to explain himself to his father who so strongly objects to his supposedly hedonistic life-style that he will not allow him to marry Agnes before he has proven his manhood in the world of business. Work, rather than leisure, is now defined as the sphere for manly activity.

This second call for action is again met with mechanical obedience. Without any real interest or knowledge, Bertie goes into business. Watson Flint, his father's broker, buys him a seat at the stock exchange. For Bertie, a seat at the stock exchange is merely a physical object, and he therefore finds the price of $100,000 rather high. Yet he is willing to do whatever is necessary to satisfy his father, and thus be allowed to marry Agnes. When she indicates her willingness to marry him, even against the will of his father, he is eager to quickly bring about the ceremony, yet leaves all the arrangements to others. The wedding gets under way in his father's house only after Rose and Agnes have taken preparations in their own hands. Bertie's subsequent failure to defend himself against Mark's accusation that he is the father of an illegitimate child, constitutes the most dramatic instance of his complete inability to take appropriate action in crucial situations, and alienates him from his wife-to-be and his father.

Bertie's isolation can only be reversed when he finally realizes his potential for aggressive self-assertion during the climactic scene at the stock exchange. Although Bertie remains ignorant about what is really going on around him, Watson Flint uses his anger about people shouting 'Henrietta' to manipulate him into action. By vigorously defending his honour against those who seem to taunt him with the name of the woman who brought about his disgrace, he saves his father, and proves himself a man, a worthy son and suitor (and at the same time Keaton proves that his violent acrobatics are a socially useful skill after all). In the end, then, anger, athletic physicality and, of course, fatherhood, rather than hedonism, notoriety and business sense, are the cornerstones of Bertie's masculine identity.[21]

Keaton's deadpan performance departed radically from the characterization explicitly outlined in the script. Here, Bertie is highly expressive, 'smiles', 'grins', 'becomes quite happy', 'is delighted', and 'stands smiling happily' on many occasions. Of these, only two smiles survive in the film, remnants of a construction of Bertie's character which Keaton otherwise rejects. Keaton's conscious choice of a deadpan performance derived from an innovative view of Bertie as a person who does not properly connect with his surroundings, his failure to understand being paralleled by his failure to respond emotionally. Keaton's deadpan performance not only serves to characterize Bertie as an intellectually and emotionally retarded young man, but also highlights Keaton's own distance from the fiction, his irreducible and transgressive presence as a comedian in the universe of serious drama. With relatively few opportunities to dominate the screen with violent acrobatics, Keaton turned his straight characterization into an excessively restrained piece of acting and thus into an extended comic turn.

The opening credits end with an oval insert showing silhouettes of the two featured actors. This dissolves into a shot, which still belongs to the credit sequence, of the two shaking hands, with Crane also putting his hand on the comedian's shoulder as if to welcome him as an actor in the world of legitimate drama. The drama then begins with a set piece for Crane. In his Wall Street office, Nick meets an old friend from his prospecting days, bringing good news about their gold mine. Crane portrays the character's excitement with expansive gestures and plenty of movements across the room. Keaton's first appearance presents a sharp contrast. While heartily tucking into his breakfast, Keaton does not make any unnecessary movement, holding his body still and keeping his face completely inexpressive, thus indicating his detachment from his surroundings.

When, in the film's climactic sequence, Bertie does learn to act vigorously in the world on his own behalf, Keaton's performance is again contrasted directly with Crane's. From his yachting trip, Nick returns to his office at a time when it is too late for him to do anything but wait for the final outcome of the trading at the stock exchange, the latest results of which are relayed to him by a ticker tape machine. Completely incapacitated, his emotions become the centre of attention. His anger and despair dominate the scene in the same way that his joy provided a key to the film's opening. In dramatic terms, however, Bertie's actions at the stock exchange are decisive, and the narrative focus soon shifts to them. Occasional cuts to Nick's office showing his reactions serve to set Keaton's athletic performance against Crane's acting. At the beginning of the film, Keaton's deadpan poses a narrative problem (Bertie's unmanly passivity) which needs to be solved. Towards the end, his slapstick speciality brings about the resolution. Bertie's dramatic transformation from passive idiot to angry fighter, which establishes him as a worthy protagonist for the narrative and a worthy suitor and son in the social world of its fiction, is pure slapstick. Running, jumping, sliding across the stock exchange, his dress disintegrating and his body bruised, Bertie's buying spree is a long-awaited return of Keaton's violent acrobatics, a reminder of his extra-fictional status as a physical comedian.

The film's conclusion does not discard Keaton's restraint, which served to define the initial narrative problem. The final two scenes of the film bring father and son, Crane and Keaton, in direct contact. In the penultimate scene, Nick goes to his son's new house to make amends. With the father rushing to Bertie and enthusiastically thanking him for the rescue of his business, Bertie's success in the story is confirmed and his new social identity is established. At the same time, the scene mirrors the end of the credit sequence, and the handshake signalling Bertie's arrival in the world of adults as an equal to his father echoes the extra-fictional welcome Crane extends to the slapstick comedian Buster Keaton. While throughout most of the film, the narrative and the extra-fictional discourse are interwoven seamlessly by matching Keaton's performance to Bertie's character, the two levels are separated out and brought into conflict towards the end. The film's last scene, which moves ahead one year to show Bertie as an expectant father receiving the news about the birth of twins, would suggest that Bertie has changed fundamentally, that he has matured and at least partly overcome his intellectual and emotional retardation. Yet, Keaton's refusal to show any response undermines the narrative resolution and the normality of Bertie's status as a father. Keaton's deadpan contrasts sharply with the way Crane uses a little dance to express Nick's joy, and foregrounds Keaton's exceptional status as a comic performer.

Reviewing *The Saphead*: performance styles, trademarks and the success of Keaton's promotion

Contemporary critical responses indicate that the simplistic and potentially dehumanized identity of 'stoneface' Keaton contradicted basic assumptions of psychological realism in feature films, and of psychological 'normality' in everyday life. This issue was explicitly and complexly addressed in the reception of *The Saphead* in New York, the largest and most influential movie market in the United States. Reviewers were also debating the merits of the film's merging of performance styles and comic traditions, the cornerstone of the campaign to launch Keaton as a featured attraction. In particular, reviewers were concerned about the marginalization of William H. Crane, who was, after all, the better known and more highly regarded of the film's two co-stars.

Some, but by no means all, New York reviewers highlighted Crane's presence in the film, seeing and judging the film primarily in relation to its origins as a stage classic, to Crane's long stage career, and to the traditions of legitimate comedy. Severely criticizing Keaton, who was seen merely as an 'additional' player, the *New York American*, for example, stated that Crane had done 'the real acting' and had 'stood out' even though his role had been 'cut down and subordinated'.[22] Critics still celebrated the sheer weight of Crane's reputation, his 'realism' and 'understanding', the nobility the old man could bestow upon the screen.[23] However, virtually all acknowledged in one way or another the datedness of play and actor, and the necessity to introduce new elements. *Variety*'s positive comments on the film's stage origins, for example, were slightly defensive, claiming that, despite the 'modern interpretation', 'the plot remains the same'. Crane was referenced 'as a comedian of the old school', and the critic quickly added that this 'does not mean that his methods are old, because they are as up-to-the-minute as those of his younger colleague'. Clearly, the writer was at pains to avoid the impression of Crane as a mere relic of the past. Yet, in the context of critical remarks on the film's reliance on theatrical tableaux ('the sparsity of close-ups and the overplus of long shots'), Crane appeared highly anachronistic.[24] The *New York Times* welcomed the fact that he 'yields place . . . to the younger Keaton'. What made Keaton's performance so appropriate for screen comedy was precisely his restraint: Unlike Crane, with his dependence on the spoken word and grand gestures, Keaton was 'a pantomimist, as all true screen actors are, . . . definitely and subtly expressive'.[25]

Keaton's centrality to the film was noted in most reviews, yet opinions about his performance differed radically. The most damning judgement came from the *New York Morning Post* which found Keaton 'downright stupid and inane'. Bertie comes across as a 'simpleton' who is both 'a menace' and 'a bore'. In this critic's view, Keaton's restraint merely proved he was not doing his job properly, causing the film to fall flat.[26] Equally, for the *New York American* Keaton's 'constant mournfulness', while initially amusing, became 'tremendously monotonous.'[27] Yet another critic, who basically liked his performance, nevertheless doubted that 'Mr. Keaton is an artist who can depict human emotions'.[28]

However, most reviews accepted and even celebrated Keaton's performance because it suited the character of Bertie, who, according to *Photoplay*, 'has always presented a problem' for actors:

> He either has to be made such a fool that the authorities would never have permitted him to roam the streets at large, and get his laughs by being a fool, or he has to be played as a reasonably normal, but quite irresponsible youth, and run the risk of being dismissed as neither funny nor interesting.[29]

Keaton solved this problem, as the *New York Globe and Commercial Advertiser* noted, by emphasizing Bertie's essential stupidity to such a degree that his performance became an ironic comment on it: 'Buster Keaton is not the only feeble-minded hero we have seen in the movies, but he is the first who has admitted it and taken no end of pleasure and merriment from his task'.[30] Here, Keaton's restraint is perceived as an indication of his professional fun, and not of his personal moroseness.

Keaton's second major contribution to the film was seen to be his physical comedy. Even the very critical reviewers of the *New York Post* and the *New York American* admitted that the climactic scene at the stock exchange 'is funny in its low comedy way', containing 'some highly ludicrous bits of business'.[31] For the *New York Journal*, this scene was 'largely responsible for the entire picture's sense of enjoyment'.[32] The *New York Herald* fit Keaton in the tradition of Fairbanks's spectacular stage and film performances, noting that he 'becomes a human rocket at the finish almost as well as Doug could have'.[33] On the whole, critics accepted the violence and 'nonsense' of slapstick sequences as effective comic entertainment, even if they cited the film's failure to achieve the realism and expressiveness of the legitimate stage.

Obviously, the film was judged according to two different standards, one applying to the sequences of physical comedy, the other to the drama.[34] The *New York Times* saw *The Saphead* as a precariously balanced union of fundamentally different concerns: 'the picture is really a two-reel comedy stretched and padded to fill some 5,000 feet of film, but its scenes that count are so full of fun that the spectator does not mind the story stuff.'[35] Story material was seen to be added to comic spectacle, potentially getting in the way of continuous enjoyment. Other critics, focussing on Crane and the legitimate tradition, approached the film differently, implying that comedy sequences were inserted into an otherwise perfectly respectable, if somewhat old-fashioned, narrative. All agreed that the film was a hybrid, resulting from the presence of Keaton and Crane, who, in their respective careers up to this point, had come to embody different comic traditions.

Whereas Crane and his followers saw his association with, and intermittent displacement by, a slapstick clown as potentially degrading, Keaton's admirers saw his teaming with the famous Broadway comedian as a new and very promising career departure from slapstick to 'the more human field of straight comedy'.[36] Genuine stardom could only be achieved in the field of feature-length comedy, and depended on a restrained performance style. The hierarchical organisation of comic forms and the sense of Keaton's upward mobility was highlighted by the *New York Journal*: Keaton 'rises to fine comedy heights here, and points distinctly to the fact that he is a player of promise as a legitimate comedian.'[37] This critical response indicates the success of Metro's promotional strategy. Yet the many criticisms of the film, especially of Keaton himself and his excessive restraint, indicated how difficult a fusion, how fragile a balancing act Keaton's rise to stardom was.

Following the release of *The Saphead* in February 1921, the first extensive articles dealing with Keaton's screen work and off-screen life were published. Elizabeth Peltret's biographical sketch 'Poor Child', for example, highlighted the possibility that Keaton's deadpan performance on screen expressed his personal sadness. 'He has a settled look of sadness, as tho [sic] from a secret sorrow', she wrote, speculating that this sadness might be atttributed to the fact that '(b)eing laughed at is a serious proposition.'[38] By May 1921, when a flurry of publicity surrounded Keaton's marriage to Natalie Talmadge, his sadness had already been so firmly established as a fundamental personality trait in the press that it now clashed with the normalized image of the comedian's private existence as a lover and husband (in the same way that Keaton's deadpan clashed with the normalization of Bertie's status as a husband and father at the end of *The Saphead*). A headline described Keaton as 'The Saddest Bridegroom in the World', and the fact that, on or off-screen, he never smiled, was seen as a unique feature of Keaton's personality, separating him from the rest of humanity, and creating a distance between him and his wife.[39]

Contemporary reviews of Keaton's later features showed that the critical remarks about his gloomy and withdrawn personality in some reviews of *The Saphead* and in the articles about his wedding also applied to his sustained dramatic roles. When Keaton returned from slapstick two-reelers to feature film production in 1923, his deadpan performance became the object of increasing criticism. It was seen as a highly inappropriate response to the task of creating characters which were rounded and believable and could sustain audience interest for the duration of a feature. Consequently, Keaton's masterpieces were not very successful commercially, and his independent status was short-lived, with Keaton in 1928 becoming a mere contract actor at Loew's/MGM, without the creative control granted to him at Joseph Schenck's studio.[40]

Notes

This chapter is a shortened and slightly revised version of an essay first published as 'The Making of a Comic Star: Buster Keaton and *The Saphead*,' in Henry Jenkins and Kristine Brunovska Karnick eds, *Classical Hollywood Comedy* (New York: Routledge, 1995), pp. 190–210.

1   Title of an important 1958 essay by Christopher Bishop (*Film Quarterly*, vol.12, no.1, pp. 10–15) and a 1970 documentary on Keaton.

2   For information on Keaton's career see Rudi Blesh, *Keaton* (New York: Macmillan, 1966); Tom Dardis, *Keaton: The Man Who Wouldn't Lie Down* (London: Andre Deutsch, 1979); Buster Keaton with Charles Samuels, *My Wonderful World of Slapstick* (New York: Da Capo, 1982). For release dates and other filmographic information, see Maryann Chach's filmography in Dardis's book, which is partly based on Sam Gill's Arbuckle filmography in David Yallop, *The Day the Laughter Stopped: The True Story of Fatty Arbuckle* (New York: St. Martin's Press, 1976).

3   There are doubts about *A Reckless Romeo*, which is usually listed in Keaton filmographies but actually seems to have been made by Arbuckle at Keystone in 1916, although it was the second Comique short released due to a special arrangement with his former studio. Cp. Gill's filmography in Yallop, op. cit., pp. 314–5.

4   See John C. Tibbets and James M. Welsh, *His Majesty the American: The Cinema of Douglas Fairbanks, Sr.* (New York: Barnes, 1977).

5   On Schenck's complex business activities, see, for example, Alan Hynd, 'The Rise and Fall of Joseph Schenck', series of three articles in *Liberty Magazine*, 28 June 1941, 5 July 1941 and 12 July 1941. On Metro, see, for example, Jackson Schmidt, 'On the Road to MGM: A History of Metro Pictures Corporation, 1915–1920', *The Velvet Light Trap*, no. 19 (1982), pp. 46–52.

6   The scripts and a summary of the play on which they were based are contained in the MGM script collection at the University of Southern California (USC).

7   Clipping in Buster Keaton file, William Seymour Theatre Collection, Princeton University Library, Princeton. The date of the contract is mentioned in an internal MGM/Loew's report written by Katherine Barnes, which is contained in the MGM collection at USC.

8   For an account of the 'vaudeville aesthetic' by which slapstick performance was informed, see Henry Jenkins, *What Made Pistachio Nuts? Early Sound Comedy and the Vaudeville Aesthetic* (New York: Columbia University Press, 1992), Ch. 3.

9   Cp, Janet Staiger, 'The Eyes Are Really the Focus: Photoplay Acting and Film Form and Style', *Wide Angle*, vol. 6, no. 4 (1985), pp. 14–23; Roberta E. Pearson, *Eloquent Gestures: The Transformation of Performance Style in the Griffith Biograph Films* (Berkeley: University of California Press, 1992); Eileen Bowser, *The Transformation of Cinema, 1907–1915* (New York: Scribner's, 1992), Ch. 6.

10 See, for example, John Emerson and Anita Loos, *Breaking Into Movies* (New York: James A. McCann, 1921), Ch. III; Tamar Lane, *What's Wrong with the Movies* (Los Angeles: Waverly, 1923), pp. 137–41.

11 Cp. entry on Crane in *Who was Who in the Theatre* (Detroit: Gale Research, 1978).

12 Unidentified newspaper clipping, dated 26 December 1915, William H. Crane biographical clippings file, Harvard Theater Collection (HTC), Cambridge, MA.

13 *New York Sun*, 28 February 1916, unpaginated clipping, Crane file, HTC.

14 Unidentified clipping, dated 5 March 1916, Crane file, HTC.

15 *David Harum* (Famous Players, 1915, 5 reels). After *The Saphead*, Crane appeared in *Souls for Sale* (1923), *Three Wise Fools* (1923) and *True as Steel* (1924).

16 *Boston Sunday Globe*, 26 July 1925, unpaginated clipping, Crane file, HTC.

17 MGM script collection, USC.

18 On 'New Comedy' and its importance for the history of comedy on stage and screen see, for example, Northrop Frye, *Anatomy of Criticism. Four Essays* (Princeton: Princeton University Press, 1957), pp. 163–86; David Grote, *The End of Comedy: The Sit-Com and the Comedic Tradition* (Hamden: Archon, 1983), pp. 17–55.

19 On Fairbanks' performance in the 1910s, see Tibbets and Welsh, op. cit., especially Chs. 1–3.

20 The Henrietta is a mine Nick co-owns with Jim Hardy, an old friend from Arizona who appears at the film's beginning to tell Nick that he has finally struck gold. Nick decides to put shares in the mining corporation on the market. At the same time, his son-in-law Mark, an unsuccessful stock broker, receives a letter from his old, now destitute love Henrietta, asking for help. When he ignores her request, she takes drastic measures: On her deathbed she sends a messenger with Mark's letters to Nick's house, asking him to take care of their child. Meanwhile, Bertie, who joins the nightlife wherever he can, displaying trophies of his (supposed) exploits in his room, has collected pictures of Henrietta, a well-known dancer. Although he has never actually met her, this apparent connection helps Mark to set him up as the addressee of the dying Henrietta's letters, and thus as the father of her child. Because Mark, who would like to have Nick's commissions, has asked Rose to put in a word for him, Nick puts him in charge of the sale of Henrietta's shares when he leaves on his trip after the disrupted wedding. Knowing that he has not much time left before his ploy will be uncovered, Mark manipulates the price

of the Henrietta shares so that he will be able to make a fortune, ruining Nick in the process. When Bertie, spending his time at the stock exchange because he was told to go into business, hears men shouting 'Henrietta', the name that brought him disaster, he naturally wants to shut them up. Nick's regular broker Watson Flint, who has realized what Mark is trying to do, tells Bertie that he can silence people by saying 'I take it' to everyone who utters the offensive name, which is precisely what he does. The share price recovers and Nick's business is saved.

21   It is possible to see *The Saphead* as a comedian comedy, which foregrounds the comedian's performance as a spectacular attraction in its own right, while at the same time narrativizing it as the expression of the comic character's unresolved personality which the film's story works to normalize. Keaton's deadpan signals the comedian's distance from the dramatic task of convincingly characterizing Bertie, and Bertie's passivity in turn appears as a refusal to fulfill the role of protagonist. In the end, these tensions are partially resolved through Bertie's decisive action at the stock exchange and his social integration through paternal acceptance, marriage and fatherhood. While I partially go along with this generic analysis, I do not believe that Keaton brought a well-known pre-established comic persona to the film – which is a requirement for comedian comedy – and instead used the film precisely to define such a persona and to develop an appropriate performance style. On comedian comedy, see Steve Seidman, *Comedian Comedy: A Tradition in Hollywood Film* (Ann Arbor: UMI Research Press, 1981); Frank Krutnik, 'The Clown-Prints of Comedy', *Screen*, vol. 25, no. 4–5 (July–October 1984), pp. 50–59; Peter Krämer, 'Derailing the Honeymoon Express: Comicality and Narrative Closure in Buster Keaton's *The Blacksmith*', *The Velvet Light Trap*, no. 23 (Spring 1989), pp. 101–16.

22   *New York American*, 17 February 1921, unpaginated clipping in scrapbook MWEZ x n.c.18,201, Billy Rose Theatre Collection (BRTC), New York Public Library at Lincoln Center, New York. This piece was probably written by the theatre critic, whereas an earlier positive review focusing on Keaton and mentioning Crane only once is likely to have been penned by a regular film critic or derived from a press release (*New York American*, 14 February, 1921).

23   *New York Evening Telegram*, 14 February 1921, unpaginated clipping, MWEZ x n.c.18,201, BRTC. Similarly, the involvement of Winchell Smith, the writer and stage director, was frequently mentioned, emphasizing the film's links to a tradition of quality in the theatre.

24   *Variety*, 18 February 1921, p. 40.

25   *New York Times*, 14 February 1921, p. 12:2.

26   *New York Morning Post*, 15 February 1921, MWEZ n.c.18,201, BRTC.

27   *New York American*, 17 February 1921, ibid.

28   Unidentified clipping, ibid.

29   *Photoplay*, May 1921, unpaginated clipping, Kevin Brownlow's personal collection.

30   *New York Globe and Commercial Advertiser*, 14 February 1921, MWEZ n.c.18,201, BRTC.

31   *New York Post*, 15 February 1921; *New York American*, 17 February 1921, ibid.

32   *New York Journal*, 14 February 1921, ibid.

33   *New York Herald*, 14 February 1921, ibid. Others simply, and approvingly, called Keaton's performance 'slapstick' or 'nonsense' designed to make people laugh. See *New York Globe and Commercial Advertiser*, 14 February 1921, ibid.; 'Buster Keaton's Nonsense Keeps You Chuckling', *New York Daily News*, 14 February 1921, ibid. Here these terms were used neutrally, if not positively; for the *New York Herald*, however, 'slapstick' had negative connotations.

34   A hint at what was at stake in this differentiation was given by the *New York Evening Mail* when it pointed out that Keaton's role and actions were basically childlike and, in their childish innocence, 'guaranteed inoffensive'. The possibility of offense, as well as slapstick's particular appeal, were related to those members of the audience who had not yet reached, and those who had gone beyond, the seriousness of maturity: 'grandma and all the children can be taken in perfect safety.' The realistic drama, which framed this infantile entertainment, however, was addressed to adults, dealing with their more mature concerns, which dominated in the end: 'as he (Bertie) winds up with a wedding and two children, it must be presumed that he is no longer a child.' (*New York Evening Mail*, 15 February 1921, ibid.)

35   *New York Times*, 14 February 1921, p. 12:2.

36   *New York Daily News*, 15 February 1921, MWEZ n.c.18,201, BRTC.

37   *New York Journal*, 14 February 1921, ibid.

38   Elizabeth Peltret, 'Poor Child', *Motion Picture Classic*, March 1921, pp. 64, 96–7.

39   Unidentified clipping in Buster Keaton file, Daniel Blum Collection, Wisconsin Center for Film and Theater Research, University of Wisconsin at Madison; cp. for example Willis Goldbeck, 'Only three Weeks', *Motion Picture Magazine*, October 1921, pp. 28–9, 87.

40   Dardis, op. cit., pp. 109–56.

Chapter 17

GAYLYN STUDLAR

"THE PERFECT LOVER"?
Valentino and ethnic masculinity
in the 1920s

AFTER HIS APPEARANCES IN *The Four Horsemen of the Apocalypse* (1921) and *The Sheik* (1921) combined to make Rudolph Valentino into a household name, the star was promoted to women as the "ideal lover," the "continental hero," "the polished foreigner," and "the modern Don Juan." Famous Players-Lasky/Paramount quickly realized that Valentino appealed almost exclusively to women audiences, a fact commented on again and again in reviews of his films.[1] Women's apparent enthusiasm for their new film idol was accompanied by the studio's carefully orchestrated strategy of stirring up interest in the star by stirring up controversy. One newspaper article (based on a publicity release) following the debut of *The Sheik* issued an explicit warning: "Don't read this if you don't like a controversy."[2]

To many observers of the 1920s, the stardom of and controversy surrounding Rudolph Valentino was not just the result of studio hype. It was created because the Italian-born star was the greatest evidenciary support of women's challenge to traditional sexual relations and American ideals of masculinity. [. . .] The implications were debated on a nationwide scale as the star became the most infamous example of screen masculinity aimed at women.

To large numbers of Americans, Valentino's emergence as an idol seemed to be the result of women's perverse search for a new model of masculinity with an erotic promise that made him much more dangerous than the physically passive mollycoddle or effeminate sissy boy. Normative manliness appeared beyond the reach of a newly emergent type of man in the 1910s and 1920s who was believed to vividly demonstrate the dreaded possibilities of woman-made masculinity, a phenomenon discussed and denounced in antifeminist tracts, general interest magazines, and popular novels. In 1914 Michael Monahan warned readers of *The Forum* that, as a result of "too much womanism," America's "tradition of great men" was lost; taking its place was "an epicene type [of man] which unites the weakness of both sexes, a sort of man-woman."[3]

While this type was sometimes simply labeled a mollycoddle, he was taking on decidedly more dangerous qualities than mere mollycoddles of the past. This new type of man was believed to be dominating fiction even as he was finding real-life counterparts in the world of dance. By the mid-1910s American women had gone "dance mad" and were consorting with "lounge lizards," "cake eaters," "boy flappers," "tango pirates," and "flapperoosters" who, for money, mindless pleasure, or the lack of anything better to do, indulged dangerous feminine desires—on the dance floor and off.[4]

This stereotype of transgressive masculinity was already well established—and much decried—by the time Valentino came to stardom. In 1919 *Photoplay* ran an article praising actor Montague Love by comparing him to the "epicene" male types, described in terms that anticipate descriptions of Valentino: "These are the male ingenues, the civilian wearers of wrist watches, the cigarstand Romeos, the disporters of pink silk handkerchiefs in a corner coyly protruding from the breast pocket, the smokers of perfumed cigarettes, and nine out of ten of them are 'dancing just simply divinely.'"[5] While there were many variations on this stereotype of sexualized and greedy masculinity, at his most dangerous he was darkly foreign, an immigrant who was ready to make his way in the New World by living off women and their restless desires. [. . .] In an era in which eugenics and notions of racial purity came to the foreground in American social discourse, these men of suspicious foreign origin were thought to be an insidious threat to the nation. Their ability to sexually entice America's women meant that the latter were weakening in their will to fulfill their primary charge: keeping the nation's blood pure.[6]

The controversy surrounding Valentino's stardom was part of a broader public debate that centered on the stereotype of the degenerate man who was "dancing just simply divinely" and, it was agreed, seducing American womanhood into rejecting (either in fantasy or reality) the sincere, stalwart American man. As a former paid dancing partner to café society matrons, Valentino was easily dismissed as one of the "menial and sensual" immigrants who made their living by exploiting women's desire for the morally and sexually dubious pleasures that surrounded nightclub and tango tea dancing.[7] His commodification as a dancer threw him into the category of "male butterflies," the ultimate in woman-made masculinity described by one novelist as "that species of male vulgarly known as 'cake-eaters' and 'lounge-lizards,' . . . young men of extremely good looks . . . [who are adopted by women] for amusement much as kings in olden times attached jesters to their persons."[8] [. . .]

Transformations of the picturesque

> The world was dancing. . . . Paris had succumbed to the mad rhythm of the Argentine tango.
> —Intertitle, *The Four Horsemen of the Apocalypse* (1921)

After playing the villainous foreign gigolo in a handful of films, Valentino's first leading role came with his casting in *The Four Horsemen of the Apocalypse* (1921), an epic family melodrama that became the biggest box-office hit of the 1920s. As a former paid dancing companion and cabaret exhibition dancer, Valentino's successful film entry into stardom suggests a compromise formula typical of Hollywood's approach in the 1920s to controversial issues, especially those involving women.[9] While *Four Horsemen* capitalizes on the socially transgressive sexual implications of dance, it balances this with elements that suggest an alignment with ideological imperatives that might guarantee the film's success.

The notion that such an epic production necessitated the casting of ethnic actors like Valentino to insure its authenticity was implied by promotion and quickly picked up by reviewers. A *New York World* review noted that "the characters [are] used primarily to give color to the picture—South American natives, Spanish, French, and German specimens—are all strikingly individualized."[10] Another reviewer remarked of Valentino: "Here is a particularly well chosen player for type. Especially so since the part calls for an adept dancer of the Argentine tango, for Valentino was a dancer before he was a movie actor."[11] Chosen "for type," Valentino was cast as Julio Desnoyers, a character described as a "romantic South-American hero" and a "picturesque figure"[12] (fig. 17.1). The film exploited the exoticism of non-Anglo ethnicity as well as the audience's familiarity with deviant forms of dancing masculinity, including the male butterfly and the tango tea gigolo. However, it also works to make Valentino's deviant masculine type acceptable to a wide audience within a xenophobic and nativist culture.

Before he is ever shown on camera, Julio is described as the spoiled heir to an Argentine ranching family. But he is not to blame, for, as the intertitles tell us: "What chance had Julio Desnoyers to be other than a youthful libertine?" His "wild ways" are encouraged by his indulgent grandfather, Madariaga. At his grandfather's death, Julio moves with his parents to Paris, where he becomes an artist whose only visible talents are collecting female models and dancing. He relies on the latter, his "boyhood pastime," to secure the funds he needs "to satisfy his extravagant tastes": he teaches aging dowagers how to tango.

The film was a complex family-centered narrative with spectacular special effects and extraordinary production values, but many of its advertisements were focused on what was assumed to be its primary box-office attraction: "You cannot have known how the tango can be danced until you have seen: *The Four Horsemen of the Apocalypse*," proclaimed one, while another declared: "It is a dance for the hot countries, a dance of tropic passion! At first seductively slow then abruptly changing to steps of lighting quickness and lithe grace."[13] Not surprisingly, Valentino's first appearance in the film occurs in a stunning dance scene that speaks to the era's fascination with (and fear of) dance as a stimulus on the sexual imaginations of American women.

Dressed in a fantasy version of a gaucho's outfit, Valentino/Julio appears in close-up, puffing on a cigarette as he stares at a woman in a Buenos Aires dance hall. The foreign setting and costuming are important because they serve to momentarily naturalize and normalize Julio's masculinity by distancing it from the potential feminizing traits (sartorial excess, love of pleasure, avoidance of work, consumption) that were associated with the tango pirate in the United States. Julio cannot be accused of being a tango pirate at this point in the narrative since he is a native son whose ability to dominate women finds a thoroughly masculine outlet in "el tango."

The disreputable low origins of the tango as a dance of Argentine pimps and prostitutes are reasserted through the setting and in the heavily made-up female with whom Julio dances. Displaying a barely constrained "primitive" sexuality, Valentino proceeds to whip the woman's dance partner into submission, then slides her across the dance floor in the sensuous maneuvers of the tango. The woman is far from beautiful, the saloon is obviously working-class: but in spite of this—or rather *because* of this—the effect is devastating: Julio's beauty and sexual appeal are inscribed in the tango's ritualized grace and blatant machismo. Julio is the master of the woman's body in the tango's controversial "hot hip contact,"[14] but just as important, he is master of his own. Valentino's body becomes the authoritative instrument through which his character's exotic menace is combined with the erotic potential of a dancer's refined physical expressivity. [. . .]

The next appearance of dance in *Four Horsemen* occurs in connection with Julio's calculating, self-interested seduction of Marguerite Laurier (Alice Terry), an attractive young woman married to one of his father's friends. The beginning of their affair is set against the backdrop of a decadent Parisian tango palace where dance-mad dowagers and their male escorts share space with lesbians in drag. In this debauched atmosphere, Julio displays the suave duplicity associated with the lascivious pan-European seducer, a stereotyped role that Valentino earlier had essayed in films like *Eyes of Youth* (1919). Julio invites Marguerite to his studio. There, after a number of her visits, he appears as usual: polite, charming, attentive, accommodating. His pet capuchin monkey amuses his guest. With teacup perched in hand, Julio makes a rather

Figure 17.1 A picturesque figure drawn from type: Rudolph Valentino in *The Four Horsemen of the Apocalypse* (1921)

effeminate figure as he sits on a low settee, his pressed knees together at an angle. He appears to be listening intently to Marguerite's conversational pleasantries. But, in a matter of seconds, Julio is on his feet. He ignores Marguerite's protests and employs a blend of physical force and verbal persuasion to initiate sexual intimacy.

Such conventionally villainous behavior was associated with the mercurial sexuality of the European. Personified in film by Erich von Stroheim, such a man was believed to masquerade his essential bestial nature behind a carefully cultivated facade of continental manners. As a result, to attain normative masculinity Julio must atone for his sexual transgression. Like John Barrymore's heroes, he must be redeemed through suffering and the realization of true love, but here, Julio's transgression requires the ultimate sacrifice. Julio and Marguerite's affair is discovered, and they are forced to part. With the advent of the Great War and the loss of Marguerite, Julio realizes a purer love for her, but also a greater responsibility. He dies on a muddy battlefield in France, but effects a ghostly return to encourage Marguerite to fulfill her duty to her now blind husband. Julio's family mourns his loss. To them it is an overwhelming tragedy, but one that can be counted only among the millions. [. . .]

Four Horsemen of the Apocalypse foregrounds a *transformation* of masculinity that closely resembles Janice Radway's description of the construction of the hero in the modern romance novel. This should not be surprising since the literary phenomenon of the romance novel for women, Carol Thurston suggests, may have had its prototype in Edith M. Hull's sensational novel, *The Sheik*, made into Valentino's most influential film in 1921.[15] Neither should this seem unusual, in light of the era's obsession with the transformative potential of masculinity. However, there are different possibilities for transformation, some foregrounding character-building values that produce stalwart manliness, and others focusing on a transformation that produces an ideal, utopian lover.

Radway argues that, in the Harlequin romances, the male object of desire must undergo "the imaginative transformation of masculinity to conform to female standards." Initially possessed of a "terrorizing effect," he must be revealed to be other than he originally seems since the narrative must prove that male behavior (and, therefore, heterosexual romance) "need not be seen as contradictory to female fulfillment."[16] This is accomplished by introducing a feature of "softness" that tempers the hero's hard masculinity in the beginning, and then, by showing that the hero has the "quite unusual ability to express his devotion gently and with concern for his heroine's pleasure."[17]

In *The Four Horsemen of the Apocalypse* the hero's "terrorizing effect" is inscribed in the opening tango scene, but it should be remembered that misogyny and sadomasochism were highly conventionalized elements in the tango and the *apache* dance. [. . .] Thus, the tango can be seen as metaphorically representing the essential reality of patriarchal relations through its dramatic exaggeration of masculine domination and female submission. Its conventions permit the female spectator to enjoyably experience a ritual confrontation with male brutality. Within the suspended time and space of the dance performance, sexual violence is carefully controlled, just as it is in the romance novel so that a reconciliation with masculinity can occur.[18]

As a consequence of this process, the female spectator of *Four Horsemen* did not necessarily participate in a simple masochistic fantasy reproducing the dance partner's submission to the dark, mysterious, brutal man. She may savor the tango as a "*safe* display"[19] of dangerously eroticized heterosexual relations because she can rely on the conventionalized patriarchal dynamics of dance to displace responsibility for her own arousal onto the powerful male dancer. The actualities of casting and presentation offer the spectator the imaginative space to enjoy being superior—in class, ethnicity, and/or physical beauty—to the woman in Valentino's arms.

Her presumed superiority also allows the spectator to reinterpret the hero's misogynistic male behavior in a sympathetic light that prepares the way for the reconciliation of masculinity with feminine ideals. For example, when Julio returns to his table with his dance partner, his grandfather suddenly collapses to the floor. Julio roughly discards the woman on his lap when she (thinking, perhaps, that the old man is drunk) laughs at him. However, the female spectator may regard Julio's rejection of the inadequate (i.e., slovenly, lower-class, insensitive) woman as appropriate. Ironically, what the film accomplishes at this misogynistic moment is the revelation of Julio's "feminine" side in his tender concern for his grandfather who, in actuality, is dying.

In romantic terms, this revelation is quite significant. It will be extended to Julio's boyish interaction with his mother, whom he unashamedly kisses and caresses on a number of occasions. The emotional and physical closeness of mother and son demonstrated in *Four Horsemen* is duplicated to great effect in Valentino's 1922 vehicle, *Blood and Sand*. A similar revelation of tenderness figures importantly in *Monsieur Beaucaire* (1924) in a moment in which the Duke of Chartres (Valentino) suddenly comforts a black child. The child, a servant to the court, has broken a delicate fan and, expecting punishment, starts to cry. When the fan is discovered, the Duke announces that he accidently broke the fan. The princess Henrietta (Bebe Daniels), who heretofore has dismissed the Duke as a worthless womanizer, has observed his interaction with the child. As a result, she is pleasantly surprised by the revelation that he may be a man of feeling and compassion. A similar strategy is evident in vehicles of other matinee idols of the era, including those of John Barrymore. This strategy resonates with Radway's claim that Harlequin narratives of masculine transformation reassure the female reader that the patriarchal system is really benign as they fulfill her deeper need to symbolically recover, through heterosexuality, a mother's love that promises that the heroine will have all her needs passively satisfied.[20]

The early demonstration of Julio's tenderness in the context of familial love in *Four Horsemen* serves to suggest the hero's capacity for such "maternal" nurturing in which tenderness is not merely a prelude to a sexual encounter focused on satisfying *his* desires. That capacity for tender nurturance will ultimately find romantic confirmation in Julio's transformed relationship with Marguerite: he becomes a war hero who reverently kisses the hem of her nurse's veil. This same quality of tenderness would be emphasized in other Valentino vehicles. An advertisement for *The Eagle* (1925) declared its hero to be "as soft as a woman when the heart rules."[21]

In *Four Horsemen of the Apocalypse* dance also provides a nuanced physical revelation suggesting that the beautiful but misogynist man possesses a latent capacity to be another kind of lover, one who combines strength and tenderness. In dance, the hero's authoritative masculinity promises sexual excitement, but women spectators, like romance readers, may see something else in his refined grace. They may see, in Radway's words, that he is also "a man who is capable of the same attentive observation and intuitive 'understanding' that they believe women regularly accord to men."[22] It is of no little interest that an interview with Valentino for *Dance Lover's Magazine* stresses some of these very same qualities in dance: "Would-be tangoers," Valentino is quoted as saying, "should remember that the good dancer gives his exclusive attention to his partner."[23] By projecting feminine qualities on the overvalued erotic object, the reader/viewer is reassured that her fantasy lover's sensitivity will preclude his transgression of the boundaries of her desire. This strategy within the context of dance anticipates Valentino's declaration to Yasmin (Vilma Banky) in *The Son of the Sheik* ("A love such as mine can do no harm") and participates in a wish-fulfilling denial of patriarchal realities. [. . .]

However, it is another type of masculine transformation that probably helped to solidify a wide audience for *The Four Horsemen of the Apocalypse*. Promotion capitalized on the more traditional, character-building spectacle of Julio's transformation from male butterfly into sacrificing war hero. One advertisement described the situation that requires a transformation: "Their [the lovers'] butterfly mentalities do not even respond at first to the sudden shock of war that breaks about them"; another declared: "And when he did enlist it was from a greater force than merely being lonely without his boulevard companions. It was the first time in his life anything but pleasure had actuated him."[24] Of course, men who danced instead of worked for a living were regarded as prime candidates for a little war service, and Julio's attainment of proper manhood certainly would have provided a measure of wish fulfillment for a broad segment of the American public: Americans had regarded the Great War as a moral crusade that, in the words of the *Washington Post*, could turn any "slacking, dissipated, impudent lout" into a man.[25]

Julio would not be the only Valentino character to require such an ideologically normative transformation. This very same approach to masculinity would be continued in publicity for another Valentino film, released the following year, *Moran of the Lady Letty* (1922), a seafaring adventure advertised as the story of "a soft society dandy whom love made a man."[26] In this so-called "Love Story with a Viking Heroine," Ramon Laredo (Valentino) is a rich young sportsman who appears to be a "softy" but needs only to be shanghaied off to sea to prove that he is actually an appropriate, manly partner to a robust female sailor, Moran.[27]

Nevertheless, such variations on the culturally familiar transformation of a mollycoddle into a man would not become a regular feature of Valentino vehicles, perhaps because his characters, as post-mollycoddle butterflies and lounge lizards, were regarded as more difficult if not impossible to transform into true American manliness. This absence may account, in part, for the difficulty of those films after *Four Horsemen* to define Valentino's image of masculinity as socially acceptable (to men) as well as sexually persuasive (to women). [. . .]

"Who said lounge lizard?"[28]

In the wake of his appearance in *The Four Horsemen of the Apocalypse*, Valentino's extratextual persona was constructed squarely within terms already applied to "divinely" dancing men, and his career as a dancer was simultaneously disavowed and exploited in fan magazines and film promotion. In particular, the early star exploitation of Valentino as yet another "young and pretty" romantic movie idol revolved around the film industry's manipulation of predictable negative reaction against the star as a woman-made dance commodity of dubious foreign origin.

As early as 1922 *Motion Picture Magazine* published an article, "The Perfect Lover," that described Valentino in terms that both catered to the fascination with the tango pirate and simultaneously attempted to defuse Valentino's (and the pirate's) transgression of American gender norms. Author Willis Goldbeck describes the actor as "suave, enigmatic, with a glistening courtesy alien and disarming." Immediately after this description befitting a gigolo, he advises the reader to "first of all dismiss the idea of the sleek and the insidious. There is nothing repellent, nothing unmasculine about Valentino. Merely a heavy exoticism, compelling, fascinating, perhaps a little disturbing."[29] Although Goldbeck plays with negating the idea that he has raised (of "the sleek and the insidious"), he goes on to hint of another characteristic often attributed to the foreign tango pirate when he notes of the young star: "His manner is always one of repression, repression—volcanic repression, one thinks nervously."[30] Valentino's continental facade hides what some might have interpreted as exciting sexual promise, but others regarded as dangerous foreign bestiality.

Valentino was not the first ethnic, romantic male star, nor was he the first male vamp, but his darkly handsome good looks and his dance background meant that he could not receive the same treatment as other notable ethnic male stars. [. . .] A Paramount-produced fan magazine reveals a direct (if heavy-handed) approach to the problematic implications of Valentino's former profession. Noting that "most screen stars [are] capable of taking up other professions," *Screenland* recites the work-centered accomplishments of other Paramount male stars, then defensively declares: "Rudolph Valentino could make a good living as a dancer, though he doesn't like it as a profession, but his real qualifications, aside from his skill as an actor, is [*sic*] landscape gardening."[31] In 1924 a letter to a newspaper summed up a view of the star that obviously continued to have currency: "And as for Rudolph Valentino, I doubt whether he could earn a living outside of a motion picture studio or a dance hall."[32]

Rather than redeeming his humble immigrant beginnings in America, the well-known facts of Valentino's multifaceted connection to dance, in combination with the circumstances of his rise to stardom, merely confirmed his status as a woman-made man. He was woman-made as a professional dancer since he partnered already-established female dancers: Bonnie Glass, and then Joan Sawyer.[33] His first wife, Jean Acker, publicly despaired of her efforts to make a man of him during their divorce proceedings and recounted, damningly, how she had been forced to support him: "I gave him money, underwear and clothes."[34] It was reported that he had been brought to film fame by a woman, screenwriter June Mathis, who was later described by fan magazines as "A Maker of Young Men." After her discovery of Valentino, it was claimed, Mathis was besieged by other "young Valentinos [who] constantly obtrude themselves into her home, over the very bodies of her servitors, imploring to be 'made' . . . [and regarding her] 'with conscientiously amorous eyes.'"[35] According to racial stereotype, these stories reconfirmed Valentino's place of public preeminence among dark, desperate, dancing young men with ambition—and good looks.

In spite of publicity pronouncements that attempted to detach Valentino from his association with dance and, therefore, with the foreign tango pirate, that connection was inevitably exacerbated by interviews and fan magazine articles in which Valentino's concern for women's pleasure as well as his ethnicity were emphasized. In an early article for *Photoplay*, "Woman and Love" (fig. 17.2). Valentino (or, more likely, a studio ghostwriter) comments on American sexual relations and speculates on the reasons why the star is disliked by American men. Echoing conservative commentary, Valentino calls American women "too restless"; he then makes statements that capitalize on his characterization of the "masterful" Sheik, Ahmed Ben Hussain, even though Valentino's Sheik was considered by most reviewers as only marginally masterful, a "Continental gentleman" in comparison with his literary counterpart:[36]

I do not blame the women for all this. I blame the American man. He cannot hold a woman, dominate and rule her. Naturally things have come to a pretty pass. He is impossible as a lover. He cares nothing for pleasing a woman. He is not master in his own house. . . . He expects to feed a woman on the husks left from business and gold and money, and satisfy her! . . .

In his blindness therefore, he despises the young European who comes here. He laughs at him, makes fun of him, calls him insulting names. Why? Because this man, versed and trained in all that goes to make everything from the lightest philandering to the deepest amour, exquisite and entertaining and delicate, this man—what do you say—shows him up? Yes.[37]

Woman and Love

By RUDOLPH VALENTINO

WHEN you ask me to write for you what I think about woman, I feel that I must produce for you something that would look like the Encyclopedia Britannica. Yet when I should be through with this great work, I shall still have said less than nothing about woman.

We cannot know woman because she does not know herself. She is the unsolvable mystery, perhaps because there is no solution. The Sphinx has never spoken—perhaps because she has nothing to say.

But since woman is the legitimate object of man's thoughts, and mine have been somewhat distilled in the alcohol of experience, I may be able to give to you a little draft of truth.

English is not my own tongue as you know. In Italian, French, Spanish, I might express myself better, for there we have such little words that have fire and understanding and delicate shades of meaning to which I know not yet the English translations.

My point of the view on woman is Latin—is continental. The American man I do not understand at all. I have lived much in Paris, in Rome, in New York, and from this traveling, which is of the finest to develop the mind and understanding soul, I have composed my little philosophy about woman.

For there is only one book in which you may read about Woman. That is the Book of Life. And even that is written in cipher.

But those who refuse to read it are generally more deeply wounded than those who digest it thoroughly.

What comes to my mind first as I try to put into some order my ideas on this all-important subject, I will tell you.

It is this. Which of the women I have known, have perhaps loved a little, do I remember instantly; and which have I forgotten, so that I must think and think to recall them at all?

The most difficult thing in the world is to make a man love you when he sees you every day. The next is to make him remember that he has loved you when he no longer sees you at all.

Strangely enough, I remember the women who told me perhaps their little lonelinesses, who spoke in close moments true and sweet and simple heart throbs.

Even the highest peak of emotion is finished. It has flamed, gone out, and told us very little about life. It was to enjoy, to drink deeply. But never is even that treasured in the heart as are those moments of simple, tender confidences, when a gentle, loving sigh opened the treasure house of a woman's heart and she spoke truly of those things within.

A man likes even the bad women he knows to be good.

To a woman who has revealed her soul, who has given a brief glimpse of her heart, no man ever pays the insult to forget; he pays her homage. I remember a little Italian girl I once knew. She was very beautiful—so young. We used to sit in a tiny cafe we knew in Naples, and hold hands quite openly. I do not think I ever kissed her. We talked little, for she was not educated. It was not her magnificent eyes, nor the glory of her hair that was like a blackbird's wing, nor the round white curves of her young body—I remember her because of those little intimate moments when our thoughts were bound together by her simple, tender, gentle words. We were intimates, and the soul is such a lonely thing that it treasures those moments of companionship.

> I do not like women who know too much.
>
> The modern woman in America tries to destroy romance. Either it must be marriage or it must be ugly scandal.
>
> No other woman can ever mean to a man what his children's mother means to him.
>
> A love affair with a stupid woman is like a cold cup of coffee.
>
> I would not care to kiss a woman whose lips were mine at our second or third meeting.
>
> One can always be kind to a woman one cares nothing about.
>
> The greatest asset to a woman is dignity.

Figure 17.2 Fan magazines stir the flames of controversy about Valentino's masculinity (1922)

Exploiting the conservative idea that America's restless women really wanted a "masterful man" to rule them, the article also recirculates the stereotype attached to the tango pirate as the "Continental gentlemen" best known (and least liked) by American men.

This kind of exploitation of the star as a controversial figure was successful, but Valentino's attacks on American men as being obsessed with business and bad lovers to boot were bound to fan the flames of negative male response. Such a publicity strategy exploited Valentino's foreignness in negative terms in much the same way as Universal promoted Erich von Stroheim as "the man you love to hate." But while the strategy for selling Valentino, like that for von Stroheim, appears as the conscious manipulation of predictable xenophobic reaction against a foreign commodity, the publicity discourses surrounding Valentino seemed unable to contain that reaction. Was it because Valentino's prototype, the tango pirate, seemed both more familiar and of more immediate danger than von Stroheim's Hunnish "cross between a crown prince and a weasel"?[38] Was it inadvertent, a result of the inability to control discourses emanating from the star system? Or was it based on Hollywood's ideological and aesthetic discomfort with Valentino combined with the country's discomfort with the immense scale of his transgressive popularity?

Hollywood's familiar strategy of attempting to give Valentino the sheen of European aristocracy failed. The facts of his immigrant life in the United States—as dishwasher, bus boy, gardener, and dance-for-hire—quickly became common knowledge. [. . .] The revelation of Valentino's background linked him also to those dark immigrants who wanted to hide what was believed to be their most dangerous characteristic: their racial/genetic inferiority. Through their false claims to aristocratic lineage, foreigners like Valentino, it was thought, tried to mask that inferiority while they attempted to appeal to the vanity and naïveté of American women.[39]

Valentino's good looks were subject to a debate that put into play racial terms familiar in the discourse surrounding both social and concert dance. [. . .] Adela Rogers St. Johns told *Photoplay* readers in 1924 that Valentino, "with his small eyes, his flat nose and large mouth, fails to measure up to the standards of male beauty usually accepted in this country."[40] Even if her opinion was not shared by millions of women, Valentino's good looks did not allow him to escape the stigma of his ethnic origins. Nor did it satisfy all female fans; the attitude of one *Photoplay* reader was simply stated: "Rudy looks wicked to me maybe because he is not an American."[41] [. . .] Racial ideology, then, may be a factor in the frequent tragic or bittersweet endings of Valentino's films that prevent romantic coupling.[42]

Race suicide discourse of the time dwelt on a fearful future world scenario resulting from those American women who chose racially inferior foreigners to be the fathers of their children. Within the context of America's racialist discourse, race was the determining factor in class, and no amount of beauty, money, aristocratic trappings, or movie fame could change racial character. It was feared that American women, duped by immigrants—especially those, like tango pirates, who achieved a masquerade of good breeding—would bear offspring who would inherit the ancestry of their dark foreign fathers, an ancestry that was considered to be tainted. [. . .]

By the mid-1920s America's susceptibility to a "foreign invasion" through sexual penetration seemed to many to be confirmed on numerous fronts: by tango teas, by movie-star marriages like Gloria Swanson's and Mae Murray's to European "princelets,"[43] and by Valentino's popularity as American women's ideal fantasy lover. Even as fan magazines appeared to acquiesce to women's perceived desire for an exotic model of masculinity, they often also worked to undercut Valentino, as if in response to a need to bring their own discussion of the star into alignment with ideological imperatives at odds with his studio and more important than he.

Instead of unequivocally endorsing him as a profitable film commodity, *Photoplay* attempted to demystify Valentino as the center of women's personal fantasy scenarios. Adela Rogers St. Johns noted that he might represent "the lure of the flesh" to women in his screen image, but in real life he was an "ordinary young man with atrocious taste in clothes, whose attributes render him devoid of physical charm." His leading ladies, she told readers, got absolutely no thrill in playing love scenes with him.[44] Similarly, Herbert Howe warned readers not to "confuse the man with his stellar shade": "He . . . is the pilgrim boy as far as trifling with hearts is concerned."[45] Such discussions implied that just as Valentino's aristocratic heritage was fake, so were his credentials as a lover. [. . .]

One fan magazine letter reacted to criticism of Valentino as a foreigner by reminding other readers that "we are speaking of actors and their acting and not of intermarriage with them."[46] Nevertheless, it seemed that the fear that America's dancing women might intermarry with darker, decadent "races" was strongly shaping the response to Valentino as the archetypal representative of those new immigrants from southern and eastern Europe who were the "slag in the melting pot" of America.[47] The "American idol" could not be made American enough. [. . .]

"A ladies' man who is a regular guy"

The tango's ethnically and sexually titillating effects were first tolerated within American social dance then tamed. Likewise, Hollywood initially exploited Valentino's decadent differences then reversed itself during the last two years of his career and worked toward a desperate reconciliation of his Otherness with masculine American norms. The reasons for this change can be traced to Hollywood's investment in numerous Valentino imitators and in disturbing rumors that the star's box-office appeal among women was slipping. In 1926 *Photoplay's* Herbert Howe declared, "The Valentino storm has blown over, leaving Rudy to paddle his bark by main strength of histrionic ability."[48]

Textually, the push toward reconciling Valentino with masculine ideological norms becomes apparent in Valentino's last three films. *Cobra* is obvious in this attempt but opened in December 1925 to poor reviews and disappointing returns. Borrowing heavily from a proven Douglas Fairbanks formula for film success, *The Eagle* followed. Demonstrating unusually high production values, *The Eagle* also attempts to mold Valentino into a more athletic Fairbanks-style Slavic hero whose first act is to ride to the rescue of a runaway coach. In contrast to *Cobra*, the film has a light, tongue-in-cheek humor characteristic of the "Lubitsch touch," due, no doubt, to the scenario-writing of frequent Lubitsch collaborator Hans Kraly. The film's emphasis on action and the hero's motivation of familial revenge give way to Valentino's transformation from masquerading hero to effete French tutor and sensitive lover.

The Eagle also comments on Valentino's matinee idol status through its hero, Dubrovsky. He, like Rodrigo in *Cobra*, must cope with the unwelcome romantic attentions of women. In this case, he draws the attention of a sexually aggressive woman who happens to be his czarina. Catherine the Great (Louise Dresser) swoons over Dubrovsky's charms. She prepares the ritual dinner that initiates young lieutenants into the sexual fast-track for generaldom. But Catherine's sexual designs are foiled by Dubrovsky's own scampish ability to evade her: "I volunteered for war duty only," he grouses after stomping out of her private quarters.

Valentino's last film, *The Son of the Sheik* (1926), released posthumously, returns to the same orientalist setting and the dynamics of kidnapping as *The Sheik*. However it, like *The Eagle*, is structured more on the order of a Fairbanks film and includes the typical Fairbanks father-son matrix typified by *Don Q, Son of Zorro*. With its exaggerated swordfights, gallery of grotesque villains, and display of the star as both stern father and robust son, the film attempts to recuperate Valentino into normative cult-of-the-body, character-building masculinity in ways similar to Fairbanks' later films. The *New York Times* reviewer noted, in fact, that the film's emphasis on revenge left little time for the matinee idol's expected screen forays into leisurely lovemaking.[49]

The relative lack of screen passion in Valentino's *The Son of the Sheik* is ironic since, by 1926, the representation of the romantic hero as ethnic erotic object had become a vogue. After recruiting ethnic actors during Valentino's standoff with Paramount in 1922, Hollywood discovered the most acceptable Latin Lover: actors who were thought to be from sturdy Anglo-Saxon stock were recruited to play swarthy, passionate foreigners, albeit within the framework of romanticized, Old World settings in films like *The Night of Love* (Ronald Colman), *The Cossacks* (John Gilbert), *The Thief of Bagdad* and *The Gaucho* (Douglas Fairbanks) and *The White Black Sheep* (Richard Barthelmess). Such stars could temporarily satisfy female desire for erotic exoticism without threatening either American men or the nation's Nordic/Anglo-Saxon purity. *Photoplay* promoted Ronald Colman in a 1924 article entitled "A Ladies' Man Who Is a Regular Guy: Ronald Colman Is a Favorite of Both Sexes." Real men, articles like this implied, would never be content to be matinee idols, but wanted to be directors, gentleman farmers, or really good actors.[50] Such stars could, like Colman in *The Night of Love*, masquerade as a vengeful gypsy chief who, in sheik-like fashion, kidnaps a princess, but they also could satisfy the need to channel women into ethnically, racially, and nationally normative models of heterosexual fantasy in a nativist culture.

Even as Anglo-American stars were capitalizing on the ethnic trends popularized by Valentino, the assignment of pejorative feminine and racist traits to Valentino intensified. One typical attack in the *New York World* described a Valentino press conference in which the star's managers told the press that men were swarming around the star because he was "magnetizing" them with his masculinity. Was Valentino aggressively seeking a male audience, as the article implies? A confirmation of this might be found in the textual shift of his last movies to a more Fairbanksian format, but the reporter suggests that the star's shift to seeking male fans is absurd: "In spite of press agents he will probably go until his death a lady's man, smiling that slow white smile, his sooty eyes watching effects."[51] The idea that this dancing foreigner, wearing slave bracelets given to him by his domineering wife, might (like a woman) watch whether he was arousing his fans, was too much to take. Dick Dorgan's classic Valentino diatribe, "Song of Hate," seemed much too mild to express the current level of feeling. It was no longer sufficient to say the obvious, that "all men hate Valentino."[52] [. . .]

Where good dancers go

In October 1926 *The Dance* satirically declared that Hollywood was the heaven of opportunity "where good dancers go when they die."[53] Valentino's sudden death of peritonitis five weeks before the magazine's appearance demonstrated a deep if no doubt unintended irony in that statement. Death would not end the debate over Valentino's symbolic place within the perceived crisis in American sexual and gender relations.

In spite of his American citizenship, his contradictory status as erotic outsider would be emphasized even in his death notices. Headlines in the *New York Times* proclaimed: "Valentino Passes with No Kin at Side; Throngs in Street."[54] Newspaper coverage reflected a distinctly unsympathetic bias toward the star. The *Times* reported at length on the fact that his hometown of Castellaneta, Italy, was "indifferent" to his death.[55] In another article it noted, "Few Floral Offerings," then disavowed the significance of the lack.[56] Coverage acknowledged tributes that poured in from Hollywood to assert for one last time that Valentino was "one of the cleanest and finest stars in the motion picture world."[57] Nevertheless, the *New York Times* felt compelled to undercut such testimony with a report that the Vatican had remarked on the need for *two* priests at Valentino's bedside: "It [the Vatican organ] regards his popularity, with a crowd of young girls crazy about him, as a sign of the decadence of the time."[58]

Valentino, like dance, had become symbolic of tumultuous changes believed to be taking place in the system governing American sexual relations. If concert and social dance confronted post-Victorian America with a "confused realm of beauty and moral uncertainty,"[59] Valentino had confronted the country with other uncertainties as well. While some of these gender-based uncertainties converged with those offered by other matinee idols, such as John Barrymore, Valentino presented a higher order of problematics that circulated around the convergence of female fantasy with the dangerous, transformative possibilities of dance and with the highly restrictive norms for constructing ethnic masculinity in a frankly xenophobic nation. Valentino, "The American Idol," generated a discourse in which he could not escape condemnation as an indolent foreign male whose beauty and grace in motion constituted a mask behind which he was thought to hide the genetic corruption attributed to all such immigrants. [. . .]

Even as Valentino embodied anxieties to some, he represented a promise to others. [. . .] Valentino had been culturally poised between a traditional order of masculinity and a utopian feminine ideal, between an enticing sensual excess ascribed to the Old World and the functional ideal of the New. Ultimately, the aesthetic implications of American efficiency, productivity, and economy brought formal changes to the arts in America, including film and dance.[60] But the wholesale textualization of the body as a kinetic machine would have to wait, for at least a moment, as Hollywood offered women the "optic intoxication" of Rudolph Valentino and generated a fantastic vision of the reconciliation of masculinity and femininity through a privileging of the dancer's body as a site of expressive knowledge and sensual understanding.

Notes

1. See, for example, review of *A Sainted Devil* (1924) in *Variety*, November 26, 1924; reprinted in *Variety Film Reviews, 1907–1980* (New York: Garland, 1983), n.p.: "Maybe it'll satisfy the Valentino rooters. Most of them are women, and this is a woman's film." Also the review of *Monsieur Beaucaire* (1924) in *Variety*, August 13, 1924; reprinted in *Variety Film Reviews, 1907–1980*, n.p.: "The women will 'go' for this one by the thousands. The girls made up three-quarters of a sweltering house when this feature was reviewed."
2. N.E.A. Service, "A Love Recipe That Is Almost Sure to Start a Controversy," *Evening Examiner–New Era*, September 29, 1921 (unpaginated clipping, New York Public Library for the Performing Arts, Theatre Collection; hereafter, NYPL–TC).
3. Michael Monahan, "The American Peril," *The Forum* 51 (June 1914): 878–789.
4. See Freeman Tilden, "Flapperdames and Flapperoosters," *Ladies' Home Journal* (May 1923): 10. See also Monahan, "The American Peril," *The Forum* 51 (June 1914). Monahan manages to connect women's influence with the tastes of immigrants. He argues that the "sexual themes" of sensational journalism "have been made possible largely by the immense immigration from Eastern Europe during the past twenty years. The taste is indeed rather Eurasian than American . . . and a decline of true journalistic power . . . seems closely related to the rise of women to influence in this field" (881).
5. Randolph Bartlett, "Speaking of Love," *Photoplay* 15 (February 1919): 71. [. . .]
6. Donald K. Pickens, *Eugenics and the Progressives* (Nashville, Tenn.: Vanderbilt University Press, 1968), 66–67. See also Paul J. Smith, *The Soul of Woman* (San Francisco: D. Elder, 1916), in which Smith says that women's "great task is to raise the level of racial quality" by being mothers who choose their "companions" carefully (60).
7. Louis Erenberg, *Steppin' Out* (Chicago: University of Chicago Press, 1984), 81–83.
8. John Wiley, *Triumph* (New York: Minton, Balch, 1926), 8.

9. For more on this, see Gaylyn Studlar, "The Perils of Pleasure? Fan Magazine Discourse as Women's Commodified Culture in the 1920s," *Wide Angle* 13, no. 1 (1991).

10. Review of *The Four Horsemen of the Apocalypse* in the *New York World*, c. September, 1921, n.p. (clipping, NYPL–TC).

11. "*Four Horsemen* Enthralls Viewers," *San Francisco Call*, June 28, 1921, n.p. (clipping, NYPL–TC).

12. Per caption for a photo of *Four Horsemen of the Apocalypse* in the *Newark American Tribune*, c. September, 1921, n.p. (clipping file, NYPL–TC).

13. *Four Horsemen* advertisement, c. 1921, n.p. (clipping file, NYPL–TC).

14. Judith Hanna, *Dance, Sex, and Gender* (Chicago: University of Chicago Press, 1988), 164–165.

15. Carol Thurston, *The Romance Revolution* (Urbana: University of Illinois Press, 1987), pp. 38–39. [. . .]

16. Janice Radway, *Reading the Romance* (Chapel Hill: University of North Carolina Press, 1984), 147.

17. Ibid., 128, 70.

18. Ibid., 71–73.

19. Ibid., 70–73.

20. Ibid., 147, 149. [. . .]

21. See *The Eagle* advertisement for the Rialto Theater, New York, c. November 1925, n.p. (clipping file, NYPL–TC).

22. Radway, *Reading the Romance*, 83.

23. Nanette Kutner, "Valentino's Own Version of the Tango," *Dance Lover's Magazine* 3, no. 5 (1925): 22.

24. Unsourced advertisements, c. 1921 (clippings, NYPL–TC).

25. Quoted in Peter Filene, "In Time of War," in Joseph H. Pleck and Elizabeth H. Pleck, eds, *The American Man* (Englewood Cliffs, NJ: Prentice-Hall, 1980), 324.

26. Advertisement for *Moran of the Lady Letty* in unidentified newspaper, c. 1922, n.p. (clipping file, NYPL–TC).

27. The phrase "Love Story with a Viking Heroine" is how the narration (synopsis) of the film's scenario is advertised for its appearance in *Photoplay*. See Gene Sheridan, "*Moran of the Lady Letty*," *Photoplay* 21 (February 1922): 49–51.

28. Caption to Valentino photo in *Screenland* (1923): n.p. (clipping file, NYPL–TC).

29. Willis Goldbeck, "The Perfect Lover," *Motion Picture Magazine* (May 1922): 40.

30. Ibid., 94.

31. "Most Screen Stars Capable of Taking Up Other Professions," *Screenland* (Dallas, Texas) 1, no. 2 (1922): 12.

32. C. Sarason (letter), *New York Daily News*, September 9, 1924, n.p. (clipping file, NYPL–TC).

33. In J. Winkler, "I'm Tired of Being a Sheik," Valentino says, "Bonnie Glass and Joan Sawyer, in turn, took me as a partner" (*Collier's* 77 [January 16, 1926]: 18).

34. "Wedded, Found Spouse Broke?" *Los Angeles Times*, November 24, 1921 (unpaginated clipping, NYPL–TC).

35. Gladys Hall, "A Maker of Young Men," *Motion Picture Classic* 19 (March 1924): 21. On Mathis's power in the studio system and her status as "the most influential screenwriter of the day," see Richard Koszarski, *An Evening's Entertainment: The Age of the Silent Feature Picture, 1915–1928* (New York: Scribner's, 1990), 239.

36. The phrase "a Continental gentleman" is from Adela Whiteley Fletcher, "Across the Silversheet," *Motion Picture Magazine* (n.d.): 108 (clipping, NYPL–TC). Fletcher says of *The Sheik*: "Remembering censorship, we wondered why they ever bought the motion picture rights in the first place." See also "Do Women Like Masterful Men?" *Baltimore News*, October 22, 1921 (unpaginated clipping, NYPL–TC). [. . .]

37. Rudolph Valentino, "Woman and Love," *Photoplay* 21 (March 1922): 106.

38. Mildred R. Hut (letter to the editor), *Photoplay* 22 (October 1922): 117, cited in Janet Staiger, *Interpreting Films: Studies in the Historical Reception of American Cinema*, ch. 6, "'The Handmaiden of Villainy': *Foolish Wives*, Politics, Gender Orientation, and the Other" (Princeton: Princeton University Press, 1992), 132. Staiger focuses on the reception of "outrage" that greeted von Stroheim's *Foolish Wives*.

39. In the 1920s many plays and books took up this subject, including Booth Tarkington's *The Man from Home* (made into a film in 1922), which told the story of how "an Italian prince makes passionate love to a pretty American girl in an attempt to win her millions" (quotation from *Shadowland*'s June 1922 issue, describing the film [clipping, NYPL–TC, n.p.]). In Arthur Tuckerman, *Possible Husbands* (New York: Doubleday, 1926), the heroine says, "American women are too adaptable when contemplating a foreign marriage, especially if there's a title at stake" (8).

40. Adela Rogers St. Johns, "What Kind of Men Attract Women Most?" *Photoplay* 25 (April 1924): 17.

41. Letter in "Brickbats and Bouquets," *Photoplay* 29 (February 1926): 118. [. . .]
42. Goldbeck suggests of Valentino: "He has been called, with tentative reservations, 'the perfect lover.' . . . It is not his fault; so let him suffer for it" ("The Perfect Lover," 40).
43. Even movie stars who married so-called princes were not beyond criticism. Mae Murray's marriage to a "princelet" who regarded his occupation as being "Mae Murray's husband" is ridiculed in "Robbing the Cradle," *Motion Picture Classic* (August 1928): 78. [. . .]
44. St. Johns, "What Kind of Men Attract Women Most?" 110–11.
45. Herbert Howe, "What Are Matinee Idols Made Of?" *Photoplay* 23 (April 1923): 41.
46. "Letters to the Editor," *Photoplay* 23 (September 1922): 113.
47. George Creel, "Close the Gates," *Collier's* (May 6 1922): 9. For a discussion of the dimensions of xenophobia in the United States during the 1920s, consult John Higham, *Strangers in the Land: Patterns of American Nativism, 1860–1925*, 2d. ed. (New Brunswick: Rutgers University Press, 1988). [. . .]
48. Herbert Howe, "Close-ups and Long Shots," *Photoplay* 29 (February 1926): 53.
49. Review of *The Son of the Sheik* in the *New York Times*, August 1, 1926; reprinted in *The New York Times Film Reviews* (New York: New York Times, 1970), n.p.
50. Arthur Brenton, "A Ladies' Man Who Is a Regular Guy," *Photoplay* 27 (December 1924): 132, 66.
51. "Rudolph Valentino to Change his Act?" *New York World*, November 22, 1925, n.p. (clipping, NYPL–TC).
52. Dick Dorgan, "I Hate Valentino," *Photoplay* 22 (June 1922): 26.
53. "A Dance Mappe of These U.S.: Culture Made Pleasant," *The Dance* 6 (October 1926): 25.
54. "Valentino Passes with No Kin at Side," *New York Times*, August 24, 1926, 1, 3.
55. "Native Town Forgets Actor," *New York Times*, August 26, 1926, 1, 5.
56. "Thousands in Riot at Valentino Bier," *New York Times*, August 25, 1926, 1, 3.
57. "Public Now Barred at Valentino's Bier," *New York Times*, August 26, 1926, 1, 5.
58. Ibid., 5.
59. Elizabeth Kendall, *Where She Danced* (New York: Knopf, 1979), 47.
60. Cecelia Tichi, *Shifting Gears: Technology, Literature, Culture in Modernist America* (Chapel Hill: University of North Carolina Press, 1987), 75.

Chapter 18

SUMIKO HIGASHI

THE NEW WOMAN AND CONSUMER CULTURE
Cecil B. DeMille's sex comedies

A N INNOVATIVE FILMMAKER DESCENDED from a famous theatrical family, Cecil B. DeMille was deservedly the only director, besides D. W. Griffith, to be inducted into the *Motion Picture News* Hall of Fame in 1922.[1] After exploiting the intertexuality of films, best-sellers, paintings, opera, theater, and historical pageants to legitimate early features in the 1910s, he set postwar trends by showcasing the "new woman."[2] Contrary to stereotypes a significant number of women in the Victorian era were college-educated activists cultivating same-sex rather than heterosexual relations. After the war young materialistic women were more uninhibited in pursuit of pleasure.[3] With characteristic flair, DeMille represented the experience of respectable middle-class wives as they were converted to belief in companionate marriage, in contrast to being sexually segregated in a supportive female culture.[4] Although he was addressing momentous social change, including a romantic definition of female sexuality, his approach was humerous and even witty. At the center of his sex comedies, specifically *Old Wives for New* (1919), *Don't Change Your Husband* (1920), and *Why Change Your Wife?* (1921), was the transformation of the sentimental heroine, piously devoted to family and community, as she became a clotheshorse and sexual playmate.[5] An inveterate consumer, she became the symbol of the modern Jazz Age.

At first, DeMille was reluctant to exploit trends that would culminate in postwar consumption accelerated by wartime restructuring of the economy.[6] But Jesse L. Lasky, Vice-President of Famous Players-Lasky and a colleague dating back to the days when they had founded the studio, was persuasive: "What the public demands to-day is modern stuff with plenty of clothes, rich sets, and action." Lasky advised the director and scenarist Jeanie Macpherson to "write something typically American . . . that would portray a girl in the sort of role that the feminists in the country are now interested in . . . the kind of girl that dominates . . . who jumps in and does a man's work. . . ." Specifically, he urged DeMille to adapt David Graham Phillips's novel *Old Wives for New* because it "is full of modern problems and conditions, and while there are a number of big acting parts, it does not require any one big star. . . . It would be a wonderful money maker and make a very interesting picture." As an alternative to Adolph Zukor's costly negotiations with Mary Pickford, the studio's biggest star, Lasky proposed all-star features capitalizing on Famous Players-Lasky's stock company. After paying $6,500 for the rights of Phillips's best-seller, a work that endorses divorce and remarriage to solve marital discord, he wrote to DeMille from his New York office: "Personally I would like to see you become commercial to the extent of agreeing to produce this novel . . . on account of the subject matter and the fame of the novel." Unrelenting, he wrote a few weeks later, ". . . you should get away from the spectacle stuff for one or two pictures and try to do modern stories of great human interest. *Old Wives for New* is a wonderful title. . . . I strongly recommend your undertaking to do it."[7]

DeMille began production in March 1918 in time for a successful mid-year release. After the film's success, Lasky encouraged the director to consider a variation of *Old Wives for New* titled *Don't Change Your Husband*. A film with elaborate fantasy sequences, this production launched Gloria Swanson on the path to stardom. Most likely, DeMille was also prodded to make *Why Change Your Wife?* another all-star feature with Swanson that completed the trilogy. Lasky argued, "It is really better that you produce this picture than William [DeMille's brother, who is credited with the story] on account of your being so strongly identified with *Don't Change Your Husband*. . . ."[8] Audience response to the trilogy and its sequel, *The Affairs of Anatol* (1921), attests to Lasky's expert reading of postwar moviegoing.[9] As he observed, there was "an entire change in the taste of the public" that manifested itself in the popularity of war pictures as well as "a decided tendency toward lighter subjects." Less than two years after the studio merged with Zukor's Famous Players to court the respectable middle-class, Lasky was encouraging DeMille to appeal to a broad audience. The director thus set an important trend both in the industry and in a burgeoning consumer culture. After the success of *Old Wives for New*, countless titles hinting at marital strife, such as *Rich Men's Wives*, *Too Much Wife*, *Trust Your Wife*, *How to Educate a Wife*, and *His Forgotten Wife*, appeared on marquee signs.

DeMille's trilogy established a light hearted tone about infidelity and divorce by updating the Victorian sentimental heroine as a frivolous consumer. But such a woman became more of a commodity herself as she acquired an expensive wardrobe to appeal to men. A fashionplate with a mansion as backdrop, DeMille's heroine set trends in clothing and interior design influenced by Orientalism, a theme relating consumption to sexuality and pleasure. As part of the rebellion against cluttered Victorian taste, women's fashion, as well as home decor, had been streamlined even before the war. After the armistice, *Theatre* announced in the flippant tone characterizing discourse on women as consumers:

> Los Angeles now fills the proud position Paris once occupied as the arbiter of fashion. . . . More women see deMille's pictures than read fashion magazines. . . . Five whole reels just crammed and jammed with beautiful creations . . . And then there are the tips on interior decoration and house-furnishing wherewith the Art Director and his staff . . . adorn each scene. It is within bounds to say that the taste of the masses has been developed more by Cecil B. deMille [sic] through the educational influence.[10]

Indeed, DeMille's mise-en-scène constituted an advice manual preaching against old habits of self-restraint, but one that only the middle and upper classes could afford. Goods such as fashion ensembles, home furnishings, and bathroom fixtures were represented in color and art deco design, informed by Orientalism, to signify modernity. A medium close-up of Swanson sleeping on a lace-trimmed, embroidered pillowcase in *Don't Change Your Husband* stressed the luxury of fine linens. Several years ahead of trends, the director had a profound influence on advertisers educating the "new" salaried, as opposed to the "old" propertied, middle class intent on self-fulfillment and upward mobility. Prescriptive literature in periodicals increasingly valued expenditure on goods symbolizing refinement.[11]

Signifying the uneven transition from a producer to a consumer economy, the middle-class self was now constructed in terms of personality rather than character. Self-realization was in effect a product of presentation and display rather than moral imperative. Advertisers exalted the acquisition of goods as the basis of personal identity by coopting the iconography and language of spiritual fulfillment. As a result, pictures acquired radiant, glowing and transcendent qualities. Particularly effective in sanctioning consumer behavior were dramatizations of the process of self-making inherent in liberal Protestantism. DeMille's mise-en-scène provided many such examples. A winning personality, well-dressed and adept in performance, could become "somebody," as Warren Sussman argues.[12] But constructing the female self in such theatrical terms had profound implications for women in a consumer culture. Admittedly, genteel middle-class women were already performers in social rituals staged in drawing rooms, and they promoted the vogue of parlor theatricals. But such performances were based on the assumption that cultural practice was a sign of proper breeding and good character.[13] As part of the modern cult of personality, however, the social construction of the female gender was now equivalent to a masquerade enhancing sex appeal. DeMille's "new woman" thus became a sexual commodity symbolizing the increasing reification of human relations, especially marital ones, in a consumer society. A spendthrift, she was now exposed, unlike the sentimental heroine in a privatized domestic sphere, to the moral dangers inherent in narcissistic consumer behavior.

The commodification of marriage: *Old Wives for New*, *Don't Change Your Husband*, and *Why Change Your Wife?*

David Graham Phillips, a best-selling novelist whose stories appeared in "new" middle-class periodicals like *Saturday Evening Post*, was prescient in contemplating the impact of modernity upon the family. Specifically, he was interested in "the bearing of the scientific revolution upon woman and the home."[14] Discord on the part of Charles and Sophy Murdock, the middle-aged couple in *Old Wives for New*, is revealed when the husband takes exception to his wife's slovenliness. An expression of her lack of personality, Sophy's disorderly and unkempt home attests to her neglect of self, husband, and two grown children. Phillips is sympathetic about her failings, attributed in part to rural origins, but DeMille mercilessly deconstructs the revered American wife and mother in favor of the "new woman."

Significantly, Jeanie Macpherson rewrote Phillips's marital squabble in terms of the exchange value of characters involved in sexual relationships. She begins *Old Wives for New* in the script as follows: "Life's Bargain Counter/Across which our destinies are bartered like/so many Sacks of Meal—to 'Fate.'/Some are sold for Dollars/Some for Ambition/Some for Love—but all—are 'Sold.'" As described in the script, "Life," costumed as Harlequin, is "constantly laughing" behind a counter with "tiny figurines of *live* people, grouped in four sections, marked . . . staples, remnants, novelties, and mark-downs. . . . Among these are the main characters of the story . . . Sophy Murdock—in 'Marked-Downs,' Murdock and Juliet in 'Staples'—Berkeley and Jessie in 'Remnants,' Viola in 'Novelties'."[15] Possibly, this sequence about the commodification of marriage was too literal a representation of marketplace transactions invading the domestic sphere. DeMille begins *Old Wives for New* instead with a didactic intertitle that could be construed as a quote from the novel but was not even a paraphrase and, moreover, could not be attributed to any character in the film:

> It is my belief, Sophy, that we Wives are apt to take our Husbands too much for granted. We've an inclination to settle down to neglectful *dowdiness*—just because we've 'landed our Fish!' It is not enough for Wives to be merely virtuous anymore, scorning all frills: We must remember to trim our 'Votes for Women' with a little lace and ribbon—if we would keep our Man a 'Lover' as well as a 'Husband'!

Such was DeMille's advice to female spectators enjoined to embrace the delights of the consumer culture, if only to retain their marital status.

Wasting no time, the film opens with the first of DeMille's celebrated bathroom sequences. Although the set design is modest compared to the spacious tiled bathroom with sunken tub and silk curtained shower in *Male and Female* (1919), the scene was surely impressive for audiences still living in homes without bathtubs.[16] A tub on the left stands opposite a door flanked by two wash basins, each with hot and cold water faucets, mirror, shelf, and pair of sconces. At right angle to the sink on the left is a stained glass window above a towel bar on the wall. Accentuating the cornice, doorway, window, and mirrors are designs in ornate molding. The flooring consists of alternate black and white tiles in a diamond-shaped pattern. Charles Murdock (Elliott Dexter), dressed in a bathrobe and assisted by a valet, opens the window so that a view of trees contrasts nature with artifice. A fastidious person, he is disgusted to find Sophy's hair clogging his basin, not to mention a messy comb and toothbrush carelessly left in his corner of the bathroom. Worse, a close-up from his point of view shows untidy toilet articles strewn on his wife's sink and vanity. Sophy (Sylvia Ashton), introduced in the credits as she is eating chocolates and reading the funnies, enters the bathroom in a grumpy mood and slams the window shut. She is wearing a loose bathrobe over her corpulent figure and has carelessly swept her hair into a knot. Deciding that a bath is not worth the effort, she seeks refuge in bed while her family breakfasts downstairs. Murdock seats himself at a table set with silverware and a glass of fruit compote but is displeased to find an orange spoon in the wrong place. The maid, who is as slovenly as her mistress, serves poached eggs with broken yolks. As he rises from the table in disgust, his daughter, who is a more sympathetic character in the novel, murmurs, "I'm sorry dear—if mother would only let *me* run the house!"

Disgruntled, Murdock retreats to his study and stares at a photograph of his wife, shown in an insert, when she was a slender young blonde (Wanda Hawley). A dissolve to a picturesque rural scene shows how he literally reeled in his bride while she was walking barefoot in the stream—a reference to fishing in the first intertitle. DeMille cleverly juxtaposes past and present as Murdock's memory of his lovely bride is intercut with Sophy, now an obese and untidy matron, bursting in on his reverie. Appalled by her aging figure, he declares, "Sophy—it's a degradation for two people to go on living who no longer care for each other! I propose that you will take half of all we've got—and that you and I shall release each other." A display of armaments on the panelled wall includes a pistol, blade, and sword. Apparently, the battle of the sexes has begun. Murdock and his son, Charley, who sides with his mother in the novel's version of the squabble, decamp on a hunting expedition. Again, DeMille associates romance with sportsmanship as the businessman falls in love with Juliet Raeburn (Florence Vidor), the owner of a boutique aptly named Dangerfield's.

Sophy is angered to learn that she may indeed have a rival. During an argument photographed in low-key lighting, she tears up the photo of herself as a young bride and exclaims, "Have all the fun you want with that younger, fresher woman—But just you remember . . . I'll never divorce you—never!" Who is at fault here? Sophy is self-indulgent. But Murdock, whose relationship with his daughter has incestuous overtones, is in love with a younger woman. Dramatic lighting is thus keyed to the emotional mood of a shot rather than the articulation of moral issues, as in DeMille's earlier films like *The Cheat* (1915) and *The Heart of Nora Flynn* (1916). Characteristic of the director's postwar visual style, set decoration, and costumes provide a more reliable sign of personal ethics.[17] Several weeks after the hunting trip in *Old Wives for New*, Murdock shops with his daughter at Dangerfield's and meets his business partner, Tom Berkeley (Theodore Roberts), accompanied by his mistress Jessie (Julia Faye) and her friend Viola (Marcia Manon). DeMille's mise-en-scène underscores the decline of separate spheres or the interpenetration of home and marketplace in that Juliet's boutique resembles a tasteful upper-class residence. A split-level design features a checkerboard black and white marbled floor, walls framed with moldings and intersected with pilasters and columns, an imposing chandelier, an elegant floor lamp and sconces, dark velvety drapery with tie backs, plush upholstered chairs, and artistic floral arrangements. Yet this well-appointed establishment, as signified by its name, is the site of transactions involving the commodification of women.

Because Juliet now shuns him as a married man, Murdock joins Berkeley, Jessie, and Viola at a supper club. An exotic dancer in a harem costume evokes Orientalist fantasies about illicit sexuality that is the focus of the plot. Unfortunately, Berkeley has a wandering eye and that evening transfers his attentions to a flirtatious blonde named Bertha (Edna Mae Cooper). Jessie, intent on revenge, intrudes on their rendezvous with a gun and retaliates with deadly aim. A sign of lower-class origins as well as loose morals, the prostitute's boudoir becomes the scene of Berkeley's unfortunate death. Bertha has a penchant for garish furniture decorated with gilt rococo curves, ruffled drapery, shiny bedspread, cheap art work on wainscoted walls, and kitsch memorabilia. Certainly, her garish room contrasts with Juliet's tasteful boutique.

After a divorce, *Old Wives for New* concludes when Sophy, flattered by Murdock's impecunious secretary, Melville Blagden (Gustav Seyffertitz), decides to undergo a torturous beauty regimen to remarry. A benign representative of the patriarchal order, Blagden educates Sophy to redefine herself as a commodity by purchasing cosmetics, gowns, and accessories. At the film's conclusion, DeMille cuts from Sophy's elegant wedding to Murdock's remarriage in Venice. After meeting at an outdoor flower market signifying nature as opposed to artifice, the businessman and dressmaker reconcile. Yet the film's affirmation of self-theatricalization emphasizes the importance of artifice in sexual and marital relations. Put another way, the reification of social relations under consumer capitalism has now invaded the boudoir to redefine matrimony. A sign of the erosion of separate spheres, even the private space of respectable homes now simulates the marketplace as a site for commodified female bodies.

According to a fan magazine article, "So many wives wrote indignant letters to DeMille about *Old Wives for New* that C. B. and his clever writer, Jeanie Macpherson, wrote a story from the wives' standpoint. . . ." The *Chicago News* described the second film of the trilogy as an attempt "to restore harmony with . . . feminine followers."[18] Although *Don't Change Your Husband* was interpreted as the wife's version of marriage, the heroine has already been transformed into a "new woman" so that her next lesson is tolerating her mate's humdrum habits. Leila Porter (Gloria Swanson), an elegant and fastidious woman, finds "several dull gray years of matrimony—getting slightly on her nerves." Blind to his wife's discontent, Jim Porter (Elliott Dexter) has an expanded waistline, buries his head behind newspapers, forgets their wedding anniversary, and eats green onions.

DeMille registers marital reversals through clever use of mise-en-scène. During a ballroom flirtation with ne'er-do-well Schuyler Van Sutphen (Lew Cody), Leila, costumed as Juliet with ropes of pearls in her hair, ascends a marble staircase featuring an ornate balustrade on screen right. After declaring that she can no longer tolerate a "'corned beef and cabbage' existence," Leila descends a marble staircase on the left in the vestibule of the house she is abandoning. While Jim, seated to her right, buries his head in the papers as the film opens, in her second marriage Leila finds Schuyler seated to her left at breakfast and equally immersed in the news. DeMille's mise-en-scène thus dramatizes the reification of marital relations: husband and wife are interchangeable parts as modern personalities signifying the dominance of exchange value in commodity production. Such a turn of events raises disturbing moral issues about the nature of consumption as practiced by the "new woman" in the marriage market. An art title shows a pyramid and sphinx symbolizing "The Eternal Feminine" to equate female self-gratification with mysterious Orientalism.

Determined to win back his former spouse, Jim shaves off his mustache, begins to exercise, and acquires a dapper wardrobe. Phillips observes in *Old Wives for New*, ". . . of those external forces that combine to make us what we are, dress is one of the most potent. It determines the character of our associations, determines the influences that shall chiefly surround and press upon us. It is a covering for our ideas no less than for our bodies."[19] Macpherson rewrites this quote in *Don't Change Your Husband* to signify the reification of human consciousness so that people are confused with things: "Of those external forces which combine to make us what we are, DRESS is the most potent. It covers our *ideas* no less than our bodies—until we finally become the thing we look to be." Indeed, a proliferation of mirror shots in DeMille's Jazz Age films attests to the increasing importance of style over substance.[20] A medium shot shows Jim standing in front of a mirror while staring at his image in a hand mirror. Although he is a business-man who handles financial negotiations, his pose resembles that of prostitutes, namely Viola in *Old Wives for New* and Toodles (Julia Faye), Schuyler's mistress in *Don't Change Your Husband*. During the credits of the former film, Viola, a "Painted Lady" with Orientalized features, sits in front of a dresser and applies rouge as she gazes in the mirror.[21] Similarly, Toodles is presented in the credits as she primps in front of a three-way mirror, turns around to face the camera, and kisses an image of herself in a hand mirror. Genteel preoccupation with appearances as a sign of character has deteriorated into narcissistic self-absorption. Accordingly, Jim wins back his former wife at the end of *Don't Change Your Husband* by transforming himself into a dinner guest wearing a tuxedo and a fur-collared coat. He has acquired personality. As part of the exchange, Leila now instructs the servants to serve him his favorite dish, green onions.

As a way of dramatizing the less inhibited nature of marriage in *Don't Change Your Husband*, DeMille conflates disparate Orientalist motifs in set and costume design. A Middle Eastern backdrop for social entertainment, Leila's living room features ornately carved pilasters, tapes-try, carpeting, and a potted palm. An Asian servant in Chinese dress provides drinks in cups carved out of precious jade. Leila, whom Schulyer addresses as "Lovely Chinese Lotus," poses in a turban (fig. 18.1) as part of the decor and carries a fan of peacock feathers. Even more exotic is Schuyler's mansion, a residence that includes a loggia with rattan furniture and a study simu-lating a display window with chinoiserie. A scroll hangs on the rear wall, and to its right an Oriental vase stands on a cabinet. A chair in the foreground is upholstered in fabric with a bam-boo pattern, and a fringed throw in floral print is artfully tossed over a nearby sofa. On the right side of the floor, partially covered with an Oriental carpet, stands an ornate table with an incense burner. Leila, responding to the pungent aroma filling the air, enters this sybaritic domain at her peril. Delighted by a beaded costume, she drapes the fabric around her body in a manikin's pose that recalls a similar moment in *The Cheat*. A description of this scene in the script implies that consumption has its dangers: "A change comes over Leila; . . . she seems suddenly to be slipping back into Orientalism; to be taking on a real, subtle, *un-American* personality. She is no longer a laughing Society Woman merely trying on a Chinese Cloak, for fun. . . ."[22]

Consumption as visual appropriation was a cultural practice already linked to exotic sites by halftones, magic lantern slides, panoramas, stereographs, and actualities, as well as by museum and world's fair exhibits and department store displays. Orientalism signified not only luxury but self-indulgence and depraved sensuality. A form of sexual license, consumption was thus interpreted as un-American, unpatriotic, or uncivilized, even as middle-class shoppers eased their consciences and loosened their purse strings. Preoccupation with bathing rituals and elegant bathrooms, as represented in DeMille's texts, belied anxiety insofar as consuming evoked the "Other," including spendthrift women.[23] Commodities that signified genteel status,

Figure 18.1 Wearing an exotic turban, Gloria Swanson converses with dinner guests in a home rich with Orientalist decor in *Don't Change Your Husband* (1919)

moreover, threatened middle-class masculinity, already beleaguered in an urban and industrial setting. Schuyler in *Don't Change Your Husband*, for example, is an effeminate voluptuary because Orientalism remains at the core of his obsession with sexuality. His exclamation about "Pleasure," "Wealth," and "Love" cues the sensational fantasy sequence of the film. A spectacle prefiguring the flashback to a Babylonian court in *Male and Female*, this footage consists of three separate scenes photographed mostly in extreme long shot: Leila seated on a gigantic swing suspended over a swimming pool adorned with masses of flowers and bathing beauties in fishnet stockings; Leila worshipped by the well-oiled bodies of black male slaves at her feet in an opulent Oriental court; and Leila clad in flimsy chiffon as she lounges in an Edenic paradise with Bacchus squeezing grapes into her mouth.

At issue in the so-called revolution in manners and morals signifying increased commodification of women was the nature of heterosexual relations. DeMille did hint at darker dealings between men and women in a disarmingly blunt intertitle in *Old Wives for New*. After Jessie shoots Berkeley, she confides to Murdock, "I killed him—he was a beast! No man ever knows what another man is with a woman!" Also revealing is a sequence in *Don't Change Your Husband* when Toodles bursts into the Van Sutphen residence to claim a share of the cash that Jim has paid Schuyler, fallen on hard times, for Leila's solitaire. Giving her husband's mistress half a wad of thick bills, Leila explains, "Don't misunderstand—he *owed* you something—and you are paid! He promised me a few things, too, such as Love and Protection—and he didn't pay!

Let's only one of us be cheated!" The use of financial language is extremely apt in a film that dramatizes the increasing commodification of matrimony. For a brief moment, the battle of the sexes takes precedence over class distinctions separating wife and mistress. Although unconventional nineteenth-century feminists like Elizabeth Cady Stanton outraged genteel society by comparing marriage with prostitution in attempts to reform divorce laws, the reification of marital relations based on exchange value, as shown in these films, implied no less.[24]

Industry discourse: old vs new morality

Significant change in the demographics of film attendance in the 1920s was related to trends established by the exhibition of DeMille's early Jazz Age films. Certainly, exhibitors distinguished between middle-class patrons of first-run theaters and working-class, ethnic audiences at neighborhood venues, as well as between urban centers and rural areas. During a decade of social strife signified by the Red Scare, labor strikes, immigration restriction, prohibition, the Sacco-Vanzetti case, the Ku Klux Klan, and the Scopes trial, the search for a national market in film exhibition was essential. The exploitation of DeMille's films showed that market segmentation based on class, race, ethnicity, religion, and geographical region could be superceded by an appeal to gender. Although reception of commercialized amusement was mediated by subcultures, the director's emphasis on set and costume design appealed to women. As his brother William noted about the democratization of luxury, "Paris fashion shows had been accessible only to the chosen few. C. B. revealed them to the whole country, the costumes his heroines wore being copied by hordes of women and girls throughout the land, especially by those whose contacts with centers of fashion were limited or non-existent." DeMille represented this obsession with style in *The Affairs of Anatol* when a farmer's wife copies a magazine illustration, shown in an insert, to trim an ordinary hat. Since the director became the industry's most important trendsetter in the late 1910s and early 1920s, his emphasis on fashion was surely related to changes in the demographics of the film audience. According to Richard Koszarski, the percentage of men in motion picture audiences began to decline in the 1910s, whereas the number of women rose from 60 percent in 1920 to 83 percent in 1927.[25]

Critical discourse, including the response of women in fan magazines, focused on controversial issues avoided by exhibitors. During the same month that critics were taking note of *Old Wives for New*, Adolph Zukor asserted that "Wholesome dramas, uplifting in character, clean comedies, comedy dramas, and plays dealing with the more cheerful aspects of life will be exclusively chosen for production."[26] DeMille recalled that Zukor, who "spent millions to plaster the country about the purity of Paramount Pictures," reluctantly released his trend-setting film.[27] Indeed, the production had been subject to in-house censorship.[28] Critics disagreed about the extent to which *Old Wives for New* violated social conventions, yet their very differences reveal a lack of consensus regarding problematic issues like divorce. R. E. Pritchard, for example, summed up his assessment in *Motion Picture News*: "There are some risque situations in the story, but these have been handled delicately." Frederick James Smith, however, objected in *Motion Picture Classic* to "scenes of disgusting debauchery" and "immoral episodes." He concluded, "It is extremely difficult to build up a pleasing romance upon a foundation of divorce." Similarly, Edward Weitzel claimed in *Moving Picture World* that "hardly any of the characters command the spectator's respect. Charles Murdock . . . has but little moral stamina, and is surrounded, principally, by well-dressed men and women of no morals at all." Weitzel even suggested censoring objectionable material: "The cabaret scene is too insistent in establishing the moral laxity of its female guests, and other scenes of the same nature would stand cutting." *Variety*'s critic also discussed censorship: "There appears to have been some doubt as to the propriety of presenting the picture in total at the Rivoli in New York [a first-run theater]. . . . cutting was no doubt considered." Clearly, critics recognized that *Old Wives for New* was questionable, but they moved their discussion to the high ground of art to appeal to respectable middle-class patrons. Pritchard asserted that "it is the kind of picture that will convince those who doubt that the photoplay has reached the artistic plane of the spoken drama." The "Exhibitor to Exhibitor Review Service" in *Motion Picture News* agreed that the "feature will prove objectionable to some of you. Nevertheless, this picture is very artistic."[29]

Don't Change Your Husband elicited another chorus of disagreement that is revealing about exhibition practices. Smith stated in *Motion Picture Classic*, "We do not agree with Miss Macpherson's philosophy, but we admire her effort . . . in approaching the realities of things as they are." *Variety* labeled the film "clean and wholesome," but *Motion Picture News* counseled exhibitors, "It suggests the divorce element without your having to go into that, and we wouldn't do so directly, because you are likely to sacrifice some of the intensely human appeal of this picture." As for the fantasy sequence, the trade journal claimed, "There is a sensuous touch here and there in the scenes that follow. They will offend no one, but they will create a lot of talk for the picture itself."[30] Aware of cultural differences, exhibitors found it difficult to market films about divorce and prostitution, especially in small towns and rural areas embracing religious fundamentalism. As a matter of fact, the Phillips novel, published a decade before the film's release, still construes divorce as socially undesirable in contrast to the blasé manner in which DeMille's characters exchange spouses. Apparently, exhibitors engaged in a high wire act by exploiting the sex appeal of a film but taking steps not to offend patrons.

Despite controversy, DeMille's early Jazz Age films played to large, enthusiastic audiences in first-run theaters in major cities. At Grauman's Million Dollar Theatre in downtown Los Angeles, *Don't Change Your Husband* broke all attendance records so that Sid Grauman held the picture over for another week. By the time *Why Change Your Wife* was released in April 1920, Smith noted the shifting moral standards of the era: "What a shock Cecil deMille's latest silken orchid drama . . . would have caused but two short years ago." But *Motion Picture News* pointed out that the feature "practically throws that which most people call part of the moral code overboard with its teaching, [and] presents its principal characters as people who have about as much regard for the sanctity of the marriage vow 'as an Arab does for a sun bath,'. . . for an exhibitor with a neighborhood or small town house it may not be an ideal attraction."[31] Constituting a parallel discourse on the evils of modernity was the trade journal's equation of sexual licence with images of Orientalism.

Sidestepping the cultural divide between rural and urban America, exhibitors showed *Why Change Your Wife?* in cities by avoiding divorce and stressing consumption. Although these two issues were interrelated, as the film's title implies, emphasis on fashion was a clever way to defuse public reaction to controversial issues. Sid Grauman, for example, simulated the screen by displaying paintings of movie stills in downtown Los Angeles shops, surely a reversal of constructing film as a plate glass window. Such advertising resulted in a special 10:45 p.m. performance that was added to the schedule to accommodate crowds at Grauman's Rialto. A similar campaign based on window tie-ups in fashionable stores was orchestrated in concert with the Memphis Chamber of Commerce. A month after the film's release, Paramount ran an ad in *Motion Picture News* to boast that "*Why Change Your Wife?* has broken records in every city in which it has been shown." Constructing an elaborate showcase for the film's premiere in New York, Adolph Zukor spent thirty thousand dollars to renovate the Criterion. Indeed, Zukor's strategy of acquiring an interest in first-run theatres resulted in publicity for Famous Players-Lasky specials shown at higher admission prices. As *Moving Picture World* noted about the record-breaking success of *The Affairs of Anatol* in the following year, "a Broadway showing is not always indicative of the attitude of the country, [but] such a run determines a great deal."[32] The exploitation of feature films at movie palaces, especially those appealing to fashion-conscious women, thus influenced nationwide trends in exhibition practices.

Although the industry still relied on small-town exhibitors and neighborhood venues in urban areas, exploitation stressing window tie-ups in department stores and movie ads in *Saturday Evening Post*, *Ladies' Home Journal*, and *Colliers* were obviously aimed at middle-class women. As for working-class, ethnic women, social historians like Elizabeth Ewen and Kathy Peiss emphasize the importance of filmgoing for a younger generation preoccupied with fashion as a mode of self-representation and assimilation.[33] Appealing to female spectators was thus an industry strategy that surmounted socioeconomic and cultural barriers. As early as 1918, *Motion Picture News* suggested that exhibitors display pictures of female stars in elegant costumes to attract women. Advertising, moreover, did not cease once the audience was seated inside the theater and began to enjoy the entertainment. As *Motion Picture News* observed about *Why Change Your Wife?*, DeMille inserted close-ups of commodities such as perfume and "a certain talking machine company's records."[34] Spectacle representing the allure of consumer goods, especially the latest fashion in apparel and home decor, was surely related to the fact that the ratio of female to male spectators continued to rise throughout the decade.

Unlike trade journals counseling exhibitors to downplay controversial issues, fan magazine discourse on DeMille's trilogy highlighted the impact of consumption on divorce as a sign of the times. During the early decades of the twentieth century, the rate of divorce almost doubled while expenditures for personal grooming, clothing, furniture, automobiles, and recreation tripled. Divorce was especially common in urban areas as hasty wartime unions were dissolved. Significantly, an increasing number of complaints involved the inability of husbands to provide wives with a more pleasurable life style. According to the *New York Times*, "if dissatisfied wives were guided by the argument of *Don't Change Your Husband*, the divorce courts would be more crowded than they are now." Postwar discourse on divorce as a sign of urbanization, secularization of liberal Protestantism, and changing patterns of wage earning and consumption focused on the "new woman."[35] Unlike the scenario of thousands of divorce cases, however, consumer behavior was touted in DeMille's films as the solution rather than the cause of marital discord.

Notes

1   *Motion Picture News*, 30 December 1922: 32.
2   See Sumiko Higashi, *Cecil B. DeMille and American Culture: The Silent Era* (Berkeley: University of California Press, 1994), chap. 1. A more complete discussion of the "new woman" appears in a slightly different version of this essay in *A Feminist Reader in Early Cinema*, Jennifer Bean and Diane Negra (eds) (Durham: Duke University Press, 2002), 298–332. On the origins of the term "new woman," see Margaret Gibbons Wilson, *The American Woman in Transition: The Urban Influence, 1870–1929* (Westport: Greenwood Press, 1979), 8. See also James R. McGovern, "The American Woman's Pre-World War I Freedom in Manners and Morals," *Journal of American History* 55 (September 1968): 315–33; Kenneth A. Yellis, "Prosperity's Child: Some Thoughts on the Flapper," *American Quarterly* 21 (March 1969): 44–64; Estelle B. Freedman, "The New Woman: Changing Views of Women in the 1920s," *Journal of American History* 61 (March 1974): 372–393; Nancy Woloch, *Women and the American Experience* (New York: Alfred A. Knopf, 1984), chaps. 12, 16; Lois W. Banner, *American Beauty* (New York: Alfred A. Knopf, 1983), chaps. 12, 13; Martha Banta, *Imaging American Women: Idea and Ideals in Cultural History* (New York: Columbia University Press, 1987); Ellen Wiley Todd, *The "New Woman" Revised: Painting and Gender Politics on Fourteenth Street* (Berkeley: University of California Press, 1993), chap. 1; Carroll Smith-Rosenberg, "The New Woman as Androgyne: Social Disorder and Gender Crisis, 1870–1936," *Disorderly Conduct: Visions of Gender in Victorian America* (New York: Alfred A. Knopf, 1985), 245–96. Unlike Todd, Yellis and Banner do not

label the Gibson girl, superceded by the flapper, as an independent "new woman." On silent screen flappers as a character-type, a concept used in early feminist criticism, see Sumiko Higashi *Virgins, Vamps, and Flappers: The American Silent Movie Heroine* (Montreal: Eden Press, 1978), chap. 6; Mary P. Ryan, "The Projection of a New Womanhood: The Movie Moderns in the 1920s," in Jean E. Friedman and William G. Shade, *Our American Sisters*, 3rd edn. (Lexington: D. C. Heath & Co., 1982), 500–18. On working-class versions of the "new woman," see Kathy Peiss, *Cheap Amusements: Working Women and Leisure in Turn-of-the-Century New York* (Philadelphia: Temple University Press, 1986), Introduction. Somewhat problematic is Peiss's assertion that working-class women influenced middle-class women. According to Billie Melman's *Women and the Popular Imagination in the Twenties: Flappers and Nymphs* (New York: St. Martin's Press, 1988), the British flapper was associated with left-wing politics and disenfranchised working-class women (chap. 1). See also Paula S. Fass, *The Damned and the Beautiful: American Youth in the 1920s* (New York: Oxford University Press, 1977).

3   The "new woman" has been subject to as many clichés as Victorianism. See Janet Staiger, *Bad Women: Regulating Sexuality in Early American Cinema* (Minneapolis: University of Minnesota Press, 1995); Gaylyn Studlar, "The Perils of Pleasure? Fan Magazine Discourse as Women's Commodified Culture in the 1920s," *Wide Angle* 13 (January 1991): 6–33; Gaylyn Studlar, "Discourses of Gender and Ethnicity: The Construction and De(con)struction of Rudolph Valentino as Other," *Film Criticism* 9 (Winter 1989): 18–35. Miriam Hansen argues that the "new woman" was not so emancipated in "Pleasure, Ambivalence, Identification: Valentino and Female Spectatorship," *Cinema Journal* 25 (Summer 1986): 6–32. Linda Mizejewski considers the "new woman" a complex phenomenon in *Ziegfeld Girl: Image and Icon in Culture and Cinema* (Durham: Duke University Press, 1999). Maureen Turim articulates a Foucauldian view of Victorianism in "Seduction and Elegance: The New Woman of Fashion in Silent Cinema," in Shari Benstock and Suzanne Ferriss, eds., *On Fashion* (New Brunswick: Rutgers University Press, 1994), but her problematic survey of women's history is extremely sketchy (dress reform, an essential subject, is overlooked), as is her discussion of DeMille's films. See also Lisa Rudman, "Marriage—The Ideal and the Reel: or, The Cinematic Marriage Manual," *Film History* 1 (1987): 327–339. Although she is aware that research on the "new woman" is lacking, Rudman has a stereotyped view of Victorian women.

4   See Smith-Rosenberg, "The Female World of Love and Ritual," *Disorderly Conduct*. See also "The New Woman as Androgyne: Social Disorder and Gender Crisis, 1870–1936," in the same volume.

5   On sentimental culture, especially its religious dimension, see Ann Douglas, *The Feminization of American Culture* (New York: Alfred A. Knopf, 1977). See also Jane Tompkins, *Sensational Designs: The Cultural Work of American Fiction 1790–1860* (New York: Oxford University Press, 1985), for a less acerbic view.

6   *The Autobiography of Cecil B. DeMille*, ed. Donald Hayne (Englewood Cliffs: Prentice-Hall, 1959), 212–213. William deMille gives his brother more credit than he deserves for starting the cycle of sex comedies and melodramas in *Hollywood Saga* (New York: E. P. Dutton & Co., 1939), 238–43. DeMille did not list his Jazz Age films, with the exception of *Male and Female* and *Forbidden Fruit*, among his best films. See George C. Pratt, "Forty-five years of Picture Making: An Interview with Cecil B. DeMille," *Film History* 3 (1989): 133–45. I am indebted to the late George Pratt for playing the tape recording of this interview for me.

7   Lasky to DeMille, 6 January 1917; Carl H. Pierce to Lasky, memo attached to Lasky's letter; Lasky to DeMille, 5 March 1917; Lasky to DeMille, 10 August 1917; Lasky to DeMille, 27 November 1917; Lasky to DeMille, 27 December 1917; Jesse Lasky 1917 folder, Lasky Co./Famous Players-Lasky, DeMille Archives, Brigham Young University (hereafter cited as DMA, BYU).

8   Lasky to DeMille, 26 March 1918; Lasky to DeMille, 6 November 1918; DeMille to Lasky, 23 January 1919; Lasky to DeMille, 23 May 1919, Jesse Lasky 1918 and 1919 folders, Lasky Co./Famous Players-Lasky, DMA, BYU.

9   In fact, DeMille discusses this particular film in relation to the trilogy and *Male and Female*. See Pratt, 139.

10 *Theatre*, February 1919, in Cecil B. DeMille scrapbook, Robinson Locke Collection, New York Public Library of the Performing Arts, Lincoln Center (hereafter cited as RLC, NYPL).

11 Roland Marchand, *Advertising the American Dream: Making Way for Modernity, 1920–1940* (Berkeley: University of California Press, 1985), chap. 6; Daniel Horowitz, *The Morality of Spending: Attitudes toward the Consumer Society in America, 1875–1940* (Baltimore: Johns Hopkins University Press, 1985), chap. 6. On distinctions between the "old" and "new" middle class, see especially C. Wright Mills, *White Collar: The American Middle Classes* (New York: Galaxy, 1951) and Harry Braverman, *Labor and Monopoly Capital: The Degradation of Work in the Twentieth Century* (New York: Monthly Review Press, 1974). On middle-

class formation, especially the role of women, see Stuart M. Blumin, *The Emergence of the Middle Class: Social Experience in the American City, 1760–1900* (Cambridge: Cambridge University Press, 1985); Mary P. Ryan, *Cradle of the Middle Class: The Family in Oneida County, New York, 1790–1865* (Cambridge: Cambridge University Press, 1981).

12   Warren Susman, "'Personality' and Twentieth-Century Culture," *Culture as History: The Transformation of American Society in the Twentieth Century* (New York: Pantheon 1984), 271–85.

13   See Karen Haltunnen, *Confidence Men and Painted Women: A Study of Middle-Class Culture in America, 1830–1870* (New Haven: Yale University Press, 1982).

14   David Graham Phillips, *Old Wives for New* (New York: Grosset & Dunlap, 1908), 100.

15   Script of *Old Wives for New*, Cinema-TV Library, Special Collections, University of Southern California (hereafter cited as USC).

16   Robert S. Lynd and Helen Merrell Lynd, *Middletown: A Study in American Culture* (New York: Harcourt, Brace & World, 1929), 256. According to the Lynds, twenty-one out of twenty-six families who owned a car were without bathtubs. See also Siegfried Giedion, *Mechanization Takes Command* (New York: Oxford University Press, 1948), Part VII.

17   See Thomas Elsaesser, "Tales of Sound and Fury: Observations on the Family Melodrama," *Monogram* 4 (1972): 2–15; repr. Christine Gledhill, ed., *Home Is Where the Heart Is: Studies in Melodrama and the Woman's Film* (London: British Film Institute, 1987), 43–69.

18   Kenneth McGaffey, "The Excellent Elliott," *Motion Picture* (January 1919): 35; W. K. Hollander, untitled article, *Chicago News*, 21 January 1919, in Gloria Swanson scrapbook, RLC, NYPL.

19   Phillips, 43.

20   See John F. Kasson, *Rudeness and Civility: Manners in Nineteenth-Century America* (New York: Hill & Wang, 1990), 166.

21   On cosmetics, prostitutes, and changing styles, see Kathy Peiss, "Making Faces: The Cosmetics Industry and the Cultural Construction of Gender, 1890–1930," *Genders* 7 (Spring 1990): 143–69.

22   Script of *Don't Change Your Husband*, USC.

23   See Mary Douglas, *Purity and Danger: An Analysis of Concepts of Pollution and Taboo* (New York; Praeger, 1966), chaps. 7–9.

24   On reification, see Georg Lukàcs, *History and Consciousness: Studies in Marxist Dialectics*, trans. Rodney Livingstone (Cambridge: MIT Press, 1971).

25   William deMille, 242; Garth Jowett, *Film: The Democratic Art* (Boston: Little, Brown), 1976, 188; Richard Koszarski, *An Evening's Entertainment: The Age of the Silent Feature Picture 1915–1928* (New York: Charles Scribner's Sons, 1990), 30.

26   Adolph Zukor, "Zukor Outlines Coming Year's Policies," *Motion Picture News* (*MPN*), 29 June 1918: 3869.

27   *The Autobiography of Cecil B. DeMille*, 214–15; the quote is from a memo by Berenice Mosk, *Northwest Mounted, Old Wives for New, Plainsman* folder, Personal: Autobiography files, DMA, BYU. DeMille claimed during a court case years later that Lasky attempted to block release of the film and to write it off as a loss. See *United States Circuit Court of Appeals for the North Circuit. Commissioner of Internal Revenues, Petitioner, vs Cecil B. deMille Productions, Inc., Respondent. Transcript of the Record. In Three Volumes. Upon Petition to Review an Order of the United States Board of Appeals* (San Francisco: Parker Printing Co., 1936), 319–20.

28   A reminder that *Old Wives for New* was condemned by the Pennsylvania State Board because it dealt with prostitution provides insight about past censorship issues. A few weeks before the film's premiere, Lasky received a detailed memo that proposed a number of cuts, including an intertitle about dowdy wives because "it is liable to be misconstrued by the average spectator. . . ." Also objectionable were close-ups of the wash basins in the bathroom and signs of Murdock's fastidiousness. Significantly, these cuts were not made in the surviving print in the director's nitrate collection at George Eastman House. But the suggestion that DeMille insert an intertitle to indicate that Murdock, contrary to the scenario, did not engage in an affair with Viola was heeded. Furthermore, risqué scenes of Berkeley's rendezvous with Bertha were cut to emphasize Jessie confronting the couple. Perhaps most interesting, given negative Catholic reception of the director's first historical epic, *Joan the Woman* (1916), was deletion of a scene in which Jessie seeks refuge in a convent. According to the New York office, this development would be "offensive to Catholics, in as much as it implies that a Catholic institution would receive and protect a murderess." (Memo to Al Lichtman, General Manager of Famous Players-Lasky, 28 June 1918, in Jesse Lasky 1918 folder, Lasky Co./Famous Players-Lasky, DMA, BYU; *Old Wives for New*, Paramount Collection, Academy of Motion Picture Arts and Sciences.)

29 R. E. Pritchard, "*Old Wives for New*," *MPN*, 8 June 1918: 3453–4; Frederick James Smith, *Motion Picture Classic (MPC)* (August 1918), in Personal: Autobiography files, *Northwest Mounted*, *Old Wives for New* and *Plainsman* folder, DMA, BYU; Edward Weitzel, "*Old Wives for New*", *Moving Picture World*, 8 June 1918: 1470 (*MPW*); "*Old Wives for New*," *Variety Film Reviews, 1907–1980* (New York: Garland, 1983), 31 May 1918; "Exhibitor to Exhibitor Review Service," *MPN*, 8 June 1918: 3400.

30 Frederick James Smith, "The Celluloid Critic," *MPC* (April–May 1920): 50

31 Frederick James Smith, "The Celluloid Critic," *MPC* (April 1919): 44; "*Don't Change Your Husband*," *Variety Film Reviews*, 7 February 1919; "Special Service Section on *Don't Change Your Husband*," *MPN*, 1 February 1919: 728; "DeMille's Film Breaks Some Records," *MPN* 9 March 1919:1353; Frederick James Smith, "The Celluloid Critic," *MPC* (April–May 1920): 50; Ad, *MPN*, 20 March 1920: 2609.

32 "Grauman's Rialto Gets Business by Use of Novelties," *MPN*, 1 May 1920: 3837; "What Brown Did for DeMille's Special," *MPN*, 10 July 1920: 403: Ad, *MPN*, 22 May 1920: 4245; Lasky to DeMille, 19 April 1920, Jesse Lasky 1920 folder, Lasky Co./Famous Players-Lasky, DMA, BYU; "Famous Players-Lasky Plans Big Campaign, *MPN*, 24 January 1920: 1083; "Getting the Woman Appeal," *MPN*, 7 December 1918: 3358; "The Affairs of Anatol," *MPW*, 24 September 1921: 446. On the cultural wars of the post-World War I decade, see Frederick Lewis Allen, *Only Yesterday* (New York: Harper & Bros., 1931); Paul A. Carter, *Another Part of the Twenties* (New York: Columbia University Press, 1973); Stanley Coben, *Rebellion against Victorianism: The Impetus for Cultural Change in 1920s America* (New York: Oxford University Press, 1991); Lawrence W. Levine, "Progress and Nostalgia: The Self Image of the Nineteen Twenties," *The Unpredictable Past: Explorations in American Cultural History* (New York: Oxford University Press, 1993), 189–205. On film exhibition during this period, see Koszarski, chap. 2; Douglas Gomery, *Shared Pleasures: A History of Movie Presentation in the United States* (Madison: University of Wisconsin Press, 1992), chaps.3–4.

33 Elizabeth Ewen, *Immigrant Women in the Land of Dollars: Life and Culture on the Lower East Side, 1890–1925* (New York: Monthly Review Press, 1985); Kathy Peiss, *Cheap Amusements*.

34 "*Why Change Your Wife*," *MPN*, 8 May 1920: 4062.

35 *Statistical Abstract of the United States* (Washington, DC: Government Printing Office, 1933), 90; Report of the President's Research Committee on Social Trends, *Recent Social Trends in the United States* (New York: McGraw-Hill, 1933), 694; William L. O'Neill, *Divorce in the Progressive Era* (New Haven: Yale University Press, 1967), 20; Elaine Tyler May, *Great Expectations: Marriage and Divorce in Post-Victorian America* (Chicago: University of Chicago Press, 1980), 51, 87; Glenda Riley, *Divorce: An American Tradition* (New York: Oxford University Press, 1991), 133; *Don't Change Your Husband, New York Times Film Reviews* (New York: Arno Press, 1970), 3 February 1919; Lynd and Lynd, chap. 10; William H. Chafe, *The American Woman: Her Changing Social, Economic, and Political Roles, 1920–1970* (New York: Oxford University Press, 1972), chap. 2.

Chapter 19

RUTH VASEY

THE OPEN DOOR
Hollywood's public relations at home and abroad, 1922–1928

HOLLYWOOD HAS ALWAYS HAD TO TREAD a fine line between the short-term profits associated with sensational material and the long-term industrial stability promised by "responsible" entertainments. The Motion Picture Producers and Distributors of America (MPPDA) became instrumental in striking this balance in the 1920s. MPPDA president Will Hays was anxious to enhance the public's image of motion pictures: he tried to persuade the affluent middle classes to adopt the movies as a form of cultural expression, and he hoped that by increasing patronage from that quarter he would be able to transform the nature of audience demand. He reasoned that if "high-class" and educational products could be sure of returning a profit, producers could reasonably be expected to abandon the controversial subject matter that threatened the industry's status as widely consumable family entertainment. Hays experimented with strategies designed to give members of the educated middle class a positive investment in the industry, promising them a measure of influence over the nature and treatment of material adapted for the screen. Although some of Hays's initial ideas proved impractical, an "open door" was created for specific lobby groups to influence aspects of motion picture production.

Meanwhile, Hollywood's representatives abroad were equally preoccupied with the problem of how to reduce resistance to their products while maintaining consumer allegiance. Playing down the broader cultural impact of the American cinema as the vanguard of consumer culture, they tried to maintain the good will of foreign governments by encouraging the studios to tailor their products more specifically to the requirements of global consumption. If motion pictures were under pressure to become more middle class within the United States, abroad they were under pressure to submerge any elements that might be politically contentious and to concentrate on "universal" themes. Both subject matter and its treatment were offered as points of negotiation in the quest for the widest possible audience.

Toward a department of public relations

The MPPDA was incorporated on 10 March 1922, with a membership comprising all the major companies involved in American production and/or distribution. Its stated objectives were "to foster the common interests of those engaged in the motion picture industry in the United States by establishing and maintaining the highest possible moral and artistic standards in motion picture production, by developing the educational as well as the entertainment value and the general usefulness of the motion picture, by diffusing accurate and reliable information with reference to the industry, by reforming abuses relative to the industry, by securing freedom from unjust or unlawful exactions and by other lawful and proper means."[1]

These aims encompassed industry-wide public and corporate relations but did not implicate the regulation of movie content in the association's industrial strategy. The omission was undoubtedly calculated. Barely a year before, the MPPDA's predecessor, the National Association of the Motion Picture Industry (NAMPI), had announced its intention to restrict content in line with community standards, only to find that its public relations were damaged rather than enhanced. NAMPI had passed a resolution known as the Thirteen Points, agreeing to avoid specific material deemed offensive, including "exaggerated sex plays, white slavery and commercialized vice, themes that make virtue odious and vice attractive, plays that would make drunkenness, gambling, drugs or other vices attractive, themes that tend to weaken the authority of the law, stories that might offend any person's religious beliefs, and stories and themes which may instruct the morally feeble in methods of committing crime or by cumulative processes emphasize crime and the commission of crime."[2] NAMPI's problems had stemmed from the fact that the Thirteen Points were openly published in the press. In the absence of any effective method of enforcing the observance of its self-regulatory code, the industry was highly vulnerable to criticism when producers were perceived to have violated its stated limits regarding themes and treatments. The public disapprobation that resulted was expressed in the passage of censorship legislation in New York State in April and May 1921, an event which signaled NAMPI's ineffectiveness in protecting the industry and ultimately led to the demise of that organization.

Will Hays decided to try a different tack in his bid to improve the industry's public image under the MPPDA. He initiated an innovative policy designed to recruit influential organizations in support of a publicly led program of motion picture reform. The cornerstone of the program was a Committee on Public Relations, made up of representatives of powerful community groups, which Hays hoped would serve to channel "destructive" censorship energies into a constructive drive toward higher movie standards. [. . .] Hays's plan was that the Committee on Public Relations should be given facilities to preview coming releases. When the members reacted favorably, they would recommend the picture to the organizations they represented; adverse reactions would receive no publicity but would be forwarded in confidence to the producer concerned. This strategy would have cast the committee in a role similar to that of the National Board of Review: it would have been a source of information and advice without wielding any binding power. But even at the committee's inaugural meeting, several delegates voiced the expectation that they would play a much more active role in the affairs of the industry. They envisaged fulfilling a function more akin to that of the early National Board of Censorship, which had had the power to request changes in movies before distribution. [. . .]

The Executive Committee insisted that the MPPDA should fund a permanent executive officer, resulting in the appointment of Colonel Jason S. Joy, a former executive assistant at the American Red Cross. Committee members claimed that the financial commitment involved in taking on a full-time employee would demonstrate that the MPPDA took the Committee on Public Relations seriously and would help to discount criticism that the producers were using the group as a public relations front.[3] [. . .]

Hays and the Committee on Public Relations were in accord on the need to elevate public taste so that "clean and artistic" pictures would meet a greater response at the box office than those that were vulgar and sensational. Achieving this goal would involve recruiting the participation of the estimated 40 percent of the American public who did not generally attend motion pictures, especially those of "cultured outlook." Committee delegates agreed to Hays's whitelisting proposals to the extent that they were prepared to preview films and encourage their members to make box office hits of those that met their standards of art and morality. However, the delegates felt that the producers should be equally prepared to follow their guidance in modifying motion pictures in the name of higher standards. [. . .]

Many of the pictures recommended by the Committee on Public Relations failed at the box office. Although the committee claimed to represent thirty million citizens, its members had to admit that the policy of "boosting" pictures was not a success.[4] [. . .] At the same time, the producers did not seem to be making "wholesome" entertainment on a completely reliable basis, and public protests were brewing about the nature of material that was being selected for picturization. The thirty million who should have been supporting the efforts of the Committee on Public Relations were instead complaining about the production of movies from salacious books and plays. Against the recommendation of the Subcommittee on Adaptations from Books, *West of the Water Tower* was bought by Lasky and made into a motion picture in revised form (Famous Players-Lasky/Paramount, 1924). *Flaming Youth* (First National, 1923), *Black Oxen* (Frank Lloyd Productions/First National, 1924), and *Lilies of the Field* (Corinne Griffith Productions/First National, 1924) all caused indignation, less because they were salacious themselves than because they advertised notorious books. Suggestive titles and advertising were a particular problem, and Hays observed that fifteen out of forty titles in the Famous Players press book were suggestive.[5] Although the producers were aware of the trouble such titles caused, there was compelling evidence that movies with suggestive titles were disproportionately successful at the box office: Warner Bros.' flop *Lucretia Lombard* (1923), for example, drew "immense crowds" when retitled *Flaming Passion*.[6]

Hollywood's unabated inclination to cater to the wider public's preferences undercut Hays's efforts to improve the industry's public relations through the committee. Some delegates began to suspect that they had been cynically duped into participating, and several, including the representative of the influential National Congress of Parents and Teachers, publicly resigned.[7] In response, the industry tried to save itself from itself by instituting cooperative controls over source acquisition. In February 1924, the MPPDA Board of Directors passed a resolution requiring the reading departments of all member companies to submit synopses of any books or plays they were considering purchasing to the scrutiny of the association.[8] If anything offensive was discovered, the material was barred from production by any participating company, and no affiliated distributor or exhibitor was permitted to handle it should it be brought to the screen by an independent producer.

By the end of 1924 the strengths and weaknesses of the MPPDA's public relations program had become apparent. Useful cooperation had been established between the industry and several influential organizations, but the broader committee structure had proved unworkable. Energy and enthusiasm had been expended on meetings, letter writing, and positive initiatives, but the association lacked a department that could tackle problems as they arose. Significantly, a precedent had been established that allowed specific objections to be met with modifications to movie content. Indeed, this approach was sometimes extended beyond the confines of the Committee on Public Relations: the National Billiard Association caused *Manhattan* (Famous Players-Lasky/Paramount, 1924) to be modified with cuts and retakes in response to protests on behalf of its "four million" members.[9] The industry required a smoother mechanism to transmit these kinds of pressures to the producers. It had to be able to accommodate professional and commercial groups and influential individuals, as well as religious and community organizations. Consequently, in March 1925, a Department of Public Relations was established within the MPPDA. It was essentially a reorganized and better focused version of the office of the Committee on Public Relations, and the department was headed by the former committee executive secretary, Jason Joy. Dubbed the Open Door, it was advertised as a direct channel of communication between motion picture producers and the public.[10] [. . .]

Jason Joy goes to Hollywood

At first the activities of the MPPDA's Department of Public Relations did not vary markedly from those of the Committee on Public Relations. Colonel Joy fielded domestic protests and generally did everything in his power to improve the status of the motion picture in the American community. His work continued to embrace the children's matinee program. He also produced various newsletters and other publications, as well as maintaining contact with the trade and religious press. Although the principle of community intervention in production had already been established, Joy's efforts to mediate between the public and the studios appear to have been haphazard until 1927, when his department transferred its operations from New York to Hollywood, where it was housed by the Association of Motion Picture Producers (AMPP). The AMPP was a West Coast association separated from the MPPDA mostly as a matter of legal convenience, in satisfaction of antimonopoly statutes.[11] The move put Joy in a far better position to negotiate with filmmakers over actual or potential causes of offense in their movies and was a logical outcome of the MPPDA's increasing vigilance over film content. The department officially moved on 1 January 1927, and throughout the year conditions on the domestic scene progressively favored tighter supervisory measures.

The most conspicuous development was a resolution adopted by the AMPP on 8 June 1927, listing eleven subjects that the producers would not, in future, represent in their motion pictures and twenty-five subjects that would only be represented with the exercise of "special care."[12] These "Don'ts and Be Carefuls" were formulated by a committee of industry executives headed by Irving Thalberg, closely guided by Hays, in anticipation of a Trade Practice Conference that would be held in October. The conference, to be conducted by the Federal Trade Commission, was primarily concerned with relations between distributors and exhibitors: the independent exhibitors hoped to be able to exert pressure on the major companies under the antitrust laws, especially in light of a recent court decision against Paramount's block booking activities. The Motion Picture Theater Owners of America, then the largest trade association for independent exhibitors, protested that block booking compelled its members to hire poor-quality and immoral movies along with the clean, high-class entertainment that they claimed their customers desired. However, the very formulation of the exhibitors' arguments left them open to the MPPDA's favorite strategy: rather than discuss the legal implications of their monopolistic business practices, of which block booking was a symptom, the producers and distributors assured the commission that their products were—or would be henceforth—entirely clean and wholesome. Through the self-regulation of movie content, they would make sure that the exhibitors would find nothing in any of the movies they were offered that could cause them or their audiences the least offense. The Don'ts and Be Carefuls were produced at the conference like a rabbit out of a hat in answer to the exhibitors' charges of salaciousness and irresponsibility, and they were incorporated into the conference's "industry fair practices" agreement. [. . .]

Following directions from Hays, Joy organized a Studio Relations Committee (SRC) consisting of himself, John V. Wilson, James B. Fisher, Douglas Mackinnon, and Miss J. Plummer, to review questionable material with studio representatives when movies were still in the preparation stage. Producers submitted synopses and scripts on a voluntary basis, although Joy could seek to intervene if a project seemed to be particularly dangerous. He based his methods of persuasion on economic rationality: he argued that any departure from the Don'ts and Be Carefuls was virtually guaranteed to cause financial loss through censorship action and/or damaging publicity. The SRC met formally with studio representatives once a fortnight, although it had more frequent contact with studios about specific projects. In January 1928 Joy reported that 349 stories and treatments had been submitted for comment. Of the 163 that had already been released, all but 2 had passed the censor boards without major elimina- tions and had "caused no difficulty among groups in this or other countries." He acknowledged that producers had not consistently followed his advice on the 186 still in production, and that the 349 represented a minority of the industry's total output. On the whole, however, his report was encouraging:

> The whole-hearted and sincere attitude evidenced by the members when they adopted the Resolution (June 8, 1927), signifying their intentions to watch their own efforts regarding the theme and treatment of pictures, has not diminished. On the contrary, to their sense of responsibility as the principal custodians of the reputation of their industry has been added a realization that in this machinery lies a means of stopping a considerable wastage in production costs and reducing to a minimum the losses due to mutilation and often costly rejection of finished pictures; and finally of removing the causes which may inspire further disastrous legislation in this country and abroad— which in the long view is perhaps the most costly and limiting obstacle this industry will ever be required to face.[13]

With the mechanisms to combat adverse legislation at the level of "theme and treatment" in place, conditions were established for the activities of Herron and Joy to converge in the system- atic accommodation of pressures arising from the domestic and foreign spheres.

Channeling foreign influences to production

The Committee on Public Relations had promoted the motion picture as "an instrument of international amity, by correctly portraying American life, ideals and opportunities in pictures sent abroad and the proper portrayal of foreign scenes and persons in all productions."[14] The foreign market only entered the committee members' considerations insofar as they were concerned about the image of the United States projected abroad; all the organizations repre- sented on the committee had constituencies within the United States. By contrast, the Department of Public Relations invited participation somewhat indiscriminately from "every organization of every description in either this country or any other country which is inter- ested in public betterment."[15] Some three years passed before the department's operations regularly incorporated foreign influences, but it is nevertheless significant that the international dimensions of the industry were recognized in the department's original charter, reflecting the fact that developments in the foreign field increasingly demanded the attention not just of the MPPDA's Foreign Department but also of the producers themselves.

The decision to send Bernon T. Woodle to Mexico in 1922 to resolve an impasse between Hollywood and the Mexican government had been taken by the MPPDA's Board of Directors; a separate Foreign Department did not become operational for at least another year. The head of this department from its inception until 1941 was Major Frederick ("Ted") Herron, who had been with Hays during his days at Wabash College in Indiana and had later joined the diplo- matic corps and served as a military attaché.[16] Herron's job at the MPPDA was to keep track of conditions affecting foreign sales and to maintain communications between the industry and the U.S. State Department. He was also responsible for persuading the foreign managers of MPPDA member companies to act cooperatively in matters in which they had a noncompetitive interest. When taxes or other trading restrictions were introduced by customer nations, Herron would confer with financial advisers, lawyers, and foreign managers to draw up the industry's response, which ranged from compliance to boycott. [. . .]

After facilitating the Mexican agreement of 1922, Bernon T. Woodle seems to have served as a kind of roving ambassador for the MPPDA. He was sent to Australia in 1924 on a mission "to find out how American films could be made more acceptable to Australian audiences."[17] A more common form of diplomatic contact took place when projects were filmed abroad. The cultivation of official favor was important in these instances both because it expedited practical matters surrounding production and because it enhanced the American industry's prestige and trading status. The MPPDA offered its assistance not through its public relations wing nor even through its Foreign Department, but through the Office of the President, with Hays himself being involved in making top-level contacts. In 1923 he personally enlisted the help of the Italian ambassador for the Rome-based production of *The Eternal City* (Madison Productions/ First National, 1923), produced by Samuel Goldwyn. [. . .]

Similarly, in 1925 Hays worked through the U.S. State Department and the French embassy to secure the cooperation of the French government in the production of the Gloria Swanson comedy *Madame Sans-Gene* (Famous Players—Lasky/Paramount, 1925). The movie, which was based on a Sardou play about a washerwoman elevated to the nobility by Napoleon, was shot in and around Paris and in the palaces of Fontainebleau and Compiègne. The French authorities reportedly even loaned Napoleonic costumes and relics from museums in Paris to the studio.[18] The cast was mostly French, and Frenchman Léonce Perret, who had worked in Hollywood from 1917 until 1921, directed.

Despite such conspicuous instances of international cooperation as these, Hollywood still had a long way to go in cultivating amicable relations with its customer nations. Apart from the underlying sensitivities attached to the American domination of the world's screens, the main stumbling block was the negative stereotyping of nations and ethnic groups in pictures routinely made in Hollywood. Cases that involved high-level protests from diplomatic missions were usually handled by Hays. The kind of negotiation conducted over such material is illustrated in the production history of *The Woman Disputed* (United Artists, 1928). In the original play by Denison Clift, set before and during World War I, the French heroine submits to the lustful advances of a German officer in order to secure the freedom of her five companions, one of whom is a French agent disguised as a priest. When her fiancé, an American soldier, learns of the reasons behind her sacrifice, the play ends happily. The MPPDA kept a close watch on current plays, seeking to be forewarned about any particularly controversial material, and *The Woman Disputed* was reviewed as a matter of course by Jerome Beatty, a member of the New York staff, in October 1926. He reported that the material was unsuitable for motion pictures for three reasons: the heroine was a former prostitute, one character was a spy disguised as a priest, and the villain was a German of the "typical Hun" variety.[19]

In 1918 the industry had turned out such virulently anti-German productions as *The Kaiser, the Beast of Berlin* (Renowned Pictures/Renowned Pictures; Jewel), *My Four Years in Germany* (My Four Years in Germany, Inc./First National) and *Hearts of the World* (D. W. Griffith/ States Rights; Road Show), but in 1926 Germany was a relatively important source of foreign revenue, providing just over 5 percent of foreign income despite its import restrictions. Moreover, as the country responsible for the original contingent, it required particularly sensitive handling. Adding these considerations to the other problematic elements in the play, Beatty's judgment of *The Woman Disputed* was not very encouraging: "It would offend the

Germans, the Catholic Church and all the women's clubs. I don't think there is any way to patch it up so that it could be made into a picture that would get by."[20]

Nevertheless, Joseph Schenck announced plans for a movie adaptation. The German consulate responded swiftly. In a letter to Hays of 20 December 1926, the acting consul general stated candidly that such a production would jeopardize the industry's commercial prospects in Germany: "Alone the fact that the proposed action would become known in Germany might easily spoil all your and our efforts to bring about peace and cooperation on the field of film production and film presentation." Hays sent the letter to Schenck on 21 December, explaining, "The negotiations to which he refers have been extending over a period of some months and touch the whole matter of developing better relations with the German Government, their nationals and the press. It is one of the most important activities which we now have on. It has to do, of course, with the ultimate handling of the Kontingent and the whole matter of the treatment of the industry in Germany." Hays urged Schenck to treat the production with the utmost care to avoid any hint of offense to Germany. Schenck assured him that there would be no problem: "The girl will be an Austrian girl, the hero an Austrian and the villain a Russian. It will be laid at the time when the Russian army marched into Austria and there will be nothing in the picture that either Austria or Germany could have any objection to."[21] In 1928 the film was finally released in this version.

While the modifications to the plot of *The Woman Disputed* doubtless offered comfort to Germany, they evinced scant regard for the feelings of the Russians. This was of little concern to either Schenck or Hays, however; in the mid-1920s Russia, unlike the capitalist nations of Europe, welcomed American films and erected no barriers to their importation. Because the Commissariat of Foreign Trade held a monopoly for the Soviet Union, it could bid unopposed for American products, acquiring them cheaply and exhibiting them at relatively high prices. [. . .] The market was never a lucrative one for the American film industry.

Thus the Russians were never in a position to influence Hollywood's field of representation because they did not attempt to introduce contingents or quotas. Other countries had to accommodate the conflicting demands of their own producer and exhibitor lobbies, which meant accepting the American product on a conditional basis. As a result, these countries gained a certain amount of bargaining power over the nature of the product they received. The position of the Russians, by contrast, was unilateral and nonnegotiable: either they admitted foreign products, as was the case in the early 1920s, or they did not, as was mostly the case in the 1930s. Because there was no basis for discussion, film content was not introduced as a bargaining chip by either side, and Hollywood producers could characterize their villains as Russians without worrying about reprisals and boycotts. Indeed, as villains the Russians offered the rare combination of minority market status and recognizable national characteristics. In most cases they also offered more feasible alternatives to European villains than did the long-suffering and increasingly troublesome Mexicans and Chinese. In dollars and cents, Russian indignation was cheap. [. . .]

By 1928 the SRC was fully operational in Hollywood, allowing Colonel Joy to accommodate the sensitivities of the foreign market in the course of his general supervision of production, not just in response to specific expressions of concern. Offenses to national groups were technically guarded against by the Don'ts and Be Carefuls, which directed that special care should be exercised in the treatment of international relations and that filmmakers should avoid "picturizing in an unfavorable light another country's religion, history, institutions, prominent people, and citizenry." This clause was something of an anomaly in the document, as it was the only stricture which did not refer to sex or crime.

Figure 19.1 Norma Talmadge's character in *The Woman Disputed* (United Artists, 1928) was originally a French girl, and Gilbert Roland was to play an American soldier, but both became Austrian to avoid fomenting trouble in the German market. The German villain became a Russian. So little profit was derived from Russia that the switch involved no financial risk; this ploy became standard for filmmakers anxious to avoid offending other European nations

In practice, national groups had more in common with other special interest groups than with moral lobbyists. Although many organizations which sought to influence the movies by way of the Open Door had a moral agenda, many others did not: the majority of contacts came from "professional organizations, unions, and individuals, who felt that their trades and professions were being shown, however unintentionally, in an unfavorable light."[22] Joy encouraged the producers to accommodate the interests of these groups during production as a matter of "industry policy," to avoid creating bad feeling in influential sections of the community. Some organizations received more consideration than others: the American Association for the Advancement of Atheism got short shrift when it complained about the prejudicial treatment of atheism in *The Godless Girl* (C. B. DeMille Productions/Pathé, 1929).[23] On the other hand, the interests of foreign nations, especially those that were important or sensitive customers, received regular consideration, the objective being less to respond to criticism than to obviate it.

Frederick Herron became an increasingly important figure in articulating the interests of the foreign market. He was in daily contact with foreign trade and diplomatic representatives in the course of his work in the Foreign Department, and he gradually assumed responsibility for much of the diplomatic negotiation that had been conducted by Hays. Hays, however, still occasionally took an active role when particularly sensitive matters were involved. Herron kept an eye on material acquired for production and alerted Joy to potential foreign hazards; he often contacted producers himself when he detected dangerous material, and he occasionally worked directly with scenarists. All productions handled by the SRC were reviewed upon completion by a member of the staff, usually James B. Fisher or Miss J. Plummer. The staff member noted any potentially contentious elements, including foreign problems, and a copy of the report was sent to both MPPDA secretary Carl Milliken and to Herron. The convergence of Herron's work at the Foreign Department with the activities of the SRC is exemplified by his contact with producers over French sensitivities in 1928.

The French also formulated aggressive quota legislation, with the intention of limiting American access to their market. Hays himself visited Paris in March 1928 and managed to have much of the sting removed from the measures by threatening to boycott the market. In reaching agreement on compromise measures, he specifically offered as a bargaining chip the assurance that the American industry would make no films presenting the French in a derogatory light.[24] It was thus essential that the treatment of French themes demonstrate appropriate tact.

An especially sensitive point was Hollywood's representation of the French Foreign Legion. *Beau Geste* (Famous Players-Lasky/Paramount, 1926) had been a great box office success, and producers saw considerable further promise in the Legion's romance and exoticism. From their point of view, the Sahara was a mythical landscape of the heart, like the American West. Unfortunately, the French were wont to interpret the movies more literally, and they saw them as insulting slights on their methods of colonial administration. Herron had difficulty communicating the French sensitivity to producers. As he explained in exasperation on the release of *Plastered in Paris* (Fox, 1928), a Foreign Legion spoof starring the comedian Sammy Cohen, "The French Foreign Legion is one thing that you cannot burlesque under any circumstances, any more than you can burlesque the English Royal Guard. We have nothing in this country that corresponds to those outfits which are old and have traditions that they consider sacred."[25]

Beau Geste had been the subject of diplomatic protests, and French officials attempted to stop its exhibition in many centers around the world. Then in March 1928 Universal brought out *The Foreign Legion*, which contained many of the elements that had caused such an uproar over *Beau Geste*. The imitation of a proven money-spinner followed the usual logic of production cycles, but from the point of view of foreign relations it was a show of exceptionally poor timing. Upon viewing it, Herron wrote urgently to N. L. Mannheim, Universal's export manager:

> I don't think it is necessary to tell you that if this film is issued with this material in it that you will not only hurt your own company in France, but will hurt the whole American industry throughout the world as a result of the agitation which will follow this. At the present time, the French are in the midst of passing a decree which gives them the privilege to do just about anything they want with the films. They can prohibit a company from doing business in their country if they feel so inclined. I feel so strongly on this film that I hate to even show it to the French Ambassador in its present condition. However, before releasing it in any condition, I would suggest that it should be sent to Washington and shown to the French Embassy, because just as soon as this is released in any form at all we are going to have a bad reaction in the French newspapers.[26]

The picture was shown to the MPPDA's European representative, Edward G. Lowry, and he advised against its release in case it jeopardized their negotiations with the French government. Robert Cochrane of Universal cabled Hays that he would reedit the film in any manner requested, even shooting new scenes if necessary, but he would not consider permanently shelving a negative worth a quarter of a million dollars.[27] Finally the changes were made, apparently to everyone's satisfaction, although the French commercial attaché could not be persuaded to put his approval in writing. Herron was particularly pleased, as he wrote to Joy in May: "Someone is certainly to be congratulated in Universal on having done a beautiful piece of work in cleaning up a very bad picture. When I say bad, I mean, of course, from the French standpoint. The work in this picture is cleverly done, and I believe they have eliminated all the points that were so strenuously objected to by the French attachés, and smoothed the edges off so that they still have a story and a film just as good as the original one which will not cause a frightful kick back."[28] [. . .]

Even when the studios chose to submit synopses for review, however, they were not strictly obliged to adopt Joy's or Herron's suggestions. *The Gallant Gringo* (MGM, 1928), also known as *The Adventurer*, treated the kind of subject that was virtually assured to run into problems in the foreign field. The movie was an action melodrama that revolved around the exploits of a U.S. hero in the context of a Latin American revolution. Latin American countries always resented the implication that they were subject to the predations of colorful and brutal dictators, especially when the restoration of order depended on the arrival of a contingent of U.S. Marines or, as in this case, the intervention of a lone Yankee visitor. Nevertheless, despite the problems inherent in the project, Herron agreed to work with the studio on a treatment that would, he hoped, be comparatively inoffensive to Latin America. To the chagrin of the SRC, however, when the picture was released it contained all the sensitive sequences that the studio had agreed to eliminate or change. The result so compromised its chances of general distribution that the film had to be withheld from circulation and modified, at considerable expense to the studio.[29] Such cases of noncooperation demonstrated the advantages of more careful selection and treatment of subject matter, not just in terms of good will but also in terms of dollars and cents.

An inevitable result of the work of the SRC was the narrowing of the field of representation normally attempted by filmmakers. After losing money on the script of *I Take This Woman*, Universal was unlikely to buy another story with equally contentious European elements. Joy or Herron would only have to request the substitution of a Russian for an Austrian so many times before scenario writers beat them to it. As Joy gathered expertise on the likely reception of different themes and treatments, filmmakers learned to limit some of the most obvious causes of agitation. [. . .]

Notes

1. Articles of Incorporation, quoted in Raymond Moley, *The Hays Office* (Indianapolis: Bobbs-Merrill, 1945), 226. Moley's book is the standard account of the MPPDA. He was highly sympathetic to the association and its progressive business methods. Because he was given access to the organization's records during the book's preparation, *The Hays Office* is a useful source of information, but it is nevertheless a frankly partial account.
2. *New York Times*, 7 March 1921, 7, quoted in Charles Mathew Feldman, *The National Board of Censorship (Review) of Motion Pictures, 1909–1922* (New York: Arno Press, 1977), 192–93. The resolution was passed on 6 March 1921.
3. James West, quoted in "Minutes of the Meeting of January Fourth of the Committee on Public Relations," 4 January 1923, Civic Committee file, reel 1, MPPDA Archive.

4. Jason Joy, "Committee Meeting Summaries: Second Annual Meeting," 6 March 1924, Committee on Public Relations file, reel 1, MPPDA Archive.

5. Ibid., p. 4, quoting Hays.

6. "Meeting of Committee on Public Relations," 8 July 1924, pp. 7–8, MPPDA Archive.

7. See Margaretta Reeve (president of the National Congress of Parents and Teachers), letter to Lee Hanmer, 18 November 1924, National Congress of Parents and Teachers file, reel 1, MPPDA Archive. Reeve's resignation came nearly a year after the controversy over *West of the Water Tower*. [. . .]

8. Courtland Smith, telegram to Fred Beetson, 26 February 1924, AMPP file, reel 1, MPPDA Archive.

9. J. J. O'Neill, memo to Courtland Smith, 14 January 1925, Protests file, November 1924, reel 1, MPPDA Archive. O'Neill suggested specific cuts and alterations and added, "At the same time, however, it might be well to let our directors know that there have been a couple of kicks about Pool Room pictures and to suggest that the directors lay off them."

10. Motion Picture Producers and Distributors of America, *The "Open Door"* (New York: Motion Picture Producers and Distributors of America, 1924).

11. Strictly speaking, both the Studio Relations Committee and the Production Code Administration came under the jurisdiction of the AMPP rather than the MPPDA. The AMPP, however, mainly rubber-stamped decisions that were taken in New York, the real center of administrative power.

12. See Motion Picture Producers and Distributors of America, "The Don'ts and Be Carefuls (1927)," in *The Movies in Our Midst: Documents in the Cultural History of Film in America*, edited by Gerald Mast (Chicago: University of Chicago Press, 1982), 213–14.

13. Joy, memo to Hays, 18 January 1928, Department of Public and Industry Relations file, reel 4, MPPDA Archive.

14. "Minutes of the Luncheon Meeting of the Executive Committee," 10 March 1923, Civic Committee file, reel 1, MPPDA Archive.

15. MPPDA, press release, "An 'Open Door' Policy in the Moving Picture Industry," 28 March 1925, Open Door file, reel 2, MPPDA Archive.

16. Herron asserted in a court deposition in February 1939 that he had held the job of foreign manager for fifteen years; see "Deposition of Frederick L. Herron," February 1939, reel 12, MPPDA Archive. He was certainly part of the organization in September 1923, when he accompanied Hays to England, although Moley claims that his first three years on the job were spent building up contacts and acquaintances. See Moley, *Hays Office*, 171.

17. See Diane Collins, *Hollywood Down Under: Australians at the Movies, 1896 to the Present Day* (Sydney: Angus and Robertson, 1987), 64–65. [. . .]

18. "Heirlooms of Napoleon for *Madame Sans-Gene*," *Morning Telegraph*, 5 October 1924.

19. Jerome Beatty, "Daily Report," 2 October 1926, Titles file, reel 5, MPPDA Archive.

20. Ibid. For documents relating to anti-German propaganda films of World War I, see Richard Wood, ed., *Film and Propaganda in America: A Documentary History*, vol. 1 (New York: Greenwood, 1990).

21. Dr. G. Heuser (acting German consul general), letter to Hays, 20 December 1926; Hays, letter to Joe Schenck, 21 December 1926; and Joe Schenck, letter to Hays, 29 December 1926, all in Titles file, reel 5, MPPDA Archive.

22. Will H. Hays, *The Memoirs of Will H. Hays* (New York: Doubleday & Co., 1955), 431–32. See also Charles R. Metzger, "Pressure Groups and the Motion Picture Industry," in *The Annals of the American Academy of Political and Social Science*, edited by Thorsten Sellin (Philadelphia: American Academy of Political and Social Science, 1947), 110–15.

23. See Hays, letter to Charles Smith (president, American Association for the Advancement of Atheism), 2 November 1927, Protests file, reel 3, MPPDA Archive.

24. Kristin Thompson, *Exporting Entertainment: America in the World Film Market, 1907–1934* (London: BFI, 1985), 119–20.

25. Herron, review, 14 September 1928, *Plastered in Paris* file, Production Code Administration (PCA) Archive, Margaret Herrick Library, Academy of Motion Picture Arts and Sciences, Beverly Hills, California.

26. Herron, letter to N. L. Mannheim, March 1928, Censor-Foreign file, reel 4, MPPDA Archive.

27. Robert Cochrane, letter to Hays, 29 March 1928, Censor-Foreign file, reel 4, MPPDA Archive.

28. Herron, letter to Joy, 16 May 1928, Censor-Foreign file, reel 4, MPPDA Archive.

29. Joy, memo to Hays, 18 January 1928, Department of Public and Industry Relations file, reel 4, MPPDA Archive.

PART VI

European cinemas

INTRODUCTION

WE HAVE FOCUSED SO FAR in this book on developments in the United States, concerning film form, style and themes, the structure of the film industry and its mode of production, film exhibition and audiences, as well as debates about the cinema and its regulation. In doing so we have consistently paid attention to the important influence of European films and companies on these developments. For example, we have seen how commercially successful film projection first developed in Europe and that it was at least partly due to the presence of European projectors in America that Thomas Edison got involved in film projection. Later, the transition from single-shot to multi-shot films was made most strikingly by British pioneers such as G. A. Smith, whose films were frequently copied in the US. Then the extended story films produced by Méliès and Pathé in France became so numerous and popular in American variety theatres that they helped transform film production – leading to an increased output of longer story films by American companies – as well as film exhibition in the US by establishing the framework for the emergence and rapid expansion of nickelodeons. This process was virtually repeated in the early 1910s when the success of ever longer films imported from Europe facilitated the shift towards multi-reel feature production in the US which in turn made the rapid growth of movie palaces possible. Thus the shift from the kinetoscope to film projection, from single-shot to multi-shot films, from actualities to story films, from projection in variety theatres to the nickelodeon, from one-reelers to multi-reelers shown in movie palaces – all these crucial developments in the US were partly dependent on the presence of European films.

Yet, by the late 1910s European imports had become very marginal in the American market.[1] As has been suggested in the preceding chapters, a number of factors contributed to this. American film companies made strenuous attempts to neutralize foreign competition. This process had started as early as Edison's attempts to highlight American subject matter in 1895 to 1896 so as to gain an advantage with American audiences over the Lumière film shows. However, the most concerted effort to marginalize foreign competition occurred from 1907 onwards, when the emergence in the US of regulatory anxieties about the effects of films on audiences frequently singled out foreign films and when, from 1908 onwards, the Motion Picture Patents Company used such anxieties alongside patent power to engineer a reduction of film imports and to curtail Pathé's dominant position in the American market.[2] Later, the mass production of feature films by American companies, beginning in 1913, together with the impact of the First World War on film production in Europe and on international film distribution, reduced the exhibition of imports in American movie theatres (as well as increasing American exports).[3] It is also quite likely that, when given the choice, American audiences did indeed, by and large, prefer domestic productions to foreign imports – especially, but not only, during times of war (more about this later).

In any case, once the major American studios had perfected their industrial mode of production as well as the classical storytelling of their feature films, while also organizing themselves into a cartel of vertically integrated companies, the impact of European developments on American cinema became negligible. As we have seen, this is not to say that Hollywood paid no attention to Europe in the 1920s. On the one hand, the American film industry was always eager to employ top European talent, ranging from cinematographers to directors, from set designers to stars.[4] On the other hand, as Ruth Vasey's chapter in this book has demonstrated, through the public relations offices of the Motion Picture Producers and Distributors of America (MPPDA), Hollywood aimed, at the earliest possible stages of film production, to avoid offending European governments, pressure groups and audiences with their output, and also to counter legislation which restricted their access to European markets. It is also worth noting that European subject matter remained important, especially in Hollywood's prestige productions, and, more fundamentally, that immigrants from Europe and their increasingly assimilated children continued to make up the majority of the American movie audience, as well as providing the industry with much of its executive and creative personnel.[5] Thus, European immigrants, markets and governments continued to play a role in the operations of classical Hollywood, yet this role was quite different from the huge and in some cases decisive impact that European films and companies had had in the first two decades of American cinema. Significantly, the major developments in 1920s American cinema – the formation of the MPPDA and its systems of self-regulation, and the conversion to sound – took place without much European input.

The basic questions we have sought to answer in this book so far, then, are: Why did cinema take the shape it did in the US? What role did European films and companies play in this development? Less centrally, we have also begun to explore why their influence was reduced so dramatically during the time that the aesthetic and industrial system of the classical Hollywood cinema was put in place. In this final section, we want to reverse our perspective, exploring developments in Europe in their own right, rather than as an influence on American cinema, and also examining the influence that American films and companies had on European cinemas. Obviously, it is impossible to offer as wide-ranging and detailed a discussion of European developments as we did with those in the US.[6] This would require another volume (at least), extending the kind of in-depth study of filmmaking under specific local conditions offered in the second section, in Frank Gray's chapter on British pioneers and Richard Abel's chapter on French genres in the years around 1900, to other countries and periods. Instead of trying to cover developments across Europe and across the whole silent period, the chapters in this section deal with aesthetic and industrial developments in three major European countries – Russia, France and Germany – in the 1910s and 1920s. Crucial questions addressed include: to what extent do film form, style, and themes vary from country to country? And to what extent do film industries, their structure and mode of production, differ?

How can we explain such differences? But also: how can we explain the many similarities between cinema in different countries?

Our focus on Russia, France and Germany is in line with the emphasis of traditional film historiography on major film movements, that is cycles of films sharing a distinctive style as well as particular thematic preoccupations, being made by an interlinked group of film artists and deriving from movements in older arts. The most written about film movements of the silent period are Soviet Montage, French Impressionism and German Expressionism, all rooted in the cinema of the 1910s, yet flowering in the 1920s.[7] The chapters collected here are not restricted in their analysis to these movements; instead they provide a framework within which to understand them better. To concentrate our case studies on the 1910s and 1920s also makes sense in another respect. An in-depth discussion of the earlier period, aiming to reconstruct the fundamental transformations taking place in European cinemas between the 1890s and the 1910s – from the kinetoscope to multi-reel features and movie palaces – would, we suspect, involve a lot of repetition of the material already presented in this book, because the crucial shifts were similar to those in the US, albeit sometimes taking place a little bit earlier or later, and the reasons for those shifts were also probably quite similar.

For example, population growth and rapid urbanization in the nineteenth century created a huge new audience for commercial entertainments in Europe as well as in the US, and variety theatres sprang up to service this demand with diverse stage acts, featuring home grown talent as well as international star attractions and including the display of technological novelties such as moving pictures. Further steps in the development of the commercial use of moving pictures – such as their circulation outside cities through travelling exhibitors, their increasing length and complexity, the special appeal exerted by longer story films, the realisation that these could be used as the focus of a new kind of cheap theatre for the urban masses, starting with small storefront venues – were taken more or less simultaneously in the US and Europe. This was partly because the external conditions that made such developments possible were similar, partly because entrepreneurs and filmmakers in different countries were likely to explore the commercial and aesthetic potential of moving pictures in similar ways, but also, simply, because the technology and the films, the showmen making and presenting them, and news about developments in other countries travelled fairly freely and certainly very fast around the globe.[8] This is not to say that there were no significant differences between countries: the travelling cinemas (*Wanderkinos*) of Germany and other European countries, for example, did not seem to have an equivalent in the US;[9] and the rapid growth and enormous size of early French film companies was not matched by companies in other countries.[10] Yet despite such differences, American and European developments mostly ran parallel during the first decade or so of cinema's history.

It is in the years between the rapid spread of storefront movie theatres (1905 to 1906 in the US, a bit later in Europe) and the end of the First World War that more pronounced developmental differences emerge. At the most basic level, it appears that the shift from a preponderance of brief actualities to the dominance of longer story films in the 1900s raised the issue of cultural specificity. While there is not much empirical research on audience responses to various types of films during this period, we can make some informed guesses.[11] Unlike earlier film shows which combined a range of brief films in such a way that their sequence and/or the showman's commentary suggested a story or an argument which could tie the films to the local circumstances of exhibition, longer story films, especially one-reel dramas, increasingly spoke for themselves. Telling a story without much or any mediation by a lecturer

in the auditorium, and thus no adaptation to local circumstances, including audience expectations and knowledge, self-contained one-reel dramas were more likely to alienate certain
audiences. Such alienation could range from lack of comprehension (because the film depended
on familiarity with an existing story that the audience simply did not have) to a more diffuse
sense of strangeness (because audiences were unfamiliar with the fashions, behaviours or social
roles displayed on the screen, or in disagreement with the values underpinning the film's story).
It is reasonable to assume that imported films were more likely to alienate audiences than
domestic products,[12] and that this divergence between the basic familiarity of domestic productions and the basic strangeness of imports increased with the transition to multi-reel features.
In any case, this would help to explain – together with the mass production and monopolistic
strategies of American companies – why, after the novelty period of European multi-reel productions in the early 1910s, such imports were very quickly displaced in the US market by American
made features, and also why, as Joseph Garncarz shows in his essay in this section, in the
1920s German audiences much preferred German films to imports, including those from
Hollywood.[13]

A particularly striking example for the distinctiveness of a country's film culture and its
incompatibility with imports and foreign markets is provided by Tsarist Russia in the 1910s.
As Yuri Tsivian shows in his chapter in this section, foreign films released in Russia were
routinely supplemented with a more downbeat ending, while Russian studios produced upbeat
endings for their films for the purposes of export. Tsivian highlights two distinctive features
of the style of Russian films of the 1910s, calling attention to the frequent occurrence of tragic
endings in these films and the deliberately slow pace of the acting and editing. Tsivian points
out that it is tempting to link these stylistic features to presumed national characteristics such
as clichéd notions of the depth of the Russian soul and its propensity for suffering. Cautioning
against this explanation, Tsivian suggests that a country's film production has to be situated
carefully in the context of traditions within the arts and mass culture in that country
and in relation to the cinemas of other countries. Russian cinema built on a tendency in parts
of Russian culture to aspire to the status of high art best exemplified by tragedy.

Tsivian's concern with how an emerging medium draws on established cultural traditions
is quite different from an alternative approach which sees all cultural forms as an expression
of national character or national identity.[14] It is worth pointing out that this alternative
approach has difficulties accounting for dramatic changes in a country's film culture (unless
one assumes that national character and identity are highly flexible entities). Russia provides
an obvious example for such changes, insofar as the most distinctive group of films released
after the revolution of 1917 were characterized, in sharp contrast to Tsarist cinema, by fast
editing and an underlying message about the progress of history. As we will see in David
Bordwell's chapter, this transformation can be explained by showing that filmmakers now drew
on a different set of cultural trends within and outside Russia.

Returning to Tsarist cinema, we can see various possible motivations for filmmakers'
tendency to aspire to the status of high art, including their class background and self image,
the film industry's attempt to elevate the status of cinema, and the established taste of target
audiences. Tsivian, however, takes his explanation in a different direction by pointing out that
Russian filmmakers did have an interest in differentiating their films from foreign imports.
Here Tsivian suggests that acting styles were an important means of such differentiation. He
also points out that the tragic endings may not be as specific to Russian cinema as it appears
at first sight, a point also borne out by Garncarz' chapter on German cinema. Indeed, it could

be argued that unhappy endings constituted the norm in Western cinema and that the establishment of the happy ending in American cinema after 1907 was an attempt to differentiate American production from the successful and influential European imports in America. This would mean that the close association of cinema and the happy end which later emerged was partly a consequence of the successful international distribution of American films.

Before exploring the reasons for the success of American exports, let's first examine the situation that other major exporters found themselves in during the 1910s. We have suggested – and the example of Tsarist cinema bears this out – that many single-reel story films and, even more so, multi-reel features were culturally specific to such a degree that they could not easily be enjoyed by audiences in foreign countries. Indeed from French film d'art to Italian epics, high profile European film production often aspired to the status of art by engaging very specifically with national cultural traditions and heritage.[15] While the cultural elites and educated middle classes who probably were the main audiences for the international distribution of these films could be expected to have some familiarity with the history and high culture of a range of countries, the majority of regular cinemagoers were unlikely to share this. However, to what extent this may have effected the international distribution of films within Europe and between Europe and the US is unclear.

It is certain, however, that the chances of export success for European films decreased when war broke out. Not only did the First World War disrupt film production and distribution materially (due to the lack of resources and disruptions of transportation) but it also increased the sense of cultural difference between hostile countries, potentially giving foreign films themselves a hostile dimension, especially, but not exclusively, where they had a propagandistic dimension.[16] The intervention of governments into the operations of their countries' film industries during the war, and the general mobilization of patriotic feelings amongst the population set the stage for post-war developments that conceived of a country's film production as an essential part of the national culture which was worth defending against foreign intrusions, especially by Hollywood.[17] Furthermore, as Kristin Thompson has argued in her chapter in the last section, the relative isolation of film producing countries from each other during the war meant that divergent developments were likely to replace the earlier tendency for filmmaking in various countries to converge due to imitation and adaptation of stylistic features and production methods. When, at the end of the war, industry insiders and outside observers across Europe compared the state of the film industry and of film art in their country with that of other countries, especially the US, they noticed substantial differences. While some saw this as a falling behind and called on filmmakers and companies to catch up, especially with Hollywood, both aesthetically and industrially, others celebrated the distinctiveness of their film culture. As we suggested above, in the wake of their extensive war-time involvement in the film industry, governments could quite easily be mobilized for the cause of defending this newly recognized national film culture.[18]

Why was Hollywood least affected by the negative impact of the cultural differentiation of films from different countries on their export chances? One suggestion is that, ever since the nickelodeon boom, American film producers, many of whom were recent immigrants, had learnt how to cater to a patchwork of European immigrant groups in their domestic market,[19] and that this increased their chances in European export markets. It is difficult to determine whether this made American films measurably different from the films that European countries exported, whether, in other words, they had indeed a multi-cultural dimension that their European counterparts lacked. However, it seems that while American producers were quite willing, especially in prestige productions, to adapt foreign books and plays, to set their films in foreign countries and in particular to deal with important moments in European history, producers in European countries by comparison may have been more inward looking. In any case, we have seen that, through the MPPDA, American companies went out of their way to take cultural sensitivities of other countries into account in their productions and systematically avoided giving offence. As Tsivian's chapter in this section and Thompson's chapter in *Feature Films and Cinema Programmes* show, it is also possible to demonstrate differences in style between Hollywood's output and European productions.[20] It has been argued that some of these differences, notably the much lower editing rate of European films, may have increased the popularity of American exports.[21]

While the above remarks suggest that export success derived from the distinctive qualities of the films themselves, other explanations can be found in the realm of corporate power and business strategy. Here one might point out the sheer size of the American companies, the co-ordination of their activities through the MPPDA, the setting up of distribution subsidiaries in foreign countries and their investment in foreign companies, their negotations with foreign governments about import restrictions, the marketing budgets for their films and their ability, where necessary, to rent out their films at cheap rates because the films had already recouped their production costs in the huge American market.[22] Following the lead of the combative rhetoric in contemporary sources, film historians have usually seen the activities of American companies in European markets in terms of a battle with local industries and governments. However, they have also pointed out that exhibitors ultimately did not care where their films came from and welcomed American films as long as they were popular and/or cheap.

We think that it is possible to take this line of argument further. The transition to multi-reel features dramatically increased the cost of film production. While European filmmakers started producing multi-reelers earlier than the Americans, the American film industry was the first to enter into mass production of such films. This required huge investments into production facilities and also produced massive on-going costs to pay numerous employees on long-term contracts as well as covering the premium salaries received by top creative personnel and stars. It seems quite likely that only countries with large domestic markets can provide the basis for a film industry on this scale. In strictly commercial terms, smaller countries simply cannot afford the mass production of feature films, and therefore depend on imports. This dependence on imports can also develop in larger countries if, for one reason or another, investors fail to support domestic production companies, as happened in the UK in the 1920s.[23] Even in major film producing countries like France, the huge demand for films by thousands of movie theatres may have required the presence of imports. Seen in this perspective, the relationship between American producers and local industries was not necessarily adversarial, but complementary. This is particularly true if many big budget or otherwise high profile productions in a given country were informed as much by artistic ambitions and ideological goals as they were by commercial imperatives (or even more so), as was the case, as outlined in Garncarz's and Bordwell's chapters here, both in Germany and in Russia in the 1920s. The power of cultural and political élites to shape important sectors of domestic film production could then be complemented by the more rigorously commercial activities of other sectors of the country's film industry and by large numbers of Hollywood imports.

Kristin Thompson's chapter in this section demonstrates that film production in France, Germany and Russia in the late 1910s and the 1920s was not, like production in the US, organized for maximum efficiency and standardization. Instead, the European mode of production gave directors a much more central and comprehensive role than they had within Hollywood's rigorous division of labour and its system of executive control by producers. Most likely modelled on other arts, in which one creative individual takes charge of the process of artistic creation, the role of the European director embraced all stages of production, from script development to editing, whereas in Hollywood directors were mostly restricted to the shooting stage, which was in turn largely determined by the instructions given in the continuity script. For Thompson, the director-centred European mode of production is an important precondition – but, of course, not the only one – for the emergence of avant-garde film movements (French Impressionism, Soviet Montage and German Expressionism) which depart significantly from the style of classical storytelling, yet are located at the very centre of their respective film industries, rather than taking place in its low budget, non-commercial margins. In fact, irrespective of their commercial success in their country of origin (which varied), such avant-garde films were often significant export successes, partly because they differentiated themselves so clearly from the mainstream output of Hollywood and other film industries, and partly because their marketing could build on the international currency of movements in the other arts with which their style was intimately connected.[24]

Like Tsivian's discussion of Tsarist cinema, Thompson aims to reconstruct the precise conditions which facilitated the emergence of a distinctive style, and she also carefully avoids equating the avant-garde movements she is so interested in with the overall film output of the countries in question. This equation has been characteristic of much traditional film historiography, which is primarily, sometimes exclusively, concerned with the outstanding artistic achievements of a country's and a period's film culture, rather than with the typical films that were produced and viewed in great numbers. As we have seen in Tsivian's chapter, there is also a temptation to relate distinctive styles and themes to something called national character. This temptation is particularly difficult to resist in the case of Weimar Germany, which has produced so many films that can easily be understood as harbingers of fascism, as was done most famously in Siegfried Kracauers aptly titled study *From Caligari to Hitler*.[25]

Joseph Garncarz's chapter on German cinema in the 1920s avoids such retrospective interpretations of both films and the national unconscious, and instead begins with an outline of the suprising normalcy of the German film industry, with its huge audience base, its own studio system, its popular genres and stars, and its dominance at the domestic box office (with German films leaving American imports far behind in the charts of the most commercially successful movies). However, by comparing German film culture with classical Hollywood, Garncarz also identifies distinctive features, which may in fact be shared with other European cinemas, as is suggested by both Tsivian and Thompson. The German film industry was not controlled by a tightly organized cartel of vertically integrated companies (although vertical integration did characterize the largest companies). Furthermore, a discourse about film as art was all-pervasive in German film culture, shaping the way that stars were publicized (as artists rather than celebrities) and, for a few years, making possible the almost total control that directors were able to command over the hugely expensive and artistically ambitious productions of Germany's largest studio, Ufa. Garncarz shows that, to some extent, this art discourse could override the commercial imperatives of the German film industry, because it failed to provide fans with the information they requested about their favourite stars, and it also led to the production of films with such enormous budgets that even an immensely popular release at home and abroad would not recoup their costs.

Although David Bordwell does not address questions of financing and popularity, his chapter on Sergei Eisenstein makes it clear that directorial control and artistic as well as political imperatives shaped many of the Soviet Union's epic film productions of the 1920s.[26] Bordwell shows that Eisenstein drew on a different set of cultural traditions than that traced out by Tsivian at an earlier moment in Russian history, principally those associated with the European avant-garde and with Russian political art. As noted earlier, Soviet Montage cinema was extremely fast-paced and so differed considerably in style from pre-Revolutionary Russian cinema. Bordwell also relates the emphasis on the mass as hero and on social change in Eisenstein's films to Marxist political theory and the ideals of the Russian Revolution. In this way, the form, style and themes of Soviet Montage cinema were connected to the specific cultural and political context of the Soviet Union, which clearly differentiated this film movement from the Tsarist tradition and from films made in other European countries and the United States.

Together the chapters in this section demonstrate the diversity of filmic practices, comprising both film styles and modes of production, in the cinemas of the 1910s and 1920s. Differences emerge between countries, but also within them. They can be tied to specific cultural traditions, to particular group interests, or to the aim of product differentiation in the international marketplace. In many cases, political discourses about the protection of domestic industries or the defence of national culture, even national identity, were mobilized in support of particular filmic practices. Yet, as we have argued, such discourses need not, and indeed should not, be taken at face value. While there is considerable evidence that from the 1910s audiences by and large preferred films made in their own country, there is no need to postulate a national identity that informed their movie choices; familiarity with the cultural traditions domestic films drew on, and lack of such familiarity in the case of imports, may be sufficient to explain such audience preferences. Also, while production and distribution companies in European countries protested against the presence of Hollywood films, and governments were willing to intervene on their behalf, it is quite likely that the exhibition sector could not have filled its schedules without American imports. Furthermore, just because domestic producers and distributors sought to curtail Hollywood's presence does not mean that this presence was overwhelming; any market share taken up by foreign companies was worth fighting for.

Finally, it is worth emphasizing that despite pockets of diversity among film practices, mainstream film cultures in the United States and across Europe also had a lot in common. In fact, at the most basic level, it is possible to say that cinema took the same shape in all of these countries. At its centre were feature films produced at considerable cost in purpose-built studios employing large numbers of highly specialized workers. These films were presented as part of a varied and intense entertainment experience in purpose-built movie theatres, and such exhibitions were surrounded by an extensive media discourse both about the films and about their stars.

Notes

1   Kristin Thompson, *Exporting Entertainment: America in the World Film Market 1907–1934* (London: British Film Institute, 1985), 26, 224; Andrew Higson and Richard Maltby, '"Film Europe" and "Film America: An Introduction', in Andrew Higson and Richard Maltby (eds), *'Film Europe' and 'Film America': Cinema, Commerce and Cultural Exchange 1920–1939* (Exeter: University of Exeter Press, 1999), 19–20; Sarah Street, *Transatlantic Crossings: British Feature Films in the USA* (New York: Continuum, 2002), ch. 1.

2 Richard Abel, *The Red Rooster Scare: Making Cinema American, 1900–1910* (Berkeley: University of California Press, 1999), chs. 4–5.

3 Thompson, *Exporting Entertainment*, 28–99, 226–7.

4 See, for example, Larry Langman, *Destination Hollywood: The Influence of Europeans on American Filmmaking* (Jefferson: McFarland, 2000); Harry Waldman, *Hollywood and the Foreign Touch: A Dictionary of Foreign Filmmakers and Their Films from America, 1910–1995* (Lanham: Scarecrow, 1996); Graham Petrie, *Hollywood Destinies: European Directors in America, 1922–1931* (London: Routledge and Kegan Paul, 1985); John Baxter, *The Hollywood Exiles* (London: MacDonald and Jane's, 1976).

5 See Neal Gabler, *An Empire of Their Own: How the Jews Invented Hollywood* (London: W. H. Allen, 1989). For a case study of the importance of Germans in Hollywood and their involvement with European-themed prestige productions see Peter Krämer, 'Hollywood in Germany/Germany in Hollywood', in Tim Bergfelder, Erica Carter and Deniz Göktürk (eds), *The German Cinema Book* (London: British Film Institute, 2002).

6 As a starting point for a more comprehensive investigation of European cinemas – as well as non-Western cinemas – we have compiled an extensive bibliography at the end of this book.

7 See, for example, Kristin Thompson and David Bordwell, *Film History: An Introduction* (New York: McGraw-Hill, 1997), Part Two.

8 See Roland Cosandey and Francois Albera (eds), *Images Across Borders* (Lausanne: Editions Payot, 1995).

9 Joseph Garncarz, 'The Origins of Film Exhibition in Germany', in Bergfelder, Carter and Göktürk (eds) *The German Cinema Book*.

10 Richard Abel, 'Booming the Film Business: The Historical Specificity of Early French Cinema', in Richard Abel (ed.), *Silent Film* (London: Athlone, 1996).

11 Material on responses, mostly in the press, to foreign films is contained in Abel, *The Red Rooster Scare*, especially 94–101; and in Yuri Tsivian, *Early Cinema in Russia and Its Cultural Reception* (Chicago: University of Chicago Press, 1994).

12 As reasonable as this assumption may be, a lot of new empirical research is required to determine which audience groups experienced such alienation from imports and under what conditions they did so. The early nickelodeon period is a case in point. As Richard Abel argues in his chapter in the third section, French films were popular with American nickelodeon audiences in 1905–06, following on from their previous success in vaudeville. However, he also suggests that this was, at least partly, due to the lack of competition from American produced 'headline' attractions. In any case, Abel has elsewhere noted the resistance against French imports after the initial boom, or what one might call the nickelodeon's novelty period. While he discusses the sustained attacks on French films starting in 1907 in relation to efforts made by American film companies to reclaim the US market from their French competitors, it is also possible to interpret them as a reflection of widespread disaffection among Americans with the cultural specificity of French imports. See Abel, *Red Rooster Scare*, 94–101.

13 Even in the UK with its notoriously weak production sector, there is evidence from a slightly later period that audiences preferred domestic quality films (but not low budget productions) to Hollywood imports. See John Sedgwick, *Popular Filmgoing in 1930s Britain: A Choice of Pleasures* (Exeter: University of Exeter Press, 2000).

14 The usefulness of the notion of national identity, and the associated concept of 'national cinema', for the writing of film history has been the subject of much debate. See, for example, Mette Hjort and Scott MacKenzie (eds), *Cinema and Nation* (London: Routledge, 2000).

15 Richard Abel, *The Cine Goes to Town: French Cinema, 1896–1914* (Berkeley: University of California Press, 1998), 246–77; Maria Wyke, *Projecting the Past: Ancient Rome, Cinema and History* (New York: Routledge, 1997).

16 See, for example, Karel Dibbets and Bert Hogenkamp (eds), *Film and the First World War* (Amsterdam: Amsterdam University Press, 1995); Andrew Kelly, *Cinema and the Great War* (London: Routledge, 1997); Leslie Midkiff DeBauche, *Reel Patriotism: The Movies and World War I* (Madison: University of Wisconsin Press, 1997); Nicholas Reeves, *The Power of Film Propaganda: Myth or Reality?* (London: Cassell, 1999), ch. 1.

17 See, for example, Thompson, *Exporting Entertainment*, ch. 4; Ian Jarvie, *Hollywood's Overseas Campaign: The North Atlantic Movie Trade, 1920–1950* (Cambridge: Cambridge University Press, 1992), ch. 4; John Trumpbour, *Selling Hollywood to the World: US and European Struggles for Mastery of the Global Film Industry, 1920–1950* (New York: Cambridge University Press, 2002). Attempts to co-ordinate

European responses to Hollywood on a transnational level are analyzed in Higson and Maltby (eds), 'Film Europe' and 'Film America'.

18   For a discussion of the arguments usually put forward in policy debates about the protection of domestic film industries in European countries, see Ian Jarvie, 'National Cinema: A Theoretical Assessment', in Hjort and MacKenzie (eds), Cinema and Nation.

19   See, for example, Miriam Hansen, Babel & Babylon: Spectatorship in American Silent Film (Cambridge, MA: Harvard University Press, 1991), chs. 2–3; Melvyn Stokes and Richard Maltby (eds), American Movie Audiences: From the Turn of the Century to the Early Sound Era (London: British Film Institute, 1999).

20   Also see David Bordwell, On the History of Film Style (Cambridge, MA: Harvard University Press, 1997), 175–210; Ben Brewster and Lea Jacobs, Theatre to Cinema: Stage Pictorialism and the Early Feature Film (Oxford: Oxford University Press, 1997).

21   Barry Salt, Film Style and Technology: History and Analysis (London: Starword, 1992), particularly 132.

22   See Thompson, Exporting Entertainment, chs. 2–4; Higson and Maltby (eds), 'Film Europe' and 'Film America'; Trumpbour, Selling Hollywood to the World; Jarvie, Hollywood's Overseas Campaign; Kerry Segrave, American Films Abroad: Hollywood's Domination of the World's Movie Screens from the 1890s to the Present (Jefferson: McFarland, 1997); Jens Ulff-Moller, Hollywood's Film Wars with France: Film-Trade Diplomacy and the Emergence of the Film Quota Policy (Rochester: University of Rochester Press, 2001).

23   Rachael Low, The History of the British Film, Volume 4: 1918–1929 (London: Routledge, 1997).

24   See, for example, Kristin Thompson, 'Dr. Caligari at the Folies Bergeres', in Michael Budd (ed.), 'The Cabinet of Dr. Caligari': Texts, Contexts, Histories (New Brunswick: Rutgers University Press, 1990)

25   Siegfried Kracauer, From Caligari to Hitler: A Psychological History of the German Film (Princeton: Princeton University Press, 1947). For a critique of Kracauer and an alternative historical interpretation of Weimar cinema see Thomas Elsaesser, Weimar Cinema and After: Germany's Historical Imaginary (London: British Film Institute, 2000).

26   For a discussion of the Soviet Union's overall cinematic output, of which montage films constituted only a small fraction, see, for example, Denise J. Youngblood, Movies for the Masses: Popular Cinema and Soviet Society in the 1920s (Cambridge: Cambridge University Press, 1992).

Chapter 20

YURI TSIVIAN

NEW NOTES ON RUSSIAN FILM CULTURE BETWEEN 1908 AND 1919

A FIRST ENCOUNTER WITH RUSSIAN FILMS of the 1910s can be puzzling: their stories seem to be moving at a wrong pace and in the wrong direction. Was this cinema out of tune with what was going on elsewhere at that time? Has this something to do with Russian culture at large? Such are the questions I will be looking at in the following notes – not to provide a detailed portrayal of 'Russian style,' but to highlight those of its features that set it apart from the general practice of the teens.

I call these notes new for the following reason. My first attempt at an essay like this took place thirteen years ago in an introduction to *Silent Witnesses*, the catalogue of surviving Russian films prepared for a retrospective at the Silent Film Festival in Pordenone[1]; it was that essay (or, rather, its extended version of 1991[2]) that I was asked to contribute to the present anthology. As I reread what I wrote I was pleased to discover how far away our field – the field of early film studies – has got from the level of knowledge we had then. Here was my chance not to revise or rewrite, but to overwrite that old essay, correcting its mistakes and challenging my own assumptions. The result is not simply a mixture of old and new. I kept the facts and quotes I found worth repeating from the first version, but on the whole the new picture is different and, I hope, more accurate than before.

Russian endings (thirteen years later)

Write the wholesome, joyous story and leave the morbid and the unpleasant to others. The temptation is strong to write the tragic plot, but the demand is for pleasant things. You may be impressed with *Romeo and Juliet*, but the greater appeal is made by the heart interest story and the demand is so much more urgent for this class of plays that you will find it profitable to hold to pleasant things and leave the tragic to others.

(Epes Winthrop Sargent, *Technique of the Photoplay*[3])

Some people – and I am one of them – hate happy ends. We feel cheated. Harm is the norm. Doom should not jam. The avalanche stopping in its tracks a few feet above the cowering village behaves not only unnaturally but unethically.

(Vladimir Nabokov, *Pnin*[4])

All is well that
Begins well
  And has no end
      (Aleksei Kruchenykh, *Victory over the Sun*[5])

In 1918 two film press organs, one Russian and one American, made – independently of one another – an identical observation. *The Moving Picture World*, after reviewing a batch of Russian pictures that had just arrived in the USA, thus summarized the general impression of its reviewers:

> As was pointed out in the first and favorable review of these films in *The Moving Picture World*, the tragic note is frequently sounded; this is in marked contrast to prevailing American methods. The Russian films, in other words, incline to what has been termed 'the inevitable ending' rather than an idealized or happy ending. That was the thing that gave the reviewers some slight shivers of apprehension as to the reception that might be accorded these films by our public.[6]

At the same time but on the Russian side the Moscow *Kino-gazeta* was informing its readers:

> 'All's well that ends well!' This is the guiding principle of foreign cinema. But Russian cinema stubbornly refuses to accept this and goes its own way. Here it's 'All's well that ends badly' – we need tragic endings.[7]

It is a fact that only a handful of Russian movies ended well, but what agency was the 'we' that needed tragic endings – the nation, the audiences, the filmmakers – is still unclear. Would Russian filmgoers leave the theatre disappointed if the hero and heroine they liked stayed alive, or, worse, ended up marrying each other? No evidence (other than films) exists to blame them for that; if critical reviews can pass as factual testimony, some facts even point to the contrary. Take the case of *Jennie the Maid* reviewed in *Kino-gazeta* (the same weekly in which, a few issues later, the above credo appeared). Unlike most Russian melodramas *Jennie the Maid* (Gornichnaya Dzhenny, 1918, written and directed by Yakov Protazanov) ended in a marriage; to support his approval, the reviewer appeals to the voice of the people:

> It was curious to observe how passionately the public desired a happy resolution, how watchful it grew as soon as it began to scent melodrama somewhere about the middle of the film – and to hear the sigh of relief when it transpired that the hero is recovering from his wound, and that the film, after all, would not end with the harmonium huskily wailing.[8]

This could be truly what the viewing-hall mood was, for it is impossible to imagine anyone watching their touching love story (a print survives) to wish anything less than a marriage for Jenny and Georges Engère; but it is also true that cautious Protazanov set his film abroad. In a Russian setting such turn of events might have seemed forced.

Whether or not audiences were happy about tragic endings, the industry thought they were. Some time in 1912 those film companies in Russia which had a market abroad, and, reciprocally, foreign companies with an eye to Russian markets got into a practice of supplementing their films with an export ending. No print of a Russian movie with such extra tail has been identified archivally – we only know about their existence from memoir sources.

Thus, a recollection left by Sofia Giatsintova, the actress that starred in *By Her Mother's Hand*, a 1913 movie shot by Protazanov (the same director who would, five years later, venture a happy end in *Jenny the Maid*) tells us she was asked to do two such scenes in a row, in the same interior and in the same white dress: 'One ending, the happy ending, was "for export": Lidochka recalls. The other, more dramatic, was "for Russia": Lidochka in her coffin.'[9]

More than one Russian memoir testifies that Russian studios did this; but as for material evidence, we are luckier with Denmark (the country whose filmmaking industry vitally depended on Russian distribution), for at least five Danish films with such lizard tails survive that we can examine to check if alternative closures were always as polarized as our historical imaginations paint them.[10] Let me dwell on Holger-Madsen's 1914 *The Life of a Priest* for a moment. Its hero (played by Valdemar Psilander), a former-convict-turned-minister, finds his mission in making local hoodlums see the light of God. One such hoodlum, a rowdy boy, happens to have a girlfriend (Alma Hinding) driven to desperation by the way he is treating her; the point in the story when the boy sees the light coincides with the moment the girl decides to hang herself. The first ending: the priest and the boy hurry up the stairs, manage to break the door leading to her room, and – the last-moment rescuers – take her out of the noose; next shot: the priest weds the couple. 'For Russia' (as handwritten across the blank lead frame sandwiched between this ending and the next): the rescuers break the door a split second late; they take the body from the noose and put it on the bed; the girl opens her eyes for the last time; as she sees her beloved in the company of the priest her eyes light up with forgiveness, and she dies with her arms around the boy's neck. Is this what we are used to think of as an unhappy ending? Come to think of it, 'the Russian ending' of *The Life of a Priest* is, too, a happy reunion, the reunion forever.

Nonetheless, the variance is there, and is waiting to be explained. The first thing that suggests itself is a cultural explanation, for isn't it plausible indeed to assume that what people like to see in art is defined by what they are in life; but explanations like this are more often than not essentialist and circular. Here is one attempt to account for Russian films in cultural terms which was made in the United States as early as November 6, 1917 (by coincidence, only a day away from the date the Socialist Revolution took place in Russia) by one Randolph Bartlet, a film critic writing in *Photoplay Magazine*: 'The Slavic emotions, the world well knows, are terrific, and these Russians have written those emotions in letters of human fire'.[11] This dictum is not a cultural theory, of course, but some cultural theories are much like this dictum. We go to cultures to explain their films, but don't we sometimes end up fitting films to a stereotypical image of their cultures? In the first version of this essay I did not do much better as I wrote:

> [o]ne has to forewarn audiences of our time: like any generalization about national psychology, the notion of the gloomy Russian soul was naïve. 'Russian endings' came into cinema from nineteenth-century Russian theatrical melodrama, which always ended badly. Unlike the Western theatrical melodrama, the Russian version derives from classical tragedy adapted to the level of mass consciousness. Hence the only conclusion that we can draw about 'Russian endings' is one that relates to Russian mass culture as a whole: the peculiarity of Russian cinema and of Russian mass culture is its constant attempts to emulate the forms of high art.[12]

Not that I wish to retract any of these parallels – as parallels go, they are relevant; but does what I said in 1989 differ much from the conclusion to which (another?) *Photoplay* critic came after seeing another Russian movie: 'These Slavs love tragedy.'[13] The difference between the film historian and the film critic is that for the former history comes before culture. Rushing to Russia for help I passed by the film history question: is it really the bad endings, and not the good ones, that need to be explained? Thirteen years ago many people – and I was one of them – tended to treat happy ends for granted; that there would be a cinema biased against them looked more like an interesting anomaly to explain. Today as we are able to examine it in relation to film history the picture appears reversed. There was a time in film history when (to repeat Nabokov's *mot a propos* literary denouements) 'harm was the norm.' In the first dozen years or so endings of the kind to be later labeled as 'Russian' were much in current internationally. 'Happy end' as a program, as Richard Abel has recently shown, began to crystallize around 1908 as part of the American film industry's effort to win its home market from the Pathé Frères. It was then that American trade papers launched a campaign to promote what they called 'clean, wholesome' subjects, in the American tradition of 'ethical melodrama' and its 'bright, happy denouements,' contrasting those to the thumb-down ends habitual to *Grand-guignol* melodramas then fashionable on stage as in films.[14] It is not cultures, as I initially thought, that give shape to film history; it is the other way round: when in need for a tool, film history resorts to culture.

The period (roughly, 1912–1914) during which the Hollywood endings became what they are, and the Russian endings became geographically Russian was linked to another film-historical process: the passage from shorts to features. This was the time when the issue of how to end the film was back on the table: having to choose only one story that would thus define the mood of your show meant that prudent film exhibitors could not any more, as many had done, balance the morbid with the wholesome. There are, I am sure, a number of ways in which the American choice can be accounted for – by linking it to general regulatory concerns, for instance (at any rate, much of the rhetoric around it was regulatory[15]), though straightforward societal explanations may be as insidious as cultural ones; as to the Russian choice, I think it was influenced – in a strange negative way – by its American counterpart. I will try to explain how in the next section.

The pace of the action

These films are amazing. They appear to have only two speeds, 'slow' and 'stop.'
(Kevin Brownlow, 1989[16])

The essential condition of life is movement; the essential condition of thinking is pause.
(Sergei Volkonsky, 1912[17])

We now turn to that other oddity of Russian film culture that amazed Kevin Brownlow (and many others who saw a selection of early Russian films shown at the Silent Film Festival in Pordenone in 1989) – the defiant immobility of their figures. But before looking into this, let me specify what I mean by Russian film culture and by film culture in general. National film culture is not (as the term may misleadingly suggest) a cinema's place on the map of its national culture, but an arsenal of cultural tools deployed by a national cinema to stake a claim on the map of international filmmaking. The Russian way of doing this was to rely on pre-existing cultural difference. 'The Three Schools of Cinematography: 1. Movements: the American School; 2. Forms: the European School; 3. The Psychological: the Russian School,' wrote Fyodor Otsep (not yet the screenwriter and the filmmaker he would soon become, but already a young trade press journalist) in an outline for a film theory book conceived in 1913.[18] The book was never written, but if it were, Otsep's attempt to make use of 'psychology' in order to dissociate Russian cinema from either of its Western sisters would look something like this: we need psychology for our films to be recognized as Russian; for what, if not 'psychology', had brought recognition to the Russian novel; and was it not 'psychology' which marked Chekhov's drama and Moscow Art Theatre acting as unique?

This line of reasoning may look neat on paper, but there remained a practical problem Russian film culture kept trying to resolve. Tolstoy enjoyed the advantage of using verbal descriptions for his readers to access the hero's mental life; likewise, the playwright and the actor can use speech and voice to bring those matters home; but how about cinema? Is silent film – that voiceless and linguistically impaired medium – a vehicle capable of carrying characters' psychology across? The 'immobility' doctrine popular among Russian trade paper theorists round about 1914–1916 was the Russian answer to this question. Here filmic 'psychology' was defined by contraries: while others invested in action and movement, immobility and inaction were declared to be native assets: 'The [Russian] film story breaks decisively with all the established views on the essence of the cinematographic picture: it repudiates *movement*,'[19] wrote a *Proektor* theorist early in 1916; and looking at film reviews that this trade magazine published that year we see how easy this immobility doctrine metamorphoses into an appreciative category, as in a review of Aleksander Volkov's *His Eyes* (Ego glaza): '[Particularly] the scenes that are devoid of traditional cinematic movement produce a great impression'.[20]

Another connection we can observe looking at the period's film literature is one between the immobility doctrine and the image of the film star. Whenever this or that critic would broach the subject of tempo, the review was likely to slip into a discussion of acting. When the notion of national style began to gain ground in film criticism and filmmaking (most energetically, around 1913[21]), it was the manner of acting – more so than the tempo of editing, or scenery and sets – that beckoned people anxious to identify movies by nationality. National cinemas crystallized around national acting schools, each with its own agenda for 'good acting.' American actors relied on little movements, like quick facial reactions and byplay with props; one could tell an Italian diva by her exquisite gestures of arms and hands; Russians valued pensive moods and introvert psychology; needless to say, all this had to do with the pace, not only with the character of acting. Much as it was done in the case of sad endings, Russian trade-paper pundits held up slow acting – that other programmatic characteristic of Russian films – as an example for American movies frequently slighted as slapdash. Note this, for instance, in a smugly condescending review of the American movie *Business is Business* (1915, dir. Otis Turner) distributed in Russian under a more loaded title *The Slave of Profit* (Raba nazhivy):

> As far as the whole pace of the action is concerned, neither the director nor the cast have managed to capture that slow tempo that is so common in the Russian feature-film play. The actors are still too fidgety, as the Americans are wont to be; their acting still derives largely from the superficial, from objects and facts rather than from experiences and emotions.[22]

The actor, indeed, was seen as cinema's ultimate metronome. Much as the Russian public may have enjoyed snappy American acting (and I am sure they did), no busybody (other than in a comedy) had much of a chance to get ahead in a Russian film of the teens. The Russian idea of good acting spelt feet and feet of stillness. To quote again from the essay that 'repudiated movement':

In the world of the screen, where everything is counted in metres, the actor's struggle for the freedom to act has led to a battle for long (in terms of metres) scenes or, more accurately, for 'full' scenes, to use Olga Gzovskaya's marvellous expression. A 'full' scene is one in which the actor is given the opportunity to depict in stage terms a specific spiritual experience, no matter how many metres it takes. The 'full' scene involves a complete rejection of the usual hurried tempo of the film drama. Instead of a rapidly changing kaleidoscope of images, it aspires to *rivet* the attention of the audience on to a single image. . . . This may sound like a paradox for the art of cinema (which derives its name from the Greek word for 'movement') but the involvement of our best actors in cinema will lead to the slowest possible tempo. . . . Each and every one of our best film actors has his or her own *style* of mime: Mosjoukine has his steely hypnotised look; Gzovskaya has a gentle, endlessly varying lyrical 'face'; Maximov has his nervous tension and Polonsky his refined grace. But with all of them, given their unusual economy of gesture, their entire acting process is subjugated to a rhythm that rises and falls particularly *slowly*. . . . It is true that this kind of portrayal is conventional, but convention is the sign of any true art.[23]

Such was Russian film culture viewed from the side of its theory. To get a glimpse of the practical side let us look, once again, at Protazanov's 1918 *Jenny the Maid*. This film, we recall, was made in Russia and set in France; its ending was happy, its tempo Russian. As it happened, many years after the film had been released two of its principal players – the former Moscow Art Theatre actress Olga Gzovskaya that did Jenny (the same Gzovskaya whom the excerpt above credits with inventing the 'marvelous' concept of 'full scenes'), and her partner Vladimir Gaidarov who played Georges – remembered the making of *Jenny the Maid* in their memoirs written, respectively, in 1948 and 1966 – so strong must have been the impress of Protazanov's voice behind the camera telling them what to do next or, to be more to the point, how long to wait before doing it. Writes Gzovskaya:

Protazanov was keen on the actor's eyes and liked to work with the glance of a character. Among all the directors only he could catch in an expression of the eyes a transition to the next step in the action, for he felt the exact duration of a glance. His famous signals during rehearsal: 'pause – looks closely – looks closely – pause – remembers – pause – pause – pause – lowers eyelids' were not prompts or dictates as to what the actress or actor must carry out but rather a perfect merger with the internal life of the performer.[24]

And this – the following quote – is from Gaidarov; his report dwells on a specific scene in which he, as convalescing Georges, is shown sitting in the armchair while Gzovskaya (Jenny the maid) is reading to him. The 'inner' action that underpins the 'outer' business of this scene was to be revealed through this by-play of glances:

Protazanov insisted on this scene being acted at a reduced pace as he dictated his famous pauses – for example, when Georges's glance lingers for a while on Jenny. There we were, face to face, and . . . pause, pause, pause . . . Jenny lowers her eyes . . . pause . . . she gets up quickly, turns and goes to leave. . . . Georges calls to her. . . . She lingers in the doorway without turning round . . . pause, pause . . . and then she turns and says, 'I must get your medicine. It's time for you to take it!' Pause

. . . she turns and leaves . . . Georges is left alone. He looks after her . . . again pause, pause, pause. . . . Then we see his elbow resting on the arm of the chair, his head bowed towards his hand, and Georges thinking to himself, 'What a strange girl she is!' Pause, pause . . . and . . . iris.[25]

Surely, this pause-pause-pause pace of action was an acquired taste, which some critics refused to succumb to. Not by chance, it was scoffed at in reviews that appeared in the 'Kinemo' section of the stage theatre periodical the *Teatralnaya gazeta* – even though (or perhaps because) in turn-of-the-century Russia, stage acting too was predicated on pausing. But stage pauses – Maeterlinckian, Chekhovian, Stanislavskian – did not necessarily entail immobility; these were made of silence, not of stillness. Yevgeni Bauer's *Silent Witnesses* (Nemye svideteli, 1914), 'moved at about three miles an hour,'[26] the *Teatralnaya* sneered; a year later the paper explained what was wrong about the slow pace of Bauer's (unpreserved) *Boris and Gleb* (Boris i Gleb, 1915):

The whole film is imbued with an irritating and unnecessary slowness. Unnecessary because the psychological climax emerges on screen in opposition to the drama, not through delays and pauses but, on the contrary, through accelerations. . . . The long drawn-out 'psychological' scenes allow the audience to start guessing and they have no difficulty in working out the subsequent course of events and the final denouement.[27]

Projectionists – that fifth column within the Russian film industry – were another group of people impatient with the slow Russian style. All over the world projectionists were known for their tendency (particularly strong during the last picture show) to project films faster than they had been shot, but I wonder how many actors other than those in Russia would stand up and act as Ivan Mosjoukine (aka Mozzhukhin, the star remembered for his long steady gaze) whose open letter published in *Teatralnaya gazeta* in 1915 called on filmgoers 'to make their protest known by banging their sticks and stamping their feet, etc.':

The poor innocent actors jump and jerk about like cardboard clowns and the audience, which is unfamiliar with the secrets of the projection booth, stigmatises them for their lack of talent and experience. I cannot convey the feeling you experience when you watch your own scene transformed at the whim of a mere boy from normal movements into a wild dance. You feel as if you were being slandered in front of everyone and you have no way of proving your innocence.[28]

Hard to tell on whose side audiences were in this debate; however, a phrase ostensibly used in the teens to yell at hasty projectionists – *Nie goni kartinu!* (Don't speed the picture!) – still exists in colloquial Russian, now meaning simply 'Not so fast!'

I cannot think of a better way to end the notes on Russian film culture than availing myself of an existing description – even if this means that I must burden the page with a particularly bulky quotation. Unlike most of the writings quoted so far, the essay I am going to cite does not come from the period, and is not authored by a filmmaker or a film critic: it was written by André Levinson, an émigré ballet critic living in Paris, as late as 1925 – some six years after the Russian cinema he remembered ceased to exist. Russian pre-Revolutionary cinema, Levinson tells in his vivid postmortem, created a style that was completely divorced from European and American experiments but enthusiastically supported by our own audiences. The scripts were full of static poetic moods, of melancholy and of the exultation or eroticism of a gypsy romance. There was no external action whatsoever. There was just enough movement to link the long drawn-out pauses, which were weighed down with languorous day-dreaming. The dramaturgy of Chekhov, which had had its day on stage, triumphed on the screen. The action of these intimate emotions was not played out against the expanse of the steppes or the steep slopes of the Caucasus, even though the steppes were as worthy as the pampas and the Caucasus as majestic as the Rocky Mountains! Russian characters dreamed 'by the hearth'. (True, at that time the sentimental heroes of the American Vitagraph film were doing the same, abandoned by their brides, making out figures from the past through a light haze of smoke.) Vera Kholodnaya and Polonsky came back from the ball in a car, facing the audience in close-up, each immersed in their own private pain; they did not look at one another and they never moved. It was in this immobility that their fate was decided. This was the drama. Nobody chased after their car. It did not gather speed. Nothing beyond its windows existed. It did not roll down a slope because the denouement did not need chance as its accomplice. However, in those years Tom Mix was already jumping from a bridge on to the roof of an express train. The 'adventure' script had triumphed. But the Russian product was preoccupied with feeling, with the vibration of the atmosphere surrounding motionless figures. The relationship between patches of black and white, the concepts of chiaroscuro were more expressive than an occasional gesture by the characters. . . . Sometimes the banality of the attitudes and ideas was striking, but only to the Russian eye. To a Western audience this banality was something inscrutably and irrationally exotic. It is for this reason, rather than technical backwardness, that the style remained a localised phenomenon – and soon afterwards war broke out.[29]

Yes, immobility looks like a strange program for the medium of motion pictures, particularly if viewed from 1925, for by this year (after the first feature-long pictures by Kuleshov, Vertov and Eisenstein) the cutting rate and acting speed of Russian films had swung to the opposite extreme, beating the fastest American movies on their own racing track, as it were. This turnabout was not an isolated phenomenon – it dovetails with an overarching makeover of taste that began to sweep Russia around 1900 when, to use John E. Bowlt's felicitous phrase, 'Russian culture moves from slow to fast lane'.[30] But, tempting though it may seem to connect film and culture causally, it is exactly at this threshold that we must watch our step. Causal explanations – vague at their best, essentialist at their worst – will creep in each time the junction is left unattended, be it between the slow pace of Russian films and Russian imperial culture, or between the cult of speed peculiar to Russian modernism and the fast-cutting craze that set in around 1924. I wish I could offer a neat workable theory of how it happens between film and culture, but at least I have a picture of how it does not. We – myself included – are often trapped into picturing a particular cinema vis-à-vis the particular culture in which it is nested as a passive, derivative, filial agency; we either picture national cinemas as 'sponging up' their respective cultures, or look for some sort of cultural genus (the mental image that I must have had in mind when I wrote, in the first version of this essay that 'the peculiarity of Russian cinema and of Russian mass culture is its constant attempts to emulate the forms of high art'), or, as I did in 1991, compare cinema to a compass needle whose dip points to where deeper things are buried:

A peripheral offshoot of the mainstream of world cinema history might be the best way to describe . . . the features of Russian cinema that I have dealt with in this essay. In fact, on the map of the world Russian endings, the immobility of the figures, the predilection of Russian cinema for titles and film recitations would all appear as an anomaly. But, just as a magnetic anomaly leads the geologist to deposits of ore, so the anomalies of Russian cinema allow us to evaluate deep-rooted layers in the psychology of Russian culture.[31]

This trope, I am afraid, is misleading. Cinema is not a culture's needle, nor is it a cultural symptom, psychological or otherwise, but rather, an active, aggressive, manipulative agency, which may, when needed, use a culture as a means to an end. Likewise, the film historian is not a geologist interested in deeper layers of culture. Culture is useful insofar as it helps us to understand films, not the other way round. In the back-and-forth between film and culture it is film that has the first serve.

In other words, there is no such thing as 'grass-root' cinema, American, Russian or Fregonian. Cinema is architecture; culture is its wallpaper. Early Russian film culture was not a blotter that absorbed the ink of Russian theatre and literature to eventually become their pale likeness; a better term to describe the workings of film cultures is not 'absorption', but 'annexation' – cinema works forcibly and aggressively to annex culture's traditional territories, to capture and enslave its innermost topoi, and does so with an eye to an international 'slave market'; a better image to understand cinema's cultural policy is to think of it as one of those science fiction aliens endowed with a gift to take the shape of terrestrial creatures not with the aim to be like them, but in order to rip them off.

Notes

1   *Silent Witnesses: Russian Films, 1908–1919* (Pordenone/London: British Film Institute & Edizioni dell' Immagine, 1989).

2   'Some Preparatory Remarks on Russian Cinema', in: Ian Christie & Richard Taylor (eds), *Inside the Film Factory* (Routledge: London, 1991).

3   Epes Winthrop Sargent, *Technique of the Photoplay* (New York: The Moving Picture World, 1916), p. 75.

4   Vladimir Nabokov, *Pnin* (New York: Vintage International, 1989), pp. 25–26.

5   Aleksei Kruchenykh's avant-garde opera libretto *Victory over the Sun* (1913), in: Aleksei Kruchenykh, *Poems, Long Poems, Novels, Opera* (St Petersburg: Akademicheskij proekt, 2001) p. 404.

6   *The Moving Picture World*, 1918, Vol. 35, No. 5, p. 640. I thank Kristin Thompson for pointing out this source.

7   *Kino-gazeta*, 1918, No. 15, p. 5.

8   A. Ostroumov, '*Jennie the Maid*', *Kino-gazeta*, 1918, No. 8, p. 3.

9   Giatsintova's interview with Tatyana Ponomareva (preserved at Ponomareva's personal archive in Moscow).

10 *Ablaze on the Ocean* (Et Drama paa Havet, 1912, dir. Eduard Schnedler Sørensen), both endings shown in Kevin Brownlow's TV film *Cinema Europe: the Other Hollywood*; August Blom's *Atlantis* (1913) whose second, 'Siberia' ending has been identified and restored by Margaret Engberg in 1992; *The Menace to Society* (En Fare for Samfundet, 1915, dir. Robert Dinesen) and Carl Theodor Dreyer's *Leaves from Satan's Book* (Blade af Satans Bog, 1919) whose variant endings have been described by Casper Tybjerg in his paper 'The Presentation of Variant Endings' given at the 2002 conference at the University of Udine on 'Cinema and Its Multiples'; there is also my own find, the 'Russian ending' made in Denmark for *The Life of a Priest* (Evangeliemandens Liv, 1914, dir. Holger-Madsen), identical copies of which are preserved at George Eastman House in Rochester and at Gosfilmofond in Moscow). I am indebted to Casper Tybjerg for helping me with this list; and I will be thankful to those who will help to make this list longer.

11   George Pratt, *Spellbound in Darkness* (New York: New York Graphic Society, 1973), p. 126.

12   'Some Preparatory Remarks on Russian Cinema' op. cit., p. 8.

13   'The Cloven Tongue', *Photoplay*, April 1918, p. 109.

14   Richard Abel *The Red Rooster Scare: Making Cinema American, 1900–1910* (Berkeley, Calif.: University of California Press, 1999), p. 99; see also p. 122. It is instructive to mention another bloomer found in my 1989 essay. I then assumed that Protazanov's 1914 *Drama at the Telephone* (Drama u telefona) was a remake of Griffith's 1909 *The Lonely Villa* with its rescue ending replaced by a Russian one, and was wrong. As Tom Gunning has more recently (and more correctly) shown, *The Lonely Villa* story is not of Griffith's invention; it stems from a French *Grand-guignol* theatre drama of 1901 whose hero, power-less to rescue his wife and children, ends up listening over the phone to the sound of them being killed (Tom Gunning, 'Heard over the Phone: *The Lonely Villa* and the De Lorde Tradition of the Terrors of Technology,' *Screen*, Vol. 32, Summer 1991, pp. 184–196.) As it appears, Protazanov's *Drama at the Telephone* was made after a Russian adaptation of De Lorde's one-acter by N. Arbenin (typescript preserved by the All Russia Theatre Society library in Moscow.)

15   'There simply must be a moral ending', wrote Henry Albert Phillips in his screenwriting manual in 1914; 'stories in which the good element is overcome by the bad, thus placing the premium on the bad, are unmoral.' *Photodrama* by Henry Albert Phillips (New York, 1914), p. 89. Compare this phrase in the quoted *Photoplay* review of the Russian film *The Cloven Tongue*: 'there is little trace of what an American producer would regard as a safe picture to offer the tender public which he is careful to shield from unhappy thoughts'.

16   Kevin Brownlow in an intervention at the round table on early Russian cinema in Pordenone, October, 1989.

17   Sergei Volkonsky, *Vyrazitelnyi chelovek. Scenicheskoe vospitanie zhesta po Delsartu* (The expressive man. Education of stage gesture according to Delsarte) (St Petersburg: Apollon, 1912), p. 69.

18   F. Otsep, *Kinematograf* (Cinema) (Plan for a book), Russian State Archive for Literature and Art, 2734/1/72.

19   I. Petrovskii, 'Kinodrama ili kinopovest?' (Film Drama or Film Story?), *Proektor*, No. 20 (1916), p. 3 (italics in the original).

20   *Proektor*, No. 19 (1916), p. 11.

21   See a good overview of the process in Tom Gunning's 'Notes and Queries about the Year 1913 and Film Style: National Styles and Deep Staging', *1895*, October 1993: 'L'Année 1913 en France' (edited by Thierry Lefebre and Laurent Mannoni), pp. 195–204.

22   *Proektor*, No. 9 (1916), p. 15.

23   Petrovskii, p. 3.

24   Olga Gzovskaya. 'Rezhisser – drug aktera' (The director, the actor's friend) in: *Iakov Protazanov. Sbornik statei i materialov* (Moscow: Iskussstvo, 1948), p. 259.

25   V. Gaidarov, *V teatre i kino* (In Theatre and Cinema) (Moscow: 1966), pp. 101–02.

26   *Teatral'naya gazeta*, No. 19 (1914), p. 11.

27   *Teatral'naya gazeta*, No. 43 (1915), p. 16.

28   I. Mozzhukhin [Mosjoukine], 'V chem defekt?' (Where Lies the Defect?), *Teatral'naya gazeta*, No. 30 (1915), p. 13.

29   A. Levinson, 'O nekotorykh chertakh russkoi kinematografii' (Some Characteristics of Russian Cinema), *Poslednie novosti* (The Latest News) (Paris), No. 1512, 29 March 1925. I am indebted to Roman Timenchik for this quotation.

30   John E. Bowlt, 'Velocity' (work-in-progress pathway for the distance learning project 'Russia: A Modernist Perspective' sponsored by the Annenberg Foundation and University of Southern California).

31   'Some Preparatory Remarks on Russian Cinema', op. cit., p. 30.

Chapter 21

KRISTIN THOMPSON

EARLY ALTERNATIVES TO THE HOLLYWOOD MODE OF PRODUCTION
Implications for Europe's avant-gardes

The concept of mode of production

WHEN UNCONVENTIONAL, EVEN AVANT-GARDE films get made within mainstream commercial industries, critics and historians often explain the anomaly by claiming that particular filmmakers – especially directors – had 'more control' over their projects. But what does 'more control' mean? What is the source of that control? My purpose here is to show how the examination of proximate institutions can help confirm that such control has existed in some circumstances and that it had a basis in the specific duties for which directors were responsible.

In studying the relationship between film style and the film industry, the concept of mode of production has proven fruitful. Janet Staiger's important study of the history of Hollywood's mode of production offers a model of how an historian could explain Hollywood filmmaking as a system, rather than simply descriptively. In Part 2 of *The Classical Hollywood Cinema*, she studies Hollywood's mode of production in the late teens and 1920s. What I would like to do is contrast the system Staiger details with certain aspects of the mode of production of three other important producing countries of the same era: France, Germany and the USSR. Each country used methods for making films which differed in significant ways from that of Hollywood. These differences will, I hope, shed some light on the filmmaking of the three countries; specifically, they may help explain why major avant-garde stylistic movements – French Impressionism, German Expressionism and Soviet Montage – were able to flourish briefly in these three countries, while the possibilities for experimentation were much more limited in Hollywood.

I would like to focus on two aspects of the Hollywood mode of production. First, Staiger emphasizes the continuity script as a 'paper record' which was crucial in allowing producers to predict costs and control the various stages of filmmaking. Second, and directly related, is the fact that the introduction of the continuity script permitted a detailed division of labour in the Hollywood studios: tasks could be assigned to specialists who would not necessarily have to work closely together, as long as they all knew from the continuity script what they were supposed to be doing. In the post-shooting phase, for example, an editor could assemble hundreds of numbered shots into a film, often with minimal input from the director, since a thorough paper record of the entire production was available to him or her. The continuity script was standardized by 1914.

According to Staiger's account, the early teens saw the introduction of a heavy emphasis on efficiency in the American studios. This emphasis became widespread by 1914, the year in which the central producer system of filmmaking was standardized. In this system, the director was no longer responsible for supervising the entire production (choosing the story and personnel, shooting the film, editing it, and so on). Rather, a producer oversaw the film from start to finish. Under this system, the director had some input at the planning and editing stages, but was mainly responsible for the shooting phase. (As Staiger points out, some directors had sufficient power to retain greater control at all stages, and the Hollywood system was often flexible enough to accommodate them. Examples would include D. W. Griffith, Charles Chaplin and Cecil B. DeMille.[1])

This move toward efficiency and control led to a greater division of labour among specialists. By the early teens, American studios not only had writing departments but also sub-specialities within those departments. Certain writers' tasks specifically involved turning stories or treatments in prose form into continuity scripts, numbered shot by shot. Formerly the director had often been responsible for writing up the numbered shooting script. Staiger's argument is that 'such a standardizing process undoubtedly controlled innovation and contributed to the overall solidification of the classical Hollywood style'.

At the other end of the process, the assembly phase, an increasingly detailed division of labour was also developing. During the early teens, cutters assembled a workprint based on a simple continuity script. Over the next few years, however, increasingly complicated continuity guidelines and the growing length of films led to greater specialization in the task of editing. By the mid-teens, there were editors as well as cutters; these people could work from the continuity script and the script clerk's notations of what happened during shooting. In some cases the director would be closely involved in the editing process, but in others he or she might only make a few decisions, or leave the task entirely up to the editing staff.[2]

If we compare these circumstances with those of the French, German and Soviet film industries, many similarities become apparent. Not surprisingly, all had some sort of division of labour involving directors, designers, camera personnel and so on. Yet one intriguing difference becomes obvious at once. None of the three industries seems to have a significant number of editors in the Hollywood sense, people responsible for following the script and making decisions about cutting. There was usually some sort of assistant, or cutter, responsible for splicing the dailies together and helping the person in charge of editing – the director. Why this lack of editors?

Following this question through along the lines Staiger used with Hollywood, it becomes clear that in all three industries the European director retained more control at every stage of filmmaking than was usually the case in Hollywood. Indeed, the continuity or shooting script was not used in exactly the same way as it was in Hollywood – though each of the three countries had a different approach to scripting. In general, in examining each country, I will be suggesting that the central producer system had not yet caught on in these three European countries after the war. Directors were still responsible for many decisions at the scripting stage. The script itself seems to have constrained the director less during the shooting phase. Directors also still had almost complete responsibility for the editing phase. There are considerable differences among the three countries, of course; Germany's system was closer to the Hollywood mode of production than were those of France or the USSR. Still, contemporary sources reveal that in all three countries, there was a recognition of a difference from Hollywood, and often a desire to imitate its system.

France: small-scale production

Late in World War I, French filmmaking seems to have been largely organized in a fashion comparable to what Staiger terms the 'director unit' system in Hollywood – a system that had flourished there from roughly 1909 to 1914. A French production company might have several filmmaking units, but each was headed by a director who was responsible for the duties we now think of as the producer's. In addition, many tiny French production firms were formed by individual directors who also acted as producers.

The strength of the French film industry had declined precipitously during the war, due partly to the loss of facilities and personnel to the war effort and partly to burgeoning competition from American films. Thus in the period when the Hollywood studio system was growing, refining its division of labour, and moving into the central producer system, the French situation discouraged parallel developments. There simply were no large, self-contained firms which could create permanent departments for writing, editing and other functions. And when, near the end of the war, Charles Pathé decided to move his company away from its earlier emphasis on vertical integration and film production in favour of a concentration on distribution, he placed further obstacles in the path of a more detailed breakdown of labour. French filmmaking remained on an artisanal level to a greater degree than in other countries. In effect, the equivalent of the director unit system remained in place, and with fewer specialized assistants at his or her disposal, the director remained responsible for more tasks.

At the same time, however, Charles Pathé seems to have realized that the resulting lack of efficiency posed serious problems for the industry. In 1917, he published an important essay, 'La Crise du cinéma', in which he blamed those problems on a 'scenario crisis'. This idea would be easy to dismiss as some sort of miscalculation of Pathé's – a simplistic notion that better stories would make for better films, and better films would be able to compete against the Hollywood product.[3] Yet it seems clear that Pathé was actually arguing in favour of an American-style continuity script that would improve production efficiency. Most scenarios he had read, he claimed, 'were, in my opinion, insufficiently developed. Nothing should be left to improvization. I estimate that the amount of work for developing a scenario for a four or five reel film would call for a book of 200 to 250 pages'. Pathé argued that such scenarios would take more time in the writing but save time on the set – exactly what Staiger sees as one goal of the American continuity script. According to Pathé, each shot should be described in detail, and all planning of camera distance, locations, lighting, and so on, should be done in advance. Such a system, Pathé argued, would help the director to make more films, as many as four or five a year. He also recommended that the director not be the author of the script – as directors frequently were in France.[4]

In 1918 Pathé wrote another article in which he discussed the role of the cinematographer, recommending that he create a careful paper record: 'Finally, he must not depend entirely on his memory, and note, in a memorandum book, all the individual circumstances, particularly the lighting, which occurred during the shooting of each shot'.[5] Given the new structure of Pathé's company, however, he was in no position to force the independent producer-directors who supplied many of the films it distributed to carry through on these recommendations.

Henri Diamant-Berger, a mainstream director who produced his own films for distribution through Pathé-Cinéma, seconded Pathé's views. In 1918, he described a meeting of the Ligue Française du Cinématographe, which brought together major French writers and film company officials: 'Opinion held that it was unlikely and materially impossible, in most cases, that *metteurs en scène* should continue to improvise. They have done it in complete freedom up to now, with obvious results. Scenarios are necessary'.[6] After a 1918 trip to the USA,

Diamant-Berger described the division of labour in the studios there and contrasted it with the French system, where the director is 'a Jack of all trades'.[7]

Another major French director, Jacques de Baroncelli, confirmed this view of the difference between the French and American systems in 1920. Reporting on his recent visit to some film studios in New York, he commented on:

> . . . the 'choral' feeling of the American companies. Each one has his precise place, plays his part with maximum efficiency, speed and conscientiousness, and the whole group can rely upon him without worrying. The human effort, intelligent, flexible, cheerful, and punctual, like a perfect machine, works until the assigned task is achieved. And that is the whole secret as to how a film is shot in America with such astonishing rapidity. We are gravely mistaken in France when we assume that it is necessary to work slowly in order to obtain the best results.[8]

On the whole, however, such recommendations for a scenario practice and a division of labour based on the Hollywood system were not adopted. In the early 1920s Louis Delluc commented on the fact that French directors were usually responsible for turning the scenario into a shooting script; as a result, scripts had good basic ideas, but were not well-written: 'Look at the importance, in America or Germany, of the "continuity writer" [phrase in English]. It is time to realize that an idea for a scenario, however good it is, is not a scenario'.[9] At about the same time, Robert Florey contrasted the efficiency of American production with that in France: 'There are twenty or thirty people just to assist the director, an omnipotent person, whose least desires are executed with an extraordinary speed; forward progression is never stopped over a *stupid detail* as often happens in France'.[10]

Throughout the silent period, the French director retained a great deal of responsibility – and control – at the scenario stage. In virtually all cases, he or she also continued to edit the film. Raymond Chirat's filmography of features of the period from 1919 to 1929 lists 973 films, of which 42 have editors credited. Of these 42 films, 18 were edited or co-edited by their directors (including Alberto Cavalcanti, Jean Renoir, Jean Epstein, and Abel Gance). Two directors – both in mainstream, commercial situations – seem consistently to have used editors. In twelve cases, Louis Feuillade's films are credited as having been edited by Maurice Champreux (who acted as cinematographer and/or co-director on all twelve). Henry Fescourt also used an editor, Jean-Louis Bouquet, on seven films. (All twelve Feuillade/Champreux films were made for Gaumont, all seven Fescourt/Bouquet films for Cinéromans, suggesting that some of the relatively large companies had a slightly more detailed division of labour.) Five more films of various types were credited as being edited by persons other than their directors.[11] Some editors may have worked uncredited, but in most cases the division of labour did not include editors. Certainly there is evidence that the Impressionist and other avant-garde filmmakers edited their own films. In 1926, for example, critic Juan Arroy described Epstein working at the studio late into the night editing *Mauprat*.[12] As we shall see, others in the group also controlled this stage of the filmmaking process.

The French system did involve an assistant, the *monteuse*. This person was apparently invariably female, and she was responsible for splicing rushes, assembling the negative, and sometimes for executing editing under instructions from the director. (Presumably some filmmakers, working very independently did not have even this much assistance.) As this 1925 description by Arroy makes clear, however, her responsibilities were quite different from those of a Hollywood editor:

The studio employee charged with this task [i.e. sorting takes] is the *monteuse*. Her work is not absolutely automatic; she must demonstrate a great deal of initiative and critical sense. In America, she must do even more, because the production is divided up in this way: the rights to some literary work are purchased, it is assigned to be adapted by an experienced scenarist, and then the decoupage is assigned to a specialist 'continuity writer' [in English], then it is given to a director to be shot, and finally the film passes into the hands of the *monteuse*. All these functions are absolutely separate, and there is no point of contact among them which would permit each of these artisans to review the work of his predecessors, to apply his critical sense, and to correct their faults. Personally, I do not believe at all in this method, which cannot create anything but mass-produced films, because the unity of the art work's creation is suppressed.

It is thus a fact that the *monteuse* in the USA has an authority and freedom which she never has in France. . . . In France, the *monteuse* has no authority except under the supervision of the director.[13]

The emphasis here on the editing as part of the overall artistic creation of the film recurs in a major 1927 article by Jack Conrad on editing. According to Conrad, the montage of a film:

. . . is done by professional *monteuses* under the director's supervision. Certain directors have their regular *monteuse* – though not many in France, except for Abel Gance, who is perfectly seconded in this work by Marguerite Baugé [sic, actually Beaugé], his *monteuse* for ten years now. When all the negative shot has been printed up as positives – and these days each shot is done in ten to twelve takes – they are projected for the director, who chooses the best to make up one, two, three or four negatives. The rest are destroyed. Then the shots are sorted and glued together one by one according to the number of the photographic order which appears at the beginning of each one, and which corresponds to the numbers indicated in the scenario. Thus the final film is created arranged in rough order. This crude film is then projected for the director, who indicates to his *monteuse* what cuts to make and what re-takes are needed in order to create a truly visual orchestration – if the said *cinéaste* is a real 'musician of silence'. The *monteuse* then cuts the negative based on the final positive version.[14]

This account makes the editing process seem reasonably systematic – not much different from the way it must have gone in some Hollywood studios.

A 1929 account by industry historian G.-Michel Coissac, however, suggests that, in some cases at least, the director simply received all the footage shot and had to sort through it him or herself; again the emphasis is on the artistic creation which remains to be done at the editing stage:

One who had never participated in the montage of a film can have no idea of the in-explicable riddle which this assemblage [of footage] contains; even the classification of these thousands of strips of various lengths is obscure, since they were exposed without apparent order; one picks them up at random, since, at first glance, they are fished back up from an enigmatic sea.

> The *metteur en scène*, however, takes a deep interest in this Herculean task – more so than the photographer watching the development of a negative. He judges and harmonizes his work. From this cacophony he creates rhythm and perfect matches; he is at the phase of orchestrating movement and life; for a second time he creates as he awaits a view of his finished work. The montage is the final gestation, or, to be more poetic, the opening of the flower, petal by petal.

According to Coissac, the director continues this process through numerous screenings and revisions, goes through once to place the intertitles, and retouches the whole thing yet again.[15]

This relatively minimal division of labour may have resulted from the French industry's continued dependence on small production companies, and upon director-producers making films for major companies. To a considerable extent, the Hollywood studios' ability to retain so many specialized employees on a permanent basis resulted from economies of scale which the French companies simply could not duplicate.

It seems clear, however, that many French filmmakers and critics considered it artistically important that the director retain a considerable degree of control over the film at prepara-tory, shooting, and post-production phases. Conrad's article sums up this view of the compositional importance of the pre- and post-shooting phases:

> There are two phases in the technical execution of a film which many still consider secondary, but which nevertheless are centrally and basically important. These two stages, which take place chronologically before and after the direction proper, are the 'decoupage' of the scenario and the 'montage' of the exposed footage . . .
>
> In every art work – book, painting, symphony, film – the subject is less important than the way in which it is treated – the style. And filmmakers all have a personal style, just as painters, composers and writers do. This cinematic style manifests itself in the way in which the director uses the technical devices at his disposal, in his way of presenting the situations, of bringing the scenes to life, and finally of visu-ally orchestrating and rhyming the images in the final montage, where the different sections of the work are created and come to have no other existence than as part of the whole.[16]

In discussing how a director can control the film of the decoupage and montage stages, Conrad sees a connection between the two:

> The montage seems to be minutely foreseen, *a priori*, in the writing of the scenario. After all, Marcel L'Herbier specifies in his decoupages the length of each shot, and this must theoretically be scrupulously respected during the shooting. In actuality this does not happen, because it is impossible practically.[17]

Still, it would appear that L'Herbier was trying to use his scenarios as a means of composing the film as a whole – a process which he would oversee and refine at every stage through to the end of the montage. Conrad also mentions that 'Germaine Dulac attaches a crucial import-ance to the montage of her films. It is, she says, the most emotional part of the creation of a film, and it is also the most delicate'[18]. Whatever the cause of the French approach to the divi-sion of labour, it is clear that the placement of so much responsibility at all stages of the production fits in with the Impressionist directors' creative methods.

Germany: development in isolation

The war placed Germany's film industry in a very different situation from that of France. During a period of nearly five years of virtual isolation, the industry grew hugely. Although there were many small production companies in Germany in the postwar years, the film industry come to be largely dominated by such firms as the Universumfilm Aktien-Gesellschaft (Ufa), Emelka and the like. Such firms had a considerable division of labour, and they used scenarios as a control over the filmmaking process. Yet, perhaps because of its very isolation, the German industry also developed a mode of production that had some distinctive traits. As in France, the differences at the scripting and editing stages suggest that many directors had considerable responsibility for controlling production.

Contemporary sources suggest that the Germans compared their system to that of Hollywood and found the latter more efficient. In 1920 the *Lichtbildbühne*'s New York correspondent described the mode of production in American studios. The article suggests that the division of labour is more systematized in the USA than in Germany. It particularly notes that in the USA everyone gets a copy of the script and hence knows what to do: 'System and organization! In our studios, one often finds either too many people, who stand around and get in each other's ways, or a lack of personnel in all areas. In this we could learn a great deal from the Americans'.[19] In 1921, the same journal published an article on how to estimate negative costs in advance and hence eliminate day-to-day waste of money. The Americans, the author claims, provide the model, and the bulk of the article is taken up with reproductions of an American-style form with boxes for estimating all categories of costs.[20] The form, by the way, is very similar to the typical mid-teens negative-estimate sheet, used by Thomas Ince, which Staiger reproduces in *The Classical Hollywood Cinema*.

The German method of scriptwriting, though similar to that of the Americans in many ways, had some notable differences. The shooting script apparently did not plan out the shot-by-shot details of the production in such a specific fashion. As late as 1926, E. A. Dupont compared the two countries' systems and found a difference in editing procedures:

> The American script is not numbered simply according to broadly outlined scenes, as is most common in Germany – where the director makes as many close-ups and changes of angle as he likes; instead the scenario is broken down as much as possible into notations of close-ups, and each of these close-ups and other changes carries a specific number. Thus, for example, when a scene has twenty-five changes according to the script, then when the director has made twenty-five shots he has also shot twenty-five numbers.[21]

Some of Dupont's own scenarios, published in his 1919 screenplay manual, confirm his description of German practice. Numbers are given only when the location changes, with all action within a given locale described with little indication as to the visual handling. Dupont distinguishes only between normal and close framings. Occasional notations of close-ups in the middles of scenes are not numbered; indeed, one courtroom scene has an establishing shot, five close shots, and three titles, yet this whole cluster of shots is given only one number.[22] Two other scenario manuals from the period make little or no attempt to describe how a writer might break a scene into separate shots or describe the camera-work; advice on scenario format is limited to how to describe locales, actors' gestures and other aspects of the staged action.[23]

An examination of shooting scripts for some of the Expressionist films suggests that they also typically used numbers to indicate a change of locale. Thus in *Siegfried*, the passage describing the intercutting between Siegfried riding in the forest and the dragon drinking uses a number for each shot; the fight with the dragon, however, consumes three pages with only one number. Similarly, the entire visit of Tsar Ivan to the poison master in *Wachsfigurenkabinett* is assigned one number, even though it goes on for pages and contains two notations of cuts to closer framings. The surviving early draft of *Das Cabinet des Dr. Caligari* follows a similar format.[24]

Other contemporary descriptions of the German mode of production in the late 1920s suggest that the director often worked on the shooting script and was capable of changing it during the shooting phase. In 1927, Dr. Kurt Mühsam described the division of labour in the studios:

> In general, the director's job begins even before the shooting of the script; this is because the production company, before it decides to acquire a film script, will usually consult with a director closely linked to it, concerning how the outline under consideration would be filmed, how the various roles would be filled, and what costs would be required beyond the normal range of expenses. If the script is acquired, then the director has to take care of it, ensuring that the various scenes are really ready for filming [*kurbelreif*] – a task which he must himself oversee, since the company in question has only a few scriptwriters at its disposal.[25]

In many cases the story would be submitted to a company in the form of a synopsis. A specialized scenario writer called a *Filmdramaturg* might turn it into a shooting script, but that task might be left to the director.

A 1928 magazine article of the 'script-to-screen' variety suggests that the director could easily add shots:

> Before studio filming begins, the director has made the author's vision, as set down in the script, his own. In the studio, however, the contact with the three-dimensional decor, with the living actors, and with the lights whirls by his fancy and alters the course of events – partly voluntarily, partly against his will. It was not foreseen that the actor of a leading role would refuse a small but important bit of psychological reaction. The director's working fancy instantly takes up the problem and obviates it; changing the motif a bit, moving a few pauses here, a small question there, he then brings in a few more close-ups and after some small detours still reaches the goal.[26]

Dupont's 1926 article on American filmmaking describes how the script clerk tells the assistant camera operator what numbered shot is to be filmed, and he marks it on the slate along with the number of the take. The result, according to Dupont, is that when the cutter and director edit the film, the director has a list of the good takes, and these shots can be located easily. In Germany, the director sits down to edit unsorted footage; he or she must search through 40–50,000 metres of film in order to choose the desired takes before beginning to edit.[27]

And indeed it seems clear that it was the director who had responsibility for editing in Germany. Gerhard Lamprecht's detailed filmography of German silent films lists extensive credits, including the make-up artists and still photographers – but no editors at all.[28] Similarly, Mühsam's study of the production roles in German filmmaking provides a detailed sample budget for a feature film, including salaries for the assistant director, hair stylist, wardrobe person, still photographer; no expenditures for an editor are listed.[29]

There was a limited division of labour in the editing phase, in that some tasks were done by '*die Kleberin*'. This term literally means 'the gluer', and it is feminine. *Die Kleberin* would be comparable to the job of 'the joiner' in the American studios and the *monteuse* in the French system: these were young women responsible for splicing dailies and positive release prints. In a 1916 essay on post-production work, popular director Max Mack described the *Kleberin* as performing similar sorts of tasks in Germany. The *Kleberin*'s duties seem not to have changed over the next decade, as this 1928 account indicates:

> In a small fireproof room sits the film's *Kleberin* and supervises the many thousand metres of negative and positive. While the director is shooting new scenes in the studio, she arranges the old ones, making from the original reels of a thousand metres usable little rolls; she preserves each of these pieces with a label and assembles the correlated parts, by act (i.e. by reel of the finished film), in cases.[30]

The *Kleberin*, then, helped keep track of the footage. She presumably labelled the shots by the numbers in the script, but it is still not clear that every shot would have had its own number.

These same sources indicate that from the teens to the late 1920s, the editing of the film was the director's responsibility. In his 1916 essay, Mack commented:

> Seasoned cinema directors know that the most difficult thing about film is the editing. Because the whole scene [i.e., shot] cannot be used for the film exactly as it was shot. Only that part that really creates a significant progression in the action should be retained. For this work are required a sure eye, artistic experience, and a sound sense of dramatic effect. Bad directors cut little. That takes away the film's tempo, its onrush of events, its inner excitement, making it into an empty spectacle.[31]

By 1928, the director still was responsible for taking the rolls of film stored away by the *Kleberin* and editing them into a film:

> When the studio and location shooting are over, then the director remains confined for weeks in this joining room. He edits the film. Adjustment by adjustment, one scene after another is cemented together, shown, edited anew, again shown, again corrected – until the whole film grows into large, round reels of two to four hundred metres.[32]

Thus the German division of labour gave the director many responsibilities for every stage of film production.

Indeed, the central producer system does not seem to have been significant in German filmmaking until 1927, when the post-stabilization crisis of the mid-1920s and the near-bankruptcy of Ufa dictated the use of strict economy measures. In late 1927, Ufa announced that it had re-organized its approach to production by introducing several '*Produktionsleiter*', or 'production chiefs'. Erich Pommer had headed the entire studio before being forced to resign in early 1926; after an unsuccessful year in Hollywood, he returned to become the foremost of its several *Produktionsleiter*: The *Lichtbildbühne* commented: 'Hence it is clear that the original organizational plans will be adhered to, and that the new, upcoming films – among which are four "Erich-Pommer-Produktion" films – should be allotted among various production heads, on the model of the American supervisors'.[33] The plan was presumably successful;

of all silent films, there are probably none that so consistently resemble those of Hollywood as the ones produced by Ufa in the late 1920s.

Even at this point, however, the director unit system seems to have remained in existence alongside the new central producer system, at least for a while. Mühsam's 1927 account described the director's position:

> Just how important the director's function is in the production of a film, however, is also clearly apparent from the fact that he has taken over all the responsibility to the corporate employer for the success or failure of the film, insofar as a so-called production chief [*Produktionsleiter*] does not relieve him of this responsibility. As a rule, however, only a large film firm can afford a production chief. Thus it remains the director who concerns himself with the best possible utilization of the capital, in the form of money, personnel and goods, placed at his disposal.[34]

Such responsibilities imply a high degree of control for the director, and that control would have been even greater in the early 1920s. In 1972, Fritz Lang commented on how much freedom he had in choosing and developing his own projects:

> In those days there didn't exist the job of producer and the director was the top man. I had all the freedom I wanted in choosing what film I wanted to do, with whom I wanted to write the script, which actors I wanted and so on . . . and I am sure the same applied to Murnau and other directors who worked under Pommer.[35]

One conclusion that can be drawn from all this is that many German directors, including those working in the Expressionist style, had a higher degree of control over their work than did most of their Hollywood contemporaries.

The USSR: the controversy over montage

In the USSR, the issue of the scenario and the division of labour were crucial for the struggling industry in the 1920s. With the loss in 1917 and 1918 of so much of the experienced personnel from the pre-Revolutionary period, the film industry often had to rely on writers who knew little about script formats and other aspects of filmmaking. By 1926, a major debate had arisen concerning the notion of applying efficiency measures in the film studios. Denise Youngblood states that a common complaint about lack of efficiency was that directors frequently departed from or even abandoned their scripts during the shooting phase; Eisenstein's wholesale changes in the filming of *Potemkin* were singled out for criticism.[36]

From the industry officials' point of view, the problem lay largely in the fact that the script process offered them little control over the director. Because so many films were based on stories by authors unaccustomed to working in the cinema, the director usually received what was called a 'libretto'. It was often the director's responsibility to break this prose synopsis down into a shooting script. Paul Babitsky, a writer who worked in the Soviet system during the 1920s and 1930s, described the situation:

> Frequently the director, considering himself the creator of the film, preferred to revise the scenario alone and to permit the writer to see the film only at its final preview, at which time most authors could not recognize their work.

In Soviet studios there was no system of joint scenario writing, by division of the work among specialists on dialogue, plot, trick effects and so on. The entire scenario depended on the invention of a single writer.

In the Moscow and Leningrad studios also, scenario editing became a routine part of the director's work. Even outstanding scripts were edited and reworked by the film director or by the scenarist himself to suit the director's tastes and methods.[37]

Thus the Soviet director had a high degree of control over the scriptwriting process.

Moreover, directors typically edited their films. In 1924, *Kino-Gazette*'s Hollywood correspondent listed the various production positions that existed in the studios there. This list included two terms given in the original English, presumably since there was no Russian equivalent: the art director and the editor.[38] A 1928 Soviet book on the mode of film production describes a production position called the '*montageur*', but, as with the *monteuse* and the *Kleberin*, the duties resemble those of an assistant editor or cutter in the Hollywood studios: sorting shots, splicing the rushes together, and eventually cutting the negative. The director makes the rough cut as well as polishing the final workprint version.[39]

In 1927, critic Viktor Pertsov described the relation of the scenario to the editing phase and suggested how little the former controlled the latter:

> A screenplay, that half-finished literary work, is the sum of the starting and finishing points for the material that is to be shot. The writer's job in cinema essentially consists in observing how the limits of the material can be drawn more closely and more precisely . . .
>
> Until work is almost completed, right up to the release of the finished film, elements of it, the exposed fragments, are still in frantic motion. What we call the stage of 'montage' is characterized by the constant shuffling of these backwards and forwards, from one part to another, taking some out, putting others in, and so on.
>
> This comparatively protracted slow stage of work on the film is the period when at long last you feel certain that one particular combination of fragments is the best and final one. Until this time the film, like an earth-worm, can be cut up into pieces and each piece can acquire a life of its own.[40]

This conception of editing differs considerably from Hollywood's approach, where the scenario ideally allowed studio personnel to predict the shape of the final edited version. Indeed, many studio officials, mainstream filmmakers, critics and others found the Soviet system less efficient than the American, and favoured reducing the director's control. From the mid-1920s on, there was much discussion in the professional literature of an 'iron' scenario, that is, a scenario which laid out the film exactly and from which the director could not depart. It was numbered shot by shot, down to estimates of the length of each shot; by following it exactly, a director would turn in a set of footage predictable in its costs and in every other respect. Essentially, the 'iron scenario' was comparable to the Hollywood continuity script.

In his 1926 book on filmmaking, Ilya Rentz pointed out that the Soviet director was overworked in comparison with his Hollywood counterpart; in the USSR, directors had to examine sets, scout locations, supervise the setting up of the lights, and so on. In Hollywood, the division of labour meant that other people did these tasks. The director, Rentz concluded, 'ought to have the commanding position only during the filming'.[41]

A 1926 Soviet scenario manual by Ippolit Sokolov pointed out that in American and German shooting scripts, the editing is worked out in advance:

The scenarist, in a purely directing way, works out the filming and montage of the picture. He determines precisely the size and sequence of the shots.

The scriptwriter is practically – the director.[42] Sokolov favoured the 'iron scenario', the development of which he attributed to American and German scriptwriters:

'An iron scenario' is a preliminary working-out of all the production details and montage in the picture. Nothing is extra, nothing is left to chance. The picture ought to be literally preliminarily edited before the filming begins. One should not film a single frame until the entire picture is mentally edited.

Noting that Soviet scriptwriters did not know how to break prose plots down into shots, he added that they should learn: 'The scenes and shots ought to have numbers'.[43]

Although many Soviet books on filmmaking written during the second half of the 1920s recommended the use of the 'iron' scenario, in practice this approach to scripting seems to have remained largely an ideal goal rather than a practical method until well into the 1930s.

In the Soviet debate over efficiency and the division of labour, artists, not surprisingly, favoured the system as it existed in the mid-1920s: with a great deal of control over the scripting and editing processes placed in the director's hands. In his 1926 book on filmmaking, director S. Timoshenko declared:

It will become clear that the American method, in which one person directs the film and another assembles it, is incorrect. This is the same as having one artist draw parts of a picture and having another put them together, determining the composition of the whole, excluding, rearranging, and throwing out various parts which had been drawn by the artist.[44]

It is notable that Timoshenko's book is entitled *Art of the Cinema and the Montage of Films*. For many filmmakers of this era, including the Montage directors, it was in the editing stage that formal qualities of the film were determined. The exposed footage was not in itself artistic; it became so only through being arranged into the whole. Hence any official attempt to control the montage at the scenario stage was resisted.

For example, in 1928, Eisenstein deplored the current push in the industry to draw more established writers from other fields into scriptwriting:

Comrade man of letters, don't write scripts!
    Force the production organizations to buy your commodities as novels.
    Sell the rights to the novel.
    You must force film directors to find the *cinema* equivalents of these works. (When required.)
    In this way we can conceive of both the renewal and the fertilization of both the formal aspect of and the opportunities for cinema, and not just of the thematic or plot aspect which, in the final analysis, is successfully implemented in other forms of literature.
    A 'numbered' script will bring as much animation to cinema as the numbers on the heels of the corpses in the morgue.
    'Writing a script is like calling out the midwife on your wedding night'. These are Babel's priceless words from the time when we were doing a script 'from' *Benya Krik*.[45]

That is, for Eisenstein, a numbered shooting script was an attempt to determine the editing at too early a stage in the filmmaking process.

In 1929, Eisenstein developed on this same idea. The script, he declared, should not be a drama but 'merely a shorthand record of an emotional outburst striving for realization in an accumulation of visual images'. Numbered scripts, he adds, are written by hacks. In place of the shooting script, he favours a prose description: 'In pursuit of a methodology for this kind of exposition we came to the film novella, the form through which we are trying to make statements on the screen with hundreds of people, herds of cattle, sunsets, waterfalls and boundless fields'. Eisenstein cites the lengthy series of shots in *Potemkin* in the scene when the sailors are under the tarpaulin and about to be executed; shots of the prow of the ship, the sea, and so on, all were inspired by one sentence in an eyewitness's memoirs: 'A deathly silence hung in the air'. Eisenstein concludes: 'That is why we are opposed to the usual form of numbered detailed script (*Drehbuch*) and why we are in favour of the film novella form'.[46] Such a format would allow the director nearly total control during the shooting phase of production.

In a similar vein, in 1926, scenarist and critic Osip Brik wrote an article which proposed a system radically opposed to that of Hollywood:

> The screenplay should be written, not before shooting, but afterwards. The screenplay is not an order to shoot, but a method of organizing what has already been shot. And we should therefore ask, not how a screenplay should be, but what should be photographed. The re-working of material in the screenplay is the last stage of the work.[47]

Brik's own screenplay for Pudovkin's *The Heir of Ghengis Khan* ran to only nineteen typed pages. The film's cinematographer recalled that 'each scene was described in at most four words. In other words, a real silent film scenario, in the old, admirable way of montage scenarios'. Sequences were added during the shooting phase; the famous scene of the ceremony at the temple did not appear in the original at all.[48]

Such a sketchy prose script fits in with Pudovkin's changing ideas about scenario format. Originally he had embraced the idea of a strong script, but he subsequently rejected it in favour of the emotional summary of the type advocated by Eisenstein. In his 1926 book *Film Technique*, Pudovkin recommended that the scenarist get as close as possible to the 'cast-iron scenario', in order to promote unity and continuity.[49] Both *Mother* and *The End of St. Petersburg* had detailed shooting scripts by Nathan Zharki. Around 1928, however, Pudovkin changed his approach; according to critic and scriptwriter Viktor Shklovsky, 'Two years after Eisenstein, Vsevolod Pudovkin made the same discovery'. He began asking for brief scenarios consisting mainly of rhythmic intertitles:

> According to Pudovkin, the author of a script must communicate to the director the rhythm of the film but he must not attempt to write the director a montage shooting plan. Pudovkin demonstrates all this in an excerpt from Rzheshevsky's plot.
>
> Pudovkin's position sins against production . . . All right, we'll have jumping and stopping titles and no montage shooting plan. But we need a montage plan in order to shoot. Consequently, between the montage lists of the director and the somersaulting titles there must be some kind of point which will in any case contain an order of scenes and their exact content. Then a script will emerge. Hence Pudovkin, instead of resolving the problem of what a script should be, is resolving another, less pressing problem of who should write the script, and he decides that the director should do it.[50]

To Pudovkin and other filmmakers, however, the problem of who would write the version of the script controlling the montage may well have been a more pressing problem than was what its exact format should be. Shklovsky mentions 'Rzheshevsky's plot', a reference to the sketchy, evocative libretto by A. Rzheshevsky for Pudovkin's *A Simple Case* (1932). Whether that film's lengthy production problems and confusing final form had anything to do with this approach to scripting is a moot point; certainly they would have made it easier for studio officials to decry the Montage directors' views.

Despite the considerable latitude allowed several of the Montage directors, and particularly Eisenstein and Pudovkin, there was still a push toward tighter controls within the film industry. When the First Five Year Plan was applied to the cinema in early 1928, one of the main goals was to improve efficiency in the Soviet studios and increase the output of films. During the late 1920s, directors were thought to be turning out too few films. According to the head of Amkino, Sovkino's New York office, during the Plan's second year, directors were expected to be up to one and a half films; in the Plan's fifth year, the average was to reach two films a year.[51] (We might recall at this point that the 1918 French debate over scenario practice also involved the idea of increasing directors' outputs.) One discussion of the mode of production written at this point mentions a 'representative of the studio administration' who would supervise the production of a film, keeping the work on schedule, checking the scenario and set designs, and coordinating the technical departments and the financial offices. This person would monitor the budget and the use of electricity. His basic job was to keep costs down.[52] It would appear that, even as early as 1928, the Soviets were trying to institute an equivalent to the central producer system as part of the Five Year Plan.

In order to improve directors' efficiency, government and industry officials sought to relieve them of control over both the scripting and editing phases. The First Party Conference on Cinema, held in March of 1928, was a crucial event in the attempts to work out a Five Year Plan for cinema. Among its resolutions were several relating to scriptwriting:

> The shortage of highly qualified workers is still exerting a very negative effect on cinema activity. This circumstance has found its most vivid expression in the so-called 'script crisis'. A number of cinema organizations explain that they cannot make films that are ideologically consistent because of the absence of script material. This reason is not insuperable and is to a significant degree conditioned by the inadequate activity of the cinema organizations themselves, by their amateurish handling of the script problem and by the absence of planning in the elaboration of themes for cinema which has, in the majority of cases, an unsystematic and fortuitous character . . .
>
> With the aim of greater productivity in creative cinema work we must maintain a much closer link between the writer, the scriptwriter, and the director.[53]

At the beginning of 1929, Sovkino published a resolution on its 'new course', declaring that the script crisis was not yet over and making some recommendations for solving it:

> . . . that the best literary sources be grouped around the film studios and they be used to devise plots;
> . . . that each studio should organize a group of qualified specialist scriptwriters to prepare scripts for particular directors;
> . . . that we should start developing script resources in the studios, strengthening the existing script workshops and adopting them to the needs of production.[54]

It is worth recalling that in this same year Eisenstein was calling upon writers to refuse to write scripts. The forces that were to help bring about the end of the Montage movement can be found in these debates over the mode of production, as well as in the more familiar ideological and formal controversies surveyed by recent historians.

Again these various recommendations were difficult to implement quickly. The debate intensified, however, in the early 1930s. In an important book written in late 1930 and published in 1932, Vladimir Sutyrin, production director of the new centralized firm Soyuzkino (and second in command under chairman Boris Shumyatski) stated the official view. Sutyrin refers to the idea of reducing filming time. Until recently, he claims, the average production time on a feature film was ten to twelve months. He hopes to reduce this to five-and-a-half months by a further division of labour, creating permanent production 'brigades', each with its own scriptwriter. The director would have no involvement in the scripting stage.[55]

Sutyrin also discusses editing as another phase at which production time could be saved. This discussion is worth quoting at length, since it demonstrates the link between changes in the division of labour and attempts to control the Montage directors:

> But let us try to go further along the road of the division of labour. Let us imagine to ourselves the following case . . . (I ask in advance the forgiveness of directors for the foolish and somewhat blasphemous example.) Let us suppose that the director is freed not only from writing the scenario, but from . . . the montage. I know that this idea is foolish, monstrous. Nevertheless, it is indisputable that the amount of time that the director spends on a picture would be shortened by the time it takes for editing. At a minimum this would be about a month, and actually, on the average, a month and a half . . .
>
> However, is the idea of freeing the director from montage work so ludicrous, monstrous, and blasphemous?
>
> We know that in the American industry, the over-whelming majority of pictures are edited not by directors, but by special workers. I asked Joe Kaufman about this in detail. He not only confirmed the existence of such a division of labour, but expressed the rather original thought that American film people feel that the qualities of a director-producer are incompatible with those of an editor [montagera]. A director, he said, ought to have fantasy, temperament, liveliness, nervousness. An editor, on the other hand, should be of a quiet nature; he should have a methodical way of working and be able to sit at his table for long periods of time. Many directors are unsuited for such meticulous, and in a certain sense, exhausting work, the kind of work which editing entails. This comment of Mr. Kaufman merits attention. The qualities that he sees in the psychology of a director and an editor may be arguable. What is important here is that various cinematic specialties require people with special qualities . . .
>
> We have become accustomed to considering that montage is the main thing, that montage is the basic thing in creative work. We must look critically at this way of thinking. We shouldn't forget that the theory of montage was taught to us either by pure formalists (for example, Shklovsky and Kuleshov) or theorists coming from formalism, but not carrying its heavy baggage (for example, Eisenstein as the author of the theory 'montage of attractions').
>
> Let us refresh our memory about the formalists' or semi-formalists' [leftists'] reasonings about art.

Sutyrin goes on to summarize the 'formalist' ideas about art, which deal with principles of the organization of material from the world into formal structures.[56]

After describing the theories of Montage filmmakers, Sutyrin attacks them, rejecting the notion that editing is the key phase of filmmaking and that content is created after shooting:

> In film production, when the editor, strictly speaking, is not able to change the composition of the montage material – that is, to add to it, and so forth – the favourable outcome of the montage of course is determined by the filming period, and the more complicated that montage becomes – and complicated not even in the sense of refinement – the more the editor becomes dependent upon the director-filmer.
>
> I believe that experience forces us to admit the indisputability of the following: a picture is edited not after filming and not even in the process of filming, but before filming, in the so-called preparatory period. In this preparatory period, the editing takes place, too. The filming and editing periods are only stages in the materialization of the picture, which is created in the preparatory period. With such an understanding of the process of the creation of a picture, the freedom of the editor – that is the possibility of varying montage constructions – is nothing other than a result of the imperfections of the director. The ideal director has nothing to do in the editing room. Ideally, filmed material is already edited material. All that is necessary is to glue it together.[57]

Sutyrin ridicules directors' desire to work in the editing room, treating this simply as a romantic image:

> I remember the cover of some brochure that we published at 'Teakinopechat': Pudovkin at the editing table – an exotic figure, dressed in a luxurious boa of countless montage pieces which curled in various directions. ('Here it is, the holy of holies of the director'![58])

Sutyrin goes on in this vein, and clearly the purpose was not simply to propose a new division of labour, but also to associate Montage directors with the old, inefficient system that equated artistic creation with the director's control over editing.

Indeed, in 1936 Shumyatsky finally systematically introduced American methods into Soviet film production in order to improve efficiency. These methods were based on work groups. Babitsky has described them: 'Each was assigned a production chief, similar to an American producer, who was responsible for the film as a whole. This step simplified the work of the film director'.[59] Presumably this new approach was comparable to the central producer system in Hollywood. Even at so late a date, however, it failed in the Soviet Union, as the low production levels in the late years of Shumyatsky's control suggest.

Implications for commercial avant-garde filmmaking

The differences among the modes of production in the three European countries and the USA may help explain why directors were able to make what we today consider avant-garde films in the three European countries. Hollywood made many extraordinary films, and these often are attributable to what we call auteurs – DeMille, Griffith, Lubitsch and others. Yet, as Staiger has suggested, the Hollywood mode of production only allowed for a limited degree of experimentation.[60]

The systems of France, Germany, and the USSR, I would suggest, briefly allowed for more. I do not wish to imply that extensive control by directors explains precisely why such movements as Expressionism, Impressionism and Soviet Montage arose between 1918 and 1933. Such control does not invariably result in avant-garde cinema movements. There are assuredly many other factors involved. Certainly these distinctive traits of filmmaking practice do not explain the particular directions in which these three national styles developed. Still, given that these stylistic movements did exist, we can reason backward to see what might have fostered them.

Similarly, I am not trying to argue that the director is the sole artist who creates a film. Other filmmakers undoubtedly had a great deal of input into the creative process. For example, in Germany the set designer was an unusually prominent production role, and certain designers often worked consistently with major directors of the Expressionist movement (e.g. Otto Hunte's collaboration with Fritz Lang). My point is simply that the division of labour in all three countries was less likely to produce the standardization of style that had resulted from Hollywood's approach to filmmaking. Assuming that a director wanted to deviate from mainstream filmmaking styles or to foster the ideas of an innovative colleague – say, a scriptwriter, designer or cinematographer – he/she would have more option to do so under these three systems.

Notes

Translations from French and German are by the author; those from Russian are by Jim Brown.

1. David Bordwell, Janet Staiger, Kristin Thompson, *The Classical Hollywood Cinema: Film Style and Mode of Production to 1960* (London: Routledge & Kegan Paul, 1985), pp. 134–136, 139–140, 147.
2. *Ibid.*, pp. 146, 152.
3. Most historians do not discuss Pathé's 'crise du scénario' claim. Sadoul summarizes Pathé's argument briefly but treats it as simply an attempt at improvements incidental to the re-organization of Pathé-Frères into Pathé-Cinéma in 1918. (See his *Histoire générale du cinéma* Vol. 2 [Paris: Denoël, 1952], pp. 44–45). Richard Abel dismisses the issue in one sentence: 'For Pathé, disingenuously, the only crisis facing the French film industry was a "scenario crisis",' presumably implying that Pathé was using it as a smokescreen to hide his real concerns. (See his *French Cinema: The First Wave 1915–1929* [Princeton: Princeton University Press, 1985], p. 12.) If I am right in suggesting that Pathé saw changes in the scenario as a means of altering the mode of production, then the 'scenario crisis' issue becomes part of Pathé's larger attempts to re-organize the French industry.
4. Charles Pathé, 'La Crise du cinéma', *Le Film* 102 (25 February 1918): 7–8. This citation is, by the way, to a reprint of Pathé's early 1917 article; the original was so much in demand that the issue sold out and *Le Film* had to print it again.
5. Charles Pathé, 'Étude sur l'Evolution de l'Industrie Cinématographique Française', Pt. 2, *Le Film* 120 (1 July 1918): 10.
6. Henri Diamant-Berger, 'Les Poètes et le Cinéma', *Le Film* 112 (6 May 1918): 5.
7. Henri Diamant-Berger, 'Pour sauver le Film Français', *Le Film* 152 (9 February 1919): 5.
8. Jacques de Baroncelli, 'Dans la Féerie des Studios Américains', *Le Journal du Ciné-Club* 1, 8 (2 March 1920): 2.
9. Louis Delluc, 'Scénarii', *Comoedia* 3763 (6 April 1923): 4.
10. Robert Florey, *Filmland* (Paris: Editions de cinémagazine, 1923), p. 258.
11. Raymond Chirat, *Catalogue des films français de long métrage: Films de fiction 1919–1929* (Cinémathèque de Toulouse, 1984).
12. Juan Arroy, 'Jean Epstein au volant', *Cinémagazine* 6, 46 (12 November 1926): 348.
13. Juan Arroy, 'La Monteuse', *Cinémagazine* 5, 39 (25 September 1925): 519.
14. Jack Conrad, 'Le Montage des films'. *Cinémagazine* 7, 3 (21 January 1927): 126.
15. G.-Michel Coissac, *Les Coulisses du cinéma* (Paris: Les Éditions Pittoresques, 1929), pp. 183, 185.
16. Conrad, 'Le montage des films', p. 123.

17. *Ibid.*, pp. 123–124.
18. *Ibid.*, p. 125.
19. 'Organisation im amerikanischen Filmbetrieb', *Lichtbildbühne* 13, 45 (6 November 1920): 26.
20. 'Sparsamkeit bei der Filmherstellung', *Lichtbildbühne* 14, 38 (17 September 1921): 31.
21. E. A. Dupont, 'Hollywood – das Filmparadies, IX: Das Schneiden des Films', *Lichtbildbühne* 20, 50 (28 February 1927): n.p.
22. Ewald André Dupont, *Wie ein Film geschrieben wird and wie man ihn verwertet* (Berlin: Reinhold Kühn, 1919), p. 76.
23. See Frank Testor, *Film Ideen: wie man sie schreibt und erfolgreich verewertet!* (Magdeburg: Burg Verlag, 1919) and Felix K. Bernhardt, *Wie schreibt und verwertet man einen Film?* (Berlin: Bauer-Verlag, 1926).
24. I wish to thank the staff of the library and script departments of the Stiftung Deutsche Kinemathek for their help during my visit to examine these scripts.
25. Dr. Kurt Mühsam, *Film und Kino* (Dessau: Dünnharpt Verlag, 1927), p. 36.
26. William H. Horwald, 'Der Weg des Films: vom Glashaus bis zur Leinwand', *Westermanns Monatshefte* 144 (June 1928): 382.
27. Dupont, 'Hollywood – das Filmparadies', n.p.
28. See Gerhard Lamprecht, *Deutsche Stummfilme* (Berlin: Deutsche Kinemathek, n.d.).
29. Mühsam, *Film und Kino*, p. 40.
30. Max Mack, 'Die Toilette des Films', in *Die zappelnde Leinwand* ed. Max Mack (Berlin: Dr Ensler & Co., 1916), p. 126; Horwald, 'Der Weg des Films', pp. 386–387.
31. Mack, 'Die Toilette des Films', p. 123.
32. Horwald, 'Der Weg des Films', pp. 386–387.
33. 'Die Organisation der Ufa-Produktion', *Lichtbildbühne* 20, 290 (5 December 1927): n.p.
34. Mühsam, *Film und Kino*, p. 37.
35. Letter, Fritz Lang to Kristin Thompson (Beverly Hills), 14 October 1972. Ellipsis in original.
36. Denise J. Youngblood, *Soviet Cinema in the Silent Era. 1918–1935* (Ann Arbor: UMI Research Press, 1985), p. 65.
37. Paul Babitsky and John Rimberg, *The Soviet Film Industry* (New York: Praeger, 1955), pp. 96–97, 102.
38. Nikolai Lebedev, *Cinema: Its Short History, Its Possibilities, Its Construction in the Soviet State* ['Kino: Ego krataia istoiia; ego voz mozhnosti; ego stroitel'stvo v sovetskom gosudarstve'] (Moscow: State Publishers, 1924), pp. 55–56.
39. V. A. Schneiderov. *The Technique and Organization of Film Production* ['Tekhnika i organizatsiia kinos'e-mochnoi raboty'] (Moscow: Tea-Kino-pechat, 1928), pp. 86–88.
40. Viktor Pertsov, 'Literature and Cinema', from *Zhizn' iskusstva* (12 July 1927), in Richard Taylor and Ian Christie, eds., *The Film Factory: Russian and Soviet Cinema in Documents 1896–1939* (Cambridge: Harvard University Press, 1988), p. 165.
41. Ilya Rentz, *On the Set* ['No s'emke'] (Moscow: Kinopechat, 1926), p. 23.
42. Ippolit Sokolov, *Film Scenarios: Theory and Technique* ['Kino-stsenarii: Teoriia i tekniki'] (Moscow: Kinopechat, 1926), p. 69.
43. *Ibid.*, pp. 68–69.
44. S. Timoshenko, *Art of the Cinema and the Montage of Films* ['Iskusstvo kino: Montazh fil'ma'] (Leningrad: Academia, 1926), pp. 74–75.
45. Sergei Eisenstein, 'Literature and Cinema: Reply to a Questionnaire', in Richard Taylor, ed. and tr., *S. M. Eisenstein: Selected Works,* Vol. 1, 'Writings, 1922–34' (London: BFI Publishing, 1988), p. 98.
46. Sergei Eisenstein, 'The Form of the Script', in Taylor, *S. M. Eisenstein: Selected Works*, Vol. 1, pp. 134–135.
47. Quoted in Richard Taylor, *The Politics of the Soviet Cinema 1917–1929* (Cambridge: Cambridge University Press, 1979), p. 34.
48. Anatoli Golovnya, 'Broken Cudgels', in Luda and Jean Schnitzer, eds., *Cinema in Revolution* (New York: Hill & Wang, 1973), p. 148.
49. V. I. Pudovkin, *Film Technique and Film Acting*, tr. and ed. Ivor Montagu (New York: Grove Press, 1960), p. 32.
50. Viktor Shklovsky, 'Beware of Music', from *Sovetskii ekran* (1 January 1929), in Taylor and Christie, *The Film Factory*, p. 252.
51. L. I. Monosson, 'The Soviet Cinematography', *Journal of the Society of Motion Picture Engineers* 15, 4 (October 1930): 521.
52. V. Shneiderov, *The Technique and Organization of Film Production*, p. 9.

53. 'Party Cinema Conference Resolution: The Results of Cinema Construction in the USSR and the Tasks of Soviet Cinema', in Taylor and Christie, *The Film Factory*, pp. 212–213.
54. 'Sovkino Workers' Conference Resolution: Sovkino's New Course (Extract)', in Taylor and Christie, *The Film Factory*, p. 243.
55. V. Sutyrin, *Problems of the Socialist Reconstruction of the Soviet Film Industry* ['Prolemy sotialistischeskoi rekonstruksii sovetskoi kinopromyshlennosti'] (Moscow: G. I. Kh. L., 1932), pp. 59–60.
56. *Ibid.*, pp. 58–59.
57. *Ibid.*, pp. 61–63.
58. *Ibid.*, p. 64.
59. Babitsky and Rimberg, *The Soviet Film Industry*, pp. 86–87.
60. For more on this subject, see my 'The Limits of Experimentation in Hollywood', in *Lovers of Cinema: Early American Avantgarde 1919–1945*. Jan-Christopher Horak, ed. (Madison: University of Wisconsin Press, 1995).

Chapter 22

DAVID BORDWELL

MONUMENTAL HEROICS
Form and style in Eisenstein's silent films

EISENSTEIN'S SILENT FILMS WERE, like those of his Left contemporaries, didactic works. Yet he saw no contradiction between creating propaganda and achieving powerful aesthetic effects. Indeed, central to his thinking was the belief that only if propaganda was artistically effective—structurally unified, perceptually arousing, emotionally vivid—would it be politically efficacious. This urge to plumb the artistic capacities of film made Eisenstein the most ambitious and innovative director of Soviet cinema.

His experiments drew on diverse sources. Certainly Constructivism, particularly its theatrical manifestations, strongly influenced his films. Yet Constructivism's moment had passed when Eisenstein began filmmaking. Moreover, the movement's reliance upon abstract design was not suited for a medium that would, in the Soviet state, have to utilize representational imagery. Kasimir Malevich quickly recognized this, criticizing film directors for plagiarizing academic realist art and refusing to use pictorial abstraction to expose the materials of "cinema as such" (Malevich 1925:228–229).

Eisenstein's films can usefully be understood as part of a broad tendency toward "heroic realism" in 1920s Soviet art. This trend had its immediate sources in the Civil War period, which generated lyrical, episodic portrayals of collective action. In agit-dramas and novels the hero became the mass, and appeal to the spectator was posterlike in its directness. By the mid-1920s, when the avant-garde had declined, most painters, writers, and theatre workers accepted the obligation of celebrating the Revolution or portraying Soviet society through some version of "realism" (although the exact meaning of this concept was hotly debated).

Several trends emerged, notably Maxim Gorky's "revolutionary romanticism," which aimed to idealize the individual, and the easel painting of the Association of Artists of Revolutionary Russia, which demanded accessible content and comprehensible form. Other artists sought to meld the imperatives of heroic realism with avant-garde experimentation. Collage and photomontage could convey a pulsating modernity; Vladimir Mayakovsky's machine-gun prosody could pay homage to Lenin; posters and typography could use Futurist design to galvanize the spectator's eye.

Like other Left artists, Eisenstein enthusiastically acceded to demands for a Soviet mythology that would stir proletarian consciousness. All his silent features start with quotations from Lenin, and the leader's image is central to the last two of them. In *Toward Dictatorship* and *The Year 1905* and the two-part *October* he conceived multi-part sagas tracing the victories of Bolshevism. These mammoth works went unmade, but the finished films did present a history of the Party's ascendency, from the turn of the century (*Strike*, 1925) and 1905 (*The Battleship Potemkin*, 1925) to 1917 (*October*, 1928) and the contemporary era (*Old and New*, also known as *The General Line*, 1929).

In constructing a cinematic mythology of the new regime, Eisenstein drew upon cultural formulas and iconography from his youth. For example, propaganda and popular legend already defined the key events of the *Potemkin* mutiny—the spoiled meat, the death of Vakulinchuk, the display of the body. (See Gerould 1989.) Public celebrations also furnished filmmakers a wealth of tales and storytelling strategies. From soon after the October revolution through the 1920s, the government sponsored mass spectacles to celebrate public holidays and commemorate historical turning points. On May Day in 1920, for instance, 4,000 participants performed in the "Mystery of Liberated Labor" for an audience of 35,000. Such spectacles, and the festivals and processions associated with them, were echoed in Eisenstein's films. The ritual of parading zoo animals dressed as class enemies finds its equivalent in *Strike*, while the mass spectacle "Storming of the Winter Palace" in October 1920 forms a plot outline for *October*.

Eisenstein was prepared to romanticize revolutionary action. In his films men (and occasionally women) fight, women and children endure, and all may die at the hands of the oppressor. The enemy slaughters innocents: the Odessa Steps are populated by mothers, infants, old men and women, a male student, and amputees. Yet these films never show a slain enemy. *October*'s Bolsheviks are murdered, but the government's side appears to suffer no casualties. In *Potemkin*, Vakulinchuk is shot, but the officers are merely tossed overboard. Sometimes the film flatly ignores the question of revolutionary justice; *Potemkin*'s priest, feigning death in the hold, is never seen again; in *Old and New*, the kulaks who poison the bull go unpunished. Eisenstein concentrates on the spectacular moments of upheaval, suffering, and victory and avoids confronting the ethical problems of insurrectionary violence.

Eisenstein's diverse aesthetic impulses find a place within heroic realism. Like the painters Alexander Deineka and Yury Pimenov, he merges monumental forms with grotesque distortions that defy verisimilitude. A "documentary" realism of locale and physiognomy can be overlaid with flagrant artifice, such as the theatrical stripe of light running down the center of the Odessa Steps (Figure 22.1). Like Malevich, whose 1927 painting *Red Cavalry* combines suprematism and illustration, Eisenstein shapes consecrated icons—fists, banners, factories, armored cars, tractors—into parts of a dynamic visual design.

The films thus explore various representational options of the New Economic Policy period (NEP) launched in 1921. *Strike*'s script emerged from Proletkult, while *Potemkin* assimilated contributions from old Bolsheviks as well as Nikolai Aseev and Tretyakov. To writers and Formalist critics who took adventure and mystery stories as the solution to the problem of plot, Eisenstein offered *Strike*, which mixes espionage intrigue with Eccentric types and conceptual abstraction. Novelists and dramatists seeking to create a pathos-drenched Soviet epic (*poema*) could find one solution in *Potemkin*. While writers were looking for a "poetic prose" that mixed revolutionary romanticism with vivid metaphoric effects, Eisenstein was at work on *October*. And in the period when *New Lef* sought to find literature in the "fact" of everyday Soviet life, he produced *Old and New*.

Eisenstein was also impelled to turn further back. Each major film, he asserted, corresponded to a text from Zola (*Germinal* for *Strike*, *La terre* for *The General Line*) (1928b:95). The Symbolism of Andrei Bely, particularly his novel *Petersburg* (1922), also seems to have influenced Eisenstein's montage practice. *Old and New*'s prayer ceremony cites Repin's painting *Religious Procession in Kursk Province* (1880–1883) in order to counterpoise that tradition to the

Figure 22.1
Battleship Potemkin

more "cubistic" rendering of the cream separator. The plate-smashing scene in *Potemkin* was derived from Daumier's figures and Myron's *Discus Thrower*.

In all, in the years before Socialist Realism became the official style, Eisenstein explored alternative aesthetic options within left cinema's montage tendency. His "Leninist formalism," that urge to extract compositional methods from diverse traditions and turn them to immediate ends, made him central to the development of heroic realism in Soviet cinema.

Toward plotless cinema

Indeed, one could argue that Soviet heroic realism was most richly realized in the new medium. Pudovkin, Dovzhenko, Ermler, and others were working in this tradition, with occasional contributions from the FEX collaborators Kozintsev and Leonid Trauberg. Whereas mainstream entertainment film was derived largely from tsarist cinema, as well as from doses of German, French, and American influence, these directors offered a distinctly "Soviet" alternative. Eisenstein helped shape this alternative, and he often took it further than his contemporaries.

In his time, Eisenstein's innovations were taken as exemplary of the trend of "plotless" cinema. This was not filmmaking that avoided narrative altogether; it was, rather, a new sort of narrative cinema. Plotless films, Adrian Piotrovsky pointed out, did not present the action as "a consequentially motivated development of individual fate." Moreover, plotless cinema relied on "exclusively cinematic means of expression," which included unrealistic manipulations of time and the use of "non-diegetic" and "associative" montage (1927:105). From these aspects of the "plotless" film Eisenstein created what Piotrovsky called his "monumental heroics" (106).

The prototypical Soviet film sought to show that history was made by collective action, and most directors provided narratives that treated characters as typical of larger political forces. Still, the characters are usually individualized, with distinctive traits and psychological motives. Often a figure is derived from an instantly recognizable type—the bureaucrat, the worker, the middle-class woman, the Red Army soldier. Although Eisenstein is associated with the practice of "typage," he did not take credit for originating it, and it is common throughout Soviet film of the period.

In Eisenstein, however, typage follows from his idiosyncratic tendency to build his plots around the "mass protagonist." A scene will employ a crowd to manifest the central role that Marxist doctrine ascribes to class action as the motor of history. Most members of the crowd who get picked out lack psychological qualities. Their actions are more often determined by their historical or organizational roles. It is as if Eisenstein took literally M. N. Potrovsky's dictum: "We Marxists do not see personality as the maker of history, for to us personality is only the instrument with which history works" (quoted in Willet 1978:106). In Eisenstein's films, history is a process—of defeat in *Strike*, of gain in *Potemkin*, of victory in *October*, of building socialism in *Old and New*—and the plot is built around stages in the unfolding of a large-scale dynamic.

By avoiding the more concrete characterization favored by his contemporaries, Eisenstein exposed himself to a problem that had already arisen in other media. Mid-1920s drama and mass spectacles commonly idealized the masses and satirized the oppressors. For instance, in the first Soviet opera, *Red Petrograd* (1925), the class enemies were given grotesque music and the positive heroes were given lyric song. The avant-gardist faced a twofold problem: how to treat the enemies seriously without heroizing them, and how to render the revolutionary forces by means of avant-garde techniques that would not mock them. In Eisenstein's case, perhaps *Potemkin* handles the matter most successfully, presenting the enemies in less caricatural terms than does *Strike* and using its montage experiments to elevate class allies. *Old and New* uses mildly modernist techniques to create moments of affirmative comedy. *October* is far more schizophrenic; as Eisenstein himself remarked at the time, intellectual montage was as yet appropriate only for satirizing the enemy (1928c:104).

In showing the masses making history, 1920s Left cinema builds its plots around social crises that trigger changes in the characters. Often an individual's dawning awareness of revolutionary doctrine furnishes major stages of the plot. In Pudovkin's *Mother* (1926), *The End of St. Petersburg* (1927), and *The Heir to Genghis Khan* (1928), the drama often hinges on the transformation of the individual's consciousness.

No such psychological conversion interests Eisenstein. His oppressed multitudes are quivering on the brink of revolt, needing only agitation, direction, and discipline. A historical crisis provides the clear-cut outlines of a momentous process, a strike or a mutiny, mounting an insurrection or building a cooperative. Even in *Old and New*, the peasant protagonist needs no convincing of the right path; she simply lacks allies.

Once one has abandoned the psychologically motivated plot, the problem is how to unify the film. We have already touched on one means of achieving unity, the conceiving of a larger process within which actions form stages. A second unifying strategy, touched on by Potrovsky, is stylistic: the film achieves a single effect partly through a dynamic organization of material and technique.

Thus, for instance, the narration will typically rely upon parallelisms to display the broad sweep of the historical process. These parallels are typically *diegetic*—that is, they liken or contrast characters, settings, or actions that are located in the fictional world of the story. In Pudovkin's *Mother*, for instance, the climactic march of the militants is compared with the thawing and cracking ice on the nearby river.

Again, however, Eisenstein goes further. First, he also utilizes *nondiegetic* material. In *Old and New*, the slaughter of pigs is intercut with spinning pig statuettes; these statuettes are evidently not in the same "world" as the pigs (22.2, 22.3). As this example indicates,

Figure 22.2 Old and New

Figure 22.3 Old and New

Figure 22.4 October

Figure 22.5 October

Eisenstein's typical cues for nondiegetic inserts are shots of objects framed in close-up and filmed against black backgrounds. Such inserts serve as a kind of abstract commentary on the action, making the viewer aware of an intervening narration that can interrupt the action and point up thematic or pictorial associations. Sometimes, however, Eisenstein's narration relativizes the distinction between diegetic and nondiegetic imagery. We find images that fall between the poles—concretely located in the story world, but treated with a freedom that "emancipates" the action from time and space (1929c:177).

Eisenstein's parallels differ from those of his peers in another way. His comparisons often emit a radiating network of graphic or thematic implications. Piotrovsky follows contemporary usage in calling this "associative montage" (105).

One of the most famous of Eisenstein's visual analogies occurs in *October*. There he intercuts Prime Minister Kerensky of the Provisional Government with shots of a mechanical peacock (22.4, 22.5). The most obvious connection is the association of peacocks with preening. Eisenstein pictorializes a figure of speech: Kerensky is as vain as a peacock. But the sequence triggers other implications as well. The peacock is mechanical, and it enables Eisenstein to reiterate the artificial pose and gesture of the man. Like motifs elsewhere in the film, the peacock's sparkling highlights and suggestion of precious metals associate Kerensky with a static opulence due to be overturned by revolutionary energy. The whirling of the bird and the spreading of its tail coincide with Kerensky's standing at a door that will not open, suggesting that the mechanical toy works better than the government. Moreover, the bird's spinning is edited so that it seems to control the door's swinging open; a toy becomes the mainspring of the palace. The peacock's mechanized dance also suggests an empty ritual, like Kerensky's grand march up the stairs and the flunkies' insincere greetings. In ways such as these, Eisenstein takes fairly dead and clichéd metaphors and enlivens them through contextual associations. His filmic figures go beyond one-for-one comparisons and acquire the penumbra of connotation that distinguishes a rich poetic metaphor.

Eisenstein's exploration of associative montage exemplifies his fascination with the concrete properties of the film material. In his theorizing, he was driven to account for all the pictorial qualities and conceptual implications of each shot. This line of inquiry gave birth to ideas of "intellectual cinema," "overtonal montage," and other concepts. His decision to make "plot-less" films committed him to a corresponding dependence upon the specific features of film technique.

Whereas most Soviet directors became identified with a severe, even laconic shot design, Eisenstein pursued sensuous lighting and intricate compositions. His cinematographer, Edward Tissé, agreed with Eisenstein's ideas about making images perceptually arresting. Tissé used large mirrors to focus sunlight, marking out hard-edged blocks of space (as in 22.1) or endowing objects and faces with sculptural gleams. His expertise with the short focal-length lens (typically 28mm) enabled Eisenstein to create dynamically deep images.

It was with the technique of editing that Eisenstein was to be most closely identified. Pudovkin, along with Kuleshov, Barnet, and others more partial to Hollywood-style drama and comedy, came to be considered the proponents of a "montage" approach to filmmaking. This style emphasized abrupt, fragmented cutting. Soviet directors broke a scene into many shots, building up a dramatic action out of many short, close-up pieces.

Although Eisenstein influenced other directors, they tended not to carry montage techniques as far as he did. Whereas most directors' films use crosscutting to convey simultaneity and parallelism, Eisenstein uses it as well to create graphic similarities and to suggest abstract meanings. He also presses the Soviet standard of rapid editing to extremes by cutting "excessively." Calculated at twenty-four frames per second, the average shot length of *Old and New* is 2.6 seconds, of *Strike* 2.5 seconds, of *October* and *Potemkin* about 2 seconds—these latter figures being lower than those for almost any other Soviet director.[1]

A montage tactic he particularly cultivates is overlapping editing. This consists of cutting so that the action on screen is prolonged beyond its presumed duration. The technique has its source in the American cinema, but Kuleshov, Eisenstein's teacher and a subtle observer of Hollywood practice, took the device further. In *The Extraordinary Adventures of Mr. West in the Land of the Bolsheviks* (1924), a brawl is rendered in four markedly overlapping shots. A year later, in *Strike*, Eisenstein refines the procedure. While overlapping the movement of a wheel striking a foreman, he shows the action from sharply different angles. The editing makes the vectors of movement clash (22.6–22.11). Later in this and other films Eisenstein experiments with lengthy prolongations, oscillations, even complete replays of events. Overlapping editing creates a nervous, vibrating rhythm and allows him to rearrange elements from shot to shot.

Such montage techniques fulfill a more general purpose. All Left directors sought to dynamize each scene, but Eisenstein often abolishes the sense that an independent, coherent fictional event is rendered by a series of shots. This strategy exemplifies that elimination of "real time" to which Piotrovsky refers. The tractor driver in *Old and New* is "matched" in the same position in two different places; the priest aboard the *Potemkin* strikes the cross into his right hand, then abruptly into his left (22.12, 22.13); the massacre on the Odessa Steps yields

Figure 22.6 Strike

Figure 22.7 Strike

Figure 22.8 Strike

Figure 22.9 Strike

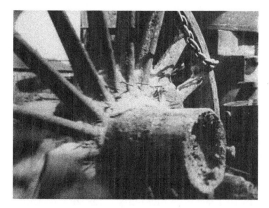

Figure 22.10 Strike

Figure 22.11 Strike

Figure 22.12 Battleship Potemkin   *Figure 22.13 Battleship Potemkin*

incompatible spatial arrangements from shot to shot; one sequence in *October* refuses to specify whether action is occurring on a single bridge or on several. In all these instances, the very idea of a consistent story event falls into question. Once again the action becomes "quasi-diegetic," hovering between the story world and a realm of abstract, emblematic significance.

In using such rapid and disjunctive editing, Eisenstein creates a narration that sacrifices strict realism to perceptual and emotional impact. As in the metaphorical ramifications of certain passages, the result, however apparently didactic, goes beyond rhetoric and becomes aesthetically complex. Eisenstein pushes dynamized style to the limits of deformation, creating a mannerist version of Soviet cinematic norms.

The emphasis upon the moment-by-moment stylistic texture calls forth one more strategy in Eisenstein's "plotless" approach to heroic realism. It goes unmentioned in Piotrovsky's discussion, but it is a significant innovation in silent film history. It involves using recurrent objects and graphic patterns as motifs to unify the film.

We are very familiar with this organizational principle today, but motivic construction of Eisenstein's sort, and on his scale, was not yet a commonplace of prestigious cinema. In dramatic cinema, both in Hollywood and Europe, the motif was typically a prop that was invested with some narrative or thematic significance. In William deMille's *Miss Lulu Bett* (1921), for instance, the title character's bedroom slipper takes on a charged dramatic significance in the course of a scene. In the course of Abel Gance's *La roue* (1923) flowers and the locomotive acquire symbolic implications by virtue of their association with the characters' feelings and experience. In such mainstream usage, the motif either enhances characterization, plays a specific causal role in the plot, or intensifies the thematic point of the scene. Moreover, the spectator is expected to notice and recall the motif upon its reappearance. Soviet filmmakers used motifs in comparable ways.

As a self-consciously modernist artist, Eisenstein took a somewhat different perspective. He was aware that imagistic motifs played a central organizing role in poetry and drama. His studies of Zola, Bely, Joyce, and other artists convinced him that a rich, truly unified art work coordinates cross-referring systems of repeated images, verbal tags, and compositional devices. He could have found in Shklovsky's essay on Bely the remark that contemporary Russian prose was largely "ornamental" in that large-scale patterns of imagery prevailed over plot structure (1925:180). Later, in a lecture to aspiring directors, Eisenstein described a motif in *La bête humaine* as "delineated in order to be remembered," like the cradle in Griffith's *Intolerance*

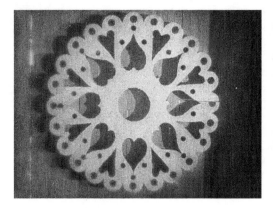

Figure 22.14 Old and New

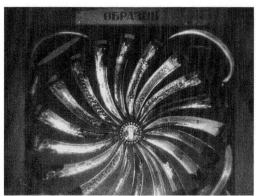

Figure 22.15 Old and New

Figure 22.16 Old and New

(1928h:102). The idea of motivic construction led Eisenstein to make the pictorial or thematic implications of an image stretch across the entire film.

Sometimes he treats his motif as a simple geometric figure. In *Old and New* the bureaucrats are linked to the kulaks by the fancy circles seen on the kulak's gate (22.14) and in the agency office (22.15). Eisenstein often dynamizes such a static motif in the course of a film, as when in *Old and New* the fleet of tractors plows in concentric circles (22.16). Less abstract motifs, such as objects and gestures, will also bind the film together, but in a way that broadens to include remotely associated items. In *Potemkin* eyes, worms, and hanging objects form a thematic cluster. The Eisensteinian motif does not simply repeat; it develops, expands its implications, and intertwines with others to create a network of visual and thematic associations.

Some films, such as *October* and *Old and New*, display a strictly binary motivic organization: a basic thematic opposition (such as "God and Country") is mapped onto a welter of constantly varied visual and dramatic items. In *Strike* motifs associated with one group of characters abruptly "change sides" at turning points in the action. *Potemkin* relies more on a "nodal" principle, in which a single event, such as the inspection of a piece of rotten meat or the gathering of a crowd at the quai, knots together several motifs.

Although the principle of large-scale motivic organization gets almost no attention in Eisenstein's theoretical writings of the 1920s, he would articulate it in later years. For instance, in 1933 he noted: "A motif of the content may be played not only in the story but also in the law of construction or the structure of the thing" (1933c:308). As in most aspects of his 1920s work, practice preceded theory.

The innovations of Eisenstein's "plotless cinema"—the construction of the action around stages of a historical process, the radiating network of motifs binding the film together, the foregrounding of style in image and montage—were not simply onetime accomplishments. Every project pushed further. This effort is particularly apparent in his last two films, which react against what he perceived as a hardening of Soviet montage conventions. After seeing *October*, Shklovsky noted that the "logical" montage of psychological analysis practiced by Kuleshov and Pudovkin had "ceased to be felt." Eisenstein's intellectual montage responded to a need for even more "perceptible" methods (1930:111). *Old and New* sought to go still further, exploring "overtonal montage" as a way of integrating intellectual stimuli with other aspects of the shots.

The urge to experiment drove him to surpass the norms of his own works. As Eisenstein repeatedly insisted, each of his silent films was an answer, a "dialectical" antithesis, to its predecessor. Each offers fresh stylistic experiments and new methods of plot construction, motivic organization, mise-en-scène, and montage. But each film can also be seen as pointing out one path for Soviet film. *Strike* borrows methods of Civil War art, using Eccentrism and mass spectacle to create an openly agitational appeal to the audience. *Potemkin* works within an epic mode, using carefully developed emotional progressions to carry away the spectator. *October*, more episodic than its predecessors, suggests that Left cinema could exploit a pluralistic "montage" of different types of filmic discourse. Finally, *Old and New* seeks not only to make the innovations of the earlier films "intelligible to the millions" but also to imbue Soviet myth with a spiritual fervor. Each film tries something strikingly new, and each offers a different model for heroic realism in Soviet cinema.

Strike (1925)

Strike sets the pattern for Eisenstein's silent features in several ways. It launches his chronicle-myth of revolutionary history; it establishes his mixture of naturalism and stylization; it initiates his research into "film language" and methods of montage. But *Strike* is unique in his oeuvre for its eclectic experimentation, its exuberant leaps of tones and style, its posterlike extremes of clownishness and romanticism. Rediscovered by Western cinéphiles in the mid-1960s, it looked far more vibrant and playful than the master's canonized classics. Its unremitting Eccentrism gives every reel a pursuit, fistfight, or gymnastic exhibition; each scene is enlivened by unexpected pictorial effects or performance flourishes. *Strike* constitutes what Eisenstein and Tretyakov called *Do You Hear, Moscow?*—an "agitguignol."

The vibrant experiments, however, are held together by a fairly rigorous structure. *Strike* seems loose only in contrast with the extraordinary unity of *Potemkin*. As in Eisenstein's next two films, the decision to create a mass historical drama impels him to devise a coherent structure and vivid motifs that will carry the propagandistic lesson.

Strike's theme is laid out in the opening quotation from Lenin: "The strength of the working class lies in its organization . . . Organization means unity of action, unity of practical operations." The film's plot traces how Bolshevik factory workers, after laying the groundwork through agitation, turn a spontaneous protest into a strike. At the moment when the strike is born, the factory workers reassert Lenin's lesson: they have power, they say in their meeting, "when we are united in the struggle against capital."

But solidarity loosens. The prolonged strike intensifies workers' family problems. A strike leader, acting in a moment of undisciplined violence, allows a spy to identify him. After police torture, he accepts a bribe to betray his comrades. At the same time, provocateurs from the lumpenproletariat provide the authorities with an occasion to attack the workers. The principal Bolshevik is captured, and the police launch a massacre that sweeps through the workers' quarters. *Strike* both pays homage to the struggles that preceded the October revolution and warns that class solidarity and Party unity must be maintained against enemies, both within and without.

The film insists on the generality of the lesson by presenting a composite of several historical strikes. The action is based upon the 1903 strikes at Rostov-on-the-Don, which spread to more than five hundred factories and involved almost a quarter of a million workers. But the film, shot in and around Moscow, makes no explicit reference to these events; indeed, Alexandrov claims that spectators did not recognize the historical source (1976:43). The film further generalizes the action with a concluding title that lists other strikes that were harshly repressed, ranging from a 1903 massacre of workers in the Urals to a 1915 strike in spinning factories. As the film's title suggests, *Strike* becomes an anatomy of the forces at work throughout several critical moments of Russian labor's struggle for socialism.

Eisenstein's habitual strategy of making every reel constitute a distinct "chapter" or "act" contributes to this generalizing quality.[2] Each part is presented as a phase through which a typical strike will pass. The first reel, starting with the title "All is quiet at the factory/ BUT—" covers the agitational phase of activity. Reel two, labeled "The immediate cause of the strike," dramatizes the theft of a worker's micrometer, the harsh response of the management, and the worker's suicide. The death triggers an uprising that bursts into a full-blown strike. The third reel opens with the title "The factory stands idle" and portrays the effects of inactivity on both the capitalist owners and the workers. Reel four, "The strike is prolonged," traces the debilitating effect of the strike on the workers. Here the turning point comes with the strike leader's betrayal of his comrades. "Engineering a massacre," the title of the next reel, becomes a parallel to the Bolsheviks' agitation in the factory: a police spy hires some provocateurs. They set fire to a vodka shop, and although the provocation fails, the firemen turn their hoses on the workers, enabling the police to seize the main leader.

Although a spy, the police chief, and the captured Bolshevik appear in the last reel, "Liquidation," the segment functions principally to expand the implications of the dramatic action. First comes a savage cossack assault on workers' tenements. Previously, the factory workers have been shown living in suburban cottages; this new locale becomes a more generalized representation of workers' homes. The tenement massacre is followed by the most abstract sequence of all, the intercutting of cossacks' firing upon an anonymous horde of fleeing workers with butchers' slaughter of a bull. The latter line of action is wholly nondiegetic, pushing the sequence into a realm of pure "attraction." The last reel is virtually a detachable short film, a showcase of Eisenstein's "free montage of attractions" that, operating independently of narrative, stimulate strong emotions and wide-ranging concepts.

Strike, then, presents an anatomy of a political process. It displays the techniques of the revolutionary underground, creating a film that, as Eisenstein somewhat obscurely suggested, paralleled the "production" of a strike with the process of industrial production itself (1925d:59–61). The plot also schematizes the typical stages, tests, and crises through which a strike must pass. In addition, the film diagnoses those forces with which the working class must contend. Seeking to dramatize the class struggle, Eisenstein builds up an enormous range of oppositions between the workers and their class enemies. And many of these call forth the sort

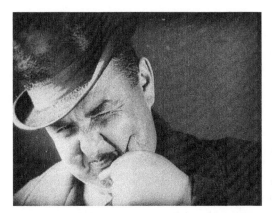

Figure 22.17 Strike

Figure 22.18

Figure 22.19

of stylization that Eisenstein associated with "theatrical October," the stage pageants during and immediately after the Civil War.

On one side are the forces of capital, personified at the outset by the obese, top-hatted factory director, who leers out at the camera (22.17). He oversees scurrying clerks, disdainful typists, a straw-hatted factory manager, and an old foreman. The director in turn answers to the factory's owners. Aligned with the capitalist and their flunkies are the police, with their herd of spies, and the lumpenproletariat, recruited by the spies. All these forces are presented as a spectrum of stylized types, ranging from the most realistic (the police) through caricature (the capitalists and their staff) and theatrical grotesquerie (the animalistic spies) to circus eccentrism (the hobo king and his retinue). Eisenstein introduces a bizarre touch into even more naturalistic moments: the bribery of the captured Bolshevik by the police administrator is accompanied by a pair of midgets tangoing on the table, their seductive dance mocking the traitor's acquiescence (22.18).

The workers, by contrast, are idealized in a manner typical of "heroic realism," with none of the bourgeois forces' exaggeration of costume or demeanor. Moreover, they are far less individualized. The film's opening depersonalizes the agitators: after the director's frontal close-up, they are presented obliquely, as silhouettes and reflections (22.19). Later, the workers are characteristically shown en masse. Individuals are momentarily picked out, but none is portrayed in depth. Indeed, any worker developed as a distinct character is likely to die soon (the suicide) or to join the bourgeoisie (the traitor). And individualization itself is used to point up thematic oppositions. The capitalist's mistress, who frenziedly urges the police agents to beat the captured worker, contrasts with the more anonymous female Bolshevik leader who battles the police to get to the fire alarm.

The contrast between the caricature of class enemies and the romanticization of class allies will become central to Eisenstein's later films, but its sources lie in Civil War art. *Strike* is indebted to the *agitki*, propaganda vehicles that emerged in the wake of the October revolution, particularly the "epic" version seen in poster art and mass festivals, with their satirically individualized rulers pitted against a mass of workers. Mayakovsky's *Mystère-bouffe* and his emblematic designs for store windows had already shown that Left art could utilize such schematic material. The boss's sadistic mistress in Eisenstein's film has a parallel in Tretyakov's *Roar, China!* in which the merchant's daughter eagerly watches two men being strangled.

Strike finds vivid motifs to sharpen its conventional opposition. From the start the workers are associated with machines; when they go on strike, so does the equipment, so that the factory director's typewriter snaps itself away from his touch. The capitalists are associated with an intricate bureaucracy, in the factory and in the police force. One sequence uses reporting and phone calls to trace the chain of command running from foreman through managers to police officers. This contrasts with the machine-centered production process in the agitators' printing shop, where a handwritten text becomes—without human intervention—a leaflet, copies of which shower down on a locomotive in the factory. Through the opposition of machines and bureaucracy, Eisenstein again moves to the abstract level, portraying the Marxist distinction between the forces and relations of production. He further shows, by the radicalization of the workers, that a revolutionary situation has come to pass. The progressive factors in the base have outstripped the institutions that they originally supported.

Such clusters of imagery are reversed in the course of the film. Initially the workers occupy the factory catwalks (22.20); but the brutal cossacks eventually take over the catwalks of the tenements (22.21). Whereas the workers are established as in the heights, the lumpenproletariat are introduced as living in huge underground barrels (22.22); soon the Bolshevik leader will be captured by being hosed into a hole and surrounded by barrels (22.23). The children associated with the strikers come to prominence in the last reel, when toddlers become victims of the cossacks' rampage (22.24).

Again and again, Eisenstein's motifs reflect the drama's progression. Three of these—animals, water, and circles—undergo particularly rich development. In each case, a motif initially associated with one side of the political struggle becomes transferred to the other.

In the early scenes the capitalist forces are likened to animals. As the factory sits idle, the factory director is intercut with a crow and a cat. More explicitly, each police spy is given an animal identity: Bulldog, Fox, Owl, and Monkey are visually linked with their counterparts and move in a roughly appropriate fashion. In the same portions of the film, the proletariat are established as being in control of animals: geese and other domestic animals are part of their milieu, and children run a goat in a wheelbarrow as their elders had turned out the factory manager. But at the film's end, it is the workers who are equated with an animal—the bull, slaughtered by a casually proficient butcher likened to the soldiers.

The motif of water develops in the same way. At the film's start, agitating workers are glimpsed in a reflecting puddle; later they plot their conspiracy while swimming. During the battle for the steam whistle during the factory uprising, workers spray water to knock the guard off balance, and a dripping worker joyously pulls the whistle cord. But as the workers'

Figure 22.20

Figure 22.21

Figure 22.22

Figure 22.23

Figure 22.24

cause wanes, water turns against them. The first leader is captured in a soaking downpour. As the hobo king spruces himself up, he sprays water from his mouth onto his mirror.

Perhaps the richest development of motifs involves a geometrical shape, the circle. Introduced in an intertitle ("HO," that is, "BUT—"), the O takes on a life of its own by becoming a circle and then a rotating wheel in the factory. It is firmly associated with the workers: they run the wheel of a turbine; a wheel turns their printing press. The agitators meet in a scrap heap of wheels (22.25). A crane operator slams the foreman to earth with a suspended wheel, which at another point aggressively hurtles at the camera (22.26). During the strike uprising, wheelbarrows roll the manager and foreman into the runoff pit, while the stopping of the factory is conveyed by a symbolic image showing workers folding their arms and a wheel ceasing to rotate (22.27). As the strike continues, Bolsheviks meet in huge pipes (22.28), another circular contrast with the barrels in which the lumpenproletariat live.

The motifs of water and circularity culminate in the sequence of the firemen's assault. One of the most sensuously arousing passages in Eisenstein's cinema, the hosing sequence uses rhythmic editing and diagonal compositions to create a pulsating movement. The water motif reaches its apogee as spray slashes across the frame in vectors that evoke El Lissitzky's Constructivist compositions (22.29). The firemen turn their hoses' punishing force on the workers. Now the wheel is on a fire truck, working against the strikers; the spume pins a worker helplessly to a cartwheel (22.30). In terms that Eisenstein would elaborate in his later theory, water and circles constitute image-based "lines" that weave through the film and "knot" in this climactic massacre.

Such opposed and transformed motifs function as associations reinforcing the film's agitational purpose. Eisenstein uses other means to drive home the lesson. To a greater degree than his contemporaries, he overtly acknowledges the audience. Most obviously, this direct address occurs in expository intertitles. Eisenstein has already perfected the ironically echoic intertitle: "Preparation" denotes the activities of the workers and the police agents; "Beat him!" recurs in scenes in which the captured worker is thrashed. More daringly, Eisenstein creates "collective" intertitles. At the workers' meeting in the factory, for instance, dialogue titles alternate with crowd shots, as if the words issue from the entire mass. Still other titles blur the distinction between diegetic and nondiegetic sources. We must often ask if a line, such as "Thief!" when the worker is accused, comes from a character or the overarching narration itself. Meyerhold approved of Eisenstein's use of such direct address: the intertitle acts directly on the viewer, he suggested, and "the director assumes the role of agitator" (Meyerhold 1925:160).

Images also assault the audience. Sometimes characters face the camera, either in shot/reverse-shot confrontations with other characters or simply in direct address to the spectator. The film concludes with a pair of staring eyes in extreme close-up and the title, "Proletarians, remember!" This final appeal to the audience was a convention of Civil War drama; at the close of *Do You Hear, Moscow?* the protagonist shouted the title line at the audience.

The engagement of the spectator arises more indirectly from Eisenstein's use of symbols and tropes. Like other art deriving from the Civil War tradition, *Strike* invokes religious iconography. The scene of the worker's suicide becomes a proletarian Descent from the Cross (22.31), and the writhing figures of demonstrators under the firemen's fusillade of hoses echo the postures of martyrs (22.32). *Strike* also shows a firm commitment to metaphorical filmmaking. Sometimes the intertitles create the linkage, as when, after the factory director petulantly kicks his wicker chair off his patio, a title remarks: "Their thrones rest on the labor of the workers." Some titles are integrated with the visual motifs more dynamically. The title "Spreading ripple," coming after the shot of workers reflected in a puddle, ties the agitational process to the water motif and suggests the expansion of the workers' discontent. At the end of the firehose

Figure 22.25

Figure 22.26

Figure 22.27

Figure 22.28

Figure 22.29

Figure 22.30

Figure 22.31   Figure 22.32

sequence, an abstract burst of spray introduces the final reel, punningly titled "Liquidation": the literal "liquidation" has been a prelude to the massacre.

Eisenstein explores an assortment of purely visual metaphors as well. Most are firmly located within the story world and are brought to our attention by means of close-ups and editing. Through crosscutting, the capitalists' squeezing juice out of a lemon becomes analogous to the harassment of strikers by the mounted police. Intercutting the machine belts with the worker's belt (22.33, 22.34) makes his suicide an ironic contrast to the machines' activity. The animal motifs we have already considered are largely metaphorical, rendering the police spies bestial through symbolic superimpositions (22.35).

In this connection, the last sequence is especially revelatory. Eisenstein has often been criticized for intercutting the final massacre with nondiegetic footage of the butchering of a bull. Kuleshov, for instance, objected that the slaughter-house footage is "not prepared by a second, parallel line of action" (Kuleshov 1967:32). A more narratively motivated treatment would situate the slaughter-house in the time and space of the story, as the pet shop contextualizes the animal imagery that characterizes the spies. But it is clear that after using so many diegetically motivated metaphors—beasts, belts, lemon-squeezer, and so on—Eisenstein experimented with a more conceptual possibility.

Eisenstein prepares for the leap into nondiegetic metaphor by a rapid series of more motivated ones. Confronted by the defiant Bolshevik leader, the raging police chief pounds his desk, knocking bottles of ink across the map of the workers' district. The shot literalizes the metaphor of "the streets running with blood" (22.36). The chief slaps his hand in the pool of ink, giving himself the gory hand of the executioner. Now comes the leap. Eisenstein cuts to connect the chief's pounding gesture (22.37) to that of the butcher coming down to stab the bull (22.38), and the nondiegetic metaphor emerges—a literal slaughter in an abstract time and space, a figurative slaughter in the story world. In context, the slaughter sequence climaxes the film's experimentation with metaphor by catapulting the event into a realm outside the time and space of the story. In *October* we will find that the nondiegetic metaphors dominate the first half of the film and become "narrativized" in the course of the action.

The wide-ranging exploration of cinema's metaphorical possibilities is typical of *Strike*'s pluralistic approach. The performances, especially in the capitalist faction, constitute an anthology of contemporary theatrical styles. A similar breadth of experimentation characterizes the film's editing. At many points Eisenstein demonstrates his command of orthodox editing

Figure 22.33

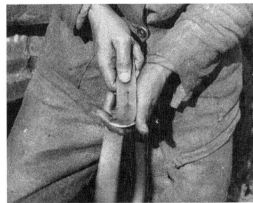

Figure 22.34

Figure 22.35

strategies: the breathless crosscutting between tumultuous strikers and the steam whistle, for instance, or the crisp shot/reverse shot when Monkey negotiates with the king. On the whole, however, the film moves a critical distance away from American-style editing and from Kuleshov's earliest work.

We have seen that Eisenstein's overlapping presentation of the wheel's assault on the foreman revises Kuleshov's reworking of American-style expansion of movement. This is only the extreme edge of a practice that pushes visual fragmentation to unprecedented limits. When Owl struggles into his pants, Eisenstein breaks the action into six shots, with slight overlaps and ellipses. As the strikers burst into the factory courtyard, seven shots of the swinging gates present graphically smooth but spatially inconsistent movement. Eisenstein often treats his sensational attractions less as discrete elements within the shot than as kinesthetic impulses to be connected by cutting. As the strikers dump the foreman and the manager into the muck, an old woman's fiercely pounding forearms continue the gesture of descent. The pulsating crowd in the hosing sequence becomes, thanks to editing, pure patterns of flowing or clashing movement.

Despite his eclecticism, Eisenstein is at pains to organize many of his editing techniques. He systematizes Kuleshov's manipulation of dissolves, superimpositions, and similar optical devices. He associates the police agents with irises and mirrors, as if to present visual analogues

Figure 22.36

Figure 22.37

Figure 22.38

of their spying (22.39). He pushes such camera tricks further when he introduces the spies as a set of animated photos (22.40), a motif that finds its parallel when the clandestine photo of the strike leader comes furtively to life. Later, the agitators meet in a cemetery (itself a token of the strike's decline), and Eisenstein superimposes the fist of the police chief hovering over a pen (22.41), not only indicating his power over them but also foreshadowing the hand that will hammer the ink-bloodied map in the last sequence.

That sequence also exhibits the most elaborate of Eisenstein's "montage of attractions." The editing certainly has some linguistic and conceptual basis. The workers are figuratively "slaughtered," and the metaphor endows the soldiers' act with the connotations of impersonal, efficient butchery. The cutting works out the conceptual parallels: as the soldiers fire, blood pours out of the bull. But Eisenstein's primary goal of provoking the spectators' emotions poses problems for the cinema. Whereas Grand Guignol theatre shocks its audience by portraying decapitations or electrocutions, the cinema, being a mediated presentation, must stir its audience to political consciousness through pictorial associations. The massacre scene can gain maximal intensity only if the filmmaker arouses the proper associations. Thus the documentary shots dwelling on the bull's torrential bloodletting and thrashing legs aim less to tease the mind than to arouse a revulsion that will take the massacre as its object. Eisenstein told a visitor that the bull's death should "stir the spectator to a state of pity and terror which would be

Figure 22.39

Figure 22.40

Figure 22.41

unconsciously and automatically transferred to the shooting of the strikers" (Freeman 1930:222).

Looking back from 1934, Eisenstein reflected that *Strike* "floundered about in the flotsam of a rank theatricality" (1934i:16), perhaps tacitly acknowledging its mixture of Eccentric and epic tendencies. It seeks to create a heroic Soviet cinema by leavening the "monumental" aesthetic of the Civil War years with elements of theatrical grotesquerie. Nevertheless, *Strike* establishes Eisenstein's creative method as one of balancing set pieces and ornamental flourishes against a pervasive unity of theme, technique, and motif. [. . .]

Notes

1. At twenty-four frames per second, Pudovkin's silent films consistently average about 2.5 seconds per shot, while Dovzhenko's range between about 3.5 and 4.5 seconds. Only Ilya Trauberg, much influenced by Eisenstein, approaches his rapid pace in *Goluboi Express* (1929), with an average shot rate of 1.7 seconds. At the same period in Hollywood, a silent film's average shot length was 5 to 6 seconds.
2. Most Soviet theatres and workers' clubs had only a single projector, so filmmakers began to construct their films in reel-length episodes. In *Strike* and *Potemkin* particularly, Eisenstein used this material constraint to demarcate stages of plot action.

Bibliography

Works by Sergei Eisenstein
1925d "The Problem of the Materialist Approach to Form." In *W*:59–64.
1928b "Literature and Cinema." *W*:95–99
1928c "Our *October*: Beyond the Played and the Non-Played." In *W*:101–106.
1928h "Zola i kino" (Zola and the cinema) *Voprosy Literatury* No. 1 (1968):98–103.
1929c "The Dramaturgy of Film Form." In *W*:161–180.
1933c "Vozvrashchenie soldata fronta" (Return of the soldier from the front). In *IP* 4:27–535.
1934i "Through Theatre to Cinema." In *FF*:3–17.
FF Film Form: Essays in Film Theory, ed. and trans. Jay Leyda (New York: Harcourt, Brace, 1949).
IP Izbrannie proizvedeniia v chesti tomakh (Selected works in six volumes) (Moscow: Iskusstvo, 1964–1969).
W Writings, 1922–1934, ed. and trans. Richard Taylor (Bloomington: Indiana University Press, 1988).

Alexandrov, Grigory. 1976. *Le cinéaste et son temps*. Trans. Antoine Garcia. Moscow: Progres, 1979.
Freeman, Joseph. 1930. "The Soviety Cinema." In Freeman *et al.*, *Voices of October: Art and Literature in Soviet Russia*. New York: Vanguard Press, 217–264.
Gerould, Daniel. 1989. "Historical Simulation and Popular Entertainment: The *Potemkin* Mutiny from Reconstructed Newsreel to Black Sea Stunt Men." *Drama Review* 33, no. 2 (Summer):161–184.
Kuleshov, Lev. 1967. "Reminiscences of Eisenstein (1967)." *Film Journal* 1, no. 3/4 (Fall–Winter 1972): 28–32.
Malevich, Kasimir. 1925. "And Images Triumph on the Screens." In *Essays on Art*, Vol.1. Trans. Xenia Glowacki-Prus and Arnold McMillan. Copenhagen: Borgen, 1971, 226–232.
Meyerhold, Vsevolod. 1925. "Intervention à la section théâtricale de l'Académie Russe des Sciences de l'Art (extrait)." In *Ecrits sur le théâtre*. Vol. 2. Trans Béatrice Picon-Vallin. Lausanne: L'Age d'Homme, 1975, 160–161.
Piotrovsky, Adrian. 1927. "Towards a Theory of Film Genres." In Eikenbaum, Boris, ed. *The Poetics of Cinema*. Trans. Richard Taylor. Special Issue, *Russian Poetics in Translation* 9 (1981), 90–106.
Shklovsky, Viktor. 1925. *Theory of Prose*. Trans. Benjamin Sher. Elmwood Park, Ill.: Dalkey Archive Press, 1990.
—— 1930. *Podenshchina* (Day Labor). Leningrad: Izdatel'stvo Pisatelei.
Willett, John. 1978. *The New Sobriety: Art and Politics in the Weimar Period, 1917–1933*. London: Thames and Hudson.

Chapter 23

JOSEPH GARNCARZ

ART AND INDUSTRY
German cinema of the 1920s

GERMAN CINEMA OF THE 1920S is often regarded as an antithesis to Hollywood. It is mainly thought of as an art cinema that produced aesthetically complex films, which may be interpreted in various ways.[1] These films include *Das Cabinet des Dr. Caligari/The Cabinet of Dr. Caligari* (1920), *Der letzte Mann/The Last Laugh* (1924) and *Metropolis* (1926). The filmmakers' self-definition seems to confirm this view. Famous German directors, screenwriters, cameramen, set designers, musicians and actors defined their task as 'making the cinema a true art form'.[2]

However, when we go beyond the established canon and analyse a larger body of films produced during this period in their historical context, we come to realize that German cinema of the 1920s was first and foremost a popular cinema, as Hollywood cinema was. Both film industries entertained mass audiences with great success by providing genre movies and star vehicles. But German cinema also differed from its Hollywood counterpart in many ways, for example concerning the special status and function of art. Striving for artistic merit was not only characteristic of the films that later became classics, but also played an important role in the German star system. Thus, it becomes possible to understand that the special characteristics of the German films of the period were not only the basis for lasting artistic recognition, but also for commercial success with contemporary audiences.

A popular national cinema

Germany had a popular cinema, which provided entertainment for a mass audience with great commercial success both nationally and internationally. No other European country produced as many films as Germany did or had as many cinemas.[3] Between 1920 and 1929, about 2,180 feature-length films (i.e. films of more than 1,000 metres in length) were produced, an equivalent of almost half of the total film output of all 33 European countries.[4] In 1920, there were already 3,500 cinemas in Germany, and by the end of the 1920s, their number had risen to over 5,000, attracting 6 million movie-goers every week.[5] Compared to other forms of entertainment, such as legitimate theatre and variety shows, cinema was the most popular pastime in Germany during the 1920s. Even in metropolitan Berlin, the centre of German theatre culture, there were twice as many cinemas as legitimate theatres and variety stages combined.[6]

In Germany, films were produced under different economic conditions than in the US. In Hollywood, only a handful of large companies shared the market. These companies formed a cartel, which operated with instruments such as the run-zone-clearance system, admission price agreements and territorial divisions.[7] There was no such cartel in Germany; instead there were a large number of small production companies, which competed fiercely. In 1926, 81 German companies produced 185 feature-length films, and 42 of these companies produced only a single film.[8] Even the two largest German film companies of the 1920s, Ufa and Emelka, only produced a relatively small number of films; in 1926, Ufa made twelve and Emelka nine films.[9] In contrast to other German film companies of the period, these two companies were vertically integrated just like the US majors were, i.e. they produced, distributed and exhibited their films. Ufa, which was founded in 1917, was the largest German film studio of the 1920s, having taken over many different production companies, for example Decla-Film, Union-Film and Messter-Film, which initially were allowed to operate with relative freedom. In 1926, Ufa produced 6.4 per cent of all films made in Germany and distributed 22.8 per cent of all films on the German market, and around 1930, the company owned 2 per cent of German cinemas. Emelka, founded in 1919, was the second largest company. In 1926, Emelka produced 4.8 per cent of all German films, distributed 2.3 per cent of all films shown in Germany and around 1930, it owned 0.8 per cent of German cinemas.

Overall, German film companies were very effective in meeting audience demand. Due to World War I, US films were not available in Germany before 1921. But even though there were years after that in which more US than German films were shown in German cinemas, it was not the US productions that German audiences favoured.[10] Data on the commercial success of films are available for Germany from the year 1925 onwards. Between 1925 and 1930, 67.6 per cent of the box-office returns were earned by German films, only 19.3 per cent by US films and 13.1 per cent by films of neighbouring European countries.[11] The great success of German genre movies and star vehicles with their domestic audience was due to their cultural specificity, not their compliance with any 'universal' standards defined by Hollywood's international productions. All societies develop specific cultural practices (beliefs, values, fashions, behaviours etc.); the less two given countries are dependent on one another, the more their cultural practices will differ.[12] Such cultural profiles are not immutable essences; some of these characteristics are relatively stable, others are in constant flux. Since people tend to find cultural representations that are familiar to them most entertaining, audiences 'naturally' prefer films produced by their own nation's film industry. German films achieved the greatest commercial success because they best reflected the values of German audiences. The economic advantage of a cartel was not sufficient for the US film industry to conquer the German export market, because US films were often incompatible with the tastes of German audiences.

Similar to Hollywood films of the period, German films used genres and stars as the two central strategies for product differentiation. The most successful German genres in the second half of the 1920s were war movies (for example *Unsere Emden / Cruiser Emden* [1926], *In Treue Stark /* Strength Through Loyalty [1926]), operettas (for example *An der schönen blauen Donau /* On the Beautiful Blue Danube [1926], *Die Försterchristl /* Christl, the Forester's Daughter [1926]), mountain films (for example *Der Kampf ums Matterhorn / Fight for the Matterhorn* [1928], *Die weiße Hölle vom Piz Palü / White Hell of Piz Palü* [1928]) and military comedies (for example *Liebe und Trompetenblasen /* Love and Trumpet-Sounds [1925]). Operettas and military comedies did not originate in the cinema, but adapted the popular traditions of musical and dramatic theatre.[13] (The star system's important role for German cinema of the 1920s will be discussed in the next section.)

Most of the contemporary US films that had been big hits with their domestic audiences, for example the Harold Lloyd vehicles *Safety Last* (released in Germany in 1924), *Girl Shy* (1926) and *The Freshman* (1926),[14] did not stand a chance with German audiences because they were culturally different. Imported productions only met with success when they could be assimilated into cultural traditions familiar to German audiences. The US films that were well-received by German movie-goers in the 1920s were set in Europe (for example *The Volga Boatman* [1926]), had Biblical themes (for example *Ben Hur* [1926]), were cast with European actors or actresses (for example *Love* [1928] with Greta Garbo) or used accepted story formulas, such as tragic endings (for example *The White Sister* [1925]).

US films were the most successful imports, but they were far from holding a dominant position in the market. Since Hollywood was the most powerful competitor, the German film industry regarded US film imports as a threat. Assuming a defensive stance against the US film industry made good sense in economic terms, because any foreign competitor, even one who was only moderately successful, cut the German film industry's share of the market. German legislation supported the national film industry by introducing import quotas and creating investment incentives. In 1925, a law was passed which restricted imports to 50 per cent. This law furthered the flow of foreign capital to Germany, because a distributor could receive an import licence for a foreign film for each German film in its programme. Consequently, US film companies produced low-budget films in Germany – some of which later became critically acclaimed classics, notably *Berlin, Sinfonie einer Großstadt/Berlin, Symphony of a Great City* (1927).

Since foreign films are only accepted by movie-goers at large when they cater to the specific preferences of their target audience, it is no surprise that German films of the 1920s were often successful in culturally closely related European countries such as Czechoslovakia, Hungary and Austria, but rarely in the US. When two given countries have film industries of unequal size (depending on the size of the population, amount of capital, legislation etc.), but have a strong cultural affinity, then the country with the larger film industry has a marked economic advantage in the export business. For example, Germany and Austria regularly distributed their total yearly film output on each other's markets; nevertheless, Germany's share of all films shown in Austria was always much larger than Austria's share of all films shown in Germany.[15] The enormous profits that Germany made with exports in the early 1920s were largely due to the general inflation during this time, but from 1924 onwards, Germany was still able to earn enough money on foreign markets to finance more than one third of its total annual film production with exports alone.[16]

The characteristics of the German star system

Apart from generic conventions, the star system was the German film industry's most effective strategy for success with its domestic audience. As in the US, stars were an important criterion for the selection of films at the box-office. Two-thirds or nine of 14 top ten films of the 1925–26 and 1926–27 seasons featured the most popular stars of the day.[17] A comparison of popularity polls shows that in Germany, over 80 per cent of the votes were allotted to the top ten stars, both male and female; in the US, by contrast, it was less than 40 per cent. This means that there was a greater consensus about favourite stars in Germany than in the US.[18] Just like US audiences, German audiences favoured stars from their own country. All German top stars, for example Henny Porten, Claire Rommer, Harry Piel, Otto Gebühr and Harry Liedtke, had made their career in German films.[19]

Even though the US and the German star system of the 1920s served the same function, namely to lure movie-goers to the cinema, the two systems reached their goal with different means. German stars displayed culturally distinctive lifestyles, attitudes and fashions. Their success was based on cultural traditions familiar to German audiences, and they represented attitudes and interests that were specific to Germany. A contemporary description of Henny Porten may serve as a striking example:

> A German woman! German not only because of her blond hair, her large eyes and her strong feminine figure! German especially because of her conception of her roles, her character, her personality, which captivatingly shines on us from the screen and touches us so appealingly and warmly, precisely because it is German![20]

In contrast to their US colleagues, German stars did not primarily define themselves through personal qualities, but through their work as actors and artists. Therefore, popular German actors and actresses disliked the term 'Star', and preferred to be called 'Filmlieblinge' (film favourites), because in their view, the US term connoted egomania, lack of talent and hype. As a contemporary observer put it: '[In the US], actors are proud finally to achieve star status, here [in Germany] they are deeply hurt by being reminded of it.'[21] The reason for this emotionally charged rejection of stardom was the fact that German actors derived their self-definition from legitimate theatre. They wanted to be respected as creative artists whose measure for excellence was the ability to play many different roles with equal brilliance.

German film actors described their work as difficult and strenuous. They frequently pointed out that they had received their training in the theatre. Eighty-one per cent of the 300 biographies of film actors in the 1926 Lexikon des Films (Dictionary of Film)[22] referred to an artistic background, with 73 per cent of the film actors claiming to have started out in the theatre. Contemporary biographical and autobiographical books on film stars also tell the life stories of artists; film acting either directly originated in the theatre or was legitimated through other links to high culture. For example, Claire Rommer, Mady Christians, Otto Gebühr, Conrad Veidt, Willy Fritsch, Ernst Hofman and Emil Jannings all claimed to have worked with Max Reinhardt, the famous German theatre director. Henny Porten and Lee Parry related that they were raised in a family of artists, and Lil Dagover liked to mention that she had been married to a stage actor.[23]

In contrast to Hollywood, which mainly differentiated its stars by disseminating information about their private lives (spouses, children, divorce, love lives, scandals),[24] German publicity gave out very little private information (birthdays, eye colour); love lives, divorce and scandals were completely taboo. German stars often refused to reveal private details, because they wanted to be respected as artists and not simply be adored for their charming personalities. 'Whenever a German film reporter wants to do something for a film star's popularity, the German film artist usually resists with all his might.'[25] In accordance with their self-definition as consummate professionals, German film actors were usually only willing to talk about private circumstances when these were in some way relevant for their professional lives, for example a spouse would be mentioned if he or she also had a connection to film or theatre. In contrast to their US colleagues, German stars were able to control their own publicity in such a rigorous manner, because they were usually not bound to a certain film company by long-term contracts, but worked as freelancers who only committed themselves to a company on a film-by-film basis.[26]

Judging by questions that readers put to the editors of fan magazines, such as Filmwoche and Film-Magazin, German audiences shared the view that stars were artists and respected their privacy to a large degree. Readers wanted to know details about the stars' physique (eye and hair colour), hobbies and families (married or single, number of children), but never touched taboo subjects (love lives, scandals). However, many questions remained unanswered. For example, a reader (named Inge) who had inquired after the name of a star's wife received the following reply: 'He does not want to reveal the name of his wife to the public . . . Alphons Fryland, dear Inge, does not at all approve of having his private affairs exposed to the public. Can you blame him for that?'.[27] Clearly, editors' policies were often more restrictive than their readers liked.

Even though, overall, German cinema of the 1920s was very successful in commercial terms, reticence about stars' private lives was not the only instance of supply not meeting demand. Even when movie-goers clearly articulated their wishes at the box-office or by fan mail, the film industry sometimes refused to cater to audience demands, especially when ethical considerations or artistic ambitions were concerned. Another example of this is the fact that no films starring children were produced in Germany during this period, even though the German audience loved child stars and there was no shortage of talented German child actors. Foreign child stars were among the German audience's absolute favourites. For example, Jackie 'The Kid' Coogan was the most popular US star in Germany (in popularity polls between 1923 and 1926 he received 2.8 per cent of the votes for the most popular male actor, reaching no. 11). German producers refused to satisfy audience demand for child stars, because allowing children to work like adults and exposing them to public attention was regarded as taboo.[28]

The special case of Ufa

The degree to which the German film industry's creative personnel were able to realize their artistic vision depended on a number of factors, including the professional group they belonged to and the structure of the company in which they worked. Actors usually had less artistic control than directors. The smaller a production company was, the more it was forced under free-market conditions to orient its production towards audience demand, because losses could not be compensated. Since most of the German production companies of the 1920s were very small, the margin for artistic innovation was narrow. Thus, the greater part of the artistically ambitious German films of the 1920s were produced by the few existing larger companies.[29]

It was Ufa that developed the greatest artistic potential. Its most famous films were produced in the short span of three years, when Erich Pommer was head of production, between February 1923 and January 1926. Pommer wanted to produce films that were expensive and artistically innovative, suitable for the international market while being typically German. His thirty productions during this period include *Michael/Chained* (1924), *Der letzte Mann/The Last Laugh* (1924), *Tartüff/Tartuffe* (1925), *Varieté/Variety* (1925), *Faust* (1926) and *Metropolis* (1926).

Ufa's directors, notably Fritz Lang, Friedrich Wilhelm Murnau, Ewald André Dupont and Ludwig Berger, enjoyed the status of auteurs. In 1920s Hollywood, the central producer supervised the shooting-script, which served as the blueprint for the finished film, before the director began to work on the picture.[30] Pommer, by contrast, only gave organisational and creative support to his directors, who planned and controlled their own films from beginning to end. With this production system, Ufa adapted the established practices of the German theatre, which had made the director the focal point of the creative process and of advertising. In the nineteenth century, the director had merely been one of the actors of the troupe who fulfilled organisational functions (for example he saw to it that the actors learned their roles properly and that they arrived on time for rehearsals and performances), but in the early twentieth century, in the most prestigious German theatres, directing became an independent, creative profession.[31] Directors like Max Reinhardt were artists who brought a unique style to their own productions, and this became the most important incentive for audiences to go to the theatre.[32] Furthermore, Ufa's directors each worked with a permanent staff, in analogy to the stock companies of German theatre.

Ufa's directors not only exercised artistic control over the production process, their artistic vision was also respected in the planning of budgets. As a member of the company's board, Pommer represented the directors' interests in financial matters. Being the largest German film company, Ufa could provide Pommer and his directors with capital as no other German company during this period could. Furthermore, Pommer was also generous in organisational matters, for example concerning scripts, production plans and dates of premieres.

These special production conditions at Ufa enabled directors to cultivate unique styles. Historiographers have consequently analysed many films of this period as oeuvres of individual artists. Since there were no companies with comparable production conditions in the US, the degree of stylistic variation was much greater in German cinema than in Hollywood at the time. The Ufa directors made films that adapted and synthesized genres and movements of the established arts, notably Kammerspiel, New Objectivity, and Expressionism, and together with their collaborators they developed new techniques, for example the unchained camera and the Schüfftan-process.[33] Expressionist films, for example, have a striking visual style, which extremely distorts everyday objects, such as houses, furniture and streets, to symbolize the inner conflicts of characters.[34] In the early 1920s, a series of Expressionist films were made by several companies, including Ufa, for example *Das Cabinet des Dr. Caligari / The Cabinet of Dr. Caligari* (1920, produced by Decla)[35] and *Das Wachsfigurenkabinett / Waxworks* (1924, produced by Ufa/Neptun). Afterwards, expressionist elements remained fashionable in many Ufa-films; for example, the eerie shape of Rotwang's house in *Metropolis* (1926) characterizes its owner as a mad scientist.

Directors not only held a special position in the production process, but also in the marketing of films, a fact that was already noted by contemporaries: 'Many companies [especially Ufa] group their productions according to the names of their directors, so that one speaks, for example, of Ufa's Lang film or Murnau film or even National-Film-Gesellschaft's Gerhard Lamprecht production.'[36] Fritz Lang was the top star among directors: some of the posters for his films *Die Nibelungen / The Nibelungs* (1924) and *Metropolis* (1926) display solely his name instead of the actors' names (see Figs 23.1 and 23.2). This, however, was an exception; for example, for the Ufa production *Ein Walzertraum / The Waltz Dream* (1925), advertisements not only used the director Ludwig Berger, but also the stars Willy Fritsch, Xenia Desni and Mady Christians.[37]

Ufa's prestigious productions were highly praised by contemporaries. They found critical acclaim in the press. And in relation to its share of the total output of German films, Ufa received the highest number of commendations by the Bildstelle des Zentralinstituts für Erziehung und Unterricht (Film Bureau of the Central Institute for Education and Teaching). Apart from organizing the exhibition of films in schools, this institute, which was founded in 1919, rated films according to their educational and artistic merit, and taxes on movie tickets with such a rating were reduced. In 1926, 185 German films were released; all 12 Ufa releases received the coveted commendation, while only four films from other companies did.[38] Thus, contemporary recognition confirmed the exceptional position as the centre of film art that Ufa held in the German film industry of the 1920s.

However, Ufa faced increasing economic problems. Its financial difficulties began as early as 1924.[39] The main reason for this was not the general crisis of the German film industry after the end of hyperinflation, which led to the demise of companies that had thrived on high profits

Figure 23.1
Metropolis poster

made by selling low-budget films to foreign countries. Ufa's troubles were primarily self-inflicted: apart from large-scale expansion both on the domestic market and abroad (i.e. the acquisition of production facilities, distributors and cinemas), the main reasons were a) the films themselves, b) production methods and c) marketing. Since it was the head of production who was largely responsible for this, Pommer left Ufa in January 1926, when it became clear that *Metropolis* would become a financial disaster.

a) Art and business were not necessarily mutually exclusive: some artistically ambitious films were very well-received by audiences at large, for example *Faust* (1926, no. 13 in the hit list of 1926/27) and *Metropolis* (1926, no. 4 in the hit list of 1927/28). However, it was not Lang's director's cut of *Metropolis* (only shown in Berlin between November 1926 and April 1927), which was such a success with audiences. When box-office returns proved to be disappointing, Ufa decided to nationally distribute the film in a new version, which was shortened by almost a quarter and significantly changed in content.[40] Overall, Ufa's strategy of producing art films was less successful in commercial terms than, for example, Emelka's strategy of producing popular entertainment without artistic aspirations. In 1926/27, for instance, Emelka released nine films (of a total of 487 films shown in German cinemas), of which three

Figure 23.2
Die Nibelungen poster

made the top ten, i.e. the romantic comedy *Ich habe mein Herz in Heidelberg verloren*/I Lost My Heart in Heidelberg (1926, no. 2), the war movie *Unsere Emden*/*Cruiser Emden* (1926, no. 6) and the operetta *Die Försterchristl*/Christl, the Forester's Daughter (1926, no. 7); Ufa, by comparison, released 12 films, but only one of them made the top ten, the operetta *Ein Walzertraum*/*The Waltz Dream* (1925, no. 10).[41]

b) Ufa's organisation of production was its main problem. Budgets were planned with too much indulgence of directors' artistic demands, not in accordance with expected box-office returns. The production of *Metropolis* (from May 1925 to October 1926) was the culmination point of this practice: the film was a financial disaster despite its popularity with audiences. As a rule, a film could break even on the German market if it cost no more than 400,000 Marks, but the budget for *Metropolis* was originally fixed at 1.5 million Marks – which means that high hopes were set on the film becoming an international success.[42] But Fritz Lang realized his artistic vision without compromise and exceeded the budget more than fourfold, so that the total cost of the film amounted to 6 million Marks. *Metropolis* was simply too expensive to break even, much less make a profit.

c) The marketing strategy of making the director the focal point of advertising was no guarantee for success with audiences at large. The strategy worked well with Fritz Lang, because his name stood for a certain type of film, i.e. films of monumental scale with striking production values, such as the science fiction films *Metropolis* (1926) and *Die Frau im Mond/Woman in the Moon* (1929, produced by Ufa/Fritz Lang-Film). But as a rule, stars proved to be bigger draws at the box-office than directors, as an analysis of the top films in 1925/26 and 1926/27 shows. Thus, using the director's prestige as a marketing tool was not a response to audience demand, but rather reflected, as a contemporary put it, 'the great significance . . . for a film's production process'[43] that German film elites attributed to the director's role.

Ufa's reorganisation

To pull itself out of its financial difficulties, Ufa borrowed 4 million dollars from Paramount and Metro-Goldwyn in 1925, and supplied 50 per cent of the screen time of its cinemas in return.[44] However, this so-called Parufamet-agreement was counter-productive for Ufa, because little money could be made with US films in Germany at the time (as explained above). An internal study by Ufa, which analyses the revenues of every film Ufa distributed in the 1925/26 season, shows that of the 53 US films distributed by Ufa 39, i.e. 73 per cent, lost more than 10,000 Marks each. Only three of the US films, *The Lighthouse by the Sea*, *The Navigator* and *He Who Gets Slapped* (all three released in Germany in 1925), made a profit.[45] Thus, by reserving screen time for US productions instead of showing its own, Ufa was actually increasing its deficit. This internal report provided the basis for the successful renegotiation of the agreement between Ufa's new management and the American companies in August 1927.

In March 1927, the Hugenberg group took over Ufa, and the company was completely reorganized by Ludwig Klitzsch. The aim was to consistently orient films towards audience demand and to make production processes economically efficient. Ufa's production subsidiaries, which had formerly operated with relative independence, now became fully integrated. Economic and creative control were strictly separated, with directors being subordinated to producers. The producer-unit system, i.e. production groups led by different producers, was thus introduced.[46] Ernst Hugo Correll became head of production in 1928; producers who worked under him were Bruno Duday, Alfred Zeisler, Arnold Pressburger, Günther Stapenhorst – as well as the re-employed Erich Pommer.

Film production was no longer organized according to the principle of artistic creation, but along the lines of economic efficiency. The experimental, innovative style of the Ufa directors was disciplined by shooting scripts, fixed production plans and strict budgets. When the director ceased to be the creative centre of production, the style of Ufa's films became more standardized. But the cultural specificity of German films continued to be cultivated, because this was the basis of the German film industry's success with its audience.

Around 1928/29, Ufa, in accordance with its new market orientation, adapted the presentation of its stars more to the audience's wishes.[47] Compared to other publications, magazines that were connected with Ufa in one way or another began to reveal more information about the stars' private lives. The new postulate was:

> Film stars do not have any 'private affairs'. They must not be allowed to have any.
> To whom they are engaged, to whom they are married, whom they divorce and why, and why there are no children – all this must be openly discussed in public.[48]

Beginning in 1929, information on spouses can be found in greater frequency even when they were not artists by profession. For example, the interested reader could learn that

Henny Porten was married to Dr. Ritter von Kaufmann, a medical doctor, and Claire Rommer was the wife of Adolf Strenger, a businessman. Nevertheless, the discourse was still centred on the star as artist, and scandals were still taboo. The new form of reporting stayed true to the basic cultural consensus between producers and audience that was the condition for stars to be accepted in Germany, but it also narrowed the gap between supply and demand that had existed before.

Thus, Ufa fell in line with the principles of consistent market orientation, which most of the German film companies had been observing all along. Ufa's new strategies were successful. In 1926–27, Emelka had produced three of the top ten films of the year, but Ufa only one. In 1930–31, however, three of Ufa's films made the top ten; the top-hit of the season, the comic operetta *Die Drei von der Tankstelle/Three Good Friends* (1930, no. 1), the national heritage film *Das Flötenkonzert von Sanssouci/The Flute Concert of Sans-Souci* (1930, no. 3) and the drama *Der blaue Engel/The Blue Angel* (1930, no. 10). No other film company could boast more than one top-ten film that season.

Conclusion

German cinema of the 1920s provided entertainment for a mass audience with great success. Many small companies, which could not afford a single flop, were forced to orient their production as consistently as possible towards audience demand. Most foreign films, including those from Hollywood, were not popular with German audiences, because they were not compatible with their expectations. The genre movies and star vehicles the German film industry produced were preferred, because they expressed the German audience's own values. The contemporary success of German cinema was due to the fact that the German film industry produced films that were culturally specific, not because they adapted 'universal' standards defined by Hollywood's international productions.

Art films, which are often identified with German films of the 1920s, only make up a small part of the total German film output during this decade. Since larger companies had greater capacities for innovation and Pommer was dedicated to furthering film art, Ufa became the centre of creative filmmaking between 1923 and 1926. But due to uncompromising artistic ideals, overly extravagant production methods and misjudgements in marketing Ufa almost went bankrupt. Ufa was successfully reorganized, and this entailed falling in line with economically efficient, demand-oriented practices. The entire scope of German cinema of the 1920s has not yet been analysed in detail.

Notes

Translation by Annemone Ligensa.

1   Lotte Eisner, *The Haunted Screen*, London: Thames & Hudson, 1969 (first published in French, 1952); Siegfried Kracauer, *From Caligari to Hitler: A Psychological History of the German Film*, Princeton: Princeton University Press, 1974 (first published 1947); Paul Monaco, *Cinema & Society: France and Germany During the Twenties*, New York: Elsevier, 1976; Thomas Elsaesser, *Weimar Cinema and After*, London: Routledge, 2000.

2   Peter Perscheid, 'Und wenn nun gar . . .!', *Die Filmwoche* 30, 1925. Cp. also the anthology Rolf Aurich and Wolfgang Jacobsen (eds), *Werkstatt Film: Selbstverständnis und Visionen von Filmleuten der zwanziger Jahre*, München: edition text + kritik, 1998.

3   John Trumpbour, *Selling Hollywood to the World: U.S. and European Struggles for Mastery of the Global Film Industry, 1920–1950*, Cambridge: Cambridge University Press, 2002, p. 5.

4   Alexander Jason, *Handbuch der Filmwirtschaft: Jahrgang 1930*, Berlin: Verlag für Presse, Wirtschaft und Politik, 1930, p. 38; Herbert Birett, Database of German feature films released between 1920 and 1929, unpublished. Analyzing a representative corpus of films is difficult: more than 50 per cent of the German films of the period are probably lost, and extant films are often only available in significantly altered versions. Cp. Martin Koerber, 'Notes on the proliferation of the film *Metropolis*', in Wolfgang Jacobson and Werner Sudendorf (eds), *Metropolis: Ein filmisches Laboratorium der modernen Architektur/A Cinematic Laboratory for Modern Architecture*, Stuttgart, London: Edition Axel Menges, 2000, pp. 209–217; Joseph Garncarz, 'Fritz Lang's *M*: A Case of Significant Film Variation', *Film History* 4.3, 1990, 219–226.

5   Alexander Jason, *Handbuch der Filmwirtschaft: Jahrgang 1930*, op. cit., p. 134; Alexander Jason, *Handbuch der Filmwirtschaft: Band II: Film-Europa*, Berlin: Verlag für Presse, Wirtschaft und Politik, 1930, p. 14.

6   Statistisches Amt der Stadt Berlin (ed.), *Statistisches Jahrbuch der Stadt Berlin*, Berlin 1923 ff: Otto Stollberg; 1926, vol. 2, p. 147; 1927, vol. 3, p. 189; 1930, vol. 6, p. 210.

7   Douglas Gomery, *The Hollywood Studio System*, London: BFI, 1986, pp. 1–25.

8   Alexander Jason, *Handbuch der Filmwirtschaft: Jahrgang 1930*, op. cit., p. 41.

9   On Ufa: Rahel Lipschütz, *Der Ufa-Konzern: Geschichte, Aufbau und Bedeutung im Rahmen des deutschen Filmgewerbes*, Berlin: 1932, pp. 33–44; Hans-Michael Bock and Michael Töteberg (eds), *Das Ufa-Buch*, Frankfurt am Main: Zweitausendeins, 1992; Klaus Kreimeier, *The Ufa Story: A History of Germany's Greatest Film Company, 1918–1945*, New York: Hill & Wang, 1996. On Emelka: Petra Putz, *Waterloo in Geiselgasteig: Die Geschichte des Münchner Filmkonzerns Emelka (1919–1933) im Antagonismus zwischen Bayern und dem Reich*, Trier: WVT, 1996.

10 Kristin Thompson (*Exporting Entertainment: America in the World Film Market, 1907–1934*, London: BFI, 1985, p. 125) measures the success of US films in foreign countries by the number of exported films. However, the supply of films is not in itself an adequate indicator for demand in films, which should be measured by the number of tickets sold.

11 *Film-Kurier* 129, 2 June 1930, p. 2, reprinted in: Alexander Jason, *Handbuch der Filmwirtschaft: Jahrgang 1930*, op. cit., p. 60. Similar conclusions are also reached by Irmalotte Guttmann, *Über die Nachfrage auf dem Filmmarkt in Deutschland*, Berlin: Gebr. Wolffsohn GmbH, 1928.

12 Cp Norbert Elias, *The Society of Individuals*, Oxford: Blackwell, 1991; Norbert Elias, *The Germans: Power Struggles and the Development of Habitus in the Nineteenth and Twentieth Centuries*, Oxford: Polity Press, 1996.

13 Malte Hagener and Jans Hans (eds), *Als die Filme singen lernten: Innovation und Tradition im Musikfilm 1928–1938*, München: edition text + kritik, 1999; Knut Hickethier and Marcus Bier, 'Militärschwänke im Kino der zwanziger Jahre', in Harro Segeberg (ed.), *Die Perfektionierung des Scheins: Das Kino der Weimarer Republik im Kontext der Künste*, München: Wilhelm Fink, 1999, 67–93.

14 Richard Koszarski, *An Evening's Entertainment: The Age of the Silent Feature Picture, 1915–1928*, Berkeley: University of California Press, 1990, p. 33.

15 Alexander Jason, *Handbuch des Films 1935/36*, Berlin: Hoppenstedt & Co., 1935, p. 109 and p. 127.

16 Alexander Jason, *Handbuch der Filmwirtschaft: Jahrgang 1930*, op. cit., p. 42; Alexander Jason, *Handbuch der Filmwirtschaft: Band II: Film-Europa*, op. cit., p. 18.

17 This can be shown by comparing the top ten lists of stars with the top ten lists of films. The top ten lists of German film stars can be found in: Joseph Garncarz, 'Made in Germany: Multiple-Language Versions and the Early German Sound Cinema', in Andrew Higson and Richard Maltby (eds), *'Film Europe' and 'Film America': Cinema, Commerce and Cultural Exchange, 1920–1939*, Exeter: University of Exeter Press, 1999, p. 264. The top ten lists of German films can be found in: Joseph Garncarz, 'Hollywood in Germany: The Role of American Films in Germany 1925–1990', in David W. Ellwood and Rob Kroes (eds), *Hollywood in Europe: Experiences of a Cultural Hegemony*, Amsterdam: VU University Press, 1994, p. 122.

18 This is one of the results of Annemone Ligensa's forthcoming dissertation on stardom.

19 Joseph Garncarz, 'Warum kennen Filmhistoriker viele Weimarer Topstars nicht mehr? Überlegungen am Beispiel Claire Rommer', *montage/av: Zeitschrift für Theorie & Geschichte audiovisueller Kommunikation* 6.2, 1997, 64–92.

20 'Henny Porten – eine deutsche Frauengestalt', *Die Filmwoche* 3, 1925.

21 'Als Komparse mit nach Staaken', *Die Filmwoche* 31, 1925.

22 Kurt Mühsam and Egon Jacobsohn, *Lexikon des Films*, Berlin: Verlag der Lichtbildbühne, 1926.

23 Henny Porten, *Wie ich wurde*, Berlin: Volkskraft-Verlag, 1919; Gustaf Holberg, *Henny Porten: Eine Biographie unserer beliebten Filmkünstlerin*, Berlin: Verlag der Lichtbildbühne, [1920]; Walter Gottfried Lohmeyer (ed.), *Das Otto Gebühr-Buch*, Berlin: Scherl, 1927.

24   Richard deCordova, *Picture Personalities: The Emergence of the Star System in America*, Urbana: University of Illinois Press, 2001.

25   *Filmwoche* 17, 1924, p. 334–335.

26   Joseph Garncarz, 'Playing Garbo: How Marlene Dietrich Conquered Hollywood', in Gerd Gemunden and Mary Desjardins (eds), *Marlene at 100*, forthcoming.

27   Collage of quotes from: 'Pazzo's Briefe', *Filmwoche* 44, 1925, p. 1046; 'Pazzo's Briefe', *Filmwoche* 28, 1925, p. 652.

28   Joseph Garncarz, 'Warum gab es im Stummfilmkino keine deutschen Kinderstars?', in Frank Kessler, Sabine Lenk, Martin Loiperdinger (eds), *KINtop: Jahrbuch zur Erforschung des frühen Films* 7, 1998, 99–111.

29   Concerning this point I differ from Kristin Thompson's position; Cp Kristin Thompson, 'Early Alternatives to the Hollywood Mode of Production: Implications for Europe's Avant-gardes', *Film History* 5.4, 1993, 386–404.

30   David Bordwell, Janet Staiger, and Kristin Thompson, *The Classical Hollywood Cinema: Film Style & Mode of Production to 1960*, London: Routledge & Kegan Paul, 1985, p. 128.

31   Michael Hays, 'Theater and Mass Culture: The Case of the Director', *New German Critique*, 29, Spring–Summer 1983, 133–146.

32   When Alfred Hitchcock worked for Ufa as a set-designer on the film *Die Prinzessin und der Geiger/The Blackguard* in 1924, he became acquainted with 'auteur-cinema' – an idea he adopted in his work in Britain and the US, where it was unusual at the time. See Joseph Garncarz, 'German Hitchcock', *Hitchcock Annual*, 2000–01, 73–99, reprinted in Sidney Gottlieb and Christopher Brookhouse (eds), *Framing Hitchcock: Selected Essays from the Hitchcock Annual*, Detroit: Wayne State University Press, 2002, 59–81.

33   For a discussion of aesthetic aspects see, for example, Kristin Thompson and David Bordwell, 'Germany in the 20s', in Kristin Thompson and David Bordwell, *Film History: An Introduction*, New York: McGraw–Hill, 1994, 105–127.

34   Jürgen Kasten, *Der expressionistische Film*, Münster: Maks, 1990; Barry Salt, 'From Caligari to Who?', *Sight and Sound*, Spring 1979, 119–123.

35   Pommer was not involved in *Caligari*'s production, only in its foreign distribution. See Wolfgang Jacobsen, *Erich Pommer: Ein Produzent macht Filmgeschichte*, Berlin: Argon, 1989, p. 39.

36   Kurt Mühsam, *Film und Kino*, Dessau: C. Dünnhaupt, 1927, p. 36.

37   See the advertisements for the premiere of this film in *Lichtbildbühne* 255, 12 December 1925, p. 7 and p. 261, 19 December 1925, p. 17.

38   Rahel Lipschütz, *Der Ufa-Konzern*, op. cit,. p. 37.

39   Ibid., p. 13.

40   Cf Thomas Elsaesser, *Metropolis*, London: BFI, 2000, pp. 30–42.

41   'Das Ergebnis der Abstimmung. 3500 Einzelurteile. Die führenden Kinos haben sich beteiligt', *Film-Kurier* 85, 9 April 1927, cover page.

42   Alexander Jason, *Handbuch der Filmwirtschaft: Jahrgang 1930*, op. cit., p. 59; Wolfgang Jacobson and Werner Sudendorf (eds), *Metropolis*, op. cit., p. 11.

43   Kurt Mühsam, *Film und Kino*, op. cit., p. 36.

44   Thomas P. Saunders, 'Rettung in den Verlust: Die Parufamet-Verträge', Hans-Michael Bock and Michael Töteberg (eds), *Das Ufa-Buch*, Frankfurt am Main: Zweitausendeins, 1992, 174–179.

45   Revisionsabteilung der Ufa, 'Bericht über Revision der Geschäftsbücher und der Bilanz für das am 31. Mai 1926 abgelaufene Geschäftsjahr', Berlin, Ufa R1091/2440 (in the Bundesarchiv, Berlin).

46   In Hollywood, the producer-unit system became standard in 1931. David Bordwell, Janet Staiger, and Kristin Thompson, *The Classical Hollywood Cinema*, op. cit., p. 320.

47   See the minutes of the Ufa board meetings on 29 May 1928 and 10 August 1928 (in the Bundesarchiv, Berlin).

48   Dr. R. Roth, 'Sind Stars Privatpersonen?', *Filmwoche* 27, 1929, 635 and 638.

Bibliography

WHILE A LOT OF IMPORTANT film historical work is published in other languages, this bibliography only lists English language publications. In addition to books, a selection of special issues of academic journals have been included; some of these deal only in parts with silent cinema. There is an extensive critical and biographical literature on many stars and directors active during the silent era; only few such books are included. Furthermore, there are a large number of film journals which regularly contain essays on the silent period, for example *Film History, Screen, Cinema Journal, Historical Journal of Film, Radio and Television, Iris* and *Griffithiana*. Such essays are not listed here, unless they are part of one of the special issues we have highlighted.

The bibliography first lists four introductions to the writing of film history. This is followed by two sections on international developments during the silent period. The first consists of publications which contain case studies from several countries or provide international overviews. The second deals more specifically with the relationship between American cinema and the world, covering both the impact of European film-makers and companies on American cinema, and the impact of American films around the world. The remaining sections of this bibliography deal with particular countries or regions, presented in alphabetical order.

Wherever possible, sections are divided into listings for secondary literature and for books reprinting primary sources. Primary sources are texts such as reviews, magazine articles and books produced during the silent period; the secondary literature consists of later publications which are based on the examination of such primary print sources and, of course, of the films themselves. Numerous silent films are available on video or DVD from a number of companies, especially Kino Video, Grapevine Video and the British Film Institute.

By and large, our bibliography is made up of recent publications, based on the most extensive and in-depth research and thus often superseding older studies, which therefore do not need to be included. However, we have listed a number of older publications which have not been surpassed by recent work. Furthermore, the paucity of recent research in some areas made it necessary to include older studies which are exploratory rather than definitive.

Film historiography

Allen, Robert C., and Douglas Gomery, *Film History: Theory and Practice* (New York: Knopf, 1985).
Thompson, Kristin, and David Bordwell, *Film History: An Introduction* (New York: McGraw-Hill, 1997).
Film History, vol. 6, no. 1 (1994), special issue on the philosophy of film history.
Usai, Paolo Cherchi, *Silent Cinema: An Introduction* (London: BFI, 2000).

International silent cinema

Primary sources

Herbert, Stephen (ed.), *A History of Pre-Cinema*, 3 Volumes (London: Routledge, 1999).
Herbert, Stephen (ed.), *A History of Early Film*, 3 Volumes (London: Routledge, 2000).
Lant, Antonia, and Ingrid Perez (eds), *The Red Velvet Seat: Women's Writings on the Cinema – The First Fifty Years* (New York: Verso, 2003).

Secondary literature

Abel, Richard (ed.), *Silent Film* (New Brunswick: Rutgers University Press, 1996).
Abel, Richard (ed.), *Encyclopedia of Early Cinema* (New York: Routledge, 2004).
Abel, Richard, and Rick Altman (eds), *The Sounds of Early Cinema* (Bloomington: Indiana University Press, 2001).
Acker, Ally, *Reel Women: Pioneers of the Cinema, 1896 to the Present* (New York: Continuum, 1990).
Armes, Roy, *Third World Film Making and the West* (Berkeley: University of California Press, 1987).
Barnouw, Erik, *A History of the Non-Fiction Film* (Oxford: Oxford University Press, 1993).
Barsam, Richard M., *Nonfiction Film: A Critical History* (Bloomington: Indiana University Press, 1992).
Bean, Jennifer M., and Diane Negra (eds), *A Feminist Reader in Early Cinema* (Durham: Duke University Press, 2002).
Bordwell, David, *On the History of Film Style* (Cambridge: Harvard University Press, 1997).
Bratton, Jacky, Jim Cook, and Christine Gledhill (eds), *Melodrama: Stage, Picture, Screen* (London: BFI, 1994).
Brewster, Ben, and Lea Jacobs, *Theatre to Cinema: Stage Pictorialism and the Early Feature Film* (Oxford: Oxford University Press, 1997).
Burch, Noël, *Life to Those Shadows* (London: BFI, 1990).
Burch, Noël, *In and Out of Synch: The Awakening of a Cine-Dreamer* (Aldershot: Scolar Press, 1991).
Camera Obscura, no. 48 (2001), special issue on early women stars.
Charney, Leo, and Vanessa R. Schwartz (eds), *Cinema and the Invention of Modern Life* (Berkeley: University of California Press, 1995).
Christie, Ian, *The Last Machine: Early Cinema and the Birth of the Modern World* (London: BFI, 1994).
Cosandey, Roland, André Gaudreault, and Tom Gunning (eds), *An Invention of the Devil? Religion and Early Cinema* (Lausanne: Editions Payot, 1992).
Cosandey, Roland, and Francois Albera (eds), *Images Across Borders* (Lausanne: Editions Payot, 1995).
Crafton, Donald, *Before Mickey: The Animated Film, 1898–1928* (Cambridge, MA: MIT Press, 1982).
Dall'Asta, Monica, Gugliemo Pescatore, and Leonardo Quaresima (eds), *Color in Silent Cinema* (Bologna: Mano, 1996).
Dibbets, Karel, and Bert Hogenkamp (eds), *Film and the First World War* (Amsterdam: Amsterdam University Press, 1995).
Dissanayake, Wimal (ed.), *Melodrama and Asian Cinema* (Cambridge: Cambridge University Press, 1993).
Drummond, Philip *et al.*, *Film as Film: Formal Experiment in Film, 1910–1975* (London: Hayward Gallery, 1979).
Dupré la Tour, Claire, André Gaudreault and Roberta Pearson (eds), *Cinema at the Turn of the Century* (Quebec: Editions Nota bene, 1999).
Dyer, Richard, *Now You See It: Studies in Lesbian and Gay Film* (London: Routledge, 2003).
Dyer, Richard, and Ginette Vincendeau (eds), *Popular European Cinema* (London: Routledge, 1992).
Elsaesser, Thomas (ed.), *Early Cinema: Space–Frame–Narrative* (London: BFI, 1990).
Fell, John L., *Film and the Narrative Tradition* (Norman: Oklahoma University Press 1974).

Fell, John L. (ed.), *Film Before Griffith* (Berkeley: University of California Press, 1983).

Film History, vol. 5, no. 4 (1993), special issue on institutional histories.

Film History, vol. 6, no. 2 (1994), special issue on exhibition.

Film History, vol. 6, no. 4(1994), special issue on audiences.

Film History, vol. 7, no. 2 (1995), special issue: 'A Chronology of Cinema 1889–1896'.

Film History, vol. 7, no. 3 (1995), special issue on film preservation and film scholarship.

Film History, vol. 8, no. 3 (1996), special issue on nation, national identity and the international cinema.

Film History, vol. 8, no. 4 (1996), special issue on international trends in Film Studies.

Film History, vol. 9, no. 1 (1997), special issue on silent cinema.

Film History, vol. 9, no. 3 (1997), special issue on screenwriters and screenwriting.

Film History, vol. 9, no. 4 (1997), special issue on international cinema of the 1910s.

Film History, vol. 10, no. 1 (1998), special issue on cinema pioneers.

Film History, vol. 11, no. 2 (1999), special issue on film technology.

Film History, vol. 11, no. 2 (1999), special issue on filmmakers and filmmaking.

Film History, vol. 11, no. 4 (1999), special issue on global experiments in early synchronous sound.

Film History, vol. 12, no. 1 (2000), special issue on oral history.

Film History, vol. 12, no. 2 (2000), special issue on moving image archives.

Film History, vol. 12, no. 4 (2000), special issue on colour film.

Fisher, Lucy, *Designing Women: Cinema, Art Deco, and the Female Form* (New York: Columbia University Press, 2003).

Forbes, Jill, and Sarah Street (eds), *European Cinema: An Introduction* (New York: Palgrave, 2000).

Franceschetti, Anja, and Leonardo Quaresima (eds), *Before the Author* (Udine: Forum, 1997).

Fullerton, John (ed.), *Celebrating 1895: The Centenary of Cinema* (London: John Libbey, 1998).

Fullerton, John, and Astrid Soderbergh Widding (eds), *Moving Images: From Edison to the Webcam* (Sydney: John Libbey, 2000).

Hecht, Hermann, *Pre-Cinema History: An Encyclopedia and Annotated Bibliography of the Moving Image Before 1896* (London: Bowker/BFI, 1993).

Hertogs, Dan, and Nico de Klerk (eds), *Uncharted Territory: Essays on Early Nonfiction Film* (Amsterdam: Nederlands Filmmuseum, 1997).

Hjort, Mette, and Scott MacKenzie (eds), *Cinema and Nation* (London: Routledge, 2000).

Hoberman, J., *Bridge of Light: Yiddish Film between Two Worlds* (New York: Schocken, 1991).

Holman, Roger (ed.), *Cinema 1900–1906: An Analytic Study* (Brussels: FIAF, 1982).

Kelly, Andrew, *Cinema and the Great War* (London: Routledge, 1997).

Kuhn, Annette, *Cinema, Censorship and Sexuality, 1909–1925* (London: Routledge, 1988).

Mannoni, Laurent, *The Great Art of Light and Shadow: Archeology of the Cinema* (Exeter: University of Exeter Press, 2001).

Nowell-Smith, Geoffrey (ed.), *The Oxford History of World Cinema* (Oxford: Oxford University Press, 1996).

Pitassio, Francesco, and Leonardo Quaresima (eds), *Writing and Image: Titles in Silent Cinema* (Udine: Forum, 1998).

Popple, Simon, and Joe Kember, *Early Cinema: From Factory Gate to Dream Factory* (London: Wallflower, 2003).

Popple, Simon, and Vanessa Toulmin (eds), *Visual Delights: Essays on the Popular and Projected Image in the 19th Century* (Trowbridge: Flicks, 2001).

Quaresima, Leonardo, Alessandra Raengo, and Laura Vichi (eds), *The Birth of Film Genres* (Udine: Forum, 1999).

Quaresima, Leonardo, and Laura Vichi (eds), *The Tenth Muse: Cinema and Other Arts* (Udine: Forum, 2001).

Reeves, Nicholas, *The Power of Film Propaganda: Myth or Reality?* (London: Cassell, 1999).

Rossell, Deac, *Living Pictures: The Origins of the Movies* (Albany: State University of New York Press, 1998).

Salt, Barry, *Film Style and Technology: History and Analysis* (London: Starword, 1992).

Smither, Roger (ed.), *This Film Is Dangerous: A Celebration of Nitrate Film* (Brussels: FIAF, 2002).

Stollery, Martin, *Alternative Empires: European Modernist Cinemas and Cultures of Imperialism* (Exeter: University of Exeter Press, 2000).

Vincendeau, Ginette (ed.), *Encyclopedia of European Cinema* (London: Cassell, 1995).

Williams, Christopher (ed.), *Cinema: The Beginnings and the Future* (London: University of Westminster Press, 1996).

Yale Journal of Criticism, vol. 7, no. 2 (1994): special issue on early cinema.

American cinema and the world

Abel, Richard, *The Red Rooster Scare: Making Cinema American, 1900–1910* (Berkeley: University of California Press, 1999).

Baxter, John, *The Hollywood Exiles* (London: MacDonald and Jane's, 1976).

Berton, Pierre, *Hollywood's Canada: The Americanization of Our National Image* (Toronto: McClelland and Stewart, 1975).

Burton, Alan, and Laraine Porter (eds), *Crossing the Pond: Anglo-American Relations Before 1930* (Trowbridge: Flicks, 2002).

Ellwood, David and Rob Kroes (eds), *Hollywood in Europe* (Amsterdam: VU University Press, 1994).

Griffiths, Alison, *Wondrous Difference: Cinema, Anthropology, and Turn-of-the-Century Visual Culture* (New York: Columbia University Press, 2002).

Higson, Andrew, and Richard Maltby (eds), *'Film Europe' and 'Film America': Cinema, Commerce and Cultural Exchage, 1920–1939* (Exeter: University of Exeter Press, 1999).

Jarvie, Ian, *Hollywood's Overseas Campaign: The North Atlantic Movie Trade, 1920–1950* (Cambridge: Cambridge University Press, 1992).

Langman, Larry, *Destination Hollywood: The Influence of Europeans on American Filmmaking* (Jefferson: McFarland, 2000).

Pendakur, Manjunath, *Canadian Dreams and American Control: The Political Economy of the Canadian Film Industry* (Detroit: Wayne State University Press, 1990).

Petrie, Graham, *Hollywood Destinies: European Directors in America, 1922–1931* (London: Routledge and Kegan Paul, 1985).

Saunders, Thomas J., *Hollywood in Berlin: American Cinema and Weimar Germany* (Berkeley: University of California Press, 1994).

Segrave, Kerry, *American Films Abroad: Hollywood's Domination of the World's Movie Screens from the 1890s to the Present* (Jefferson: McFarland, 1997).

Street, Sarah, *Transatlantic Crossings: British Feature Films in the USA* (New York: Continuum, 2002).

Thompson, Kristin, *Exporting Entertainment: America in the World Film Market 1907–1934* (London: BFI, 1985).

Trumpbour, John, *Selling Hollywood to the World: US and European Struggles for Mastery of the Global Film Industry, 1920–1950* (New York: Cambridge University Press, 2002).

Ulff-Møller, Jens, *Hollywood's Film Wars with France: Film-Trade Diplomacy and the Emergence of the Film Quota Policy* (Rochester: University of Rochester Press, 2001).

Vasey, Ruth, *The World According to Hollywood, 1918–1939* (Exeter: University of Exeter Press, 1997).

Waldman, Harry, *Hollywood and the Foreign Touch: A Dictionary of Foreign Filmmakers and Their Films from America, 1910–1995* (Lanham: Scarecrow, 1996).

Africa and the Middle East

Diawara, Manthia, *African Cinema: Politics and Culture* (Bloomington: Indiana University Press, 1992).

Gutsche, Thelma, *The History and Significance of Motion Pictures in South Africa, 1895–1940* (Cape Town: Howard Timmins, 1972).

Issari, Mohammad Ali, *Cinema in Iran, 1900–1979* (Metuchen: Scarecrow, 1989).

Malkmus, Lizbeth, and Roy Armes, *Arab and African Film Making* (London: Zed Press, 1991).

Australia and New Zealand

Collins, Diane, *Hollywood Down Under: Australians at the Movies, 1896 to the Present Day* (Sydney: Angus and Robertson, 1987).

Dennis, Jonathan (ed.), *Aotearoa and the Sentimental Strine: Making Films in Australia and New Zealand in the Silent Period* (Wellington: Moa Films, 1993).

Long, Joan, and Martin Long, *The Picture That Moved: A Picture History of the Australian Cinema, 1896–1929* (Richmond: Hutchinson, 1982).

Martin, Helen, and Sam Edwards, *New Zealand Film, 1912–1996* (Auckland: Oxford University Press, 1997).

O'Regan, Tom, *Australian National Cinema* (London: Routledge, 1996).

Pike, Andrew, and Ross Cooper, *Australian Film, 1900–1977: A Guide to Feature Film Production* (Melbourne: Oxford University Press, 1980).

Reade, Eric, *Australian Silent Films: A Pictorial History of Silent Films from 1896 to 1929* (Melbourne: Lansdowne, 1970).

Reade, Eric, *History and Heartburn: The Saga of Australian Film, 1896–1978* (Sydney: Harper and Row, 1979).

Shirley, Graham, and Brian Adams, *Australian Cinema: The First Eighty Years* (Sydney: Angus and Robertson, 1983).

Tulloch, John, *Legends on the Screen: The Australian Narrative Cinema, 1919–1929* (Sydney: Currency Press, 1981).

Belgium and the Netherlands

Blom, Ivo, *Jean Desmet and the Early Dutch Film Trade* (Amsterdam: Amsterdam University Press, 2003).

Mosley, Philip, *Split Screen: Belgian Cinema and Cultural Identity* (Albany: State University of New York Press, 2001).

Canada

Armatage, Kay, *The Girl from God's Country: Nell Shipman and the Silent Cinema* (Toronto: University of Toronto Press, 2003).

Gittings, Christopher E., *Canadian National Cinema: Ideology, Difference and Representation* (London: Routledge, 2002).

MacKenzie, Scott, *Screening Québec: Québécois Cinema, National Identity and the Public Sphere* (Manchester: Manchester University Press, 2003).

Morris, Peter, *Embattled Shadows: A History of Canadian Cinema 1895–1939* (Montreal: McGill-Queens University Press, 1978).

China

Hsiao-Lu, Sheldon (ed.), *Transnational Chinese Cinema: Identity, Nationhood, Gender* (Honolulu: University of Hawaii Press, 1997).

Leyda, Jay, *Dianying: Electric Shadows, an Account of Films and the Film Audience in China* (Cambridge, MA: MIT Press, 1972).

Pang, Laikwan, *Building a New China in Cinema: The Chinese Left-Wing Cinema Movement, 1932–1937* (Lanham: Rowman and Littlefield, 2002).

Zhang, Yingjing (ed.), *Cinema and Urban Culture in Shanghai, 1922–1943* (Stanford: Stanford University Press, 1999).

Eastern Europe (without Soviet Union)

Bren, Frank, *World Cinema: Poland* (Trowbridge: Flicks Books, 1986).

Burns, Bryan, *World Cinema: Hungary* (Trowbridge: Flicks Books, 1996).

Dewey, Langdon, *Outline of Czechoslovakian Cinema* (London: Informatics, 1971).

Ford, Charles, Robert Hammond, and Grazyna Kudy, *Polish Film: A Twentieth Century History* (Jefferson: McFarland, 2003).

Haltof, Marek, *Polish National Cinema* (Oxford: Berghahn, 2002).

Hames, Peter, *The Czechoslovak New Wave* (Berkeley: University of California Press, 1985).

Nemeskurty, Istvan, *Word and Image: History of the Hungarian Cinema* (Budapest: Corvina Press, 1968).

Nemeskurty, Istvan, *Short History of Hungarian Cinema* (New York: Baseline, 1981).

Skvorecky, Josef, *All the Bright Young Men and Women: A Personal History of the Czech Cinema* (Toronto: Peter Martin Associates, 1971).

Taylor, Richard, Nancy Wood, Julian Graffy and Dina Iordanova (eds), *The BFI Companion to Eastern European and Russian Cinema* (London: BFI, 2000).

France

Primary sources

Abel, Richard (ed.), *French Film Theory and Criticism, 1907–1939. A History/Anthology, Volume 1: 1907–1929, Volume 2: 1929–1939* (Princeton: Princeton University Press, 1988).
Hammond, Paul (ed.), *The Shadow and its Shadow: Surrealist Writing on the Cinema* (London: Polygon, 1991).
Lumière, Auguste and Louis, *Letters: Inventing the Cinema* (London: Faber and Faber, 1995).

Secondary literature

Abel, Richard, *The Ciné Goes to Town: French Cinema, 1896–1914* (Berkeley: University of California Press, 1994).
Abel, Richard, *French Cinema: The First Wave, 1915–1929* (Princeton: Princeton University Press, 1984).
Bordwell, David, *French Impressionist Cinema: Film Culture, Film Theory, and Film Style* (New York: Arno, 1980).
Brownlow, Kevin, *'Napoleon': Abel Gance's Classic Film* (New York: Knopf, 1983).
Crafton, Donald, *Emile Cohl, Caricature and Film* (Princeton, NJ: Princeton University Press, 1990).
Ezra, Elizabeth, *Georges Méliès* (Manchester: Manchester University Press, 2000).
Flitterman-Lewis, Sandy, *To Desire Differently: Feminism and the French Cinema* (Urbana: University of Illinois Press, 1990).
Frazer, John, *Artificially Arranged Scenes: The Films of Georges Méliès* (Boston: G. K. Hall, 1979).
Gordon, Rae Beth, *Why the French Love Jerry Lewis: From Cabaret to Early Cinema* (Stanford: Stanford University Press, 2001).
Hayward, Susan, *French National Cinema* (London: Routledge, 1993).
Hayward, Susan, and Ginette Vincendeau (eds), *French Film: Texts and Contexts* (London: Routledge, 1990).
King, Norman, *Abel Gance: A Politics of Spectacle* (London: BFI, 1984).
Kovacs, Steven, *From Enchantment to Rage: The Story of Surrealist Cinema* (London: Associated University Presses, 1980).
Kuenzli, Rudolf E., *Dada and Surrealist Film* (New York: Willis Locker and Owens, 1987).
McMahan, Alison, *Alice Guy Blaché: Lost Visionary of the Cinema* (London: Continuum, 2002).
Monaco, Paul, *Cinema and Society: France and Germany during the Twenties* (New York: Elsevier, 1976).
Robinson, David, *Georges Méliès* (London: BFI, 1993).
Sesonske, Alexander, *Jean Renoir: The French Films, 1924–1939* (Cambridge, MA: Harvard University Press, 1980).
Slavin, David Henry, *Colonial Cinema and Imperial France, 1919–1939: White Blind Spots, Male Fantasies, Settler Myths* (Baltimore: Johns Hopkins University Press, 2001).
Williams, Alan, *Republic of Images: A History of French Filmmaking* (Cambridge, MA: Harvard University Press, 1992).

Germany

Primary sources

Kracauer, Siegfried, *The Mass Ornament: Weimar Essays* (Cambridge, MA: Harvard University Press, 1995).
Screen, vol. 42, no. 3 (Autumn 2001), special issue reprinting in parts Emilie Altenloh's sociological study of German movie audiences from 1914.

Secondary literature

Barlow, John D., *German Expressionist Film* (Boston: Twayne, 1987).
Bergfelder, Tim, Erica Carter, and Deniz Göktürk (eds), *The German Cinema Book* (London: BFI, 2002).
Brouwer, Stephen Eric, and Douglas Kellner (eds), *Passion and Rebellion: The Expressionist Heritage* (London: Crown Helm, 1983).
Budd, Michael (ed.), *'The Cabinet of Dr. Caligari': Texts, Contexts, Histories* (New Brunswick: Rutgers University Press, 1990).
Calhoun, Kenneth S. (ed.), *Peripheral Visions: The Hidden Stages of Weimar Cinema* (Detroit: Wayne State University Press, 2001).

Coates, Paul, *The Gorgon's Gaze: German Cinema, Expressionism and the Image of Horror* (Cambridge: Cambridge University Press, 1991).

Eisner, Lotte H., *The Haunted Screen: Expressionism in the Cinema and the Influence of Max Reinhardt* (Berkeley: University of California Press, 1969).

Elsaesser, Thomas (ed.), *A Second Life: German Cinema's First Decades* (Amsterdam: Amsterdam University Press, 1996).

Elsaesser, Thomas, *'Metropolis'* (London: BFI, 2000).

Elsaesser, Thomas, *Weimar Cinema and After: Germany's Historical Imaginary* (London: Routledge, 2000).

Gunning, Tom, *The Films of Fritz Lang: Allegories of Modernity and Vision* (London: BFI, 2000).

Hake, Sabine, *Passions and Deceptions: The Early Films of Ernst Lubitsch* (Princeton: Princeton University Press, 1992).

Hake, Sabine, *The Cinema's Third Machine: Writings on Film in Germany 1907–1933* (Lincoln: University of Nebraska Press, 1993).

Hake, Sabine, *German National Cinema* (London: Routledge, 2002).

Hardt, Ursula, *From Caligari to California: Erich Pommer's Life in the International Film Wars* (Oxford: Berghahn Books, 1996).

Jung, Uli, and Walter Schatzberg, *Beyond Caligari: The Films of Robert Wiene* (Oxford: Berghahn Books, 1999).

Kracauer, Siegfried, *From Caligari to Hitler: A Psychological History of the German Film* (Princeton: Princeton University Press, 1947).

Kreimeier, Klaus, *The Ufa Story: A History of Germany's Greatest Film Company, 1918–1945* (New York: Hill and Wang, 1996).

Leitner, Angelika, and Uwe Nitschke (eds), *The German Avant-Garde Film of the 1920s* (Munich: Goethe-Institut, 1989).

Levin, David J., *Richard Wagner, Fritz Lang and 'The Nibelungen': The Dramaturgy of Disavowal* (Princeton: Princeton University Press, 1998).

McCormick, Richard W., *Emancipation and Crisis: Gender, Sexuality, and 'New Objectivity' in Weimar Film and Literature* (New York: Palgrave, 2002).

Minden, Michael, and Holger Bachmann (eds), *Fritz Lang's 'Metropolis': Cinematic Visions of Technology and Fear* (Rochester: University of Rochester Press, 2001).

Monaco, Paul, *Cinema and Society: France and Germany during the Twenties* (New York: Elsevier, 1976).

Murray, Bruce, *Film and the German Left* (Austin: University of Texas Press, 1990).

Oksiloff, Assenka, *Picturing the Primitive: Visual Culture, Ethnography, and Early German Cinema* (New York: Palgrave, 2001).

Petro, Patrice, *Joyless Streets: Women and Melodramatic Representation in Weimar Germany* (Lawrenceville, NJ: Princeton University Press, 1989).

Plummer, Thomas *et al.*, *Film and Politics in the Weimar Republic* (New York: Holmes and Meier, 1982).

Silberman, Marc, *German Cinema: Texts in Context* (Detroit: Wayne State University Press, 1995).

Usai, Paolo Cherchi, and Lorenzo Codelli (eds), *Before Caligari: German Cinema, 1895–1920* (Pordenone: Edizioni Biblioteca dell'Imagine, 1990).

Wager, James B., *Dangerous Dames: Women and Representation in the Weimar Street Film and Film Noir* (Athens: Ohio State University Press, 1999).

India

Barnouw, Erik, and S. Krishnaswamy, *Indian Film* (New York: Columbia University Press, 1980).

Chabria, Suresh, and Paolo Cherchi Usai (eds), *Light of Asia: Indian Silent Cinema, 1912–1934* (Bombay: Wiley Eastern, 1994).

Dwyer, Rachel, and Dina Patel, *Cinema India: The Visual Culture of Hindi Film* (London: Reaktion, 2002).

Gokulsing, K. Moti, and Wimal Dissanayake, *Indian Popular Cinema: A Narrative of Cultural Change* (Stoke-on-Trent: Trentham, 1998).

Prasad, Madhava, *Ideology of the Hindi Film: A Historical Reconstruction* (New Delhi: Oxford University Press 1998).

Rajadhayksha, Ashish, and Paul Willemen (eds), *An Encyclopaedia of Indian Cinema* (Oxford: Oxford University Press, 1999).

Ramachandran, T. M. (ed.), *Seventy Years of Indian Cinema (1913–1983)* (Bombay: Cinema India, 1983).

Vasudevan, Ravi (ed.), *Making Meaning in Indian Cinema* (Oxford: Oxford University Press, 2001).

Willemen, Paul, and Behroze Gardhy (eds), *Indian Cinema* (London: BFI, 1982).

Ireland

Gray, Michael, *Stills, Reels and Rushes: Ireland and the Irish in Twentieth Century Cinema* (Blackrock: Ashfield, 2000).
McIlroy, Brian, *World Cinema: Ireland* (Trowbridge: Flicks, 1988).
Rockett, Kevin, *Irish Filmography* (Dublin: Red Mountain Press, 1996).
Rockett, Kevin, and Eugene Finn, *Still Irish: A Century of the Irish in Film* (Upland: Diane Publishing, 1993).
Rockett, Kevin, Luke Gibbons, and John Hill, *Cinema and Ireland* (London: Routledge, 1988).

Italy

Bruno, Guiliana, *Streetwalking on a Ruined Map: Cultural Theory and the City Films of Elvira Notari* (Princeton: Princeton University Press, 1992).
Film History, vol. 12, no. 3 (2000), special issue on early Italian cinema.
Hay, James, *Popular Film Culture in Fascist Italy: The Passing of the Rex* (Bloomington: Indiana University Press, 1987).
Landy, Marcia, *Italian Film* (Cambridge: Cambridge University Press, 2000).
Reich, Jacqueline, and Piero Garofalo (eds), *Re-Viewing Fascism: Italian Cinema, 1922–1943* (Bloomington: Indiana University Press, 2002).
Sorlin, Pierre, *Italian National Cinema 1896–1996* (London: Routledge, 1996).
Wyke, Maria, *Projecting the Past: Ancient Rome, Cinema and History* (New York: Routledge, 1997).

Japan

Anderson, Joseph, and Donald Richie, *The Japanese Film: Art and Industry* (Princeton: Princeton University Press, 1982).
Bernardi, Joanna, *Writing in Light: The Silent Scenario and the Japanese Pure Film Movement* (Detroit: Wayne State University Press, 2001).
Bordwell, David, *Ozu and the Poetics of Cinema* (Princeton: Princeton University Press, 1988).
Buehrer, Beverly Bare, *Japanese Films: A Filmography and Commentary, 1921–1989* (Jefferson: McFarland, 1990).
Burch, Noël, *To the Distant Observer: Form and Meaning in the Japanese Cinema* (London: Scolar Press, 1979).
Kirihara, Donald, *Patterns of Time: Mizoguchi and the 1930s* (Madison: University of Wisconsin Press, 1992).
Noletti, Arthur, and David Desser (eds), *Reframing Japanese Cinema: Authorship, Genre, History* (Bloomington: Indiana University Press, 1992).

Latin America

Chanan, Michael, *The Cuban Image: Cinema and Cultural Politics in Cuba* (London: BFI, 1985).
Johnson, Randal, and Robert Stam (eds), *Brazilian Cinema* (New York: Columbia University Press, 1995).
King, John, *Magical Reels: A History of Cinema in Latin America* (London: Verso, 2000).
Mora, Carl J., *Mexican Cinema: Reflections of a Society, 1896–1988* (Berkeley: University of California Press, 1989).
Noriega, Chon A. (ed.), *Visible Nations: Latin American Cinema and Video* (Minneapolis: University of Minnesota Press, 2000).
Stam, Robert, *Tropical Multiculturalism: A Comparative History of Race in Brazilian Cinema and Culture* (Durham: Duke University Press, 1997).

Russia and Soviet Union

Primary sources

Eisenstein, Sergei, *Selected Works. Volume 1: Writings, 1922–34* (London: BFI, 1988).
Levaco, Ronald (ed.), *Kuleshov on Film: Writings of Lev Kuleshov* (Berkeley: University of California Press, 1974).
Kuleshov, Lev, *Selected Works: Fifty Years in Film* (Moscow: Raduga, 1987).

Michelson, Annette (ed.), *Kino-Eye: The Writings of Dziga Vertov* (London: Pluto, 1984).
Taylor, Richard, and Ian Christie (eds), *The Film Factory: Russian and Soviet Cinema in Documents* (London: Routledge, 1988).

Secondary literature

Bordwell, David, *The Cinema of Eisenstein* (Cambridge MA: Harvard University Press, 1993).
Christie, Ian, and Julian Graffy (eds), *Protazanov and the Continuity of Russian Cinema* (London: BFI, 1993).
Goodwin, James, *Eisenstein, Cinema and History* (Urbana: University of Illinois Press, 1993).
Gillespie, David, *Early Soviet Cinema: Innovation, Ideology and Propaganda* (London: Wallflower, 2000).
Historical Journal of Film, Radio and Television, vol. 11, no. 2 (1991), special issue on Russian and Soviet cinema.
Kenez, Peter, *Cinema and Soviet Society: From the Revolution to the Death of Stalin* (London: I. B. Tauris, 2001).
Kepley, Vance, *In the Service of the State: The Cinema of Alexander Dovzhenko* (Madison: University of Wisconsin Press, 1986).
LaValley, Al, and Barry P. Scheur (eds), *Eisenstein at 100: A Reconsideration* (New Brunswick: Rutgers University Press, 2001).
Lawton, Anne (ed.), *The Red Screen: Politics, Society and Art in Soviet Cinema* (London: Routledge, 1992).
Leyda, Jay, *Kino: A History of the Russian and Soviet Film* (London: Allen and Unwin, 1983).
Mayne, Judith, *Kino and the Woman Question* (Columbus: Ohio State University Press, 1989).
Nesbet, Anne, *Savage Junctures: Images and Ideas in Eisenstein's Films* (London: I. B. Tauris, 2002).
Petric, Vlada, *Constructivism in Film: 'The Man With the Movie Camera' – A Cinematic Analysis* (Cambridge: Cambridge University Press, 1987).
Roberts, Graham, *Forward Soviet! History and Non-Fiction Film in the USSR* (London: I. B. Tauris, 1999).
Roberts, Graham, *'The Man With the Movie Camera'* (London: I. B. Tauris, 2001).
Sargeant, Amy, *Vsevolod Pudovkin: Classic Films of the Soviet Avant-Garde* (London: I. B. Tauris, 2001).
Stites, Richard, *Russian Popular Culture: Entertainment and Society since 1900* (Cambridge: Cambridge University Press, 1992).
Taylor, Richard, *The Politics of the Soviet Cinema, 1917–29* (Cambridge: Cambridge University Press, 1979).
Taylor, Richard, *Film Propaganda: Soviet Russia and Nazi Germany* (London: I. B. Tauris, 1998).
Taylor, Richard, *'The Battleship Potemkin'* (London: I. B. Tauris, 2001).
Taylor, Richard, *'October'* (London: BFI, 2002).
Taylor, Richard, and Ian Christie (eds), *Inside the Film Factory: New Approaches to Russian and Soviet Cinema* (London: Routledge, 1991).
Taylor, Richard, and Ian Christie (eds), *Eisenstein Rediscovered* (London: Routledge, 1993).
Tsivian, Yuri *et al.* (eds), *Silent Witnesses: Russian Films 1908–1919* (London: BFI, 1989).
Tsivian, Yuri, *Early Cinema in Russia and Its Cultural Reception* (Chicago: University of Chicago Press, 1998).
Youngblood, Denise J., *Soviet Cinema in the Silent Era, 1918–1935* (Ann Arbor: UMI Research Press, 1985).
Youngblood, Denise J., *Movies for the Masses: Popular Cinema and Soviet Society in the 1920s* (Cambridge: Cambridge University Press, 1992).
Youngblood, Denise J., *The Magic Mirror: Moviemaking in Russia, 1908–1918* (Madison: University of Wisconsin Press, 1999).

Scandinavia

Bordwell, David, *The Films of Carl Theodor Dreyer* (Berkeley: University of California Press, 1981).
Fullerton, John, and Jan Olsson (eds), *Nordic Explorations: Film Before 1930* (Sydney: John Libbey, 1999).
Forslund, Bengt, *Victor Sjostrom: His Life and his Work* (New York: Zoetrope, 1988).
Mottram, Ron, *The Danish Cinema Before Dreyer* (Metuchen: Scarecrow, 1988).
Soila, Tytti, Astrid Soderbergh Widding and Gunnar Iverson, *Nordic National Cinemas* (London: Routledge, 1998).

Spain

Morris, C. B., *This Loving Darkness: The Cinema and Spanish Writers, 1920–1936* (Oxford: Oxford University Press, 1980).

Store, Rob, *Spanish Cinema* (London: Longman, 2001).
Triana-Toribio, Nuria, *Spanish National Cinema* (London: Routledge, 2003).

United Kingdom

Primary sources

Harding, Colin, and Simon Popple (eds), *In the Kingdom of Shadows: A Companion to Early Cinema* (London: Cygnus, 1996).

Secondary literature

Barnes, John, *The Beginnings of the Cinema in England, 1894–1901*, 5 volumes (Exeter: University of Exeter Press, 1998).
Barr, Charles, *English Hitchcock* (Moffat: Cameron and Hollis, 1999).
Burrows, Jon, *Legitimate Cinema: Theatre Stars in Silent British Films, 1908–1918* (Exeter: University of Exeter Press, 2003).
Burton, Alan, and Laraine Porter (eds), *Pimple, Pranks & Pratfalls: British Film Comedy Before 1930* (Trowbridge: Flicks, 2000).
Burton, Alan, and Laraine Porter (eds), *The Showman, the Spectacle and the Two-Minute Silence: Performing British Cinema Before 1930* (Trowbridge: Flicks, 2001).
Burton, Alan, and Laraine Porter (eds), *Scene-Stealing: Sources for British Cinema Before 1930* (Trowbridge: Flicks, 2003).
Chanan, Michael, *The Dream That Kicks: The Pre-History and Early Years of Cinema in Britain* (London: Routledge, 1996).
Dickinson, Margaret and Sarah Street, *Cinema and State: The Film Industry and the Government, 1927–1984* (London: BFI, 1985).
Dixon, Wheeler Winston (ed.), *Re-Viewing British Cinema, 1900–1992* (New York: SUNY Press, 1994).
Fitzsimmons, Linda, and Sarah Street (eds), *Moving Performance: British Stage and Screen, 1890s-1920s* (Trowbridge: Flicks, 2000).
Higson, Andrew, *Waving the Flag: Constructing a National Cinema in Britain* (Oxford: Oxford University Press, 1995).
Higson, Andrew (ed.), *Young and Innocent? The Cinema in Britain, 1896–1930* (Exeter: University of Exeter Press, 2002).
Historical Journal of Film, Radio and Television, vol. 13, no. 2 (1993), special issue on "Britain and Cinema in the First World War."
Low, Rachael, *The History of the British Film, Volumes 1–4: 1896–1929* (London: Routledge, 1997).
Pronay, Nicholas, and D. W. Spring (eds), *Propaganda, Politics and Film, 1918–45* (London: Macmillan, 1982).
Reeves, Nicholas, *Official British Film Propaganda during the First World War* (London: Croom Helm, 1986).
Ryall, Tom, *Alfred Hitchcock and the British Cinema* (London: Athlone, 1996).
Sopocy, Martin, *James Williamson: Studies and Documents of a Pioneer of the Film Narrative* (Cranbury: Fairleigh Dickinson University Press, 1998).
Street, Sarah, *British National Cinema* (London: Routledge, 1997).
Swann, Paul, *The British Documentary Film Movement, 1926–1946* (Cambridge: Cambridge University Press, 1989).

United States

Primary sources

Amberg, George (ed.), *The New York Times Film Reviews. A One-Volume Selection, 1913–1970* (New York: Arno, 1971).
Bowser, Eileen (ed.), *Biograph Bulletins, 1908–1912* (New York: Farrar, Straus, and Giroux, 1973).
Bromley, Carl (ed.), *Cinema Nation: The Best Writing on Film from 'The Nation', 1913–2000* (New York: Thunder's Mouth, 2000).

Brownlow, Kevin, *The Parade's Gone By . . .* (London: Secker and Warburg, 1968).

Cardullo, Bert *et al.* (eds), *Playing to the Camera: Film Actors Discuss Their Craft* (New Haven: Yale University Press, 1998).

Denby, David (ed.), *Awake in the Dark: An Anthology of American Film Criticism, 1915 to the Present* (New York: Vintage, 1977).

Deutelbaum, Marshall (ed.), *IMAGE on the Art and Evolution of the Film: Photographs and Articles from the Magazine of the International Museum of Photography* (New York: Dover, 1979).

Elley, Derek (ed.), *The Variety Movie Guide 2000* (New York: Perigee, 2000, abbreviated reprints of original reviews in leading film industry trade paper).

Grau, Robert, *The Theatre of Science: A Volume of Progress and Achievement in the Motion Picture Industry* (New York: Benjamin Blom, 1914).

Hochman, Stanley (ed.), *From Quasimodo to Scarlett O'Hara: A National Board of Review Anthology, 1920–1940* (New York: Ungar, 1982).

Kauffmann, Stanley (ed.), *American Film Criticism: From the Beginnings to 'Citizen Kane'* (New York: Liveright, 1972).

Koszarski, Richard (ed.), *Hollywood Directors 1914–1940* (London: Oxford University Press, 1976).

Lindsay, Vachel, *The Art of the Moving Picture* (New York: Liveright, 1971, originally published in 1915).

McClure, Arthur F. (ed.), *The Movies: An American Idiom* (Rutterford: Fairleigh Dickinson University Press, 1971).

Mast, Gerald (ed.), *The Movies in Our Midst. Documents in the Cultural History of Film in America* (Chicago: University of Chicago Press, 1982).

Münsterberg, Hugo, *The Photoplay: A Psychological Study* (New York: Dover, 1970, originally published in 1916).

Musser, Charles (ed.), *Thomas A. Edison Papers: A Guide to Motion Picture Catalogs by American Producers and Distributors, 1894–1908: A Microfilm Edition* (Frederick: University Publications of America, 1985).

Niver, Kemp (ed.), *Biograph Bulletins, 1896–1908* (Los Angeles: Locare Research Group, 1971).

Pratt, George C. (ed.), *Spellbound in Darkness: A History of the Silent Film* (Greenwich: New York Graphic Society, 1973).

Ramsaye, Terry. *A Million and One Nights: A History of the Motion Picture Through 1925* (New York: Simon & Schuster, 1926).

Semenor, William Wurtzel, and Carla Winter (eds), *William Fox, Sol M. Wurtzel and the Early Fox Film Corporation: Letters, 1917–1923* (Jefferson: McFarland, 2001).

Slide, Anthony (ed.), *They Also Wrote for the Fan Magazines: Film Article by Literary Giants from E. E. Cummings to Eleanor Roosevelt, 1920–1939* (Jefferson: McFarland, 1992).

Wood, Richard (ed.), *Film and Propaganda in America: A Documentary History*, vol. 1 (New York: Greenwood, 1990).

Secondary literature

Addison, Heather, *Hollywood and the Rise of Physical Culture* (London: Routledge, 2003).

Allen, Mike, *Family Secrets: The Feature Films of D. W. Griffith* (London: BFI, 1999).

Allen, Robert C., *Vaudeville and Film 1895–1915: A Study in Media Interaction* (New York: Arno, 1980).

Austin, Bruce A., *Immediate Seating: A Look at Movie Audiences* (Belmont: Wadsworth, 1989).

Bachman, Gregg, and Thomas J. Slater (eds), *American Silent Film: Discovering Marginalized Voices* (Carbondale: Southern Illinois University Press, 2002).

Balio, Tino, *United Artists: The Company Built by the Stars* (Madison: University of Wisconsin Press, 1975).

Balio, Tino (ed.), *The American Film Industry* (Madison: University of Wisconsin Press, 1985).

Barbas, Samantha, *Movie Crazy: Fans, Stars, and the Cult of Celebrity* (New York: Palgrave, 2002).

Barrios, Richard, *Screened Out: Playing Gay in Hollywood from Edison to Stonewall* (London: Routledge, 2002).

Barsam, Richard, *The Vision of Robert Flaherty: The Artist as Myth and Filmmaker* (Bloomington: Indiana University Press, 1988).

Basinger, Jeanine, *Silent Stars* (Hanover: Wesleyan University Press, 1999).

Beauchamp, Cari, *Without Lying Down: Frances Marion and the Powerful Women of Early Hollywood* (New York: Scribner's, 1997).

Bernardi, Daniel (ed.), *The Birth of Whiteness: Race and the Emergence of United States Cinema* (New Brunswick: Rutgers University Press, 1996).

Black, Gregory D., *Hollywood Censored: Morality Codes, Catholics, and the Movies* (Cambridge: Cambridge University Press, 1994).

Bordwell, David, Janet Staiger, and Kristin Thompson, *The Classical Hollywood Cinema: Film Style & Mode of Production to 1960* (London: Routledge and Kegan Paul, 1985).

Bowser, Eileen (ed.), *The Slapstick Symposium* (Brussels: FIAF, 1988).

Bowser, Eileen, *The Transformation of Cinema, 1907–1915* (New York: Scribner's, 1990).

Bowser, Pearl, and Louise Spence, *Writing Himself Into History: Oscar Micheaux, His Silent Films, and His Audiences* (New Brunswick: Rutgers University Press, 2000).

Bowser, Pearl, Jane Gaines, and Charles Musser (eds), *Oscar Micheaux and His Circle* (Bloomington: Indiana University Press, 2001).

Brownlow, Kevin, *Behind the Mask of Innocence – Sex, Violence, Prejudice, Crime: Films of Social Conscience in the Silent Era* (London: Jonathan Cape, 1990).

Buscombe, Edward, and Roberta E. Pearson (eds), *Back in the Saddle Again: New Essays on the Western* (London: BFI, 1998).

Butsch, Richard, *The Making of American Audiences: From Stage to Television, 1750–1990* (Cambridge: Cambridge University Press, 2000).

Butters, Gerald R., Jr., *Black Manhood on the Silent Screen* (Lawrence: University Press of Kansas, 2002).

Campbell, Craig W., *Reel America and World War I: A Comprehensive Filmography and History of Motion Pictures in the United States, 1914–1920* (Jefferson: McFarland, 1985).

Carr, Steven A., *Hollywood and Anti-Semitism: A Cultural History up to World War II* (Cambridge: Cambridge University Press, 2001).

Cohen, Paula Marantz, *Silent Film and the Triumph of the American Myth* (Oxford: Oxford University Press, 2001).

Couvares, Francis G. (ed.), *Movie Censorship and American Culture* (Washington: Smithsonian Institution Press, 1996).

Crafton, Donald, *The Talkies: American Cinema's Transition to Sound, 1926–1931* (New York: Scribner's, 1997).

Cripps, Thomas, *Slow Fade to Black: The Negro in American Film, 1900–1942* (New York: Oxford University Press, 1977).

Dale, Alan, *Comedy is a Man in Trouble: Slapstick in American Movies* (Minneapolis: University of Minnesota Press, 2000).

DeBauche, Leslie Midkiff, *Reel Patriotism: The Movies and World War I* (Madison: University of Wisconsin Press, 1997).

deCordova, Richard, *Picture Personalities: The Emergence of the Star System in America* (Urbana: University of Illinois Press, 1990).

Diawara, Manthia (ed.), *Black American Cinema* (New York: Routledge, 1993).

Dick, Bernard F. (ed.), *Columbia Pictures: Portrait of a Studio* (Lexington: University Press of Kentucky, 1992).

Dick, Bernard F., *City of Dreams: The Making and Remaking of Universal Pictures* (Lexington: University of Kentucky Press, 1997).

Donahue, Suzanne Mary, *American Film Distribution: The Changing Marketplace* (Ann Arbor: UMI Research Press, 1989).

Eckhardt, Joseph P., *The King of the Movies: Film Pioneer Sigmund Lubin* (Cranbury: Fairleigh Dickinson University Press, 1998).

Everett, Anna, *Returning the Gaze: A Genealogy of Black Film Criticism, 1909–1949* (Durham: Duke University Press, 2001).

Everson, William K., *American Silent Film* (New York: Oxford University Press, 1978).

Fell, John L. (ed.), *Before Hollywood: Turn-of-the-Century American Film* (New York: Hudson Hills Press, 1987).

Fielding, Raymond, *The American Newsreel 1911–1967* (Norman: University of Oklahoma Press, 1972).

Finler, Joel, *The Hollywood Story* (London: Wallflower, 2003).

Fleener-Marzec, Nickieann, *D. W. Griffith's 'The Birth of a Nation': Controversy, Suppression, and the First Amendment as it Applies to Filmic Expression 1915–1973* (New York: Arno, 1980).

Francke, Lizzie, *Script Girls: Women Screenwriters in Hollywood* (London: BFI, 1994).

Friedman, Lester D. (ed.), *Unspeakable Images: Ethnicity and the American Cinema* (Champaign: University of Illinois Press, 1990).

Fuller, Kathryn H., *At the Picture Show: Small-Town Audiences and the Creation of Movie Fan Culture* (Washington: Smithsonian Institution Press, 1996).

Gabler, Neal, *An Empire of Their Own: How the Jews Invented Hollywood* (London: W. H. Allen, 1989).

Gaines, Jane, *Fire & Desire: Mixed-Race Movies in the Silent Era* (Chicago: University of Chicago Press, 2001).

Gledhill, Christine (ed.), *Home is Where the Heart Is: Studies in Melodrama and the Woman's Film* (London: BFI, 1987).

Gledhill, Christine (ed.), *Stardom: Industry of Desire* (London: Routledge, 1991).

Gomery, Douglas, *The Hollywood Studio System* (London: BFI, 1986).

Gomery, Douglas, *Shared Pleasures: A History of Movie Presentation in the United States* (London: BFI, 1992).

Green, J. Ronald, *Straight Lick: The Cinema of Oscar Micheaux* (Bloomington: Indiana University Press, 2000).

Grieveson, Lee, *Policing Cinema: Movies and Censorship in Early Twentieth Century America* (Berkeley: University of California Press, 2004).

Gunning, Tom, *D. W. Griffith and the Origins of American Narrative Film: The Early Years at Biograph* (Urbana: University of Illinois Press, 1991).

Haberski, Raymond J., Jr, *It's Only a Movie! Film and Critics in American Culture* (Lexington: University Press of Kentucky, 2001).

Hansen, Miriam, *Babel and Babylon: Spectatorship in American Silent Film* (Cambridge, MA: Harvard University Press, 1991).

Hark, Ina Rae (ed.), *Exhibition: The Film Reader* (London: Routledge, 2002).

Higashi, Sumiko, *Virgins, Vamps and Flappers: The American Silent Movie Heroine* (St. Albans: Eden Press Women's Publications, 1978).

Higashi, Sumiko, *Cecil B. DeMille and American Culture: The Silent Era* (Berkeley: University of California Press, 1994).

Hilmes, Michele, *Hollywood and Broadcasting: From Radio to Cable* (Urbana: University of Illinois Press, 1990).

Horak, Jan Christopher (ed.), *Lovers of Cinema: The First American Avant-Garde, 1919–1945* (Madison: University of Wisconsin Press, 1995).

Izod, John, *Hollywood and the Box Office, 1895–1986* (London: Macmillan, 1988).

Jenkins, Henry, *What Made Pistachio Nuts? Early Sound Comedy and the Vaudeville Aesthetic* (New York: Columbia University Press, 1992).

Jowett, Garth, *Film: The Democratic Art* (Boston: Little, Brown, 1976).

Jowett, Garth S., Ian C. Jarvie and Kathryn H. Fuller (eds), *Children and the Movies: Media Influence and the Payne Fund Controversy* (New York: Cambridge University Press, 1995).

Karnick, Kristine Brunovska, and Henry Jenkins (eds), *Classical Hollywood Comedy* (New York: Routledge, 1995).

Keil, Charlie, *Early American Cinema in Transition: Story, Style and Filmmaking, 1907–1913* (Madison: University of Wisconsin Press, 2002).

Keil, Charlie, and Shelley Stamp (eds), *American Cinema's Transitional Era* (Berkeley: University of California Press, 2004).

Kerr, Paul (ed.), *The Hollywood Film Industry: A Reader* (London: Routledge, 1986).

Kerr, Walter, *The Silent Clowns* (New York: Knopf, 1975).

Kindem, Gorham (ed.), *The American Movie Industry: The Business of Motion Pictures* (Carbondale: Southern Illinois Press, 1982).

Kirby, Lynne, *Parallel Tracks: The Railroad and Silent Cinema* (Exeter: University of Exeter Press, 1997).

Koszarski, Richard, *The Man You Loved to Hate: Erich von Stroheim and Hollywood* (New York: Oxford University Press, 1983).

Koszarski, Richard, *An Evening's Entertainment: The Age of the Silent Feature Picture, 1915–1928* (New York: Scribner's, 1990).

Krutnik, Frank (ed.), *Hollywood Comedians: The Film Reader* (London: Routledge, 2003).

Lang, Robert (ed.), *The Birth of a Nation* (New Brunswick: Rutgers University Press, 1995).

Lovell, Alan, and Peter Krämer (eds), *Screen Acting* (London: Routledge, 1999).

Marks, Martin, *Music and the Silent Film: Contexts and Case Studies, 1895–1924* (New York: Oxford University Press, 1996).

Maland, Charles J., *Chaplin and American Culture: The Evolution of a Star Image* (Princeton: Princeton University Press, 1989).

May, Lary, *Screening Out the Past: The Birth of Mass Culture and the Motion Picture Industry* (New York: Oxford University Press, 1980).

McLean, Adrienne L., and David A. Cook (eds), *Headline Hollywood: A Century of Film Scandal* (New Brunswick: Rutgers University Press, 2001).

Merritt, Greg, *Celluloid Mavericks: A History of American Independent Film* (New York: Thunder's Mouth, 2000).

Merritt, Russell, and J. B. Kaufman, *Walt in Wonderland: The Silent Films of Walt Disney* (Baltimore: Johns Hopkins University Press, 1993).

Miller, Blair, *American Silent Film Comedies: An Illustrated Encyclopedia of Persons, Studios and Terminology* (Jefferson: McFarland, 1995).

Musser, Charles, *The Emergence of Cinema: The American Screen to 1907* (New York: Scribner's, 1990).

Musser, Charles, *Before the Nickelodeon: Edwin S. Porter and the Edison Manufacturing Company* (Berkeley: University of California Press, 1991).

Musser, Charles, *Thomas A. Edison and His Kinetographic Motion Pictures* (New Brunswick: Rutgers University Press, 1995).

Musser, Charles, *Edison Motion Pictures, 1890–1900: An Annotated Filmography* (Washington: Smithsonian Institution Press, 1997).

Musser, Charles, and Carol Nelson, *High-Class Moving Pictures: Lyman H. Howe and the Forgotten Era of Traveling Exhibition, 1880–1920* (Princeton: Princeton University Press, 1991).

O'Leary, Liam, *Rex Ingram: Master of the Silent Cinema* (New York: Barnes & Noble, 1980).

Pearson, Roberta, *Eloquent Gestures: The Transformation of Performance Style in the Griffith Biograph Films* (Berkeley: University of California Press, 1992).

Phillips, Ray, *Edison's Kinetoscope and Its Films: A History to 1896* (Trowbridge: Flicks, 1995).

Rabinovitz, Lauren, *For the Love of Pleasure: Women, Movies, and Culture in Turn-of-the-Century Chicago* (New Brunswick: Rutgers University Press, 1998).

Robinson, David, *From Peep Show to Palace: The Birth of American Film* (New York: Columbia University Press, 1996).

Rogin, Michael, *Blackface, White Noise: Jewish Immigrants in the Hollywood Melting Pot* (Berkeley: University of California Press, 1996).

Rosenbaum, Jonathan, '*Greed*' (London: BFI, 1993).

Ross, Steven J., *Working-Class Hollywood: Silent Film and the Shaping of Class in America* (Princeton: Princeton University Press, 1998).

Schaefer, Eric, *"Bold! Daring! Shocking! True!" A History of Exploitation Films, 1919–1959* (Durham: Duke University Press, 1999).

Schatz, Thomas, *The Genius of the System: Hollywood Filmmaking in the Studio Era* (New York: Pantheon, 1988).

Singer, Ben, *Melodrama and Modernity: Early Pulp Cinema and the Social Contexts of Sensationalism* (New York: Columbia University Press, 2001).

Sloan, Kay, *The Loud Silents: Origins of the Social Problem Film* (Urbana: University of Illinois Press, 1988).

Staiger, Janet, *Interpreting Films: Studies in the Historical Reception of American Cinema* (Princeton: Princeton University Press, 1992).

Staiger, Janet (ed.), *The Studio System* (New Brunswick: Rutgers, 1995).

Staiger, Janet, *Bad Women: Regulating Sexuality in Early American Cinema* (Minneapolis: University of Minnesota Press, 1995).

Stamp, Shelley, *Movie-Struck Girls: Women and Motion Picture Culture after the Nickelodeon* (Princeton: Princeton University Press, 2000).

Stanfield, Peter, *Horse Opera: The Strange History of the 1930s Singing Cowboy* (Urbana: University of Illinois Press, 2002).

Stempel, Tom, *FrameWork: A History of Screenwriting in the American Film* (New York: Continuum, 1991).

Stokes, Melvyn, and Richard Maltby (eds), *American Movie Audiences: From the Turn of the Century to the Early Sound Era* (London: BFI, 1999).

Studlar, Gaylyn, *This Mad Masquerade: Stardom and Masculinity in the Jazz Age* (New York: Columbia University Press, 1996).

Uricchio, William, and Roberta A. Pearson, *Reframing Culture: The Case of the Vitagraph Quality Films* (Princeton: Princeton University Press, 1993).

Usai, Paolo Cherchi, and Lorenzo Codelli (eds), *The Path to Hollywood, 1911–1920* (Pordenone: Edizioni Biblioteca dell'Imagine, 1988).

Usai, Paolo Cherchi, and Lorenzo Codelli (eds), *The DeMille Legacy* (Pordenone: Edizioni Biblioteca dell'Imagine, 1991).

Valentine, Maggie, *The Show Starts on the Sidewalk: An Architectural History of the Movie Theatre* (New Haven: Yale University Press, 1994).

Waller, Gregory, *Main Street Amusements: Movies and Commercial Entertainment in a Southern City, 1896–1930* (Washington, DC: Smithsonian Institution Press, 1995).

Waller, Gregory (ed.), *Moviegoing in America* (Oxford: Blackwell, 2002).

Walsh, Frank, *Sin and Censorship: The Catholic Church and the Motion Picture Industry* (New Haven: Yale University Press, 1996).

Wasko, Janet, *Movies and Money: Financing the American Film Industry* (Norwood: Ablex, 1982).

Williams, Linda, *Playing the Race Card: Melodramas of Black and White from Uncle Tom to O. J. Simpson* (Princeton: Princeton University Press, 2001).

Wyatt, Justin (ed.), *Film Marketing: The Film Reader* (London: Routledge, 2003).

Wyke, Maria, *Projecting the Past: Ancient Rome, Cinema and History* (New York: Routledge, 1997).

Zimmermann, Patricia R., *Reel Families: A Social History of Amateur Films* (Bloomington: Indiana University Press, 1995).

Zucker, Carole (ed.), *Making Visible the Invisible: An Anthology of Original Essays on Film Acting* (Metuchen: Scarecrow, 1990).

Index

Italic page numbers refer to illustrations.

#0281 - 220217 - C0 - 246/174/24 - PB - 9780415252843